Recreational
Handicapping

Recreational Handicapping

A Comprehensive Introduction
to the Art and Science of
Thoroughbred Handicapping

JAMES QUINN

WILLIAM MORROW AND COMPANY, INC.
New York

In Memory of
JOHN LUCKMAN

Who believed playing the races
to be a form of adult recreation,
best engaged by individuals equally
well-informed about the rules of the
games as racing's insiders . . .

Library of Congress Cataloging-in-Publication Data

Quinn, James, 1943–
    Recreational handicapping: a comprehensive introduction to the
art and science of throughbred handicapping / James Quinn.
        p.   cm.
    Includes bibliographical references.
    ISBN 0-688-08964-X
    1. Horse race betting. I. Title.
SF331.Q555 1990
798.401—dc20   90-6140
                                                            CIP

Printed in the United States of America

First Edition

1 2 3 4 5 6 7 8 9 10

BOOK DESIGN BY BERNARD SCHLEIFER

Contents

- Turn time
- Class ratings
- Improving and declining horses
- Recording trips and track biases
- Late speed on the turf
- Evaluating trainers and jockeys
- Evaluating sires
- The post-parade inspections

- Sprints and routes
- Long sprints
- One-turn miles
- Bullrings
- Claiming races
- Claiming races restricted to three-year-olds
- Maiden races
- Maiden-claiming races
- The nonwinners allowance series
- Claiming horses in nonwinners allowance races
- Classified allowance races
- Overnight handicaps
- The stakes menagerie
- Overnight horses in stakes races
- Turf races
- Starter races
- Juveniles

- Fillies vs. colts
- Three-year-olds & up
- State-breds vs. open competition
- The earnings box
- Peaking form
- Off tracks
- Contentious races
- Unpredictable races
- Small fields
- Local information services

How to Play
the Races Today

A MERE TWENTY-TWO SEASONS have lapsed since the most comprehensive authoritative guide to playing the races was published to enthusiastic acclaim.

A millennium might as well have glided by.

For thoroughbred racing's audience, the beleaguered cadres of customers known optimistically as handicappers, the sport since 1975 has undergone successively startling changes.

The more radical alterations have included year-long racing calendars, the faster development of younger horses, a proliferation of stakes races, unprecedented purse inflation, an upsurge of state-bred breeding programs, the increased importation of foreign horses, the advent of exotic wagering, the inauguration of the Breeders' Cup championship series, and the most futuristic change of all, the legislation of intertrack wagering and off-track betting parlors.

Of hallowed tradition, all that remains, I dare say, is the daily double.

Of the great game of handicapping, the transformation has been equally dramatic, just as complete. Here, to be sure, the news has been exciting. New and demonstrably effective methods of speed handicapping, class handicapping, pace analysis, form analysis, trip handicapping, pedigree evaluation, and trainer evaluation have fundamentally altered the general practice.

Conducted successfully, too, and on a national scale, have been the first scientific investigations of every meaningful piece of data in the *Daily Racing Form*'s past performances.

Which characteristics of handicapping have been related significantly to horses' chances of winning? Which have proved incidental? Which meaningless?

The national probability studies have provided stimulating answers and a wealth of handicapping knowledge not previously available to racetrack customers. Here, too, tradition has suffered an overdue setback.

Factor in the blandishments extended to small racetrack bettors by the comings of the exacta, quinella, trifecta, serial triple, pick-six, and pick-nine, and a neutral observer can readily feel the psychological turbulence richocheting across the modern practitioner's typical day at the races.

As a novice handicapper in 1970 I was a disciple of *Ainslie's Complete Guide to Thoroughbred Racing*. The book contributed excellent chapters on class appraisal and form analysis, the latter a classic.

It's instructive to consider how conservative and dated a majority of the author's selection and elimination guidelines would be in the contemporary milieu.

The book held, for example, that horses should be unacceptable on form unless they had raced and worked out within the past 17 days or, if unraced, had worked out repeatedly during that period. Claiming-class barriers were set at 20 to 25 percent of prior selling prices, up and down, or bettors were advised to eliminate the horses.

Nowadays, horses unraced for months can be accepted on form if they show a single five-furlong workout (or longer) within the past couple of weeks. Rises and drops in claiming class, routinely outrageous now, can nevertheless be bet.

To invoke traditional guidelines on class and form today would mean eliminating far too many winners, not to mention serious contenders for the newly valued place hole.

The same shortcoming haunts the implementation of classical guidelines associated with other fundamentals of handicapping, notably distance, age, and sex. Traditional standards eliminate too many eventual winners. Of the remainder that do win, too many pay miserly mutuels.

It's a brand-new ballgame, racing in the 1990s, and fresh approaches are needed.

The new methods, and new knowledge, have rubbed together for a time already, igniting an information explosion among modern handicappers, just in time to accommodate the age of information sweeping across the broader society. The role of personal computers in the handicapping process, as this is composed, remains an elusive, troublesome issue.

In consequence, the real problem for regular racegoers has become the effective management and selective use of the various innovative methods and multiple-information resources. Newcomers are often overwhelmed at the deluge.

Are some rating methods better than others? Which deserve priority? In which kinds of races might the various methods apply best? Is there anything that approaches a panacea? What about technique? Which procedures are valid? Which are faulty?

What about specialized information that is circumstantial—about trips, surface biases, track conditions, body language? What of information that is subjective—about trainers, jockeys, owners, the odds board?

How should descriptive types of information be treated? When do they take precedence over numerical ratings that estimate the real abilities of horses?

What to do? How best to do it?

How to play the races today?

In fact, the new methods, knowledge, and information resources—all of it—can be fully integrated with the familiar processes of handicapping.

That process, as outlined anew in this guide:

- begins with a few simple routines for marking the past performances
- proceeds to identifying the main contenders and ratable races
- features a number and diversity of basic methods for rating horses' abilities
- underscores the interpretation of numerical ratings and any descriptive information in a context of everyday applications
- considers a number of special topics that can influence the interpretation and evaluation of handicapping data
- concludes, as do handicappers, with making selections, and making decisions, in accordance with the recommended principles of parimutuel wagering, here called recreational betting.

The integrative aspect of the handicapping process is emphasized. Methods of speed handicapping, class handicapping, pace handicapping, trip handicapping, and the rest, for example, apply variously, and perhaps in combination, depending upon the kinds of races under study and the circumstances surrounding today's competition.

A critical mistake a majority of recreational handicappers commit instigates the fruitless search for a best method, or a singular approach, as a potential cure-all applicable to all handicapping events and purposes. Figure handicappers too attached to a favorite brand of speed figures constitute the most notorious contemporary species.

I like to refer, a bit disdainfully, to the varieties of self-styled figure handicappers as method players. Method players stand an extraordinarily good chance of identifying horses well-suited to their methods—assuming technique has been appropriate, hardly an elementary assumption—but of missing just about everything else.

As crucial as speed figures and pace ratings may be in the contemporary game—and they are—the numbers are far from everything. The finest figures in the land merit only limited application, if any, in grass races, nonclaiming routes, certain races for developing three-year-olds, and top-grade stakes races at classic distances.

Users getting less than the highly touted nourishment from their numbers, without understanding why, might be willing to concede the argument for an integration of the whole.

Regardless of basic convictions, disciples of this modern guide will be prepared to combine various rating methods, comprehensive knowledge, and multiple-information resources in the day-to-day challenge that is handicapping.

They will become accomplished method players, and information managers besides.

They will implement different methods of analysis under different circumstances.

After putting it all together, they will have a splendid chance of evolving into racetrack winners.

Occasional racegoers face a serious impediment beyond the maintenance and use of multiple methods and information. The problem boils down to access. Attending the races irregularly, infrequently, and intermittently, casual handicappers cannot stay up to snuff on the information fronts. They rarely possess updated numerical ratings of horses, and will be missing trip, bias, and trainer information that often may be decisive.

This guide has been prepared with those tens of thousands of individuals, racing's casual customers, clearly in mind. It presents methods of obtaining satisfactory numerical ratings of performance on the speed, pace, and class factors that can be implemented by reliance strictly on the *Daily Racing Form's* past performances. No excessive expenditure of time and energy will be required.

Other guidance, if pursued, can equip the casual audience with updated trip, bias, and trainer information, if not practically everything the recreational handicapper needs to know.

The ambitious purpose is to deliver to recreational handicappers everywhere a complete, state-of-the-art, integral treatment of modern handicapping's leading ideas, methods, and applications. Interested readers should come away with fundamental, in-depth knowledge, as well as strategies and procedures they can implement immediately.

The sequence of sections and topics in the book are intended to simulate the actual practice of handicapping. That is, the guide begins at the earliest stages of the handicapping process, proceeds through the steps that successful handicappers routinely complete, and concludes as racegoers of all stripes inevitably do—with the bets, and how to place them intelligently.

I dare not pretend the book's message and guideposts will place recreational handicappers on equal footing with professionals, who exist at all major tracks, or with regular dedicated hobbyists. But I do not hesitate to promise these contents will afford practitioners a precious edge on the racing crowd.

The possibility of making handsome seasonal profits while enjoying a stimulating, exciting, and interesting hobby is also real, and not a minor incentive.

No doubt many experienced racegoers will exceed their previous best efforts as handicappers after a careful reading.

Novices will receive a fast head start toward the unraveling of a complicated intellectual challenge game which nevertheless is not as complex as many beaten sages have proclaimed.

And several especially inspired devotees, I can state categorically, will end the discourse armed to the teeth for the battles to come at the racetrack, and will emerge from the bloody experiences as big brave winners. My firm salute, in advance.

We are almost ready to begin. But first a glimpse at a few of the more unpleasant realities standing staunchly in the recreational customer's path to success.

CHAPTER I

The Casual Customer's
Day at the Races

To BEGIN, let me revive an illustration of the racing customer's main problem from personal acquaintance and experience. I recall the occasion vividly.

Five years ago a now-professional but then-casual handicapper joined me for lunch and the afternoon's action in the Santa Anita Turf Club.

On arrival, and before so much as seating himself, my colleague announced he was prepared to make a major wager in the seventh race. He referred to his choice, I do not exaggerate, as the best bet of the season.

It was an allowance race at a mile for fillies & mares, 4up, that had not won once other than in maiden or claiming races. In other words, the field was restricted to older horses that had never won an allowance race.

From previous conversations and readings, my friend understood that in winter races for older nonwinners of an allowance race, consistent winners of medium-priced claiming races can sometimes enter an allowance field and win impressively. It's a fine point of class handicapping, and well taken, notably when fillies & mares are the menu.

My friend pointed to a recent winner of a $40,000 claiming race, at a mile, and pronounced the filly a standout. He suggested the odds might be generous besides, the filly switching from the claiming division to an allowance race today, an apparent rise in class.

Why do you like the filly so much? I inquired.

The class disguise aside, his excitement had been aroused because the filly had run 1:36.2 (a minute, thirty-six and two-fifths seconds) in winning the $40,000 claiming mile. Other contenders in the field were exiting an allowance contest having a final time of 1:38.2. The difference in lengths can be estimated at ten to twelve. Among horses of comparable class, the advantage seemed insurmountable.

Throwing water on his fire, I noted that the day the filly had won, the track surface at Santa Anita had been playing fast in relation to normal times. My handy notebook indicated the track indeed had been five lengths faster than normal. I suggested the filly's adjusted final time was closer to 1:37.2.

In addition, I continued, now dousing the flames completely, on the afternoon the other fillies had lost under non-winners allowance conditions similar to today's, the Santa Anita track surface had been playing slow. The surface that day had been exactly opposite, five lengths slower than normal.

That meant the other fillies' adjusted final times were closer to 1:37.2 as well.

Merely by adjusting a pair of actual times to reflect track-surface speed for the two days under study, an apparent difference of ten to twelve lengths had been reduced to no difference at all. My colleague absorbed the new information without comment, and ate his lunch.

When the seventh arrived, my friend strolled to the window and bet his much-admired filly. Instead of risking the $250 he had intended, however, he bet $20 to win.

The public odds on the $40,000 filly had leveled at 5–2, down from a morning line of 7–2.

Entering the stretch, my friend's well-placed filly launched a mild bid along the inside that fizzled just inside the eighth pole. She finished a dull fifth of seven.

It happens every race day at every racetrack in the nation.

My colleague, an abnormally bright racegoer, had no means of distinguishing the horses accurately on speed. He did not keep a file of daily track variants, a vital piece of information for handicappers. He therefore could not know that Santa Anita had been Fast 5 on one day and Slow 5 on another.

Had he not scheduled lunch with a diligent daily handicapper who did possess a file of track variants, my friend would have squandered a sizable bet on a filly having no real advantage. When the filly failed miserably, and inexcusably, my friend would have been more than disappointed. He would have been discouraged, perhaps disillusioned.

Another recreational handicapper is knocked down for the count, and has no clue as to why. Many do not come back.

THE RECREATIONAL HANDICAPPER'S MAIN PROBLEM

Casual occasional customers, alongside their more serious counterparts, here called recreational handicappers, approach a day at the races with relatively equal concerns for fun and profit.

In anticipation of the potential profit, many buy the *Daily Racing Form*. Unaware of certain complications embedded in the past performances, they pick the horses they like best, based upon the printed records.

Among various objectives, recreational handicappers want to know how fast horses have run in the past. All observe the actual times provided in the past performances. Most examine the speed ratings and track variants that appear alongside.

Unknown to racing's casual occasional customers, the clockings and speed ratings of the *Racing Form* bear only coincidental resemblance to the true speed of racehorses. More often than not, the actual times and speed ratings will be misleading, maybe grossly misleading, as with my guest.

This is the casual customer's main problem.

Using the *Form's* raw data to guide handicapping and wagering decisions, recreational customers dive headlong into confusion and error. Best bets of the day, week, and month routinely finish up the course. Recreational handicappers haven't a clue as to why.

Among the problems racegoers confront in this complicated game, none supersedes the typical customer's inability to evaluate the horses on speed.

How fast have horses in today's race run in the past? Casual racegoers just do not know.

Final times of races can be influenced by several factors, but in fundamental ways by three: (1) relative class, (2) pace, and (3) track surface. When track-surface speed predominates, final times fluctuate wildly. Abnormal times must be adjusted. Handicappers need to know how.

The early portion of Santa Anita's winter season of 1989 featured an extraordinarily fast track surface. In anticipation of winter rains that otherwise would muddy the surface, the main track had been "sealed" repeatedly by maintenance crews— meaning heavy rollers had packed down the topsoil. The effect is a hard, glib racing surface, resulting in abnormally fast running times.

Conventional track-surface speeds deviate from typical times by one, two, or three fifths of a second, but when large deviations from typical times predominate, even professional handicappers become susceptible to the biases and distortions that result. My file of daily track variants, the measure of track-surface speed, for the initial 18 racing days at Santa Anita 1989, show the track was faster than normal by a full second or more on 13 days.

When horses that won or finished close on those days returned to competition, recreational handicappers were virtually lost.

For a dramatic illustration of the casual customer's main problem, consider the past performances of the five-year-old mare Humasong, active at Santa Anita 1989.

Humasong			Gr. m. 5, by Drone—Raja's Song, by Raja Baba				
PINCAY L JR		119	Br.—Daley-Daley-Dley-WltenbrgSt (Ky)	1989 2 1 1 0			$26,250
			Tr.—Shulman Sanford	1988 16 3 4 5			$110,275
Own.—Clear Valley Stables			Lifetime 19 4 5 5 $136,525		Turf 2 0 0 1		$7,350
20.Jan89-7SA	6f :212 :434 1:083ft	*2½ 117	2½ 1½ 12 15	Pincay LJr 2 ⑥Aw35000	95-13 Humasong,FunAtTheSle,MissTwpie 8		
7.Jan89-5SA	6f :214 :444 1:093ft	2½ 117	2½ 1½ 1¹ 22½	StevensGL⁶ ⑤Aw35000	87-14 APnnylsAPnny,Humsong,SlwJnFll 10		
26Nov88-7Hol	6f :221 :46 1:123m	*9-5 115	3¹ 2½ 2hd 32½	StevensGL² ⑦Aw25000	77-25 WrningZone,Pirte'sAngel,Humsong 7		
16Nov88-8Hol	7f :214 :451 1:224ft	6½ 116	3¹ 3¹ 2hd 2hd	StevensGL³ ⑥Aw26000	90-22 NeverCeeMiss,Humasong,FlorlMgic 6		
2Nov88-5SA	a6½f ①:213 :4441:16¹fm	3 116	75½ 66½ 55½ 44½	StevensGL⁶ ⑤Aw30000	74-22 Mrn'sCourg,NvrCMss,Bolgr'sSprng 9		
20Oct88-5SA	6½f :214 :45 1:16¹ft	3 117	3¹ 41½ 31½ 31½	Baze R A¹ ⑥Aw30000	87-14 AnnvrsryWsh,Bolgr'sSprng,Hmsong 9		
20Oct88—Crowded. checked 3/16							

The record shows that Humasong won the seventh race at Santa Anita on January 20, 1989, in a final time of 1:08.3. The second-call fractional time is recorded as 43.4, absolutely blazing. Not shown, the five-furlong time was recorded as 55.4.

When Humasong returned to competition, casual racegoers at Santa Anita were influenced enormously by the rapid times. Those customers were badly misled.

Humasong did not run 1:08.3 on January 20. The mare did not even approach that clocking.

The track variant for the sprints of January 20 at Santa Anita was Fast 10, meaning final times on average were two seconds faster than normal. The pace variant was Fast 8, meaning fractional times on average were four lengths faster than normal.

Humasong actually ran closer to 1:10.3 on January 20, and set a pace to the quarter pole of 44.3.

Dozens of horses and races were characterized by the same kind of abnormally fast track variants during December and January at Santa Anita 1989. No doubt casual racegoers attending Santa Anita during February and March that season absorbed a harsh beating while attempting to sort the horses on speed and pace.

Modern speed handicapping has solved the problems inherent in the variable speed of track surfaces day to day. Updated regular handicappers can resort to concepts such as par times, projected times, track variants, adjusted times, and speed figures to estimate the true speed of racehorses. The speed and pace figures modern handicappers calculate even permit the comparisons of horses competing at different distances and at different racetracks.

The adjusted times, and associated figures, restrain informed handicappers from betting on horses that appear to have run six furlongs in 1:08.3, when in truth the horses actually ran closer to 1:10.3.

The recreational handicapper's main problem becomes a relentless predicament. The running times, speed ratings, and track variants supplied to racing's customers by the *Racing Form* simply do not signify real values. Thus the data estimate the abilities of horses poorly, permit no reliable comparisons among horses that have competed at different distances or different racetracks, and generally contribute to uninformed, unintelligent handicapping and betting, the salient reasons so many bright, alert, motivated horseplayers lose so much money so often.

The recreational customers, to extend a consolation, do not suffer alone in the maelstrom of misinformation. The unreliability of published times and speed ratings has contributed to massive confusion and misjudgment as well among racing's famous insiders.

Horsemen seem peculiarly susceptible to drawing the wrong conclusions.

When Alysheba was still immature, age three, trainer Jack Van Berg became another in a long line who would dismiss criticism of the colt's dismal times, notably at 1¼ miles, America's classic distance, by asserting loudly that final time doesn't mean a thing.

Alysheba completed the Kentucky Derby in 2:02.4, the fourth-slowest final time on record. In explanation, Van Berg assumed a predictably defensive posture regarding the horse's brilliance, or lack of it.

When Alysheba matured, age four, and recorded no fewer than three 1¼ mile clockings below two minutes, in southern California, New York, and New Jersey, emerging as an authentically brilliant champion, Van Berg apparently had changed his mind. In reaction to choruses of hurrahs saluting Alysheba's brilliant times, the trainer did not discount the praises by reminding the nation's revelers that final time doesn't mean a thing.

In fact, comparative studies of race times reveal an indisputable relationship between class levels and final times. Better horses run faster. Whether extracted from claiming races or graded stakes, the data reveal similar patterns. A perfect positive correlation exists between class and speed.

On average, claiming horses valued at $16,000 will run faster than the $12,500 kind. Stakes horses will run faster than classified allowance horses, on average. The patterns recur at every racetrack in North America. Thus a perfectly legitimate handicapping technique for assessing relative class relies upon comparisons of final times.

Unfortunately, adjusted final times estimate true speed, and therefore class, far better than actual times. The adjusted times are not readily available, not to casual racegoers, not to horsemen, not to racing officials, and not to regular handicappers without daily track variants and the savvy to use them appropriately.

Curiously, when his all-time champion was retired, in 1988, trainer Van Berg asserted his opinion that Alysheba's best race had been the Kentucky Derby, the sluggish final time notwithstanding. In that 1987 classic, Alysheba had overcome insufferable traffic trouble and near calamity in the upper stretch before gathering himself impressively and prevailing in a long, hard drive.

Here, too, Van Berg was badly mistaken.

As the adjusted times, and speed figures, of the horse's key races indicated, Alysheba was merely a good three-year-old. He was a brilliant four-year-old.

OTHER PROBLEMS FOR THE CASUAL CUSTOMERS

The unreliability of published running times and speed ratings creates a web of derivative problems for recreational handicappers.

Unable to understand why the fastest horses (seemingly), or best horses (seemingly), lose so frequently, track customers conclude (wrongly) the racing game is inherently unpredictable and unbeatable, a jumble of inconsistencies and contradictions. A sport fantastically formful, and therefore predictable, in its essential patterns, is popularly misapprehended.

Repeated attendance only serves to harden the perception that the game is a crazy quilt. Trackside conversations among veteran racegoers solidify and reinforce an attitude of haphazard results.

Soon a cultural value of the racetrack takes hold. The best means of beating the races is not with fundamental knowledge and skill, but with inside information and clever angles. The track degenerates into a rumor-and-whisper mill more outrageous than society ladies doing lunch.

A disintegrating pattern of behavior inevitably develops. Ill-equipped to distinguish horses on real abilities, recreational handicappers preoccupy themselves instead with the secondary and tertiary factors of handicapping. They bet on jockeys. They bet on trainers. They bet on weights. They bet on post positions. They bet on tote action. They bet on hunches, whim, and whisper.

Jockeys are especially overrated as handicapping aides, and terribly overbet by casual customers. The observation that racegoers are betting on horses almost begs the question.

Sometimes situational factors do rule. Understanding trainers can be equally important as judging horses. Track conditions can predominate. It's convenient to know which jockeys are hot and which are cold. But even though the circumstances of races can be decisive, as standard handicapping procedure, situational factors shrink in comparison to horses' native abilities.

Regarding special situations generally, another problem thwarting recreational handicappers is the absence of meaningful information, readily available, whenever uncommon circumstances prevail.

When it rains, horses compete in slop and mud. Pedigree data could inform racing's customers as to the sires that transmit mud-running ability and sires that do not. Mud starts, and win percentages, would fill the bill. Would that be a fundamental kind of assist?

When turf races are carded for younger developing horses—the three-year-olds and juveniles—pedigree data is greatly relevant. Which sires win with first and second starters on the grass? Recreational handicappers get no access to that information either.

When the dashes for juvenile maidens appear, both pedigree and trainer data apply. Which sires and horsemen are especially effective with first-starting two-year-olds? Recreational customers cannot obtain that information at racetracks.

Trainer effectiveness data would be prized for several major categories of performance—first starters, repeaters, stretching out, following lengthy layoffs, following claims, significant rises and drops in class. Number of starts and win percentages for the preceding calendar year would suffice. How about the instances and win percentages of particular trainers and jockeys in tandem?

That information—all of it, and much more besides—is easily accessible, but so far recreational handicappers of the information age have access to none of it.

Besides overreliance on minor handicapping factors, and a lack of telltale information about situations that arise frequently enough to matter, the casual customers suffer another problem, one so devastating in its consequences, it virtually assures the demise of the untutored majority within five years.

Recreational handicappers receive no instruction on the fundamental principles of parimutuel wagering; are provided no official means of distinguishing good bets from bad bets. The omissions have contributed to a dreadful situation whereby typical wagering habits at the nation's racetracks could not be more pitiful, more self-destructive, if the customers were betting blindfolded.

Unknown to casual customers, the handicapping purpose is to estimate horses' relative chances of winning, such that minimum fair-value odds can be established, at least with ball-park accuracy.

Morning lines published in track programs are not sufficiently serviceable. These predict how the crowd should wager, not how the horses in a field compare to one another on fundamental full-dress handicapping. Most morning lines are elaborated by racetrack employees who are not qualified as handicappers and are routinely embarrassing.

A professional, state-of-the-art betting line established for each horse in each race by an authentically talented handicapper, and published in the track's daily program, would be ideal. Recreational handicappers would be provided a basis for successful handicapping and parimutuel wagering at last.

And last, not least, there is the general and overarching ignorance. Attempting to get a grip on a difficult mental-challenge game, casual racegoers comprehend too little about the basic ingredients of handicapping—class, speed, pace, form—and how they relate to one another under varying race conditions.

It's no exaggeration to assert that American horseplayers remain the most poorly educated fans in the country on their favorite sport. Here the industry bears a terrible responsibility. The ignorance not only has cost recreational handicappers a princely sum to pursue the pastime, but also has detracted heavily from the long-applauded fun. No one of normal emotions departs the racetrack exalting in the pleasures of the pastime while simultaneously tallying the day's financial losses.

The widespread ignorance has contributed as well to a lamentable circumstance curiously indulged by the casual racing audience. The racetrack qualifies as a mine field of misinformation. Recreational handicappers can scarcely escape the booby traps.

The whispered tips and secondhand opinions dished out daily by racing's famous insiders are irredeemably worthless. No adult of the slightest intelligence, maturity, or worldliness can possibly believe otherwise. Yet the quick surreptitious conversations gather on a day at the races as does mold on living plants. A disinterested observer might conclude the shallow exchanges persist only because the legions of bewildered bettors want the infamous information to be true.

It's painfully clear how many obstacles the recreational handicappers who want to improve their knowledge, skill, and results must be prepared to overcome.

Nonetheless, the goals are noble enough. And hundreds of talented, dedicated recreational handicappers have already succeeded, at least much of the time. No one should imagine for a moment that it cannot be done.

TOWARD SUCCESSFUL RECREATIONAL HANDICAPPING

From the problems, the solutions. Of the casual customer's main problem, an ambition here is to provide a satisfactory means of estimating horses' true speed. The recommended rating procedures can be implemented by anyone with access to the past performances, supplemented by a piece of information called a par variant, which will be provided for all major racetracks.

Of the several handicapping procedures promoted in this book, only the par variants cannot be found in the *Daily Racing Form*'s past performances. These will be crucial for estimating daily track variants, indispensable to obtaining accurate estimates of speed and pace.

More broadly, on the information fronts, the latest knowledge is fully communicated here, and various original means of deciphering the past performances in a context of systematic, state-of-the-art handicapping, will be detailed. New methods of class appraisal, pace analysis, and form analysis will be described. So will procedures for recording track biases and trips. And recreational handicappers should benefit from the book's fresh techniques for analyzing turf races, an area of widespread incompetence.

This book stresses the relational character of handicapping tools, revealing which methods should work best in the various kinds of races. And the sections on everyday applications, special topics, and familiar situations guide recreational handicappers in the interpretation of handicapping ratings and other descriptive information under a comprehensive array of conditions that are standard fare in major-league racing.

The guidance on recreational betting sets the casual audience on a straight course to the windows of parimutuel wagering. It provides positive practical approaches to playing the present-day exotic wagers that afford casual racegoers an opportunity to make a healthy financial gain in the short run of a few races, a day, or a weekend. Most important, recreational handicappers learn a simple means of distinguishing good bets and bad bets, the only way skillful handicappers can beat the races in the long run.

A few definitions are important, as the text refers to the terminology repeatedly:

Good race. A finish in-the-money, or within two lengths of the winner in a sprint, within three lengths in a route

Acceptable race. A finish that beats half the field, and/or within six lengths of the winner

Big win. A win by three lengths, or more

Where additional definitions of terms are appropriate, they will be provided in the adjoining text.

For newcomers, and novices, the appendices show how best to interpret the data items contained in the past performances and results charts of the *Racing Form*, stressing their meanings for handicapping purposes.

For all recreational handicappers, other appendices supply reasonably current lists of sires that do especially well in the mud or on the turf, and of selected stakes races that draw higher quality horses than the hundreds of others.

This guide is intended as a lasting reference for racing's casual followers who believe effective handicapping is largely a function of knowledge and skill. It tells what to do, and how to do it well.

CHAPTER II

Simple Routines

A HANDICAPPING HABIT shared by racegoers is marking the past performances of the *Daily Racing Form*. The markings provide clues to the abilities of horses, as perceived by the handicapper. The habit becomes deeply instinctive. Most handicappers begin the handicapping process by marking the *Form* with numbers and symbols that represent mental codes understood solely by the individual.

The shorthand serves a number of practical purposes. It organizes a mass of data in ways meaningful to the handicapper. It guides the later phases of handicapping. It reminds practitioners of pointers they intend to emphasize. The routine is elementary, and amazingly helpful.

We begin in the same routine style.

FINDING THE "GOOD" RACES

Below are five simple routines recommended as starting points for effective handicapping. They are intended to provide first impressions of horses' relative class, early speed, current form, and trainer-jockey connections. The markings are few and minimal, and I urge recreational handicappers to afford them a tryout.

Let's consider a few of the entries for the first at Hollywood Park, May 27, 1989. It's a $10,000 claiming race at six furlongs for horses 4up, the kind of race that appears on every card in the nation. Review the conditions of eligibility first, a keenly important habit, and examine the markings for Cracksman, a seven-year-old gelding.

1st Hollywood

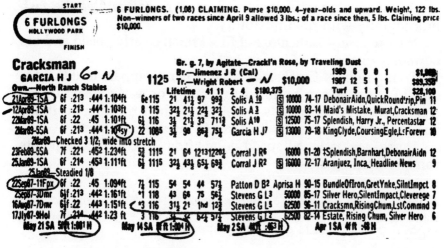

Mimic these procedures:

First, from top to bottom, review the past performances and draw a line under the running line of the most recent winning race. Cracksman last won on August 16, 1987, at Del Mar. He beat $62,500 horses that summer.

Second, move up the past performances from the latest win, and in the margin use a hash mark to identify any race that has been "good." A good race means a finish in the money, or within two lengths in sprints, within three lengths in routes.

Following its latest victory, Cracksman's next good race occurred on April 12, 1989. Note the hash mark in the left margin.

By completing two small steps, handicappers have identified the "good" performances in a horse's recent record. For horses 4up, the procedure captures each horse's relative class fairly well. Cracksman once beat $62,500 claiming horses, but now struggles against the $10,000 kind. Obviously, the gelding's relative class has plunged. Most older horses will reveal more comparable class boundaries. Regardless, handicappers get a quick fix on a horse's relative class and how closely that range of ability fits today's competition.

Also, when rating methods are used, the ratings will usually be extracted from the "good" races. These races best represent the horses' abilities and preferences. Handicappers prefer to rate horses when they have performed well, not when they have disappointed, or finished up the course.

We explore the problem of identifying contenders and finding ratable races in the next section. For now, understand that the initial markings of wins and good races handles the task procedurally with high reliability.

Next we want indicators of Cracksman's early speed and his current form.

To the right of Cracksman's name handicappers find the numeral 6. Horses can be rated accurately on early speed by assigning them speed points, based upon their running positions and beaten lengths at the first call of three recent races.

Horses are assigned speed points from zero to 8. The points can be interpreted easily:

7–8 points means high early speed

5–6 points means good early speed

4 points means acceptable early speed

0–3 points means poor early speed

Cracksman, handicappers now know, has shown good early speed. The technique for rating horses on early speed is simple to use, and will be explained later in this section.

Regarding Cracksman's form, the letter N in the designation 6–N means "neutral," and indicates Cracksman has demonstrated acceptable current form.

If the designation had been 6+, the plus sign would have suggested positive current form. More than one plus sign suggests highly positive current form, or peaking form.

If the designation had been 6–0, the zero would have suggested questionable current form. More than one zero suggests highly questionable current form.

Form standards for assigning horses a plus sign, letter N, or a zero will be explained later in this section.

Additional markings used as indicators of form are the circles drawn around the most recent race, April 21, as well as the circles drawn around the workouts Cracksman has recorded on May 2, May 14, and May 21.

The circle around April 21 indicates it has been longer than a month since Cracksman's last race. Similarly, track down the left column of the past performances and circle the dates of races that have occurred more than 30 days prior to the succeeding race. Cracksman's record indicates only one extensive layoff, a whopper, from September 22, 1987, to January 25, 1989.

Circles also signify the workouts that have occurred since the last race. Cracksman has recorded three workouts since April 21. Each is circled.

The pattern of circles embedded in a horse's past performances reflects its cycles of racing and training. Handicappers achieve a first sense as to how frequently a horse has been running and working out, whether extended layoffs have occurred, and how well horses have performed following absences of varying intervals. A horse's form cycle begins to take shape.

Handicappers will assign pluses, zeros, and the neutral letter designations to certain indicators in the racing and workout patterns, but none of the relevant plus and minus indicators appear in Cracksman's record.

Now handicappers understand that Cracksman possesses good early speed and acceptable form. The seven-year-old would not be eliminated on either fundamental.

Next to trainer Robert Wright's name in the past performances, handicappers find another letter N, for neutral. The marking indicates the horse's trainer is acceptable, and the horse should not be eliminated or discounted due to its trainer.

Trainers can also be designated as positive (+), acceptable (N), or negative (0). So can jockey switches. So can sires, owners, and breeders, whenever the situation invites marks for those contributions.

The remaining marking on Cracksman's record is the circle drawn around the *Form* symbol for the sloppy track surface of March 2. Go down the track-condition column and circle the off-track performances. A pattern of good or bad performances on off tracks often becomes immediately plain.

Employing routines and markings that can be applied mechanically in less than thirty seconds, recreational handicappers accumulate a wealth of vital information. Cracksman, handicappers know, has run well against $10,000 claiming horses at Santa Anita, possesses good early speed, is in acceptable form, and has an acceptable trainer.

Having passed muster on several fundamentals, Cracksman looms as a contender today, and must be rated in relation to other contenders in the field. As claiming horses are best evaluated by referring to the most recent wins, or good races, handicappers also know already they will rate Cracksman using his good race of April 12.

Almost invariably, the ratable races will be those getting an underline or hash marks in the first few seconds of the handicapping.

The mental activity underlying the procedures and markings handicappers apply during the earliest stage of the handicapping amounts to impressions—some strong, some weak, many ambiguous. Strong first impressions usually mean the horses do qualify as strong contenders, if not probable winners, but not always. Weak impressions usually mean the horses ultimately will be discarded, but not always. Much more spadework must be completed.

In addition, the simple routines that ignite successful handicapping and point recreational handicappers in the proper directions are decidedly simple to master. A practice effect occurs quickly. Anyone who cares can comprehend the techniques.

The remainder of this section not only provides familiarity with the recommended procedures and markings, but also the standards and logic that make the procedures meaningful. The past performances have been taken from the same race as Cracksman's.

Examine the records of La Jolla Speedster and Splendish.

La Jolla Speedster. Last won on April 1, 1988, at Santa Anita versus state-bred $10,000 claiming horses, but last four outings qualify as good races.

Good early speed. Positive form. Acceptable trainer. No workouts since last race, May 13, just 14 days ago. Last race is ratable. But so are previous two. Rating multiple races often reveals patterns of improving or declining form.

Splendish. Last won on March 22, 1989, at Santa Anita, against state-bred $12,500 claiming horses. No good races since.

Poor early speed. Acceptable form. A plus sign for trainer Noble Threewitt, among the most effective claiming trainers in southern California. No workouts since last race on May 6.

The ratable race for Splendish is the win on March 22, not the disappointing efforts against better on April 1 and May 6.

La Jolla Speedster is clearly a contender here, but is Splendish?

La Jolla Speedster

NAKATANI C S   ↙↗   **1125**
Own.—Greek Stables Inc

B. g. 6, by La Jolla Booster—Higuerita, by Figonero
Br.—Brizendine C R & Jean (Cal)   1989   4   0   3   1 $8,200
Tr.—Peterson Douglas R— ∧⌣ $10,000   1988   5   1   0   0 $7,450
Lifetime   16   2   5   1 $26,100

3May89-2Hol	6f :221 :443 1:101ft	*7-5 1115	11 11 12 2hd	Nakatani C S2	10000 90-11 RcknghrsDrm,LJllSpdstr,MtthT.Prr 8
25Apr89-1Hol	6f :221 :451 1:10 ft	*21 1105	1hd 11 11 213	Nakatani C S7	10000 89-10 FillUp,LaJollaSpeedster,LsForever 11
3Apr89-1SA	6f :212 :441 1:093ft	41 1115	33 311 22 211	Nakatani C S3 Ⓢ	10000 88-15 StrOrphn,LJollSpedstr,SilntImpct 11
3Mar89-1SA	6f :213 :443 1:094ft	83 116	631 33 331 361	Sibille R4 Ⓢ	10000 83-17 StrOrphn,SilentTrust,LJollSpedstr 12
31Mar89—Bobbled start					
20May88-5Hol	6f :222 :454 1:112ft	20 116	513 533 54 67	Meza R Q2 Ⓢ	12500 78-16 FairlyOmen,MasoBlue,Pyramiding 11
30Apr88-1Hol	6f :22 :452 1:104ft	9 118	421 531 651 561	Castanon A L4	10000 81-14 Bold Topsider, CleverCoin,Hawkley 8
13Apr88-1SA	6f :213 :443 1:104ft	3 116	54 561 67 781	Velasquez J10 Ⓢ	12500 76-22 IrishIllusion,Pyrmiding,MrkThLrk 12
13Apr88—Bobbled start, lugged in stretch					
1Apr88-1SA	6f :22 :451 1:111ft	31 116	1hd 1hd 1hd 11	Castanon AL1 Ⓢ	10000 82-21 LJllSpdstr,RmbIngMnt,SnrpyBnd 12
1Apr88—Bobbled start					
22Jan88-5SA	61f:213 :443 1:163ft	105 116	431 34 910111153	Deitrick D R3	16000 71-17 GoldenBeu,ClssicQuickie,BumBRy 12
20Dec87-1Hol	6f :22 :443 1:09 ft	55 117	21 54 711 817	Pedroza M A8	25000 80-08 IdelQulity,LodThWgon,RdwoodBoy 8

Splendish   2-∧

↑ **VALENZUELA P A**   **117**
Own.—Johnson W R

B. g. 4, by Splendid Courage—French Dish, by Beau Brummel
Br.—A J B Associates (Cal)   1989   7   1   2   1 $15,175
Tr.—Threewitt Noble — ⌣↗ $10,000   1988   15   1   2   1 $17,063
Lifetime   23   2   4   2 $33,663

6May89-1Hol	61f:22 :444 1:16 ft	7 1105	523 52 68 781	Garcia H J2	14000 87-09 WellInTheAir,ExplodedJr.,BickrBr 11
6May89—Lugged out late					
1Apr89-1SA	6f :22 :451 1:104ft	31 116	841 861 803 8131	Stevens G L8 Ⓒ c16000 70-16 HarryJr.,John'sRetret,LstCommnd 10
1Apr89—Wide					
22Mar89-1SA	6f :22 :45 1:101ft	*21 116	513 311 21 11	VlenzuelPA3 Ⓢ c12500 87-17 Splendish, Harry Jr., Percentastar 12
4Mar89-9SA	11f:454 1:102 1:424ft	21 116	751 741 751 55	Sibille R4	20000 82-12 Frisk Me Not, Aranjuez, Sun Club 9
4Mar89—Wide into stretch					
23Feb89-5SA	7f :221 :452 1:234ft	11 116	74 211 11 1nk	† Valenzuela P A1	16000 81-20 †Splendish,Barnhart,DebonairAidn 12
23Feb89—Disqualified and placed second; Lugged out drive					
1Feb89-1SA	7f :222 :451 1:23 ft	41 113	853 863 551 36	DominguzRE 12 c10500 79-15 Unrepressed,J.C.Architct,Splndish 12
12Jan89-1SA	6f :214 :444 1:093ft	15 113	853 851 35 2nd	DominguzRE 8 Ⓢ 10500 90-12 Notable Host,Splendish,StarOrphan9
29Dec88-1SA	6f :22 :444 1:092ft	45 113	853 541 351 231	DominguzRE 3 Ⓢ 10000 87-12 NkdJybird,Splndish,SwtwtrSprings 9
29Dec88—Troubled trip					
11Dec88-1Hol	61f:22 :453 1:172ft	15 113	5311051 9811101	Dominguez RE 2 10000 78-17 Alaskan Jim, CoastalLove Bortino 12
4Dec88-2Hol	1 :453 1:11 1:37 ft	15 112	121 111 411 451	DominguezRE 11 10000 73-13 Silor'sTle,NkedJybird,BoldDecree 12
Apr 27 Hol 5f ft 1:01 H	Apr 20 SA 4f ft :47 H	Apr 14 SA 5f ft :593 H		

Yes!

Any horse that races "up close" to the pace (second call) of better horses qualifies as a contender on form when dropped in class. This is a crucial form guideline which recreational handicappers routinely ignore.

Notice that on May 6 Splendish raced within two lengths of the leader at the second call of a $14,000 claiming race. Entered today for $10,000, a double drop in claiming class, Splendish's "up close" position at the pace call against much better horses qualifies it here on form. Many casual handicappers would eliminate Splendish at an early stage of the handicapping, citing two consecutive awful finishes, but that would be premature.

The standard of form called "up close" refers to a horse's beaten lengths at various points of call and varies according to distance and class. The technique is simple to comprehend, as is the procedure for rating early speed.

Before examining additional past performances, it's convenient to explain the techniques for qualifying horses initially on early speed and current form.

EARLY-SPEED POINTS

The procedure for rating horses on early speed depends upon horses' running positions and beaten lengths at the first point of call in three of their most recent five races.

The technique is called "speed points." It is surely the best procedure for evaluating horses' early speed yet developed. Speed points was invented and tested successfully by mathematician Bill Quirin, arguably the most important figure in handicapping instruction in this country. Quirin's test data revealed the importance of early speed in racing everywhere, and the likelier chances of horses having greater numbers of speed points.

The rating procedure concentrates on the running positions and beaten lengths of horses at the first call, because Quirin's studies revealed these factors far superior to fractional times as indices of reliable early speed. Three qualifying races are rated, but without referring back to more than the latest five races. Three races are rated because a series of performances represents a far better predictor of what should happen today than does any single performance.

The rules differ slightly for sprints and routes. Each horse is assigned 1 point to begin. At the end horses will have been assigned between zero and 8 speed points.

For horses in sprints, award speed points as follows:

1 point   for any sprint in which the horse ran 1–2–3 at the first call

and

1 point   for any sprint in which the horse led or ran within two lengths at the first call

0 points   for any other sprint performance

0 points   for any route performance, unless the horse led or ran within one length at the first call in which case the race is passed (not rated)

1 point   is awarded as a bonus, for any horse that led or raced within a neck of the leader in each of its rated races

–Note   any horse that did not beat half the field in any of its rated races loses the original point, for a total of zero

Exception: at seven furlongs a horse gets a point for position only if it led at the first call, but not if it ran 2nd or 3rd.

That's all. Review the rating rules and apply them to the past performances of La Jolla Speedster.

La Jolla Speedster gets two points for position and beaten lengths on May 13, and again on April 26. It gets a point April 13 for position (3rd), but not for beaten lengths (3). The total is 5, plus the original 1, or 6.

Now rate Splendish on early speed.

Splendish gets no points May 6 or April 1. He gets 1 point for beaten lengths (1¾) on March 22. The 1 point is added to the original point, for a total 2.

For horses in routes, award speed points as follows:

1 point   for any route in which the horse ran 1–2–3 at the first call

and

1 point   for any route in which the horse led or ran within three lengths of the leader at the first call

or

1 point   for any sprint in which the horse ran 1–2–3 or within six lengths of the leader at the first call

0 points   for any other route performance

1 point   is awarded as a bonus, for any horse that led or ran within one length in each of its rated races.

Note: any sprint in which the horse neither ran 1–2–3 nor raced within six lengths at the first call is passed, and the handicapper goes to the next race, never going back more than five races

As stated, the rules are easy to apply. With practice, the procedure becomes automatic, completed within seconds. A complication concerns younger, lightly raced horses having only one or two starts. Speed-point totals can be projected from the number of points already earned. Quirin recommends the following projections:

Career Starts	Speed Points					
	0	1	2	3	4	
one start	0	3	5	5	7	Projected Points
two starts	0	1	3	4	5	

Recreational handicappers are now equipped to rate all thoroughbreds on the prime factor of early speed. In the next section, on identifying contenders, we will discuss a statistically valid approach to isolating probable winners, based solely upon early speed. The profits are surprisingly generous.

THE LAST RUNNING LINE

Whether in sprints or routes, horses in sufficiently sharp form to challenge for the victory usually reach contention between the prestretch and stretch calls. Turf routes excepted, one-run winners from behind depend upon a ruinous or collapsing pace to get ahead in time.

Thus handicappers can qualify horses on form by invoking a standard of "up close" performance in the last race. The race should have occurred within the past 30 days. The "up close" position refers to the stretch call, which at all distances is the point of call before the final call.

The "up close" standard varies by distance. Here are the benchmarks:

Distance	"Up Close" Standard
up to 6½ furlongs	within 2¾ lengths
at 7F or one mile	within 3¾ lengths
at 1¹⁄₁₆M or farther	within 4¾ lengths

Two exceptions are warranted, for class and distance:

- If horses are down in class today, up close at any call in the race against better qualifies.
- If horses are entered at a shorter distance today, up close at the prestretch call of the longer race qualifies. The prestretch call is the point of call prior to the stretch call.

Horses that satisfy the "up close" standard are designated by the N symbol, for acceptable form.

To qualify for a plus designation (+) for recent performance, horses must have been "up close" at each call of the last running line.

Horses not "up close" the last race out can be assigned a zero to indicate a form defect. Handicappers should be lenient. If horses fail to qualify as "up close" by a small margin, but the last running line appears satisfactory otherwise, award the N, not a zero.

If the last running line is not representative—wrong distance, wrong footing, a troubled trip, mud—use the next-to-last running line, provided that race occurred within 30 days of the last race. Whenever the next-to-last running line is used, horses earn only an N for recent performance, never a plus.

The last running line is used to assess form as a function of recent performance. Races that occurred more than a month ago may be unreliable as predictors of current form. When evaluating form following layoffs, handicappers best concentrate on workouts.

Here the qualifying standards can be liberal, a dramatic change from a traditional conservative past.

THE WORKOUT LINE

If horses have been absent for 31 to 45 days, or four to six weeks, a four-furlong workout in the past seven days can be accepted as a sign of positive form. Award the N symbol.

Long layoffs are treated even more leniently.

If horses have been away more than 45 days, accept them on form if they show a workout of five furlongs or longer within the past 14 days. Speed of the workout is irrelevant. Slow workouts are perfectly acceptable. Length of layoff is also irrelevant.

Layoffs of six months to a year can be accepted provided horses show the five-furlong workout within the past two weeks.

If horses show a pattern of regular workouts—every five or six days, for example—the five-furlong (or longer) exercise can have occurred anytime within the past 28 days.

Furthermore, if a workout of five furlongs or longer has been best-of-morning at the operating track, as indicated by the bullet in the *Racing Form*, award a plus for form. If that kind of longer bullet workout has occurred following an improved race, award two pluses. The improved race–improved workout pattern is a strong predictor of sharp form.

Do not award the plus sign for a five-furlong workout if the conditioning occurred at a sister track on the circuit, or at a local training center. Not enough horses record longer workouts at the off-track sites to render the best-of-morning designation meaningful.

For the same reason, bullet workouts on the training track or the turf often result from a lack of action on the courses. But if the longer workouts appear relatively fast on the deeper surfaces, credit the exercise as a positive sign of form.

Horses can earn a zero for a poor workout line. If horses have been away longer than six weeks, and do not show a five-furlong workout in the past 14 days, assign them a zero, to indicate a form defect. The exception, as mentioned, is a regular series of workouts, with the five-furlong drill embedded in the pattern more than two weeks ago.

Underlying the liberal standards of acceptable form in the early stages of the handicapping is the desire not to eliminate the eventual winners prematurely. Far too many recreational handicappers, and numerous regulars as well, commit serious mistakes with the form factor. Eager to pare the field to its ultimate contention, they invoke overly strict standards of form. The rigorous standards unfortunately eliminate too many eventual winners.

Empirical investigations of form conducted by several practitioners indicate horses exhibiting merely acceptable form regularly win. Impressively improving or peaking form is a telltale ingredient of impending victory, but it is not necessary. Acceptable form wins frequently enough.

Later in the handicapping, when evaluating contenders closely, horses will be discarded on the finer points of form analysis. But early eliminations on form will be sadly mistaken too frequently. Many of the horses not only win regardless, but at generous odds, a contribution of the thousands of racegoers still attached to conservative standards of current form.

Keeping in mind the standards of "up close" performance and workouts, examine two additional past performances from the $10,000 claiming race containing Cracksman, La Jolla Speedster, and Splendish. To recall, it's May 27.

Las Forever has been away 31 days, but shows a five-furlong workout May 15 as part of a regular pattern. Moreover, the four-year-old gelding raced up close at every call of the last running line, April 26. I awarded Las Forever a plus for recent performance and an N for its workouts during the 31-day respite. No form problems here, obviously.

Master Galaxy has been absent exactly 30 days. Its last running line, April 27, occurred at an unrelated distance. The next-to-last running line occurred just eight days prior to April 27, a qualifying race at seven furlongs. The five-year-old was not "up close" at the stretch call by one-quarter length.

But Master Galaxy was up close at the prestretch call and at the finish. The horse fell back at the stretch call, due to a troubled trip, as the *Form's* notes tell.

In close situations, if horses have finished "up close" as part of a fall-back, come-again pattern, credit the performance. Master Galaxy deserves the N for acceptable recent form. The gelding also shows the required four-furlong workout for horses away four to six weeks.

The subtle variations of the form standards applied to the recent races of Las Forever and Master Galaxy introduce a fundamental precept of successful handicapping. Flexible thinking beats rigid rules. Handicappers can ill afford to be careless or capricious when applying basic guidelines, but they cannot remain stuck-in-cement either.

Notice, too, that Master Galaxy does not show a winning race or a good race in its past performances. The effort April 19 has been underlined as a ratable race because the fall-back, come-again pattern suggests the horse might have finished within two lengths of the winner if the trouble had not happened. Flexible thinking beats rigid rules.

CHECKING THE TRAINERS AND JOCKEYS

Examine the records of Las Forever and Master Galaxy again.

Next to jockey A. L. Castanon find a zero (0), to indicate Las Forever gets an unfavorable jockey switch.

Master Galaxy not only suffers an unfavorable jockey switch, the gelding has an ineffective trainer, as indicated by the zero to the right of the trainer's name.

In the early stage of handicapping, trainer-jockey defects do not eliminate horses. The circumstances are merely noted for later consideration. Ineffective trainers that win with fewer than 5 percent of their starters are truly negative factors, but the horses might earn competitive ratings regardless and be offered at tantalizing odds. Look for pluses on the form and jockey factors as compensations, especially if a weak trainer's horses will be dropping in class.

Unfortunately, Master Galaxy has earned no pluses, is not dropping in class, and arrives at today's race in marginal form. Handicappers can fairly eliminate the horse from further consideration.

Trainers and jockeys merit a plus under certain circumstances. Splendish in the example race shows a plus next to trainer Noble Threewitt for his prowess with recent claims, and a plus next to jockey Pat Valenzuela, a positive switch, especially in combination with the drop in class.

Award trainers a plus sign under these circumstances:

1. Ranks among the leaders at the meeting, as indicated by a win percent of 20% or better.
2. Has been especially effective in situations like today's, that is, with recent claims, with first starters, double jumps in claiming class on the turf, following lengthy layoffs.
3. Has been hot, as indicated by a recent win percentage roughly twice as high as normal.

Inversely, if trainers win with 5 percent of their starters, have been ineffective in situations like today's, or have been cold lately, assign them a zero.

All other trainers can be assigned the N, for acceptable, or a U, for unknown.

Award jockeys a plus sign under these circumstances:

1. Ranks among the leaders at the meeting, as indicated by a win percent of 20% or better.
2. Represents a favorable jockey switch, particularly in combination with a drop in class.
3. Has been hot lately, as indicated by a win percentage roughly twice as high as normal.
4. Is the leading apprentice, especially if employed by a trainer who wins with apprentices consistently.
5. Has a specialty well suited to today's race, such as winning on the turf, getting two-year-olds out of the gate, or riding for a specific stable when its horses are well intended.

Be cautious when assigning jockeys a zero. Riders are not nearly as significant in handicapping as are trainers, and are notoriously overcriticized. If jockeys, especially leaders, have been unequivocally cold, give them a zero. Clearly unfavorable switches also deserve a zero. So does a weak rider under testing circumstances, as in important stakes, in contentious grass races featuring classy horses, or exiting the far outside posts at middle distances on mile ovals.

Otherwise, jockeys can be assigned the N, for acceptable. Under questionable or unknown circumstances, afford jockeys the benefit of the doubt, an N.

Weak jockeys, and minor jockeys, win races every day, and many pay juicy mutuels.

Now examine a final entry in the sample race for older $10,000 claiming horses.

What do the markings reveal to handicappers about the six-year-old Gold Timbre?

It last won five and a half months ago, when favored to defeat $12,500 maiden-claiming horses at Bay Meadows.

Since the December 8 win, Gold Timbre shows one "good" race, finishing third March 19, against today's claiming class at Golden Gate Fields. If Gold Timbre is rated, its performance March 19 will be used as most representative.

Gold Timbre has 1 speed point, or poor early speed.

Gold Timbre has been away 50 days, but has acceptable form, barely, as indicated by the six-furlong workout at the Galway Downs training site on May 12.

Gold Timbre has been away from the races for 30 days or longer five times since July 1988, three times since its lone victory. Irregular races and workouts among claiming horses suggest minor, nagging ailments that prevent steady training and racing.

Gold Timbre has an acceptable trainer.

Gold Timbre has an acceptable jockey.

Is Gold Timbre the kind of contender that deserves to be rated further?

Absolutely.

With a good race at the class and no defects for form, trainer, or jockey, the horse has a right to win. Its poor early speed suggests Gold Timbre will need assistance on the pace, but that determination must be delayed until later.

No doubt numerous recreational handicappers would dismiss Gold Timbre as a tossout.

The lesson is plain. The complexities of handicapping involve the effective interpretation of information, not merely the implementation of procedures. Procedure never substitutes for thought. Procedure facilitates thought. At times procedure clarifies thought.

Now examine the past performances below, which have been marked according to the simple routines promoted here.

Is Rakaposhi a contender against $12,500 claiming horses, 4up, at 1$\frac{1}{16}$M? It's June 4, 1989.

Rakaposhi ✳
ᴧ/NAKATANI C S /‑ᴧ/ **1105**
Own.—Success Stables

B. g. 5, by Lord Avie—Hope She Does, by Mr Leader
Br.—Jones A U (Ky)
Tr.—Shulman Sanford— ᴧ/ $12,500
Lifetime 46 8 10 7 $172,800

1989 7 0 3 1 $28,925
1988 20 7 2 2 $108,050
Turf 2 0 0 0 $600

18May89-9Hol	1$\frac{1}{16}$:46³ 1:10³ 1:48³ft	6 115	6⁵ 44¼ 68¼ 610¾	Davis R G 1	20000 83-07	Addie's Bro, Mispu, KentuckyStar 12
18May89-Wide						
8Apr89-9SA	1$\frac{1}{16}$:46¹ 1:10² 1:43¹ft	*7-5 116	55½ 55½ 55 8⁸	Stevens G L 5	c25000 77-12	PlesRmit,SpndTwoBucks,K.'sChrgr 8
12Mar89-9SA	1$\frac{1}{16}$:46¹ 1:11 1:43 ft	6½ 114	54½ 31½ 2hd 2½	Stevens G L 8	45000 85-14	Ascension, Rakaposhi, My Partner 11
5Mar89-9SA	1$\frac{1}{16}$:46 1:10² 1:42 ft	4 117	65½ 64½ 63¾ 3nk	Pincay L Jr 9	c32000 91-07	Adios Girl, Armin, Rakaposhi 11
25Feb89-9SA	1$\frac{1}{16}$:46⁴ 1:11¹ 1:42¹ft	*2½ 115	2hd 1¹ 1½ 2½	Stevens G L 9	c25000 89-14	MgnumPlus,Rkposh,SpndTwoBcks 9
28Jan89-9SA	1$\frac{1}{16}$:46¹ 1:10³ 1:42³ft	3½ 116	42 3nk 2hd 22½	Stevens G L 3	25000 85-14	BooBoo'sBckroo,Rkpsh,K.'sChrgr 12
7Jan89-9SA	1$\frac{1}{16}$:46² 1:10⁴ 1:43¹ft	*2 120	43½ 53½ 42 43½	Stevens G L 1	c20000 81-14	KmpOut,ImprssvRslt,EmotonlFlyr 10
26Dec88-9SA	1$\frac{1}{16}$:46¹ 1:10³ 1:42⁴ft	*2½ 116	2hd 2hd 11½ 22	Stevens G L 2	25000 85-13	Shafy, Rakaposhi, Remar 8
9Nov88-9Hol	1$\frac{1}{16}$:46¹ 1:10² 1:42 ft	4 116	53½ 44 47½ 38¾	Baze R A 4	25000 81-11	Bizeboy, Emperdori, Rakaposhi 12
9Nov88-3Hol	1$\frac{1}{16}$:46 1:11 1:43²ft	(*1 115	31½ 2½ 1½ 11¼	Stevens G L 5	20000 83-11	Rakposhi,ExoticArbitor,K.'sChrger 8
May 5 Hol 5f ft 1:02 H						

Last victorious on November 9, 1988, Rakaposhi has disappointed four times since when favored at the $20–25,000 claiming levels. Yet Rakaposhi was beaten just a half length March 12, when entered for $45,000. He lost by a neck versus $32,000 horses in the race before that.

What to do?

First handicappers can rely on procedure.

Up close (within 4¾ lengths at 1$\frac{1}{16}$M) at the prestretch call against better on May 18—notice the underlined portion of the

May 18 running line—Rakaposhi has acceptable form (N) against $12,500 horses today.

The point is crucial, as careless handicappers might discard Rakaposhi on form here. The five-year-old has clearly declined since the $25,000 claim on April 8, but he satisfies the recent form standard nonetheless.

Rakaposhi shows numerous good races against better in recent months, and its trainer and jockey are acceptable.

Rakaposhi has poor early speed, but we prefer to discount horses having poor early speed only following a later pace analysis, not early in the handicapping. To be sure, horses can qualify as contenders by possessing good early speed and little more, but poor early speed is not an early elimination factor.

Acceptable on form versus better, Rakaposhi qualifies as a contender here and deserves to be rated.

Which "good" race should handicappers rate?

The most recent good race occurred on March 12, a second-place finish and half-length loss.

But is the March 12 race representative of Rakaposhi today?

Clearly not. The $45,00 claiming level is too far removed from the $12,500 level. If the March 12 performance were rated, the horse would certainly get the high ratings. But if Rakaposhi could duplicate those ratings, he would not be entered for $12,500.

A practical solution depends upon the most recent good race at a class level closely related to today's.

Handicappers who consider the $20–25,000 claiming levels essentially interchangeable at Santa Anita—where these horses are—would likely rate the second-place finish of February 25. If the $25,000 claiming class were judged too steep, handicappers might rely on the winning race at $20,000 at Hollywood Park on November 9. Recency counts with claiming horses, but reliance on recency has been complicated here by a pattern of deteriorating form.

To find the ratable races, look first at the most recent good race.

If that race is not representative of today, find the most recent good race versus a class level closely related to today's.

Ah, the complexities! Identifying the contenders and finding the ratable races endures as one of the thorniest problems recreational handicappers confront.

Rakaposhi won the $12,500 race, despite the horse's declining form. Consult the result chart.

FIRST RACE
Hollywood
JUNE 4, 1989

1 1/16 MILES. (1.58) CLAIMING. Purse $12,000. 4-year-olds and upward. Weight, 122 lbs. Non-winners of two races at a mile or over since April 16, allowed 3 lbs.; such a race since then, 6 lbs. Claiming price $12,500; if for $10,500, allowed 2 lbs. (Races when entered for $9,000 or less not considered.) 31st DAY WEATHER. CLOUDY TEMPERATURE 68 DEGREES.

Value of race $12,000; value to winner $6,600; second $2,400; third $1,800; fourth $900; fifth $300. Mutuel pool $348,413.

Last Raced	Horse	Eqt	A.	Wt	PP	St	1/4	1/2	3/4	Str	Fin	Jockey	Cl'g Pr	Odds $1
18May89 ^{9}Hol^{6}	Rakaposhi	b	5	110	7	3	3^{hd}	3^{1}	2^{1}	1^{hd}	1^{hd}	Nakatani C S^{5}	12500	2.60
17May89 ^{1}Hol^{5}	Prince Hoedown	b	5	115	4	5	7	6^{1}	$6^{3\frac{1}{2}}$	2^{3}	2^{6}	Stevens G L	12500	5.50
18May89 ^{9}Hol^{8}	Beret Scout	b	5	117	1	7	6^{hd}	7	7	6^{7}	$3^{2\frac{1}{2}}$	Pincay L Jr	12500	4.60
18May89 ^{2}Hol^{1}	Percentastar		6	121	2	6	5^{3}	$5^{3\frac{1}{2}}$	$3^{\frac{1}{2}}$	3^{2}	4^{2}	Valenzuela P A	12500	3.30
17May89 ^{1}Hol^{2}	Mt. Erin		4	118	3	4	$4^{1\frac{1}{2}}$	4^{1}	$5^{1\frac{1}{2}}$	5^{hd}	$5^{4\frac{1}{2}}$	Black C A	12500	3.70
18May89 ^{10}GG^{6}	Famillion		8	118	6	2	2^{1}	$2^{\frac{1}{2}}$	1^{1}	4^{1}	$6^{8\frac{1}{2}}$	Davis R G	12500	8.90
7May89 ^{1}Hol^{10}	Chili Hill	b	6	115	5	1	$1^{1\frac{1}{2}}$	$1^{\frac{1}{2}}$	4^{hd}	7	7	Cedeno A	12500	25.80

OFF AT 1:33 Start good. Won driving. Time, :23 3/5, :47 1/5, 1:11 3/5, 1:37 2/5, 1:57 3/5 Track fast.
New track record.

Official Program Numbers

$2 Mutuel Prices:			
7-RAKAPOSHI	7.20	4.40	3.20
4-PRINCE HOEDOWN		5.40	3.40
1-BERET SCOUT			3.00

B. g, by Lord Avie—Hope She Does, by Mr Leader. Trainer Shulman Sanford. Bred by Jones A U (Ky).

RAKAPOSHI, close up early, battled for command through the final furlong while inside PRINCE HOEDOWN and narrowly prevailed. PRINCE HOEDOWN, devoid of early speed, rallied to take on RAKAPOSHI a furlong out, battled for command through the last furlong while outside that rival and lost a close decision. PRINCE HOEDOWN'S rider lost his whip a furlong out when it was inadvertenly knocked out of his hand by the rider of RAKAPOSHI. BERET SCOUT, devoid of early speed, improved his position after six furlongs but failed to menace and was four wide into the stretch. PERCENTASTAR, outrun early but not far back and wide down the backstretch, was close up around the far turn, continued close up in the upper stretch, then gave way in the last furlong. MT. ERIN, close up early, gave way. FAMILLION, prominent through the early stages, faltered. CHILI HILL had early speed, stopped and was five wide into the stretch.

Owners— 1, Success Stables; 2, X J Stable; 3, Blincoe M D; 4, Winkleman A P; 5, Stanford Ranch Statle; 6, Johnson-Kuebler-Zeis; 7, Lentz D P & Christine.

Trainers— 1, Shulman Sanford; 2, Lewis Craig A; 3, Blincoe Tom; 4, Mitchell Mike; 5, Ellis Ronald W; 6, Washington William; 7, Lentz David P.

To complicate the situation even more, I must now advise recreational handicappers everywhere that Rakaposhi, and horses like him, are notoriously poor bets.

Should handicappers have rated Rakaposhi? Absolutely.

Should handicappers have bet Rakaposhi to win. Absolutely not.

The horse was overbet—the favorite, no less—and given Rakaposhi's suspicious form, he cannot be supported at the odds. For now, to explain, recreational handicappers should simply understand that for every Rakaposhi that wins, four manage to lose. Thus, to bet at low odds is to bet an underlay, a horse whose chances are not as strong as its odds suggest.

If Rakaposhi had been 5–1 on June 4, 1989, he would have represented a fair bet. If he had been 8–1 or greater, Rakaposhi would have represented an excellent bet. So horses like Rakaposhi must be rated, but they need not be bet.

The complexities of handicapping include a balancing act between the chances horses will win and the odds offered on those probabilities. It's an underestimated aspect of the casual practitioner's game, and a serious one, which we will deal with at length in the section on money management and betting.

As the handicapping process continues, additional markings will be recommended.

First, we turn full attention to the initial phase of handicapping, and a disturbing source of confusion, not only among recreational handicappers, but among too many veteran handicappers besides.

CHAPTER III

Identifying Contenders
and Selecting Ratable Races

SEVERAL SEASONS PAST, I received an emergency call from Howard Sartin, leader of a national club of pace analysts whose ultimate influence on the practice of handicapping in this country may be profound.

The group, Sartin said, was using a pair of computer programs to separate contenders with extraordinary reliability. Win percentages of some members proved abnormally high, 63 percent or better, when the top two horses in a ranking of five were bet to win.

The problem bothering too many members was identifying the real contenders to begin with, and selecting the races in the recent record to be rated. The computer programs performed most efficiently when ranking five contenders, but numerous Sartin practitioners had trouble isolating the likeliest five. Often the eventual winners had been left out. Sartin had read *The Handicapper's Condition Book* and thought the material pertinent to the problem.

Would I talk to the membership on identifying contenders and selecting ratable races?

Gladly.

The task seemed elemental. After all, the trick of successful handicapping was separating contenders, not finding them. All outstanding handicappers of my acquaintance qualified as experts on identifying contenders. With experience, competent practitioners could apply the skill intuitively with 80 percent proficiency, at least for the bettable races. These leading practitioners sorted themselves out on the art of picking winners, not contenders.

It intrigued me that the Sartin experience had transposed the dual objectives of handicapping so diametrically. Here was a practical situation where the winners might be isolated with remarkable consistency, if only the authentic contenders could be similarly identified.

How many grizzled handicappers would benefit by an exchange of that kind? Solve my headaches by sorting the winners, they would propose, and I'll supply you with the contenders of every predictable race.

On this dichotomy of recreational handicapping, I have changed my mind. A task that registered at first as readily manageable proved annoyingly difficult. The presentations proved wide-ranging and repetitive, yet the problems persisted. As my acquaintance with the Sartin practitioners lengthened, I became increasingly aware the crucial objectives of identifying contenders and selecting ratable races elude many recreational handicappers to a degree I had not before imagined. The mistakes, furthermore, are basic.

Mistakes of class appraisal and form analysis are especially nettlesome. Horses that fit the race conditions well are eliminated as outgunned. Perfectly acceptable rises in class are disallowed. Suspicious drops in class are overlooked. Horses in acceptable form, particularly following layoffs, are summarily discarded, presumably not in winning condition. Alternately, clearly deteriorating form is accepted, perhaps on the basis of races completed months ago.

The interaction of class levels and form cycles arouses a seemingly ceaseless outpouring of interpretation problems.

Special circumstances are routinely bungled as well. Sprinters stretching out are forsaken as unsuited to the distance.

Claiming horses moving into allowance conditions, and the converse, nonclaiming horses dropping into claiming races, are not comprehended well.

The peculiarities of developing three-year-olds, notably in relation to horses 4up, become problematic.

The relative quality of stakes races, and of stakes races in relation to overnight races, is misjudged. The consequences of troubled trips, positive and negative, are not carefully evaluated.

The laundry list is large. The pratfalls are hardly characteristic of a private club of Sartin handicappers, but of casual practitioners at large. Numerous factors and circumstances can combine to complicate the handicapper's chore of isolating contenders and of finding the races that best represent those contenders' abilities.

The multiplicity of handicapping factors and situations that apply also explains the elusive nature of the problem. No formal set of guidelines covers the bases. No systematic method can be applied relentlessly. No strict rules will be unswervingly serviceable, except as they might be broken.

The task is far less susceptible to systematic procedure than to the application of a broad, diverse array of knowledge and skill in handicapping. The more handicappers understand about the multitudinous topics of handicapping, the more effectively they will isolate the authentic contenders consistently.

In the Sartin surroundings the computer programs perform most powerfully in the hands of the most complete handicappers. Even as the programs enhance competence, competent handicappers enhance the programs' effectiveness. Those practitioners would flourish by implementing any demonstrably effective methodology, if more so with the powerful Sartin tools.

The Sartin methodology attracts a large number of less complete, relatively uneducated, unsophisticated practitioners as well. Those practitioners struggle, notwithstanding the power of the method's computer programs. They stumble about repeatedly when identifying contenders, or selecting ratable races, or interpreting the printouts.

Impressively, Sartin's methodology can be potent enough to protect even untalented, uncommitted practitioners from a ruinous downside. Untutored practitioners may even win, for a time. But the only lasting solution to the problem of identifying contenders and ratable races with 80 percent proficiency is a better, broader education in handicapping. Rigid rules do not apply, only general knowledge and skill.

And so it is with recreational handicappers everywhere.

The sections that follow deal carefully with the significant factors handicappers will most frequently rely upon to identify a race's main contention. Selection guidelines will be promoted. The nuances and subtle variations of the basic guidelines, however, are plentiful. Those subtleties will be understood best by recreational handicappers who combine these contents with additional study and repeated experiences.

THE IMPORTANCE OF EARLY SPEED

All racegoers sense the advantages of early speed. Few appreciate how decisive the factor can be. The advantage is not merely tactical, avoiding traffic and trouble, but substantive. Speed is the hallmark of thoroughbred class, by far the crucial attribute of a racehorse. Early speed may prove cheap, stopping when pressed, but horses having it win significantly more than their fair share of the races. In cheap races, to be sure, cheap speed prevails. Where speed biases or rail biases predominate, early speed predominates. When closers encounter traffic or trouble, speed horses benefit.

The facts, as revealed by probability studies of thousands of races nationwide, are provocative.

1. Horses alone on the lead win 2½ times their fair share of the races, regardless of distance.
2. Horses alone on the lead of sprints at six furlongs (or less) win three times as many races as they should.
3. Horses alone on the lead in long sprints at 6½ and seven furlongs win half again as many races as they should.
4. Horses alone on the lead of routes from a mile to 1¼ miles win more than twice as many races as they should.
5. In sprints of six furlongs (or less) horses that are running 1–2–3 at the first call win twice as many races as they should.
6. In long sprints and routes, horses that are running 1–2–3 at the first call win slightly more than 1½ times the number of races they should.

These statistics are dynamite. Even more. The same studies reveal horses that won after taking a clear lead returned average odds of 4–1.

The figure is deceptive, as predicting which horses will be clear on the lead can be problematic. Speed horses can experience mishaps out of the gate, break sluggishly and be outrun early, or simply not fire. The anticipated pace duel does not develop. Another horse, or one horse, inherits an easy lead, unpredictably, and pays an unexpected dividend.

Although the guts of the early speed invariably figures as

part of a race's main contention, recreational handicappers entertain a number of common practices with speed horses that qualify as myths.

First, early speed is most predictable as a function of position and beaten lengths at the first call. It is *not* predicted reliably from prior fractional times.

The surface speeds of racetracks differ. A fractional time of 22.2 at Calder might be faster than 21.4 at Hialeah or Gulfstream, to cite the Florida circuit. In New York, Aqueduct's circumference is 1⅛M, Belmont Park's 1½M, and Saratoga's 1M. In Chicago, Arlington Park is 1⅛M, Hawthorne 1M, and Sportsman's Park a ⅝M bullring. In southern California, Hollywood Park is now 1⅛M, Santa Anita 1M, and Del Mar 1M.

Do handicappers imagine track circumferences might contribute to variations in fractional times among the same population of horses? They do.

Moreover, changes of weather or changes of track-maintenance procedures contribute to variations in running times at the same track week to week, if not more frequently.

Reliance on fractional times to predict the early speed, or the speed of the speed, results too often in upset. Handicappers best rely on position and beaten lengths at the first call, as does the speed-points technique recommended in this book.

By this technique horses possessing "good" early speed, 5 speed points or greater, qualify as contenders.

A second myth about early speed, far more serious, regards the presence of speed duels and the supposed results. Most racegoers believe that horses engaging in speed duels will weaken one another, such that each reduces the chances of the other. This is patently untrue.

Studies of horses paired in speed duels, within a half length of each other but at least two lengths clear of the pack, revealed that one of the two wins approximately 40 percent of the races, almost twice as many victories as probabilities would expect.

In addition, winners surviving speed duels pay generous mutuels. The crowd expects the two will destroy one another, but they do not. One of the two frontrunners survives the duel and wins the race.

Distance does make a difference when analyzing speed duels. Sprints of six furlongs have proved twice as advantageous to horses in speed duels as routes. Fighting frontrunners win slightly more than their fair share of routes, but not significantly more.

Handicappers cannot dismiss routers that should tangle in speed duels, but no extra credit is warranted. Long sprints are not as accommodating to speed duels as sprints of six furlongs, but a real advantage remains.

A third myth suggests the speed of the speed, or fastest horse, should be preferred when a rapid early-speed duel figures to be contested by three horses or more. Wrong.

The likeliest winner in a hotly contested speed duel engaging several horses is the horse whose running style throughout its past performances shows (a) it has won when pressed during the first two calls, and (b) it has won when rated behind the early speed for the first two calls.

If speed types insist upon securing the early lead as a matter of running style, if they cannot be rated kindly as the pace demands, their chances diminish whenever several frontrunners will battle for the lead. Faster three-year-olds of winter, spring, and summer are especially prone to this fate. Not as a result of two-horse duels, remember, but a strongly contested early duel that features more than two horses.

Horses that earn 8 or 7 points by the speed-points technique, as a result of continually dashing for the lead at the first call, can be presumed susceptible to severe prolonged challenges by other frontrunners. If more than a single horse in the field has earned 8 or 7 speed points, examine the total records.

Has the horse won when pressed early?

Has the horse relaxed behind the early speed when the race has been rapidly and severely contested throughout the first two calls?

The versatile, competitive speed horses deserve extra credit. Alternatively, frontrunners that have never lasted when pressed, winning only when unmolested at every call, can be discounted. So can speedballs that have indicated they cannot be rated behind other horses.

Another miscue casual handicappers commit every racing day regards horses without early speed. The obstacles closers must overcome is reflected undeniably in their probability statistics.

In sprints of six furlongs, horses composing the rear half of the field win approximately 35 percent of their rightful share of the races.

In long sprints and routes, the rear half wins 50 percent of its fair share. In these cases, handicappers who insist the closers possess a compensating edge on class or pace, sometimes both, will be working with the percentages, not bucking them.

No early speed, however, does not amount to a disqualification. One convenient double-check determines whether horses exhibiting poor early speed (zero to 3 speed points) should be accepted for further study.

Examine the past performances for the pair of sprinters below? Which is the authentic contender? It's June 4.

5th Golden Gate

6 FURLONGS. (1.07⅗) ALLOWANCE. Purse $20,000. 4-year-olds and upward, which have not won $3,000 other than maiden, claiming, starter or classified handicap. Weight, 122 lbs. Non-winners of a race other than claiming since March 15 allowed 3 lbs.

Rusty Attitude
B. g. 4, by Rusty Rooster—Mystic Mood, by Exalted Rullah
Br.—English J (Cal)
MAELFEYT B J   119   Tr.—Johnson Robert H
Own.—English J
Lifetime   12 3 1 1 $30,663

1989 4 0 1 1 $9,900
1988 8 3 0 0 $20,763

Tabletown
B. g. 4, by Never Tabled—For Seen, by Anticipating
Br.—Klein-Sarkowsky-Wygod (Ky)
WARREN R J JR   119   Tr.—Utley Doug
Own.—Ward Trust-Hockaday-Utley
Lifetime   8 1 2 2 $18,525

1989 1 0 0 1 $2,400
1988 7 1 2 1 $16,125

Ninety-nine of a hundred recreational handicappers would accept Rusty Attitude as a contender, but not Tabletown. The ninety-nine got it backward.

The casual handicapper recognizes an impressive stretch drive last out by Rusty Attitude, resulting in a second, beaten a half length, a good race. That performance was as recent as May 21, two weeks ago.

Tabletown has not competed since January 6, five months ago. He has beaten only maidens. Out.

The conventional practice is desperately wrongheaded. Rusty Attitude has little chance here, but Tabletown might win in a breeze.

To appreciate the reasoning, handicappers must first understand the stretch gain is greatly overrated. As persuasively shown by probability statistics, neither the stretch gain nor the stretch loss are very significant as signals of improving and declining form. Not many practitioners have internalized the point. The impressive stretch gain, in particular, is notoriously misapprehended.

Now to the present point. With zero speed points, or a few, sprinters are not redeemed by a stretch gain resulting in a good race, unless they were up close—within 2¾ lengths of the leader—at the prestretch call.

The "up close" position at the second call represents striking position. Closers prevail in sprints from there, but not from far back. To set a standard, look for 4 speed points at the prestretch calls in the last three ratable races.

Reexamine Rusty Attitude's positions at the prestretch calls of its races, as indicated by the vertical lines. For his last three sprints, Rusty Attitude earns 2 speed points at the prestretch calls. Not enough. And not a likely winner.

Tabletown advances to striking position in most of his sprints. Not counting the January 6 race, when he stumbled, Tabletown earns 5 speed points at the prestretch calls for the previous three sprints. Away since January 6, Tabletown not only qualifies on form (N) by showing a five-furlong workout or longer within the past 14 days, he gets a plus for recording a best-of-morning workout at six furlongs on May 29 at the host track. Contender.

Beginning now, recreational handicappers can discount the stretch gains of come-from-behind horses in sprints, and instead evaluate their positions at the prestretch calls. Closers that reach striking position by then qualify on early speed. Those that do not are best abandoned.

The same reasoning applies to closers in routes, but with a fascinating twist. Examine the pair of past performances below. Which horse might stay, which must go? It's June 4, 1989.

1st Hollywood

1 3-16 MILES
HOLLYWOOD PARK
START FINISH

1 3/16 MILES. (1.58) CLAIMING. Purse $12,000. 4-year-olds and upward. Weight, 122 lbs. Non-winners of two races at a mile or over since April 16, allowed 3 lbs.; such a race since then, 6 lbs. Claiming price $12,500; if for $10,500, allowed 2 lbs. (Races when entered for $9,000 or less not considered.)

Beret Scout
PINCAY L JR 115
Own.—Blincoe M D
B. g. 5, by Don Roberto—So Pleasant, by Djakao
Br.—RittenberryRS&DoubleEglStb (Ky)
Tr.—Blincoe Tom $12,500
Lifetime 14 1 1 3 $17,800
1989 7 1 1 2 $11,875
1988 5 M 0 1 $6,325
Turf 1 0 0 0

18May89-9Hol 1⅛ :463 1:103 1:483ft 15 115 99½ 87¼ 911 811¼ Baze R A 8 20000 83-07 Addie's Bro, Mispu, KentuckyStar 12
18May89—Wide into stretch
22Apr89-10SA 1 1/16 :463 1:113 1:443ft 16 120 99¾ 75½ 44½ 31 Sibille R 1 12500 77-17 Mt. Erin, Tricky Lad, Beret Scout 9
9Apr89-10GG 1⅜ Ⓣ:481 1:383 2:174fm 11 111 913 85¼ 87 77¾ Lambert J 1 H12500 69-21 GllntHwk,Chinoiserie,IHerdAVoic 10
9Apr89—Jumped dark spot entering stretch both times
17Mar89-10GG 1⅛ :472 1:111 1:482ft 15 110 53 53¼ 32½ 21½ Lambert J 8 H12500 81-16 GallantHwk,BeretScout,Chinoiserie 8
17Mar89—Lugged in 3/16
3Mar89-4GG 1⅛ :461 1:121 1:53 ft *1 119 917 79 32 13½ Lambert J 8 M12500 60-23 Beret Scout, Barnstormer,Ol'Elmo 10
15Feb89-2SA 1 1/16 :471 1:122 1:45 ft 17 118 1110 109½ 97¼ 910¼ Toro F 8 M45000 66-17 TurnAndPrss,CorondoBy,RmboSt 12
15Feb89—Wide
3Feb89-6GG 1 :461 1:111 1:38 sy 7¾ 119 67 57 44½ 33¾ Lambert J 5 Mdn 71-26 CscdeGold,SuperSurgeon,BrtScout 6
15Dec88-6Hol 1 :45 1:101 1:36 gd 63 119 1015 912 77½ 44½ Ortega L E2 M45000 77-18 Exclr'sSpcl,CorondBy,MjstcSght 10
7Dec88-1Hol 1 1/16 :47 1:124 1:453ft 50 121 107½ 85¼ 77¼ 510½ Gryder A T12 M32000 61-17 AbleMove,ApacheMagic,Winecpde 12
7Dec88—Wide stretch
27Feb88-4SA 1 1/16 :471 1:113 1:443ft 99 1145 89 711 614 514¾ Ortiz M F Jr6 Mdn 63-17 ThirtyGrand,Daloma,FortunteHour 10
May 16 SA 3f ft :37 H May 10 GG Ⓣ 5f fm 1:014 H (d) May 3 GG Ⓣ 3f fm :372 H (d) Apr 19 SA 4f ft :482 H

Prince Hoedown
STEVENS G L 115
Own.—X J Stable
Ch. g. 5, by Elegant Prince—Miss Hoedown, by Dance Lesson
Br.—Thatcher Christine C (Cal)
Tr.—Lewis Craig A $12,500
Lifetime 22 4 3 7 $58,610
1989 5 0 2 0 $8,725
1988 10 2 0 4 $29,613
Turf 2 1 0 0 $9,350

17May89-1Hol 1⅛ :464 1:102 1:493ft *3¼ 115 810 88¼ 511 510 Solis A 5 12500 79-11 SpedyShnnon,Mt.Erin,Convincing 11
17May89—Bumped 1/8
30Apr89-3Hol 1 1/16 :463 1:11 1:431ft 4¾ 116 88¼ 65¼ 39½ 24 Solis A 9 12500 88-13 Mispu,PrinceHoedown,WellInThAir 9
22Mar89-9SA 1⅛ :463 1:11 1:502ft 4¾ 116 78 68 56½ 68 Baze R A 7 c[illegible] 72-17 Sweetest Song,Tablado,Ack'sReply 8
22Mar89—Bobbled start
20Feb89-9GG 1⅛ :481 1:122 1:503ft 3¼ 119 1hd 2hd 1hd 2nk Kaenel J L 6 [illegible] 72-21 Nl'sAffir,PrincHodown,WondrPlum 7
4Feb89-9SA 1 1/16 :47 1:123 1:47 sy 4¾ 118 713 57½ 47 410¾ Baze R A 2 20000 55-30 Hagley'sLion,Bigbdndmen,ChryJoy 8
4Feb89—Wide into stretch
17Dec88-7BM a1⅛ Ⓣ 1:491fm 15 117 42½ 41½ 2½ 1¾ Kaenel J L 7 A25000 89-15 PrincHodown,Plottng'sHost,Monro 9
1Dec88-8BM 1 :462 1:111 1:372ft 10 117 75½ 74¾ 33 41½ Lambert J 1 32000 80-25 FrstOnThLn,Scrpbook,FlyngLutnnt 7
1Dec88—Awarded third purse money; Ducked out start
13Nov88-6BM 1 1/16 :47 1:113 1:44 ft 6¼ 117 2hd 2hd 2½ 3nk Lambert J 7 25000 72-25 HotMetl,YehMeDo,PrinceHoedown 7
4Nov88-10BM 1 :454 1:10 1:354ft 11 117 95¾ 87¾ 813 712¾ Lambert J 4 Aw18000 76-19 DimondBnk,VrietyExprss,Brb'sRlic 9
4Nov88—Crowded 1/4
22Oct88-7BM 6f :223 :452 1:093ft 11 117 99¼ 98¾ 78 65¼ Lambert J 2 25000 86-16 Stn'sBower,GllntShootr,SuprmStnd 9
May 24 Hol 5f ft 1:003 H Apr 16 SA 6f ft 1:143 H Apr 8 SA 4f ft :483 H

Each five-year-old gelding raced two weeks ago, unimpressively. Each has an acceptable trainer. Each switches to a leading rider today. Neither possesses early speed or an acceptable last running line. Checking the prestretch calls, neither horse establishes satisfactory striking position (4 speed points or better). Each earns zero speed points. A tough call for handicappers?

Prince Hoedown is the reject.

Beret Scout rarely establishes striking position at the prestretch calls of routes. Beret Scout is an authentic closer, and the closers of routes should not be penalized on early speed for running style. Closers of routes often have enough time to get there.

Prince Hoedown is a different sort. Not an authentic closer, the horse merely shows no run to the prestretch call lately. He gets zero speed points at that call for his last three routes.

But prior to that, Prince Hoedown in four of six routes did establish favorable striking position at the prestretch calls. His lack of prestretch speed of late can be accepted as an expression of declining form, not as a function of running style. The declining form should be recognized. Out.

As a rule, if come-from-behind horses in routes often establish striking position at the prestretch call, but in recent tries have been far back there, throw them out. The stretch gain does not redeem them. They have tailed off.

So horses without early speed (zero to 3 speed points) can qualify on early speed if they race up close at the prestretch call.

If not, and the race is a sprint, handicappers can eliminate them.

If not, and the race is a route, check the prestretch calls to see whether the condition represents declining form or running style. Bad form goes, running style stays, until a pace analysis can be completed.

Several horses that qualify as contenders on early speed, of course, can be eliminated from further consideration once a few appropriate standards of acceptable form and relative class have been applied. Below are the initial guideposts.

STANDARDS OF ACCEPTABLE FORM

Anxious to relieve recreational handicappers of the unwieldy complications inherent in thoroughbred form cycles, this book takes a firm liberal stance. In the initial stage of the handicapping, when identifying contenders, standards of form must be relaxed. Bad-form horses must virtually eliminate themselves.

The purpose is to avoid discarding the eventual winners because they fail to satisfy narrow, rigid standards of fitness. Empirical studies that have observed the characteristics of form associated with winners indicate many of them triumph even when current condition appears far from peaking or improving by traditional standards.

Moreover, horses in obviously good form, the peaking and impressively improving types, are notoriously overbet. Many win as underlays, the handicappers who hold the tickets not receiving fair value from the cashiers. Horses in acceptable but undistinguished form win enough, and pay more, often more than they should.

Applying strict standards of form early on has never made convincing handicapping sense besides. A tremendously dynamic factor, thoroughbred form varies subtly or substantially numerous times throughout a horse's career, and several times a season. The changes—negative patterns especially—are difficult to decipher with confidence.

Trainers differ markedly in their conditioning regimens as well. Many take an individualized approach to a barnful of horses. Some horses prefer to work fast, some slow. Some frequently, some infrequently. Some in company, some alone. Some short, some long. The variations are impossible to assimilate or to organize into predictable patterns. Strict standards and conservative guidelines will be unable to account for the exceptions, which will be manifold, resulting in a cavalcade of premature errors.

The appropriate place for a rigorous assessment of current form is late in the handicapping, when contenders closely matched on speed, class, pace, and other fundamentals must be distinguished further.

At that point, horses in peaking, improving, and acceptable form can be classified respectively, the horses in the best condition obtaining greater respect. Other horses in questionable, obscure, or inconclusive form can be discounted.

An in-depth practical understanding of form cycles contributes to a kind of final decision-making. A journeyman's knowledge of form is sufficient to begin.

In the preceding section, an "up close" requirement for recent performance, and workout standards following layoffs, were presented as indicators of acceptable form. Horses that satisfy those loose requirements qualify as contenders on form. If recreational handicappers will implement the guidelines, they will eliminate few winners prematurely, without becoming careless or capricious.

Here again are the broad guidelines that apply. Among horses that have competed in the past 30 days, any are acceptable on form if they:

a. Have been up close at the stretch call against the same or a lower class
b. Have been up close at any call against a higher class
c. Are entered in a sprint and have been up close at the prestretch call of a route race

The definition of the "up close" standard varies with distance, and can be found on page 36.

Among returnees from layoffs of four to six weeks, form is acceptable if horses have worked out twice in the interval, or once at four furlongs (or longer) within the past 7 days.

Among horses returning from layoffs longer than six weeks, regardless of duration, form is acceptable for any that show a five-furlong workout or longer within the past 14 days. The speed of the workout is not relevant.

A five-furlong bullet workout deserves extra credit. The extra attention will be significant at medium-sized and smaller tracks, where a longer workout represents a more vital sign of health and readiness. Horses at major tracks train at five furlongs or longer routinely. Bullet workouts are reassuring, but better horses can train speedily whenever asked to do so.

What about horses tagged with a form defect (zero) for recent performance or layoffs? Does the zero mean instant elimination?

Lengthy layoff horses that do not flash the five-furlong workout in the past two weeks can be eliminated. Horses returning from four to six weeks of rest can be tolerated, provided they have impressed following similar respites.

The last running line and "up close" standard can present a few complications.

To recall, if the last running line is unrepresentative, due to class barriers, troubled trips, mud, and so forth, handicappers can accept up close in the next-to-last race, provided that race occurred within six weeks.

Also, the fall-back, come-again performance is acceptable, provided the horse finished up close.

Sometimes the last running line will be atypically awful. Perhaps the horses finish last, or near the rear, at the first call, and never raise a gallop. Consider the past performances below, of a horse in a $6250 claiming route.

Icouldatoldyouso — Ch. g. 4, by Singular—Mrs Holiday, by Gun Song
GHAPMAN T M — 117 — Br.—Siegel Jan (Fla) — Tr.—Paasch Christopher — $6,250
Own.—Curless N & Mary
Lifetime 23 4 3 3 $22,101

1989	8 1 1 1	$9,238
1988	14 3 2 2	$12,863
Turf	1 0 0 0	$275

29Apr89-9GG	1⅛	:47^4	1:12	1:51^{1}ft	5	119	11^{13} 11^{10} 11^{13} 11^{13}	Warren R J Jr 3	6250	56-18	ShadowsFll,StrVesco,NordicLight	11
29Apr89—Bumped start												
16Apr89-1GG	1$\frac{1}{16}$	:47^1	1:11^3	1:44^{1}ft	4¾	119	7^9 7$^{7\frac{1}{2}}$ 4$^{5\frac{1}{2}}$ 4^3	Warren R J Jr 7	8000	75-13	Dncr'sBuck,MiSuR,Grgg'sCommnd	7
16Apr89—Steadied 1/4												
6Apr89-5GG	1½ Ⓣ	:49	2:07^2	2:33^{3}fm	6¼	115	7^{13} 8$^{5\frac{3}{4}}$ 9$^{5\frac{3}{4}}$ 5$^{9\frac{3}{4}}$	Warren R J Jr 6	H6250	59-25	MelncolieFllow,Fluctut,MusiclWltz	9
24Mar89-9GG	1½	:47^2	2:06^1	2:34^{1}gd	6¼	115	9^{12} 5^5 3^2 2^2	Warren R J Jr 6	H6250	74-27	MlncolFllow,Icouldtoldyoso,FlyUp	10
8Mar89-3GG	1$\frac{1}{16}$	:47	1:11^4	1:45^{1}sy	7	119	6^{13} 6$^{8\frac{1}{2}}$ 6^6 4$^{2\frac{3}{4}}$	Patton D B 6	10000	70-21	HaloExpress,GumFleet,DnielDoone	7
26Feb89-6GG	1$\frac{1}{16}$	:48^2	1:12^3	1:44^{2}ft	9¾	110^5	7^9 7$^{6\frac{3}{4}}$ 7^7 6$^{8\frac{1}{2}}$	Wooten J W 3	10500	68-18	Plum Rich, Renzo, Cactus Clipper	7
26Feb89—Bobbled start												
5Feb89-1GG	1	:46^3	1:12^1	1:39^{2}gd	13	117	6^{14} 5$^{9\frac{1}{2}}$ 2^4 1no	Warren R J Jr 5	10000	68-24	Icouldtoldyouso,MSR,AwrdForAlln	7
20Jan89-10BM	1	:47^3	1:12^1	1:38^{1}ft	5¾	114^5	7$^{4\frac{3}{4}}$ 6^6 4^6 3$^{4\frac{1}{2}}$	Gann S L 1	c6250	73-26	DltSm,Wstrtdsomthng,Icoldtoldyos	8
20Jan89—Ducked out start												

The four-year-old ran last of eleven all the way on April 29. In its next-to-last start, April 16, the horse finished up close against a higher class. That qualifies.

Usually, especially with claiming horses, the bogus line, such as the April 29 race, will be followed by reentry as soon as possible. If such a horse reappears in two weeks or thereabouts, disregard the awful line.

Finally, nonclaiming three-year-olds regularly throw in inexplicably poor efforts. The bad race often coincides with a new experiment—change of distance or footing, new kind of handling by the jockey, a change of running style. If the total record and training pattern look otherwise acceptable, disregard the dismal line.

Beyond these special circumstances, form defects for recent performance can often be interpreted in relation to considerations of class, trainer, and track surface. Recreational handicappers can learn to detect the meaningful relationships. For now, they will be wise to retain a decidedly liberal posture.

A SUITABLE CLASS LEVEL

Class is no more important in handicapping than speed, pace, and form, the other fundamentals. No less important either. The four factors deal directly with the basic abilities and performance capacities of thoroughbreds. A working knowledge of each is indispensable.

Of the four, at least two prove seriously troublesome to recreational handicappers: class and pace. Egregious errors on the class factor are committed every day. The worst mistakes find casual handicappers thinking horses will be outgunned when they surely belong. Once again, too many eventual winners can be discarded prematurely.

When identifying contenders, the practical question asks whether horses qualify as suited to today's class level. Two common situations confuse recreational players repeatedly.

1. Which rises and drops in claiming class are acceptable? Which are not acceptable?
2. How can horses be compared accurately on class when changing from claiming races to the allowances and stakes? Conversely, when nonclaiming horses are entered to be claimed, at which levels should they be expected to win?

As complicated as these problems appear, the practical solutions have been found. National studies of claiming races have revealed how frequently claiming horses can be expected to win on the rise and drop. Handicappers can anticipate what kinds of rises and drops are perfectly normal. Abnormally large rises and drops can be comprehended more reliably than ever.

Research from speed handicapping has revealed as well the average times of all classes of horses at all North American racetracks. The average times are called par times. Par times permit comparisons between claiming classes and nonclaiming classes.

By combining the knowledge provided by the several studies of class and speed, handicappers can erect a class hierarchy for the local racetracks. Class levels can be arranged in ascending order of difficulty, as indicated by typical times, and the comparisons between claiming and nonclaiming class levels can be made plain.

The class hierarchy services the fundamental task of determining whether today's competition represents a suitable class level for a horse. It tells whether claiming horses rising and dropping in selling prices are acceptable.

It tells whether claiming horses entering nonclaiming races, and vice versa, are acceptable.

Recreational handicappers who rely on the class hierarchies presented here will have no excuses in the future for making the grossest errors when evaluating class.

Consider the class hierarchy below, which represents the

relative class levels in southern California, but can be generalized reasonably well to other major U.S. racetracks.

Class Hierarchy/Major Racetracks

Level	Claiming	Nonclaiming
1	$10,000 & below	
2	12,500–16,000	
3	20,000–25,000	Maiden
4	32,000–40,000	Alw, NW1X
5	50,000–62,500	Alw, NW2X
6	Above $62,500	Alw, NW3X4X
		Clf Alw
		R Stk/Open Stk Below $100K
7		Listed/Gr. 3
8		Gr. 2/Gr. 1

The class hierarchy for major tracks consists of eight class
levels, with $10,000 claiming horses and below at Level 1, and
Grade 2 and Grade 1 stakes horses at Level 8. At four classes,
levels 3 to 6, claiming horses are juxtaposed with nonclaiming
horses, meaning the par times of the respective classes are virtually equivalent.

Notice that all claiming classes and several nonclaiming
classes have been clustered into brackets. For example, Level 3
brackets the $20,000 and $25,000 horses, and sets those claiming classes equal to maiden winners.

In the nonclaiming division, at Level 6, advanced nonwinners allowances, classified allowance races, restricted stakes
horses, and open stakes below a purse of $100,000-added have
been bracketed. These several nonclaiming classes have been
set comparable to claiming horses valued above $62,500.

Probability data indicate that among horses showing a "good
race," a step-up of one class level or a step-down of one class
level is perfectly acceptable. Horses move up and down one
level equally successfully and win their rightful share.

In other words, horses exiting a good race can be expected
to move about within levels of the class hierarchy with no hes-
itation. A horse delivering a good race for a claiming tag of
$20,000 would be accepted on class if entered for $25,000 next.

Similarly, horses that have won under allowance conditions, for nonwinners three times other than maiden or claiming, would be acceptable in a classified allowance race, a restricted stakes, or an open stakes having a purse below $100,000.

Horses exiting good performances in classified races would also be accepted in restricted stakes or any open stakes below $100,000.

Nonclaiming horses that cannot proceed to the next higher class level can be expected to win next at the claiming class corresponding to the latest nonclaiming success.

Where should handicappers expect maidens that cannot proceed successfully in the allowance division will win next?

At the $20,000 to $25,000 claiming level.

Where should winners of two allowance races be expected to win in the claiming division?

At the $50,000 to $62,500 claiming level.

Now, the kicker. Regardless of claiming prices, a step-up of one full bracket is acceptable for any horse exiting a winning race at the preceding level.

Thus, victory against $12,500 claiming horses (Level 2) qualifies a horse on class as high as the $25,000 claiming level (Level 3).

"Good" races allow step-ups too. Use these guidelines.

A good race at the lower end of a class level qualifies a horse on class at the lower end of the subsequent level.

So a good race for $32,000 at a major track qualifies the horse on class at the $50,000 claiming level.

A good race at the upper end of a class level qualifies a horse on class at the upper end of the subsequent level.

So a good race for $25,000 claiming qualifies a horse on class at the $40,000 claiming level.

In the nonclaiming division, a winning race qualifies a horse on class at the subsequent class level. A good race can often qualify horses at a higher level as well, as when stakes horses prepare for bigger objectives in lower-level races.

Recreational handicappers should pause to review the recommended guidelines for qualifying contenders on class. If handicappers suspect the guidelines on rises in class too lenient, a brief rationale is appropriate, and, I trust, persuasive.

Since the early 1980s, when racing calendars were expanded to their end points to combat the economic ravages of inflation, the demand for racehorses to fill hundreds of additional races at a greater number of racetracks has resulted in an inevitable decline in the quality of the competition. Numerous races at major tracks are embarrassingly bad. At the same time, the longer season disrupts horses' form cycles intermittently. In concert, horses climb and descend the class ladders incessantly. Claiming horses especially move up and down in class more dramatically than ever.

Handicappers must be more flexible on class maneuvers than ever. Traditional class barriers have been knocked down. The conventional 20 percent guideline for permissible rises in claiming class is no longer serviceable. Neither is the notion that nonclaiming horses should move ahead in class one gradual step at a time. Trainers enjoy unparalleled options and unbridled flexibility in placing horses in suitable races. Shipping and scratching have therefore increased terrifically, even in the overnight races.

Class drops can be treated even more leniently. Horses dropping in class win twice as often as probabilities would expect, and a 30 percent plunge in claiming class wins almost three times as frequently.

Now an acceptable performance (beats half the field *and* finishes within six lengths) at a higher level in the hierarchy qualifies a horse on class at the preceding level.

Thus, an acceptable race for $40,000 claiming qualifies on class at the $25,000 to $20,000 claiming level.

"Good" races qualify horses better on the drop in the nonclaiming division. Acceptable races at levels 8 and 7 are transportable to any lower level.

A caution here. Large drops emcompassing multiple claiming-class levels can be tricky and must be handled on a case-by-case basis. Many are acceptable, but many are frauds. More on this in the section on rating methods.

The majority of thoroughbreds, of course, compete regularly at the same class level, especially when class levels have been defined as clusters of classes embracing a range of competitive quality. Older claiming horses, 4up, sometimes compete at a specific level for an entire season, notably at medium-sized and smaller tracks.

At the same class level, use the following pair of guidelines to determine if today's race represents a suitable class level.

1. Accept any horse whose last performance was a good race.
2. Accept any horse whose last performance was an acceptable race, provided it raced up close at the prestretch call.

Other horses entered at the same level today can be eliminated as outclassed.

Recreational handicappers benefit by recording any contender's relative class on the *Daily Racing Form*. Use numerical markings above the class column. Examine the previous six races in the record. Identify the lowest class level and highest class level at which the horse has run a good race. Record the class levels by their numbers, such as 2–3, meaning a claiming horse has impressed from $12,500 to $25,000 in its last six races. If a horse has won twice at the upper end of today's class level or higher, add a plus.

The markings look like this (it's June 10):

2nd Hollywood

6 ½ FURLONGS. (1.15) CLAIMING. Purse $18,000. 4-year-olds and upward. Weight, 122 lbs. Non-winners of two races since April 23 allowed 3 lbs.; of a race since then, 5 lbs. Claiming price $25,000; if for $22,500 allowed 2 lbs. (Races when entered for $20,000 or less not considered.)

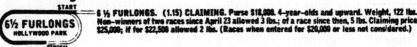

Well In The Air

Golden Gauntlet

```
21Aug88-2Dmr  6f :214 :444 1:092ft   3½ 116  43  41¼ 2hd 13½  Stevens G L 2  c62500 91-12 GoldenGuntlet,LnsMnus,Rosi'sK.I. 8
     21Aug88—Wide into stretch
25Jun88-7Hol  6f :22  :45  1:101ft *7-5 118  21  3nk 31  32½  Stevens G L 4  Aw42000 88-13 LuckyMsddo,Pewter,GoldenGuntlet 6
     25Jun88—Steadied start
11Jun88-3Hol  7f :222 :45  1:221ft    4 118  31  31½ 2hd 2hd  Toro F 3       Aw42000 93-13 Oricao, Golden Gauntlet, Pewter 7
   May 21 SA 5f ft 1:002 H         ●May 14 SA 3f ft :35 H

Under And Over                        Dk. b. or br. g. 5, by Far North—Belle Bottom, by Hoist the Flag
  DELAHOUSSAYE E   24      119        Br.—Winick A & DelrayTrngCntr (Fla) +   1989  8  3  2  1        $45,580
Own.—Glickman & Success Stables       Tr.—Shulman Sanford         $25,000      1988 17  1  5  1        $58,925
                                      Lifetime  26  4  7  2  $104,425   3-4    Turf  2  0  0  0         $2,550
13May89-3Hol  7f :214 :441 1:223ft   3½ 118  41½ 31  22½ 2½   Baze R A 5      32000 90-11 TimToSmok,UndrAndOvr,KnKnight 7
29Apr89-1Hol  7f :213 :442 1:223ft   4½ 117  42½ 42¾ 2hd 1no  DelahoussayeE 5 32000 91-10 UnderAndOver,Crftmster,Invoking 10
     29Apr89—Drifted out, wide in stretch
2Apr89-2SA    6f :214 :45  1:102ft   3½ 120  64  62¼ 32  32   Pincay L Jr 3   25000 84-15 Desperte,Mcemobile,UnderAndOver 8
     2Apr89—Wide into stretch
22Mar89-5SA   7f :222 :45  1:224ft   4¾ 117  52½ 32  32  22¾  Pincay L Jr 5   32000 83-17 RedAndBlue,UnderAndOvr,Mr.Spd 10
26Feb89-2SA   6½f:213 :442 1:161ft   3½ 117  53½ 44½ 48  54¾  Pincay L Jr 8   32000 84-14 Pop'sRuling,RdAndBlu,HrdToMiss 10
18Feb89-2SA   6½f:213 :443 1:171ft   2½ 118  74¾ 65½ 42½ 11   Pincay L Jr 4   c25000 84-19 UnderAndOvr,NoMonyDown,Dsprt 12
22Jan89-1SA   6½f:212 :443 1:162ft   5¾ 117  65  53½ 41  12   Pincay L Jr 5   25000 88-14 UndrAndOvr,RdAndBlu,Bubb'sBlt 11
13Jan89-7SA   7f :22  :444 1:223ft    15 120  32  42½ 87¾ 89½  Meza R Q 1     Aw31000 77-15 RoylEgl,OurNtivWish,Excllr'sSpcil 10
     13Jan89—Bobbled start
31Dec88-7SA   6½f:211 :433 1:153ft   6¾ 120  66  55  66½ 52½  Sibille R 4    Aw31000 90-10 MgicLeder,SnowPrch,OurNtivWish 8
     31Dec88—Steadied 3/4
10Dec88-5Hol  7f :221 :451 1:233ft   2½ 117  3nk 4nk 32½ 22   Sibille R 9     32000 84-17 BrginStndrd,UnderAndOvr,Gossron 9
   May 24 Hol 5f ft 1:013 H        ●Apr 19 SA 5f ft :584 H        Apr 12 SA 5f ft 1:002 H
```

A $25,000 claiming sprint for horses 4up, today's class is Level 3.

The three horses above qualify on class. Under And Over enjoys a class edge, having delivered good races at Level 4 and having won twice at Level 3 or higher in its last six races (notice the plus sign).

If a horse fails to qualify on class as a contender, enter a zero above the class column on the *Form*, as below:

```
Bright And Right *                    B. g. 7, by Search for Gold—Airy and Bright, by Olympiad King
  DAVIS R G   0-0          117        Br.—Hawn W R (Cal)                        1989  5  0  1  0        $10,175
Own.—Currie D & Trish                 Tr.—Goodin Mike             $25,000       1988  9  6  1  1       $117,775
                                      Lifetime  37 13  7  9  $263,150    0      Turf  7  2  3  0        $55,460
31May89-5Hol  6f :22  :444 1:093ft    15 115  77  75¾ 75¼ 76   Baze R A8    35000 87-15 Third Census, Pialor, Hard To Miss 9
21May89-5Hol  6½f:214 :44  1:151ft   4¾ 117  65  65¼ 55¼ 46½  Baze R A3    32000 92-05 KevinsDefens,HrdToMiss,HdlinNws 8
19Feb89-2SA   6f :213 :444 1:104ft   3½ 116  84¾ 84¾ 52¼ 2½   Baze R A3    45000 83-21 WindwoodLn,BrightAndRight,Plor 10
     19Feb89—Crowded, altered path, bumped 1/8
8Feb89-7SA    6½f:213 :441 1:16 m    3½ 115  53½ 55  45½ 45½  Baze R A4    55000 84-23 PresidentsSummit,KenKnight,Ordr 9
29Jan89-5SA   6f :211 :441 1:10 ft   5½ 1135 77½ 98½ 76  64½  Corral J R12 40000 83-16 Pialor, EightyBelowZero,QuipStar 12
     29Jan89—Lugged in, bumped 1/2; rider lost rein momentarily
30Nov88-5Hol  6f :221 :452 1:101ft   *1 122  63¼ 42  52  1nk  Stevens G L7 c50000 91-15 BrghtAndRght,KnKnght,LckyMsdd 8
     30Nov88—Wide into stretch
7Nov88-5SA    a6½f(T):211 :4411:152fm*6-5 116 64 52¾ 42½ 1½  Stevens G L6 70000 82-18 BrightAndRight,Cstnilli,Complicte 12
     7Nov88—Bumped 1/16
23Oct88-3SA   6½f:213 :443 1:161ft *9-5 116  44  42¾ 42  12   Stevens G L3 62500 89-16 BrghtAndRght,CnstntBnt,J.R.Jhnsn 7
     23Oct88—Steadied 1/8
```

Formerly the classiest claiming sprinter on the grounds in southern California at Level 5—$50,000 to $62,500 claiming—and a strong contender at Level 6—above $62,500 claiming—Bright And Right does not qualify on class for $25,000 claiming (Level 3) six months later.

With no early speed of late, and a form defect for its last running line, Bright And Right shows a trio of zeros. Recreational handicappers can disqualify any horse from contention when three conditions coincide:

a. poor early speed
b. unacceptable current form
c. unsuited to today's class level

Class Hierarchy at Minor Tracks

A situation that befuddles recreational handicappers at major tracks is shippers from minor tracks.

A less puzzling situation at minor tracks involves shippers from major tracks. Alert handicappers at smaller tracks learn quickly enough how to spot the big-league shippers that threaten.

A class hierarchy for minor tracks can be elaborated, the class levels corresponding to a degree with those of the major tracks. Guidelines can be formulated for recreational handicappers to follow whenever the cross-track shipping occurs. Shipping from minor tracks to major tracks happens more frequently than ever, and much more of it succeeds.

Consider the class hierarchy below as representative of numerous minor racetracks throughout the U.S.

Class Hierarchy/Minor Racetracks

Levels	Claiming	Nonclaiming
1	$ 3,500 and below	
2	4,000–5,000	
3	5,500–7,500	
4	8,000–10,000	
5	10,500–12,500	Maiden
6	13,000–19,500	Alw, NW1X, NW2X
7	20,000 and above	Alw, NW3X
		Clf Alw
8		Stakes and Handicaps

Mdn Clm $5000 and Above
Mdn Clm $3500 and Below

As at major tracks, maiden-claiming horses are assigned no class level to begin. Winners of maiden-claiming races can be expected to compete effectively versus winners at approximately one half the selling price of the maiden-claiming contest. Exceptions are not numerous. More about them later. Not many maiden-claiming graduates should be expected to conquer allowance conditions, no matter how sharp the maiden-claiming win.

The class hierarchy for minor tracks consists of eight levels too.

At minor tracks maiden races can be considered comparable to $10,500–12,500 claiming races. Maiden graduates that cannot proceed in the allowance division should be expected to win next there.

Winners of one and two allowance races at minor tracks can be accepted as comparable to winners of $13,000–19,500 claiming races. Conversely, claiming horses valued between $13,000 and $19,500 that enter the allowance races can be accepted at times in races for nonwinners once other than maiden or claiming, or even nonwinners twice other than maiden or claiming, but no higher.

Claiming horses valued at $20,000 and above are comparable at minor tracks to advanced nonwinners allowance conditions (NW3XMC) and classified allowance horses.

Rises and drops of a class level are perfectly acceptable, too, at minor tracks. Winning races, good races, and acceptable races can be elaborated into guidelines for identifying contenders on class, precisely as described for major tracks on pages 43–45.

Nonclaiming horses that impress at minor tracks will often be shipped for the bigger purses at the majors. Winners and horses exiting good races at the minors can often be accepted on class. Assign them a class level in the hierarchy of major tracks, depending upon the conditions of eligibility at the sending and receiving tracks. The appropriate translation is on page 68.

Thus shippers exiting stakes at minor tracks and entering stakes at major tracks will be assigned Class Level 6, and no higher. Exceptions are the few graded stakes at minor tracks, which deserve the same class level assigned the respective graded stakes at major tracks. That is, Grade 3 or Grade 2 stakes at minor tracks are accepted as the equivalent of Grade 3 or Grade 2 stakes at major tracks.

Conditions of Eligibility	Class Level, Minor Tracks	Class Level, Major Tracks
Maidens	5	3
Alw, NW1	6	4
Alw, NW2	6	5
Alw, NW3	7	6
Clf Alw	7	6
Stakes and Handicaps	8	6

If nonclaiming horses ship from minor tracks and enter claiming races at major tracks, assign them the class level for claiming prices at the major tracks that correspond to the nonclaiming conditions the shippers exited at the minor tracks.

So if a minor-track winner of an allowance race, for nonwinners once other than maiden or claiming, enters a claiming race at a major track, it would be acceptable up to Level 4, for $32,000 to $40,000 claimers. It would not be acceptable at Level 5, for $50,000 to $62,500 claiming horses.

If claiming horses 4up ship from minor tracks to major tracks, accept winners and horses exiting good races at one class level lower in the hierarchy for major tracks. Assign the shippers the class-level numeral of the major track.

So if the runner-up of a $25,000 claiming race at a minor track ships to a major track, it's acceptable at the $16,000 level (Level 2) but not the $25,000 level (Level 3).

Smaller Tracks

To an extent at minor racetracks, but pervasively at even smaller tracks housing the horses least likely to win, low-end claiming races are carded with a diverse array of restrictions in the eligibility conditions.

A $2500 claiming race at six furlongs for horses 4up, for example, might be limited to horses that have never won two races lifetime. Recent maiden graduates would be preferred against chronic nonwinners. The restricted race can be contrasted to the open kind, where $2500 horses could compete regardless of how often they have won in the past.

Another $2500 race might be open only to horses that have never won three races. Horses that have won two races would be preferred. The fewer attempts, the better.

Another kind of restriction might bar horses that have won a race this season; for example, nonwinners of a race this year.

Another might bar horses that have won two races this year. Admitting horses that have won once recently, that race would be more difficult to win than one that barred previous winners for a longer time line.

Another might bar horses that have not won a race since a specified date, perhaps 120 days ago. Horses that last won within 121 to 150 days, but have not raced frequently since, would enjoy a real edge against horses that have raced repeatedly for 120 days but remain eligible.

Another $2500 race might be a route that bars previous winners at a mile or over for a lifetime, a year, or a specified date. Consistent sprinters can stretch out more effectively, as consistent routers tend to possess tactical speed, and these have been barred. The more recently the sprinters have won, and the better the fields, the better.

The point should be plain.

Racing secretaries at small tracks provide opportunities to win for every animal on the grounds by restricting the competition to horses of comparable records.

As a rule, the more frequently and recently claiming horses have won, the better horses they are. And the likelier they will be barred from certain low-end claiming races intended to provide chronic nonwinners a sturdier chance.

Recreational handicappers need to be keenly aware of the claiming restrictions, and capable of interpreting their implications.

Restrictions in claiming races can be graded, from A to Z, so to speak, such that A races are usually superior in competitive quality to B races, B races superior to C races, and so forth.

The higher grades are assigned to races whose eligible horses have won more frequently and recently. The lowest grades go to races whose horses have not won once in a long time.

At any claiming level in the class hierarchy for minor tracks, recreational handicappers can use the following grading system whenever restrictions are embedded in the conditions of eligibility:

A. nonwinners twice since a specified date
B. nonwinners since a specified date

C. nonwinners twice during the calendar year
D. nonwinners during the calendar year
E. nonwinners twice during the past two years
F. nonwinners during the past two years
G. nonwinners of three races lifetime
H. nonwinners of two races lifetime
I. nonwinners of a race lifetime

Which of the following $2500 six-furlong claiming races for 4up should bring together the best field? It's June 15.
"Nonwinners of a race since April 15."
"Nonwinners of two races this year."
"Nonwinners of three races lifetime."
Using the recommended grading system, the trio of $2500 races (Level 1) would be graded as follows:

"Nonwinners of a race since April 15."　　　　　1B

"Nonwinners twice during the calendar year."　　1C

"Nonwinners of three races lifetime."　　　　　1G

The restriction barring winners since April 15 admits multiple winners prior to April 15 that might have finished close since, or have not raced in the 60 days since April 15.

The restriction barring multiple winners this year admits horses that have won no more than once in five-and-a-half months. Claimers competing regularly, but still eligible, will not be as talented as the horses eligible to the race carrying the April 15 specified date.

Yet the restriction barring multiple winners this year would also admit consistent claiming horses returning from lengthy layoffs. These winners may pulverize the less consistent types that could be the main contenders in the April 15 field.

So might a consistent winner that has won once this year only because it has been relatively inactive. Such a horse might have returned from vacation two weeks ago, won big or finished close, and press an undeniable advantage today against the inconsistent platers that have not won twice in almost six months.

The gradings for the restrictions of claiming races will be reliable, therefore, but not impeccable. Recreational handicappers must remain on guard.

Other claiming-race restrictions can be even trickier. If multiple winners at a mile or over (routers) have been barred, two horses should be considered at advantage: (a) routers that have won once recently, finishing well enough otherwise, and eligible today due in the main to inactivity, and (b) impressive sprinters stretching out.

If previous winners at the route have been barred, sprinters enjoy even a stronger advantage. But they may confront a consistent router that recently returned to the races, or will be returning today. The horse will be eligible because it has been inactive. If the horse has won just prior to the specified date in the restriction, it figures. The impressive sprinters and the returning routers may be the only legitimate contenders in the field.

Another aspect of claiming-race conditions affecting eligibility is the exemption. Lower-class claiming horses are usually exempted from today's restrictions, providing horsemen with incentives to move cheaper horses ahead in class.

The conditions of a $5000 claiming race specify: "for nonwinners since the current meeting began . . . (races for $3500 horses and below are exempted)."

Now horses that have won multiple races since the start of the season when entered at $3500 or less can move up to $5000 competition, and face the leftovers at the higher level.

And the cheaper horses do move up, successfully. Recreational handicappers should understand the situation for what it is. The contenders on class will include impressive $5000 horses barely eligible, as well as consistent winners jumping up from the exemption prices.

In the $5000 example, characterized by restrictions at a higher claiming level but exemptions at a lower level, the appropriate class levels will be recorded as 2B (for $5000 claiming, nonwinners since a specified date) and 1 (for $3500 claiming).

Stay close to this general guideline. At the same class level, as well as one level up or down, an open race is usually preferable to any restricted race. Thus 1 (open $3500) claiming is preferable to 2B, restricted $5000 claiming.

The fewer the number of victories permitted over the longest duration by the claiming-race restrictions, the more attractive the open race at a lower class level. Where claiming races at particular class levels contain various restrictions, prefer the higher class level and better grade in combination, such that 2A is preferable to 2B, 2C to 2D, and so forth. Where class levels and gradings are mixed, such as 2A, 3B, and 1, treat the respective horses as contenders on class, and separate them later in the handicapping process.

Recreational handicappers, of course, do not compile the results charts that specify the exact restrictions in the eligibility conditions of claiming races. No *Daily Racing Form* symbols advise handicappers as to the recency and consistency of the eligible horses' previous competition.

Experience provides the practical remedy. If today's claiming race features class-consistency restrictions in the conditions of eligibility, the recent races of several horses in the field will have too. Identify the class levels and grades of restrictions as best these can be known. Mark them, as recommended, above the class column of the form.

Recreational handicappers stationed at smaller tracks will be familiar with the worst problems, if not the solutions. Recreational handicappers at major tracks, but visiting smaller tracks, should beware of the problem at least. What handicappers see in the class column of the *Racing Form*, such as a $5000 claiming race, may not necessarily be what they get. As casual handicappers now realize, $5000 claiming races at smaller tracks can come in several distinct varieties.

Recreational handicappers sufficiently intrigued by the class advantages to be uncovered that they collect the results charts of claiming races at minor and smaller tracks, will be rewarded for the extra effort many times a season.

Nonclaiming Horses Moving Through Their Conditions

Certain allowance races, referred to as the nonwinners series, are carded for specific kinds of horses. Practitioners should expect those kinds of horses to win, and discount the others, but most recreational handicappers haven't a clue. I have always imagined that more uninformed money is lost on nonwinners allowance races than any other kind. And I know that few casual handicappers can beat these races. As I have written before, the nonwinners allowances are racing's toughest nuts to crack.

To explain.

Nonwinners allowance races are carded for promising horses that have not yet won one, two, three, or four races other than maiden or claiming races. The idea is to expose developing horses of positive but undetermined potential to a limited kind of competition while they develop and refine their basic abilities.

Thus nonwinners allowance races are nicely suited to recent impressive maiden graduates who are younger, lightly raced, and improving impressively.

The likeliest winners will therefore be three-year-olds, not four-year-olds, and certainly not horses five years old and older.

The likeliest winners tend to be better horses, not horses that have already defined themselves as claiming horses.

The likeliest winners tend to be horses having 15 or fewer starts, not horses that have raced 20 times or more already but still remain eligible.

The menu of nonwinners allowance races in major racing will be more diverse than presented here, and the contention sometimes more diverse, but recreational handicappers can slice numerous losses from their racetrack experiences by honoring the basic principles underlying these races. The ideal prospect in any nonwinners allowance field is a lightly raced three-year-old that has been improving impressively lately and now is taking another logical step ahead in the order of competition. The fewer the horse's races, the better.

To spare recreational handicappers the headaches that result from the gross mistakes most racegoers repeat in analyzing allowance races, it's helpful to set down strict guidelines as to which horses merit the handicapper's full attention, depending on the exact conditions of eligibility.

Here are the basic array of nonwinners allowance conditions to be alert to, and the kinds of horses that fit them well.

1. Nonwinners of a race other than maiden or claiming races.

Handicappers should accept:

1.1 any lightly raced three-year-old that recently won a maiden race and has finished close in few tries under allowance conditions similar to today's.

1.2 any impressive three-year-old maiden winner last out.

1.3 any nicely bred three-year-old whose recent performances and clockings indicate dramatic or continued improvement.

1.4 foreign horses of Europe that have run in-the-money in a graded or listed stakes.

    1.5 foreign horses of South America, Australia, New Zealand, or South Africa that have run in-the-money in a Grade 1 stakes.

    1.6 a nicely bred, lightly raced, late-developing four-year-old from a leading stable, provided the horse has never been entered in a claiming race.

Regular eliminations on class include four-year-olds and older that have been entered in claiming races with unimpressive results and have lost six races under today's allowance conditions; three-year-olds that have lost six consecutive races under today's conditions; unimpressive maiden winners; maiden-claiming winners last out; and three-year-olds that have been entered for a claim without success.

The same guidelines apply when the conditions specify "nonwinners of two races," a restriction that bars previous winners of claiming races.

The guidelines apply, too, when the conditions specify "nonwinners of $3000 other than maiden or claiming," or a similar winner's share, a restriction that permits winners of allowance races at smaller tracks to ship impressive horses to major tracks and remain eligible there to a limited kind of allowance competition.

    2. Nonwinners twice other than maiden or claiming races.

Handicappers should accept:

    2.1 a lightly raced, improving three-year-old that in a few attempts has won an allowance race smartly in fast time and now is moving ahead in class by one logical step.

    2.2 foreign horses of Europe that have won or placed in a graded or listed stakes.

    2.3 a lightly raced, late-developing four-year-old that once won an allowance race, has not since been entered to be claimed, and has never been beaten when favored under today's conditions (without an excuse).

In the absence of the above, accept:

    2.4 consistent high-priced claiming-race winners age four or five that previously won an allowance race.

Regular eliminations include older horses that have lost six races under similar conditions; three-year-olds that have been entered to be claimed since winning an allowance race; unimpressive recent winners (weak ratings) under nonwinners-once allowance conditions; horses whose claiming races look dramatically better than their allowance races; horses aged six and older; and any three-year-old that has been trounced in a stakes race after winning its first allowance race, unless the stakes is listed or graded and the badly beaten three-year-old has had a period of six weeks to recuperate.

Where winter racing occurs, January through March and November-December, nonwinners allowance races will be carded for horses 4up, and handicappers must treat these contests differently.

Now, impressive claiming horses can be accepted as contenders on class. Any horse four years old or older and still eligible to races for nonwinners of one or two allowance races is no great shakes. Many of them will be chronic nonwinners that should be forsaken, notably among fillies and mares. The females are protected from being claimed for breeding purposes, but cannot survive in allowance races.

Claiming horses of winter in sharp form can enter the preliminary nonwinners allowances, as nonwinners-once and -twice conditions can be termed, and win convincingly. The class hierarchy for major tracks indicates the nonwinners-once allowances for 4up can be taken by older claiming horses valued from $32,000 to $40,000. The nonwinners-twice conditions for 4up can be captured by older claiming horses valued from $50,000 upward.

At minor tracks in winter, nonwinners-once and -twice allowance conditions (4up) can be completed by older claiming horses valued from $13,000 to $19,500 or better.

Three-year-old claiming horses of winter are a far cheaper brand. Do not expect they will reenter the allowance division and win, even following lopsided triumphs in claiming races. Most cannot.

After developing horses have won a pair of allowance races, many stables try them next in stakes. Thus a decent performance in a stakes race becomes a vital credential for winning a third allowance race. The conditions of these races can be referred to as advanced nonwinners allowances, as the fields will contain several winners of multiple allowance races. The guidelines for accepting horses as contenders on class get tighter.

3. Nonwinners three times (or four times) other than maiden or claiming races.

Handicappers should accept:

3.1 a lightly-raced three-year-old that has been a powerful winner of two allowance races and has run evenly or better while beating half the field in a graded or listed stakes.
3.2 the same kind of three-year-old that has placed in an open or restricted stakes.
3.3 multiple allowance race winners, lightly raced, age three or four.
3.4 foreign horses of Europe that have won graded or listed stakes; other foreign horses that have won a Grade 1 or Grade 2 stakes and placed repeatedly in similar races.

At this juncture in a racehorse's career the competitive quality of the opposition escalates, and sometimes soars. The advanced nonwinners allowance races feature the faster nonclaiming horses on the grounds. If the conditions specify "nonwinners four times other than maiden or claiming," the likeliest winner should already have won a stakes.

Appropriately, eliminations on class make sense whenever two or more of the following circumstances present themselves in a horse's past performances.

1. Has lost six races under similar conditions.
2. Last out won a nonwinners-twice race in ordinary time or manner.
3. Was beaten soundly in a restricted stakes that bars former stakes winners.
4. Has run rank, and is unseasoned at the distance or on the footing.
5. Has been entered to be claimed since its second allowance win.
6. Is a shipper from a minor track and has not won or placed in an open stakes having a good purse there.
7. Started in a maiden-claiming race, regardless of its record since.

8. Is a three-year-old and has been entered to be claimed more than once.

The nonwinners allowance races are not hospitable to recreational handicappers. Unless the horses have looked extraordinary, handicappers know less about these horses real abilities than any other kind of racehorse.

Will they handle the new distance? Will they like the footing? Can they run faster? What will happen when the pace quickens and other impressive horses contest the outcome throughout the late stages? No one really knows.

Be strict. The nonwinners allowances invite good horses to participate. Handicappers should restrict their enthusiasms to those prospects.

This concludes an opening discussion of the class factor for purposes of identifying contenders suited to the quality of the race. Results charts notwithstanding, all the details can be mastered by recreational handicappers. Study the class hierarchies presented here. Modify them to suit local tracks, if necessary. Use the recommended guidelines to evaluate relative class and rises and drops.

Identifying contenders nicely suited to the quality of the race is the province of class handicapping. With practice, recreational handicappers should seldom be fooled.

POSITIVE AND NEGATIVE PERFORMANCE PATTERNS

Effective handicapping to a degree becomes an exercise in pattern recognition. Practitioners notice familiar patterns of performance, some positive, some negative. These inform problem-solving and decision-making.

When identifying contenders, a number of performance patterns signify a strong upcoming effort. Others arouse suspicions of a dubious effort. Still others represent standard operating procedure, as when three-year-olds stretch out from sprints to routes. Positive and negative trainer patterns raise white or red flags for handicappers who recognize them. Positive and negative track-surface biases encourage handicappers to move horses up or knock them down.

Here we identify twelve familiar performance patterns as

positive or negative. Neither condition means the horses in question qualify as automatic contenders or eliminations. Pattern recognition merely enhances or detracts from the case.

Positive patterns indicate horses deserve the benefit of any doubts that might have been generated following first evaluations of early speed, current form, and relative class. Negative patterns reinforce suspicions aroused by the same considerations of early speed, current form, and relative class. They also can dampen enthusiasms associated with first impressions.

These performance patterns are well known to be associated with positive and negative effects. They involve distance changes, form cycles, trainer intentions, and track biases. Doubtful contenders associated with a positive pattern no longer should be doubted. Doubtful contenders associated with a negative pattern should no longer be considered.

On Distance

Changes of distance appear in the past performances of many horses every day. Distance switches are needlessly troublesome to recreational handicappers. The evidence is clear on the following.

1. With two exceptions, sprinters can be accepted when stretching out to routes. All ages qualify.

Sprinters win their rightful share of the routes they contest, and many of them pay generous mutuels. Do not throw them out early as unsuited to the distance.

One exception is the all-out frontrunner that is virtually a prisoner of its running style. The horses consistently burn up the course, earning 8 and 7 speed points. They cannot be rated kindly.

When switched to routes, speedballs expend too much energy in the six-furlong run to the prestretch call, and normally expire.

Naturally, if frontrunners are older, mature, seasoned sprinters that have demonstrated they can be rated when routing, accept them.

The second exception is the unmanageable frontrunner's opposite number, the one-run, come-from-behind sprinter. These lag at the rear of sprints and attempt to overhaul a tiring pace.

Late-running sprinters also remain hostages to their running styles. When switched to routes, they lag again, and try to punch, but the extra distance robs them of the punching power they retain at six furlongs. One-run sprinters are poor bets to route successfully. Throw them out.

2. With one exception, routers should not be accepted when attempting to sprint.

Statistics are dreary here. Horses changing from routes to sprints win less than 50 percent of the races they are entitled to win. Lack of early speed prevents them from reaching striking position soon enough. They do not arrive at the wire in time, class advantages notwithstanding.

The exception is the distance horse that demonstrates high early speed for the first two calls of its route races. The horses should have been on the lead or within a length of the leader in recent routes. Even so, the route horse has a much better chance if the switch is to a long sprint of 6½ or seven furlongs. Six furlongs tends to be too short.

In addition, the faster the fractional times of the recent routes, the better.

3. The worst stretchout pattern for distance horses after a layoff is one sprint.

4. The best stretchout pattern for distance horses after a layoff is two sprints.

One sprint and one route is also an effective stretchout pattern for distance horses following layoffs, but not as attractive as a pair of sprints. And the paired-sprints pattern gets better prices.

Recreational handicappers are not encouraged to split hairs when confronted by other conventional changes of distance. When identifying contenders, the concept of related distances carries the cause very well.

Sprints to seven furlongs are related, as are routes from a mile to 1³⁄₁₆ miles, the middle distances. Good races, at times acceptable races, qualify horses at all related distances.

Unappreciated caution about distance regards stakes horses. Abundant evidence shows that stakes performances at middle distances are not strongly correlated with performances at classic distances (1¼ miles and 1½ miles). A track-record performance at 1⅛ miles does not translate to victory at 1¼ miles.

The classic distance requires a different combination of speed and stamina that many top horses do not possess. They disappoint, often at miserly odds.

Three-year-olds are especially vulnerable. They have not acquired seasoning at the classic distance. The Kentucky Derby stands as the irrefutable illustration. Smashing performances at middle distances in Derby preps are not repeated in the Derby. Favorites collapse year after year. Why? Derby favorites are projected primarily as a result of performances at middle distances. The ratings do not stand up.

On Form

The patterns of highest intrigue involve the form cycles of horses following lengthy layoffs. Sprinters and routers both can win fresh. No problem accepting fresh horses, as we have noted, and the workout standards presented earlier cover these bases. Two familiar patterns can be spotted, one positive, one negative. Both contribute to the general finding that a racehorse's best efforts following long layoffs will be its third and fourth attempts.

1. Among sprinters returning from lengthy layoffs, if the second start is clearly an improved performance in relation to the first, the third race back is often a win.

Statistics indicate the pattern wins twice as frequently as probabilities would expect, a significant advantage. The first race after a layoff will often be dull or nondescript, the second clearly an improvement, and the third a victory. Prices are sometimes surprisingly good, as the crowd notices two consecutive losses, but not an improving form cycle.

2. When the first race following a long layoff results in an overexertion, horses either winning or finishing close in rapid time, the second race will often result in a disappointing loss.

This circumstance is curiously negative, often referred to as the "bounce" pattern.

The horses overextend themselves too soon, depleting energies and straining muscles. If raced again within 30 days, perhaps six weeks, they "bounce." That is, they finish up the track unexpectedly.

Fortunately, on the third comeback race, the horses bounce back. The general pattern represents an outstanding source of opportunities for handicappers in the know.

In the second race, when expected to impress following a strong comeback, the horses lose, usually at low odds.

In the third race, when expected to lose, following the disappointing second start, the horses rebound and win, now at generous odds.

Even top horses, stakes stars, are susceptible to the "bounce" pattern, though many better horses regress following two strenuous comeback efforts, not one. Which horses will regress following two overexertions and which following one can be predicted only on a case-by-case basis. The most familiar pattern consists of one all-out comeback race and a bounce.

Nonclaiming three-year-olds, top stakes prospects included, are particularly susceptible to the bounce pattern. Handicappers can distrust three-year-olds next time whenever they return from vacation following the two-year-old campaign and deposit a tremendous race.

The colt D. Wayne Lukas called his best three-year-old ever returned at three in New York's Grade 2 Bay Shore stakes, at seven furlongs, and earned a figure five lengths superior to its ratings as a juvenile.

Houston next appeared in the Grade 1 Santa Anita Derby in a ballyhooed confrontation with Sunday Silence. So, what happened?

Houston bounced badly in the Santa Anita Derby. His uncharacteristic performance at 4–5 is characteristic of the negative "bounce" pattern. Houston wins huge on March 25, following a long layoff, bounces April 8, and rebounds to win on April

29. Only the odds on April 29 do not fit the pattern. They are normally bigger.

Another negative pattern of form that is badly understood by recreational handicappers follows a claim of a sharp horse by a decent stable.

3. Following a claim of a positive-form horse by a competent trainer, if the horse is absent for more than 30 days and then returned for a selling price below the claiming price—that is, dropped in class—forget the horse.

The amount of money squandered by bettors on an obviously negative pattern is inexplicable. No competent horseman is giving away the goods. On February 1, 1989, clever claiming trainer Mike Mitchell haltered the gelding below for $45,000. Recreational handicappers should pay attention to the pattern that ensued.

Away 44 days, Spicy Yellowtail reappears March 17 carrying a lower sales tag. The horse is bet like a good thing to win, and finishes in the toilet. Dropped sharply on April 7, and bet as the favorite again, Spicy Yellowtail loses again. Dropped again, and bet again on April 20, Spicy Yellowtail disappears again.

How long has this been going on? Forever, it seems. The paradox is that racegoers are betting in support of a claiming trainer who has posted blaring warning signs the horse is no longer the commodity he claimed. The dropdown after a layoff by a competent barn following a claim of a sharp horse constitutes a negative pattern. If handicappers rate the horse, the rating will be high, based upon a strong performance against better. But the horse is no longer dependable. Stay away.

On Trainer Intentions

Certain patterns are positively indicative that trainers intend to win today. Award the plus sign when any of the following patterns appear.

1. A drop in class, accompanied by a switch to the leading rider.

This class-drop, jockey-switch angle has been well documented and is well known. Less well known, the class drop is normally of one level and leading jockeys are those currently winning at 20 percent or better. Precipitous class drops do not count. Neither do famous jockeys presently off their best form.

2. A quick return to action, of five days, or seven.

The horse is extra sharp. The trainer knows it. He finds the best available slot. If the last race features a troubled trip, or merely an inexplicable line, forgive it. Trust the trainer's intentions. The fast comeback is a positive pattern.

3. An impressive claiming win, followed by a class rise of multiple levels.

Racegoers shy from lofty rises in claiming class. But if a competent trainer suddenly gets ambitious with a claimer, he thinks the horse can deliver. Here the ratings will ultimately decide the horse's fate. For now, however, early in the handicapping, accept the class climber as a contender.

4. Poor dirt form, turf breeding, first time on grass today, perhaps against better.

Bred-for-grass wins on grass, frequently at first asking, or second. If horses show dull dirt form but a successful turf sire, accept them on grass. If a competent trainer enters this kind of horse against better, that's a positive pattern, and a long-shot pattern that wins. The trainer expects results, and recreational handicappers can too.

On Track Biases

Of the several track biases that wield a severe impact on race outcomes, one is susceptible to exploitation by casual handicappers. A positive speed bias on the rail amounts to a post-position bias that propels horses exiting the No. 1 hole.

Recreational handicappers need only check the post-position studies currently published astride the past performances by the *Racing Form*. If horses are winning in bunches from the one-hole, assume a positive speed bias inside and prepare to support anything that looks like it will benefit from the bias.

In sprints, horses having 4 speed points or better will be advantaged.

In routes, horses with mere traces of speed can be dangerous, notably in cheaper races.

In any event, inside speed horses will be contenders. If their ratings or figures suggest they can prevail, the bet often makes sense, absolutely at long odds. Positive inside speed biases will be decisive.

On a recent trip to a Las Vegas race book, I opened the central edition of the *Racing Form* and glanced at the post-position studies for Louisiana Downs. In routes, after 90 races, the No. 1 post had won 38 percent of the races. In sprints, after 140 races, the No. 1 post had won 25 percent, and the three inside posts 54 percent.

The first four races that day were sprints. The four were won by the three inside posts. In the fifth, a route, a horse exhibiting poor speed and poor form exited the No. 1 post, led all the way, and paid $48.60.

I decided to back anything out of the one-hole in routes, as well as any attractive speed inside in sprints.

In the seventh, an awful maiden-claiming affair, and second route of the afternoon, another horse with no speed in five previous races exited the No. 1 post, dashed to the front, led all the way, and paid $23.60, thank you.

In the next race, a sprint, a mildly attractive frontrunner came charging out of the one-hole, led all the way, won literally by half a furlong, and paid $10.40.

The bias prevailed throughout the week at Louisiana Downs, though less intensely. Only a dearth of routes prevented a landslide of profits. An inexperienced but observant racegoer at Louisiana Downs might have leaped upon the opportunities presented.

The Louisiana inside post-position bias was abnormally powerful, but many others are severe. If unexceptional horses that exit from the rail speed toward the front, pull away inexorably, and win cruising, get on the bandwagon. If rail horses shape up as potent contenders on the fundamentals, too, the handicapping has ended. Take the gift horses handed to you.

Negative post-position biases are different, and difficult for recreational handicappers to exploit.

Now the bias will be exploited best on the comeback, when speed horses that ran strongly against a negative rail bias, but stopped, return. If the bias has disappeared, the impressive speed horses do not stop. By now, however, recreational handicappers have gone home. Few of them collect the data or keep records that allow them to prosper from negative rail biases later in the season.

5. First-time Lasix, plus blinkers on, often translates to dramatically improved form.

The last running line or two may look dismal, but if a competent trainer uses equipment and medicine simultaneously, handicappers can anticipate a positive change. A professional of my acquaintance at Santa Anita has supported this double-edged maneuver almost invariably for two seasons, and reports an enviable profit. It's understandable. With their recent running lines ugly, when these horses pop up, they pop with fanciful odds.

Blinkers on has long been appreciated by handicappers as a positive equipment change that can steer horses forward. On green, rank, and insecure horses, the blinkers restore concentration, such that the capacity to run straighter and faster is improved. Two-year-olds, in particular, have been known to behave better in the gate, come out quicker, and demonstrate greater early speed with blinkers on.

First-time Lasix helps horses reverse poor recent form that has resulted from improper breathing due to minor bleeding in the respiratory tract. If the condition has persisted for a few races, the medical treatment can cause quite a transformation.

When horsemen use blinkers and Lasix concurrently, either a happy coincidence or clever manipulation has occurred. In either case, handicappers can accept the situation as a positive pattern, and prepare to rate a previously impressive performance.

Horses whose past performances contain any of the positive patterns recounted here can be accepted as contenders. No matter how the horses have measured up so far, on matters of early speed, current form, and suitable class, they project a positive pattern.

Handicappers benefit by including the horses in the surviving group of contenders, and rating them on performance.

EARLY ELIMINATIONS

The lofty purpose of identifying contenders should not be confused with the low instinct to eliminate horses.

An overwhelming majority of recreational handicappers suffer a tendency to reduce a horse race to artificial remains. The likeliest contenders draw too much attention. Other real possibilities are too quickly disowned. The regimen whereby public selectors brandish their top three choices as if the winner were inevitably included instigates, reinforces, and perpetuates an unfortunate and self-defeating habit. Practitioners imitate the pros adversely by picking three contenders only, regularly overlooking a genuine threat or two. The tactic amounts to sloppy procedure.

Identifying contenders is a positive, assertive art. Horses that satisfy the requisite standards qualify, whether two, three, seven, or eight. Four to six contenders in an eight-horse field is not atypical. Any horse that might win 15 of 100 attempts under today's conditions belongs, even when another horse might win 35 of 100 attempts. The latter would be approximately 2–1, the former 6–1. Not a long shot, by any means.

Furthermore, the position staked out here is unequivocal and opposite. Liberal standards, flexible thinking, and a mindset to include marginal horses for added scrutiny carry the cause. We reject the superficial, conditioned handicapping that thumbs the eventual winners prematurely.

In practice, early in the handicapping uninteresting horses must virtually eliminate themselves. These fall apart on each of the fundamentals. No positive patterns resurrect them.

Where horses look marginal, qualifying on some factors, disappointing on others, casual handicappers, novices absolutely, are urged to stretch the handicapping net to include them. When in doubt, do not throw horses out. Later, during the phase utilizing rating methods, weak sisters will be unmasked as pretenders.

Notwithstanding the liberal standards and flexible thinking, certain eliminations not only make perfect sense early on, but also contribute to greater efficiency in handicapping. The relevant guidelines will be broad, admitting all intriguing exceptions.

We have already noted that horses combining poor early speed, unacceptable current form, and unsuitable class can be deserted. Three strikes and you're out, so to speak.

Two additional negative combinations on the fundamentals will be only slightly less deadly.

Questionable form in combination with an incompetent trainer does not rise up in triumph. Even peaking or impressively improving form becomes ambiguous in the hands of an ineffective horseman. If a trainer wins with 5 percent or thereabouts, and the horse's condition looks unappetizing, why bother?

Poor early speed in combination with unsuitable (or inferior) class do not mix well either.

Superior class can overcompensate for a tardy running style. Inferior class complicates the come-from-behind horse's problems enormously. Unless the field drifts back to this kind of latecomer, no prize today.

In sum, the deadly combinations fully deserving of an early heave-ho are:

1. Poor early speed, unacceptable form, and unsuitable class in combination.
2. Unacceptable form in combination with an ineffective trainer.
3. Poor early speed in combination with unsuitable or inferior class.

To protect recreational handicappers from their own worst instincts, here are five broad guidelines for affording many horses a closer look:

1. Any horse having a good race at the relative class (class level) in the recent past (six to eight weeks), and no defects for form or trainer, deserves a longer look.
2. Any horse having a good race against a higher class in the past 90 days, and no more than a single defect (0) for form and trainer, look again.
3. Any horse having good early speed (5 speed points) and an acceptable race at today's class level, look closer, even

when the horse has multiple defects for form, trainer, and other factors of handicapping.

4. Any horse having acceptable early speed (4 speed points) and a good race against a higher class since the latest win, check further.

5. If a horse will be running against a mildly negative track bias but shapes up on the fundamentals otherwise, rate the horse.

In the last circumstance, even if the horse is not bet, the effects of the bias can be monitored against expected performance. Biases change from severe to subtle, and come and go within days. Tracking the course of a bias is not only easy, but also fascinating—and instructive.

When the last running line looks negative but the preceding races acceptable to good, recreational handicappers must decide whether the horses have begun a descent or might recuperate today.

If the last running line can be explained by a legitimate excuse—outclassed badly, troubled trip, an off track, negative bias, uncharacteristic running style, poorly judged ride—concentrate on the preceding races. Be wary, however, of excusing a pair of recent races. This may be warranted, but infrequently.

The psychologist and handicapper Sartin tells his club members flagrantly troubled by the problem that the skill of identifying contenders becomes intuitively precise with practice. I agree heartily.

In fact, the best of handicappers, the true experts, do not often misfire on the matter of identifying the authentic contenders. Wide, repetitive experience draws them to the leading contenders, as if instinctively.

The expert's breadth of knowledge and experience cannot be replaced by standards, guidelines, and procedures. Until recreational handicappers transform themselves into experts, they can cope admirably enough with the problem of identifying contenders. This book's procedures serve the purpose well. The standard of excellence is 80 percent accuracy. In other words, of five bettable races, one might be stolen by a handicapper's noncontenders, but no more.

Sartin's promise that the skill becomes intuitive will be delivered in the end, even to customers that remain casual, but careful. At that fabulous moment, occasional handicappers will realize they have progressed. They will have scuttled a debilitating problem that hovers about too many of their colleagues like a toxic cloud.

FINDING THE RATABLE RACES

Once horses have been identified as contenders, handicappers next find the races in the recent record that best represent real abilities. The task is not complex; it is much more elementary than identifying contenders.

Already, handicappers have marked the latest win in the past performances and the good races since. Almost always the ratable races will be those. If the last running line is representative, use it.

Adhering to a few trusty guidelines secures the successful completion of the task.

First, prefer races at today's relative class, or one class level up or down. If today's race is a $16,000 claiming race, 4up, at a major track, good races from these related class levels qualify:

$10,000 and below
$12,500–16,000
$20,000–25,000

I trust recreational handicappers have begun to appreciate the array of class levels that apply. Discounting an excellent performance at $10,000 claiming because a horse has been entered for $16,000 would be a mistake. An "acceptable" race for $20,000–25,000 claiming would also qualify.

Use the class hierarchies in this book to evaluate performances at related class levels.

Second, prefer races at related distances, but exact distances are unnecessary. If today's race will be at seven furlongs and the most recent good race occurred at six furlongs, use the shorter race, and vice versa.

Related distances means:

Sprints up to seven furlongs
One mile to 1¾₁₆ miles
1¼ miles and farther

Among routers that have been racing regularly, prefer performances at distances within one sixteenth of a mile whenever available. Also, performances at a mile are not readily compared to performances at 1⅛ miles, or even 1¹⁄₁₆ miles. The early pace of the mile tends to be significantly faster than those of the longer middle distances.

Sprints can be used to rate horses entered today in routes. An adjustment will be mandatory, as explained in the section on rating methods.

Routes can sometimes be used to rate horses entered today in sprints, provided the horses have demonstrated high early speed for the first two route calls. The appropriate adjustments will be discussed in the section on rating methods. Recreational handicappers can implement them easily.

Third, in claiming races, the most recent good performance usually will be the most representative. The current form of claiming horses is dynamic. Recency matters more. Recent performance does not necessarily mean the last running line. The next-to-last running line satisfies, if the last race must be excused or for some reason is not representative.

An exception in claiming races regards horses returning from layoffs of 60 days or longer. Now the last running line is often problematic; the cause, in fact, of the lay up. Handicappers can prefer the most recent good race or winning race in the previous form cycle. Occasionally, this kind of representative performance will have occurred five or six races back.

Among claiming horses that have been competing regularly, every couple of weeks, handicappers can often select the race in the recent series that is precisely representative of today's particular conditions, such as the same class, exact distance, probable race, and exact footing.

Fourth, among nonclaiming three-year-olds, if the last race looks unrepresentative, as often it will, prefer the best performance against the most advanced competition in the past six attempts. Nonclaiming three-year-olds differ from other racehorses. Handicappers who have accepted the horses as contenders want to know what the three-year-olds can do when they deliver their best blows. Find that performance and rate it.

Fifth, multiple performances often represent horses' current abilities better than a single selective race. Where a series of good races appears, handicappers benefit by rating a few performances instead of one. Patterns of improvement and decline become palpable. At times, a horse's top performance will be rated below a performance of another horse, or two, marking the first horse down.

And double-advantage horses, or runners whose two top ratings are each higher than any other rating in the field, can be spotted only after rating multiple performances.

Recreational handicappers as a group suffer three main failings when selecting ratable races:

1. Confusion about the last running line; that is, is it representative.
2. Thinking good performances are not representative of today—when they indeed are—due to class differences or distance changes not as meaningful as handicappers believe.
3. Searching too far back in a claiming horse's record to select a "representative" race, either because the horse won against the same class or at the same distance. But weeks or months have expired, and the claiming horse is an animal of a different color now.

The recommendations and guidelines presented here have been elaborated with those pratfalls in mind. Guideposts are intended to prevent the grossest errors. Practice helps enormously. Again, the final authority is experience.

Let's find the ratable races of a number of interesting contenders under a variety of eligibility conditions:

The first examples were entered in a $32,000 claiming race at Hollywood Park, June 7, 1989.

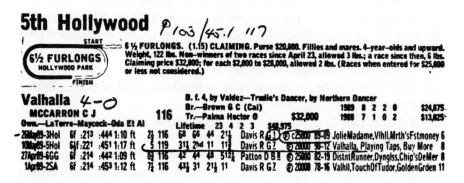

5th Hollywood P /o3 /45./ "7

24Mar89-1SA 7f :222 :454 1:251ft 11 1115 11½ 12 11 21¾ Garcia H J 2 Ⓕ 16000 72-20 RobertsReglGirl,Vlhll,NoSePorque 12
4Mar89-1SA 6f :213 :451 1:102ft 5¼ 116 2hd 1hd 31 58¼ ValenzuelPA 1 Ⓕ 20000 78-12 DefndYourMn,GrySptmbr,MlynLdy 7
20Feb89-1SA 6½f :214 :451 1:18 ft 10 1115 2½ 1hd 21 97¼ VlnzulFH 1 ⒻⓈ c16000 73-19 MostDrmtc,AShdFstr,RbrtsRglGrl 12
14Jan89-1SA 6f :213 :444 1:101ft 36 115 42½ 43 55½ 65¼ Gryder A T 6 Ⓕ 25000 82-11 ManyPasses,Madhuri,NastyPaster 12
28Dec88-5SA 1 :441 1:091 1:361ft 76 114 68½ 811 1014 1015½ Gryder AT 8 ⒻAw34000 71-10 Lyphrd'sFlg,BrghtStl,DsgnngChrls 10
28Dec88—Wide 7/8
1Dec88-5Hol 6f :22 :454 1:114ft *8-5 1105 75½ 83¾ 62¼ 32 VlenzuelFH 4 Ⓕ c25000 81-17 Heed To Speed, Tell Kel, Valhalla 10
1Dec88—Jostled early
●Jun 4 Hol 4f ft :471 H May 23 SA 4f ft :472 H May 7 SA 3f ft :353 H Apr 22 SA 5f ft 1:003 H

Oh Marie * 2-N
DELAHOUSSAYE E **116**
Own.—Friendly E

B. m. 6, by Quick Dance—Verna Marie, by Bravest Roman
Br.—Benford R M (Cal) 1989 7 1 0 1 $16,950
Tr.—Fulton Jacque $32,000 1988 13 2 1 2 $44,765
Lifetime 62 10 5 10 $160,867 Turf 3 0 0 1 $5,250

23Apr89-1SA 6f :214 :45 1:111ft 3¼ 118 53 43½ 43½ 31¼ DelhoussyeE7 Ⓕ 32000 81-17 SumthingRare,JolieMadme,OhMrie 8
23Apr89—Off slowly; wide 3/8 turn
9Apr89-1SA 6f :214 :444 1:102ft 17 116 77½ 67½ 57 65¾ DelhoussyeE6 Ⓕ 40000 80-14 DelwreStret,ShowtimLdy,MissTwpi 9
15Mar89-5SA 7f :222 :45 1:223ft 4¼ 116 61¾ 43 99¼ 912 DelhoussyeE4 Ⓕ 40000 75-14 Taybree, Alfitz, Defend Your Man 10
15Mar89—Broke slowly; wide into stretch
3Mar89-3SA 6½f :212 :441 1:17 gd 3¼ 116 65 46 32 13 DelhoussyeE4 Ⓕ 32000 85-19 Oh Marie, Heed To Speed,MayFirst 8
10Feb89-5SA 7f :221 :453 1:26 m 5½ 118 86 98¼ 95¾ 711 Douglas R R9 Ⓕ 32000 59-25 Pretty Lake North,Afloat,Barmera 12
10Feb89—Steadied 4 1/2
3Feb89-5SA 6f :21 :434 1:101ft 25 114 87¼ 96¾ 87¼ 73½ Douglas R R7 Ⓕ 45000 83-17 DelwreStreet,FlyingCountss,ZhZhn 9
20Jan89-7SA 6f :212 :434 1:083ft 16 117 87 89 812 814¼ DouglasRR4 ⒻAw35000 81-13 Humasong,FunAtTheSle,MissTwpie 8
20Jan89—Wide final 3/8
7Dec88-7Hol 6½f :214 :443 1:164ft 6¼ 114 55½ 44½ 33½ 1½ Douglas R R1 Ⓕ 37500 91-17 OhMrie,DelwreStreet,MuchoPicnte 7
16Oct88-4SA 6f :214 :444 1:10 ft 6¾ 116 53 57½ 58½ 510¼ Solis A1 Ⓕ 40000 78-16 LaSierra,DistntRunner,EnggingBeu 7
21Sep88-11Fpx 6f :221 :45 1:101ft 4½ 119 42½ 43 33 42½ Olivares F1 Ⓕ 40000 93-10 Ona Lucky Road,MissTawpie,Afloat 6
Jun 5 Hol 3f ft :362 H May 27 Hol 5f ft :593 H May 18 Hol 4f ft :471 H May 2 Hol 4f ft :482 H

Either the May 26 or May 10 races of Valhalla qualify. The $25,000 performance is more closely related to $32,000 claiming, so that might be preferred. Yet Valhalla exited the one-hole May 26, and as even recreational handicappers were aware, Hollywood Park featured a prominent negative rail bias in sprints during its spring-summer season of 1989. Ah, the complexities of real life. What to do?

Rate both races, and use the better rating today.

Oh Marie has been away 45 days, but is a contender, acceptable on current form (five-furlong workout in the past 14 days), relative class, and trainer-jockey connections.

The mare shows good races on April 23 and March 3, the former following a troubled trip, the latter on an off track. Both races featured $32,000 claiming horses.

Which race should be rated?

When in doubt, as here, rate both races, and use the better rating as most representative.

Try the pair of females on the next page, which were entered in the same race at Hollywood on June 7, 1989. Both are tricky.

Afloat does not qualify as a contender today, eliminated on current form (zero) following a lengthy layoff. If the mare did qualify, its performances on off tracks prior to the respite inter-

```
Afloat                          Ch. m. 5, by Relaunch—Engagingly, by Quack
  MEZA M D                      Br.—Glen Hill Farm (Fla)                      1989  4  2  1  0     $29,000
                          1115  Tr.—Peterson Douglas R—       $32,000         1988 15  1  4  5     $38,670
Own.—Mitrevich M P             Lifetime   27  5  6  7   $92,465               Turf  1  0  0  1      $2,200
10Feb89-5SA   7f  :221 :453 1:28 m  *3½ 121   96½ 64¾ 1½  22   Stevens G L 6 Ⓕ c32000 68-25 Pretty Lake North,Afloat,Barmera 12
22Jan89-4SA   6½f :213 :443 1:162ft  7 1115   65  75½ 68½ 711  Olguin G L 3  Ⓕ 55000 77-14 Ona Lucky Road, Toulange, Beseya 9
    22Jan89—Steadied 5/8
13Jan89-8BM   6f  :222 :453 1:11 gd  7½ 114   22  21½ 22  1¾   Douglas R R 5 ⒻHcp0  83-32 Afloat, Miss Quilla Illa, Keen Lady 6
 6Jan89-7SA   6½f :22  :451 1:18 gd  3½ 116   21½ 1hd 13½ 11¾  Stevens G L 9 Ⓕ 32000 80-20 Afloat,PlayingThrough,Suspiciously 9
22Dec88-3Hol  6f  :223 :464 1:12 gd  2½ 114   3½  54¼ 43½ 33½  Stevens G L 4 Ⓕ c22500 71-27 AShadeFster,WetherEyeOpen,Aflot 8
 1Dec88-3Hol  7f  :214 :443 1:233ft  3½ 116   12  11½ 12½ 2nk  ValenzuelPA 1 Ⓕ 25000 86-17 To The Dancer, Afloat, Zha Zhana 10
    1Dec88—Broke in a tangle
30Oct88-3SA   6f  :213 :444 1:093ft  7½ 116   44  44½ 43  56½  ValenzuelPA 3 Ⓕ 50000 84-13 ShowtimLdy,MissTwpi,Suspiciously 7
16Oct88-4SA   6f  :214 :444 1:10 ft  5½ 116   42½ 35½ 47  46¾  Black C A 2  Ⓕ c40000 81-16 LaSierra,DistntRunner,EngingBeu 7
21Sep88-11Fpx 6f  :221 :45  1:101ft  21 119   54  57  56  31¾  Skinner K 6  Ⓕ 40000 94-10 Ona Lucky Road,MissTawpie,Afloat 6
10Sep88-4Dmr  6f  :223 :452 1:10 ft  17 118   43  54½ 46½ 66½  Gryder A T 4 Ⓕ 50000 81-12 OnLckyRod,Sspcesly,Lt'sDrnkDnnr 9
  Jun 2 Hol 4f ft :491 H      May 29 Hol 4f ft :48 H      May 8 Hol 4f ft :483 H      Apr 26 Hol 5f ft 1:021 H

Lady Belief                     B. f. 4, by Believe It—Lucky One Axe, by The Axe II
 PINCAY L JR                    Br.—Raintree Farm (Fla)                       1989  1  0  0  0
                           116  Tr.—Ner Fabio                 $32,000         1988 10  1  6  0     $39,275
Own.—Trzcinka W                Lifetime   11  1  6  0   $39,275
12Jan89-5SA   6½f :212 :44  1:161ft  14 119   1011 911 89  76½  StevensGL9 ⒻAw31000 82-12 CstlCmmssn,ChcltJmbl,BrghtStyl 10
23Dec88-8Hol  7f  :22  :451 1:25 gd *2½ 118   25  27  23½ 2hd  Pincay LJr4 ⒻAw24000 77-25 MuchoPicante,LadyBelief,Durbility 6
25Nov88-7Hol  7f  :214 :45  1:242sy  12 119   54½ 44  33  42¾  StevensGL2 ⒻAw24000 79-23 Brmer,GlowingResum,Lyphrd'sFlg 10
 7Nov88-6SA   6f  :21  :442 1:102ft   7 118   77¾ 45½ 1½  13½  Stevens G L8  ⒻMdn  86-15 LdyBlf,CostlCommsson,BrknSlppr 10
23Sep88-7Fpx  6½f :21  :451 1:163ft  3½ 113   32½ 32  32½ 2¾   Gryder A T9   ⒻMdn  92-06 DifferentLook,LadyBelief,QueenGil 9
    23Sep88—Bumped start
 2Sep88-6Dmr  1 1/16 :46 1:113 1:441ft 15 1115 2hd 42½ 54½ 78   Corral J R2   ⒻMdn  71-15 Art College, Ann's Motel, Dancrit 10
26Aug88-6Dmr  6f  :22  :451 1:102ft *9-5 116   1hd 21½ 31½ 22½  StevnsGL11 ⒻMc50000 83-16 TeeterTotter,LdyBelief,LuckyRod 12
    26Aug88—Veered out start
11Aug88-6Dmr  6f  :214 :453 1:112ft   4 117   53  41½ 4¾  22½  Black C A10 ⒻM50000 78-21 FlowersKrisS.,LdyBelief,TetrTottr 12
    11Aug88—Very wide into stretch
28Jly88-6Dmr  6f  :22  :452 1:11 ft   4 116   42  42½ 31  2¾   Black C A6  ⒻM50000 82-13 YouBttrBliv,LdyBlif.FoundThScrt 12
26Jun88-4GG   6f  :212 :442 1:094ft  3¾ 114   21  31½ 512 59½  Warren R J Jr7 ⒻMdn 81-10 Sweet Tryst,AgitatedGirl,EstherEl 11
  Jun 1 Hol 4f ft :491 H      May 27 Hol 4f ft :491 H      May 21 Hol 6f ft 1:14 H      May 15 Hol 4f ft :483 Hg
```

fere with handicappers' finding a ratable race. I would settle—reluctantly—on the December 1 sprint at Hollywood Park, but the bad break at the gate and special distance weakens the rating.

Lady Belief qualifies as a contender, and the presence of Laffit Pincay, Jr., in the saddle for the comeback race adds. The good races prior to the layoff are December 23 and November 7, the former on a "good" surface.

The nonwinners-once allowance race of December 23, when Lady Belief finished second, beaten a head, is comparable in the class hierarchy to $32,000 claiming conditions. This is the race to be rated, unless the off-going proves too distorting.

The maiden race of November 7 qualifies as well, at one class level below today's, but ratings achieved at lower levels in nonclaiming races transfer less reliably, and should be avoided whenever feasible. Using the races risks inflated ratings that cannot be duplicated against the better horses.

The following horses entered a $16,000 claiming sprint, also at Hollywood Park, June 17, 1989. Examine the ratable races (marked) since the latest win. Find the most representative performance.

The $10,000 sprint of May 21 is most representative. Do not use routes to rate horses entered in sprints, if avoidable.

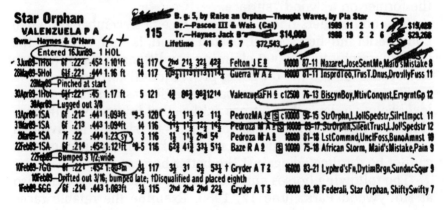

A sharp horse, the kind that often represents a double advantage. I would rate the last two performances.

Star Orphan

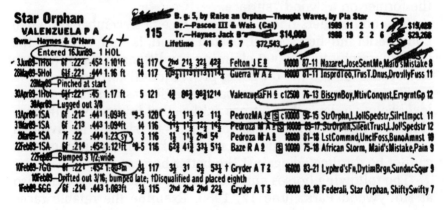

Star Orphan's last line: is the performance attractive enough to be rated? Look closely at it again.

Neither in-the-money nor within two lengths, Star Orphan's June 3 sprint does not fit snugly the definition of a good race. But the horse finished fourth and within 2¾ lengths, after tracking the pace throughout, an impressive effort. Flexible thinking beats rigid rules.

Michael D. Man also presents a variation of the norms earlier presented.

An "acceptable" race versus better beats half the field *and* finishes within six lengths.

Michael D. Man did not beat half the eleven horses in the $25,000 sprint of June 10. Yet the performance is clearly an improvement, and the colt has swung back in seven days, a plus factor. Today's claiming price will be the cheapest Michael D. Man ever carried. When on a fence, include the horse, and let the ratings inform final decisions.

An infinite array of similar situations can be provided. No matter. The point has been stated before. Identifying contenders and selecting ratable races depends for its success on the practitioner's knowledge and skill in handicapping. Until that knowledge and skill has accumulated into expertise, the benefit of the doubt belongs to the horses.

CHAPTER IV

Basic Methods

To SEPARATE CONTENDERS, sophisticated practiced handicappers depend upon a fantastic array of rating methods. Some estimate true speed, others relative class, others pace, others form, and several rate combinations of these factors. Basic methods, in addition, yield values commonly adjusted by values attached to other related factors, perhaps trips, trainers, or track conditions.

The rating methods tend to be technical and arithmetical, complicated but not complex, and producing numbers. Horse racing is a data-based activity, superbly susceptible to numerical manipulation, and contemporary handicappers by large consensus imagine themselves as numbers merchants. A common conceit among regular handicappers of the late 1980s, certain to extend to the 1990s, is the thoughtful post-race reference to the efficacy of one's figures.

No one should doubt, however, the pivotal role in handicapping of accurate numerical ratings.

The numbers can be invoked to quantify horses' chances to win in efficient, objective manner, organizing a mass of disjointed data items into a meaningful coherent rating.

The numbers can compare horses competing at different distances, even at different racetracks, a convenient comparative function.

Numbers can rank contenders from high to low on specific dimensions of performance, such as final time (speed), fractional time (early pace), fractional time and final time in combination (pace), and even quality of opposition (class).

A sequence of numbers sometimes can reflect horses' current form cycles, or indicate patterns of improvement and deterioration from season to season.

Numerical rating methods of greatest value have in common a reliance on data that is not contained in the past performances. The information so produced is thought to bestow on its users a sharp-edged sword not available to the crowd, which it does. Or may not, depending on whether users are sufficiently enlightened about the handicapping process as a whole to interpret the numbers accurately and to apply them sensibly, which thousands of racegoers are not.

It's crucial to understand at the outset the numbers produced by rating methods represent the means to an end, but not the end. A pair of melancholy thoughts for numbers wizards: (a) high-rated horses lose races every day at every track, and (b) the finest numbers in the kingdom contain sizable grains of error.

To state it differently, numerical ratings of horses do not represent reality, but estimates of reality, and the estimates contain small to moderate to gross degrees of error. Any dedicated figure handicapper who has attempted to beat the races with a blind ambition hinged to the numbers can testify eloquently to the point. The numbers are necessary, all right, but they are not sufficient.

Exactly where does this leave recreational handicappers, racing's casual audience without access either to the raw data or to the information ultimately produced?

A fair reply is: (a) definitely in arrears of excellent figure handicappers, but (b) not out in the cold.

The material presented in this section is intended to bring recreational handicappers into competitive handicapping shape. It describes an array of numerical rating methods that will put casual handicappers, not on equal footing with professionals, but on solid footing nonetheless.

To get moving, recreational handicappers can borrow a few ideas from the branch of modern handicapping that has blazed the new pathways for the past fifteen years.

Modern speed handicapping has solved the problems of estimating the true speed of racehorses, a monumental contribution to the theory and practice of handicapping. As explained, users of the *Daily Racing Form* cannot gauge the true speed of horses from the actual times and speed ratings provided, the customer's main problem.

But savvy speed handicappers can.

The solution involves new means of evaluating the influences on running times of two critical factors, relative class and track-surface speed. Recreational handicappers can adapt the procedures of modern speed handicapping to clarify the running times printed by the *Racing Form*. One piece of vital information, and a few procedural steps, amount to a quantum leap.

First, recreational handicappers must comprehend the following pair of terms of speed handicapping:

Par time. The typical final time of a specific class of thoroughbred at a regularly run distance at a particular racetrack, such as $25,000 claiming horses, 4up, at six furlongs at Santa Anita

Daily track variant. A measure of track-surface speed on a particular racing day, normally calculated as the average deviation from pars of the actual final times on that day

Pars are averages, not unlike pars for golf courses or for a specific hole on a golf course. Like golfers, horses of the same class will perform better than par, and others will perform worse. But when the running times for a specific class of horses at a specific distance throughout a season have been averaged, the result is a par time.

Daily track variants are merely typical deviations from par of the running times at a particular track on a specific day. To note that the track variant for Santa Anita on April 15 was Fast 2 means the nine races that day on average were two lengths (or two fifths of a second) faster than normal.

Daily track variants can be calculated for sprints and routes, respectively, and up-to-snuff speed handicappers prefer to possess both variants.

The daily track variant indicates how fast or slow a track surface has been in relation to what is expected. If handicappers know the track variant, they can adjust the actual times for that day to reflect the combined effects of relative class and track-surface speed.

So if those $25,000 claiming horses at Santa Anita have run six furlongs in 1:10.2 seconds on a day when the track variant was Fast 3, the adjusted time would be three fifths of a second slower, or 1:11 flat. If the track variant that day had been Slow 3, the adjusted time of the 1:10.2 race would be 1:09.4.

Now the significance of the daily track variant can be appreciated by even the most casual racegoers.

Suppose a pair of $25,000 claiming horses have run six furlongs in 1:10.2 seconds each, but Horse A competed on a Fast 3 surface and Horse B on a Slow 3 surface. Which horse ran the faster race?

Not only did Horse B run faster, he ran faster than A by six lengths, hardly an inconsequential distinction. The daily track variant is an indispensable consideration whenever handicappers intend to evaluate running times, which is often.

Without par times, which can vary from season to season, recreational handicappers have no means of calculating the daily track variant. They therefore cannot determine how fast or slow a track surface has played on a specific day, and cannot adjust raw times accordingly.

In practical terms, moreover, daily track variants must be calculated daily, a regimen not compatible with the timetables, tastes, or temperaments of occasional recreational handicappers.

The approach to be recommended here substitutes the concept of a par variant for the par times from which daily track variants are customarily calculated. The par variant will be a single number—for sprints and routes, respectively—that describes the normal track-surface speed of a racetrack in relation to the par times and track records of that track. A par variant can be used in conjunction with the daily track variants published by the *Daily Racing Form*, these determined in relation to track's best times in the past three seasons.

The deviation between a track's par variant and the *Racing Form*'s daily track variant for a particular day would indicate whether the track surface was atypically fast or slow on that day. Thus:

Daily track variant = *Racing Form* Variant *Minus* the Par Variant

Let this be the daily track variant utilized by recreational handicappers. Par variants for 62 racetracks, sprints and routes, will be provided in the next section.

The resulting estimates of horses' true speed will contain greater error at times than the author would prefer, but they will also position recreational handicappers in possession of the numbers far ahead of the crowd.

ADJUSTING FINAL TIMES

The *Daily Racing Form*, as mentioned, prints a daily track variant that describes the average deviation between the actual final times of races and track records for the distances, sprints and routes, respectively, on that day. In the past performances below, the track variants for the three-year-old Lightning Port's last eight races appear in the column below the arrow:

The numeral 11 (circled) means that on May 13, 1989, at Hollywood Park, the final times of the sprints (on average) were 2⅕ seconds slower (11/5ths) than the existing track records for the sprint distances that were run that afternoon.

In the same record, on December 24, 1988, on a sloppy track, the numeral 23 means the final times (sprints) at Hollywood were (on average) 4⅗ seconds slower (23/5ths) than the track records for the distances that were run that afternoon.

In theory, the lower the *Form's* track variant, the faster the track surface that day. The higher the *Form's* track variant, the slower the track surface that day.

But it ain't necessarily so, and can be terribly misleading. A parade of authors have exposed the flaws in the *Form's* track variants. Recreational handicappers need to be versed on the subject. Here are three vital flaws:

1. The form's track variants are totally insensitive to relative class levels.

Because the form's track variant is based upon track records, or best times within the past three years a lower variant may result merely because classier horses were running closer to record times, as on a Saturday, and a higher variant may result because cheaper horses were running slower than record times, as on a Thursday.

The track-surface speed might not have changed at all. Or, the track surface might have been faster on Thursday, slower on Saturday, the opposite conditions reflected by the variants supplied by the *Racing Form*.

2. The use of local track records renders comparisons between distances and racetracks meaningless.

At major tracks all-time champions have established the track records for the distances, routes especially. Ordinary horses cannot approach those records. Track variants at those tracks therefore will be larger, notably for routes, not because the track surface was slower, but because the track records were faster.

At Belmont Park the track record at 1⅛ miles is a remarkable 1:45.2, set in 1973 by the great Secretariat.

At Hollywood Park the same track record is 1:47.2, set in 1985 by the local filly Fran's Valentine.

Is Belmont Park ten lengths faster than Hollywood Park? In fact, Hollywood Park has a faster surface than Belmont Park. Both feature one-turn routes. But Hollywood Park has a track surface just six years mature, its time records established by parochial division leaders, not by all-time champions. Form variants will be lower at Hollywood Park than at Belmont Park as a rule, regardless of track-surface speeds.

3. When sprints predominate on a program, sprint variants will be lower, route variants will be higher—perhaps flagrantly higher—regardless of track-surface speed.

Ordinary horses can run closer to the track records of sprints than of routes. If just one route is carded, for cheaper claiming horses, the route variant will be ridiculously high. The track surface is neither faster for sprints nor slower for routes.

No modern speed handicapper worth his numbers bothers with the daily track variants published by the *Daily Racing Form*, sad to say.

But if the par times for a racetrack are compared to the track records for the same distances, the deviations indicate how much slower than the track records ordinary local horses normally run. If those deviations are averaged, the resulting figure is a best estimate of how much slower than the track records are the combined classes of horses at the local track. This average can be termed a par variant.

Consider the par-time chart for Santa Anita during 1988–89, below. The track records at Santa Anita during the period were:

Sprints		Routes	
6F	1:07.3	1M	1:33.4
6½F	1:14	1¹⁄₁₆M	1:40.2
7F	1:20	1⅛M	1:45

Santa Anita Pars 1988–89

Class	Distance					
	6F	6½F	7F	1M	1¹⁄₁₆M	1⅛M
Stakes	1:09	1:15.2	1:22	1:35.3	1:42.2	1:48.4
clf Alw	1:09.2	1:15.4	1:22.2	1:36	1:42.4	1:49.2
NW 3–4	1:09.3	1:16	1:22.3	1:36.2	1:43.1	1:49.4
NW 2	1:09.4	1:16.1	1:22.4	1:36.3	1:43.2	1:50
NW 1	1:10.1	1:16.3	1:23.1	1:37	1:43.4	1:50.2
Mdn	1:10.3	1:17	1:23.3	1:37.2	1:44.1	1:50.4
Mdn Clm 50	1:11	1:17.2	1:24	1:38	1:44.4	1:51.2
Mdn Clm 32	1:11.3	1:18	1:24.3	1:38.4	1:45.2	1:52
Above 50	1:09.2	1:15.4	1:22.2	1:36	1:43	1:49.3
Clm 50	1:09.4	1:16.1	1:22.4	1:36.3	1:43.2	1:50
Clm 40	1:10	1:16.2	1:23	1:36.4	1:43.3	1:50.1
Clm 32	1:10.1	1:16.3	1:23.1	1:37	1:43.4	1:50.2
Clm 25	1:10.2	1:16.4	1:23.2	1:37.1	1:44	1:50.3
Clm 20	1:10.3	1:17	1:23.3	1:37.2	1:44.1	1:50.4
Clm 16	1:10.4	1:17.1	1:23.4	1:37.4	1:44.3	1:51
Clm 12,5	1:11	1:17.2	1:24	1:38	1:44.4	1:51.2
Clm 10	1:11.1	1:17.3	1:24.1	1:38.1	1:45	1:51.3

When the sprint pars at Santa Anita are subtracted from the track records at the regularly run distances, and the deviations averaged, the average sprint deviation is 15. The average route deviation is 17. Thus the Santa Anita par variants are set equal to 15 for sprints and 17 for routes.

When a track's par variant is compared to the Form's daily track variant, the deviation is a better estimate as to how fast or slow the track surface played on a particular day. That is, a track's typical deviation from record times is contrasted with a particular day's average deviation from the same times.

Look again at the past performances for Lightning Port (page 100). On April 20, 1989, at Santa Anita, the Form's track variant is 16. The race is a sprint. The par variant at Santa Anita for sprints is 15. Recreational handicappers can estimate the Santa Anita track surface that day was Slow 1, as $16/5$ is one fifth of a second (one length) slower than $15/5$.

The par variants become handy tools for rating horses' speed more accurately.

If Santa Anita were Slow 1 for sprints on April 20, 1989, the final time for Lightning Port's six-furlong race can be adjusted from 1:09.4 to 1:09.3. As Lightning Port was beaten a half length that day, his adjusted final time becomes 1:09.4. The adjusted times now reflect the effects of track-surface speed.

Adjusting final times becomes a simple matter of adding to or subtracting from actual times the deviation between the par variant for the distance and the Form's track variant.

The examples of this book deal mainly with Santa Anita and Hollywood Park, where the 1989 par variants were:

	Spr	Rte
Santa Anita	15	17
Hollywood Park	13	13

A list of 1988–89 par variants for 62 racetracks in North America is presented in Table 1.

Unless the track surface has changed substantially, or the local racetrack is new (Arlington Park), par variants should remain relatively stable for a time, lasting upward of five seasons perhaps.

Recreational handicappers can begin to use par variants for local tracks immediately to estimate daily track variants and obtain adjusted final times. Adjusted final times will provide better estimates of true speed than the raw times printed in the *Daily Racing Form*.

Here are a few additional horses from Lightning Port's race at Hollywood Park on May 13, 1989. For each horse, use the par variants above to calculate the daily track variant for the last running line, and to adjust the final time of the race.

6 FURLONGS. (1.08½) CLAIMING. Purse $14,000. 3-year-olds. Weight, 122 lbs. Non-winners of two races since March 26, allowed 3 lbs.; a race since then, 6 lbs. Claiming price $20,000; if for $18,000 allowed 2 lbs. (Races when entered for $16,000 or less not considered.)

Coupled—Island Legacy and Lightning Port.

I trust recreational handicappers will agree that adjusting final times by applying daily track variants is elementary arithmetic.

The results are invariably striking. The sprint Lightning Port exited, no longer rates a full second or five lengths faster than the sprint exited by Telephone Khal, but three-fifths slower.

To be sure, the swiftest adjusted time is the sprint Telephone Khal engaged in as a juvenile during fall 1988. That day Hollywood's daily track variant was Slow 9, changing the final time from 1:10.4 to 1:09 flat.

Recreational handicappers here confront the nasty problems generated by extreme track variants.

Normally, track surfaces will be fast or slow by one to three lengths. As daily track variants become more extreme, the adjusted times and numerical ratings they engineer become less reliable.

A daily track variant greater than a second represents a large deviation from the norm. During the 1988–89 winter season at Santa Anita, the daily track variant was faster or slower by a

Table 1. Best Times, and Par Variants (PV), Sprints and Routes, for 62 North American Racetracks

Track	Sprint	PV	Route	PV
Ak-Sar-Ben	1:07.2	19	1:40.3	28
Aqueduct (main)	1:08	16	1:47	24
Aqueduct (inner)	1:08.4	14	1:41.4	20
Arlington Park	1:08	20	1:32.1	27
Assininoia Downs	1:09.1	18	1:35.4	26
Atlantic City	1:08.2	15	1:41	14
Bay Meadows	1:07.4	11	1:38.2	20
Balmoral	1:11.3	9	1:45	17
Belmont Park	1:08	15	1:40.2	16
Beulah Park	1:08.4	11	1:41.2	20
Birmingham	1:09.2	14	1:43.4	16
Blue Ribbon	1:09	14	1:44.3	14
Calder	1:10.1	11	1:43.4	20
Caliente	1:07.4	11	1:41	13
Canterbury Downs	1:09.1	10	1:42.1	13
Charles Town	1:17	21	1:44	25
Churchill Downs	1:08.3	15	1:41.3	24
Delaware Park	1:08.1	14	1:41.3	14
Del Mar	1:07.3	12	1:40	12
Detroit	1:08	24	1:40.3	41
Ellis Park	1:09	18	1:34.3	24
Exhibition Park	1:15.1	10	1:42.1	12
Fair Grounds	1:09	13	1:42.2	21
Fairmount Park	1:08.3	26	1:42.1	33
Fairplex Park	1:09.2	7	1:42.1	10
Finger Lakes	1:09.2	15	1:43.1	18
Garden State	1:08.2	16	1:41.3	22
Golden Gate	1:07.4	10	1:39.4	14
Greenwood	1:17.1	17	1:42	26
Gulfstream Park	1:07.4	19	1:40.1	29
Hawthorne	1:08.1	16	1:39.3	33
Hialeah Park	1:08	15	1:40.2	21
Hollywood Park	1:08.2	9	1:40	15
Keeneland	1:08.2	18	1:41.1	26
Laurel	1:08.3	13	1:41.3	18
Longacres	1:07.1	12	1:39.4	13
Los Alamitos	1:08.3	12	1:41.3	17
Louisiana Downs	1:08.2	15	1:42.2	15
The Meadowlands	1:08.2	8	1:40.3	15
Monmouth Park	1:08	13	1:41	14
Oakland Park	1:08	16	1:40.1	23
Penn National	1:08.4	16	1:40	19
Philadelphia Park	1:08.1	13	1:40.4	15

Table 1.

Track	Sprint	PV	Route	PV
Pimlico	1:09.1	15	1:40.4	22
Portland Meadows	1:09.2	16	1:43.1	17
Remington Park	1:08.1	11	1:41	14
River Downs	1:08.3	18	1:36.1	22
Rockingham Park	1:08.4	14	1:42	22
Ruidoso Downs	1:09.2	10	1:45.2	11
Santa Anita	1:07.3	15	1:40.1	17
Saratoga	1:08	9	1:47	20
Sportsman's Park	1:10	17	1:42.4	22
Stampede Park	1:09.2	13	1:43.1	13
Suffolk Downs	1:08.1	18	1:41.4	21
Sunland Park	1:08.2	16	1:42	16
Tampa Bay Downs	1:09	17	1:43.4	14
Thistledown	1:08.2	18	1:41	18
Timonium	1:15.2	10	1:43	12
Turf Paradise	1:06.4	17	1:39.1	24
Turfway Park	1:08.4	18	1:42	23
Woodbine	1:08.3	15	1:41.4	25
Yakima Meadows	1:08.2	15	1:42.2	13

*Par times of local racetracks change annually. Researcher and author William L. Quirin updates the par times for some 91 racetracks, dirt and turf, each January. Current pars can be obtained from Quirin at Box 701, Department of Mathematics and Computer Science, Adelphi University, Garden City, New York 11530.

Prices are $3 for any par table, $5 for any two tables; $50 for the entire set of dirt pars, $25 for the entire set of turf pars.

**Where track records change, add a point to the par variant for each one fifth of a second faster the best time has become.

***Where the *Daily Racing Form*'s track variants consistently and significantly deviate from the above par variants, user must identify the current "best times" being utilized by the *Form* to calculate speed ratings and variants, and modify the local par variants accordingly.

Lightning Port

GUERRA W A		**116**

Dk. b. or br. c. 3, by Hyannis Port—I'm Not Cheap, by Count Recess
Br.—Foonberg & Shulman (Cal)
Tr.—Shulman Sanford

Own.—Shulman & Wild Oak Ranch

1989	4	0	1	2	$9,337
1988	3	1	0	0	$8,250

$20,000

Lifetime 7 1 1 2 $17,587

20Apr89-1SA 6f :21⁴ :45¹ 1:09⁴ft 4 116 1² 11½ 1½ 2½ Stevens G L ⁴ 20000 88-16 GrkMyth,LightningPort,W'tzingSss 7
23Mar89-1SA 6½f:21³ :45 1:18³ft 4½ 117 2ʰᵈ 2² 3¹ 3³ Pincay L Jr ² 20000 76-19 WltzngSss,MgcJhnsn,LghtⁿⁿgPrt 11
2Feb89-5SA 6f :21³ :45 1:11¹ft *3½ 116 112⁴111⁷111¹⁵10¹⁴³ Hawley S ¹⁰ 32000 67-18 GingrSocks,Ptzcuro,Homb⁻Hombr 11
   2Feb89—Reared at start
20Jan89-2SA 6f :21² :44³ 1:10²ft 39 113 2ʰᵈ 2ʰᵈ 21½ 32½ ♦ Hawley S ½ 35000 83-13 Gntlmn'sStyl,MgcJhnsn,BtOtOfHll 10
   420Jan89—Dead heat
24Dec88-7Hol 6f :22² :46³ 1:13³sy 3 111⁵ 1ʰᵈ 2ʰᵈ 5⁸ 620½ Valenzuela F H⁶ 40000 53-23 BucksForBob,AegenKing,CkeForOn 7
10Dec88-6Hol 6f :22 :45¹ 1:10²ft 7½ 116 42½ 42½ 88³ 812³ Delahoussaye E⁸ 50000 77-15 BlckJckAttc,MgcJhnsn,Gn'lmn'sStl 8
1Dec88-4Hol 6f :22 :45¹ 1:11 ft *8-5 118 11½ 2ʰᵈ 1ʰᵈ 1ⁿᵏ Pincay L Jr¹² M32000 87-17 LghtnngPrt,MrclMystry,SctOfFrtn 12
Apr 15 Hol 4f ft :51 H

```
Telephone Khal                       B. g. 3, by Blue Eyed Davy—Khal Dr Kehr, by Dr Marc R
  MCCARRON C J                 116   Br.—Sledge Stable (Cal)             1988 3 1 0 0        $9,500
Own.—Sledge Stable                   Tr.—Perdomo Pice          $20,000
                                     Lifetime  3 1 0 0  $9,500
17Nov88-7Hol  6f :223 :454 1:104ft  *2½ 116  2½ 31 45 78¼  DelahoussayeE7 50000 80-22 Morlndo,MgicJohnson,Tnc'ousTom 9
22Sep88-12Fpx 6½f:204 :45 1:164ft  13 114  31½ 35½ 56 69½  Ortega LE5 Beau Brml 82-12 Gum, Might Be Right, Loaded Juan6
8Sep88-4Dmr  6f :22 :453 1:112ft  4¼ 117  1hd 11½ 12½ 13½  DlhoussyE11 [S]M32000 81-15 TelphonKhl,Agrssion,FrwllPromis 12
  May 11 Hol 3f ft :353 Hg   May 6 Hol 5f ft 1:002 H   Apr 30 Hol 4f ft :50 H   Apr 21 Hol 5f ft 1:012 H

Believe It To Me                     Dk. b. or br. g. 3, by Believe It—Janets Kindy, by Bold Joey
  VALENZUELA P A               116   Br.—Round Meadow Fm & Vienna (Cal)  1989 6 1 0 1       $11,750
Own.—Bloom Jr–Otteson–Vienna Jr      Tr.—Vienna Darrell        $20,000   1988 2 M 0 0
                                     Lifetime  8 1 0 1  $11,750
3May89-5Hol  6f :22 :451 1:104ft  2½ 117  42½ 32 32 33  Pincay L Jr 8  25000 84-15 ChiefRunninBlze,Telvizd,B'ivItToM 8
     3May89—Veered out start; lugged in stretch
7Apr89-5SA  6f :22 :46 1:113ft  5 117  41¼ 31 64½ 77  Pincay L Jr 4  25000 73-19 GrkMyth,SpcyYllowtl,PcktflOfAcs 10
     7Apr89—Troubled trip
16Mar89-9SA  1 :461 1:104 1:372ft  *2¾ 116  11½ 2½ 44½ 611½  Valenzuela P A 7  32000 69-16 PrccsKnght,MrclMystry,MlcsPrtnr 8
15Feb89-5SA  6f :213 :45 1:103ft  6½ 116  63¼ 64½ 89½ 813¼  Baze R A 5  40000 72-17 Pttn'ForEgl,MgcJohnson,ClrflHttr 8
     15Feb89—Bumped start
27Jan89-6SA  6½f:213 :44 1:17 ft  34 117  75¼ 88¼ 814 817½  Baze R A 2 [S]Aw32000 67-21 MyLuckyLynnie,ShadyPine,Mr.Bolg 8
     27Jan89—Broke slowly
2Jan89-4SA  6f :213 :444 1:101ft  *2¼ 118  1hd 1hd 13½ 17½  Baze R A 11  M32000 87-13 BlvItToM,MrclMystry,ScotOffFrtn 12
2Dec88-6Hol  6f :214 :443 1:104ft  39 118  42 43 45 74½  Baze R A1  [S]Mdn 83-15 DistntPowr,BluEydDnny,BggrBoy 10
5Nov88-8SA  6f :213 :443 1:092ft  46 1125  64 64¾ 59 613¾  ValenzuelFH10 [S]Mdn 77-13 Mr.Bolg,DonutsToDollrs,FistDlSol 16
  Apr 29 Hol 5f ft 1:00 H   Apr 23 SA 5f ft 1:021 H   Apr 16 SA 5f ft 1:012 H   ●Apr 5 SA 3f ft :344 H

Muscle Bound                         B. c. 3, by Turn to Mars—Figure Conscious, by Determine
  MEZA R Q                     116   Br.—Rancho Jonata (Cal)             1989 5 0 0 0        $1,000
Own.—Four Four Forty Farms           Tr.—Borick Robert         $20,000   1988 5 1 2 0       $14,762
                                     Lifetime  10 1 2 0  $15,762
26Apr89-3Hol  1 :452 1:104 1:361ft  11 116  11½ 2½ 46 510¾  Solis A 7  25000 71-10 SrosFntsy,MlcosPrtnr,WtTllTmrrw 7
7Apr89-5SA  6f :22 :46 1:113ft  44 1115  51¾ 84¾ 86¾ 88¾  Garcia H J8  25000 71-19 GrkMyth,SpcyYllowtl,PcktflOfAcs 11
30Mar89-3SA  1 :453 1:104 1:371ft  15 117  11 21 45½ 511¼  Pincay L Jr10  25000 71-16 GrekMyth,SumDndy,MurtMunson 10
23Mar89-1SA  6½f:213 :45 1:183ft  11 116  63¼ 109¾ 77½ 66  Pedroza M A3  c20000 71-19 WltzngSss,MgcJhnsn,LghtnngPrt 11
     23Mar89—Lugged in early
2Jan89-1SA  6f :22 :452 1:104ft  4½ 114  2½ 3nk 42 67  Stevens G L5  28000 77-13 Targo, Bally Car Road,GingerSocks 8
9Dec88-5Hol  6f :221 :454 1:111ft  6 116  1hd 2hd 2hd 43  Stevens G L4  28000 83-16 Bye Bye, Upinthesky, Targo 9
26Oct88-3SA  6f :214 :452 1:111ft  5½ 1115  1hd 22 46 69¾  Valenzuela F H8  28000 72-16 Waltzing Sass, Rip Curl, Morlando 9
     26Oct88—Bobbled start
7Oct88-4SA  6f :22 :453 1:113ft  2¼ 115  11½ 1hd 1hd 1no  Stevens GL2 [S]M28000 80-19 MusclBound,PntdTgr,BrllntEqton 11
5Aug88-6LA  6f :222 :462 1:124ft  9-5 118  1hd 44½ 35 21½  Gryder A T5  M32000 77-13 ChromSilvr,MusclBound,HyWinnr 10
26Jly88-4LA  6f :222 :474 1:143ft  *9-5 118  73½ 54¾ 22 2½  Pedroza M A7  M32000 69-21 ChnsDsrtSong,MsclBond,ABtOfOb 10
  May 11 SA 3f ft :372 H   May 5 SA 5f ft 1:05 H   Apr 21 SA 4f ft :493 B   Apr 14 SA 4f ft :472 Hg
```

full second or more no less than 45 of 90 racing days. Figure handicappers will testify that season stands among the most difficult ever.

Slow 9 is obviously a gross deviation from par. When using par variants to estimate daily track variants from *Form* variants,

Date	*Horse*	*Track*	*Variant*	*Final Time*	*Adjusted Final Time*
May 3	Island Legacy	Hol	Slow 2	1:10.4	1:10.2
Apr 20	Lightning Port	SA	Slow 1	1:09.4	1:09.3
Nov 17	Telephone Khal	Hol	Slow 9	1:10.4	1:09
May 3	Believe It To Me	Hol	Slow 2	1:10.4	1:10.2
Apr 26	Muscle Bound	Hol	Fast 3	1:36.1	1:36.4

as this guide recommends, extreme variants will be even more prone to error. The correction, perfectly rational, pushes extreme variants toward the norm. Two alternative strategies are explained in the sidebar opposite. Review the procedures now.

Unless track surfaces have been "off" due to weather, or running times have proved inordinately sluggish, or rapid, due to track-maintenance peculiarities, handicappers can modify extreme track variants as they prefer. Slow 9 becomes Slow 4. Fast 12 become Fast 6. Expediency rules. Practice, plus experience, forms the best guidelines on the matter, which in any event will be more subjective and artistic than mechanical.

Recreational handicappers need not be upset by the intricacies and adaptations. Figure handicapping is imprecise, characterized by error estimates, even in the best of situations.

The colt Muscle Bound in the sample exits a route. The adjusted final time of 1:36.4 at a mile is not readily compared to the adjusted final times of sprints. By applying a portion of the daily track variant to the internal fractions of a route, an adjusted six-furlong time can be constructed.

The arithmetic, again, will be elementary, but is best discussed in conjunction with the next topic.

ADJUSTING FRACTIONAL TIMES

To obtain pace ratings, handicappers relate fractional times to final times. Pace analysis considers the relations among fractional times, final times, and running styles an intricate slice of the handicapping art. Fractional times are central both to the ratings and the analysis that follows.

Pace methods concentrate on the second calls of sprints and routes. In sprints, horses will have traveled four furlongs. In routes up to 1¼ miles, the horses will have traveled six furlongs.

In all instances, as Tom Brohamer has emphasized, the horses will have completed significantly more than half the race at the pace call.

Track-surface speed affects fractional time as well as final time, an obvious observation. But a telescoping effect occurs, the daily track variant gathering less impact at the shorter distances.

As a small concession to imprecision, adjusting fractional

WHEN FORM VARIANTS FLUCTUATE WILDLY

For a variety of reasons, the *Daily Racing Form*'s track variant may fluctuate wildly in relation to a track's par variant. The situation arises frequently for routes, when just one or two routes have been carded, and these of the cheaper kind.

Two strategies make sense.

If the *Form*'s sprint variant appears normal, but the route variant a gross distortion, adjust the route variant. Use a two-to-three ratio of sprint variant to route variant. Thus a sprint variant of Fast 4 translates to a route variant of Fast 6.

If the sprint variant is Slow 2 in relation to the track's par variant, but the route variant a suspiciously Slow 14, change the route variant to Slow 3.

If sprint and route variants both appear exaggerated or inexplicably out of balance with prior days' variants, or expected variants, another adjustment helps. For every two points the *Form* variant deviates from the track's par variant, equate that to one length. That is, a two-point deviation of the *Form* variant from the par variant equals a one-point adjusted deviation from the par variant.

If the *Form* variant for routes is 25, but the track's par variant for routes is 13, the best estimate of the daily track variant is Slow 6, not Slow 12. A twelve-point spread is adjusted to a six-length deviation. Extreme *Form* variants that appear irrational must always be adjusted or discarded.

times to reflect track-surface speed can adhere to one golden rule, sprints and routes. Assign one half the daily track variant to the fractional time at the pace call. If the daily track variant is Fast 4, the fractional variant is Fast 2.

Half lengths on the split variant are translated to an additional full length. Thus Fast 5 translates to Fast 3 (2½ lengths) at the fractional call.

Reconsidering the actual times of Lightning Port's sprint on April 20, handicappers see: 45.1   1:09.4.

The daily track variant is Slow 1.

The adjusted times are: 45   1:09.3.

Using the daily track variants provided (pages 105–106) to adjust the fractional times of the other horses in the Lightning Port field, handicappers get:

Horse	Variant	Fractional Variant	Adjusted Fractional Time
Island Legacy	Slow 2	Slow 1	45.1 to 45
Telephone Khal	Slow 9	Slow 5	45.4 to 44.4
Believe It To Me	Slow 2	Slow 1	45.1 to 45
Muscle Bound	Fast 3	Fast 2	1:10.4 to 1:11.1

Horses exiting routes can be rated for sprints by adjusting the four-furlong and six-furlong fractions of the route.

Consider Muscle Bound's last running line, the mile at Hollywood Park on April 26. The daily track variant is Fast 3, and one half of that is assigned to the six-furlong call, Fast 2. To adjust the four-furlong fractional time, use one half of the six-furlong variant, Fast 1.

The adjusted fractional times of Muscle Bound's race are: 45.3   1:11.1.

Now, using the adjusted fractional times of routers, to adjust further for rating the horses in sprints, follow these procedures*:

1. Subtract two fifths from the four-furlong time.
2. Subtract two fifths from the six-furlong time.
3. Divide the beaten lengths at the six-furlong time by one half.

To rate Muscle Bound in today's sprint, the adjusted times and new beaten lengths are: 45.1   1:10.4   beaten ¼ length.

As with all rating methods, the explanation is more labored than the procedure itself.

The four-year-old maiden filly below was entered at 6½ furlongs May 13, 1989, at Hollywood Park. Use the techniques and information presented above to adjust its last running line, so that it might be rated in a sprint.

* When evaluating one-turn miles, no further adjustments are necessary.

Priceless Candy
Ch. f. 4, by Debonair Roger—Hello Doily, by Irish Castle

JAUREGUI L H

Br.—Velasquez J–R–Lydia (Cal) 1989 4 M 0 0 $2,850
Tr.—Velasquez Robert A 1987 0 M 0 0

Own.—Velasquez R A

1185

Lifetime 4 0 0 0 $2,850

14Apr89-6SA	1	:461 1:113 1:372ft	39 120	66 64¼ 43½ 59	Patterson A9	⑤Mdn 72-12	PennyLegnd,Dhli'sImg,Lyphrd'sSnp 9
24Mar89-6SA	6f :22	:454 1:12 ft	60 120	1011 910 53 43½	Patterson A1	⑤Mdn 74-20	ForvrGorgos,SwtWtrL,SplndrDncr 12
24Feb89-6SA	6f :214	:451 1:102ft	139 118	1111 96¾ 88½ 813¼	Cedeno A4	⑤Mdn 73-16	SummrTrsr,Shddbot,Dncncnthprk 12
6Jan89-6SA	6f :22	:46 1:113m	84 1145	1114 1117 91² 913¼	Corral J R6	⑤⑤Mdn 67-20	Callet Time, Settle It,AlomasCase 12

6Jan89—Broke in, bumped

May 8 Hol 5f ft 1:013 H   ● Mar 17 Hol 5f ft :58³ H

The par variant for routes at Santa Anita is 17. The *Racing Form's* track variant of April 14 is 12. Thus the daily track variant for Santa Anita on April 14, 1989, is an estimated Fast 5.

The adjusted final time of Priceless Candy's race on April 14 is 1:38.2.

One half the daily track variant (Fast 3) is applied to the six-furlong fractional time, changing 1:11.3 to 1:12.1 seconds.

One half the six-furlong variant (Fast 2) is applied to the four-furlong fractional time, changing 46.1 to 46.3.

Finally, to adjust for today's sprint, two fifths of a second is subtracted from the adjusted fractional times, changing 46.3 and 1:12.1 to 46.1 and 1:11.4. Beaten lengths at the six-furlong call are divided by half, changing 4¼ lengths to two lengths.

Once daily track variants have been applied and other adjustments completed, the adjusted times and beaten lengths provide a new look at the same race. Below is the revisionist view of the five contenders in the Lightning Port field.

Which horse ran the fastest race last out? Adjusted final times clearly favor Lightning Port. The colt ran approximately four fifths of a second faster than Telephone Khal, and faster still than the others.

What about the probable pace?

Telephone Khal ran against the fastest pace, a 44.4 to the

Horse	Adjusted Times		Beaten Lengths	Horse's Adjusted Final Times
Island Legacy	45	1:10.2	6	1:11.3
Lightning Port	45	1:09.3	½	1:09.4
Telephone Khal	44.4	1:09	8	1:10.3
Believe It To Me	45	1:10.2	3	1:11
Muscle Bound	45.1	1:10.4	¼	1:10.4

quarter pole. If chasing, or setting, a slower pace today, the gelding may not fade as badly.

If forced to run faster to the pace call today, what will Lightning Port do? Weaken? Or win handily just the same?

Do either Telephone Khal or Lightning Port enjoy a pace advantage here? If so, which horse is it?

Might another horse actually have an advantage here, a class edge maybe? If so, which horse is it?

Ah, the persistent challenges of full-dress handicapping. The prickly queries that endow the pastime with its unquenchable mental appeal.

Recreational handicappers will be interested to discover they can find clear-cut answers much of the time by converting adjusted times to numerical pace ratings, and pretty damn quick at that.

Which brings us to PDQ (pretty damn quick) pace ratings, a rating procedure that has taken on a number of conventional formats but which has been successful with unprecedented consistency when implemented with the twist promoted in this book's variation.

PDQ PACE RATINGS

A convincing argument for pace analysis might be entered at several points. The practical imperative, that recreational handicappers can use the associated rating procedures effectively, and without recourse to information outside of the contents of the past performances, serves the present purpose splendidly.

The substantive reasons are hardly less persuasive.

Studies of professional speed and pace figures in combination have revealed that when fractional times increase, final times regularly decrease.

The converse happened as well.

When speed, or final times, improved, pace, or fractional times, often declined.

For many horses a faster pace does not contribute to a faster final time, but slower. For other horses a faster pace does result in a faster final time. It's crucial to understand the interactions.

In practice, expert pace analysts have always comprehended why ordinary horses that had recorded an impressive final time

two weeks ago against similar horses dispensed a dull performance yesterday. The internal fractions—pace—quickened, and
the horses were unable to duplicate prior final-time feats.

Claiming horses are notoriously prone to the phenomenon.
So are maiden graduates. Maiden-claiming winners that will face
a faster pace versus former open winners today almost always
expire. Younger nonclaiming horses as a class are sadly susceptible to a quickening pace as well, disappointing their hopeful
owners, curious trainers, and confident bettors.

The most occasional recreational handicappers will bear
witness to the phenomenon of the uncontested frontrunners. Left
alone on the lead, the horses win waltzing, and can achieve
dazzling final times. When contested for the early advantage,
throughout similar or slightly accelerated fractional times, many
frontrunners weaken and lose, often in final times slower than
they had completed in the recent past.

In recent years empirical investigations of energy distribution among winners at various distances and racetracks have
demonstrated provocatively that the energy demands of racetracks at the pace call can be highly predictive of the eventual
outcomes. Horses that have displayed the requisite pace capacities and running styles regularly win. Horses that expend too
much energy early, or too little, in relation to a track model of
recent winners at the distance, are less likely to be winners
themselves.

Similar studies of sprinters, 3up, stretching out to routes,
indicate the likeliest survivors will be horses that do not release
too much energy too soon.

Reliance on pace offers pragmatic advantages as well. Racegoers by the thousands rally after superior class, high speed figures, rapid early speed, positive form, and leading trainers. Far
fewer clamor after pace standouts. Of the fundamentals, pace
probably reveals itself at the windows the least.

Yet the irresistible argument for pace is that it allows recreational handicappers to cope with the complicated realities and
subtleties of class-within-a-class.

Within class levels, claiming and nonclaiming, the best horses
will run faster fractional times, faster final times, and both. At
any level, the classiest horses can complete the fastest fractional
times en route to the fastest final times.

Handicappers in possession of accurate pace ratings will be
equipped to identify the best of class, not only between levels,

but within levels. Adjusted final times, and the associated speed figures, can be badly mistaken on the matter.

PDQ pace ratings deal with fractional time, final time, and beaten lengths. In sprints, beaten lengths at the pace call take precedence; in routes we emphasize beaten lengths at the finish.

The rating method is intended to determine which horses can set and sustain the fastest pace, or track and overtake the fastest pace. A single number, or pace rating, is calculated.

Sprint ratings are comparable to other sprint ratings, route ratings to other route ratings. When rating horses at related distances, as between six furlongs and seven furlongs, or between a mile and 1⅛ miles, a simple one-step adjustment will be recommended.

Sprint ratings are not comparable, alas, to route ratings, a limitation recreational handicappers can abide.

We begin by assigning a numerical rating of 100 to the following standard times at the regularly run distances, regardless of racetrack.

4F	44	1M	1:34
6F	1:08	1¹⁄₁₆M	1:40
6½F	1:14	1⅛M	1:46
7F	1:20		

A fractional time of 44 flat in a six-furlong sprint, or any other race, is set equal to 100. Any slower fractional time will be assigned a rating lower than 100.

A final time of 1:46 at 1⅛ miles also is set equal to 100. Any slower final time at the distance will obtain a rating lower than 100.

The six-furlong standard time of 1:08 (100) is also invoked when rating the fractional times of routes.

Three numerical ratings are obtained for sprints: at the pace call of the race, at the pace position of the horse, at the final position of the horse. The method therefore combines one rating for the race and two ratings for the horse.

The first step concentrates on the fractional time and final time of the race, *after these have been adjusted by the daily track variant.*

Subtract one point for each one fifth of a second the adjusted times of the races have been slower than the standard times of the method.

For example, if a six-furlong sprint has been completed in 45 flat to the pace call and 1:10.3 to the finish, the tabulations are:

$$44 = 100 \qquad 1:08 = 100$$
$$45 = 95 \qquad 1:10.3 = 87$$

Next, examine the horse's beaten lengths to rate its running position at both the pace call and finish.

Subtract the horse's beaten lengths at the pace and finish from the race's rating at the pace call and finish, respectively. If Horse A were beaten two lengths at the pace call of the sample race (95) and one length at the finish (87), its ratings for position would be 93 at the pace call and 86 at the finish.

PDQ pace ratings are equal to the sum of the three ratings: pace of the race (95), pace of the horse (93), and finish of the horse (86).

The PDQ pace rating of Horse A in the example would be equal to $95 + 93 + 86 = 274$.

Each contender's PDQ pace rating is calculated in the same way. In routes, to repeat, the fractional time is the six-furlong time.

For practice, obtain the PDQ pace ratings for the five contenders in the claiming race featuring Lightning Port (pages 105–106).

Here are the appropriate numerical ratings for the pace of the race, and for each horse at the pace-finish positions, plus each contender's combined PDQ pace rating.

Island Legacy	$95 + 89 + 82 = 266$
Lightning Port	$95 + 95 + 91 = 281$
Telephone Khal	$96 + 95 + 87 = 278$
Believe It To Me	$95 + 93 + 85 = 273$
Muscle Bound	$94 + 94 + 86 = 274$

If recreational handicappers obtained different ratings, they probably forgot to begin by adjusting actual times by the daily track variants. Go back and repeat the procedure.

A cautious interpretation of the ratings equates a length to two rating points. One point amounts to a half length.

Lightning Port shapes up as a probable winner on pace, after all. The upset possibility is Telephone Khal, earning a higher rating than suspected, due to a slow track variant, and plunging two levels in claiming class. If Lightning Port is backed to win, an exacta box with Telephone Khal makes sense as well, if only as a protective measure.

By rating horses' positions at the pace call, the PDQ method penalizes closers for their running style. Closers will inevitably earn lower ratings for position at the pace call.

But the bias is less pronounced than imagined. Closers that win sprints normally do so by reaching contention at the second call. They then sustain their punch to the finish. Late runners in sprints, the one-run closers, do not arrive in time, unless (a) the early pace has collapsed, or (b) the closers possess a tremendous class edge.

The correction occurs in the interpretation. Pace analysis supersedes pace ratings. If a swift, hotly contested pace should defeat its combatants, or a monstrous closer looks irresistible on class, a pace analysis can concede the case, and pace ratings can be junked.

A more problematic weakness of the method is structural. It concerns the standard times to which the arbitrary rating of 100 are assigned.

It's easier for unexceptional horses to run closer to 1:08 at six furlongs than to 1:20 at seven furlongs. Unexceptional routers can approach a 1:34 miles much easier than they can a 1:46 at 1⅛ miles.

PDQ pace ratings can be biased in favor of faster horses at shorter distances. The correction is an adjustment to the final ratings. When comparing horses at related distances, examinations of the par times of $10,000 claiming horses indicate the following adjustments:

6F to 6½F	−4
6½F to 7F	−7
6F to 7F	−11
1M to 1¹⁄₁₆M	−10
1M to 1⅛M	−15
1¹⁄₁₆M to 1⅛M	−6

When comparing the rating of a horse at six furlongs to the rating of a horse at seven furlongs, subtract 11 points from the six-furlong rating. Inversely, add 11 points to the seven-furlong rating.

When comparing a rating earned at a mile to a rating earned at 1⅛ miles, subtract 15 points from the mile rating.

It's prudent to avoid extreme rating adjustments, such as 11 to 15 points. Recreational handicappers should prefer to rate horses using races at closely related distances, and wherever feasible, at the same distance.

I wish to stress the point. The method works well for the same and closely related distances. The adjustments from six to 6½ furlongs, from 6½ to seven furlongs, and from 1¹⁄₁₆ miles to 1⅛ miles are tenable; larger adjustments are a stretch.

Also, if daily track variants are unknown, or cannot be estimated using this book's par variants, the power of the method might be compromised. To correct, handicappers must insist on larger numerical differences in ratings between horses.

To appreciate the point, let's attach a typical daily track variant of Fast 2 to hypothetical running times of 45 flat and 1:10.3 for a frontrunner beaten two lengths. Unadjusted, the PDQ pace rating will be $95 + 95 + 85 = 275$.

With a track variant of Fast 2 applied, the adjusted times are 45.1 and 1:11 flat. Beaten two lengths, the horse's adjusted final time is 1:11.2. The PDQ pace rating is now $94 + 94 + 83 = 271$.

The difference of four ratings points amounts to roughly two lengths. How many races are won by margins of two lengths or less?

To dramatize the situation further, examine what happens to the unadjusted PDQ pace rating of a $10,000 claiming-race winner that goes wire to wire on days when the daily track variant is a perfectly typical Fast 1, Fast 2, or Fast 3.

Santa Anita $10,000 clm	PDQ Pace Ratings			
	Unadjusted	F1	F2	F3
Pace 45.2	93	92	92	91
Pace (horse) 45.2	93	92	92	91
Final (horse) 1:11.1	84	83	82	81
PDQ Pace Ratings	270	267	266	263

The importance of the daily track variant should be clear, a difference of 3 to 7 ratings points, and frequently more. In beaten lengths, two to four lengths is the conservative tradeoff. If the track were a full second fast, the PDQ pace rating for the mythical frontrunning $10,000 claiming winner would be 259, or 5½ lengths slower than the unadjusted rating.

Recreational handicappers are urged to rely on daily track variants in making pace ratings, as promoted here. The small extra effort will be rewarded numerous times a season.

When daily track variants cannot be applied, unadjusted PDQ ratings must reveal a spread of 5 to 6 points in sprints, 7 to 8 points in routes, to be accepted confidently. As wider differences in ratings will be required, the utility of the method will be reduced.

PDQ pace ratings can be a remarkably functional tool for separating contenders quickly and reliably. Skill with the method can be acquired with a week's practice.

The method is also transportable. When they visit unfamiliar racetracks, recreational handicappers can carry the par variants and rating method with them.

For full-blown figure handicappers, the method can be a handy crutch at the beginnings of new seasons, when speed and pace figures have not been updated. A few weeks of PDQ pace ratings bridge the gap in the figure file. I employ the method myself in that way.

To conclude the topic on a sober thought, PDQ pace ratings at times will be susceptible to the same demons that bedevil the Form's speed ratings and track variants. On racing days when only a single route has been carded, or two, notably if the races feature cheaper claiming horses, the Form's route variant may be excessively high.

Be cautious. If the Form's route variant looks uncomfortably, awkwardly extreme, it probably is. The correction depends upon the sprint variant for the same day, which recreational handicappers must identify or find. The route variant should be set equal to the sprint variant plus the difference between the track's par variant for sprints and its par variant for routes.

Consider Santa Anita, where the par variant for sprints is 15 and for routes 17, a difference of two. If the Form variant for routes on a particular day is 28, but the sprint variant for the same day is 14, handicappers should distrust the route variant as too extreme in relation to the day's sprints.

The adjusted route variant for the day at Santa Anita would be 14+2, or 16. Now the route variant has been balanced with the sprint variant sensibly.

As before, the explanation is worse than the operation. A little practice sharpens the skill. The same observation suits the next topic, a skill virtually lost to recreational handicappers, until now.

PACE-RATING SHIPPERS

In rating shippers, one adjustment to the PDQ ratings can control reasonably well for differences due to track class and track-surface speed.

Here recreational handicappers can borrow from the practices of professionals.

Professional handicappers first identify a class level at the local track where comparable-class horses from the shipping track have won consistently. In California, for example, $12,500 to $16,000 claiming horses that ship to southern California from northern California win repeatedly at the same $12,500–16,000 levels at Santa Anita and Hollywood Park. Relative class at those claiming thresholds between the circuits is negligible.

Next, the pros examine the average times (pars) for the comparable classes of claiming horses at the receiving and sending tracks. The differences can be accepted as an index of track-surface speed. Looking at the typical times for $12,500–16,000

PDQ PACE IN SPRINTS

The PDQ pace ratings promoted here favor early pace in sprints. Where final times are relatively close, horses that have set or pressed a rapid pace will be advantaged. By this approach, horses that have won might be rated inferior to, or below, other horses they have beaten.

Consider the seven-furlong September 1 sprint of the pair on the next page. Daily track variant is Fast 1 to the pace call, Fast 4 to the final call. Adjust the raw times, and calculate PDQ pace ratings for each horse.

Just Deeds — B. g. 3(May), by Beau's Eagle—Shaky Footing, by Shecky Greene
NAKATANI C S — 1115 — Br.—Dilbeck Ray (Cal) — 1989 10 2 0 3 $30,400
Tr.—Mason Lloyd C — $50,000 — Turf 2 0 0 0
Own.—Dilbeck R — Lifetime 10 2 0 3 $30,400

120ct89-8SA 1 Ⓣ:46 1:093 1:34 fm 43 1115 55 67½ 77¾ 89¼ Nakatani CS9 Aw37000 92 — ImmrtlScrpt,LvThDrm,Bbtscldtsd 10
1Sep89-3Dmr 7f :222 :45 1:214ft 4¾ 1115 3½ 2½ 2hd 32¼ Nakatani C S6 62500 91-11 Its Royalty, Comical, Just Deeds 6
24Aug89-3Dmr 1 Ⓣ:491 1:124 1:37 fm 22 117 62¼ 43 63¾ 63½ Pincay L Jr5 Aw38000 82-09 Friendly Ed, Strung Up, One Drink 8
24Aug89—Wide throughout
11Aug89-8Dmr 7f :214 :441 1:213ft 42 115 65½ 76¼ 65 65½ Black C A7 ⓈRl Gd Dl 88-15 Mr. Bolg, Timeless Answer, Bruho 7
11Aug89—5 wide into lane
9Jly89-9Pln 6f :224 :452 1.103ft *1 117 41½ 53¼ 57 56½ Chapman T M3 HcpO 82-18 BearInMind,Doncreer,PlusOrMinus 6
24Jun89-7GG 6f :214 :45 1:101ft 6½ 117 42½ 41½ 31 1¾ ChapmanTM6 Aw20000 88-16 Just Deeds, Comical, Bin Of Ice 7
24Jun89—Bumped start
10Jun89-8GG 6f :212 :44 1:093ft 8½ 117 43 31½ 31½ 32 ChapmanTM6 Aw20000 89-11 Desert Rival, Vote, Just Deeds 8
27May89-7GG 6f :214 :443 1:092ft 9¾ 117 95 63¾ 54¾ 34½ Kaenel J L5 Aw20000 87-15 Mr. Don, Rip Curl, Just Deeds 10
6May89-6GG 1 :461 1:094 1:351ft 33 109 21½ 22 26 48¼ Gryder A T2 HcpO 81-14 AvengingForce,BseCmp,Beu'sAllinc 7
23Apr89-4GG 6f :221 :453 1:113gd 29 118 11 2hd 1hd 1½ ChapmnTM4 ⓈM20000 81-17 JustDeeds,KingoftheByou,GryWhl 12
23Apr89—Broke in a tangle

Speed Index: Last Race: –5.0 1–Race Avg.: –5.0 1–Race Avg.: –5.0 Overall Avg.: –0.5
Oct 18 SA 3f ft :363 H Oct 6 SA 7f ft 1:301 H Sep 30 SA 6f ft 1:143 H Sep 20 SA 3f gd :37 H

Its Royalty — B. c. 3(Mar), by Native Royalty—Cuidado Jan, by Introductivo
SIBILLE R — 116 — Br.—AIBAIncThbd&OwnsRE&Sns (Ky) — 1989 4 1 1 0 $25,250
Tr.—Mulhall Richard W — $50,000 — 1988 7 M 0 2 $10,975
Own.—Arnold & Fulmer — Lifetime 11 1 1 2 $36,225

1Sep89-3Dmr 7f :222 :45 1:214ft 15 116 59 57 33 12¼ DelahoussayeE 5 62500 93-11 Its Royalty, Comical, Just Deeds 6
20Feb89-5SA 1 1/16 :474 1:121 1:433ft 39 115 1110 106¾ 75¼ 68 Sibille R 9 Aw35000 75-19 ExemplryLeder,Copet,BrtcChief 11
3Feb89-3SA 1 1/16 :461 1:112 1:444ft 4¼ 116 811 76½ 43 2nk DelahoussayeE 6 40000 77-17 ScoutOfFortune,ItsRoylty,DimeTim 8
3Feb89—Bumped start
11Jan89-2SA 1 :462 1:114 1:381ft *7-5 117 43 31½ 1½ 13 † DelahoussyeE 1 M32000 77-14 ItsRoyalty,Naskra'sWltz,Dr.Hughes 9
11Jan89—Disqualified from purse money; Broke out, bumped
14Dec88-3Hol 1 1/16 :472 1:122 1:454ft 5½ 118 75¼ 64¼ 34 3¾ DelahoussyeE 4 M32000 70-16 LuckIsSweet,Dramtized,ItsRoylty 12
14Dec88—[illegible]
3Nov88-4SA 1 1/16 :464 1:123 1:451ft *2 117 43 32½ 37 310 Stevens G L 4 M40000 65-18 LeliaLove,TropicWarrior,ItsRoylty 12
3Nov88—Veered out, bumped start, again at 7 1/2
16Oct88-6SA 1 1/16 :462 1:113 1:454ft 9½ 117 79 56¾ 49 410¼ Baze R A 6 Mdn 62-16 SnowsInPris,Pster'sImge,PcerRex 12
16Oct88—Broke in a tangle
5Oct88-?SA 1 :47 1:12 1:38 ft 16 117 813 59 56½ 47½ Ortega L E 5 Mdn 69-21 [illegible] 6
5Oct88—Steadied start

The adjusted times for the race are 45.1 to the half, and 1:22.3 at the finish. And the ratings are:

		Pace/ Race	Pace/ Horse	Final/ Horse	PDQ Pace
Just Deeds	Adjusted times	45.1	45.2	1:23	
	Ratings	94	93	85	272
Its Royalty	Adjusted times	45.1	46.3	1:22.3	
	Ratings	94	87	87	268

Despite winning the September 1 sprint, Its Royalty has been rated four points, or approximately two lengths, behind the third-place finisher Just Deeds, beaten two lengths.

In sprints, the rating method rewards horses' ability to set or press a swift pace and still finish strongly. Horses trailing by several lengths at the pace call, like Its Royalty, will be penalized for a poor pace position, notwithstanding an impressive finish.

The reasoning is sound. Horses trailing by several lengths at the pace call of sprints normally will require (a) a collapsing pace, or (b) a tremendous class edge, to finish the job.

In the subsequent meeting between Just Deeds and Its Royalty, a $50,000 claiming race at a mile, Just Deeds finished second, beaten a length. Its Royalty finished up the course.

It happens all the time.

PDQ PACE IN ROUTES

In races at 1¹⁄₁₆ miles and farther, the fractional times at the pace call can vary widely, depending upon track class, track configuration, and even riding tactics. Moreover, the ability to finish well, as from the prestretch call to the wire, counts significantly more than in sprints.

Moreover, most contending horses will have reached contention by the prestretch call, or second call. From there, the field spreads itself out widely until the finish.

PDQ pace ratings might better reflect the race's final time in relation to the horse's position at the finish, as opposed to its position at the pace call. This can be particularly indicative of nonclaiming horses and higher-priced claimers.

Thus, in better routes PDQ pace ratings can include the pace call of the race, the final time of the race, and the final position of the horse. Standard times remain the same, and as before, the three ratings are added to form a final pace rating.

Consider the October 9 performance of Pirate's Hoorah at Santa Anita:

Pirate's Hoorah — **Dk. b. or br. f. 4, by Pirate's Bounty—Northerly Glow, by Pass the Glass**
CHAPMAN T M **116** — **Br.—Sarkowsky H (Ky)** — **1989 12 2 3 4 $59,025**
Own.—Asistio L A — **Tr.—Seguin Yves M** — **Turf 5 1 0 1 $18,525**
Lifetime 12 2 3 4 $59,025

9Oct89-9SA 1 1/16 :463 1.12 1:443ft *9-5 117 75½ 21 2½ 23 Pincay L Jr 5 Ⓕ c32000 75-19 NoRomnc,Prt'sHoorh,ComplitAccrd 9
31Aug89-3Dmr 1 1/16 :461 1:104 1:423ft 2¾ 116 52½ 21 21½ 22 Stevens G L 4 Ⓕ 40000 85-14 CrftyDrl,Pirte'sHoorh,Soonermoon 7
31Aug89—Fractious gate
16Aug89-9Dmr 1 :46 1.11 1:363ft *2½ 116 59 55 43 3½ VlenzuelPA 4 Ⓕ c32000 82-16 CraftyDarla,PlyingTps,Pirte'sHoorh 7
16Aug89—Wide into stretch
7Aug89-8Dmr 1⅛ Ⓣ:48 1:13 1:512fm 9½ 117 44½ 43 54 64¾ Sibille R 3 ⒻAw38000 71-24 Edge Of Heaven, Bracorina Mornin 9
7Aug89—Bumped 1/4
13Jly89-9Hol 1 1/16 Ⓣ:4631:1031:42 fm 5¾ 112 118¾ 97 54½ 3¾ Davis R G 9 Ⓕ 45000 83-20 AssumedTrits,Goldrry,Pirt'sHoorh 11
13Jly89—Off slowly
10Jun89-4Hol 1 1/16 Ⓣ:4621:11 1 42 fm 7 1175 47 34½ 45 54 NakatniCS 3 ⒻAw33000 80-15 BbCoo ChickenDinner,Lyphrd'sFlg 6
18May89-7GG 1⅛ Ⓣ:4841:14 1:521fm*6-5 118 84¼ 52¼ 41¼ 11¾ Lambert J 5 ⒻAw21000 87-12 Prt sHoorh Dsv sFlng,ForgtTnD rt 9
30Apr89-9Ho 1⅛ Ⓣ:47 1:1041:48 fm 6½ 116 64½ 43 42½ 44¾ Davis R G 8 ⒻAw28000 83-06 Brcorin,Dncingintpprk Cn.ckn D rnr 9
30Apr89—Wide into stretch
9Apr89-7SA 1 1/16 :463 1:104 1:433ft 7½ 117 54 46½ 45½ 34¾ Davis R G 7 ⒻAw36000 76-14 SummerAmbo SssySlw,Pirt sHoorh 6
9Apr89—Broke out, bumped
31Mar89 5 . . 1 1/16 464 1 12 1 45 . *4 5 12 54 44 21½ 13 D . . R G 3 ⒻW5000 76 1 Pirte sHoorh BronzeRb' SnowSpr . 6
31Mar . F . . . .
Speed Index Last Race -5 . 3-Race Avg -2.. 5-Race Avg . Overall Avg -4
0 . h 4 . 4 Se. 3 St . . . Sa . SA 5f h . . Se 1 . Dmr 5

First, the par variant for routes at Santa Anita is 17. The *Daily Racing Form*'s variant for Santa Anita routes of October 9 is 19. Thus the estimate of the track variant for routes at Santa Anita that day is Slow 2.

The adjusted times of Pirate's Hoorah's race are therefore 1:11.4 to the pace call (Slow 1), and 1:44.1 at the finish (Slow 2). Beaten three lengths, Pirate's Hoorah's final time is 1:44.4.

What is Pirate's Hoorah's PDQ pace rating for the race? At the route we rate the race's fractional time (1:11.4), the race's final time (1:44.1), and the horse's final time (1:44.4).

The three ratings, and combined PDQ rating, would be:

Race's fractional time	1:11.4	81
Race's final time	1:44.1	79
Horse's final time	1:44.4	76

Pirate's Hoorah's PDQ pace rating on October 9 is 236. Whenever relative class at the route amounts to a greater concern than the pace of the race for the first six furlongs, recreational handicappers can prefer this procedure. At major tracks the procedure is highly recommended, as it is for top-of-the-line horses everywhere.

Pace ratings so obtained are not interchangeable with the ratings obtained in sprints, regardless of any adjustments applied.

claiming horses at Hollywood Park and Golden Gate Fields, the Gate is faster by two lengths.

Claiming horses that ship from Golden Gate to Hollywood Park would have their PDQ pace ratings reduced by two points.

In the nonclaiming division, relative track class can be estimated by examining the pars either of maidens or classified allowance horses, perhaps both. This book prefers the classified horses, as these races variously include higher-priced claiming horses and stakes horses as well.

As with comparable claiming classes between tracks, partime differences can be observed, and these invoked to adjust the numerical ratings of shippers.

In the claiming divisions, recreational handicappers are urged to rely upon the convenient finding of Bill Quirin's computer studies of thousands of races nationally that $10,000 claiming horses are pretty much the same caliber everywhere.

That is, a $10,000 horse is a $10,000 horse is a $10,000 horse, at any track. Thus the $10,000 claiming pars can be compared, and the time differences judged a serviceable reflection of track-surface speeds.

To illustrate, below are the $10,000 claiming pars and classified allowance pars for the major tracks on the southern California circuit: Santa Anita, Hollywood Park, and Del Mar.

Track		6F	6½F	7F	1M	1¹⁄₁₆M	1⅛M
SA	$10K	1:11.1	1:17.3	1:24.1	1:38.1	1:45	1:51.3
	Clf	1:09.2	1:15.4	1:22.2	1:36	1:42.4	1:49.2
Hol	$10K	1:11.1	1:17.3	1:24	1:36.4	1:44.3	1:51
	Clf	1:09.2	1:15.4	1:22.1	1:34.3	1:42.2	1:48.4
DM	$10K	1:10.4	1:17.1	1:23.2	1:37.2	1:43.4	1:50.2
	Clf	1:09	1:15.2	1:21.3	1:35.1	1:41.3	1:48.1

Using the most frequently carded distances of six furlongs and 1¹⁄₁₆ miles as barometers, handicappers notice that in claiming sprints Santa Anita and Hollywood Park do not differ, but Del Mar is two lengths faster than both.

In claiming routes, Hollywood Park is two lengths faster than

Santa Anita. Del Mar is six lengths faster than Santa Anita and four lengths faster than Hollywood Park.

The same patterns characterize the nonclaiming races at the sister tracks, making southern California a reasonably symmetrical circuit.

The mile pars, however, are vastly dissimilar, as Hollywood Park's circumference is 1⅛ miles, and that track cards one-turn miles. Hollywood Park is seven lengths faster than Santa Anita at the mile, under claiming and nonclaiming conditions, and three lengths faster than Del Mar.

When the claiming horses of southern California change to another track on the circuit, handicappers would adjust their PDQ pace ratings for track-to-track comparisons as follows:

Receiving Tracks

		Santa Anita			Hollywood Park			Del Mar		
		Spr	Rte	1M	Spr	Rte	1M	Spr	Rte	1M
Sending Tracks	SA	x	x	x	0	+2	+4	+2	+6	+4
	HOL	0	−2	−7	x	x	x	+2	+4	−3
	DM	−2	−6	−4	−2	−4	−3	x	x	x

When the horses ship in late July from Hollywood Park to Del Mar, within a few weeks handicappers will be comparing $20,000 claiming routes at Del Mar with the same class of routes completed weeks ago at Hollywood Park.

If a $20,000 Hollywood Park route winner earned a PDQ rating of 260, the adjustment to the rating to facilitate comparisons with similar ratings earned at Del Mar is +4, or 264. The adjustment (+4) accommodates the circumstance that Del Mar is typically four lengths faster than Hollywood Park in claiming routes.

To compare nonclaiming races at sending and receiving tracks, differences between classified allowance pars are observed, and PDQ ratings adjusted accordingly. Recreational handicappers might anticipate larger par-time differences among classified allowance horses at different tracks, especially as distinctions in track class are palpable.

Tables 2 and 3 below present the 1988–89 par times of $10,000 claiming horses and of classified allowance horses, respectively, at the regularly run distances for 62 racetracks in North America.*

Recreational handicappers can find the pars of racetracks that ship regularly to their local tracks. Calculate the adjustments appropriate to PDQ pace ratings obtained by shippers from the sending tracks.

Table 2. Par Times at Regularly-Run Distances for Older $10,000 Claiming Horses at 62 North American Racetracks

Tracks	6F	6½F	1 Mile	1¹⁄₁₆M
Ak-Sar-Ben	1:11.1			1:46.3
Aqueduct (main)	1:12	1:18.2	1:38.3	
Aqueduct (inner)	1:12.3			1:47
Arlington Park	1:12.1	1:18.3	1:38.1	
Assiniboia Downs	1:12.1		1:40.1	1:47
Atlantic City	1:10.1			1:44
Balmoral	1:13.2	1:20	1:40.1	1:48.2
Bay Meadows	1:10.2		1:37	1:43.3
Belmont Park	1:11.4	1:18.1	1:38.2	1:45
Beulah Park	1:10.4			1:45.1
Birmingham	1:12.2		1:40.3	1:47.1
Blue Ribbon	1:11		1:32.4	1:45.3
Calder	1:12.2	1:19.1		1:48.2
Caliente	1:09.3		1:36	1:43
Canterbury Downs	1:11.2	1:17.4	1:38.3	1:45.2
Charles Town		1:20.4		1:48.3
Churchill Downs	1:11.4	1:18.3	1:38.4	1:47
Delaware Park	1:10.4			1:44.3
Del Mar	1:10.4	1:17.1	1:37.1	1:43.4
Detroit	1:12.3		1:42.1	1:49
Ellis Park	1:12.1	1:18.4	1:39.1	
Exhibition Park	1:10.2	1:17		1:44.3
Fair Grounds	1:11.4			1:47.1
Fairmount Park	1:13.1			1:48.1
Fairplex Park	1:10.4	1:17.1		1:44.2

*Note. Pars for racetracks not listed can be obtained for $3 per track beginning in February of each year from William L. Quirin, c/o Department of Mathematics and Computer Science, Adelphi University, Box 701, Garden City, New York, 11530.

Of the tracks listed, pars are subject to change annually due to surface changes, weather patterns, and variations in track maintenance procedures. Updated pars are strongly recommended.

Table 2.

Tracks	6F	6½F	1 Mile	1¹⁄₁₆M
Finger Lakes	1:12		1:39.4	1:46.3
Garden State	1:12		1:40	1:46.4
Golden Gate	1:10		1:36.3	1:43.1
Greenwood		1:20.4	1:40.3	1:47.2
Hawthorne	1:11.3	1:18.1	1:46.3	
Hialeah Park	1:11.2	1:18		1:45.3
Hollywood Park	1:11		1:37	1:44.2
Keeneland	1:12	1:18.4		1:47
Laurel	1:11.3	1:18.1	1:38	1:45.4
Longacres	1:09.3		1:36.3	1:43.1
Los Alamitos	1:10.4	1:17.1		1:43.2
Louisiana Downs	1:11.4	1:18.1		1:46.2
The Meadowlands	1:10.4		1:38	1:44.3
Monmouth Park	1:11		1:38	1:44.3
Oaklawn Park	1:11.3		1:39	1:45.3
Penn National	1:11.2		1:39.2	1:46
Philadelphia Park	1:10.4	1:17.1	1:37.4	1:44.1
Pimlico	1:12.2			1:46
Portland Meadows	1:12.1		1:39.2	1:46
Remington Park	1:10.3	1:17		1:44.2
River Downs	1:12		1:40.2	1:47.1
Rockingham Park	1:11.3			1:46.2
Ruidoso Downs	1:11		1:40	1:47
Santa Anita	1:11	1:17.2	1:38	1:44.3
Saratoga	1:11.2	1:17.4		
Sportsman's Park	1:13.2	1:19.2	1:41	1:47.2
Stampede Park	1:11.2		1:38.1	1:45
Suffolk Downs	1:11.3		1:39.1	1:45.4
Sunland Park	1:11.1	1:17.4	1:38	1:44.4
Tampa Bay Downs	1:12			1:46.3
Thistledown	1:12			1:47
Timonium		1:17.1	1:38.4	1:45.3
Turf Paradise	1:10	1:16.2	1:37.1	1:44
Turfway Park	1:12.2	1:19.1	1:39.4	1:46.4
Woodbine	1:12	1:18.4		1:47.3
Yakima Meadows	1:11.1		1:38	1:44.3

*Whenever possible, compare shippers at six furlongs in sprints and 1¹⁄₁₆ miles in routes.
**The par times indicate that Turf Paradise, for example, is 10 lengths faster than Thistledown in sprints and 15 lengths faster in routes. PDQ pace ratings for shippers from Turf Paradise at Thistledown would be adjusted 10 or 15 points downward to compensate for typical differences in track-surface speeds.

Table 3. Par Times at Regularly-Run Distances for Classified Allowance Horses at 62 North American Racetracks

Tracks	6F	6½F	1 Mile	1¹/₁₆M
Ak-Sar-Ben	1:10			1:44.4
Aqueduct (main)	1:10.1	1:16.3	1:36.1	
Aqueduct (inner)	1:11.1			1:45
Arlington Park	1:10.4	1:17.1	1:36.1	
Assiniboia Downs	1:12.2		1:40.2	1:47.1
Atlantic City	1:09			1:42.1
Balmoral	1:12.2	1:19	1:38.4	1:47
Bay Meadows	1:09		1:41.3	
Belmont Park	1:10	1:16.2	1:36	1:42.3
Beulah Park	1:10.2			1:44.2
Birmingham	1:11.1		1:38.4	1:45.2
Blue Ribbon	1:11		1:32.4	1:45.3
Calder	1:11	1:17.4		1:46.2
Caliente	1:09.1		1:35.1	1:42.2
Canterbury Downs	1:10.1	1:16.3	1:36.4	1:43.3
Charles Town		1:20.1		1:47.3
Churchill Downs	1:10.3	1:17.2	1:37	1:45.1
Delaware Park	1:09.4			1:43.1
Del Mar	1:09	1:15.2	1:34.4	1:41.2
Detroit	1:11.3		1:40.4	1:47.3
Ellis Park	1:11.3	1:18.1	1:38.1	
Exhibition Park	1:09.4	1:16.2		1:43.3
Fair Grounds	1:10.3			1:45.2
Fairmount Park	1:12.4			1:47.4
Fairplex Park	1:09.4	1:16.1		1:43
Finger Lakes	1:11.1		1:38.4	1:45.3
Garden State	1:10.4		1:38.1	1:45
Golden Gate	1:08.3		1:34.3	1:41.1
Greenwood		1:19.2	1:38.3	1:45.2
Hawthorne	1:10.2	1:17		1:44.4
Hialeah Park	1:09.3	1:16.1		1:43.1
Hollywood Park	1:09.1		1:34.3	1:42
Keeneland	1:10.3	1:17.2		1:45
Laurel	1:10.2	1:17	1:36.1	1:44
Longacres	1:08.3		1:35.1	1:41.4
Los Alamitos	1:10	1:16.2		1:42.1
Louisiana Downs	1:10.3	1:17		1:44.3
The Meadowlands	1:09.1		1:35.4	1:42.2
Monmouth Park	1:09.1		1:35.3	1:42.1
Oaklawn Park	1:10		1:36.4	1:43.2
Penn National	1:11		1:38.3	1:45.1
Philadelphia Park	1:09.3	1:16	1:36	1:42.2
Pimlico	1:11.1			1:44.1

Table 3.

Tracks	6F	6½F	1 Mile	1¹⁄₁₆M
Portland Meadows	1:11.4		1:39	1:45.3
Remington Park	1:09.3	1:16		1:43
River Downs	1:11.3		1:39.3	1:46.2
Rockingham	1:10.4			1:45.2
Ruidoso Downs	1:10.4		1:39.4	1:46.4
Santa Anita	1:09.1	1:15.3	1:35.3	1:42.1
Saratoga	1:09.3	1:16		
Sportsman's Park	1:12.3	1:18.3	1:39.4	1:46.1
Stampede Park	1:11.1		1:38	1:44.4
Suffolk Downs	1:11.1		1:38.3	1:45.2
Sunland Park	1:10.3	1:17.1	1:37.1	1:44.1
Tampa Bay Downs	1:11.2			1:45.4
Thistledown	1:11			1:45.3
Timonium		1:16.1	1:37.2	1:44.1
Turf Paradise	1:09.1	1:15.3	1:36.1	1:43
Turfway Park	1:11.4	1:18.3	1:38.4	1:45.4
Woodbine	1:10.2	1:17.1		1:45.2
Yakima Meadows	1:10.2		1:37.1	1:43.4

Recreational handicappers now are equipped to rate practically any horse in the country on pace. Two sources of new information facilitate satisfactory ratings and comparisons: par variants for local tracks, and the standard adjustments for shippers.

Regrettable experience shows the comparisons between bullrings and major ovals do not withstand the change of scenery. Essentially, par-time differences of the sending and receiving tracks are too gross to permit reliable comparisons.

Before leaving the treatment of pace and methods of pace analysis, recreational handicappers will be delighted to discover another potent means of separating close contenders. The elementary calculation not only isolates numerous probable winners, the data is fully contained in the *Racing Form's* past performances, and the technique has been scarcely distributed.

It remains conveniently outside the repertoire of racegoers everywhere. That's a formula for overlays.

TURN TIME

Contemporary pace analysts, the Sartin followers notably, have persuaded hundreds of handicappers, including me, that in sprints among unexceptional horses, which is virtually all, the critical point of call is the second.

Not the first call, which reveals early speed. Not the stretch call, which reflects late speed.

The second call measures early pace. In sprints of six furlongs, as hinted, the race at the second call is two-thirds complete. At the mile's second call the race is three-fourths complete. At no distance up to 1½ miles is the race less than half complete at the second call.

Do recreational handicappers imagine that an appreciation of what has transpired throughout more than half the race might prove significant on occasion?

In certain common situations a component of the early pace qualifies as a direct wiring to the finish.

To illustrate, which of the maidens below do handicappers prefer at six furlongs?

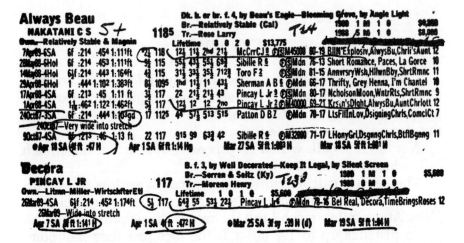

Sexy Slew competed against the swiftest final time. The top three fillies exhibited high early speed. The bottom pair finished second last out, highly predictive among maidens of victory next time.

A crucial question among closely matched sprinters, rarely posed, is which can run the fastest turn time.

Turn time refers to second-quarter time, typically recorded on the far turn.

At six and 6½ furlongs turn time is often decisive. It's calculated simply, as the difference in seconds between the first call and second call, modified by lengths gained or lost. Recreational handicappers need only perform the arithmetic.

Horses that accelerate on the far turn can be credited with an advantage on early pace. The horses customarily grab the lead while turning into the stretch. Closers will narrow the gap, gaining striking position. If past performances indicate the horses can sustain the rapid turn of speed, they will be awfully difficult to defeat.

To practice, recreational handicappers should calculate the turn times of the maiden fillies above. For your information, the turn times have been recorded on the past performances, above and slightly to the right of the jockey column; for Sexy Slew, turn time is 23.2 seconds.

Of interpretation, handicappers prefer a turn time faster than par. Or, par unknown, a turn time clearly superior to others in the field.

Par on the turn for maiden and claiming sprinters at Santa Anita is 23.2. Discount any turn time slower than par. Extra credit favors any horse capable of completing the second quarter mile in less than 23 seconds.

Turn times for the fillies in the maiden example are:

Sexy Slew	23.2
Debs Angel	23.1
Moonriver And Me	22.4
Always Beau	24
Decora	23.3

Debs Angel and Moonriver And Me have completed the turn faster than par, and Moonriver And Me has rushed around two-fifths faster than Debs Angel.

Slower than par, Always Beau and Decora can now be dismissed. Sexy Slew cannot keep pace in the second quarter, either, an unlikely candidate from the rail.

By conventional handicapping, curiously, Decora looks seductive.

If the three frontrunners weaken one another, the proverbial wisdom argues, Decora will be along in time. The magnificent rider Laffit Pincay, Jr., stays aboard, a plus sign. Forget it. With a sluggish pace time, and more dismal turn time, these kinds gain no striking position and disappoint desperately, even if the early pace staggers.

Sexy Slew is the most interesting of the group, and represents a common nonclaiming contender frequently misunderstood by casual handicappers.

With high early speed, and exiting the race having the fastest final time, this nicely bred, well-trained youngster will be strongly supported by the crowd. On March 30, Sexy Slew indeed was favored, after dispensing a turn time of 23.2 (par) at 2–1 on February 19.

Yet to keep abreast today, Sexy Slew will be forced to run faster than par around the far turn. Unable to complete an average turn time without disappointing, Sexy Slew cannot be expected to complete the second-quarter mile faster than par without collapsing.

In fact, Sexy Slew is prototypical of the lightly raced contenders handicappers want to avoid as nonclaiming prospects. Impressive final times, high early speed, but ordinary to slow turn times. The second quarter betrays these horses for the villagers they are. Prepare to upset them with horses registering competitive final times but faster turn times.

Turn time amounts to hidden speed. Even more than in maiden races, it can be absolutely the key to profits in the non-winners allowance series. The public will fancy rapid final times and high early speed, but pace analysts can dig deeper for the contenders possessing the swiftest turn times. Any that can negotiate the far turn in 22-and-change may represent the best bet of the day or week.

On a far wider plane, turn time can distinguish closely matched contenders in claiming races too. Certainly, claiming races limited to three-year-olds, or two-year-olds, should always be submitted to inspections for impressive turn times. Many short-priced contenders in these poorly sorted fields will exhibit below-average turn times and can be discarded.

Regarding older claiming contenders, the pair below were entered at 6½ furlongs for $32,000 at Santa Anita on April 12, 1989. The past performances illustrate a number of issues hinged to turn time.

Both geldings circled the far turn of the last running lines in a rapid 22.3 seconds. Par on the turn for better horses at Santa Anita is 23 flat.

Desperate has improved on the turn by one fifth of a second in each of its previous three sprints, a definite sign of positive form. The steady improvement supports a continuing rise in class. No surprise to pace fanatics, Desperate did continue to perform well, both on the far turn and at the finish. It won, April 12, at 4–1, and handily, by 3½ lengths.

Not surprising, either, Desperate's turn time April 12 was 22.2, another one-fifth improvement. Be alert for similar patterns among older claiming horses. The veteran campaigners with accelerating turn times are rampantly on the upgrade and can rise in class successfully. Desperate would be challenging $60,000 and $70,000 claiming stars in southern California within weeks of its April 12 upset, and even attempted to whip handicap horses.

The upstart rated as a solid contender in every race, and did okay.

Donner Party is a late-rallying sprinter. Also, at age eight, a bit of an in-and-outer.

Turn time is most effective in distinguishing frontrunners, pressers, and horses possessing tactical speed, such that they can relax within three to five lengths of the leaders at the first call.

Closers should be expected to gain ground around the far turn of sprints, their turn times not pregnant with meaning, unless sensational.

But a poor turn time by a late-running sprinter is bad news. If a rallying type shows tardy turn times, handicappers should mark them down as unlikely to gain favorable striking position in time to launch a successful bid.

In the April 12 sprint at Santa Anita, Donner Time was dropping a class level, from $50,000 to $32,000, a double drop actually, supported by a turn time last out of 23.3. A contender, to be sure.

Yet Donner Time, a 2–1 choice, did not come close to catching the improving Desperate, up from $25,000 competition. Donner Time finished fourth, beaten a cozy seven lengths.

Recreational handicappers who preferred Donner Time as the class of the field were mistaken, as deputies of this guide by now understand. Late closers inherit the front in sprints, provided they show impressive turn times, only when the leaders and pressers back up, as turn-time freaks like Desperate do not.

To repeat a delectable scenario for the emphasis it deserves, recreational handicappers are advised that many maiden graduates, as well as recent winners of a first allowance race, step ahead in nonclaiming class burdened by a hidden pace defect. They cannot negotiate the far turn in par, or better than par. The shortcoming will prove deadly whenever they encounter competitive allowance types that can.

CLASS RATINGS

The class, or talent, or ability, a racehorse exhibits depends upon the interaction of three attributes: speed, stamina, and competitive spirit.

By competitive spirit I mean the animal's willingness, determination, and courage under pressure or in the face of adverse circumstances, intangibles widely remarked.

The element of stamina, or endurance, suggests the class factor will become more influential as distances lengthen, and this is demonstrably true.

The complexity of the concept—what is this thing called class?—is the first of three reasons the class factor proves difficult to assess. Intangibles, after all, are hardly easy to quantify. Of the attempts to do so, a majority have proved not only fruitless, but embarrassingly bad. It's fool's play, perhaps, to take a performance that is essentially qualitative and describe it numerically.

A second reason is that class is dynamic. It matures. It changes. It declines.

In not inconsiderable measure, class is a function of form, though the correlation today is weaker. In like measure, form is a function of soundness, of conditioning. Physical development plays a role, as does competitive seasoning, surely among the young. So do the cyclical patterns of racing and training on a grinding schedule. The mix of ingredients is stirred relentlessly by trainers and handlers, whose horsemanship and management skills vary tremendously.

A third explanation is that class is relative. It's expressed in relation to the abilities and competitive qualities of other horses.

The typical progression involves increasingly fast and challenging horses, competing at longer distances under increasingly demanding conditions of eligibility. Only the strong will survive, are meant to survive. Thus a horse's class improves and declines in concert with the relative circumstances of major-league racing.

A perfectly legitimate approach to rating class eschews the attributes of horses and concentrates on the specific types of races where those attributes must be expressed.

As race conditions become more exacting, so the expression of the combined qualities of class must be correspondingly pronounced.

Recreational handicappers can benefit from the accuracy and simplicity of the rating method promoted here.

A taxonomy, or classification scheme, of the types of races can be drawn, and a numerical sequence of values attached, as in the class hierarchy described earlier for major tracks. That hierarchy of class levels is represented again now, and two new higher-order class levels attached, forming a ten-level hierarchy of thoroughbred class.

Class Levels at Major Racetracks

Levels	Claiming	Nonclaiming
1	$10,000 & below	
2	$12,500–16,000	
3	$20,000–25,000	Maiden Special Weight
4	$32,000–40,000	Alw, NW1XMC
5	$50,000–62,500	Alw, NW2XMC
6	Above $62,500	Alw, NW3X4X Clf Alw, Overnight Handicaps Stakes, Open & Restricted
7		Stakes, Listed and Grade 3
8		Stakes, Grade 2 and Grade 1
9		Multiple Grade 1 Stakes Winners
10		Champions, Classic Winners, and Outstanding Division Leaders

Levels 9 and 10, added, are intended to distinguish the best horses of each generation.

In today's climate of smaller, less competitive stakes fields, horses that have won two or more Grade 1 titles deserve distinction apart from winners of a single Grade 1 race. Champions, classic winners, and outstanding division leaders, of course, merit the handicapper's highest praise.

Horses can be rated variously on class, invoking the numerals for the class levels, based upon the rater's best judgment as to quality of performance.

Quality of performance might be assessed according to the following definitions:

Good race, or unexceptional win	Same class level
Big Win, or win following a fast-fast pace	Class level, plus 1 or 2
Acceptable race	Class level, minus 1
Poor race	Class level, minus 2

A horse displaying a good race, for example, when entered for $25,000 claiming, would be rated a 3.

A good performance by a maiden warrants the same 3, as maidens compare to $25,000 claiming horses in the class hierarchy.

A good race under classified allowance conditions rates a 6.

A Big Win means a margin of victory of three lengths or greater, preferably in a field of seven or more horses.

A fast-fast pace refers to obviously rapid fractional times in *combination with* a fast final time.

Any other victory defaults to an unexceptional win.

A good race, to rehash the operational definition, is a finish within two lengths in sprints, within three lengths in routes.

An acceptable race is a finish within six lengths that beats half the field.

If a horse entered for $50,000 claiming wins by five, what class rating is awarded?

The Big Win deserves a 6, a level above $50,000 claiming.

If a three-year-old is entered under allowance conditions, for nonwinners of a race other than maiden or claiming, and prevails in ordinary time and manner, what is the class rating?

The horse rates a 4, indicating it would be competitive on class against $32,000 to $40,000 claiming horses (4), but should be stretched, beyond limits perhaps, against nonclaiming prospects gunning for the second allowance purse (NW2XMC), a class rating of 5.

Suppose a $20,000 claiming horse has been whipped by six lengths while finishing fifth of eleven. What class rating should be assigned?

It's a 2, suggesting a class drop.

If another $20,000 horse in the field finished third, beaten two lengths, what class rating is deserved?

It's a 3, suggesting a potential win at the level.

By this rating technique, recreational handicappers can classify every horse on the grounds. As each class level in the hierarchy embraces a range of classes, a one-point distinction can signal a real edge. A two-point spread can be decisive.

Maiden-claiming graduates are assigned a class rating equal to the class level 50 percent below the selling price of the maiden-claiming race. Thus the winner for $32,000 maiden-claiming is assigned a class rating equal to the $16,000 claiming level, a 2.

Recreational handicappers at minor tracks also can extend the local class hierarchy by two new levels.

Level 9 honors consistent winners in the stakes division, notably of better purses on the local schedule. The horses might have annexed a graded stakes as well, probably Grade 3 or Grade 2.

Level 10 acknowledges the superiority of multiple graded stakes winners, or of horses talented enough to win a Grade 1 race.

To implement the rating procedure, recreational handicappers must learn how to identify the exact conditions of eligibility from the information provided in the class column of the past performances. Two obstacles interfere, but can be circumvented.

The *Daily Racing Form* does not publish the exact conditions of allowance races, but the paper does publish the pertinent purse values. Handicappers must associate purse values and eligibility conditions.

What is the standard purse at the local track of an allowance race, for nonwinners of a race other than maiden or claiming?

Class Hierarchy / Minor Racetracks

Levels	Claiming	Nonclaiming
1	$3,500 & below	
2	$4,000–5,000	
3	$5,500–7,500	
4	$8,000–10,000	
5	$10,500–12,500	Maiden
6	$13,000–19,500	Alw, NW1X, NW2X
7	$20,000 and above	Alw, NW3X Clf Alw
8		Stakes and Handicaps
9		Consistent winners, ungraded stakes, relatively
	(New)	large purse values
10		Multiple graded stakes, or a single Grade 1 event

For nonwinners twice other than maiden or claiming? For nonwinners three times?

What are the highest and lowest purses of classified allowance races?

What are the purse values of stakes on the local schedule?

The detective work is hardly complicated. On request, racegoers can obtain official condition books from the racing office, and observe the purses associated with the various races. Observation skills also help. When studying the *Racing Form*, pay attention to the purse values listed for each type of nonclaiming race.

Regarding the stakes programs, the *Racing Form* publishes grade designations for graded stakes; that is grades 1, 2, 3, and the symbols R (restricted) and S (state-bred) for stakes races limited to certain categories of horses.

All other stakes races are open—as in, open to all comers—including an important subcategory of open stakes called listed stakes.

The *Form* does not yet designate listed stakes symbolically. Yet for handicapping purposes, listed stakes can be considered interchangeable in quality and prestige with Grade 3 stakes, and they are clearly superior to open but unlisted stakes. Listed stakes are sufficiently prestigious in quality and value to be "listed" on the pages of international sales catalogs. Owners and breeders yearn for their horses to achieve Listed stakes status, meriting black type.

An appendix presents the listed stakes of North America through January 1989. Graded and Listed stakes are evaluated as to competitive quality annually, resulting in a few changes each season.

Handicappers should consider the reference list important. Horses exiting a win or strong performance in a listed stakes, can be preferred when entered next in an open but unlisted stakes, notably if the open unlisted purse is below $100,000. The Listed stakes is almost invariably the better race.

By this book's class-rating method, a Big Win, or fast-fast win, in a Listed stakes, earns a rating of 8, placing the winners on equal footing with Grade 2 and Grade 1 horses.

Below are a half-dozen horses of varying talents. Assign each a class level, based on recent performances.

Honolulu Honey Ch. f. 4, by Hawaii—Dorothy Gaylord, by Sensitive
Br.—Rose Hill Farm (Ky) 1989 7 3 1 0 $86,168
Own.—Stronach F 110 Tr.—Sedlacek Michael C 6 1988 10 2 4 1 $58,867
Lifetime 19 6 5 1 $145,955 Turf 5 1 0 1 $7,340
15May89-8Bel 1 1/16 :451 1:092 1:432ft 8 1/2 1177 58 49 35 11 Carle J D3 (F)Aw47000 85-14 HonoluluHoney,BoldWench,TollFee 6
22Apr89-6Aqu 1 1/16 (T):48 1:1311:451fm 11 113 64 76 612 611 1/4 Samyn J L6 (F)HcpO 68-24 Wakonda, Aquaba, Far East 7
8Apr89-11GS 1 1/16 :463 1:12 1:46 ft 6 1/2 112 815 76 1/4 56 1/2 46 1/2 VlttMJ4 (F)Btsy RossH 71-20 LdyAnnbll,Emly'sHill,SummrScrtry 9
8Apr89—Grade III
12Mar89-7Aqu 1 1/16 [•]:48 1:1341:47 ft 2 111 55 3/4 43 1/2 13 1/2 110 1/4 Krone J A5 (F)HcpO 74-29 HonollHony,AWnkAndANod,D'rEtl 7
11Feb89-8Aqu 1 1/8 [•]:49 1:1321:511ft 12 108 53 1/2 66 510 513 1/2 BlntJF5 (F)Rare Trt H 72-20 ScornedLss,Rose'sCntin,ToThHunt 7
11Feb89—Grade III
13Jan89-8Aqu 1 1/8 [•]:4531:1041:491gd *6-5 115 312 36 24 28 1/4 Maple E5 (F)Aw41000 88-13 GlwySong,HonolulHony,SbrnStorm 7
5Jan89-8Aqu 1 1/16 [•]:4831:1321:461ft 2 1/2 117 2hd 22 11 15 1/2 Maple E4 (F)Aw29000 78-28 HonoluluHoney,Podeic,HouseWine 7
9Nov88-8Grd 1 :471 1:131 1:41 sl 7 1/2 118 65 21 1/2 22 2no Attard L7 (F)Aw25500 75-32 RomntcStory,HonllHny,PrprEvdnc 8
Jun 7 Aqu 4f sy :504 B (d) May 9 Aqu 5f ft 1:024 B ●May 3 Aqu 4f sy :483 H (d) ●Apr 17 Aqu 3f gd :381 B

Rose's Cantina Gr. m. 5, by Naskra—Soft as Satin, by Promised Land
Br.—Gentry Tom (Ky) 1989 6 2 2 0 $181,392
Own.—Icahn C 117 Tr.—Jolley Leroy 8 1988 16 3 1 2 $187,102
Lifetime 33 8 6 4 $456,950 Turf 7 0 1 2 $30,280
13May89-8Bel 1 1/16 :444 1:09 1:404ft 30 117 717 73 1/2 32 22 1/4 CrugtJ6 (F)Shuvee H 95-16 Bnker'sLdy,Ros'sCntin,GrcinFlight 7
13May89—Grade I
23Apr89-8Aqu 1 1/8 :491 1:134 1:511ft 11 119 34 1/2 32 1/2 46 46 MapleE5 (F)Top Flight 73-27 Banker'sLady,ColonilWters,Aptostr 5
23Apr89—Grade I
25Mar89-12Lrl 1 1/8 :471 1:112 1:50 ft 2 122 814 712 47 48 3/4 MplE4 (F)SnowGooseH 84-20 ThrtyEghtGoG,ClnlWtrs,LdyAnnbll 8
25Mar89—Lugged in
4Mar89-8Aqu 1 3/16 [•]:4811:1311:594ft 8-5 118 513 510 13 16 MplE5 (F)Next Move H 78-30 Rose'sCantin,ToTheHunt,NoButter 5
4Mar89—Grade III
11Feb89-8Aqu 1 1/8 [•]:49 1:1321:511ft *4-5e119 42 31 1/2 23 24 1/2 MpleE7 (F)Rare Trt H 82-20 ScornedLss,Rose'sCntin,ToThHunt 7
11Feb89—Grade III
14Jan89-8Aqu 1 1/16 [•]:46 1:11 1:424ft 4 1/2e114 1016 74 3/4 2 1/2 15 1/4 MapleE9 (F)Affctnly H 95-15 Ros'sCntn,TpsInTps,ThrtyEghtGG 10
14Jan89—Grade III
20Nov88-8Aqu 1 1/4 :474 1:363 2:02 sy 6 1/2 114 65 1/2 46 411 415 3/4 MapleE3 (F)Ladies H 70-20 Bnkr'sLdy,MkChng,ThrtyEghtGoGo 7
20Nov88—Grade I
4Nov88-9Med 1 1/8 :47 1:104 1:48 ft 7 1/2 116 96 1/2 74 43 43 3/4 MplE1 (F)Long Look H 89-16 Bnker'sLdy,WithoutFthrs,MkChng 10
4Nov88—Grade II
Jun 6 Bel 3f sy :371 B Jun 2 Bel 4f ft :512 B May 26 Bel 5f ft 1:012 B May 9 Bel 5f ft 1:02 B

Sand Crystal

Dk. b. or br. g. 5, by Never Tabled—Crystal Tree, by Windy Sands
Br.—Drake & Wygod (Cal)

DOOCY T T   **117**

Own.—St Francis Stable   Tr.—Knight Terry $6,250

		1989	5 1 2 1	$6,775
		1988	8 2 1 1	$18,075
Lifetime	38 8 6 5	$71,325	

```
27May89-5GG   6f :22  :45 1:094ft    3 119   11 1hd 1hd 23     Doocy T T2        6250 87-15 TouchTime,SndCrystl,Tobin'sWish 11
2Apr89-2GG    6f :22  :45 1:10 ft   *3-5 119   11 1hd 2nd 331  Doocy T T10    Sⓑ6250 85-16 Tiz Stealin,EagleDive,SandCrystal 12
17Mar89-7GG   6f :214 :443 1:093ft  *3-5 119   21 11 111 2nd   Doocy T T7        6250 91-16 La Bean, Sand Crystal, Tiz Stealin 8
8Mar89-9GG    6f :22  :452 1:113sy  *3-5 117   2nd 1hd 12 11    Doocy T T1        6250 81-21 SandCrystl,HerrHeinz,LuckyEdition 9
4Feb89-7GG    6f :214 :452 1:163m    81 117   21 1hd 21 771⁄2  SchvneveldtCP3  c8000 79-20 Paul'sRampge,TizStelin,RceyRichie 9
   4Feb89—Ducked out start
23Apr88-9GG   1  :464 1:114 1:39 gd  *21 119   11 111 22 661⁄2  Doocy T T4        6250 66-19 Carocrest,AgentsHeart,SteadyPrty 8
13Apr88-9GG   1  :451 1:094 1:35 ft  *31 119   21 12 31 761⁄2   Gonzalez R M1    8000 65-10 Bemidgi,CircleErly,Albob'sPlesure 10
   13Apr88—Broke in a tangle
24Mar88-7GG   1  :461 1:104 1:371ft   31 117   11 12 211⁄2 26   Gonzalez R M10  10000 76-21 ToB.ARuler,SandCrystal,HomeRun 10
12Mar88-4GG   11⁄2:463 1:102 1:424ft  61 117   13 13 12 131⁄2   Gonzalez R M2    8000 85-10 SndCrystl,AnotherGuy,FltingHour 11
26Feb88-6GG   6f :213 :443 1:181ft    9 117   31 321⁄2 44 34    Doocy T T2       8000 84-20 Runagate,AnotherGuy,SandCrystl 10
   26Feb88—Lugged out
Jun 6 BM 4f ft :483 H      ●May 28 BM 6f ft 1:134 H      May 12 BM 5f ft 1:011 H      May 6 BM 3f ft :353 H
```

Lyphard's Flag

B. f. 4, by Lyphard's Wish—Lady's Flag, by Fifth Marine
Br.—Parrish Hill Farm (Ky)

SIBILLE R   **118**   4-5

Own.—Hartstone & ParrishHillFarm   Tr.—Hartstone George D

		1989	5 0 0 1	$11,100
		1988	10 2 1 3	$46,400
Lifetime	16 2 1 4	$57,500	Turf 2 0 0 1	$3,750

```
21May89-3Hol  6f :221 :45 1:094ft   10 118   79 751⁄2 441⁄2 46  Sibille R7      ⓕAw28000 91-05 Debs Angel,YugoMarie,ManyPasses 7
   21May89—Wide
11Mar89-3SA   1  :464 1:104 1:354ft   61 119   571⁄2 571⁄2 581⁄2 610  DlhoussyE2 ⓕAw41000 79-14 Chrmnte,ComedyCourt,DnceRenee 6
18Feb89-5SA   1  :451 1:112 1:373ft   71 117   711 531⁄2 42 33   McCrrnCJ5  ⓕAw40000 77-19 Voila, Petalia, Lyphard's Flag  9
25Jan89-7SA   11⁄2:464 1:112 1:431ft   41 117   761⁄2 771⁄2 431⁄2 431⁄2  DlhoussyE7 ⓕAw48000 82-17 Vive, Comedy Court, Dancing Halo 7
   25Jan89—Bumped 3/16
11Jan89-5SA   11⁄16ⓣ:4711:1131:511yl   8 117   531⁄2 47 917 9201⁄2  Meza R Q12 ⓕAw38000 50-29 Beat, Maison Close, ComedyCourt 12
   11Jan89—4 wide 7/8 turn
28Dec88-5SA   1  :441 1:091 1:361ft   3 116   912 60 24 15     DlhoussyE2 ⓕAw34000 87-10 Lyphrd'sFlg,BrghtStll,DsgnngChrls 10
   28Dec88—Wide 3/16
8Dec88-8Hol   1 ⓣ:47 1:1121:352fm  *31 116   118 109 76 331⁄2  DlhoussyE5 ⓕAw25000 83-13 ComdyCort,Lor'sLght,Lyphrd'sFlg 12
25Nov88-7Hol  7f :214 :45 1:242sy   3 116   10141012 56 31    DlhoussyE4 ⓕAw24000 81-23 Brmer,GlowingResum,Lyphrd'sFlg 10
   25Nov88—Broke slowly
12Nov88-5Hol  6f :213 :444 1:101ft  20 116   10111061⁄2 75 2no  DlhoussyE4 ⓕAw24000 91-08 SlwJunFll,Lyphrd'sFlg,DffrntLook 10
26Oct88-7SA   61⁄2f:213 :443 1:161ft  23 116   910 991⁄2 881⁄2 80  DlhoussyE9 ⓕAw27000 81-16 FlorlMgic,DifferentLook,SlwJunFll 9
   26Oct88—Wide into, through stretch
Jun 6 Hol 3f ft :353 H     May 31 Hol 5f ft 1:002 H     May 13 Hol 5f ft 1:014 H     May 8 Hol 6f ft 1:134 H
```

Barnhart

Dk. b. or br. g. 5, by Dandy Binge—Passion Play, by Candy Spots
Br.—Moncure & Mac Kenzie (Tex)

BAZE R A   **115**   3

Own.—Riggle Ora S & Virginia L Jr   Tr.—Miller Peter $22,500

		1989	8 1 2 3	$21,750
		1988	2 0 0 0	
Lifetime	26 7 4 5	$74,910	Turf 1 0 0 0	

```
14May89-2Hol  61⁄2f:221 :444 1:162ft  *3 117   42 421⁄2 42 2no  Valenzuela P A6  20000 93-09 John'sRtrt,Brnhrt,JournyThruTim 11
27Apr89-5Hol  6f :221 :451 1:094ft   31 117   641⁄2 53 221⁄2 22  Valenzuela P A4  18000 90-10 Vancealot, Barnhart, Bugarian   8
14Apr89-9SA   11⁄16:471 1:111 1:421ft  4 116   31 211⁄2 24 37   Davis R G9       20000 83-12 ImpossiblStrm,LmmonJuic,Brnhrt 11
   14Apr89—Wide 7/8 turn
25Mar89-7GG   6f :213 :441 1:091ft   61 119   75 751⁄2 551⁄2 531⁄2  Gryder A T3    Aw18000 89-13 Idmized,WesternRegent,FletHombr 9
11Mar89-9SA   7f :223 :453 1:224ft  15 116   321⁄2 42 411⁄2 31   Baze R A8        20000 85-14 Craftmaster,DrouillyFuisse,Brnhrt 12
   11Mar89—Crowded in drive
23Feb89-5SA   7f :221 :452 1:234ft  10 115   85 531⁄2 21⁄2 2nk  Baze R A2       14000 81-20 ‡Splendish,Barnhart,DebonairAidn 12
   23Feb89—Placed first through disqualification; Floated out drive
4Feb89-1SA    61⁄2f:214 :451 1:174sy  51 116   1073⁄4 861⁄2 541⁄2 7101⁄2  Baze R A2  16000 71-30 RunCougrRun,MuiMelody,LsForvr 12
   4Feb89—Broke out, bumped
21Jan89-1SA   6f :214 :444 1:101ft  14 116   741⁄2 531⁄2 331⁄2 31   Baze R A12    12500 86-12 ShowerDecr,Empror'sTurn,Brnhrt 12
31Jan88-5SA   7f :223 :451 1:231ft  59 114   11121013 981⁄2 991⁄2  Patton D B9   62500 74-21 BrghtAndRght,QpStr,J.R.Johnson 12
10Jan88-5SA   7f :222 :444 1:221ft  25 115   55 751⁄2 751⁄2 85   Sibille R3     Aw35000 84-15 ReEnter,Fanticola,Buckland'sHalo 10
Jun 5 Hol 5f ft 1:012 H
```

Desert Rival

B. c. 3, by Desert Wine—Ruling Lark, by One-Eyed King
Br.—Agnew D J (Ky)

WARREN R J JR   **120**   4

Own.—DanDar Farm   Tr.—Fanning Brett C

		1989	1 1 0 0	$6,000
		1988	0 M 0 0	
Lifetime	1 1 0 0	$6,000	

```
26May89-5GG   6f :212 :441 1:10 ft   21 115   1hd 11⁄2 11⁄2 131⁄2  Warren R J Jr2  Mdn 89-13 Desert Rival, Bankster, Calvinist  9
Jun 4 SA 6f ft 1:142 H     May 29 SA 5f ft 1:002 H     May 16 SA 6f ft 1:141 H     May 10 SA 6f ft 1:133 H
```

Class ratings can be recorded in the past performances, as in the examples, atop the class column.

I hope recreational handicappers agreed that Desert Rival had earned a 4, for its Big Win at the maiden level. The colt qualifies on class when matched against allowance horses, nonwinners other than maiden or claiming.

Lyphard's Flag proved difficult to classify, as do many thoroughbreds. A mixed rating (4 or 5) can be assigned to reflect the ambiguity.

The May 21 sprint can be discounted as an uncomfortable distance. Three back, Lyphard's Flag dispensed a good race versus nonwinners of two allowance races (5). As far back as December 28 the filly also registered a Big Win against nonwinners of one allowance race (5), but since has shown primarily poor and acceptable races at the next level (4).

Where does Lyphard's Flag figure to win next? Versus nonwinners of two allowance races; maybe. Versus $40,000 claiming horses; maybe.

Class ratings should be more meaningful to handicappers in nonclaiming races, where barriers to advancement can be severe. They gain added recognition in longer races, too, including claiming routes.

In routes among better horses, class ratings deserve a weighting roughly half again as important as speed. When in doubt here, go to the class.

Class ratings are definitely germane on the turf, where stamina and competitive desire come forcefully into gear. If grass horses boast class ratings superior by two points under nonclaiming conditions, an authentic class advantage probably exists. The horse will be difficult to deny.

Class ratings are not altogether unimportant in claiming races, especially routes, but now speed figures and pace ratings dominate by a two-to-one weighting at least. In claiming sprints, early speed, even cheap speed, can outrun classier horses, and regularly does.

Class Stickouts

All experienced handicappers elaborate a personal vision of the best bet at the racetrack. I advocate mine.

Under any conditions, horses that combine the top class rating and top pace rating in the field will be doubly difficult to defeat. And the class horse alone on the lead and carrying the highest pace rating in the field is virtually a cinch, unless the animal inadvertently self-destructs.

In claiming races, too, certain drops in selling price stand out as significant, the actual prices varying from circuit to circuit.

In southern California, for example, a drop from $32,000 to $25,000 claiming is associated with more winners than any other. The drop from $12,500 to $10,000 likewise is associated with an upsurge of winners.

When similar critical drops occur, award a plus sign.

So if a four-year-old of southern California drops from a good performance (not a win) at $32,000 to $25,000 claiming, its class rating can be 4+, not 4.

Local tracks at large feature similar dividing lines in the claiming division. Recreational handicappers on alert can exploit the telltale class maneuvers.

In rating horses 4up on class, concentrate on recent performances, not deserting the last two running lines unless clearly appropriate. If recent races appear unrepresentative, go further back in the record, but carefully, to the most recent representative performance.

A few situations do not lend themselves to distinguishing contenders reliably by numerical class ratings: (a) races at classic distance, ten furlongs or farther, especially among stakes horses, unless the prior class ratings were achieved at the same distances; (b) two-year-old sprints, certainly the dashes; and (c) even classified allowance races, notably routes, which can differ markedly from one another, so much so they beg a deeper discussion.

Classified Allowance Races

Classified allowances have been forever confusing and troublesome for recreational handicappers.

Understandably so, as the eligibility conditions typically bring together vastly dissimilar horses. The typical classified field is crowded with stakes horses, allowance horses, and claiming horses, the diversity affording the races their peculiar charm.

Numerical class ratings can be misleading not only because the horses in classified races gather together from poles apart, but also with divergent intentions. The ratings may not transfer as readily as do the horses.

The practical solution is to comprehend the conditions of eligibility intelligently. The task is not as complicated as it sounds. Classified races can be divided conveniently into two categories.

Imagine a continuum, having opposite poles.

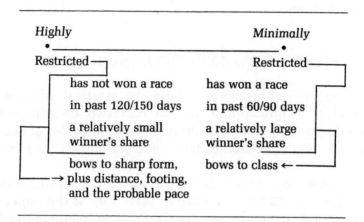

At one pole, on the left, most rewarding to handicappers, are classified contests for horses that have not accomplished anything of late. I call them highly restricted. Classy horses do not dominate these fields, because they have been effectively barred.

In fact, in highly restricted classified races, the best horses lose. Recreational handicappers should expect that. Class bows to sharp form, especially when the sharp horses are also nicely suited to today's distance, footing, and probable pace.

If the conditions of eligibility bar horses that have not won a single race during the past 120 days or longer, handicappers can fairly assume the sharper, classier horses on the grounds will have been excluded. Prefer the horses in positive form, even claiming horses. Give extra credit to any horse that will be advantaged by the distance, footing, and probable pace.

Numerical ratings do not reveal those circumstances, but fundamental comprehensive handicapping does.

At the opposite pole, on the right, classified conditions admit horses that boast a victory, maybe multiple victories, and multiple impressive performances, perhaps in graded stakes, within the past 90 days or thereabouts. I call them minimally restricted.

Now the purses tend to be richer, attractive stakes performers remain eligible, and a few will be aiming at the money. Authentic stakes performers, in form, will be tigers under advanced classified allowances.

Now the best horse regularly wins. Lean to the class. Here the class ratings do apply. Favor horses that have managed a two-point spread.

IMPROVING AND DECLINING HORSES

No longer is thoroughbred form the mystical, elusive fundamental of handicapping. In the past two decades several qualified researchers have examined the form cycles of successful horses, and the findings have emerged clearly and conclusively.

No longer, as a result, can allusions to the mystique of the unpredictability of the racehorse be served up as the impenetrable excuse for losing. I enjoy casual-to-close relationships with a number of professional handicappers, and I can testify that none of them is baffled by form cycles. Neither need recreational handicappers be baffled any longer.

In the preceding section, on identifying contenders, recreational handicappers learned the standards of acceptable form. Of recent performance, horses up close at key points of call were accepted. Of layoffs, horses that had worked out at five furlongs within the past 14 days were accepted. Qualifiers were acceptable on form, that is, to be evaluated more closely later.

Acceptable form is not interchangeable with improving form. Paradoxically, acceptable form does not mean that form is not declining. In the thick of the handicapping process, when rating contenders, those are two operative questions.

Which contenders are improving? Which are declining?

The traditional notion that improving horses might be observed to run closer to the leader at the prestretch, stretch, and final calls following layoffs still applies. The pattern has always been more meaningful the longer the layoff. Three to six months away often will be followed by precisely this incremental pattern of improvement.

Now the guideline has been buttressed by numerous indicators of improving form that might be observed in the last running line, the last two races, or the past three. I shall mention ten, and each deserves the handicapper's attention, if not some extra credit. Each portends a better performance next time, and in combination, the indicators of improving form can be decisive.

The first is controversial in its logic, and not easily discussed, without averting to qualifications and exceptions.

1. Improved adjusted final times, speed figures, or pace ratings.

The logic that improved running times, figures, or ratings necessarily reflect improving form collapses on the alternative explanations.

It's fact, not opinion, that improved final times (and the numerical ratings that derive from them) can be a function of pace. Faster pace, slower final time. Slower pace, faster final time. Form perseveres intact.

Or dramatically improved final times can be a function of uncontested early speed.

Or of inept opposition.

Or of a strong positive speed bias.

Form remains the same.

Where running times remain unadjusted, track-surface speed accounts for improved times as frequently as a positive change of form.

So recreational handicappers must be careful when interpreting improving final times, speed figures, or pace ratings. The association with form is not linear, but multivarious.

In recent seasons professional speed-figure merchants have increasingly marketed their numbers to horsemen, jockey agents, owners, breeders, and regular handicappers—at inflated prices—as a means of understanding horses' current condition. But the proposition can be seriously flawed.

Recreational handicappers benefit by sticking close to these guidelines: among horses 3up, unless the horse won uncontested wire to wire, no severe bias assisted, and the early pace was not abnormally slow, pay attention to final times (adjusted) that have suddenly improved from three to five lengths.

Occasionally older racehorses reflect improving form with adjusted final times that improve successively by a length in consecutive races, a positive pattern. Far more typical is the sudden dramatic improvement. Expect the horse will repeat the much-improved final time in its next, or exceed itself, even if jumped in class.

This is even likelier if the horse has engaged in a long, taxing stretch drive. The fight sharpens improving older horses to the razor's edge.

On the other hand, if much-improved horses stay away for 30 days or longer, discount the impressive improvement. Something has interrupted the positive flow. The terrific improvement is unlikely to be resurrected, at least not immediately.

Better nonclaiming three-year-olds normally will reveal gradually improving final times and ratings as the competition stiffens and their personal seasoning develops, but at some point an unanticipated dynamite performance stuns the audience. The final time, speed figure, and pace rating soar. Trust that performance. Such a three-year-old may regress temporarily, but expect a repeat performance in the next two starts. If it is not forthcoming, forsake the colt or filly just as quickly. Three-year-olds are tricky, and so are their form patterns.

During the winter season of 1989 at Santa Anita, a pair of three-year-olds suddenly recorded stratospheric speed figures. The good colt Music Merci hit the ceiling in the San Raphael Stakes (Grade 2) at a mile, on the lead, but could not deliver an encore in his subsequent performances. The huge figure probably resulted from a track bias, a hard racetrack.

Kentucky Derby winner Sunday Silence delivered the same first act, reserving his virtuoso performance for the Grade 1 Santa Anita Derby. Until then Sunday Silence's times and figures had improved gradually, but never exceeded the ordinary for stakes horses.

Sunday Silence did repeat his dramatically improved performance, of course, and did so in the 1989 Triple Crown classics.

An exception to the pattern, an important exception to appreciate, is the nonclaiming three-year-old that earns a fantastically improved numerical rating on its inaugural start at three. That kind of performance is usually not repeated next time. The three-year-old "bounces," or regresses badly, due to premature overexertion. More on the bounce pattern later in the section.

2. The horse "bid and hung" last out, but finished in front of half the field.

Second in line here, this improvement factor deserves high priority among all handicappers. Probability data indicate the pattern has earned a surprisingly strong impact value. "Bid and hung" horses win half again as many of their rightful share of their next starts, and pay generous odds.

The pattern, in fact, tosses statistical profits—meaning that a wager on all bid-and-hung horses results in long-term profits, one of the few positive form patterns capable of amassing winnings.

The generous odds can be affiliated with handicappers' chronic contempt for horses that "hang," meaning the horses have surrendered their acceleration and drive and merely try to stay even.

But if in the last race a big move occurred between the first two calls, or between the prestretch and stretch calls, and then horses tired, but finished well enough to beat half the field anyway, that's a positive sign of improving form. Expect the big move again, but now the horses are prepared to win. They do not hang.

3. Engaged in an all-out stretch drive in its last race.

Whether the horses won or not, the all-out exertion reflects positive form.

Traditional guidelines in relation to all-out stretch drives have been negative, an expectation that the prolonged, punishing exertions will deplete the energy reserves. Probability data convinces modern practitioners the opposite effect is likelier. The positive form is repeated.

4. The horse won by three lengths or more last time.

The margin of victory defines a Big Win, notably if horses have tracked a rapid pace to the prestretch or stretch calls before drawing off. A Big Win is particularly indicative in stakes races, where handicappers regularly see them.

5. The five-day return.

Any horse swinging back to the races in five days is well intended by its connections. The pattern is even more appealing if the last race (five days ago) resulted in a win, or a much-improved effort. Extra credit should be extended to successful stables.

If a five-day return accompanies any of the positive patterns above, prepare to bet. These are among the best bets of the day, week, or month. The seven-day return is almost as hospitable to improving horses, and to form analysts.

6. Improved race last out, improved workouts since.

As a rule, workouts are overemphasized by recreational handicappers, especially the speed of workouts. But if a workout merits special notice, and that workout occurred a week to 10 days following a dramatically improved race, that's a pattern of improving form.

We will return to this positive pattern at greater length later, when discussing peaking form as a special topic of interest.

7. Third start for a sprinter following a long layoff, provided the second start was a dramatically improved race.

Probability data also uncovered this positive pattern. It applies only to sprinters, not routers. The first race following a layoff will be dull to ordinary. The second race will be much improved. The third race begs success. The fourth race is a strong performance too.

8. Freshened router, a pair of sprints, stretch out to a route.

How many recreational handicappers realize that one sprint is the worst stretchout pattern for a distance horse following a layoff, but two sprints is the best?

The impact value for a pair of sprints, in fact, is greater than two (twice as likely to win as probabilities would expect), and the payoffs are generous. If the second sprint is a good race, the route mutuels are even juicier, approximately a three hundred percent profit!

Keep the two-sprint stretchout pattern in mind.

Remember, too, that the one-sprint stretchout following a layoff is the worst pattern for a distance horse. The statistics here are gloomy. These routers win roughly half as frequently as they should, and return dollar losses upward of 70 percent.

Another negative pattern is a poor race at a route following a long layoff, and reentry in another route. This pattern can continue for weeks without noticeable improvement. Watch the horses lose, without wagering.

9. Exits a fast-fast claiming race with an acceptable performance.

"BID AND HUNG," A SIGN OF PEAKING FORM

```
*Stop The Fighting           Ch. h. 6, by Cure the Blues—Fighting, by Aggressor
 DELAHOUSSAYE E  ¯ +    116  Br.—Kildangan Stud (Ire)                 1989  3 0 0 1      $10,200
                             Tr.—Frankel Robert ¯ +  $32,000          1988  7 1 1 1      $78,200
Own.—Summa Stable            Lifetime  25 6 4 2  $200,236             Turf 16 5 2 2     $113,686
21Jun89-9Hol  1 1/16 :474 1:114 1:43 ft     3  116  62¼ 4¾ 42 46    Davis R G6      40000 79-17 Ascension,Sinforoso,TimeForSkrto 8
   21Jun89—Lost whip 1/4
15Apr89-7SA   1 (T):4621:1041:354fm         2  116  106½ 84¼ 63¾ 32½ Davis R G6     100000 89-08 Inddlst,HtAndSmgg,StpThFghtng 10
   15Apr89—Steadied 3/8
24Mar89-8SA   1 (T):4721:1041:353fm         3¾ 115  41 41¼ 32½ 56   Davis R G3     Aw60000 87-12 PoliticalAmbition,TheMedic,Neshd 6
   24Mar89—Wide 3/8 turn
19Jun88-8Hol  1 1/16(T):47 1:10 1:402fm     4e 115  87¾ 77¾ 811 79¼ Sibille R 8  Inglwd H 83-10 Steinlen, Deputy Governor,Galunpe 9
   19Jun88—Grade II; Wide 3/8 turn
15May88-8Hol  1 1/8(T):4631:10 1:46 fm     19  115  89½ 74 43 32½   Sibille R 6 Jn Hnry H 95-05 DputyGovrnor,Stnln,StopThFghtng 8
   15May88—Grade I
1May88-8GG    1 1/16(T):4921:1311:432fm     3½ 115  2hd 2hd 1½ 2nk  Toro F 6    All Amer H 85-18 Ifrad, StopTheFighting,NickleBand 7
   1May88—Grade III; Drifted out 3 1/2
10Apr88-3SA   1 1/8(T):4831:1231:491fm      2¾ 116  11 11 11½ 1¾    Day P 4        Aw54000 81-12 StopTheFighting,Uptothehilt,Motly 6
27Mar88-7SA   1 :462 1:101 1:352ft          8  116  32 46 48½ 611½  Day P 3        Aw60000 79-16 Sebrof, Talinum, Nostalgia's Star 6
   27Mar88—Bumped start
27Feb88-7SA   1 :453 1:102 1:371ft          4¾ 117  46 54¾ 54¾ 54   DelhoussyeE 2  Aw60000 78-17 StaffRiot,Sebrof,MasterfulAdvocte 5
   27Feb88—Fanned wide into stretch
30Jan88-3SA   1 :47 1:112 1:364ft           3  119  21 31 43 46½   Hawley S 4     Aw60000 77-20 High Brite, Sabona, Lord Grundy 7
 ●Jun 14 Hol 7f ft 1:27 H     Jun 8 Hol 7f ft 1:274 H     Jun 3 Hol 6f ft 1:142 H     May 29 Hol 5f ft 1:002 H
```

On July 1, 1989, the six-year-old above was entered at Hollywood Park at a mile, $32,000 claiming, 4up.

Stop The Fighting won by five lengths, and paid $8.20.

Ten days earlier, Stop The Fighting bid and hung against $40,000 claiming horses at 1¹⁄₁₆ miles, beating half the field of eight. It's a classic illustration of a positive pattern of improving form misunderstood by thousands of handicappers.

The contempt horseplayers rain down on horses that "hang," or refuse to extend themselves fully in the drive, should not be confused with the bid-and-hung pattern. Between the first two calls, as above, or between the prestretch call and stretch call, a horse passes at least two horses and gains at least a length, as above, or gains two lengths and passes one horse, but tires, still managing to finish ahead of half the field.

The next race often represents peaked form, resulting in an easy romp at underbet odds.

For me, anytime a claiming horse exits a fast-fast race and will be the only horse of its kind in the field, it's virtually an automatic play. The pace has been fast, the final time has been fast, and the horse finished within six lengths, while beating half the field.

Not a large number of claiming races will be fast at every call. Admire the participants of the few that are, even if moving ahead in class following the loss. The odds sometimes will be splendid. A fair number of the horses will win as overlays.

I like this pattern, and recommend it heartily.

Some recreational handicappers support horses exiting impressively fast races, regardless of performance. I do not recommend that practice. The horses must have been up close at some point of call, or have finished in an acceptable position. A sizzling pace is most impressive among horses that have pressed it, tracked it, or even chased it. Only horses outrun all the way should be discarded.

10. Surprise early speed, dull recent form, back class.

Surprise early speed can be a predictor of improving form and brighter moments ahead. It counts much more among horses that once handled classier horses. Now the interactions of class and form can contribute to dramatically improved performance next out.

If the odds are inviting next time, accept the proposition that significant improvement can be expected.

The pattern does not represent horses whose surprise early speed amounts to a change of running style. Instead of improving, after flashing surprise early speed, these horses merely revert to familiar running styles.

Recreational handicappers should register mentally any positive indicators of improving form they observe, and can record pluses in the past performances as they please. By all means, record a plus for any of the following combinations of positive indicators:

- Significantly improved final time (adjusted), up close at every call
- Obviously improved performance, five-furlong bullet workout to follow
- Big Win, improved numerical rating, double jump in class, good trainer, claiming race
- Rapid turn time, back class, same class today

Many variations of improving form are tenable. Positive patterns by themselves are attractive, but in combination they are downright dangerous.

Alternately, here are a half-dozen signals of declining form. Any combination of these can be deadly.

1. Not a good race in past three.

If horses have not finished in the money, or close to the winner, in three consecutive attempts, mark them down on form. If drops in class have attended the dull performances, without improvement, the case for declining form can be closed.

A future positive form reversal will probably entail a precipitous drop in class, or a thirty-day rest, or both.

A variation of the negative pattern is two consecutive poor races, without an excuse for either. Do not expect a form reversal.

The next pattern of decline qualifies as a serious form defect. It's a distinctly negative pattern overlooked by large segments of the crowd.

2. A dismal performance following a 30-day recuperative rest.

Many regularly running horses will be afforded 30-day rest periods whenever trainers imagine the respite will rejuvenate spirit and limbs. If the rest proves productive, the horses respond.

But should rested horses disappoint, a sudden reversal next time is infrequently forthcoming. The pattern looks like this:

Restless Galaxy next ran on July 3, 1989, at seven furlongs against $32,000 claiming horses, a small retreat to the claiming class it had bested before the 37-day vacation began on May 18. Naturally, the crowd overbet. The result chart tells the tale.

1454—FOURTH RACE. 7 furlongs. 3 year olds. Claiming prices $32,000-$28,000. Purse $20,000.

Index	Horse and Jockey	Wt.	PP	ST	¼	½	¾	Str.	Fin.	To $1
**1399	By No Means, Solis	116	7	3	1¹½	1¹	-	12½	1¹¾	22.90
*1372	American Force, Delahoussaye	116	8	1	4½	3½	-	2¹½	22¾	11.30
1320	Colorful Hitter, Pedroza	116	9	2	6¹½	5¹½	-	3²	33½	3.50
1342	Sum Dandy, Baze	116	4	6	2ʰᵈ	2¹	-	5¹	4¹	9.00
1399	Restless Galaxy, Davis	115	1	8	8	7³	-	4½	5¾	3.80
1253	Agiwin, Stevens	119	2	7	7ʰᵈ	8	-	6¹½	6⁵	13.70
1372	Catfish Purdy, Black	116	5	4	3ʰᵈ	4ʰᵈ	-	7¹½	7¹¾	2.50
1339	Classy Player, Pincay	119	6	5	5¹½	6½	-	8	8	6.20
1166	Waltzing Sass, Sibille	116	3	lst rdr	-	-	-	-	dnf	22.00

Scratched—None.
Claimed—Catfish Purdy by F & Sharon Alesia (trainer Peter Eurton), for $32,000.

```
7—BY NO MEANS................47.80  20.20  9.80
8—AMERICAN FORCE ................11.80  5.60
9—COLORFUL HITTER .....................4.20
```

Time—22. 44 3/5. 1.09 2/5. 1.22 2/5. Clear & fast. Winner—ch.c.86 Miswaki—Zenelope. Trained by Jerry Fanning. Mutuel pool—$324,022. Exacta pool—$375,778. Daily Triple pool—$272,451.

Restless Galaxy's loss was entirely predictable. Recreational handicappers fall prey to this declining form pattern all the time. No more, please. Throw them out.

3. Declining final times (adjusted), speed figures, or pace ratings, same or slower pace.

Declining numbers can reflect deteriorating form, provided nothing about the pace, class, footing, etc., suggests the horse might have declined anyhow. In sprints, rating points lower by two to three might be attributable to normal fluctuations of pace. In routes, four or five points down can also reflect normal fluctuations of pace, which are wider at the slower, longer distances.

But if the pace and class look acceptable, and the numbers have declined, so usually have the horses.

The next negative form pattern is a subtle variation of the above, and another rarely appreciated by recreational handicappers.

4. Stakes winners, next season, after a layoff, declining numbers.

Stakes winners are notoriously overbet the next season. Three-year-olds returning for the four-year-old season, and four-year-olds returning for the five-year-old season, are susceptible to the pattern. No longer the same added-money stars, the horses are supported nonetheless off their marquee value. But they have deteriorated, and the numbers sound the alarm.

Developing horses, the twos and threes, should be expected to mature from the juvenile or sophomore seasons to the next. If they regress instead, mark them down.

Following a prep or two, older stakes winners should be expected to earn the same numerical ratings at five as at four. If the ratings decline, so have the horses.

Recreational handicappers cannot benefit by avoiding this negative pattern, unless they are willing to calculate multiple ratings for returning stakes contenders. It takes time and effort, besides the know-how. Is it worth it? Emphatically, yes! It's nice to know when overbet horses figure to lose.

5. Winning race, or good race, followed by an illogical drop in class.

No one is giving away the goods. Racehorses are valuable assets. They run where they belong, or thereabouts. An irrational, illogical plunge in class means damaged goods. At low odds, forget the horses. They figure to lose. Shop for the overlays as substitutes.

An exception is the claiming horse lowered slightly in class following a good race (occasionally a winning race) to grab another purse. This is striking with a hot iron, so to speak. The drop is rational, and current form impressive, but neither sensational.

Also, toward the end of race meetings, claiming trainers will often drop ready horses to steal another purse before vacation begins or before a change of scenery accommodates a change of stable plans. Regular handicappers experience the late-season dropdowns every season. Recreational handicappers can partake of the picnic. The horses go postward at low but not miserly odds, yet they are ready to win, and many do.

6. Overextension first out following a lengthy layoff, the much-remarked "bounce" pattern.

This guide has described this negative form pattern elsewhere and will illustrate it later, but so much money is squandered on seemingly impressive horses that "bounce," the guideline warrants renewed emphasis here.

The return engagement qualifies as overextension if it resulted in a win, or close finish, in good time. Expect the horses will "bounce" if they return within three weeks, perhaps a month.

Some better horses, mainly older stakes performers, will

bounce following two exertions after a layoff.

The third race after the layoff represents the positive form reversal. Horses that bounced now bounce back. Several win at generous prices, the public unaware of the pattern. Savvy recreational handicappers will want to anticipate these golden opportunities. They will savor having the odds on their side.

Other signs of negative form include front bandages (first time), lugging in or bearing out continually through the stretch, and an uncharacteristic lack of position at the pace call, notably in sprints.

Handicappers can assign a zero, for a form defect, to any negative pattern they observe. In combination with zeroes allocated earlier, when identifying contenders on form, the truly risky form horses now begin to reveal themselves in all their tattered clothes.

Multiple form defects present a shaky case, especially in reference to the liberal standards promoted in this book. Unless the horses demonstrate clearly overcompensating pluses on class and pace, handicappers have every right to be unforgiving.

At paltry odds, cast the horses adrift.

RECORDING TRIPS AND TRACK BIASES

Recreational handicappers cannot imitate racing's regulars on collecting for future reference the trips of racehorses and biases of racetracks, but they need not capitulate on the factors. Trips and biases represent plentiful sources of overlays. Casual customers can convert several of them.

First, official sources of information have extended a rare helping hand to the practitioner. Racetracks now televise race replays in many major markets. Weekend customers and occasional racegoers can tune to the local independent station, or to the local cable service, and conduct an amateur's style of trip handicapping for thirty minutes an evening.

Local information services in major markets provide trip and bias information to handicappers—for a modest fee. Assuming the charges are low and the providers genuine, tapping the services makes sense. The investment pays dividends several times a season.

The *Daily Racing Form* has pitched in on this front, now

supplying trip notes in the past performances, though not in a very enlightened way. Brief, descriptive phrases offer an assist of a sort, illuminating curiously dull or dreadful running lines, or explaining atypical positions at various points of call.

For casual handicappers willing to perform light on-the-job observation duties on their occasional excursions to the races, and to complete the homework with reasonable tenacity, trips and biases can become a reasonably updated slice of the recreational handicapping regimen. The guidelines below supply the basic ammunition.

Trip handicapping refers to the scheduled observation of horses' positions, problems, and maneuvers at various stages of the races.

The stages of the race include: the start (gate), first turn (routes), backstretch, far turn, entering the stretch, upper stretch, mid-stretch, and nearing the finish. A commonly deployed notation helps handicappers record positions, trouble, and moves at each successive stage. The notation, a shorthand, summarizes a horse's performance as a narrative having a beginning, middle, and end.

Before presenting the recommended notation, recreational handicappers should understand that trip handicapping deals only indirectly with the abilities of horses. Trips deal directly with the circumstances of races. The distinction is vital. Logical leaps from the circumstances of races to the abilities of horses can be acrobatic and entertaining but unsubstantial. The reasoning is associative and inferential but not causal.

Thousands of trip fanciers succumb to the "post hoc, pro hoc" fallacy of logical thinking. That is, if it happened after this (losing race), it must have happened because of this (troubled trip).

Leading figure handicappers, for example, customarily juxtapose speed and pace figures with trip notes, and evaluate the total situations analytically. But if a horse is forced four wide on the far turn, expert speed handicappers do not improve the figures by three points, technically an incorrect procedure.

Other speed handicappers do modify the figures numerically to reflect horses' trips, adding or subtracting points. Each adjustment, it must be understood, represents an additional source of error. Intended to strengthen the figures, trip adjustments often weaken them.

As trip information is inherently descriptive and qualitative, it's more sensible to evaluate the data in a context of adjusted times, speed figures, or pace ratings that are intended to quantify real abilities, and themselves contain degrees of error. The interrelationships merely suggest whether the numbers can be improved or should decline. Quality complements quantity. Thought supersedes procedure.

So recreational handicappers are implored to evaluate trip information analytically, not to rely on it to adjust other data numerically. It is no small point.

Below is a standard notation that recreational handicappers can depend upon to summarize and describe horses' trips, either on track programs—the conventional procedure—or on individual notepads.

Stages of the race:

G	gate	S	in the stretch
FT	first turn	US	upper stretch
B	backstretch	MS	mid-stretch
T	far turn	NF	near the finish
E	entering the stretch		

Position of the horse:

R   along the rail, on the rail
2-   in the 2-path, or second path out from the rail
3-   in the 3-path, or third path out from the rail
4-   in the 4-path, or fourth path out from the rail
GP   good position, in the clear
BP   behind the early pacesetters
LF   a lone frontrunner; recorded also as Lone F, a pace maneuver
2P   one of two frontrunners
3P   one of three frontrunners
W   wall; situated behind a string of horses, either on the far turn, entering the stretch, or in the stretch

---

Pace Maneuvers:

Duel   engaged in a hotly contested pace duel
stalk   situated just behind a pace duel, prepared to strike as soon as the leaders tire or weaken
Move   any obvious acceleration at any point of call; recorded in combination with a stage of the race
MM   a strong middle move in the race
Inherit overtook the pacesetters through no effort of its own, but because the frontrunner(s) tired

B & H	Bid and hung, usually on the far turn or into the upper stretch, but finished in front half of field
Lone F	a lone frontrunner
Rank	cannot be rated kindly by the jockey, usually in the early stages of a race
Green	has not learned the mechanics of racing; does not respond properly to the jockey, the traffic of other horses, or routine racing situations
Lag	stays at the rear of the field
FW	finished well
FF	finished fastest

Trouble:

Slo-1	slow out of the gate by approximately one length
Rush	broke slowly, and rushed up under the jockey's urging
V	ran into a vise, or blind switch, often after accelerating into the pace of the race
St	steadied; meaning the jockey was forced to slow a horse's natural stride and momentum, due to traffic
Ck	checked; meaning the jockey was forced to brake a horse's stride and momentum momentarily, without losing significant ground or position
Up	took up; meaning the jockey was forced to brake a horse's stride and momentum completely, now losing significant ground and position before regaining stride and momentum
Alter	altered course; meaning the jockey was forced to change a horse's direction and running path, usually in the stretch
Wall	blocked behind a wall of horses while attempting to find running room
Lug	lugged out; meaning the jockey could not maintain a straight course as the horse drifted to the outside, due to tiredness, soreness, or being "green"
Bore	bore in; meaning the jockey could not maintain a straight course as the horse drifted to the inside, due to tiredness, soreness, or being "green"
Stumble	stumbled out of the gate, losing stride, position, and momentum

In recording trips, the notation for position, pace maneuvers, and trouble can be combined with the stages of the race from the start to finish in a logical progression that mimics the running. For example:

Slo-1, 3FT, 3B, MM, Ck-FT, 5E-US, Lug-NF

describes the horrendous experience of a horse that exited the gate sluggishly, roughly one length in arrears, raced three wide around the first turn, remained three wide down the backstretch, made a middle move to gain striking position, checked on the far turn, wound up five wide entering the stretch and in the upper stretch, and lugged out near the finish.

The illustration is slightly ridiculous, but those below are routine:

R-B,T,E: describes a sprinter that raced along the rail down the backside, around the far turn, and into the stretch.

6FT,B: describes a router that raced six wide into the first turn and continued six wide down the backstretch.

4T,E: describes the everyday situation of a horse racing four wide around the far turn and entering the stretch.

R-Trip: describes a horse that raced on the rail all the way.

Slo-2, Lag, B & H-5FT: describes the troubled odyssey of a horse that broke slowly enough to surrender two lengths, then lagged at the rear, and finally delivered a bid-and-hung move while five wide around the far turn.

3P-Duel: describes a horse involved in a three-horse pace duel.

Slo-1, Rush, V, FW: describes a sprinter slow by a length out of the gate, rushed up, entered a blind switch, then finished well.

GP-BP, B, T: describes a horse that raced in good position behind the pace down the backstretch and around the far turn.

Recreational handicappers will want to record the trips of winners, runners-up, and close finishers in contentious races. Also qualifying for trip notes are horses that deliver unusual moves or encounter significant problems, not minor mishaps, during the running.

Noncontenders and uninteresting or uninspiring runners can be ignored. Their trips are not meaningful.

The vexing problem of evaluating trip data lends itself as well to amazingly simple but crucial notation. Three symbols can be instructive and should be used deliberately, and sparingly, only as reality demands:

X   Excuse. The horse would have delivered an undeniably sharper performance otherwise.

X1   An excuse that clearly prevented a horse from winning; would have won otherwise.

P   A perfect trip. Good position, no trouble spots, at every stage of the race.

Legitimate excuses imply the horses will improve, provided form has remained intact.

A perfect trip sometimes explains the surprisingly facile victory of unanticipated horses, or exceptionally high numerical ratings, notably if other contenders in the field experienced troubled trips.

Of excuses, the tipoff that the X or X1 designations are indeed pertinent can be observed following mishaps.

Do bothered horses try to overcome obstacles? Do troubled horses finish well regardless?

If horses sulk, waver, refuse to continue, or quit in the path of a troubled trip, refusing to extend themselves afterward, the trip information may be legitimate, but its meaning will be difficult to determine. It's reassuring to observe that horses stopped in traffic, or interfered with, persevere willingly, and finish eagerly anyhow.

Certain trips invariably qualify as excusable. Stay on the lookout for victims of the following:

1. Frontrunners in a claiming route have been kept wide all the way.

One of the most difficult trips to overcome, the horses must be urged throughout, and as ordinary as they are, ultimately tire before the wire, as early as the far turn perhaps.

If these frontrunners persevere into the stretch, prepare to support them next time. The trip will be smoother, and the odds higher.

2. Deep closers, regardless of the class, that have been forced to take up on the far turn, or entering the stretch, while moving, provided they appear willing to persevere following the incident.

Few latecomers can overcome relatively severe interference and win regardless. The horses deliver one long run, and that has been interrupted. If troubled closers attempt to regroup, gaining ground and momentum anew after taking up, excuse the loss, and expect an improved performance next out.

Minor traffic problems do not qualify. Steadying, checking, bumped, blocked, forced wide, the several annoying mishaps that regularly accompany the trips of come-from-behind horses might be registered mentally, but not as legitimate excuses for failure. The implications of routine minor incidents in the running are tentative and inconclusive. Some bothered horses will improve, but many others will not.

3. Stumbling at the gate, no push by the jockey afterward.

Several unfortunate horses lose races at the start, and the lackluster performances that follow obviously must be excused. Usually, the poor start has sacrificed several lengths, such that the rider decides it's foolhardy to waste the horse's limited energies.

The admissible excuse, a truly poor break, does not extend to normal kinds of bumping, bobbling, breaking sideways, or even stumbling but recovering quickly. On this matter the *Racing Form* has not served its customers well, recording as trouble ad nauseam routine gate mishaps that bear on the outcomes of races not at all.

Just as certain trips can be excused unequivocally, others are irrationally exaggerated.

Racing wide is a phenomenon easily submitted to the trip handicapper's abuse.

Off-pace runners will be wide in the late stages naturally, a function of running style, as they circle lifeless horses and tiring pacesetters.

Do the wide swings qualify as bad trips? It depends.

If horses are urged while wide, they lose ground and energy simultaneously. If wide but under restraint, or under control, the jockey not pumping or urging, no extra energy has been squandered. When set down, the horses retain ample time, with ample energy conserved, to prevail in a long, strong stretch run.

Trip fanciers avoid a nettlesome dilemma by noticing whether horses running wide are simultaneously being urged. If they are, the trip has been plagued by lost ground in concert with heavy expenditures of energy. Often, wide-running horses will lose momentum as the centrifugal force of taking the turn abruptly ends, the wide-running horses now bearing in slightly, perhaps severely, until the riders can shift weight and reestablish a straight course.

Linear-regression studies of the racing-wide phenomenon reveal horses forced wide on the swings of turns surrender one length for each path out from the rail. If these horses fall short by a length, perhaps two, after racing wide while urged—in the 4-path, 5-path, or farther out—trip handicappers can conclude they figure to improve next time—assuming they are not the kinds of closers very likely to be forced wide again.

Minor mishaps in the early stages of races normally will be incidental to race outcomes, in the same way that weight, jockey, and post position tend to be incidental. An exception is the frontrunner or presser forced to the outside while pressing for advantage around the clubhouse turns of routes. That can be debilitating.

Traffic congestion in the middle stages of races is also incidental, provided an opening appears prior to the stretch call. Three sixteenths of a mile, even one eighth, is enough distance for horses trapped in typical traffic situations to gather their rapid stride and outrun the opposition.

At times, while the bettor's desperate hope is trapped in traffic, another horse draws away and cannot be caught in time. Award an excuse, and curse the fates.

Before awarding the X1 designation, however, and after watching the replay—objectively, not in a passionate defense—be convinced the troubled horse would have triumphed. If the situation is murky, or inconclusive, accept the uncertainty and assign an X.

Among horses caught in traffic around the far turn and entering the stretch, a scenario worse than the blockage is the impatient altering of stride and course by the anxious jockey. Unless much the best, horses subjected to sudden premature maneuvers by rattled riders have a splendid chance of expiring near the finish. The horses run out of gas. Another late runner slips by. That other horse, as often as not, stayed put behind the traffic tie-up on the turn. When a hole appeared in the stretch, the patient horse crashes through, having saved position and energy earlier.

In nonclaiming races, too, trips as a group can be seriously overrated. Real problems in the stretch, or entering the stretch, no doubt can be viciously difficult to surmount, but whatever happened prior to that routinely can be forgotten.

To invoke the extreme case, when Grade 1 horses race head to head through the late stages of races, the better horse usually wins, regardless of what happened beforehand. If Horse A noses Horse B following an all-out stretch battle, but B was tardy out of the gate, raced wide down the backside, steadied on the far turn, and came wide again into the stretch, trip handicappers will conclude the outcome would have been reversed if the circumstances had been gentler to B.

Next time B drops four pounds, while A picks up three pounds. Horse B now enjoys a perfect trip, while A experiences trouble. The two engage in another furious stretch duel. Guess what? Horse A wins by a nose, a head, a neck, or by a length. It happens all the time.

To less extent, the better horses can be expected to prevail in hotly contested stretch drives in lower-level nonclaiming races as well, regardless of what has occurred prior to the stretch fight. Unless the trouble has been inordinately prolonged and severe, poor trips tend to be incidental among nonclaiming horses, once the decisive racing, the late racing, begins. If nonclaiming contenders have been clear while battling for the final one eighth of a mile and finish close, recreational handicappers can be confident the best horses have triumphed. They will usually be correct.

Expert trip handicappers never fail to scrutinize the race replays, and many digest them repeatedly.

When Andrew Beyer invaded Santa Anita in winter 1983, he watched the replays twice immediately following each race, again at night, on television, and insisted on arriving early the next racing day, to see the race replays for a fourth time. No doubt familiarity breeds contempt, but it also illuminates hidden form in vaguely disguised but troubled trips. No doubt Beyer finds winners his companions overlook, however few.

That's the rationale of trip handicapping, of course. The information so collected will not be widely distributed: a greater chance to locate a fugitive overlay that figures. Several times a season dedicated trip handicappers do uncover solid attractive trip overlays, and a fair share of them win. By paying a fraction of the price, recreational handicappers can pursue the same objective and achieve reasonably good results.

To wrap up on a somber thought, trip information, or circumstantial evidence, cannot be used to beat the races alone, notably when evaluating closely matched, low-priced contenders, where trip data would appear to count but does not.

Probability data shows irrefutably that horses exiting troubled trips win no more than their fair share of their next starts. Not only that, the victims of poor trips are themselves victims of a familiar racetrack theme—overbetting. Statistically, as a group, excused trips throw losses upward of 35 percent on the invested dollar. Ouch!

Track Biases

Track biases enhance the chances of horses whose running styles or post positions are favored, and retard the chances of horses whose running styles or post positions are not favored. Biases, that is, can be positive or negative. Biases can also be subtle or severe.

Recreational handicappers are best served by biases that are both positive and severe. It's a far more efficient task to spot horses favored by a strong bias. Identifying horses not favored by the bias still leaves the not unsubstantial task of finding the probable winners.

Severe biases are frequently decisive. They can overcome significant class disadvantages, and can nullify powerful speed and pace advantages. Not only that, severe biases can be characterized as making surprise winners of probable losers. By that standard, in fact, are severe biases best recognized. Handicappers notice horses winning that do not figure. No tenable explanation for race outcomes exists, other than a severe track bias wreaking its havoc.

Of subtle biases, racegoers appreciate that track surfaces contain natural biases. The composition and texture and maintenance of the course favors speed, or perhaps stamina. It favors inside posts, or perhaps outside posts.

In southern California, for example, the surface at Santa Anita favors early speed, but Hollywood Park favors sustained speed, requiring endurance. Hollywood Park penalizes inside posts in sprints rather severely, but does not necessarily favor outside posts, as does Del Mar.

Del Mar formerly favored inside speed rather strongly, but now does not. Thus track biases change, even as surface compositions change and maintenance procedures change.

When rain threatens at Santa Anita in winter, the track surface is sealed repeatedly. A surface that favors speed to begin with, now propels it. Then the rains come down. If storms persist, eventually the Santa Anita surface will be drenched. On drying out, it favors stamina, penalizes speed.

In short spans of play, recreational handicappers must intuit the implications of subtle track biases and adapt their thinking to the conditions. Credit is awarded, debits charged, but the handicapping process as a whole is not unduly sabotaged.

Severe biases pose problems, and opportunities, that are altogether different. Now the reality is harsh. Horses unable to win on conventional handicapping, but abetted by a severe bias, win powerfully. Horses that stand out on conventional handicapping, but retarded by a severe bias, lose embarrassingly.

The recreational handicapper's task is to recognize when normal biases have become severe enough to control race outcomes, and adapt to the possibilities.

Have unfathomable horses been winning, and handily?

Have strong contenders been losing, and inexplicably?

Severe biases can be presented in eight varieties. These are:

Running Styles	Post Positions	
	Inside	Outside
Early speed	+ / −	+ / −
Late speed	+ / −	+ / −

Of the eight, the most advantageous to handicappers is the severe positive speed bias inside, or on the rail. The positive inside speed bias propels any horse with a trace of speed to the front, and sustains them there. Several romp by half a furlong.

The opposite bias, a severe negative speed bias inside, defeats horses exiting the rail post, but leaves handicappers to grapple for the winners still. Outside biases, positive or negative, can be equally as severe as inside biases, and impact several post positions. The far outside posts might be advantaged atypically, but other horses toward the outside might benefit as much.

Post-position studies published by the *Daily Racing Form* astride the past performances can clue casual handicappers to the inside-outside biases currently operating. Below is the post-position study of Hollywood Park sprints and routes through 51 of 67 racing days during spring/summer of 1989.

What, if any, severe biases can handicappers detect?

WINNING POST POSITIONS

HOLLYWOOD PARK
(April 26 to June 29, Inclusive)

	(Main Track)							(Turf Track)					
	....SPRINTS.....			....ROUTES......				....SPRINTS.....			....ROUTES......		
	(Under One Mile)			(One Mile & Over)				(Under One Mile)			(One Mile & Over)		
P.P.	STS	WINS	PCT.	STS	WINS	PCT.	P.P.	STS	WINS	PCT.	STS	WINS	PCT.
1	215	10	.05	133	11	.08	1	5	2	.40	70	9	.13
2	215	14	.07	133	13	.10	2	5	2	.40	70	8	.11
3	215	24	.11	133	13	.10	3	5	0	.00	70	11	.16
4	215	25	.12	133	11	.08	4	5	0	.00	70	13	.19
5	215	29	.13	133	22	.17	5	5	0	.00	70	8	.11
6	211	30	.14	124	17	.14	6	5	0	.00	69	10	.14
7	187	22	.12	112	19	.17	7	4	0	.00	55	5	.09
8	154	12	.08	83	12	.14	8	3	0	.00	43	4	.09
9	121	17	.14	56	4	.07	9	2	1	.50	26	1	.04
10	99	16	.16	40	8	.20	10	1	0	.00	17	0	.00
11	61	11	.14	30	2	.07	11	1	0	.00	7	1	.14
12 & UP	50	5	.10	17	1	.06	12 & UP	2	0	.00	6	0	.00

Inside posts in sprints have been severely disadvantaged. Following 215 starts, post 1 represents more than 10 percent of the starters but less than 5 percent of the winners, an impact value below .50. The inside claims less than half as many winners as posts 3, 4, and 5, which have the same percentage of starters.

Hollywood sprinters fought a negative speed bias along the rail the entire summer meeting of 1989. Recreational handicappers there who ignored low-priced sprinters on the rail were courting the percentages.

A corresponding outside post-position bias in sprints at Hollywood 1989 proved real, but not overwhelming. Post 10, for example, contained 5 percent of the starters and 7 percent of the winners. A positive trend, but insignificant. The extreme outside, post 12, won only its fair share. Sprinters at Hollywood that summer won equally well from posts 3 through 12.

Not revealed by the *Racing Form*'s post-position studies, since one-turn miles are grouped with two-turn routes, was the nearly impossible task faced by Hollywood horses of 1989 exiting the inside post at a mile. Through 50 racing days only two horses exiting the No. 1 spot at one-turn miles managed to prevail. A convenient statistic well within the grasp of casual customers.

To be considered severe, inside-outside biases should be twice as strong or weak as probabilities would expect, and preferably stronger. The correct procedure for estimating the intensity of the bias divides the percentage of winners exiting each post position by the percentage of starters exiting the same post. A bit of arithmetic will be required, but not much.

Of speed biases, positive or negative, that may be severe, casual handicappers must depend upon observation skills, bolstered by handicapping skills. If a bias assists speed horses when other horses clearly figure best, it's severe enough to matter. If a bias defeats speed horses when they figure to romp, it's severe enough to matter.

In all situations, discount underlays opposed by a bias, and credit overlays having a reasonably strong chance and supported by a bias. Severe biases represent outstanding sources of financial gain in the short run of a day, a weekend, a week, a few weeks, or occasionally a month. It pays to scrutinize biases closely enough to detect when a predominant pattern may be settling in.

Both speed and post biases can be recorded conveniently, and immediately, following each race, on the track program or a sheet of looseleaf. Draw a tic-tac-toe arrangement, as represented below:

Posts

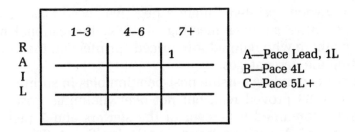

Pretend a handicapper is standing atop the starting gate. Posts are arrayed from inside to out. Pace styles are identified to the right as A-B-C, for frontrunners, off-pace horses, and closers.

The A-Pace includes horses on the lead or within a length at the first call.

The B-Pace includes horses behind the frontrunners by more

than a length but no more than four lengths.

The C-Pace includes horses behind the frontrunners by five lengths or more.

Only the winners of races are rated.

Watching the replay, or observing the actual race, determine the winner's running position at the first call. Mark it A, B, or C. Check the winner's post position.

Put a hash mark (/) in the space that reflects the winner's post position and pace style in combination. In the figure above, a hash mark can be found in the upper right space, meaning the winner of the sample race exited post 7, or farther out, and demonstrated the A-Pace style, by racing on the lead or within a length at the first call.

The first call of sprints occurs after the horses have run two furlongs.

The first call of routes occurs after the horses have run four furlongs.

As races proceed, and hash marks accumulate, casual handicappers can tell how frequently specific posts and running styles have been winning. Double-check the odds and records of horses that have been part of a provocative pattern.

Are severe biases affecting the race outcomes?

Consider the opposing speed and post biases represented in the pair of figures below.

Use First Call Of Winner's Race

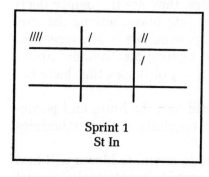

Sprint 1
St In

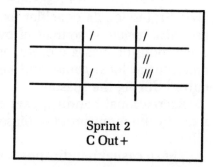

Sprint 2
C Out+

On the left, Sprint 1, seven of eight races have been won by speed horses. Four of those seven exited the inside posts. The pattern represents an extra-strong speed bias (S+) that favors, somewhat, the inside posts (In).

On the right, Sprint 2, six of eight races have been won by horses exiting the outside post positions. Five of the six were horses racing behind the pace at the first call. The pattern represents an extra-strong outside post-position bias (Out +) that favors off-pace types (C).

Late in the racing day recreational handicappers on site for the Sprint 1 menu would support overlays featuring inside speed.

Late in the racing day recreational handicappers on site for the Sprint 2 menu would support overlays featuring a strong close from the outside.

Speed and post biases for any racing day can be recorded using the following notation:

S   bias that favors speed horses

S+   extra-strong bias favoring speed horses

C   bias that favors closers

C+   extra-strong bias favoring closers

In   bias that favors the inside posts

In+   extra-strong bias favoring inside posts

Out   bias that favors the outside posts

Out+ extra-strong bias favoring outside posts

To repeat, when biases are severe, they are frequently decisive. Professionals consider extra-strong biases among the surest, most generous sources of overlays available at any racetrack. They monitor biases closely, as do regular practitioners up-to-date on the local game, and keep a log of biases that have occurred during the season.

Recreational handicappers should join the hunt, and participate in the monitoring of biases as regularly as their schedules allow.

Those casual handicappers who do attend to biases will find playbacks when horses have competed impressively against negative biases.

In the Hollywood Park situation illustrated earlier, horses that ran strongly on the front out of post-position 1 but tired and lost, will have returned to action before the meeting closes.

If they draw an outside post, regular handicappers will expect an even stronger performance, and if the odds dictate, those handicappers will readily wager to win. Playbacks that impressed against a negative speed bias on the rail are routinely among the most conspicuous generous winners at the same racetracks a few weeks later.

LATE SPEED ON THE TURF

Grass races are distinctly different, vastly dissimilar from races on the dirt.

The palpable, observable difference is pace. The explanation is class.

Turf courses are softer, deeper, more tiring. Horses and riders quickly settle into a relaxed, slower stride. The early pace resembles an orderly procession. Classified allowance types typically will run middle-distance fractions of 23.2, 46.4, 1:11-and-change, the pars for the class at Santa Anita 1989. Winners will have expended roughly half of their energy after six furlongs, significantly less than counterpart route winners on the dirt.

Around the far turn, off-pace contenders maneuver for striking position, either inside or outside. When the procession has curved into the upper stretch, and the runners have straightened, the final decisive stampede to the finish line is under way.

Late speed on the turf gathers its vital force, and when late speed alone is not enough, the qualities of determination and endurance rule.

Thus three factors dominate on the grass:

1. Late speed
2. Class
3. Pedigree

Late speed means the ability to finish faster-than-par from the prestretch call to the wire, not a familiar concept even to regulars.

On grass, too, the desirable qualities of class are stamina and determination, overarching brilliance, especially as demonstrated against horses comparable to, or better than, today's.

Irrefutable evidence has persuaded handicappers also that

sires prepotent for grass racing pass on special attributes, including wide, dishlike feet, angular pasterns, a long extended stride, and greater endurance.

When the conditions of racing invite grass horses 4up, handicappers can emphasize measures of late speed and relative class, as reflected by the past performances. When the conditions limit the competition to three-year-olds, or the juveniles, handicappers can emphasize pedigree, running style, and demonstrated class.

No one should doubt the significance of class handicapping on the turf. Early speed is incidental, and often suicidal. Early pace can be irrelevant, or self-defeating. Final time can be entirely misleading, and so, too, the accompanying figures.

Late speed, and the capacity to prolong a late burst without let-up against horses of comparable or superior ability, is the distinguishing attribute. Whether the early pace has been relatively fast or relatively slow, turf contenders prepared to finish with a cannon blast of speed are most likely to prevail.

One of the greatest turf runners of all time, of course, was the venerable gelding John Henry.

John Henry lacked brilliance or intense speed. He was incapable of taking a lower-grade stakes field wire to wire in rapid time on the dirt, though he might easily pass them in the late stages.

But John Henry did possess tactical speed, and could readily attend a typical turf pace for a mile, 1⅛ miles, 1¼ miles, or longer, and then ignite the after-burners, finishing with an authentic late punch, fueled by unmatched endurance and determination. The all-time grass champ simply persevered with a kick of late speed for as long as it took to beat his foes into submission and defeat. John Henry was the prototypical grass champion.

Modern speed handicappers endure as many headaches on the turf as anybody, and probably more. No surprise. Conventional speed methods do not apply. Early speed, brilliance even, certainly if slightly out of control, regularly tires, and regularly loses. Final times fluctuate abnormally, pace times madly. Daily track variants are unreliable commonly, and at times impossible to calculate. The resulting speed and pace figures cannot distinguish grass horses accurately enough.

I have witnessed a few of the soundest, savviest figure handicappers in the nation desert their figures in frustration when confronted by an uneven, unpredictable grass course. And few of their comrades in speed figures spot the prime bets of the day, week, or month on the turf.

Recreational handicappers can benefit on the turf by turning standard operating procedure on end.

Identify the horses particularly well suited to today's class (not outclassed), or bred for grass. Calculate the late speed of each, using grass lines only. Be relatively strict about distance, using closely related distances whenever possible. Late speed at a mile may fizzle at 1⅛ miles.

Of the experienced runners, which horses have finished fastest? Which can finish similarly fast, or faster, and in a determined manner, against the classiest field? Credit stables and trainers that concentrate on winning turf races. Unless a speed bias predominates on the turf, and this happens, forget the rest.

A complicating factor for recreational handicappers on grass is the presence of shippers, of which the turf sees many. Below graded-stakes conditions, among horses 4up, a perfectly legitimate technique is to rank the horses by average grass earnings.

Purse values do not fluctuate grossly on grass as on dirt, even from track to track. The proliferation of stakes on the main track has not extended to the turf. And the relative class of grass runners at major tracks can be considered homogeneous, at least in relation to the widely diverse population of dirt runners. Gross earnings and average earnings will be more strongly correlated with real abilities.

Rely on the lifetime turf record published in the earnings box of the *Daily Racing Form*. Among horses 4up, divide the total turf earnings by the number of turf starts. Divide that average by today's purse. Accept as contenders on class any horse showing an earnings index of 1.0 or better. If one horse boasts a turf-earnings index considerably higher than any other horse in the field, pause to consider whether the animal shapes up as a class standout.

Among 3YOs, prefer gross earnings on the grass to average earnings, as a single stakes share can distort averages wildly. Any young horse that already has earned more money on grass than today's purse size probably outclasses today's conditions. Contender.

The calculation of late speed is elementary arithmetic.

At middle distances subtract the second-call fractional time from the final time. Add or subtract lengths gained or lost.

At the classic distances of 1¼ miles and 1½ miles, calculate the final-quarter time. Adjust for lengths gained or lost.

At 1⅜ miles calculate the final three eighths of a mile. Adjust for lengths gained or lost.

Consider the past performances of Impossible Stream and Mind Master below. Using the last running lines, what is each four-year-old's late speed?

On June 18, 1989, Impossible Stream completed the final five sixteenths of a 1¹⁄₁₆ mile allowance race in 29.3 seconds. The colt gained two lengths against a 30-second fractional time.

On June 25, 1989, at the same distance and racetrack, Mind Master completed the final five sixteenths in 29.4 seconds. The gelding gained 3½ lengths against a 30.2 fractional time. When calculating late speed, a change in conventional procedure, half lengths should be rounded upward.

The examples crystallize a few important considerations when comparing horses on the grass.

First, try to compare horses by using running lines at today's exact distance at today's racetrack.

Second, in picking pace lines, if the most recent race is not representative, choose an alternative race from the past six races on the turf. Use a good race if rating a race at today's relative class. Use a winning race if rating a race at a lower class level. Use an acceptable race if rating a race at a higher class level.

Third, when unable to compare horses at exact distances, demand related distances, or distances within one sixteenth of a mile.

If related distances are rated, an adjustment to the final times of the inexact distances will be necessary. The adjustment is simple. Add or subtract 6.3 seconds, depending upon whether the related distance is longer or shorter than today's.

If Mind Master's May 20 running line were compared to Impossible Stream's June 18 line, handicappers would subtract 6.3 seconds from 1:48.2, adjusting the final time at 1⅛ miles to a 1¹⁄₁₆ mile time of 1:41.4.

The fractional time is not adjusted. Thus the adjusted late speed of the race would be 30.1 seconds. Mind Master gained 1¾ lengths. So the horse's late speed on May 20 is adjusted to 29.4 seconds. Precisely the late speed Mind Master delivered on June 25, at today's exact distance.

The recommended adjustment of 6.3 seconds corresponds to typical time differences at middle distances among classified allowance horses at major tracks. Classified allowance pars reflect the relative class of nonclaiming horses at major tracks well enough. The adjustment serves recreational handicapping admirably.

Unless the early pace will be abnormally slow, a contender with the fastest late speed is a probable winner.

Early pace on grass can be wickedly difficult to predict, as the jockey's intent is to save energy for later. Early-speed tactics are virtually abandoned. A clear lead of a length or more on grass may be just as valuable as on dirt, but scarcely as predictable. Horses and jockeys conserve energy, as speed duels on grass prove suicidal.

When the contention has been evaluated on late speed, but the puzzle persists unsolved, prefer the classiest horses. The old maxim, "when in doubt, go to the class," has long since been unfaithful in dirt races, but perseveres on the turf. Besides late speed, the more abstract attributes of endurance and determination must rise to the occasion, else the grass race is usually lost.

The class of the field on grass is often the horse boasting the best performance against the most advanced competition in its recent turf races. The last six turf starts form an index of recent consistency.

On grass, too, the conventional levels of the class hierarchy are not as much compressed, or squeezed into narrow brackets. Class barriers on the turf remain distinct, even though customary margins of victory are shorter. When separating contenders, rely on the following grass hierarchy:

Relative Class Levels on Grass

Level	Claiming		Non-claiming
1	$25,000 & below		
2	$32,000–50,000	↔	Maiden Nonwinners allowance
3	Above $50,000	⟵⟶	Classified allowance Restricted stakes Open stakes below $100,000
4			Open stakes of $100,000 or higher
5			Listed Stakes—Grade 3 stakes
6			Grade 2 stakes
7			Grade 1 stakes

A separation of one class level can now be considered significant. Within the nonclaiming turf division as well, especially in the classified allowances and stakes, the richer the purse, the better the race.

As on dirt, stay alert for winners and close runners-up of listed and graded stakes dropping into open stakes. Not as many prestigious stakes are carded on the turf. For that reason, too, on grass Grade 1 is clearly superior to Grade 2.

Though far fewer in number, certain turf stakes can be considered classics, the winners and impressive graduates deserving of extra credit. The Breeders' Cup Turf and Breeders' Cup

Mile (on turf) qualify, of course, as does the Arlington Million.

The Budweiser International, at Laurel, during fall, formerly the Washington D.C. International, often attracts a stellar cast. The Turf Classic at Belmont Park during fall has traditionally drawn the upper crust of grass runners in the stakes, though it now competes for stars with the Breeders' Cup races, and may suffer a loss of talent.

In southern California, the 1¾ mile San Juan Capistrano Stakes at Santa Anita, in April, beginning down the unique hillside turf course, no doubt attracts the best grass horses in the west, but no longer the international set it once boasted, or even the leading grass horses of the east and midwest. The San Juan has declined, sadly, into a regional title bout.

The best grass race in the country for older fillies and mares is Santa Anita's Yellow Ribbon Stakes, in fall, during the Oak Tree meeting. In this Grade 1 event, a glamorous, murderous, international field travels 1½ miles, after starting midway down the hillside course. Several graduates of the Yellow Ribbon win repetitively afterward, long into the winter and spring seasons. Watch for them.

As always, the younger developing horses must be treated distinctly.

Nonclaiming three-year-olds sort themselves out as grass runners beginning in late spring and throughout the summer and fall. The handicapping must be adaptive, as many of the horses will have no experience, or little experience, on the lawn.

Pedigree matters most. And running style matters considerably more than most handicappers realize.

Breeding for grass is instrumental whenever inexperienced horses switch from dirt to turf. Among developing horses having effective turf sires, studies show handicappers can make steady substantial profits by backing the horses on their first two grass attempts. Dirt form is not relevant. Dull form is acceptable, provided the successful turf sire looms menacingly in the background.

Moreover, higher odds can be preferred, as fewer racegoers proceed knowledgeably about pedigrees on the grass. If three-year-olds switching from dirt to grass descend from effective turf sires, and the odds beckon, recreational handicappers should by all means court the horses. Turf breeding top and bottom enhances the profit margin.

In the appendices of this book can be found a list of sires

whose progeny win roughly 20 percent of their turf starts. Their three-year-olds can be supported the first and second time they try the turf.

Another group of grass sires not only succeed at a high percentage, but pay odds generous enough to toss substantial profits. Recreational handicappers can commit the names to memory at once.

Sires that Win Regularly and Pay Generously on the Turf
(First and second grass starts only)

Acaroid	Green Dancer	Spectacular Bid
Advocator	Grey Dawn II	Stage Door Johnny
Affirmed	Hail The Pirates	Stalwart
Air Forbes Won	Halo	Stutz Blackhawk
Ambernash	His Majesty	Sunny's Halo
Assert	Icecapade	Superbity
Bailjumper	Irish River	The Bart
Big Spruce	J.O. Tobin	Top Command
Buffalo Lark	Kris S.	To The Quick
Cannonade	L'Enjoleur	Transworld
Caro	Little Current	Tri Jet
Caucasus	London Company	True Colors
Coastal	Lyphard	Tunerup
Codex	Lyphard's Wish	Valdez
Czaravitch	Majestic Light	Vent Du Nord
Dance Bid	Marshua's Dancer	Verbatim
Danzig	Mr. Leader	Vigors
Darby Creek Road	Nijinsky II	
Diplomat Way	Nodouble	*Top 10 of 1989:*
Empery	Northern Baby	Darby Creek Road
Exclusive Native	Northern Dancer	Diplomat Way
Explodent	One For All	Explodent
Fappiano	Our Native	Green Dancer
Five Star Flight	Quack	J.O. Tobin
Forever Sparkle	Riverman	Little Current
Forli	Roberto	Majestic Light
Galaxy Libra	Rock Talk	Roberto
Great Above	Sharpen Up	Stage Door Johnny
Great Neck	Sovereign Dancer	Transworld

And another group of grass sires regularly fail their reputations and progeny on the turf, winning less than 10 percent of their grass starts. At low to moderate odds, the progeny of the following sires should be abandoned on grass:

Sires that Fail to Win with 10 Percent of Their Grass Starters

Ack Ack	Linkage	Sensitive Prince
Believe It	Mac Diarmida	Shelter Half
Ben Fab	Mr. Justice	Sir Ivor
Blushing Groom	Naskra	Stop The Music
Conquistador Cielo	Nikoli	Summing
Cougar II	Noble Dancer	Super Concorde
Effervescing	Northern Fling	Teddy's Courage
Far North	Northern Jove	Temperance Hill
Fire Dancer	Pleasant Colony	The Minstrel
Florescent Light	Proud Birdie	Topsider
General Assembly	Quiet Fling	Upper Case
Give Me Strength	Rich Cream	Upper Nile
Highland Blade	Run The Gauntlet	Vaguely Noble
Hostage	Salutely	Vatza
Key To The Mint		

For handicappers' information, each year in late January, William L. Quirin updates the roster of grass sires combining success rates and profitable mutuels. The computer printout costs $10 and can be obtained from Quirin at the Department of Mathematics and Computer Science, Box 701, Adelphi University, Garden City, New York, 11530. I recommend the service absolutely.

Evaluation of younger horses' running styles also contributes to a tactical procedure on the grass strongly recommended. Violation of the procedure can cost the individual a couple of hundred dollars annually, as the tendency it resists wagers too much on grass underlays that predictably finish up the course.

The leading three-year-olds of every generation display an abundance of speed and early speed, brilliance actually, and many of them do not learn to conserve it kindly while running freely toward the front on the dirt.

When switched to the turf, the brilliance and free-running style collapse in a kind of exhaustion the young unseasoned horses have not previously experienced.

Expected to win, or to contend strongly, the impressively fast, pace-pressing three-year-olds instead fall back in the late stages. Until the developing colts and fillies learn to control their speed, and to dole it out conservatively, they represent dire prospects in turf routes.

Alternatively, off-pace three-year-olds and stronger closers unable to get up on the dirt track often move ahead dramatically on the grass. If a nonclaiming three-year-old has been finishing from behind impressively on the dirt, with obvious reserves of energy and power, it might be a clever bet against faster sophomores when first they try the turf.

Moreover, whenever a nonclaiming three-year-old wins powerfully, or improves impressively, especially from behind, when first turned loose on the grass, handicappers should expect an encore. The horses prefer the turf, and should continue to flourish on that gentler surface.

If recreational handicappers can discount early pace and avoid the conventional preoccupation on dirt with early-speed horses, they can position themselves to concentrate on late speed and relative class, the two factors that operate decisively over long stretches of grass. Late punch is a knockout punch on the turf.

None of the above discussion transports well, however, to sprints on the grass.

Shorter turf races are susceptible to the same kind of speed and pace calculations that preoccupy handicappers on the dirt, but with a ringing qualification. The fastest grass sprinters to the prestretch and stretch calls had better be prepared to punch just as hard to the wire.

Expiring speed does not often survive on the grass, whether across six furlongs or twelve.

EVALUATING TRAINERS AND JOCKEYS

Ill-equipped to assess the relative abilities of racehorses, recreational handicappers allocate an inordinate amount of mental energy at the races to the machinations of trainers and jockeys. On this they err, and grievously.

Some of the silliest mistakes involve speculations as to why trainers have selected certain jockeys to ride certain horses. The changes are numerous, but so are the explanations. Speculating on trainers' motives, however clever, circumspect, provocative, or sinister they appear, is a waste of time.

It's true that horsemen tend to be creatures of habit, notably successful habits, and the manners extend to riders they believe fit horses well. Yet the routine changes are daily occurrences, even to occasional racegoers, and can be encapsulated in a solitary guideline for purposeful handicapping.

Whenever an effective trainer switches to a leading rider, stable rider, or hot apprentice, handicappers can assume the intentions are positive, notably if the rider change is accompanied by a class maneuver, a change of distance, a new footing, or an equipment change.

Jockey switches are invariably more meaningful in a broader context of change. Multiple changes in concert beg the player's attention. That is, authentically meaningful jockey switches tend to be part and parcel of a larger scenario.

A leading rider means a jockey currently winning with approximately 20 percent of his mounts.

The class drop–jockey switch maneuver, for instance, has long qualified as a twin-pack of positive trainer intentions. Statistics have indicated the maneuver produces profits, provided the new jockey has been scoring at a 20 percent rate. The 15 percent winner is not nearly as successful, regardless of reputation.

It's true, too, that trainers elaborate other, systematic, more complicated methods of placing horses at advantage that involve jockeys, and if recreational handicappers can recognize the successful patterns, they operate on the edge. Few recreational handicappers can participate in the capers, however, unaware as they are of the specifics that must be coordinated to signify the big try.

Not to worry. The successful trainer patterns, literally, are very few, and far between, and successful only sometimes. Digging for accurate inside information regarding trainer intentions on today's program normally arouses only misinformation, faulty opinion, and disappointing results. Who needs it? It's far more efficient, and rewarding, for recreational handicappers to focus on the talents and preferences of racehorses.

Notwithstanding that, the casual customer's notion that trainers play a vital role in the outcomes of numerous races proceeds from a sound sensibility. Trainers manage horses' racing careers, and exercise full responsibility for their daily conditioning and readiness.

Practically all experienced handicappers appreciate the general situation whereby competent trainers can be expected to defeat incompetent trainers, assuming the horses are comparable, or perhaps the more accomplished trainer's horse is merely slightly inferior.

Is the trainer competent? That is always the first question. The answer is a dichotomous decision: yes or no. If a trainer is judged competent, the horse is acceptable on the trainer factor.

A competent trainer wins approximately 11 percent of his starts, which is roughly equivalent to his percentage of the starters in the races he enters. Normal fluctuations around the baseline during a shorter time interval, as of a race meeting, can be higher or lower by 50 percent. But at year's end the competent trainer's win percentage settles at upward of 11 percent.

If a leading trainer wins approximately 20 percent of the time, an incompetent trainer wins approximately 5 percent. Those are useful benchmarks. A 5 percent trainer can be dismissed, unless the horse figures solidly *and the odds will be greater than 10–1.*

As a rule, leading trainers—the 20 percent bunch—can be supported whenever they present handicappers with a contender at attractive odds, and incompetent trainers cannot be backed whenever they present handicappers with a contender at low odds. The former is an overlay, the latter an underlay.

The *American Racing Manual* is a useful source of information about trainers. It is published annually and available at the state breeders' associations libraries each fall. The manual publishes the win percentages of all trainers for the preceding calendar year. Recreational handicappers who take the time to consult the data will be stunned at the number of local horsemen unable to succeed with 5 percent, or less, of their starters.

Beyond general competence, recreational handicappers can limit their preoccupation with trainers to a few situations where trainer performance, or trainer intentions, really count.

A trio of questions can be posed as part of the handicapping routine:

1. Is today's situation, or conditions of eligibility, among the trainer's strengths (20 percent) or weaknesses (5 percent)?

In particular, as earlier noted, handicappers want to know a leading trainer's weaknesses, and a minor trainer's strengths.

2. Is today's trainer especially hot or cold?

All horsemen experience extended periods of inordinate success and failure. Recreational handicappers can exploit the streaks, provided they have attended to them.

A hot trainer has been winning regularly at approximately twice the rate as normally. A cold trainer has been winning with no horses, or just a few, across several weeks of steady racing. The losing run, in particular, can persist for months, even among genuinely competent horsemen. Abandon them, until they rebound.

3. Is this particular horse in this specific race part of a successful trainer pattern?

Again, a number of peculiar factors will suddenly be arrayed in a discernible pattern the handicapper intuits as vaguely familiar and previously successful. The odds will be generous, not miserly.

Where trainers are competent, and any of the three questions has been answered affirmatively, award an additional plus (++) astride the trainer's name in the past performances. Each year, surprisingly frequently, the actual bet will be predicated on the extra credit awarded a competent trainer prepared to pull the trigger again today.

Where trainers are incompetent, but any of the three questions has been answered positively, award a plus alongside a zero next to the trainer's name in the past performances (0 +). The negative has been cancelled by the positive. Evaluate the horses finally on their own merits. Pay strict attention to the odds. High odds are preferred, low odds unacceptable.

Regarding strengths, weaknesses, and successful patterns, certain familiar situations lend themselves to manipulation and exploitation by a trainer's peculiar expertise. Give greater emphasis to well-documented trainer performance:

1. Immediately following a claim
2. Following lengthy layoffs
3. When rising or dropping more than one class level
4. When switching from sprints to routes
5. With first starters

The occasional racegoer's problem, of course, is the practical constraint: access to the pertinent information. The *Daily Racing Form* does not publish categorical data that describes trainer performance in detail. The *American Racing Manual* does not help either.

Local information services represent a convenient practical remedy. Now common at major tracks, and at many minor tracks, most handicapping-information suppliers emphasize detailed information about trainer performance and trainer patterns. Annual surveys of performance supersede compilations for a race meeting only. Three-year baselines are probably optimal. If the providers' professional reputations are intact, and the fees moderate to low, the information is worth the expense.

The future of thoroughbred handicapping includes comprehensive data bases whereby racegoers having personal computers and modems (or access to them at racetracks and OTB sites) will enter the names of trainers and quickly obtain their performance data in several categories of interest. If the local trainers have been listed on a spreadsheet application—the rows containing the win percentages for performance categories of concern to handicappers—high-tech recreational racegoers will arrive at the local track armed at last with the kind of valuable inside information they forever have extracted from unreliable touts.

That eventuality cannot be far away.

While the trainer deserves a reasonable emphasis in the recreational handicapper's regimen, the jockey does not. No blunder has burdened the casual racegoer's day at the races as the overbetting of jockeys. The inclination is virtually universal, and almost as universally unproductive.

If a trainer switches from a minor rider, or journeyman, to a leader, handicappers can mark the occasion (+). The interpretation of the change, as mentioned above, depends upon other, broader contexts. Jockey changes will be understood best in a context that underscores trainer intentions.

Outside of that purposeful context, this book urges recreational handicappers to ignore jockey assignments as incidental to race outcomes. That is, jockeys can be accepted routinely as professionals who will accord a decent ride to virtually any horse in the barns.

It's fortifying, and reassuring perhaps, to see that Laffit Pincay, Jr., has been named to handle a horse the racegoer intends to bet. If traffic accumulates, Pincay will more likely elude it. If trouble occurs, Pincay will more likely avoid it. If a vicious stretch battle develops, Pincay will more likely win it. Pincay, and his peers, commit few mistakes, and deliver few uninspiring performances. For these persuasive reasons Pincay stands among the most popular, and therefore most overbet, jockeys in the sport.

The unfortunate, unvarnished truth is that none of Pincay's virtuoso talents or special skills can be anticipated prior to the races, except in the most generalized sense. All things considered, far more often than imagined, Pincay will not sit erect aboard the best horse. The premier jockey of his time, Pincay loses approximately four of every five races he contests. When he wins, moreover, Pincay returns significantly less than the compensating profits of 4–1. All other leading riders do even worse.

The bottom line on jockeys is painstakingly plain. No one can bet consistently on jockeys and hope to prosper at the races.

The following advice on jockeys can be accepted as gospel among recreational handicappers:

1. Jockeys are relatively unimportant as handicapping factors.
2. Never bet on the jockey factor alone.
3. Leading jockeys, and hot apprentices, are notoriously overbet. Avoid their mounts as underlays.
4. Overweights among jockeys are meaningless.
5. Hot and cold jockeys are not nearly as instrumental to handicappers as their counterpart hot-and-cold trainers.
6. Apprentices can win routes as frequently as they win sprints, but the large majority of apprentices do not win as frequently on the turf or in stakes.
7. Riding specialties, that is, Toro on the turf, Pat Valenzuela out of the gate, Eddie Delahoussaye on deep closers, sometimes can be meaningful, but the full context counts most, and the most successful patterns tend to be overbet.

As with leading trainers, although not as salient, it's convenient to know when leading riders are off their game. When top riders have been losing abnormally, their favorites and low-priced contenders in contentious and unpredictable races can be forsaken. Handicappers can pursue the contenders and ripe overlays mounted by other talented jockeys.

Two of the finest riders in the nation—indeed, in the sport's history—are Chris McCarron and Eddie Delahoussaye. During Santa Anita's long winter season of 1989—for the first time ever, I suspect—McCarron rode at a journeyman's 13 percent winners. Months later, through 56 of 67 summer racing dates at Hollywood Park, McCarron's win percentage had resurged to 25 percent, tops in the southern California colony.

In close situations, certainly when discriminating finely among underlays and overlays, McCarron might have been discounted at Santa Anita and preferred at Hollywood Park.

Alternately, third-leading rider throughout 90 racing days at Santa Anita 1989, Delahoussaye, through 56 days and 50 mounts at Hollywood Park the same season, rode at an uncharacteristically poor 8 percent winners on the grass.

In close situations Delahoussaye might have been discounted on the Hollywood Park turf in 1989. Yet leading trainer Neil Drysdale uses Delahoussaye first call on many outstanding grass horses. When Drysdale named Delahoussaye on the turf during Hollywood Park 1989, should handicappers have abandoned the horse?

Of course not.

That's the closing argument when evaluating jockeys. So many other factors take precedence in handicapping, the jockeys in the main merely tag along for the ride.

As always, the exceptions deserve fair notice.

In distance races on the grass, and in pressure-packed stakes events, the talent, experience, poise, and confidence of the jockey takes on special dimensions. Handicappers should insist on a competent rider. Such jockeys will not blow the opportunity by making silly mistakes.

And the Kentucky Derby qualifies as the ultimate challenge of horsemanship, where the jockey is even more important than the trainer. Only truly talented jockeys can get home first in the country's most popular horse race.

As for the races filling tomorrow's card, and the next day's, and the next, accept the jockeys. The best horse may self-destruct due to a stumblebum ride, after all, but the cause and effect will not be predictable beforehand.

EVALUATING SIRES

Information about horses' pedigrees becomes useful to handicappers in three situations where conventional methods often disappoint:

1. first and second attempts on the turf
2. two-year-old first starters
3. in the mud

In each situation, handicappers want to know which sires can be expected to perform successfully about twice as frequently as probabilities would expect. A statistical study of a sire's progeny's win percentages in the situations sometimes clears the air.

In the tabulations summarized in this book's appendices, which describe successful sire performance on the grass and in the mud, the sires have been represented by a reliable number of starts and have produced a success rate near or above 20 percent. Their progeny can be strongly preferred on grass or in mud.

Successful sires with first-starting two-year-olds vary from season to season. The *Daily Racing Form* tabulates win percentages, and prints them periodically. Tote action here also supports the handicapping cause. Until the juveniles actually perform, their potential is largely the private property of stables and clockers. These people might prefer to bet on the fast ones.

Dams pass on racing aptitude equally well as sires, to be sure, but the small number of their sons and daughters prohibits effective statistical evaluation.

A critical mistake repeated daily by recreational handicappers in situations where breeding applies confuses a sire's racing aptitudes with the tendency to pass it on. Because a horse performed well on grass, or in mud, does not mean its sons and daughters will, too, and the majority do not.

Prepotency is a condition whereby a sire transfers its racing aptitudes to progeny unusually well, in comparison at least with sires that are not prepotent. The most productive grass sire of the past two decades, Stage Door Johnny, never raced on the turf. Not many sires achieve prepotency, though thousands persist in trying. When evaluating pedigree, it's crucial to distinguish the sires that have passed along their aptitudes from those that have not.

In addition, because a sire's progeny win approximately 20 percent of the time in certain situations (grass, mud) does not mean handicappers can support the horses reflexively. In the same circumstance, another horse may figure on cold dope by a wide margin, and proceed to dominate the field.

The odds also play a determinant role. In close analyses, in contentious or indecipherable races, the 20 percent statistic strengthens the possibility that a favorably bred horse may win. At low odds, however, as below 4–1, the 20 percent chance surrenders a great deal of its force. But if the odds are generous, 5–1 to 12–1 perhaps, and the horse has a fundamental handicapping attraction as well, a prepotent sire intensifies the basic appeal.

Of course, whenever horses figure firmly on speed, class, pace, and form, a successful sire in today's situation adds the icing. Now maybe the horse is offered at 7–2, when it should be 2–1. That's a fundamental kind of overlay proposition, more seductive because of the successful sire in the background.

THE POST-PARADE INSPECTIONS

No aspect of evaluating thoroughbreds eludes the typical practitioner's comprehension as thoroughly as inspecting horses' body language. A small minority of handicappers qualify as astutely primed on the topic, and the rest remain swamped in ignorance, frustration, and contradiction.

My personal aptitude for applying the skill has persisted as despairingly poor, despite several seasons of interlocking readings, applications, observations, and consultations. Having observed irrefutably negative signs, I throw them out, and more than a few return in glory to the winner's circle.

The years of contradiction have contributed to new perspectives on body language, and how recreational handicappers might benefit from the factor. One tale of woe I shall regret forever sets a tone for the no-nonsense discussion that follows.

In 1984, when the champion Precisionist was three, I observed the colt closely through the winter, spring, and summer of the season. I like to follow brilliantly fast nonclaiming three-year-olds that have been losing while learning how to race. The losses can be attributed to inexperience, lack of competitive seasoning, inadequate training, or merely the inability to be rated, the last a consequence of the first three.

Precisionist was that kind of three-year-old. Exhausted, after running away with the riders in blazing fractions, Precisionist would expire in the shadow of the finish line, succumbing to ordinary horses I knew he would annihilate later, once the experience, maturity, and instructive seasoning took hold.

In April, Precisionist blew the Santa Anita Derby to an outsider in that same self-defeating style. Not for the first time his betting public had been burned. Precisionist had rated more kindly in the Santa Anita Derby, nonetheless. The colt finished tired, but not exhausted. He was learning.

Santa Anita ended. I stopped playing the races. The spring classics proceeded. Precisionist earned no fame or fortune during the period, lost in the national commotion.

I dutifully tracked Precisionist's progress on the track and in the morning workouts. The colt at last learned to be rated out of the gate, due not inconsiderably to the talents of jockey Chris McCarron.

In July, at Hollywood Park, comes the Grade 1 Swaps Stakes, at 1¼ miles. Precisionist is entered.

I bought the *Racing Form* on the eve of the Swaps Stakes and found Precisionist lined up against a field of overblown, overraced contestants exiting the classics. The brilliant colt should win as he pleased, I determined, and set myself to make the major wager I had been formulating for half a season.

The next afternoon I drove across town, sat idle during the overnight program, and teased my companions on the good fortune of being present at the best parimutuel opportunity of the season.

When the feature arrived, I walked to the paddock, not my routine procedure. Precisionist was a horrid sight.

Tugging backward, head and neck stretched high, whirling, the colt fought its handler relentlessly. Nervous sweat poured down both flanks and between the hind legs. Eyes rolled, the whites flashing.

The fracas persisted throughout the saddling and walking, intensifying by the minute.

The colt was now wet from front to rear, shaking its head repeatedly, the eyes dancing wildly, the ears flicking about, the torso bucking the ceremonies.

During the post parade kidney sweat ran down the legs of Precisionist in small streams. The jockey swiped the sweat off the colt's shoulders and belly repeatedly.

With ten minutes to go the odds on Precisionist hovered at 9–2, a fabulous overlay on objective facts. On the track, however, Precisionist looked the embodiment of defeat. A serious wager shaped up as pathetic as Precisionist himself.

Late betting supported Precisionist some, lowering the final odds to 7–2. I sat still, moaning the wasted afternoon.

The gate opened and Precisionist sped to the front, as usual. The brilliant colt increased his lead at every call. Precisionist demolished the Swaps Stakes opposition by ten lengths. He came back dry as toast. The rest is racing history.

It was a formative experience for a regular handicapper. The hunt for negative signs when observing body language gets the untrained eye nowhere but lost in the thicket. No horse has looked worse than Precisionist, and few have won more powerfully. The contradiction cannot be denied, and occurs more frequently than rational debate allows. The circumstance begs for a new set of conclusions.

First, washiness alone, however severe, does not defeat horses, and washiness and fractiousness in combination will often end in victory regardless.

In sprints, if horses figure, but appear washy and fractious, handicappers can accept the horses anyway, certainly at attractive odds. Before the energy lost to nervousness is required, the race is over.

The possible exception is the frontrunner imprisoned by its running style—cannot be rated. If the horse should be contested in the early stages, its prospects are dim. Out of sorts to begin, and pressured, that kind of speed horse is likelier to squander excessive energy in a futile dash for the front.

Route horses can be treated separately. If routers look a mess and act badly in combination, the negative body language may exact a toll over longer distances. The cheaper the horses, the more serious the condition. Certain precautions make sense.

First, inspect the horses during the post parade, not at the paddock. Horses unnerved by crowds of people can unravel in the paddock and walking ring, but settle down quietly on leaving. Too many paddock handicappers gather a false impression. Negative body language in the post parade may constitute a real problem.

Two additional checks serve the purpose.

If the odds on a messy, misbehaving horse are relatively low, and alternative contenders beckon at higher prices, favor the alternative contenders.

If the odds on a messy, misbehaving horse are moderate to high, postpone any serious bet. Observe the prerace warm-ups. Inspect the horse as it approaches the starting gate. Many horses, à la Precisionist, quiet down and relax once they have been removed from the combustion and glare of the crowd.

Is the horse finally calm and dry?

If strong contenders pass the final inspection at the gate, and the moderate to high odds have persevered, carry out the intended wager.

If strong contenders at attractive odds remain plainly out of sorts as the start approaches, either reduce the bet size or pass altogether. Once again, if the distressed horse is a frontrunner that will be pressed early, it's prudent to pass.

Negative body language has its opposite number, of course, and many contemporary handicappers prefer to bet on sharp-looking horses, for that reason alone, at landslide prices. It's an instinct I unhesitatingly reinforce, as sharp horses customarily deliver sharp performances. Sharp horses will consistently outrun high odds, and some of them win at boxcars.

If horses do not shape up as contenders on the homework, but can be seen prancing on their toes, neck arched, coat dappled, muscles pronounced, ears pricked, handicappers can conclude the horses will be ready to run as best they can. If sharp horses stride out strongly to begin the prerace gallops, the readiness has turned to eagerness. Whenever the odds are extraordinarily generous, handicappers might indulge them, especially in lower-class claiming races.

Sharp horses should not be bet for that reason alone, however, at moderate to low odds, notably in nonclaiming races. The horses do not win frequently enough to generate profits.

Naturally, when strong contenders on fundamental handicapping look sharp on the track as well, bet-size can be increased.

And mild washiness, or slight fractiousness, should not be a deterrent for supporting strong contenders. As often as not, the mild sweat, and nervous energy, are part of a positive profile of eager anticipation.

Here are a few further guidelines on the post-parade inspection:

1. Back wraps are acceptable, but front bandages are not, unless the horse has won with fronts in the past.

Long front bandages for the first time are particularly negative signs on juveniles, three-year-olds, maidens, and stake horses. The horses are unsound, sore, or both, and cannot be expected to withstand the competition.

Of prior winners adorned in front bandages, a serious wager is inevitably risky. The horses are no doubt competitive, but still unsound, and possibly sore today. If the horses are feeling lousy, they probably will not extend themselves.

Consistency here counts. The more consistent the runners

in front wraps, the more sensible a prime bet.

On the other hand, if a consistent winner that wears front bandages runs terribly, a bet next time at attractive odds is immediately plausible. Alert handicappers can profit surprisingly well from this angle in claiming races. The public will shy from bandaged horses following a dull effort. Yet the horses have proved their consistency. Feeling bad last out but healthy today, many unsound but courageous claiming horses will bounce back with a gem of a performance.

Ankle wraps in front can be accepted, unless the horses show a high-stepping, choppy gait as well, head bobbing up and down or left to right. Many trainers use ankle wraps up front to prevent horses from "running down," the tendency to rub sloping pasterns and ankles in the scratching sand.

2. In the slop, or mud, beware of horses showing short, high, or choppy strides during the post-parade and prerace warm-ups.

Prefer a fully extended, fluid gallop in the mud, similar to gallops on dry ground. Gait and stride should appear secure. Horses tentative, uncomfortable, or uncertain, during gallops or warm-ups, are less likely to run straight and aggressively throughout a mud race.

3. If horses leave the post parade under the jockey's control, it's a positive sign, but inconclusive.

If body language is positive, leaving the post parade early suggests the horses are full of themselves and eager to compete.

If body language is negative, the rider is probably trying to settle the horse, or work out the kinks.

Running off from the post parade is a negative, but also inconclusive. If the situation worsens, the horse running off ridiculously, throw them out. But if the jockey regains control following a hundred-yard dash, not to worry.

Likewise, refusing to load is usually nothing more serious than a fear of the starting gate. The delay may cause as much discomfort among the horses standing in the gate or waiting to be loaded as it does the perpetrator.

Breaking through the starting gate, however, is bad news, and tickets should be refunded, though usually they are not. The incident ruins concentration, robs energy, and disturbs temperament. The horses become badly distracted. Trainers abhor the scene. So should handicappers. A few of these victims survive and win, but most of them perish long before the wire.

4. Dull coats, drooping heads, and listless strides are not reliable bases for eliminating contenders during the post-parade inspection.

When the gates spring open, numerous dull horses suddenly respond as if charged at a gas station. They run their race absolutely, and if good enough to win, they do.

Broadly speaking, body language will be more meaningful as a fundamental in handicapping at minor tracks, where horses in far greater number are seriously unsound and sore. There, a paddock inspection is fully warranted, and post-parade inspections can be sufficiently crucial that recreational handicappers in possession of the observational skills that apply will enjoy a definite advantage.

At major tracks, in the main, the kind of cursory post-parade inspection promoted here will suffice. If contenders look washy and fractious, and the odds are low, prefer other contenders. If horses look sharp, and the race is otherwise indecipherable, the odds extremely generous, take a chance on readiness.

Recreational handicappers can cope with body language on those spare terms and do all right.

CHAPTER V

Understanding Speed, Class, and Pace Relationships

AMONG THE MOST SIGNIFICANT, well-documented relationships of thoroughbred racing is the positive correlation between speed and class.

Better horses run faster. Studies of par times, or typical times, or average times, demonstrate that final-time differences among classes of racehorses are standard and small. Consider the 1988–89 six-furlong par times for claiming and nonclaiming races, respectively, at Santa Anita:

	Claiming		*Nonclaiming*	
	$10,000	1:11.1		
	12,500	1:11	Maiden	1:10.3
	16,000	1:10.4	Alw, NW1	1:10.1
	20,000	1:10.3	Alw, NW2	1:09.4
	25,000	1:10.2	Alw, NW3	1:09.3
	32,000	1:10.1	Clf Alw	1:09.2
	40,000	1:10	Stakes	1:09
	50,000	1:09.4		
Above	50,000	1:09.2		

Without exception, the typical time differences between classes is one fifth or two fifths of a second, and normally one fifth. It's the same at all racetracks. Empirically, speed and class are interlocking.

Conceptually, speed and class should be just as closely related, viewed as complementary aspects of horses' natural ability. Arguments among handicappers as to the relative importance of speed vis-à-vis class are entirely specious and always have been, a monumental waste of time.

At any particular class level, of course, final times will be faster or slower than par by as much as a second, even more—the phenomenon referred to as class within a class. That is, at any specific class level, some horses will be more talented than the norm, some less talented.

Another explanation is pace. Among ordinary horses, as studies demonstrate, when fractional times improve, final times decline. The patterns are highly symmetrical:

	Pace	Final Time
Horse A	45.3	1:10.3
Horse A	45.1	1:11

If Horse A travels two fifths of a second faster to the pace call, it finishes two fifths of a second slower. The patterns repeat themselves among older, mature horses, the claiming horses especially.

A third explanation depends upon the intangible attributes of class. These are (a) endurance and (b) competitive spirit, meaning qualities of willingness, determination, and courage.

When the early pace or late drive or both become unusually fast and prolonged, only horses that can summon the optimal degrees of speed, stamina, and determination in combination can prevail. The others fall behind, either outrun, tired, or unwilling. Not surprisingly, the qualities of endurance and determination normally matter most among better horses and at longer distances.

Why, handicappers ask, do horses still in form lose in the same final time (adjusted), or slower final time, as they have completed previously against a comparable class?

The answer is either a faster early pace or a more prolonged stretch duel or both.

Why, handicappers wonder, do horses that have won impressively in faster time at a lower level often fail to duplicate the clocking, while losing at a higher level?

Again, it's invariably a faster pace, sustained farther. If the swifter pace is being sustained by more determined horses, the demise of the class rise can be sudden and sure.

Yet horses that can attend the faster pace and respond to the stiffer challenge can leap ahead in class successfully, duplicating the prior final time or exceeding it. The candidates likeliest to rise in class successfully therefore are younger, improving horses, still unclassified, or mature horses, 4up, now in improving or peaking form, or benefitting from providential circumstances, such as a new trainer, a track bias, a soft early lead, or a perfect trip.

In general, horses exiting a race featuring a fast pace in combination with a fast final time not only move ahead in class successfully, they can dominate horses exiting a race having an average or slow pace and fast final time, or a race having a fast pace but an average or slow final time. In claiming races, horses exiting a fast-fast race, if they are the only horse of the kind in the field, possess a tremendous advantage.

Such are the naked statistical facts and the patterns that represent them.

A perfectly legitimate way to understand the relations among speed, class, and pace as fundamentals of handicapping is to comprehend well the characteristics of class, the broadest, most inclusive, of the factors.

As noted, the attributes of thoroughbred class are three: brilliance (speed), endurance, and determination.

Speed can be cheap or one-dimensional but still outrun unexceptional horses without speed, especially at shorter distances, as happens frequently. Cheap or early speed wins when uncontested, or abetted by a positive speed bias or by track surfaces that extract little energy.

As distances lengthen, stamina and competitive spirit are drawn inexorably into battle. So are the effects of pace, or the rates of speed at the various points of call, intensified by the number and quality of the pace combatants.

Long sprints, for instance, demand far greater expressions of endurance and determination than do sprints of six furlongs, which are more hospitable to the cheaper speed. Numerous sprinters cannot stretch their swift an additional half furlong, notably when challenged in the late stages.

Nonetheless, brilliance, or speed, the essential attribute of class, dominates in sprints. All other handicapping factors are secondary (not unimportant), as are the intangible attributes of class. Thus the factor most likely to defeat one-dimensional speed in sprints is rate of speed or pace.

In routes, speed counts significantly to nine furlongs, but usually must be buttressed by stamina, a willingness to persevere against obstacles, and, frequently enough, a noticeable measure of late determination.

At ten furlongs, the classic 1¼ miles, or farther, the stamina to sustain speed throughout the distance becomes very significant. Among unexceptional horses—practically all—speed, stamina, and competitiveness will be equally salient, unless undisciplined pace spoils the plot. If a pressured pace weakens or collapses, late speed, stamina, and determination will dispute the verdict. If the pace slows to a steady gallop, a seeming crawl, ordinary frontrunners can steal ordinary races at classic and marathon distances, and regularly do.

At ten furlongs among stakes horses, surely the highest-grade winners, speed and pace regularly will be subordinate to endurance, late brilliance, and high determination. In Grade 1 races at classic distances, class laughs at pace, a reckoning too few experienced handicappers appreciate.

Class is also dynamic—meaning natural ability changes—and relative, meaning natural ability will be expressed variously against different classes of opposition. As noted, better horses dispense a keener pace and simultaneously exhibit greater degrees of endurance and determination to win. Racehorses tend to deliver career-best times when matched against animals of relatively equal ability. When pitted against superior runners, the same horses fall short, stop, or quit.

The class, or natural talent, of younger developing horses— the nonclaiming three-year-olds absolutely—changes, at times dramatically, as a result of physical maturation, training, and competitive seasoning. As a result, better three-year-olds can advance in class sensationally, then disappoint inexplicably, then rise anew. Ordinary three-year-olds advance and decline more gradually, but many climb up and down the local class ladders throughout the core season.

Two-year-olds tend to improve tremendously, or to deteriorate radically. A negative reversal by an impressive juvenile should be accepted at face value. A positive rebound should not be expected.

The relative class of fully mature horses, 5up, or of four-year-olds during the second half of the season, is altered primarily as a function of form. Form refers to current condition, soundness, or readiness, the latter dependent upon trainers. The contemporary longer season has resulted in improving and declining form cycles several times a year, as horses are subjected intermittently to overwork, overexertion, rest, and reconditioning.

Relative class can be reflected often by improving or declining final times (adjusted), pace ratings, or speed figures. The numbers are intended to reflect reality, not to substitute for it.

A logical sequence of consecutive clockings, or numerical ratings, is always preferable to a single rating. An isolated final time, pace rating, or speed figure, high or low, may reflect an abnormal pace, or severe bias, or perfect trip, or a lone front-running romp.

But if the track surface has been normal, the pace typical, and the opposition comparable, a slower adjusted final time or corresponding numerical rating intimates declining form. Tailing horses that record a slower pace and slower final time in combination can be forsaken.

Finally, among horses of established and comparable class that are in form, speed or final time will usually play second fiddle to an astute pace analysis. When separating closely matched contenders in sprints and at middle distances, handicappers should routinely elaborate the probable pace. If one horse should benefit from the probable pace by controlling it or overtaking it, that horse deserves the bettor's nod, and very often justifies it. If no horse should benefit from the probable pace or several might, go to the class.

Recreational handicappers who aspire to expertise in handicapping, and to successful seasonal play, should resign themselves to mastering the intricacies and interrelations of speed, class, and pace. The individual's countdown to success cannot commence until these fundamentals are firmly in place. No one should be mistaken about it.

CHAPTER VI

Everyday Applications

ONCE HANDICAPPERS HAVE identified the contenders and evaluated them variously utilizing rating methods, the task at hand is slightly more than half complete.

Which factors take precedence today? In this race? Should handicappers emphasize speed over class, class over speed, track bias over all else? How does the trainer fit in? And so forth.

After the rating methods have been applied and a preliminary analysis of the race conducted, the pieces must be reassembled into visions of the probable outcome.

The practitioner surveys a diverse array of information pertinent to several contenders. Which information deserves priority, or emphasis? How should the information be combined to complete the puzzle such that the pieces fit together properly?

It's this stage of handicapping, putting the pieces of the puzzle together, that separates the experts from the journeymen. Success depends upon applying a comprehensive array of knowledge about races and horses, as well as practical experience in handicapping, to the hard data the basic methods have already produced. Presumably, handicappers combining the widest know-how and experience with accurate data supplied by reliable methods will be best equipped to solve the puzzles.

It's at this advanced stage, too, where method players carelessly stumble into trouble. Method players are those who belong to an amazingly large, nationwide club of handicappers almost blindly submissive to the procedures and output of pet methods.

Speed handicappers entranced by the magical power of their figures.

Class handicappers dedicated to the proposition they have discovered the best horse.

Pace analysts unable to imagine the race might be run in any other way.

Trip handicappers persuaded that horses running into trouble last out will convert the mishaps into clear sailing to victory today.

Trainer specialists clinging stubbornly to personal convictions that what a trainer intends to happen today amounts to direct access to reality.

And the rest.

Closer to reality is the proposition that handicapping factors and rating methods obtain priority and emphases variously, depending on the conditions of racing and the circumstances surrounding the races.

No method, however wonderful, applies effectively all of the time, or should be considered appropriate under all circumstances. Handicappers prepared to relate the output of pet methods to the conditions and circumstances of races proceed from a frame of reference attuned to the dynamic conditions of a changing game.

The typical race analysis will produce information, some quantitative, some qualitative, in relation to several fundamentals of handicapping and the ubiquitous circumstances of races. Consider:

Fundamentals	Circumstances
Early speed	Trips
Final speed	Track biases
Pace	Trainers
Class	Jockeys
Form	Post position

Putting the pieces together obviously involves relating the abilities of horses to the circumstances of races.

Which is more important?

It depends.

But a generality can be set forth: excepting track biases that are severe enough to overwhelm the abilities and preferences of

horses, the abilities of horses invariably deserve first consideration over the circumstances of races. The fundamentals themselves can be equally important, but variously applicable. Class
is superfluous in maiden-claiming races. Final speed is much
less meaningful on the turf. Pace does not easily separate top-
grade horses at classic distances. Early speed is sometimes difficult to predict, sometimes uninteresting to predict. Form is
significantly less decisive in nonclaiming races than in claiming races.

In the end, in tight situations certainly, handicappers may
judge a horse best due to its trip or trainer, but from an evalua-
tive point of view, the first consideration belongs to the abilities
of horses: their early speed, speed figures, pace ratings, relative
class, and current form.

The following sections relate the information obtained by
rating methods to types of races, classes of horses, and the general conditions of racing. Numerous applications will be discussed, but briefly.

The purpose is to present basic principles, statistical facts,
broad guidelines, and specific recommendations as to the factors and methods that deserve priority or emphasis in specific
situations or under familiar circumstances.

If effective, recreational handicappers will not only suspend
faith in the everlasting power of a particular handicapping
method, but also gain a deeper understanding of how to apply
the various methods they prefer to use.

Let's begin with the broadest categories of races, sprints and
routes.

SPRINTS AND ROUTES

At tracks of one mile in circumference, sprints are races contested around one turn. Routes are races contested around
two turns.

At tracks 1⅛ miles in circumference, the frequently carded
one-turn mile is actually an elongated sprint, far more comfortable for sprinters than routers.

Sprints are relatively short distances hospitable to speed
horses and less susceptible to the influences of stamina or the
intangibles of class, such as determination and courage. Early
speed, final time, early pace, and turn time represent the hand-

icapping factors of greatest persuasion, with speed variables at least twice as significant as any other.

In sprints, in the timeless equations balancing speed and class, how fast horses have run is twice as important as the kind of opposition they have defeated. That is, speed supersedes class by a two to one weighting. Accurate speed figures, or pace ratings, are indispensable to evaluating contenders.

Furthermore, whenever the figures or ratings justify the maneuver, claiming horses in sprints can leap ahead in class and win decisively.

The point cannot be overstated. Recreational handicappers need to know how fast horses have actually run in sprints. The pace ratings promoted in the methods section of this book satisfy that purpose reasonably well.

Occasional racegoers imagine the No. 1 post position performs at a disadvantage in sprints, but probability studies dispel that perception absolutely. The No. 1 post wins slightly more than its rightful share of the races. The finding generalizes to all racetracks.

Thus recreational handicappers should not shy from horses in sprints because they will exit the inside post. Some rail horses in sprints undoubtedly get shuffled back due to troubled trips, but the incidents are too infrequent to alter the general circumstance.

The only factor capable of altering the impact of speed in sprints is a strong track bias.

A positive speed bias, of course, propels speed horses even more in sprints. Prefer the fastest horse, or the speed of the speed, as the punters put it.

A positive rail bias assists frontrunners inside, and casual racegoers can sense the presence of the bias from a cursory study of post-position win percentages printed in the *Daily Racing Form*. Look for a win percentage twice as great as the middle posts. A win percentage twice as great may indicate a positive rail bias, or may be a statistical fluctuation. The more races in the sample, the better.

A negative rail bias tires the frontrunners in sprints, and handicappers might then prefer speed horses toward the outside. An outside bias boosts speed horses in the outer posts in sprints, where the run to the far turn is extensive.

A negative rail bias has been present whenever the rail position shows a win percentage less than half as high as the middle post positions. Insist on a hundred races as an adequate sample. As a race meeting progresses, if a negative rail bias persists, alert handicappers will await speed horses that ran strongly against the bias from the No. 1 hole, not winning, but lasting until the upper stretch, or perhaps inside the eighth pole. The odds can be quite generous.

A strong bias favoring closers alters the conventional sprint scenarios dramatically. Now the speed horses tire and a majority stop. Handicappers notice the come-from-behinders rallying to win an inordinate number of sprints.

Whenever a positive closers' bias dominates in sprints, the class horse with an off-pace running style shapes up as possibly the best bet of the day. If a speed duel should occur on a track favoring closers, any legitimate off-pace contender looms as dangerous.

As mentioned earlier, as significant as any single guideline apropos to sprints, recreational handicappers must understand that typical speed duels do *not* result in another off-pace horse winning the race. As often as not, one of the battling frontrunners survives the duel and wins. The facile race analysis in sprints, that frontrunners will weaken one another into defeat, is not substantiated by the facts. Only when the pace to the second call will be abnormally fast, and the pressure severe, does the speed duel result in a suicide.

Weight, jockey, and pedigree are irrelevant in sprints.

Class handicappers wedded to their ideas and methods will be consistently frustrated in sprints. Early speed, adjusted final time, early pace, and turn time can easily upset the best horses at the shorter distances, and do. In contemporary racing, moreover, more races than ever are being captured by the speed horses, and the trend approaches its zenith at the customary six furlongs.

Routes are vastly dissimilar from sprints. Speed is not unimportant, but now class and pace begin to exert their powerful influences. As distances lengthen and the competition stiffens, endurance and determination must inexorably be summoned. Early swift must be carried. It's no wonder the cream of each generation are brilliant types that can stretch the high speed across classic distances.

In cheaper routes, to be sure—the claiming races up to $20,000 selling prices—early speed and adjusted final times still stake a heavy claim on the winner's circle. Cheap speed steals cheap routes consistently.

When the speed tires, as following a pace contest, other low-priced horses near the front inherit the lead and prevail. The laggards in cheaper claiming races lack talent, not just speed. They do not often rally successfully from far behind.

The same is characteristic of claiming races limited to three-year-olds during winter and spring, and for two-year-olds of fall. These are cheap commodities. The speed horses dart to the lead or follow closely, and the winners regularly emerge from the front tier. Younger claiming horses that stay at the back do so because they lack the ability to run closer, even when the front-runners and pace-pressers get tired.

In better routes, for high-priced older claiming horses—the allowances and the stakes—the equation changes. Now speed, endurance, and determination strongly interact, and class is half again as important as speed, by a three to two weighting. Up to 1³⁄₁₆ miles, unless a horse sticks out on the numbers, a careful pace analysis regularly reveals the probable winners, as pace separates closely matched nonclaiming horses more reliably than any other factor.

The pace of routes at the fractional call (six furlongs) will be more variable than the pace of sprints. Recreational handi-cappers should be flexible. If nonclaiming horses typically run 1:11.3 to the six-furlong call of races at 1¹⁄₁₆ miles, a devia-tion of two to three lengths faster or slower should raise no eye-brows.

But if the route pace will be abnormally fast, or abnormally slow, pace immediately becomes the telltale clue. An abnor-mally fast pace among better horses favors off-pace running styles, and often closers, as pace-pressers will have tracked the inor-dinately swift leaders and tire from the effort.

An abnormally slow pace among better horses favors the frontrunners. Having conserved their energy, they now release it, and other horses, however swift, cannot easily catch up. The exception regards frontrunners that struggle against the rider's rating throughout the slower fractions. The fight saps energy needed later. But the phenomenon is extremely difficult to pre-dict prior to the start.

If a frontrunner will be the lone speed horse in a nonclaim-ing race, and handicappers sense the horse can be rated and will therefore relax on the lead, the bet is almost automatic, unless the odds are prohibitively low. These speedy nonclaiming horses can relax early, set sluggish fractions, and then draw away, winning handily.

The fastest frontrunner in a nonclaiming route limited to three-year-olds should be among the best bets at the racetrack, but is not, simply because few nonclaiming three-year-olds demonstrate enough maturity and competitive seasoning to relax on the lead. Many cannot be rated kindly. The minority that can will be hounded on the front by other impatient three-year-olds.

In any route race among better horses, if the pace should be contested by three horses or more, find the contender that has demonstrated the ability to be rated behind the front flight. A fast nonclaiming horse that doesn't need the early advantage will surge to the front once the others weaken. That's a tough individual to defeat.

If a pace analysis proves inconclusive when analyzing contenders in nonclaiming routes, prefer the horse having the highest class rating. The rating should be recent, within 60 days, unless form is clearly on the improve and the animal boasts back class. "When in doubt go to the class" is a cliché that has become passé in modern racing, but it makes stricter sense in closely competitive routes.

In one situation, uncommon, pace analysis is less meaningful than many experienced handicappers appreciate. In Grade 1 stakes at classic distances, prefer the best horse. Pace now is incidental. The class of the field overpowers the pace, and wins.

Also, at 1½ miles prefer the horse that can finish the final quarter mile the fastest. Stamina and late drive dominate in these marathons. Horses unable to finish strongly at ten furlongs, or any shorter distance, should not be expected to survive at twelve furlongs, however sluggish the pace. This does not mean frontrunners cannot prevail at twelve furlongs, as the results of the Belmont Stakes regularly show. If the frontrunners can finish fastest, they figure at 1½ miles.

As many recreational handicappers appreciate, the inside post positions at middle distances present a tactical advantage to speed horses angling for position around the clubhouse turn. The outside posts, numbers 10 through 12, suffer a corresponding disadvantage. Frontrunners on the outside often must be urged to gain either the lead or a favorable inside lane before the first turn appears. Closers on the outside at middle distances proceed at no disadvantage.

Frontrunners outside at middle distances, even in middle posts, often experience traffic on the inside in the rush to the first turn, and end up wide. Trip handicappers insist the wide swings of frontrunners at middle distances rank among the worst of trips for contenders. If the wide frontrunners persevere to the top of the lane before tiring, a smooth trip probably would have ended in a much closer finish. The horses can be supported next time, notably if reactivated quickly.

Biases in routes can be similar to biases of sprints, but two deserve special consideration.

A strong positive inside speed bias literally propels the frontrunners around the clubhouse turn. If the rail remains favorable, the speed horses merely continue on a merry jaunt.

A negative speed bias in routes penalizes the frontrunners that do too much too soon. If a negative speed bias exists, and any sort of pace duel looms apparent, handicappers can prefer the closers. The crowd prefers early speed, and pacesetters often will be overbet. If a closer on a biased surface also enjoys a class edge, prepare to support the horse.

Many recreational handicappers believe routers will be unable to tally at familiar distances following a long layoff. Statistics prove the opposite. Routers do significantly better than sprinters following an absence. The slower pace of the route does not exhaust horses as badly.

Related routes are middle distances of a mile to 1¾₁₆ miles. Versatile runners can adapt to the switches. Many routers, however, require 1⅛ miles, and others prefer a mile, to demonstrate their best. In close calls, prefer the authentic milers at that distance, and the genuine middle-distance specialists at nine furlongs.

As noted, sprinters that do not exhaust their energies on the front end can stretch out to middle distances effectively. Routers do not drop back to sprint distances effectively unless they can stay within a length of the four-furlong call in routes, and preferably show superior speed to the six-furlong call.

One of the tastiest distance changes for experienced handicappers who know what to look for are the hard-knocking pricier claiming sprinters stretching out to a flat mile. The "bulldogs," as a handicapping friend calls them, can get the mile impressively, and many of them upset at fanciful odds.

LONG SPRINTS

Long sprints are carded at distances of 6½ furlongs and seven furlongs.

A logical paradox hovers about the long sprints. Although frontrunners and pace-pressers dominate, and the speed factors of handicapping merit priority, now the late-running sprinters enjoy a significantly greater chance. Oddly enough, late-running sprinters, the closers, often find better opportunities to catch up at 6½ furlongs than at seven. The explanation is pace. Studies of fractional pars reveal that frontrunners record the same fractional times at 6½ furlongs as they do at six, but typically slow the pace at seven furlongs. Here are the 1988–89 sprint pars, final and fractional, for $20,000 claiming horses at Santa Anita:

Clm $20,000 Pars, Santa Anita

6F	45	1:10.3
6½F	45	1:17.
7F	45.2	1:23.3

A similar phenomenon occurs at most major tracks. Riders instinctively slow the pace of seven-furlong races, anxious to conserve the limited energies of sprinters. The phenomenon repeats itself among classier horses. Here are the 1988–89 Santa Anita pars for stakes sprinters:

Stakes Pars, Santa Anita

6F	44.1	1:09
6½F	44.1	1:15.2
7F	44.4	1:22

Because the fractional times at 6½ furlongs normally will be as fast as fractional times at six furlongs, frontrunners will tire as badly in the longer sprints, but closers will have an extra sixteenth of a mile to exploit the situation. Many do.

At 6½ furlongs, therefore, handicappers benefit by paying added attention to the probable early pace. Two circumstances, in particular, should serve notice the closers will be a dangerous late factor.

First, the early pace will be contested among three or more frontrunners. A trio on the lead accelerates the pace and intensifies the conflict, as none of the horses can settle into an accommodating stride, and sets up the closers' late charge.

Second, the early pace will be controlled by cheap speed, the types that regularly expire at six furlongs, or tire noticeably, barely lasting. Or a pair of ordinary to common frontrunners will contest a fast early pace for four furlongs, weakening one another before the eighth pole arrives.

At seven furlongs the pace analysis should determine whether the early pace (start to second call) might be inordinately fast or inordinately slow. If too fast, the late-running sprinters will inherit a marvelous opportunity to rule in the stretch. If too slow, the front flight will merely draw away after passing the prestretch call. Closers will be unable to overtake the pace.

An ordinary pace at seven furlongs does not interfere with the frontrunners' statistical advantages in sprints.

A problem peculiar to races of seven furlongs regards the routers attempting to sprint. Numerous recreational handicappers believe routers should be preferred at seven furlongs. The belief is unsupported by facts. Routers do not transfer to sprints of any distance and win a fair share of the races. But the situation at seven furlongs is more complicated.

A useful practical guideline discounts routers at seven furlongs, if they cannot stay within a length of the leader at the first call of routes. Alternately, any running style slower than a few lengths behind a route pace eliminates the horses at seven furlongs. The running lines look something like this:

**AT
SEVEN
FURLONGS:**

NOT ACCEPTABLE

ACCEPTABLE

But if a router can run within a length of the route pace at the first call, and complete the second call in par, accept the horse on distance at seven furlongs. Better still is the router that displays high speed to the second call of routes, notably if the speed has been carried to the stretch call. These intriguing sprint prospects possess the router's speed and endurance. They can track a sprinter's pace at seven furlongs and finish strongly. If the sprinters tire, the routers roar by in the lane.

Numerous lightning-fast sprinters possess the stamina and willingness to persevere at the same high speed for six furlongs, 6½, or seven furlongs. They often display obvious reserves of speed and power at the finish of six furlongs, almost an eagerness to do more. These powerful sprinters outrun the late-runners and routers dropping back, regardless of the sprint distance.

Other lightning-fast sprinters do not possess the stamina and willingness to persevere at the same rate of speed beyond six furlongs. They finish at six furlongs noticeably tired, perhaps lugging out in the final sixteenth. In long sprints, unless the early pace softens, they can be expected to perish.

Younger horses, the nonclaiming three-year-olds and juveniles that win impressively at six furlongs will almost invariably continue to impress in long sprints, especially as they progress through the conditions of eligibility against their own age group.

Younger claiming sprinters are cheaper, slower, and less reliable. They regularly lack the stamina and willingness to extend a cheap brand of six-furlong speed another half furlong, and are therefore susceptible to the same pace patterns that bedevil their older counterparts.

And the lone frontrunner whose calling card is cheap speed and cheap speed alone, will be far more susceptible to collapse in long sprints. The commoners get tired as usual, and absolutely yearn to call it quits.

Certain sprinters are particularly terrifying at seven furlongs. They often track the pace for four furlongs and then explode. Final times are fast, and the rapid acceleration on the turn is unmistakable.

Here are two striking illustrations:

Sewickley had also broken its maiden at seven furlongs—by six lengths in dazzling time. Look for similar seven-furlong patterns.

So while long sprints are substantially interchangeable with sprints of six furlongs, the distances differ enough so that handicappers must be alert to the nuances, shadings, and degrees of change that surround the pace preferences, running styles, and competitive willingness of the horses under scrutiny today.

ONE-TURN MILES

Is the one-turn mile an elongated sprint? Is the distance an authentic route?

Treated as a route, in practice the one-turn mile plays like a sprint. That is, sprinters are far more likely to negotiate the distance effectively than routers.

As at seven furlongs, the routers entered in one-turn miles should have demonstrated genuine route speed, staying within a length or two of a normal route pace and carrying the speed at least six furlongs, preferably longer.

The truly appealing horse in any one-turn mile is the tactical speed type, the kind that can lay a few lengths behind the early pace, relaxed, and then accelerate powerfully turning for home.

Another attractive prospect in a one-turn mile is the consistently contentious sprinters, the "bulldogs," or horses that finish at conventional sprint distances with ample reserves of speed and power. These competitors crave to do more, and in one-turn miles the opportunity arrives.

Off-pace running styles in routes, closers especially, normally cannot arrive in time to prevail in one-turn miles. Unless the early pace will be fast and contested, and figures to collapse, and the horses usually launch their bid in the routes between the prestretch and stretch calls, mid-pack routers and closers can be eliminated reliably in one-turn miles.

One-turn miles are carded daily at Aqueduct, Arlington Park, Belmont Park, and Hollywood Park, as well as other tracks greater than a mile in circumference.

At none of the tracks does the No. 1 post hold an advantage or suffer a disadvantage. Contrary to conventional trackside wisdom, one-turn miles are not susceptible to post-position biases of any kind. The run to the far turn is four furlongs, at least, and statistically the twelve post positions perform equally well. I implore recreational handicappers to accept that assertion as factual, which it is, and avoid the confusion in one-turn miles aroused by apparent post-position biases that do not exist.

Figure handicappers must perform an impressive juggling act in one-turn miles, as sprinters, routers, and two-turn milers join in the pursuit. Professionals, and clever regulars, make numerical adjustments to sprint and route figures by observing the par-time differences at the fractional calls of the various distances and calculating the deviations.

If $20,000 claiming horses typically travel to the six-furlong call of a one-turn mile in 1:10.2, and the six-furlong call of a two-turn route at 1$\frac{1}{16}$ miles in 1:11.4, a router's pace adjustment when entered at a one-turn mile would be Slow 7, an addition of seven points to the ratings or figures. The same procedure adjusts the final times or numerical ratings at the separate distances.

The adjustments are essentially unreliable. The comparative pace calls of the unrelated distances are fundamentally distinct, altering riding tactics and changing running styles such that numerical comparisons between sprints, one-turn miles, and routes can amount to a kind of parlor game.

The firm position here is that recreational handicappers are not equipped to make adjustments to numerical ratings or final times at unrelated distances, or two-turn routes, when analyzing one-turn miles. Do not adjust this book's pace ratings in that way.

If horses have never attempted the one-turn mile but have won at distances both shorter and longer than a mile, accept the horses as contenders. Armed with a sprinter's speed and a router's stamina in combination, these versatile runners may represent the best bet of the day, or week, and at generous odds too.

BULLRINGS

Even where good horses gather to compete for sizable purses, as at Fairplex Park, outside of Los Angeles, or at Sportsman's Park, in Chicago, bullrings are sites for minor-league racing. This does not imply the bullrings operate without their special charms.

Numerous handicappers are drawn irresistibly to these ovals of four or five furlongs, which afford them a distinctively fascinating handicapping experience.

Besides that, bullrings can be digested as smoothly and sweetly as vanilla pudding by talented handicappers. Moreover, the customary demands for specialized handicapping information, paradoxically, do not apply. Knowledgeable recreational handicappers can do very well merely by consulting the past performances of the *Racing Form*.

Here, in descending order of importance and utility, are the handicapping factors to emphasize:

1. A double drop in claiming class.
2. Any drop in claiming price, abetted by tactical speed and an inside post position.
3. Inside early speed.
4. Talented bullring riders.
5. High-rated horses in featured stakes and allowances.
6. Track class.

That's all, actually. Regarding form, unless the recent running lines appear downright awful, as many do, or the horses have shipped from major tracks where form has been lackluster, the current form of numerous bullring horses approaches the inscrutable. Inscrutable form amounts to acceptable form, however, and the horses are best evaluated on other fundamentals. Do not throw out horses entered at bullrings on form unless the case is clear-cut. Among the ambiguous situations the odds will be juicier, and several of the horses will surprise.

To dispense with the final factor on the list, track class, bullrings are magnets for various horses representing every minor racing emporium in the region. Numerous horses from the major tracks on the local circuit show up too.

Know your racetracks.

When Los Alamitos, in Orange County, conducts twenty-one programs of thoroughbred night racing each summer, the fields below $10,000 claiming will be stocked with representatives of the northern California racing fairs; of Turf Paradise, in Phoenix, Arizona; of Prescott, in Arizona; of Caliente, in Mexico; even of Hollywood Park, just ended, and Del Mar, just begun.

Impressive Prescott horses can be discarded blindly, but the Caliente sharpies cannot, and often will whip ordinary horses that arrived from Turf Paradise and northern California. Caliente sends its top prospects at low levels, the other tracks do not.

Yet a bottom-level Hollywood Park shipper might trounce the assorted minor-league opposition, or may not, depending upon current condition. In this special context—evaluating shippers from major tracks to bullrings—form counts. If the major leaguer is not in ripe condition, discount it, notably at miserly odds, and favor a fast, sharp minor-league prospect. If the major leaguer retains acceptable form, it regularly wins.

The same is true of bullrings located anywhere in the vicinity of a major racetrack. Handicappers need to evaluate the relative track class of the shipping centers. Use the average purse indexes printed periodically in the *Racing Form* in conjunction with a careful perusal of the results at the bullring so far.

Once the contenders have been isolated, favor the following guidelines in the final separations.

1. A double drop in claiming class.

Class drops in claiming races below $10,000 are far more meaningful than similar drops at higher selling prices. At the lower levels, class barriers are severe, and more impenetrable.

A class drop from $6000 claiming to $4000 claiming is a huge descent. The corresponding class rise is almost insurmountable. The sharpest $4000 animal on the grounds cannot handle a $6000 horse in acceptable form.

The claiming-class hierarchy below $10,000 at bullrings might be depicted as follows:

1. $8500
2. 7500
3. 6000
4. 5000
5. 4000
6. 3200
7. 2500
8. 2000
9. 1500

As the claiming prices become cheaper, the gradations become tighter. Any double drop amounts to a real change in the pecking order and often will be decisive.

2. Any drop in claiming price, abetted by tactical speed and an inside post position.

As the previous discussion alerts, a claiming-class drop at bullrings can represent a genuine edge. If the horse will benefit as well from a favorable post position, the twin advantage will be difficult to defeat. The dropdowns can position themselves behind the early pace on the inside, sweep around the sharp turns unmolested, and strike at will on the backstretch or rounding the far turn.

3. Inside early speed.

Speed horses on the inside at bullrings, as most racegoers quickly appreciate, operate at tremendous tactical advantage. "On the inside" refers to posts 1 through 4 in sprints, and post-position No. 1 in routes.

Sprints from five furlongs to seven furlongs will be run around two turns. Inside speed horses can negotiate the turns smartly, without losing ground or encountering traffic that forces them to swing extra wide while being urged. Below $10,000 claiming, if no horse from a major track has been entered and appears prepared to dominate, the lone speed horse on the inside will often be the best bet of the day or week.

Use the speed-points technique described in the methods section of this book to anticipate the early speed, and hunt for low-level claiming horses having a two-point spread on the field. If the odds beckon, make the play.

Among classier sprinters at bullrings, inside speed matters noticeably, but not as decisively. The inside speed horse suited to the class, or superior to it, is always a top contender.

Routes at bullrings are run around three turns. Statistics indicate only the inside lane offers speed horses a favorable post-position bias, but the advantage is significant. The rail post in bullring routes wins approximately 30 percent more races than probabilities would expect.

If the rail horse in a bullring route possesses early speed and shapes up as a contender, the circumstances are near to ideal. If the odds beckon, by all means plunge.

4. Talented bullring riders.

Jockeys are incidental to successful handicapping, but not as incidental at bullrings. Horses must be guided around multiple sharp turns, while under urging. Late maneuvers begin on the backside.

Riders that understand the configuration of the course well enough to establish inside position on turns, as well as striking position down the backside, without robbing their mounts of enthusiasm or energy, go to the top of the standings immediately. Handicappers at bullrings should not fail to identify the jockey leaders and appreciate their special talents.

Alternatively, jockeys that cannot take the turns impressively or cope with the pace intelligently or establish striking position satisfactorily, should be avoided at bullrings. They make routine mistakes, and disappoint.

5. High-rated horses in featured stakes and allowances.

With few exceptions, handicappers do not need technical information to unravel the competition at the nation's bullrings. Besides, recreational handicappers will rarely possess accurate numerical ratings or modern speed figures for the several racetracks represented.

But if a highly rated horse at a major track enters the featured event at a bullring, the horse can be expected to prevail. If fewer customers have access to the ratings or figures, perhaps the odds will be acceptable. It's a solid opportunity, to be sure, for horses and bettors.

Not much more about the bullrings is pertinent.

Superior class, inside early speed, a decent jockey, an overwhelming rating or figure—positive factors that preside.

Handicapping at the bullrings is fun, a refreshing change of pace from the bigger tracks, and seductively profitable.

TURF HORSES AT THE BULLRINGS

One of the least remarked, scarcely understood oddities of thoroughbred racing regards the surprisingly strong performances of turf horses at the bullrings.

Present for the running of the Orange County Handicap, $75,000-added, 3up, during August 1989 at Los Alamitos, I hardly afforded the six-year-old below a second look. Neither did either of two companions, astute handicappers who wagered serious money on the outcome.

Review the past performances of the eventual winner:

11th Los Alamitos

1 ⅛ MILES. (1.46⅘) 13th Running of THE ORANGE COUNTY HANDICAP. $75,000 added. 3-year-olds and upward. By subscription of $50 each to accompany the nomination; $370 to pass the entry box, with $75,000 added, of which $12,500 to second, $8,600 to third, $5,250 to fourth, $3,750 to fifth, $1,500 to sixth and $750 to seventh and eighth. Weights Wednesday, August 9, 1989. Starters to be named through the entry box by the closing time of entries. A trophy will be presented to the owner of the winner. Closed Monday, August 17, 1989, with 13 nominations. (The winner of this race will receive an invitation to the $150,000 Invitational Pomona Handicap run at the Los Angeles County Fair.)

*Individualist

PEDROZA M A   115
Own.—Red Baron's Barn

B. h. 6, by Viking—Lusaka, by Wolver Hollow
Br.—Limestone Stud (Eng)
Tr.—Vienna Darrell
Lifetime 33 6 5 3 $134,110

1989 7 1 3 1 $76,725
1988 3 0 0 0 $8,975
Turf 32 6 5 3 $130,660

[detailed past-performance running lines]

Few practiced handicappers will fail to recognize Individualist as a middle-distance turf specialist, one asserting few claims to fame in recent stakes, though current form is sharp.

At 9–1, Individualist came bounding around the third turn of the Los Alamitos handicap route and promptly overhauled a game frontrunner that had controlled the pace throughout and, by conventional logic, figured to win. Needless to say, the upset soiled the evening for a number of surprised handicappers.

Shortly following the finish, a bit late, it occurred to me that trainer Darrell Vienna had completed the same maneuver a year ago, taking the Orange County Handicap of 1988 with turf specialist Conquering Hero.

"Didn't Vienna win this same race last year with the turf horse Conquering Hero?" I asked my associates.

All immediately agreed Vienna had indeed performed the same trick last season.

No one, however, could shed a shining light on the propensity of turf horses toward winning better routes at the bullrings. The handicappers began naming the similar upsets they previously had observed, and the roll call proved longer than expected.

Why do turf horses win so frequently at the bullring, where they seem peculiarly out of place?

The turns are extra sharp on both courses, but that explanation hardly satisfies.

Besides, closers on the grass appear to be the real threats at the bullrings. These hardly resemble the inside speed types that benefit from the three sharp turns of bullring routes.

Pace analysts may provide an insight. Numerous turf horses score highly on measures of sustained pace, the ability to carry speed farther than six furlongs. Where the surfaces of bullrings demand a decent combination of speed and stamina, especially at the route, turf horses may not be as ill-suited to the surroundings as traditionally believed.

Perhaps this is just another peculiarity of racing, where the explanation need not intrude upon the situation. The bald facts find turf horses winning richer routes at bullrings frequently enough to legitimize the horses as contenders. Recreational handicappers at least have been warned.

CLAIMING RACES

As most racegoers understand, claiming races call together racehorses for sale at relatively equal market values. The comparable selling prices assure that the order of competition will be more or less equitable as well. Horsemen that enter claiming horses at unrealistically low selling prices risk losing them at unfair values. Horsemen who enter claiming races at inflated prices risk a steady diet of negative results. Neither circumstance is appetizing to horse owners.

In handicapping terms, claiming races are characterized by horses having low to moderate levels of ability. Many of them are severely pressed to carry a fair portion of speed across six furlongs. Fewer still can perform that feat consistently. And fewer still can combine the speed, stamina, and competitive spirit that distinguishes claiming horses at the route.

In consequence, the effective handicapping of claiming races as a group can proceed from the following assumptions:

1. Speed, and rates of speed (pace), will generally be more important than relative class, as indicated by the kinds of horses a horse has beaten in the past.
2. Inconsistent horses will be far more prevalent than consistent horses.
3. Positive form is a prerequisite of continuous success.

On the matter of positive form, handicappers quickly understand that claiming form can improve or deteriorate radically and intermittently, depending upon physical soundness, the stresses of continuous training and racing, the seasoning developed in competition, the recuperative powers of rest and medicine, and the nurturing talents of trainers. Across the longer contemporary racing seasons, form cycles of claiming horses will be positive (improving) or negative (declining) several times a year.

All things considered, recreational handicappers should understand clearly that the most effective evaluation of claiming races involves a style of numerical handicapping that describes how fast the horses have actually run. A numerical approach can be considered axiomatic in sprints.

Speed handicapping, pace analysis, and the evaluation of the early speed—these must be the essential components of the practitioner's approach to claiming races.

How fast have the main contenders actually run in the recent past?

Which horse(s) can set and maintain, or track and overtake, the swiftest pace?

Which horse(s) might secure the early lead, and run to victory uncontested?

It's no heresy to assert that a first-rank figure handicapper needs only a supply of accurate updated speed figures, pace ratings, or adjusted final times to get by satisfactorily in the claiming division—although a wider array of know-how and skill will surely assist.

The procedures for adjusting final times, obtaining pace ratings, and evaluating early speed promoted in the methods section of this book form the first line of attack in claiming races.

Recreational racegoers who shy from numerical approaches to handicapping should master the rating methods nonetheless, and apply them with unwavering fidelity in analyzing claiming races. The methods are not overbearing. As a rule, the top-rated horse on final speed, the high-rated horse on pace, and the lone or surviving frontrunner represent the fastest horses in the claiming field, and one of those horses figures to win.

Something else. Among the best, most serviceable applications of numerical ratings is the reliable evaluation of claiming horses on the rise.

Recreational handicappers notoriously eliminate claiming horses rising in class. Wrong. If a claiming horse on the rise has been improving, and brandishes the high rating in the field, it not only qualifies, the upstart is very, very likely to win. If that kind of claiming horse also reveals back class, handicappers should never hesitate to demonstrate their support.

So influential are the speed factors of handicapping in claiming races that considerations of relative class and form are secondary. Acceptable form qualifies. So do class maneuvers, up or down, that satisfy the liberal guidelines promoted in this book's methods section.

The bottom line is plain. If a claiming horse is the high-rated contender in the field, on speed, on pace, or early speed, the horse figures. Conversely, if its numerical ratings are poor, the horse is unlikely, notwithstanding a drop in class, a good effort last out, a top jockey, or a competent trainer.

To complicate matters, it's clear the speed factors can conflict with one another annoyingly. Claiming horses showing the fastest adjusted final times may not have the highest pace ratings. Early-speed leaders may reveal neither the fastest adjusted final times nor highest pace ratings, or they may possess the fastest adjusted times but not the highest pace ratings.

Or, in many claiming races the main contenders may have similar numbers.

What to do? It depends.

First, in sprints, examine the turn times of the contenders. If one horse has a superior turn time, by two lengths or more, prefer that horse. Many claiming horses flashing attractive adjusted times or exciting early speed cannot handle an unaccustomed fast pace throughout the second quarter mile, which includes the far turn. When the turn time accelerates, the final time declines.

Second, if the probable pace appears normal or unusually fast, prefer horses having the highest pace ratings. Pace ratings embrace significant relationships that adjusted final times do not reflect.

If the probable pace is unclear, will be abnormally slow, or the field appears paceless, prefer the horses having the fastest adjusted final times. Horses and jockeys will adapt to the circumstances as best they can. The fastest horses usually adapt best of all.

And when early-speed horses appear to enjoy clear sailing into the stretch, many of them will relax throughout the early stages and then dash to the finish line successfully.

In claiming routes the case for the speed ingredients is often less convincing. When the numerical ratings are unclear, inconclusive, or contradictory, prefer claiming horses whose running styles and relative class might dictate the final circumstances.

Other handicapping factors that apply frequently when analyzing claiming races include trainers, trips, and impressively improving form.

Competent claiming trainers surely deserve extra attention following a claim.

Some claiming trainers impress on the rise, others on the drop, and a few in both directions. Certain trainers win claiming races following lengthy layoffs, and others bring selling horses to peak performances using the traditional sequencing of regular races and workouts, each of them improving. It pays to know who's who among the claiming trainers, including those that rarely win a race.

Troubled trips suggest claiming horses can improve previous ratings today. The numerical ratings and trips are best juxtaposed and considered analytically. Do not use trip notes to modify numerical ratings numerically.

Impressively improving form among claiming horses is invariably reflected by dramatically improving numbers. The numerical ratings can literally stun the handicappers that compute them, who now wait eagerly for the horses to reappear. The positive pattern usually means the claiming horses can leap ahead in class by several levels and win impressively anyhow.

So the vast majority of claiming races in major racing can be dissected using an array of handicapping tools that resembles this pattern:

1. Numerical ratings of final times, pace, and early speed, preferably in combination.

2. Competent claiming trainers.
3. Troubled trips, of the kind that suggest a claiming horse's prior ratings can be improved today.
4. Impressively improving form.

Claiming races represent approximately 70 percent of the horse races on the national calendars. Recreational handicappers must learn how to cope with them successfully. The alternative is depressing.

CLAIMING RACES RESTRICTED TO THREE-YEAR-OLDS

Claiming races open to 4up, or 3up, are radically dissimilar from claiming races limited to 3YOs.

A $50,000 claiming sprint for older horses of spring will feature established runners at that selling level or thereabouts. Three-year-olds of spring entered to be claimed for the same $50,000 may be worth less than half the amount. And at no track during spring can $50,000 three-year-olds that win against their own kind finish in the shadows of their older claiming counterparts.

The reason is largely economic. Three-year-olds are adolescent racehorses. Those that cannot proceed in the allowances and stakes must compete with claiming tags. But younger, still-developing athletes may suddenly mature and begin to soar. Owners figure that if other horsemen would risk that happenstance, they might as well pay a premium for the adventure.

Unexceptional three-year-olds enter the claiming division with unrealistically high price tags. Once they disappoint badly, the commoners will be lowered successively in selling price, until a claiming level is found where they can earn a portion of a purse. Trainers next make a best guess as to where the creatures can actually win.

Handicappers notice the shopping sprees and stay on alert for the three-year-old claimer's much improved performance. The next start, up or down, is the barn's best estimate as to where the win will occur. Once a three-year-old claiming horse does succeed, depending upon the time and manner of victory, it may be sent up the claiming escalator again. If the improvement continues, the horse belongs, and moves ahead again. If the horse falters miserably, down it comes again, until another purse is snatched. The alternating cycles continue throughout the spring, summer, and fall of the three-year-old season.

Examine the record of the three-year-old claiming horse Versatile Leader.

The sequence of events is practically prototypical. Following a good race March 8, at $30,000 claiming, the colt is lowered a notch in spring to $25,000 claiming, where it wins by three on May 11 in the mud.

Six days later Versatile Leader is claimed for $32,500 by New York's outstanding Gasper Moschera.

Moschera jumps his new three-year-old to $70,000 claiming and puts it on the grass. Under turf specialist Jean Cruguet, Versatile Leader finishes up the course. The Moschera shopping spree begins.

Where should Versatile Leader win again, wonders its excellent trainer: $45,000 (May 28), $35,000 (June 18), $30,000 (July 1)? Today (July 14) Versatile Leader has been entered for $25,000 claiming, following a good race versus slightly better, which brings handicappers full circle to May 11, the previous $25,000 claiming win.

If Versatile Leader now beats the $25,000 claiming caliber, the colt will likely be lifted in class again, the patterns repeating themselves as if on schedule.

Casual racegoers can be knocked off balance by the ups and downs embedded in the records of three-year-old claiming horses. But handicappers need not be unduly confused. Here are a few trusty guidelines for coping with the alternating cycles.

1. Assume the three-year-old first entered to be claimed will be overvalued, and will probably blow.

The outstanding exception is the three-year-old that has run a good race under nonwinners allowance conditions, or an acceptable race under the same conditions in rapid time last out. If the class maneuver appears realistic, and the claiming price relatively high on the local schedule, but not outrageously high, the barn is merely dropping to win with a ready horse. If such a horse has already won an allowance race at a major track, the case is closed. No doubt, these kind beat the brains out of the typical three-year-old claiming specimens they encounter.

2. On the drop, rely on a three-year-old claiming horse's recent adjusted final times, or final figures, to predict whether it can withstand today's competition.

3. On the rise, discount final times and final figures, and rely instead on pace ratings and turn times to predict whether the escalation is warranted.

Nothing thwarts the ambitions of 3YO claiming horses on the rise as much as faster interior fractions. The claiming horses cannot accelerate earlier, notably on the turns, and repeat the previous final times. This is especially true of three-year-old claiming horses of winter, spring, and summer.

For this reason, too, three-year-old claiming horses invariably cannot be trusted when they attempt a return to the allowances following a credible claiming victory.

Recreational handicappers should not fail to grasp the situation represented here, and many regular handicappers can heed the point as well. Several three-year-old claiming-race winners revisit the allowance ranks following fast victories against the platers, but few of them succeed. The faster early pace dispensed by better nonclaiming horses, sustained farther as well, defeats the claiming horses' best efforts. They fall back, usually prior to the stretch call.

The situation is so misunderstood by handicappers, let's establish a fresh guideline to protect the defenseless.

4. No three-year-old can be accepted under allowance conditions following a win in a 3YO claiming race unless the claiming race reveals an early pace and turn time superior to the early pace and turn times of today's main contenders.

In addition, beware of three-year-old claiming horses that also ran for a claim as two-year-olds. Improvement is still a possibility, but gradual improvement, not the rapid dramatic kind characteristic of younger, nonclaiming horses.

Beginning in late spring, surely by summer, claiming races will be carded for three-year-olds and older horses together. Until November casual handicappers can eliminate the three-year-olds in mixed claiming company without mercy.

Studies show that claiming sprints limited to three-year-olds of winter and spring are completed on average three fifths of a second slower than comparable races open to older horses. By fall the time differences have been reduced to two fifths, or to one fifth.

Routes open to older claiming horses are typically completed at least a full second faster than comparable races limited to three-year-olds. Often, the contrast is even greater. By fall the time differences have been reduced to three fifths, or two fifths.

Another unforgiving guideline serves the discussion.

5. Until November, do not play three-year-olds in claiming races open to older horses.

It's true, too, that following the three-year-old season, most claiming horses turning age four will need a drop in selling price in order to compete effectively in the older claiming division.

The class maneuvers that occur at this special career juncture open a few fantastic wagering opportunities to informed handicappers each season. In January, February, and March, look for claiming horses, age four, that have impressed at the same selling prices in races open to 4up and now have been entered in races limited to 4YOs.

The claiming races open to the older runners will have proved far more rugged. This represents a serious class drop. The other four-year-olds in the line-up may run at the dropdown's command. This is especially true of claiming races below $20,000 or such, where the older horses are established commodities but the new four-year-olds have been washouts.

By late fall three-year-old claiming horses can topple their older counterparts, particularly in sprints, provided they have earned the fastest adjusted final times, speed figures, or pace ratings.

Obviously, three-year-olds that do slay the older claiming horses of fall will not require drops in selling price when they turn four on January 1 and now confront similar older claiming horses of winter.

MAIDEN RACES

Apparently, the casual racing audience loses a bundle a season while chasing after the maidens. In the corridors and boxes of racetracks, the general whining among insiders about the unpredictability of races for older maidens never ceases.

The complaints are unjustified, and have been ever since 1974, when a researcher named Fred Davis resolved the only real dilemma attaching to maiden races. I had been dangling on the wrong horn of the dilemma myself for several seasons, until Davis changed my mind.

Which horses should be preferred in races for older maidens: first-starters that have impressed in the morning, or horses that have raced previously and, in an improved performance, finished second or third last out? It's the experienced maidens, by a landslide. The second-place finish last out is particularly powerful.

Davis showed that first-starters (3up) win less than half the percentage of maiden races probabilities would expect them to win, a staggering statistic. Inexperience defeats first-starters, notwithstanding the lickety-split workouts, fashionable pedigrees, and leading jockeys.

On the other hand, experienced maidens that finished second last out win approximately 274 percent their fair share of the races. Almost three times as many races as probabilities would expect! Third-place finishers last out win roughly 174 percent their rightful share of maiden races. The close placings are more meaningful when reflecting an improved performance. They are superfluous among maidens that have finished second and third repetitively, without winning next out.

The upshot for all handicappers is tantalizing. No more the undue anxiety about the potential charms of those well-bred, fast-working, nicely connected first-time starters. Throw them out. At low odds, which happens frequently, spare none of them.

At decent or attractive odds, practiced handicappers can contemplate two exceptions.

First, during winter racing, many authentically talented three-year-olds will make their long-awaited debuts. Several older maiden fields will be crowded with first-starters. The racetrack will be buzzing with tales of the horses' prerace exploits. Before bets are placed, however, first-time older maidens should satisfy these standards:

1. Regular workouts, every five or six days, with at least one recent workout completed in sharp time, preferably at five furlongs or longer.

Faster, longer workouts are preferred, as virtually all nicely bred, relatively sound, mature maidens can deliver fanciful clockings for three or four furlongs.

The longer workouts are most impressive at racetracks outside of New York or southern California. A blowout in rapid time a day or two before the debut is meaningless. And a prerace training regimen extending beyond ten to fifteen workouts is uncomfortably problematic.

2. Mounted by a leading jockey, or hot apprentice, or regular stable rider.

Jockey agents scramble furiously for the "live" maidens on the grounds. The horses might be any kind. If maidens can run fast but top riders are absent, presumably neither the jockey agents nor clockers nor anyone else knows it yet. When the first-starters cakewalk to the wire in dazzling time, the insiders will be just as surprised as local handicappers.

3. Not adorned in long front-leg bandages.

Front wraps spell poison on first-starting older maidens. The horses are probably unsound, unwilling, and unable already.

The second exception considers the performance patterns of older maidens' trainers, especially during winter, but throughout the core season as well.

Certain trainers specialize in winning with first-starters. If a maiden's trainer triumphs with 20 percent or thereabouts of his first-starters, his beginners might be supported, but the odds should be 4–1 minimum.

Similar standards attach to sires whose progeny win approximately 20 percent of their first starts. The odds must overcompensate for the statistical risk, a 4–1 minimum.

If the sire wins with 20 percent of its first-starters, but the trainer performs poorly in the category, forget the maidens. If the trainer scores with 20 percent of his first-starters but the sire performs poorly, accept the horses as contenders. Training usually beats breeding, in these circumstances as well.

Much of the discussion circumscribing the second exception will be academic to recreational handicappers. Few members of the casual audience have access to updated performance data on trainers and sires. Yet even occasional customers develop a keen sensibility as to the trainers that win most frequently with first-time starters. Trust that sensibility, all right, but insist upon an adequate price.

Among experienced older maidens, find the contenders boasting the fastest adjusted final times at the distance. In close situations, prefer the early-speed leaders. With several outstanding exceptions, of course, maiden races tend to be won early and late, with only mild competitive pressures in between.

Naturally, if the experienced contenders each show dismal times and ratings, the first-starters' chances improve, notably during the winter. This happens nowadays more frequently than ever. The fastest experienced maiden shapes up as a sluggish racehorse. First-starters coming equipped with successful trainers and sires may warrant a second glance, after all.

Troubled trips of maidens should never be readily excused, especially if the problems occurred in the gate or on the turns. Untutored, unseasoned maidens instigate the majority of their own troubles. If the odds will be low, and the maiden in question has been trouble-prone, forget it.

If a maiden has been tardy out of the gate, however, and will be adding blinkers today, the equipment change normally moves them up. If the change to "blinkers on" has resulted in a much improved effort, the improvement should continue. The next start, second with blinkers on, regularly ends in victory.

As a rule, any dramatic improvement in a maiden's record, as from a noncompetitive race to a good race, should be interpreted to mean the improvement will progress, with victory merely a race or two away. The pattern is especially provocative among maidens having fewer than seven races. If that kind of maiden was heavily bet in its first start, perhaps its first two, the dramatic improvement indicates an unready horse may be prepared at last to run to its reputation.

Older maidens that appear on the grass, either against other maidens or nonwinners allowance horses, are invariably bred for turf. Stables intend to press whatever advantages the grass pedigrees afford them.

If dirt form has been dull, and the odds sparkling, say 10–1, handicappers should give prudent consideration to accepting the risks. Form reversals on the turf among horses bred for grass are commonplace in major-league racing. Several of the reversals each season will be accounted for by three-year-old maidens of spring and summer.

If experienced maidens have looked lackluster, and the first-starters indistinguishable, maiden races remain unplayable. Do not guess.

As the core season progresses, many maiden races for older horses will be clearly decipherable. Recreational handicappers have ample reason to be sanguine about their financial prospects among the older maidens. The handicapping guidelines contained here are simple to implement, they perform, and they provide positive results. Mutuels are rarely gigantic, but they are not often niggardly either.

Elsewhere I have stated that knowledgeable handicappers can expect to win roughly 40 percent of the maiden races they attack. I see no reason to desert that position now.

MAIDEN-CLAIMING RACES

The sheer weight of maiden-claiming races on major racing cards has increased terrifically during the past decade, a consequence of the expansion of racing calendars to combat the general and severe inflation of the late seventies and early eighties.

No one should misapprehend the decadence these developments have wrought. Maiden-claiming races contain the cheapest, slowest, least reliable horseflesh in the barns. Before establishing any semblance of market value by winning a race, the horses are for sale, inevitably at markups bordering on 50 percent.

The in-depth handicapping of maiden-claiming races can be despairingly displeasurable, since so many of the animals reveal nothing resembling the outermost limits of acceptable form. What busy handicappers need more than anything, to dispense with these contests in the few minutes they warrant, is a quick fix.

Not long ago that ready-made formula could be provided confidently, consisting of two negative rules (never to be broken under penalty of a heavy fine), and one positive catchall guideline.

I reprise the rigid rules and famous guideline here, with the qualification that nowadays the rules must sometimes be broken, and a concession that additional guidelines will occasionally prove meritorious.

Negative rules:
1. Never bet a horse that has lost a maiden-claiming race.
2. Toss out all first-time starters in maiden-claiming races.

Catchall guideline:
1. Wagers in maiden-claiming races shall be restricted to horses exiting an acceptable race against straight maidens, as indicated by early speed, an even effort, a competitive move at any point of call, tracking a reasonably fast early pace to the prestretch call, a faster adjusted final time, or a close finish.

If the maiden dropdown has not competed for a while, perhaps for months, it need only display acceptable current form, and it figures regardless. The opposition, to repeat, will be awfully slow of foot. Straight maidens just run so much faster.

The negative rules were constructed originally in honor of the proposition that if racehorses were possessed of any genuine quality or potential they would (a) not be able to lose a maiden-claiming race and (b) not be offered for sale until their true market value were understood at a high level of probability.

The negative rules and positive guideline still work admirably well, but they have suffered a loss of utility. With so many maiden claimers on the scene, a depressing proportion of their races will be filled with first starters and chronic losers of prior maiden-claiming races. No maiden dropdowns conveying a hint of positive form can be found to carry the cause.

An alternative approach that makes sense is required to deal with the worst of maiden-claiming races, lest handicappers must sit on their hands, or guess, whenever these processions comprise a leg of the daily double, trifecta, serial triple, or pick-six, as they invariably do.

There is hope. Par-time charts of typical times at local racetracks usually indicate that certain subclasses of maiden-claiming horses run significantly faster than others. Consider the following pars from the 1988–89 season at Santa Anita:

	Sprints			Routes		
Maiden	45	1:10.3	1:17	1:11.2	1:44.1	1:50.4
$50 Mdn-Clm	45.1	1:11	1:17.2	1:11.4	1:44.4	1:51.2
$32 Mdn-Clm	45.2	1:11.3	1:18	1:12	1:45.2	1:52

Aware handicappers have realized for years that maiden-claiming races are normally completed a full second slower than nonclaiming maiden races in sprints, and seven-fifths slower in routes. The Santa Anita pars for maidens and $32,000 maiden-claiming horses, respectively, reflect those realities.

But at Santa Anita, happily, $50,000 maiden-claiming horses typically run significantly faster than $32,000 maiden-claiming horses. The difference is three fifths of a second in sprints, a similar three fifths in routes. In all instances the pace of $32,000 maiden-claiming races is slower too.

At Santa Anita the drop from $50,000 maiden-claiming to $32,000 maiden-claiming, the only subclasses of maiden-claiming competition carded, represents a real change. Close finishers at $50,000 maiden-claiming can regularly outrun close finishers at the $32,000 level. Speed horses that set, or track, the early pace at the higher subclass are likely to draw away at the lower subclass. Savvy handicappers at Santa Anita can exploit the discrepancies weekly.

A professional handicapper named Ron Cox has done the same on the northern California circuit for years, exploiting what he has called the "gaps" in the average times (pars) of the regular subclasses of maiden-claiming races carded at Bay Meadows and Golden Gate Fields.

All recreational handicappers can mimic Cox and other pros on the point, provided they can identify the gaps in the local maiden-claiming pars, or average final times. Numerical differences of two fifths of a second are sufficient.

As not too many subclasses of maiden-claiming races will be carded, a perfectly plausible strategy divides the maiden-claiming competition in half. A top half and bottom half, if you will, or high and low.

A month's experiment provides an objective basis for the line of separation. Simply record for 30 days the actual times of the local track's maiden-claiming races. It takes a few minutes a day, relying on the local newspaper as a data source. In the end, for each maiden-claiming subclass, average the final times. Examine the differences. Where should the logical exploitable drops occur?

In analyzing maiden-claiming events, the class dropdown, whether from straight maiden conditions or from a higher subclass of maiden-claiming races, always takes top priority. If no dropdowns impress, prefer first-starters to previous maiden-claiming losers at today's price level. One of the nastiest sucker bets in racing is the recent close finisher in a maiden-claiming race at today's selling level. The horses are slow, inveterate losers at the level, and wonderful candidates for the dust bin again today.

Of first-starters in maiden-claiming races, leading trainers and jockeys are not prerequisites. In fact, minor stables and journeymen riders enjoy relative advantages in the cheaper events. Minor stables handle more maiden-claiming types, and leading jocks do not scramble impatiently for the mounts. As always, minor connections will be untrusted, and therefore underbet, but they can shine brightly in maiden-claiming affairs.

Another tricky circumstance regards the graduates of maiden-claiming races, especially of the highest-priced subclass at the track. Some winners of maiden-claiming races will have earned adjusted times, or final figures, or pace ratings comparable to, maybe superior to, winners of open claiming races at similar prices, or occasionally of a nonwinners-once allowance race.

Where should the maiden-claiming graduate be expected to win next?

My position remains firm. Cut the selling price of the maiden-claiming race in half, and expect the winner to repeat there, or thereabouts. I have watched a few of the shrewdest figure handicappers in this nation support impressive maiden-claiming winners against legitimate open company next time, because the figures convinced them the horses could get the job done.

The maiden-claiming graduates usually disappoint, and roughly half of them quit before they reach the stretch call. The reason—again—is pace. The interior fractions will be faster, and carried farther, and the low-brows cannot keep up. Prior ratings are not repeated. The scenario is especially common whenever maiden-claiming graduates try to enter the nonwinners allowances. A few of them each season survive, but the great majority are immediately exterminated.

To conclude the discussion on an optimistic tone, whenever a contender in a maiden-claiming field combines the capacity to control the early pace with a slight edge in ability—dare I say class—victory is virtually preordained. Slow horses, lacking as well in endurance and competitive spirit, do not catch up. At the route, it's a marvelous wager.

THE NONWINNERS ALLOWANCE SERIES

Allowance races baffle recreational handicappers as a group, and not a few regular handicappers besides. To an extent, the confusion is rational.

Because claiming horses win allowance races, and allowance horses win stakes races, but allowance horses lose claiming races, and stakes horses lose allowance races, the inconsistent patterns serve to grab struggling racegoers by the neck and plop them down in the middle of a maze. But the potpourri of seemingly contradictory results makes perfectly logical sense, and an ambition of this book is to set racing's customers on a straight course in the nonclaiming races.

Allowance races come in two basic varieties, nonwinners allowance races and classified allowance races.

The nonwinners allowances are carded as a series of progressively more testing races restricted to relatively inexperienced, unseasoned, and unclassified horses. The "nonwinners" label is attached, because the eligibility conditions specify that the horses may not yet have won one, two, three, or perhaps four, nonclaiming races. The purpose is to restrict the competition to better horses of high potential at comparable stages of development, so that the horses can sort themselves out, some moving ahead to the stakes, most repairing to the claiming division.

Classified allowances are carded for mature, experienced horses that, while unable to prosper in the stakes division, are nonetheless too talented to be offered for a claim, and deserve opportunities to earn richer purses. Within that frame of reference, the diversity of classified allowances can be fascinating and instructive, a subject to be taken up with enthusiasm in a later section.

Recreational handicappers should be warned that the nonwinners allowance races can be rugged, arguably the most challenging on the daily programs, even when they appear elementary. Upsets and unanticipated outcomes are standard fare.

The explanation should be plain. After all, the races are written for relatively inexperienced, unseasoned horses still in the formative stages of development. The intended winners will be younger and lightly raced. Thus handicappers access less information about basic abilities and preferences. The reliability of the information at hand is less than ideal.

Which horses can run to a sizzling pace and still repeat a splendid final time? As the going gets tougher, which can summon the qualities of willingness, determination, and courage, to complement the more obvious speed? Which will be similarly fast and competitive across longer distances? Which can be rated effectively behind a suicidal pace and then unleash a powerful finish?

The questions will be many, the clues few. Handicappers regularly can resort to just a handful of races, with a few of those inexplicably dull, but others persuasively bright. Among the main contenders, as often as not, early speed will be high and adjusted times too close to call. Not even their trainers and owners, the famous insiders, can predict which of the horses will prove genuine and which will be revealed as fakes.

What to do?

Having posed the problems, I can now admit the solutions are not overly complex. A conservative mind-set is mandatory and appropriate as a first line of defense. The key to coping well with nonwinners allowance races is to limit action, almost exclusively, to the kinds of horses whose records remain nicely suited to the restrictions in the conditions of eligibility.

That is, horses that fit the conditions and purposes of the nonwinners allowances are accepted as contenders, horses ill-suited to the conditions are summarily rejected. It's an aspect of class handicapping, apropos to all practitioners, regardless of pet methods.

Below is arrayed the sequence of nonwinners races, and the kinds of horses in each that qualify as main contenders. Some comments will be directed at horses poorly suited to the allowances, qualifying for instant elimination.

Before horses win two allowance races, they can be described as competing under "preliminary" nonwinners allowance conditions. At the first stop beyond the maiden ranks, horses compete under conditions elegantly summarized as:

". . . nonwinners once other than maiden or claiming . . ."

No eligible entrant, obviously, has won an allowance race or stakes race, though several may have finished close. Just as obvious, horses might have won several claiming races, but now are invited to try stiffer competition.

Claiming horses, I hope recreational handicappers will concede, are normally unattractive contenders here. The nonwinners-once allowance race was not written with claiming horses in mind. Weeks ago, any owner at the track could have purchased the horses. How much potential can there be?

The main contenders of nonwinners-once allowance races emerge from three groups:

1. Any lightly raced 3YO that has finished close in good time in few attempts under today's conditions or better. An acceptable finish in a stakes race is especially attractive, but not definitive.

2. A recent impressive 3YO maiden graduate, with extra credit to the nicely bred types from leading stables.

"Lightly raced" means fewer than a dozen starts. If the race is restricted to horses 4up, prefer the 4YOs.

Two variations of the nonwinners-once allowance races are carded commonly:

". . . nonwinners of two races," and

". . . nonwinners of $3000 other than maiden or claiming . . ."

The first bars winners of claiming races, a more restrictive race.

The second admits not only claiming-race winners, but also winners of allowance races at tracks having a relatively small purse structure. The $3000 refers to the winner's share of the pie.

This is a less restrictive race. Horses might have won several allowance pots at a minor track, ship to a major, and still remain eligible for a nonwinners-once allowance purse. Accept these shippers as contenders. The connections at the minor plant believe they have a good one, and are eager to find out.

Recreational handicappers that limit the contention in these preliminary allowance fields to the types of horses above will be working with the percentages and will have eliminated errors of the grossest kind. Chucked aside as unworthy will have been horses 4up, claiming horses, repeated losers under similar conditions, and horses still eligible despite fifteen starts or more. All are inveterate failures under preliminary nonwinners allowance conditions.

And a common practitioner's mistake, eliminating recent maiden winners, will have been corrected. Attractive maiden graduates that enter the nonwinners-once allowance race merely are taking the next logical step in their progress. It is hardly a giant step.

A third kind of contender for the nonwinners-once purse is often more difficult to spot. Many three-year-olds stumble about clumsily before breaking maiden conditions. They repeat the awkwardness at the nonwinners-once allowance stage. They may lose a handful of the races, but suddenly deliver a dramatically improved performance. The adjusted time has been convincing, and so has the manner of victory.

Accept the horses, and evaluate them further on the much-improved performance. The improvement may not always intensify, but that should be expected. The third kind of contender:

3. Younger horses (3YOs) whose recent efforts or clockings under similar allowance conditions indicate continued or dramatic development.

One step removed from horses' introduction to the allowances are the next eligibility conditions in the sequence:

". . . nonwinners twice other than maiden or claiming . . ."

This represents a second preliminary allowance experience, not a large step-up in class. The main distinction, of course, is that now younger, developing horses will be confronted by contenders that already have won an allowance race, or perhaps an open stakes.

Stakes winners normally will be aimed at additional stakes, but runners-up in stakes, and horses supplying an acceptable stakes performance, will routinely return to the nonwinners allowance series for seasoning, not to mention the purse.

The main contenders for the nonwinners-twice race come together from four distinct groups:

1. Younger, lightly raced 3YOs that have already demonstrated a good race, or an acceptable finish, in a stakes.

2. The same kind of 3YOs that recently have won an allow-

ance race, and in few attempts have finished close in rapid time under conditions similar to today's.

If the nonwinners-twice race is restricted to 4up, prefer the 4YOs.

3. Late-developing, lightly raced, nicely bred 4YOs that recently won an allowance race, and were not disgraced in an open stakes.

In recent years foreign-raced horses have entered the preliminary nonwinners allowance races of southern California and New York with consistent success. Imports from Europe, in particular, tend to be talented, relatively expensive horses. If the imports have finished in the money, or close enough, in a graded or listed stakes of France, England, Italy, or Ireland, they presumably outclass preliminary unexceptional allowance competition in the states.

If no U.S. horse in the nonwinners-twice field shapes up as the genuine article, favor the European imports. Be lenient about current form, distance, and footing. Where the competition is lean, a decisive class edge overcompensates for shortcomings on other fundamentals, absolutely when the odds are generous. The fourth contender:

4. Any import from Europe that has finished close in a graded or listed stakes overseas, particularly horses that have won such a race and remain eligible for nonwinners allowances here.

Regarding imports from South America, Australia, New Zealand, and South Africa, prefer horses that have competed consistently in Grade 1 and Grade 2 stakes with some success. Discount the others, until they demonstrate local form.

The main contenders in preliminary nonwinners allowance races should almost always emerge from one of the groups described above.

Claiming horses can sometimes be threats in nonwinners-twice allowance races, especially if they formerly won one allowance race, but preferably at certain times of the season. In the next section, we discuss these exceptions briefly.

Once the contenders of nonwinners-once or -twice allowance races have been identified, the task of separating them on final speed, early speed, pace, and relative class remains complicated. Too often, adjusted times and numerical ratings will be close and inconclusive. More problematic, often adjusted final times will be fast and early speed sharp, but the horses falter badly on a careful pace analysis.

An outstanding, easily implemented strategy for separating closely matched contenders in preliminary nonwinners allowance races relies upon early pace, in particular on the interior fractions between the first and second calls. Calculate the contenders' turn times. So often a younger developing thoroughbred's final time and early speed will be sensational but its turn time unimpressive.

The unimpressive turn time inevitably defeats the horses. Forced to accelerate throughout the second quarter against higher-quality allowance runners, many developing horses cannot do it and still deliver their previous best. Claiming horses are greatly susceptible to the pattern. Maiden-claiming graduates ordinarily collapse. The accelerated pace weakens the pretenders. Only the strong survive.

An uncompromising triple-edged approach is recommended for evaluating the fields of preliminary nonwinners allowance contests:

1. Identify the contenders on class as nicely suited to the eligibility conditions.

2. Evaluate contenders variously on final time, early speed, pace, and relative class.

3. Separate closely matched contenders on early pace by calculating turn times, and preferring contenders' having the fastest interior fractions.

Once two allowance victories have been stashed away, horses have arrived at advanced nonclaiming territory. No more easy pickings. The nonwinners allowance series has progressed to:

". . . nonwinners three times other than maiden or claiming . . ." or

". . . nonwinners four times other than maiden or claiming . . ."

These are "advanced" nonwinners allowances. Not only has the contention already won a pair of allowance races, but several eligible horses will have impressed in an open or graded stakes. Ordinary horses hit the brick wall. For that reason, handicappers are advised to prefer contenders whose credentials include a snappy stakes performance.

In descending order, here are the possibilities to anticipate:

1. Impressive winners of two recent allowance races that have impressed in a graded or open stakes.

2. Imports from France, England, Ireland, or Italy that have won, or finished close, in any Grade 1 or Grade 2 stakes overseas.

3. Any impressively improving lightly raced three-year-old that has done everything asked, and despite a lack of stakes experience, is merely taking the next logical step-up in class.

The guts of any advanced nonwinners allowance race can be unearthed in those three profiles. If no horses qualify, duck the race. Of three-year-olds without stakes credentials, the pace ratings obtained by the second allowance win should have been sparkling, and the horses should never have run for a claim.

If the restrictions specify "nonwinners four times other than maiden or claiming," handicappers will be prudent if they insist the main contenders already have *won* an open stakes. The most advanced nonwinners races are carded for the cream of the nonclaiming division, and not for common horses.

Dominated ultimately by class or sheer brilliance, every other fundamental of handicapping must be tightened once horses have reached the advanced nonwinners allowances. Nonwinners three times is racing's dividing line. The quality of competition has improved tremendously.

Whereas handicappers might be liberal when analyzing the contenders of preliminary nonwinners allowance fields, strict standards now apply. If acceptable form satisfies against fields that have not yet won one or two allowance races, now positive form is demanded. If horses will be tired, dull, rank, or green, they will almost certainly lose.

If inexperience at the distance is permitted against preliminary allowance opposition, under advanced allowances, horses' comfort at the distance can be decisive. Good performances at related distances is a reasonable standard. Stretching out from sprint to route while simultaneously advancing from nonwinners-twice to nonwinners-three-times allowances, or to an open stakes, is one of the steepest double jumps in the sport. Only authentically leading three-year-olds can complete the dual maneuver at first asking. All others should be discounted.

Under nonwinners-three-times allowances as well, contenders best be comfortable with the footing and probable pace, and boast a competent trainer. And they should not be expected to overcome a strong negative speed or rail bias.

Which escorts the discussion full circle, back to an original proposition about the nonwinners allowance series. These are tricky, complicated races, flanked with hazards for beginning or casual handicappers. The several red flags have been unfurled because unsophisticated racegoers lose hundreds of dollars annually chasing phantoms in the nonwinners allowances, without in the slightest understanding why.

Handicappers may not beat the nonwinners allowances by sticking exclusively to the kinds of contenders for which the races have been written, but they will avoid financial catastrophe, I promise.

And here's a tip that will help put the allowance ledger in the black. Several times each season trainers place truly promising three-year-olds "above their conditions," to use the vernacular. Horses eligible for nonwinners-once allowances are entered under nonwinners-twice conditions. Nonwinners-twice eligibles are entered for nonwinners three times. Purse values, printed in the class column of the *Daily Racing Form*, provide the telltale clues to the manipulations.

If horses lose impressively while racing "above their conditions," and next out are entered at the appropriate lower station, hooray! That's the magical turn. Win or lose, it's a clever bet, and gets good odds too.

CLAIMING HORSES IN NONWINNERS ALLOWANCE RACES

Nothing so befuddles racegoers as the transpositions of claiming horses in allowance races, and vice versa.

In fact, the problems can be readily resolved. Concrete guidelines can be posted, alerting handicappers to the friendlier nonwinners allowances for claiming types.

Although nonwinners allowance races are programmed specifically for nonclaiming horses on their way to celebrity status in the stakes, claiming horses can prosper under the conditions at two periods of the season.

By mid-fall the authentically talented three-year-olds and late-developing four-year-olds that dominate the nonwinners allowances will have graduated. Left over will be the chronic losers and least impressive contenders of previous fields. The past performances will feature anywhere from six to twelve prior failures under the same conditions, intermingled perhaps with a couple of hapless attempts in higher-priced claiming races.

Hard-knocking older claiming horses in receipt of strong numerical ratings of late can now crash the nonwinners allowances and succeed.

The situation reaches a crowning point in winter. Now certain nonwinners allowance races will be restricted to horses 4up. A four-year-old that has not yet won one or two allowance races can be no great shakes. Five-year-olds and older that still are eligible should be dismissed.

Older claiming horses have earned tenure at moderate-to-high-priced levels where they have won, run in-the-money, or finished close. Several will have hammered horses that formerly won an allowance race, perhaps two. Unless a respectable late-developing four-year-old remains on the scene, consistent older claiming horses in sharp form can humiliate the depleted nonwinners allowance ranks.

If older consistent claiming horses formerly have won an allowance race but remain eligible for nonwinners-twice conditions, the hard-knockers can steal that second allowance purse in the dead of winter.

At what selling levels will recent claiming-race winners be best prepared to complete the allowance gambit? Let's resurrect a portion of the class hierarchies of major and minor tracks delineated earlier in the book, illustrating the classes of claiming and nonclaiming horses that dispense comparable running times.

Major Tracks

$32,000–40,000 Clm	Alw, NW1XMC
$50,000–62,500 Clm	Alw, NW2XMC

Minor Tracks

$13,000–19,500 Clm	Alw, NW1X2XMC
$20,000 Clm & above	Alw, NW3XMC

The parameters are explicit. Claiming horses transferring from the specified claiming levels to the corresponding allowance conditions during late fall and winter can sometimes clobber the chronic nonwinners they regularly challenge there.

At major tracks, at the designated intervals only, the toughest horses at the peak end of the claiming ladder can sometimes even trespass in advanced nonwinners allowance territory and upset. But the horses' numerical ratings should be best, or second best, in the field, and nothing about the probable pace—notably, how hotly it might be contested—should suggest the claimers might unravel from a case of weak knees.

The circumstances can be even more advantageous to older consistent claiming horses in nonwinners races restricted to fillies and mares. Females, 4up, and many 3YO fillies, too, reveal themselves as woeful racehorses, but owners prize them as broodmare prospects nonetheless. The ladies compete as virtual prisoners in the nonwinners allowances, preventing claims but forsaking victories. The past performances show pitiful strings of losses, without a change of venue.

Recreational handicappers can adhere to these two guidelines:

1. Beginning mid-fall, accept impressive older claiming horses in preliminary nonwinners allowance races, provided no impressively improving, nicely bred, lightly raced, three-year-olds enter the fray and figure to dispose of the eligible opposition.

2. In winter, prefer older consistent claiming horses entered in preliminary nonwinners allowance races for 4up, especially if the claiming horses have formerly won an allowance race and have won convincingly since the high-priced claiming races.

A stark warning is appropriate here. Although older claiming horses that impress can complete nonwinners allowance chores, as indicated, three-year-old claiming horses usually cannot.

In winter, especially, three-year-olds competing in claiming races have persuaded their handlers to relinquish all hope of a blossoming career. Very few of the horses can follow a claiming-race score with successful reentry in the nonwinners allowances. Most will be gobbled up helplessly by the faster pace and more determined three-year-olds they confront in the nonclaiming division. Do not be fooled by the claiming races, especially at low odds.

The reverse side of the transposition finds heretofore regular allowance runners finally entered to be claimed.

Which horses should win, and at what claiming levels?

As the class hierarchy indicates, horses that have won one allowance race at a major track can be expected to handle $32,000 to $40,000 claiming horses there as well.

Horses that have won a pair of allowance races at major tracks can be expected to handle all but the highest-priced claiming horses on the circuit. Winners of three allowance races, or perhaps two allowance races and a minor stakes, can challenge the highest-priced claiming horses as well. Keep in mind the highest-priced claiming horses at major tracks once completed the nonwinners allowance series themselves, but ultimately descended to claiming conditions when they could not prosper in the stakes.

Maiden winners that cannot manage to win the nonwinners-once allowance race can be expected at major tracks to level off at the $20,000 to $25,000 claiming levels, or lower.

If recreational handicappers cling closely to those price guidelines at major tracks, the worst predicaments will have been avoided, at least.

The nonclaiming three-year-olds of winter and early spring again must be treated differently. Several of these will leave the maiden ranks for the nonwinners allowances but fail to progress further.

A good race, or acceptable finish, in a nonwinners allowance race limited to three-year-olds of winter and spring translates to the highest-priced three-year-old claiming races on the programs. Any three-year-olds exiting the nonwinners-once allowances proudly, even without winning, should annihilate their claiming cousins.

To appreciate the unevenness, recreational handicappers need only understand that high-priced claiming races for older horses of winter and spring are filled with well-established, hardknocking breadwinners, but the same levels of claiming competition limited to three-year-olds are filled with the equivalents of high school dropouts.

By mid-spring, and throughout the summer and early fall, the nonwinners allowance picture shifts. Better nonclaiming three-year-olds, and occasional late-developing four-year-olds, now preside, and handicappers should expect those horses to win. In nonwinners allowances open to horses 3up, the improving three-year-olds are greatly preferred.

Should claiming horses enter these races accompanied by high numerical ratings, handicappers should insist the horses can cope with the probable pace and will fight to the finish. Most claiming horses cannot do either.

CLASSIFIED ALLOWANCE RACES

Imagine a long line of racehorses strung together at opposite poles. Toward each pole a distinct set of competitive circumstances are dangled. The horses have arranged themselves in concert with the circumstances most suitable for them. Bettors are encouraged to look for relatively classy horses at one pole, but especially sharp horses at the other.

The polar extremes can be characteristic of classified allowance races, whose elemental charm resides in the diversity and variety of competition the race conditions call together. Formulated on the whole for high-quality horses a cut below stakes caliber, classified races are ravaged nonetheless by previous stakes winners, and just as frequently captured by high-priced claiming horses.

Can casual, occasional racegoers hope to decipher classified allowance races? Yes, absolutely. Classified races offer skilled recreational handicappers some of the best betting opportunities of any season.

A figurative representation of the contrasting classified races features the uncomplementary elements of each pole:

Classified Allowances Races

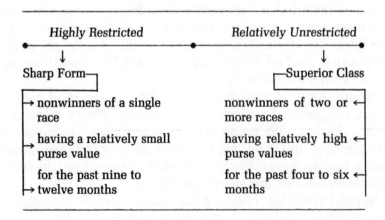

Highly Restricted	Relatively Unrestricted
Sharp Form—	—Superior Class
→ nonwinners of a single race	nonwinners of two or ← more races
→ having a relatively small purse value	having relatively high ← purse values
→ for the past nine to twelve months	for the past four to six ← months

The drawing shows that classified allowance races range from highly restricted to relatively unrestricted. The latter bows to class, the former to current form.

Highly restricted classified races are closed to any horse on the grounds that has accomplished anything of note for a long duration, even as long as a year. Thus, recent stakes winners, plus recent winners of other classified races, will be effectively barred. The idea is to afford somewhat inferior nonclaiming stock a better chance to swipe an excellent purse.

Relatively unrestricted classified races, in contrast, are open to any horses below the cream of the division. Only the most current stakes stars will be barred. The classified purse is valuable, and the idea is to offer perennial runners-up in stakes a slightly softer opportunity to win.

Here are illustrations of the contrasting classified conditions:

July 1989

HIGHLY RESTRICTED

8th Belmont

1 ⅛ MILES. (Inner Turf). (1.46⅘) ALLOWANCE. Purse $47,000. 3-year-olds and upward which have not won a race of $21,500 at a mile or over in 1988–89. Weight, 3-year-olds, 116 lbs. Older, 122 lbs. Non-winners of a race of $19,000 at a mile or over since March 1 allowed 3 lbs. Of such a race since January 1, 5 lbs. Of such a race since November 1, 7 lbs. (Maiden, claiming, starter and restricted races not considered.)

July 1989

RELATIVELY UNRESTRICTED

7th Hollywood

6 FURLONGS. (Turf). (1.07⅘) ALLOWANCE. Purse $50,000. 4-year-olds and upward, which have not won $19,500 twice other than closed or claiming since January 23. Weight, 121 lbs. Non-winners of $22,000 twice since March 15, allowed 3 lbs.; a race other than closed or claiming since then, 5 lbs.; such a race of $22,000 since December 25, 7 lbs. (Claiming races not considered.)

The highly restricted classified race at Belmont Park bars any horse that has won a stakes or classified route in the past eighteen months. Claiming-race winners have been exempted.

Probable winners include a diverse population: winners of multiple sprint stakes; runners-up of recent graded and open stakes; improving three-year-olds that recently have bested nonwinners allowance races having winner shares below $21,500;

winners of a recent classified allowance race at a mile or over; winners of multiple classified races, or stakes, having winner shares below $21,500; and high-priced claiming horses in sharp form.

The diversity should be unmistakable.

The relatively unrestricted classified race at Hollywood Park bars local horses that have won multiple stakes, or two classified races, in the past five months. Claiming-race winners have been exempted, as usual, but it's farfetched to suppose a claiming horse can actually win. The Hollywood Sprint will be spoils for a recent stakes winner, or grabbed by a close runner-up in stakes.

The effective handicapping of the contrasting classified races is itself contrasting. The relatively unrestricted race bows to class, meaning the best horse is the likeliest victor. That will normally be a stakes winner.

Handicappers merely find the most impressive contenders exiting recent stakes, and prefer the horses earning the strongest numerical ratings. As the horses run rapidly throughout, final times (adjusted), and the corresponding final figures, can separate the contenders admirably. The handicapping task has been reduced to bare essentials. Find the best horse; prefer the high number.

The highly restricted classified race presents a much different puzzle. The handicapping now must be comprehensive, can be difficult, and should proceed from the assumption that the class horse is likely to lose. Highly restricted classified conditions are intended to offer slightly inferior runners at the higher echelons a better chance. Handicappers should cater to that grand purpose.

The likeliest winner—and best bet—in any highly restricted classified allowance event is the horse in particularly sharp current form and simultaneously well-suited to the distance, footing, and probable pace. The horses benefit today from a confluence of factors, not to mention the deliberate absence of the racetrack's top achievers of recent months.

Regarding numerical ratings or final-time figures in highly restricted classified races, the numbers may apply but usually will not suffice, and often can mislead. Classified horses arrive at the starting line from different distances, on different surfaces, at disparate class levels, and in varying degrees of positive form. It's preposterous to imagine a simple numerical rating can eradicate the variety and diversity in all their ramifications. If the numbers look suspiciously foul, handicappers should discount them and depend upon full-dress handicapping instead.

A timeless sucker horse in a highly restricted classified allowance race is the graded stakes horse returning from a lengthy layoff. Almost always, the previous stakes winners are prepping for later bigger stakes. Certain trainers crack down with stakes horses in minor classified races, and if handicappers recognize these individuals, by all means trust the horse.

But anytime a Grade 1 or Grade 2 stakes performer shows up in a classified allowance race, handicappers should assume the stable leader is out for conditioning. No Grade 1 stakes star is well-intended under classified allowance conditions. The odds may be desperately low, but these standouts are destined to disappoint. Avoid the pratfalls.

Classified allowance races have numbered fewer than ever in recent seasons. Many of the more interesting classified events are now carded on grass. The classified allowance sprint is practically extinct.

Close adherence to the handicapping principles delineated here represents the sum and substance of what the recreational handicapper needs to know.

OVERNIGHT HANDICAPS

In overnight handicaps, as racegoers know, the racing secretary weights the combatants according to his estimate of their relative abilities, as indicated by recent records. The best horses carry the highest weights, purportedly to afford the low weights a fairer chance.

The same procedure, and principle, applies in stakes races programmed under handicap conditions. The relative weights are supposed to bring them all together, which they do not.

The burden of high weight has been a controversial topic in racing circles during modern times, contributing to differing philosophies in various jurisdictions. Overnight handicaps, for example, are programmed regularly in New York, but are rarely seen in southern California. Similar hopscotch patterns occur in the various racing states.

Handicappers differ from horsemen curiously regarding a number of basic influences on race outcomes, including the rel-

ative importance of speed, jockey, and post position, but nowhere can the disagreements be trumpeted as loudly as on the
relevance of the weights. Horsemen respond to extra pounds as
petulantly as the vainest starlets. Handicappers abandon the
factor as next to meaningless. Across fifteen seasons, I have yet
to meet a first-cabin handicapper who assigns weight even a
perfunctory position in the handicapping arsenal. No one pred-
icates a serious wager on weight, unless perhaps a trainer.

The scientific evidence, too, supports the handicappers, and
without qualification or exception.

Probability studies have revealed irrefutably that high-
weighted horses in stakes win a fantastically disproportionate
share of the titles. Low weights get virtually nothing. Moreover,
high-weights in overnight races win significantly more races than
probabilities would expect. And weight shifts do not alter prior
results, however close.

Finally, in a provocative sample of stakes races programmed
under handicap conditions, the winners triumphed by safer
margins than did the winners of similar stakes where weight
differentials were not as gross. The highest-weighted horses, in
fact, won by the largest margins.

So biased is the evidence in favor of the high-weights, mathematician Bill Quirin has suggested that if racegoers had access
to no other information about the horses, they would do best by
playing the top-weighted horses every time.

Should recreational handicappers clutch these findings to
their breasts and apply them unflinchingly to overnight handicaps? Simply support the high-weights?

The inference is tempting, but overnight handicaps can be
deceiving, precisely on the matter of weight.

A colleague of mine in New England formerly attended the
New York simulcasts to Suffolk Downs faithfully, and looked
beseechingly at outstanding Big Apple stakes winners that recently disappointed in an overnight handicap. He knows such
a horse may be a good thing on the rebound today.

That's the rub. New York trainers use the overnight handicaps to warm up stakes winners for the next added-money objectives on the agenda. They enter overnight handicaps with the
not-so-hidden intention of failing, thereby getting weight off.

Recreational handicappers must understand that if stakes
performers enter overnight handicaps and win smashingly, as
they are capable of doing, the racing secretary will pile on ad-

ditional pounds next time. Trainers hate that. So they bother to enter top horses in overnight handicaps, and lose. Weight comes off, or at least extra weight is not the unpleasant consequence of snatching the cheaper purse.

Whenever a graded stakes winner enters an overnight handicap, handicappers should assume, correctly, the horse will be privileged to lose. It therefore enters the upcoming graded stakes with lighter weight. Trainers love that. The same is true of ungraded but impressive stakes winners and fussy trainers on all circuits.

Of overnight handicaps themselves, a platoon of horses consistently populate these races, from which they can extract a very decent living indeed. One such horse is New York's Dr. Carrington, and the past performances will resemble his:

An overnight handicap specialist, Dr. Carrington and the like do not often prosper under graded stakes conditions—as the good doctor did not on January 28, at Aqueduct—but can scrape together a couple of hundred thousand in the overnight game.

The handicapping of overnight handicaps is straightforward, provided handicappers know what to do with the legitimate stakes stars in the lineup. After eliminating the better stakes horses as unintended, find the horse with the highest numerical rating, or final figure, based upon its latest two starts.

That's the probable winner, irrespective of weights.

THE STAKES MENAGERIE

In the swath of the 1980s, and forevermore, the stakes programs of thoroughbred racing have been altered radically. Competition among racetracks for horseflesh of a quality that might attract local audiences and national recognition has resulted in an unprecedented proliferation of stakes.

Other forces have complicated a delicate situation, such that by 1990 the majority of stakes races in the United States were being won by exceedingly common racehorses.

In a healthy initiative, the Breeders' Cup Ltd. originally allocated industry-financed premium awards to owners and breeders whose horses won or placed in a fantastic spectrum of stakes on the national calendar. In a thoughtful, fair, egalitarian program, all racetracks were served proportionately well.

But in a revisionist gambit not nearly as healthy, the Breeders' Cup joined hands with the brewers of Budweiser beer, withdrew several premium awards from traditional stakes, and attached the money to a new series of "stakes" brandished commercially as the Budweiser Breeders' Cup Stakes Program. This ensured the already crowded stakes schedules would be squeezed some more, lowering quality and reducing field sizes all around.

Local racing associations have chipped in dubiously with an innovation euphemistically called the supporting stakes. Whenever a big-ticket prominent stakes is scheduled, the support stakes, or another stakes, is believed to enhance the attractiveness of the card, thereby boosting the day's attendance. In the hands of unthinking imitators, or impetuous marketing experts, this is the kind of idea that can run amok.

In late July, Monmouth Park, in New Jersey, presents the $500,000-guaranteed Grade 1 Haskell Invitational, for leading three-year-olds. In 1987, when Bet Twice nipped Alysheba and Lost Code in a stirring finish, every other race on the program was billed as a support stakes. On the same day in 1989, on a twelve-race program, Monmouth Park featured six support stakes. The added-money of each was the same, a regrettable $35,000.

In Kentucky, Florida, Maryland, New York, and other racing centers, on the days of the big races, the support stakes are trotted out in depressing numbers. In the long run—and here the future is now—there are not enough authentic stakes horses to pass around. The unwanted, unanticipated, unfortunate legacy is a lowering of competitive standards, a reduction of quality.

In the support stakes, and in numerous traditional established stakes, handicappers of the nineties will encounter fields of ordinary horses masquerading as stakes runners. When one of the ordinary horses wins, as happens frequently, everyone has been sadly misled. The horses are not nearly as talented as their trophies intimate, and recreational handicappers benefit by being skeptical of unexceptional one-shot stakes winners.

Fortunately, there is a logical order to the contemporary stakes madness, and stakes winners can be classified by handicappers at gradations of a national stakes hierarchy.

Since 1973, in a brilliant stroke intended to regulate the lives of owners and breeders—but of tremendous help to handicappers, coincidentally—the richest, most prestigious stakes in the country have been evaluated by formal committees of horsemen and racing officials as Grade 1, Grade 2, and Grade 3, respectively, the Grade 1 designation limited to fewer than one percent of the total and signifying its bearers as the leading representatives of each succeeding generation.

Since the *Daily Racing Form* prints the grade designations of stakes in the past performances, as well as notations that identify lesser stakes, modern handicappers can imagine both local and national stakes programs as a logically arranged sequence of races that fit into discrete categories of a stakes hierarchy.

In ascending order of importance and prestige, stakes races can be classified at one of six levels:

1. Restricted
2. Open
3. Listed
4. Grade 3
5. Grade 2
6. Grade 1

Restricted stakes, lowest in the pecking order, bar former stakes winners, or horses that have won a specified amount of first money since a specified date. Restricted stakes are indicated in the *Racing Form* by the symbols R, or S, the S meaning the race was limited to state-breds.

Open stakes, by definition, are open to all comers. Owners merely pay nomination fees, entry fees, and starting fees, all of which will be redistributed to the winning owner, and the proud possessions can compete in stakes. The racetrack adds a hefty purse, referred to as added-money. Open stakes traditionally have been differentiated by the amounts of added-money, a perfectly reliable index of competitive quality, as horsemen are attracted to stakes races in exact proportion to the money added.

Listed stakes, unknown to racegoers and to most regular handicappers as well, are considered by racing's establishment of sufficient prestige to be "listed" on the pages of international sales catalogs. Owners and breeders hold winners of listed stakes in higher esteem than they do winners of open but unlisted stakes, and handicappers should too. The purses are richer, the competition keener, and the winners praiseworthy.

Grade 3 races involve even bigger purses and better horses, but the competition is less than definitive. At the highest echelons of the sport, at major tracks, Grade 3 stakes are often engaged as stepping-stones to Grade 1 objectives. In Europe Grade 3 races historically have been programmed as equivalent preps for Grade 1 events, and the Grade 3 purse values of France barely vary.

Winners of the nation's Grade 3 stakes deserve notice and applause, but they accumulate little reputation and scarce breeding value.

Grade 2 stakes provide prestigious titles, $100,000-plus purses, and happy hunting grounds for horses of truly outstanding speed and competitiveness that simply cannot overtake the Grade 1 superstars. Grade 2 winners might become important horses, and multiple Grade 2 winners often will be rewarded with breeding syndications of the pedestrian kind. Grade 2 horses can be considered a prime cut above the lower-grade stakes varieties, and can usually beat those horses into humble submission.

Grade 1 stakes, 120 in number, call together the fastest horses of a generation, and ultimately define the sport's champions, near-champions, and division leaders. Purses are extravagant, distances longer, and the competition supreme, at least much of the time. Until 1989, the lonesome Grade 1 sprint in North America was Belmont Park's Vosburgh Stakes, at seven furlongs.

Breeding value accrues automatically to Grade 1 stakes winners, the primitive motive of owners and breeders. Multiple Grade 1 winners stand by for the fabulous syndication offers from Kentucky farms, and the majority will not be disappointed.

For handicapping purposes, the preceding discussion can be regarded as rather formalized and theoretical, a basic kind of orientation to the modern stakes menagerie, but frequently impractical.

In practice, the categories of the stakes hierarchy can be annoyingly overlapping. Many common horses win listed and graded stakes. Small fields, consisting of one or two prized specimens, plus a remainder of ordinary horses filling up the starting gates, predominate. As a result, such a dizzying number of unexceptional horses wind up with stakes credentials, it's more painstaking than ever for handicappers to separate the genuine articles from the costume jewelry.

In identifying the contenders of stakes races, it's crucial that novices and recreational handicappers begin to assign the horses to a level of the stakes hierarchy. The procedure can clarify real class differences. For practical purposes, as in the contenders section, we condense the six levels of the stakes hierarchy into three:

Restricted / Open Stakes below $100,000
Listed / Grade 3
Grade 2 / Grade 1

Handicappers should recognize the breakdown as levels 6, 7, and 8 in the class hierarchy for major tracks presented in the contenders section. In practice, handicappers can consider open stakes at $100,000-added and above the equivalent of listed stakes.

And to distinguish authentically outstanding stakes horses from the multitudes, we add levels 9 and 10.

9. Multiple Grade 1 Winners
10. Classic Winners

Each entry in a stakes race deserves a class rating, 6 to 10. Staying pragmatic, before stakes winners are assigned a class rating of 7 (Listed and Grade 3) or 8 (Grade 2 and Grade 1), handicappers might demand they have won at least two stakes at the level. All other stakes winners are assigned a 6 (Restricted and Open Stakes). Good races at higher-grade levels receive a 6+, acceptable races a 6.

Class barriers between the levels can be considered dense but not impenetrable. That is, horses earning a class rating of 7 should scuttle stakes winners carrying a class rating of 6, especially if the higher rating has been earned by winning multiple listed or Grade 3 stakes, but upsets will occur. Class differences among stakes horses connote an edge, but not rigid boundaries.

Within class levels, stakes horses can batter one another variously, depending on matters of form, soundness, suitability to distances, footing, and pace.

Not long ago Grade 1 horses could be expected to slaughter Grade 2 horses, but not now. For the reasons alluded to at the top of the section, small fields of Grade 1 horses, containing one or two genuine Grade 1 runners, have become commonplace. If the bigshots do not run, a lower-grade horse wins. That horse instantly joins the exclusive Grade 1 fraternity, pretender or not.

A standard of multiple victories at the top levels limits the pretensions to a degree, but not absolutely.

As a rule, closely matched contenders within stakes categories can be separated reliably by numerical ratings: adjusted final times, speed figures, and pace ratings. Pace ratings in combination with final-time figures might be preferred, as stakes horses should rate highly at both ends of the races. Stakes horses having come-from-behind running styles can be exempted from a fast-pace standard, as the horses will score relatively low on a pace scale.

In certain situations the numerical ratings of stakes horses have limited or fraudulent application.

Numerical ratings obtained at middle distances are worthless at classic distances. Abundant evidence supports the assertion. The extra quarter mile of the 1¼ mile classics places a tremendous premium on added outlays of stamina and competitiveness, not speed. Numerical ratings earned at middle distance primarily reflect brilliance or speed. For that reason, graded-stakes performances at middle distances are not strongly correlated with similar performances at classic distances.

If anyone cares to dispute this, they might first consider that studies of the pedigrees of open stakes winners up to 1⅛ miles reveal that approximately 40 percent possess a relatively high ratio of speed to stamina. At ten furlongs, just 5 percent reveal similar ratios of speed to stamina. The differences are huge, too wildly disparate to be mistaken.

This does not mean stakes horses at classic distances cannot be evaluated by numerical ratings. But the numerical ratings should have been obtained at classic distances, not at middle distances. Moreover, at 1½ miles, try to evaluate stakes horses by comparisons among races at the same distance—not an easy assignment. Twelve furlongs demand outlays of late speed and stamina that even ten furlongs do not. As spectacular a racehorse as Spectacular Bid was not as imposing at 1½ miles, and did not win at the distance.

None of this helps recreational handicappers predict season to season which three-year-olds will win the Kentucky Derby or Belmont Stakes, but it does explain why experts who rely solely on numerical ratings obtained by developing horses at middle distances fall flat on their classic predictions every spring.

Also, numerical ratings earned by three-year-olds while competing against their own age group will almost always decline when the younger stakes horses face older stakes horses during summer and fall. The pace will be swifter and more stubbornly disputed, and the late-speed requirements go up— fantastically up. Keep in mind that routes for three-year-olds, on average, are completed a full second slower than similar routes open to older horses. The statistical findings apply to stakes races too. Truly outstanding three-year-olds are excepted, and will maintain their typical ratings.

In another anomaly, numerical ratings of stakes horses obtained in one-turn routes should not be used to evaluate the horses in two-turn routes. The practice is notoriously misleading if the distance will change from a mile to a longer middle distance. Specifically, the pace ratings promoted by this book, as emphasized in the methods section, cannot be used to compare stakes horses switching from sprints to routes, or vice versa.

For recreational handicappers without numerical ratings in stakes races at Grade 3 or below, the size of the purse is a fairly reliable index of relative quality. The greater the discrepancies among purse values, the likelier the horses will differ correspondingly as well.

Since the *Daily Racing Form* does not print the purse values of stakes races, recreational handicappers must collect results charts, or more readily, record purse sizes in a notebook. The data is easily transferred from the conditions of eligibility in the past performances, and can include grade designations and eligible ages. It's a vital edge well worth the time and effort.

Certain dropdowns in the stakes division will be more meaningful than others, resulting regularly in class standouts that win. Be alert for two:

1. A listed stakes winner, or close finisher, drops to an open, but unlisted, stakes.

In New York and southern California the maneuver is frequently engineered among imports from France, England, and Italy. Handicappers will find winners, and prices, by monitoring these clever switches.

2. Multiple Grade 2 stakes winner, or close runners-up, drop to any lower-grade stakes.

Genuine Grade 2 horses are superior to the Grade 3 kind, or anything lower.

Here are some additional useful guidelines for recreational handicappers grappling with a stakes menagerie confusingly out of balance.

- Multiple Grade 1 winners, classic winners surely, are not well meant in any stakes below Grade 2, and sometimes use Grade 2 races as preps for upcoming Grade 1 events.
- Grade 3 horses should not be considered superior to open stakes winners, or close runners-up, that have competed well for purses of $100,000-added, or better.
- An impressively improving three-year-old that has won a pair of allowance races may be a stickout in a restricted stakes, and is acceptable in an open stakes below $100,000-added, even if the race is open to older horses.
- In any graded sprint stakes, prefer speed horses that have also won Grade 1 or Grade 2 stakes at middle distances.
- In any open stakes, or better, throw out previous stakes winners whose numerical ratings have declined in successive races.
- In any graded stakes featuring a small field, and containing just a couple of genuine graded stakes horses, prefer the genuine graded winner offered at the higher price; if either of the graded horses smacks of questionable current form, throw it out, and key the other graded horse in exactas to any attractive overlays.
- In Grade 1 races at classic distances, class laughs at pace.

Finally, the following is a golden nugget about leading stakes horses that few racegoers appreciate. Follow the rule, and get a pari-mutuel prize. Whenever leading stakes horses engage one another in a furious stretch drive, the winner, however close the margin, a neck or a head or a nose, is almost inevitably the better horse.

Nothing else matters. Not the early pace—unless it is ridiculously abnormal—not the weights, and not the trips. If the stakes star that lost by a head experienced trouble on the clubhouse turn, was blocked on the far turn, and swung wide into the stretch before losing by a head in an all-out driving finish, the conventional wisdom will conclude the horse would have won without the trouble and can reverse the verdict next time.

Almost always, that conventional wisdom is wrong. Long stretch battles in top-grade stakes are definitive. The likeliest outcome in the future is that the horse beaten by a head will lose again by a head, or by a wider margin. In all-out graded-stakes finishes, the better horses win, regardless of what has happened earlier.

Secretariat outruns Sham. Affirmed beats Alydar. Spectacular Bid defeats Flying Paster. Alysheba outlasts his pursuers. Sunday Silence edges Easy Goer. And Horse A beats Horse B.

As usual in racing, there is a glorious exception. Throughout the winter, spring, and summer, leading three-year-old stakes horses will be advancing at various stages of development. Competitive seasoning of the most demanding, exhausting kind does matter.

The first time eventual Kentucky Derby heroine Winning Colors, alone on the lead, was tested by the excellent filly Goodbye Halo, from the quarter pole to the finish of a Grade 1 stakes at Santa Anita, Goodbye Halo won by a neck.

Was Goodbye Halo the better filly?

In the ensuing confrontation, weeks later, Winning Colors, no longer surprised, decapitated Goodbye Halo, leaving her former conqueror exhausted and flying the white flag at the eighth pole.

Goodbye Halo would never match Winning Colors again. But she beat the champion once, while Winning Colors still lacked that exhaustive kind of competitive seasoning.

With that exception, involving those developing inexperienced three-year-olds, recreational handicappers can accept the all-out stretch drives in graded-stakes races as definitive. The better horses win, by a neck, by a head, by a nose.

Nothing about the evolving changes of contemporary thoroughbred racing prevents recreational handicappers from getting a firm grasp on the stakes divisions, local or national. Respectful adherence to the precepts of class handicapping isolates the main contenders, and solid numerical ratings evaluate them, with the several exceptions noted.

OVERNIGHT HORSES IN STAKES RACES

Claiming horses carrying the richest selling prices at the local track are fully capable of winning stakes races there, whether the locale is New York or New Hampshire. Certain boundaries can be drawn, forestalling anarchy in the stakes division.

Those boundaries reveal themselves in the much-touted class hierarchy of major tracks:

Claiming	Nonclaiming
Above $62,500	Alw, NW3X4X
	Clf Alw
	Restricted/Open Stk
	below $100,000

The highest-priced claiming horses on the grounds must be taken seriously in restricted stakes and in open stakes having purses below $100,000. The actual claiming prices will vary from track to track, with $62,500 a floor in New York and southern California. Local handicappers can readily substitute the price tags at their place.

At minor tracks the highest claiming prices might be $40,000 to $50,000, and the standouts there can tackle open stakes having purses below $50,000. But $20,000 claiming horses should be a bit cheap to upset the stakes, unless the field is barren or the purse less than $20,000-added.

To win in a stakes, claiming horses should arrive in improving or peaking form, and they should demonstrate one of the top two numerical ratings in the field, based upon their two latest outings. The last out is much preferred, unless not representative due to a legitimate excuse.

When evaluating claiming horses in stakes, do not dig back

into the past performances to find a best effort. The most recent outlays count most. Moreover, if claiming horses should meet with an uncomfortable experience on the pace, forget it.

In addition, it's reassuring if the trainer is competent—better still, excellent. Claiming horses in stumblebum hands rarely upset in a stakes. Not only are most of the horses outgunned, so are their trainers.

Claiming horses should also have impressed at today's exact distance, and when on turf or in the mud, should favor the footing. And the odds should attract the handicapper's interest, at least a point higher than the number of nonclaiming contenders in the field. Do not support claiming horses in stakes races at regrettably low odds.

Can claiming horses win in listed, graded, and richer open stakes?

Not ordinarily.

Grade 1 and Grade 2 events are out of bounds. Occasionally, a Grade 3, Listed, or rich open stakes represents a legitimate target. Not only must the ground rules above be satisfied in regard to the claiming horse's recent record, the established stakes runners in the field must be suspect. The circumstance often accompanies unusually large fields, as in the absence of a real live stakes star, horsemen shoot for the purse with a panoply of minor-stake and overnight horses.

Any sharp claiming horse in a restricted or open stakes that will be advantaged by a strong positive track bias deserves close scrutiny, and if the horse possesses one of the top two numerical ratings, figures to win.

The class hierarchy indicates that classified allowances and the advanced nonwinners allowances can be considered interchangeable with restricted and open stakes below $100,000. Winners of the allowance races often finish as fast as the winners of the lower-order stakes, justifying the equivalence in the scheme of things.

In a restricted stakes that bars former stakes winners, or even winners of specified first shares for extended periods, the lightly raced, impressively improving three-year-olds that have recently overpowered a pair of nonwinners allowance conditions and now debut in a stakes, shape up as potential standouts. The colts, or fillies, are clearly en route to glamorous races, with today's opposition merely a way station. Accept them in open stakes below $100,000 too.

That same lightly raced, impressively improving three-year-old would be unacceptable in a Grade 1 or Grade 2 stakes open to older horses, and may be humiliated in a Grade 1 or Grade 2 stakes limited to its own age. A Grade 3 stakes would provide a warmer welcome. Many impatient, overly aggressive horsemen advance impressively improving three-year-olds toward the mountaintop too soon. The division leaders can complete the transition remarkably well, but others suffer a setback. Shellacked while trying their utmost, the young thoroughbreds recoil from the whipping, and many surrender form and spirit, at least for a time.

Classified allowance winners aged five or older that have never won an open stakes at $100,000 or above should not be expected to crack that class barrier now. In lesser stakes, perhaps, provided the distance, footing, and probable pace will be comfortable, and the trainer competent.

Unless the early pace has been fast and contested, the numerical ratings of classified races do not transfer well to the stakes. A front-running victory in a classified allowance route, for example, is almost never duplicated in an open stakes worth $100,000-added, unless the winner had previously annexed that kind of stakes.

Lightly raced, late-developing four-year-olds can exit highly rated nonwinners allowances and classified allowances and run on to victory in open, Listed, and Grade 3 stakes. Numerical ratings should be tops. The pedigrees should be fashionable. And the trainer should be demonstrably effective in the stakes division.

Overnight horses rarely win Grade 1 or Grade 2 stakes titles, and if they do, it's an anomaly, unpredictable by both horsemen and handicappers.

TURF RACES

Only yesterday, on Del Mar's grass, the Grade 1 Eddie Read Handicap was featured, dangling a quarter million in front of 3up at 1⅛ miles. Twelve lengths in arrears after six furlongs, the $12.80 winner stands as testament to much of what recreational handicappers need to know about turf racing.

Its past performances looked like this:

Saratoga Passage ✻ — Ch. g. 4, by Pirateer—Loridown, by Barrydown
DELAHOUSSAYE E **115** — Br.—Beck M & Helen (Wash) — 1989 6 2 0 2 $117,250
Tr.—Frankel Robert — 1988 1 0 0 0
Own.—Saratoga I Stable — Lifetime 13 5 2 2 $430,962 — Turf 1 1 0 0 $30,250

31Jly89-6Dmr 1 Ⓣ:48 1:12^{2}1:36^{4}fm *2 116 7$^{3\frac{1}{4}}$ 6$^{2\frac{1}{4}}$ 5$^{1\frac{3}{4}}$ 1^{nk} DelhoussyeE 7 Aw55000 87-13 SaratogPssge,TrulyMet,LoylDouble 9

4Jun89-8Hol 1⅛ :46^2 1:10^1 1:46^{4}ft 26 115 3^4 5^4 6$^{5\frac{1}{4}}$ 6$^{8\frac{3}{4}}$ DlhoussyE6 Clfrn 94-14 Sabona, Blushing John, Lively One 6

4Jun89—Grade I

13May89-9Pim 1$\frac{3}{16}$:46^2 1:10 1:53^{1}ft 24 116 10^{14}10^{11} 9^{13} 6$^{7\frac{1}{2}}$ DlhssyE 5 Pim Specl H 93-10 BlushingJohn,ProperRelity,Grncus 12

2Apr89-8SA 1⅛ :45^4 1:09^1 1:47^{1}ft 6½ 116 6^{11} 5^9 4$^{5\frac{1}{2}}$ 3$^{4\frac{3}{4}}$ DlhssyE 2 Sn Brndn H 88-15 Ruhlmann,LivelyOne,SaratogPssge 6

2Apr89—Grade II

5Mar89-3SA 1 :45^4 1:09^1 1:33^{2}ft 2¼ 120 3^3 3$^{2\frac{1}{2}}$ 3^5 3$^{4\frac{1}{4}}$ DlhssyE 5 Ⓡ Vkng Sprt 97-07 Ruhlmnn,ProveSplendid,SrtogPssg 5

5Mar89—Wide backstretch

1Feb89-7SA 1 :45^1 1:09^4 1:35^{3}ft 6¾ 116 8$^{6\frac{1}{4}}$ 6^4 4^2 1^{hd} DelhoussyeE 3 Aw60000 90-15 SaratogaPassage,Gorky,He'sACjun 9

1Feb89—Broke slowly, steadied start, bumped 1/8

20Mar88-8SA 1$\frac{1}{16}$:46^2 1:10^4 1:42^{1}ft 14 119 8^5 6$^{6\frac{1}{2}}$ 6^{10} 6$^{16\frac{1}{4}}$ SteinerJJ 6 Sn Flpe H 74-15 Mi Preferido, Purdue King, Tejano 8

20Mar88—Grade I

31Oct87-8SA 1$\frac{1}{16}$:46^3 1:11^2 1:48 sy 13 118 4$^{6\frac{1}{2}}$ 3^3 3^1 1$^{2\frac{1}{4}}$ Steiner J J 7 Nrflk 76-25 SrtogPssge,PurdueKing,BoldScond 7

31Oct87—Grade I

11Oct87-9Lga 1$\frac{1}{16}$:46^2 1:11 1:43^{2}ft *7-5 121 5^3 1½ 1$^{1\frac{1}{2}}$ 1^5 StinrJJ 13 Ⓢ J Gtsn Fut 82-19 SrtogPssge,TortlliniRom,Khootny 14

27Sep87-9Lga 1$\frac{1}{16}$:45^1 1:10^2 1:42^{3}ft 3 122 8$^{9\frac{3}{4}}$ 2$^{1\frac{1}{2}}$ 2$^{3\frac{1}{2}}$ 2^2 Steiner J J3 Lads 84-19 Nohwbee,SrtogPssge,MobiusStrip 14

27Sep87—Wide 2nd turn

●Aug 7 Dmr Ⓣ 5f fm 1:01^3 H (d) Jly 25 Dmr 5f ft 1:00^2 H Jly 20 Hol Ⓣ 7f fm 1:29^3 B ●Jly 14 Hol Ⓣ 5f fm :59^4 H (d)

A Grade 1 winner in the slop in Santa Anita's Norfolk Stakes at two, Saratoga Passage did not impress again until last out, the four-year-old's first attempt on turf.

Saratoga Passage was not bred for grass, but its running style suggested a more agreeable passage over a deeper, softer surface. Closers like Saratoga Passage do not often catch up against ranking opposition on the dirt, but they often outrun the same kind in the late stages on grass.

On most turf courses, speed horses tire, as they do not on the dirt. Speed on the grass must be complemented by the qualities of endurance and competitiveness—the three components of class—in order to survive. On the numerous occasions when speed on the turf does not survive, the fastest-finishing closers regularly win.

Late speed, in combination with class, dominates on the turf. Not early speed, not pace, not tactical speed, and not improving form. When the real grass racing begins, shortly following the prestretch call, class and late speed tell the tale.

The fractions of the Eddie Read Handicap that Saratoga Passage overruled were:

23.3	46.4	1:11	1:36.3	1:49

A lonesome frontrunner set the pace for three quarters, traveling the second quarter mile in 23.1, two ticks faster than an ordinary first quarter mile, not altogether unusual on the turf.

The six-furlong par for nine-furlong stakes horses at Del Mar is 1:11.2. Final stakes par at the distance is exactly 1:49. So stakes horses on the grass at Del Mar normally complete the final three eights in 37.3 seconds.

Twelve lengths back after six furlongs, Saratoga Passage completed the final three furlongs of the Eddie Read in a fast, hard-charging 35.3 seconds, nine lengths faster than the stakes par. Late speed wins on the turf.

The lesson is transferable to middle-distance grass races as a group. Evaluate grass contenders on late speed and class. Whenever possible, use exact distances to compare horses. At 1⅛ miles, Saratoga Passage can be rated as follows:

Final Time	Late Speed	Class
1:49	33.3	Grade 1 (8)

The 8 in parentheses, to recall, is the numeral assigned to Grade 1 races in the class hierarchy for major tracks.

If recreational handicappers add the final time and late speed in seconds, and from that sum subtract the class level numeral, the resulting figure estimates how well horses can close on grass at various class levels.

Saratoga Passage would be rated as 109 (final time in seconds) + 35.3 (late speed) − 8 (class level), or 136.3. The lowest figure is best.

When comparing grass horses at inexact distances, but no more than one-sixteenth mile apart, add or subtract 6.3 seconds from the inexact distance. The adjustment is a gross estimate as to how fast classified allowance horses will run an additional sixteenth of a mile in the late stages. It's serviceable.

Grass horses 3up can be evaluated surprisingly well using late speed and class in combination, up to nine furlongs. At 1¼ miles and beyond, use only late speed. Ignore final time, as the pace up to a mile can vary ridiculously. Besides, at the classic distances on turf, closing speed matters most.

Return to the past performances of Saratoga Passage. Two additional comments.

In the gelding's only turf try, July 31, Saratoga Passage picked up a slow pace of 48 (4F) and 1:12.2 (6F). Against similar fractions on dirt, Saratoga Passage would surely have been defeated, no matter how fast he finished. Most handicappers would concede the comparison.

Pace is not exactly irrelevant on the grass, but it is far less decisive an influence. The softer footing saps enormous energy, regardless of running times. Frontrunners without stamina tire on the turf, no matter how slow the early going. Pace duels ruin the participants. Impressive closers possess the endurance required. Closers can relax early, settle into a slower stride and, as the jockey desires, unleash a burst of late speed. The strongest closer represents a serious contender on turf; always.

Horses that have an extraordinary chance of succumbing on the grass:

- Frontrunners that cannot relax, or cannot be rated kindly
- Horses engaged in a pace duel, notably if three horses or more will be involved
- Nonclaiming three-year-olds in their first attempts on turf, if they routinely run on the front, press the pace, or run green

As a general rule, handicappers can throw out heavily bet, front-running three-year-olds when first they switch to the turf. The inexperienced horses exhaust themselves, and lose. Do not expect they will finish second either.

The second point illustrated by Saratoga Passage concerns horses that win from behind on the first turf attempt. Invariably, the horses duplicate the finish the next start on turf, or excel themselves, especially if that's the very next race. Many will be repeat winners, even if raised in class. Saratoga Passage jumped from classified allowances to a Grade 1 stakes, but was a previous Grade 1 winner himself. Normally that escalation will be too steep, but any reasonable climb can be accepted.

The colt that set the pace in the Eddie Read Handicap looked like this:

***Halcyon Days** — B. c. 4, by Kris—Summer Bloom, by Silly Season
BLACK C A — 115 — Br.—Norelands Stud (Ire) — 1989 5 3 1 0 $67,100
Tr.—Gregson Edwin — 1988 4 2 1 1 $8,329
Own.—Hand E J — Lifetime 10 5 2 1 $75,429 — Turf 10 5 2 1 $75,429

15Jly89-9Hol 1 1/16 Ⓣ:46^{4}1:10^{1}1:40^{1}fm*3-2 117 1^1 1$^{1\frac{1}{2}}$ 1^2 1$^{\frac{1}{2}}$ Black C A^6 Aw35000 93-07 Halcyon Days, Bon Vent, Quiet Boy 6
25Jun89-9Hol 1 1/16 Ⓣ:48^{1}1:11^{1}1:41^{3}fm *2¾ 118 1$^{\frac{1}{2}}$ 1$^{1\frac{1}{2}}$ 1$^{1\frac{1}{2}}$ 1^{nk} Black C A^3 Aw33000 86-08 Halcyon Days, Ramonda, Dramatis 10
14Apr89-7SA 1¼Ⓣ:46^{2}1:35^{2}2:01^{3}fm *1 119 1$^{2\frac{1}{2}}$ 2^{hd} 1^{hd} 1^{nk} Black C A^2 Aw36000 79-21 HalcyonDays,Henbane,PlnToBrter 10
29Mar89-5SA 1⅛Ⓣ:46^{1}1:10^{4}1:49^{4}fm*8-5 120 1^4 1^3 1^2 2^{hd} Black C A^8 Aw36000 78-18 Quvo,HlcyonDys,HowVryTouching 11
18Feb89-7SA a6½f Ⓣ:21^4 :44^{4}1:15^{4}gd 5½ 115 5$^{5\frac{1}{2}}$ 5^4 4^3 4$^{3\frac{3}{4}}$ Black C A^6 Aw36000 76-20 GrndTier,Exceller'sSpecil,BrveCpd 10
5Sep88♦4Nottingham(Eng) 1¼ 2:03^{3}gd*2-3 128 Ⓣ 2$^{\frac{3}{4}}$ CchrnR Can Pac Nwsprt SanDomenico,HalcyonDys,MillLoft 8
27Aug88♦7Windsor(Eng) a1¼ 2:09 gd*2-3 133 Ⓣ 1^3 CchrnR Rd Spner Grad HalcyonDys,HrvestDnce,CspinMist 12
30Jly88♦5Goodwood(Eng) 1 1:43^{3}gd 3¼ 131 Ⓣ 3$^{\frac{3}{4}}$ CochrnR SurpliceGrad Literati,HibernianGold,HalcyonDys 6
1Jly88♦1Haydock(Eng) 1 1:42^{4}fm*1-2 126 Ⓣ 1^2 CchrR Stve Dnghe(Mdn) HlcyonDys,DringTimes,FrnchPolish 7
25Sep87♦5Ascot(Eng) 7f 1:32 gd 3 123 Ⓣ 5^4 CchrnR MorningtonGrad ShriffsStr,AncintFlm,SmrtRobrto 12
25Sep87—Off slowly
Aug 9 Dmr Ⓣ 5f fm 1:03 H (d) Aug 3 Dmr Ⓣ 7f fm 1:32^4 H (d) Jly 28 Dmr 5f ft 1:00^3 H Jly 23 Hol 4f ft :48^1 H

Winner of three straight grass routes on the lead, as long as 1¼ miles, Halcyon Days has demonstrated late speed, and competitive spirit, too, completing the final five sixteenths of its latest middle-distance victories in 30.2 and 30 seconds flat.

Notice the faster closing time of 30 seconds was delivered after Halcyon Days had completed a significantly swifter pace at the same distance. Impressive.

If speed horses like Halcyon Days can relax on the front, uncontested, no doubt they can outfinish numerous closers. They complicate the handicapping of grass races and must be boxed in exactas, whenever possible, with the strongest closers.

In addition, the texture of the turf course matters. In the situation at hand, Del Mar presents a deeper, softer grass course than either Hollywood Park or Santa Anita, and Hollywood's grass can be exceptionally glib.

Can a persevering frontrunner such as Halcyon Days complete a longer distance on a softer turf while up in class? The answer is usually negative. The softer grass is particularly bothersome, as it drains extra energy. If frontrunners have been winning barely, while all-out, as had Halcyon Days, a softer grass will probably defeat their best effort, at least for a time, especially if the horses move up in class.

Conventional speed figures and pace ratings are unreliable, and in numerous instances useless, in the handicapping of grass routes. The pace varies tremendously, and so do the corresponding final times, the configurations reflecting poorly on horses' basic abilities.

Moreover, conventional track variants are painstakingly difficult to calculate on grass. The *Daily Racing Form* variants are worthless. Professional speed handicappers who rely upon projected times at both the pace call and final call to obtain accurate variants can stay abreast of the turf programs, but the labor is arduous, and technically difficult. No one else can duplicate the practice, not regular handicappers, and certainly not occasional racegoers.

Highly experienced professional speed and pace handicappers have abandoned their grass figures in frustration during many meetings throughout the seasons. Recreational handicappers should not rely on this book's speed and pace handicapping techniques on the grass. They will not work.

Turf specialists can move ahead in class at fancier leaps than is permissible on dirt. Among nonclaiming horses, the class barrier that remains erect separates preliminary nonwinners allowance graduates from open stakes at $100,000 or above, mainly because the allowance winners will not yet have developed a closing kick. But experienced, tested, high-priced claiming horses can mix with classified horses on grass, and both can tangle effectively with stakes horses below Grade 2. Find the fastest finishers. Adjust for class, as recommended here.

Among claiming horses, the $20,000 to $50,000 range represents an acceptable bracket. So does below $20,000.

In all claiming cases, horses that finished fastest last out from the prestretch call to the wire will be difficult to handle.

Jockeys are more significant on the turf. The worst abuse grass horses prematurely, running low on the precious energy that must be summoned late. Prefer intelligent, waiting-style riders, and discount the impatient, aggressive, can't-wait types that consistently move boldly into the far turn and around the far turn, but fall short in the drive.

Inside post positions are also helpful on the grass. Statistically, the inside outperforms the outside on all turf courses. The sharper turns place a premium on saving ground. But if the classiest horse having the best closing time will exit from the outside, that's the likeliest winner regardless. The horse can take back, drop over, and save its kick for the end. If the jockey doesn't rush the horse to secure early position, or arouse it too soon for striking position, the long late kick will be satisfactory, at least much of the time.

Among horses trying the turf for the first and second times, pedigree is the overarching asset. Dirt form is unimportant. When introduced to the scene, horses bred for grass win on the surface with amazing consistency. They repeatedly pay high mutuels. In maiden races, nonwinners allowances, and 3YO stakes, all of which involve younger, lightly raced horses, prefer horses boasting effective grass sires.

Among horses 4up, too, any switching to grass for the first or second time and having an effective turf sire become automatic contenders. The selective list appears in the appendices.

Foreign imports also deserve special consideration on grass. As the 1990s come into focus, racing in Europe can be considered five pounds superior to comparable racing in the States. The superiority reveals itself undeniably in American grass racing, where European imports shine. Other things being relatively equal, prefer the imports of England and France, more so at inflated mutuels. And if graded or listed imports from Europe remain eligible to preliminary nonwinners allowance contests, or highly restricted classified races, or restricted stakes here, the horses stand out on class.

Turf races can be upsetting to handicappers who fail to adapt to the grassy surface. Conventional figure handicappers have been heard to denounce the races as inexplicable. But turf races can be as predictable as any. Different kinds of horses prosper on turf, and different handicapping factors apply. Just as versatile runners are more likely to transfer their talents to grass racing successfully, so are versatile handicappers.

STARTER RACES

Starter races bring a warm, confident glow to the countenances of handicappers who comprehend the possibilities. They make no impression upon racegoers who cannot perceive their distinctive charms.

Starter races are written for horses 4up that have "started" for a specified claiming price during a specified time interval. Eligible horses cannot be claimed. This wrinkle assures the races will become hideouts for trainers in possession of consistent breadwinners they do not care to lose.

The conditions of eligibility below are typical. Examine them carefully. It's March 31, 1989.

3rd Golden Gate

1¼ MILES. (1.58⅗) STARTER HANDICAP. Purse $11,000. Fillies and mares. 4-year-olds and upward, which have started for $6,500 or less since November 1, 1988. Weights, Sunday, March 26, 1989. Horses must re-enter by closing time of entries. High weights, preferred. Closed Sunday, March 26, 1989 by 11 a.m.

Any claiming horse that has started for $6500 in the past five months is eligible to this race. The horse might have won for $20,000 two weeks ago, but if it started for $6500 three months ago, it qualifies.

Do handicappers begin to see the possibilities?

Trainers certainly do. The starter game becomes a chessboard of trainer maneuvers and manipulations. Purses of starter races are more generous than purses of open claiming races at the same levels. The Golden Gate purse of $11,000 is 75 percent greater than the starting price. Typical purses at the Gate for $6500 claiming horses are $7500.

The trainer's purpose is to enter a horse that has won for a selling price above the starting price, but still remains eligible. The trainer knows the horse might outclass the others near the starting price and might dominate the races repeatedly.

Aware handicappers simply play along. In the Golden Gate situation, handicappers would shop for horses that recently won open claiming races above $6500 but remain eligible today because they once started for a lower price. A major contender in any starter race is the claiming horse that has been trouncing the highest-priced open opposition lately.

The overnight favorite at 2–1 for the Golden Gate starter handicap was the four-year-old Poncelle, runner-up last out under the same conditions. I present Poncelle's past performances, along with another four-year-old's, a 7–2 shot overnight.

Poncelle — Ch. f. 4, by Messenger of Song—Marlborough Set, by Acroterion
KAENEL J L — 116 — Br.—Ridder Georgia B (Cal) — 1989 2 1 1 0 $6,125
Own.—Buckley-Enbom-Enbom — Tr.—Jenda Charles J — 1988 15 2 1 6 $15,175
Lifetime 17 3 2 6 $21,300

24Feb89-3GG	1¼	:47^1	1:38	2:03^{3}ft	3¼	117	3$^{1\frac{1}{2}}$	1^1	1^{hd}	2^2	Kaenel J L^3	Ⓕ H6250	71-18	Helleborus, Poncelle, Fightin Lil	5
1Feb89-2GG	1	:45^2	1:10	1:36^{2}ft	5¼	116	5$^{4\frac{1}{2}}$	3½	1^{hd}	1$^{1\frac{1}{2}}$	Doocy T T^1	Ⓕ 8000	83-10	Poncelle, Spirit Lodge, Basic Grey	10
14Dec88-7BM	1	:46^4	1:11^1	1:36^{4}ft	8	116	5^5	5^4	5^8	8$^{13\frac{1}{4}}$	Doocy T T^5	Ⓕ 12500	71-20	Deal'nGirl,NonHitter,PhntomBlood	8
23Nov88-9BM	1	:47^2	1:12^3	1:39 gd	3¾	116	3^1	1^{hd}	1½	3$^{1\frac{1}{4}}$	Doocy T T^2	Ⓕ 10000	72-18	NonHitter,Meghn'sMence,Poncelle	9
2Nov88-1BM	1$\frac{1}{16}$	:46^2	1:12^1	1:46 ft	8	116	3$^{4\frac{1}{2}}$	3^1	1^3	1^7	Doocy T T^4	Ⓕ 6250	62-27	Poncelle,MauiTan,SweetActionPlus	8
5Oct88-10Fno	1	:45^4	1:11^4	1:37^{3}ft	10	117	1$^{1\frac{1}{2}}$	1^2	1^2	4^4	Nicolo P^7	Ⓕ 6500	77-12	NonHitter,ThePantry,VlentineRose	9
21Sep88-4BM	6f	:22^3	:45^4	1:11 ft	17	116	2^{hd}	3$^{2\frac{1}{2}}$	7$^{9\frac{1}{2}}$	9^{17}	Hummel C R^1	Ⓕ 8000	67-24	BlueMoonBay,BusyDay,OpheliMine	9
30Aug88-11Sac	1	:45^4	1:10^2	1:37^{1}ft	3	115	1$^{1\frac{1}{2}}$	1½	2^3	3$^{7\frac{1}{4}}$	Caballero R^7	Ⓕ 6250	80-11	PlainOrFncy,CrownCtcher,Poncelle	7
23Aug88-2Sac	1	:45^3	1:12	1:40 ft	*8-5	114	1½	1^{hd}	1^1	1$^{2\frac{1}{2}}$	CblleroR^{10}	Ⓕ[S]M12500	73-12	Poncelle, Brudi, Mc Cou	10
10Aug88-4Bmf	1$\frac{1}{16}$	:47^3	1:13	1:46 ft	5½	117	5^3	4^2	5^5	7$^{11\frac{1}{4}}$	MaelfeytBJ^6	Ⓕ M12500	51-22	AdaMoon,L'Astrgle,HighflyerJmie	12

Mar 27 GG 4f ft :48^4 H — Mar 21 GG 1 ft 1:43 H — Mar 14 GG 1 ft 1:42^2 H — Mar 5 GG 4f ft :48^1 H

Crown Catcher *
GONZALEZ R M **115**
Own.—Diederichsen & Medieros

Gr. f. 4, by Ali Oop—King's Destiny, by Clandestine
Br.—King H G III (Ky) 1989 5 2 1 1 $11,275
Tr.—Delia William 1988 15 3 2 0 $17,775
Lifetime 24 6 4 1 $38,900

17Mar89-4GG	1 1/16	:46	1:101	1:432ft	*2	116	2½	2½	11½	16	GonzlezRM 4	Ⓕ c10000	82-16	CrownCatcher,GottCopy,DppleDwn	7
10Mar89-9GG	1	:464	1:122	1:403m	3¼	116	21½	16	16	18	Gonzalez RM 1	Ⓕ c6250	62-26	CrownCatcher,BjQueen,MgiclGrden	8
16Feb89-4GG	1	:464	1:12	1:373ft	6¾	1135	43½	53¾	46	37	Hubbard N J 4	Ⓕ 8000	70-22	SpiritLodg,RichAdvoct,CrownCtchr	8
1Feb89-2GG	1	:452	1:10	1:362ft	4¾	118	43½	51¼	51¾	75	Hansen R D 4	Ⓕ 8000	78-10	Poncelle, Spirit Lodge, Basic Grey	10
1Feb89—Forced wide into drive															
20Jan89-3BM	1 1/16	:472	1:124	1:453ft	3	1115	24	3½	2hd	22	Hubbard N J 6	Ⓕ 10000	62-26	FlseCourtesies,CrownCtcher,BjQun	6
29Dec88-3BM	1 1/16	:481	1:143	1:481m	3½	116	31½	32	43½	56½	Lamance C 4	Ⓕ 10000	44-30	NonHitter,BajaQueen,Shron'sSight	7
21Dec88-4BM	1 1/16	:47	1:122	1:452sy	*2¼	118	33	32	1hd	11	Lamance C 4	Ⓕ 8000	65-21	CrownCtchr,Shron'sSght,TrdngWtr	8
23Nov88-9BM	1	:472	1:123	1:39 gd	4	117	41½	42	42	43¾	Kaenel J L 6	Ⓕ 10000	69-18	NonHitter,Meghn'sMence,Poncelle	9
11Nov88-4BM	1 1/16	:463	1:13	1:464ft	*8-5	117	86¾	51¼	1hd	11½	Kaenel J L 8	Ⓕ c8000	58-21	CrownCtchr,BontyLss,Crntnsndlc	11
11Nov88—Off slowly															
20Oct88-7BM	1 1/16	:463	1:12	1:453ft	7¾	116	87½	55½	31	21	Kaenel J L 4	Ⓕ 8000	63-23	UpToHrTricks,CrownCtchr,MuiTn	11

Mar 27 GG 4f ft :481 H **Mar 7 GG 4f m :523 H (d)** **Mar 1 GG 4f ft :492 H**

Crown Catcher blasted $10,000 claiming horses last out, and had started for $6250 seven days prior to that, winning by eight. Crown Catcher became eligible that day for the $6500 starter series. Before that, Crown Catcher had challenged $8000 and $10,000 horses exclusively, winning her share.

Crown Catcher is precisely the type that sneaks into starter races and thrives. The open $10,000 romp indicates the filly will be too sharp for the $6500 brand. Poncelle looks attractive, too, and handicappers should have noticed she became eligible for the $6500 starter races at Golden Gate on November 2, 1988, one day after the specified date of today's eligibility conditions. Poncelle won that day herself, by seven.

But Crown Catcher has beaten stronger open competition, and that's the primary clue. Relative class rules in the starter series. Find the best horse in sharp form.

Because a significantly classier horse still eligible can enter starter races, the series is sometimes dominated by a single horse. Repeated victories under the conditions characterize the past performances. That horse is obviously a second major contender.

To combat this tendency, racing secretaries alter the conditions of starter races in various ways. Some of the races, as with the Golden Gate example, will be carded under handicap conditions. The racing secretary can assign punishing weights to repetitive winners.

The distance and footing can be altered. The Golden Gate race is carded at 1¼ miles. Other races in the series will occur at middle distances. One might go on the turf.

None of this does much to deter the wily claiming trainer. As best he can, the trainer merely maneuvers a hard-knocking versatile runner into the series. The results remain predictable.

A third automatic contender in a starter race is any horse that was dropped precipitously to the starting price last out. Even if the horse blew the race on the drop, it warrants close inspection in the starter race. Many racegoers interpret the class drop negatively, as a sign of decline, but the situation instead encompasses a positive trainer maneuver. If the dropdown has beaten better open competition in the past four months or so, it's a contender.

The maneuver just explained is part and parcel of a particularly positive trainer angle if the conditions of eligibility specify that horses may not have won a claiming race since last being entered for the starting price. Be on the lookout for this one.

If handicappers approach starter races as a kind of cat-and-mouse game between racing secretaries and trainers, which they are, with clever trainers presiding by obtaining eligibility for solid, versatile, higher-priced claiming horses—which they do—the paths to the major contenders will have been cleared.

All that is left is identifying the best horse in sharp form today.

JUVENILES

Two-year-old dashes and sprints are won by juveniles that have recorded the fastest adjusted final times. Actual times, of course, must be modified by the day's sprint variant. Use the procedures promoted in the methods section of this book. An advantage of one fifth of a second can be conclusive.

Juveniles of spring and summer run as fast as they can for as long as they can. The fastest horses win. Pace is relatively unimportant. If a two-year-old can settle behind the unrestrained swift of a couple of speedballs, and then accelerate strongly at the quarter pole, winning in brilliant time, that's the most impressive kind of juvenile victory. That suggests the youngster can be rated. It will not necessarily be burned out on the uncontrollable pace of a crucial juvenile stakes.

Jockey, weight, and post position are virtually meaningless in juvenile sprints. Gate ability helps, but the finer riding skills of handling and timing hardly matter. Before weight is felt, the race is over. And the fastest juveniles will quickly recover any ground lost to a wide post position.

Form is similarly secondary. Juveniles are relatively sound, trim, and in sharp competitive condition. Workouts should be regular, with a few of them promising genuine speed. If juveniles train out of the gate, subtract a second from the workout time. Repeated gate works may indicate a problem in the gate. Do not bet on two-year-olds that appear in front-leg bandages.

Although effective speed handicapping gets to the guts of two-year-old sprints quickly and reliably, the races are normally complicated by the appearance of well-connected, nicely bred, fast-working first starters.

Handicappers can evaluate debuting juveniles in four ways:

1. Sires' win percentages with first-starting 2YOs
2. Trainers' win percentages with first-starting 2YOs
3. Workout patterns
4. Tote-board action

Prefer sires that win with 15 percent or better of their first-starting two-year-olds. If a sire wins impressively with juveniles but the trainer does not, credit the sire. Unlike the conditioning of first-starting three-year-olds, the trainer's task with juveniles is straightforward and uncomplicated, at least in preparation for the early sprints. A select list of the most productive juvenile sires can be found periodically in the Daily Racing Form. Local sires are equally as crucial to evaluate as the national leaders.

A few trainers specialize in polishing the speed of precocious two-year-olds. They win the dashes and sprints of spring and summer season after season. Credit these trainers during those times. That the aggressive refinement of juveniles' inherent speed may interfere with the horses' later and better development is of no concern to handicappers, until that later time.

Workouts, of course, should be regular and sharp. The best is a five-furlong move of genuine speed. If shorter works have been fast but longer workouts slow, that's a red flag. When asked to do so, almost all nonclaiming juveniles can deliver a fancy turn of speed for three or four furlongs.

If racegoers know that juveniles worked in company and finished in front, that's a positive sign.

Betting action on first-starting juveniles should always be regarded seriously. Until the juveniles reveal themselves on the racetrack, they remain the exclusive property of horsemen, clockers, and stable hands. These people may want to wager on their good ones. So will associates, friends, and loved ones that have been tipped. It's a glorious tradition.

As a standard of respectable time, the adjusted final times of juvenile sprinters should fall within three seconds of the track-record for the distance. If that standard is invoked, impressive first-starters will be required to run reasonably fast to win, after all.

If a two-year-old has already run within 2⅖ seconds of the track record for the distance (adjusted time), it should be expected to withstand the challenge of first starters. The fast experienced horse is even likely to improve its final time, notably if it started sluggishly or raced wide around the far turn.

By midsummer, two-year-olds will be competing at six furlongs. If the front end will be contested by three or more juveniles, prefer the horse that can be rated behind the pace. If just two two-year-olds will contest the early pace, prefer the fastest horse.

If the pace at six furlongs will be hotly contested, and none of the juveniles can be rated kindly, prefer horses that have been closing strongly from behind at 5½ furlongs but running out of room. A come-from-behind running style does not flatter juveniles, unless the stretch run has been conspicuously powerful and today's pace will be faltering. The brilliant filly Open Mind rallied from far back as a juvenile, and won eight consecutive Grade 1 or Grade 2 events with the style. But she got there late, and the front half of the field had sputtered.

The divide between the sprints and routes for two-year-olds is enormous. Excepting the top layer of the division—potentially outstanding racehorses that impress tremendously as juveniles, and normally will accomplish whatever is asked of them—two-year-olds that win the routes generally will not be the same horses that won the sprints.

It's a critical distinction, for two-year-old routes are largely unpredictable.

Handicappers can expect the leading two-year-olds to collect the nonclaiming routes, the stakes races, but the claiming routes can be elusive propositions.

A perfectly rational strategy in juvenile routes prefers the early speed. As mentioned, the majority of two-year-olds will run as fast as they can for as long as they can. Few juveniles of fall will have learned how to conserve speed and energy while running relaxed behind the pace. Instead, most juveniles chase.

Few of them arrive in the stretch with a final kick. Early-speed horses may be tiring, but many of them continue on to victory.

The cheaper the juvenile route race, the more likely early-speed horses will control the race from wire to wire. If the price looks inviting, so do juvenile route contenders with high early speed.

Of two-year-old form, the juveniles share a tendency to improve tremendously or deteriorate dramatically. If a two-year-old dispenses an inexplicably dull performance, do not expect a form reversal. Unlike the consistently inconsistent three-year-olds, two-year-olds should always be rated off the latest race unless clearly excusable.

Among two-year-olds in acceptable form, days away between races should be of no concern. Juvenile form perseveres. The rested two-year-olds will run as fast, or faster, than they had prior to the respite.

"Blinkers on" can be a positive sign among juveniles, especially among horses that have been demonstrating improved early speed or increasingly faster final times. The blinkers focus concentration, and the horses respond by running straighter and faster. If juveniles have been breaking poorly when bet strongly, and put blinkers on, several will now break smoothly, and at higher odds.

Not much more about the juveniles is pertinent. The handicapping is relatively uncomplicated and quick, but several of the races will prove too unpredictable to challenge. Once the fastest juveniles have shown what they can do, however, they can be supported confidently, because two-year-olds notoriously repeat their final times, or improve them. Many of the winning mutuels may be low, but the risk even smaller.

To end on a scarcely understood point, on January 1, when the juveniles become three-years-old, the jewels of the division can be expected to proceed uninterrupted to even greater heights. And the plodders can be expected to continue recording their milkwagon times. But all other juveniles will effectively be starting over. Among ordinary horses, the two-year-old record does not transfer very reliably to the three-year-old season.

Patient handicappers can wrangle seasonal profits out of the juvenile divisions. Emphasize adjusted final times in sprints the early speed in routes, but wait until the requisite evidence has been scattered on the racetrack.

CHAPTER VII

Special Topics

WHAT IS STANDARD, formful, and predictable in thoroughbred racing is routinely countermanded by the exceptional. To every general principle, broad guideline, and basic method, an opposite logic applies such that the game's loyal practitioners can be confounded and seemingly disabused by the numerous exceptions to the rules.

Furthermore, in everyday application, the principles, guidelines, and methods of effective handicapping interact in fantastical patterns, such that nuances, subtleties, and variations continually intrude. Opposite logics do apply. Speed wins, speed loses, class wins, class loses, pace wins, pace loses, same track, same day, and nothing is the same. The mental challenge that is handicapping's soaring high never ceases. The game is exciting, stimulating, and rewarding; the game is unforgiving.

In this section and the next, recreational handicappers are exposed to several of modern racing's subtlest complexities and blatant contradictions. The material deals with special topics and familiar situations that racing fans experience as confusing or altogether elusive. Although practitioners will entertain the familiarity of the situations and topics discussed, and maybe even the value of the book's advice, compiled from seasons at the front, the final teacher on the subjects will be personal experience.

Only personal experience juxtaposes the pratfalls and the penalties attached, and the corrective measures that might enlighten the future. It's at the sensory, visceral levels where the multitudinous interactions of the handicapping factors are felt, and where in-depth, practical learning occurs.

The intent here, however, is noble enough—to introduce the issues and to reduce the confusion, thereby alleviating the oppression associated with wholesale ignorance.

FILLIES VS. COLTS

The issue is not whether fillies can topple colts, because they do, but under what circumstances do fillies have an especially favorable chance to upset, and under what circumstances do they confront a negligible chance.

The quintessential horseman who has posed these questions and answered them persuasively is the colorful trainer D. Wayne Lukas. Admired for his ministrations with the weaker sex, Lukas enters fillies against colts every season, but judiciously.

Lukas will enter Winning Colors in the Kentucky Derby because he senses the brilliant filly can handle Forty Niner and company, but he will not enter Lady's Secret in the Breeders' Cup Classic because he knows the brilliant mare cannot withstand Turkoman and company.

Handicappers must comprehend the differences in the same confident way.

A precocious filly possessed of brilliance (high speed) and competitive spirit can outrun comparably talented but immature underdeveloped males until those males develop and mature. A brilliant, fully mature mare cannot outduel comparably talented, fully mature males. A Winning Colors can outrun a Forty Niner. A Lady's Secret would be squashed by a Turkoman.

An interesting variation of the theme has been transported to U.S. handicappers from Europe, where older fillies and mares regularly defeat leading males at marathon distances on the turf.

The reason is a lazy pace. Females possessed of abundant endurance, but with a brilliant burst of speed in reserve, can relax into an ambling stride for a mile or longer, squandering little energy, and then rush to the wire as fast as latent power allows. If the late burst is sufficiently fast and powerful, the ladies win. As the races involved are normally stakes bringing together the outstanding horses on the continent, no one should be surprised at the results.

The phenomenon occurs less frequently in the States, where the pace is comparatively brisk and often savagely debated. The American fillies and mares expend greater amounts of energy early, with less in reserve for the furious finish. On U.S. main tracks, the typical longer nonclaiming route demands far greater expenditures of speed and stamina during the first six furlongs, and now females do not often endure against the stronger, more powerful males.

Better fillies and mares deserve full attention against non-claiming males under contrasting conditions:

1. In sprints and routes for two-year-olds, and three-year-olds of spring and early summer, provided the fillies possess abundant speed and have earned a higher numerical rating than any colt in the field.
2. In routes on the turf, provided the females will not be required to set or contest the pace during the first six furlongs or mile, and have already defeated horses comparable to, or better than, today's class.

In other nonclaiming circumstances, the males predominate such that fillies and mares are rarely even tempted. And among younger, still developing three-year-olds, once the males have matured, the fillies will be pounded. As soon as three months following the 1988 Kentucky Derby, for example, Winning Colors would have been stretched to steal a Grade 2 stakes open to colts. She could not have beaten Forty Niner in the Travers Stakes in August, and if Winning Colors had attempted to compete with handicap males 4up in the fall championship stakes, she would have been slaughtered.

In major-league claiming races, fillies vs. colts is virtually a moot question, as females stay in their own division. When females do challenge males in claiming races, a single operating principle guides the handicapping: fillies and mares must have completed a good race against clearly superior female claiming horses, and while doing so have earned a numerical rating at least comparable to today's male contenders.

Under $10,000 claiming, handicappers can be more flexible. Not-as-cheap females can overhaul cheap males. It happens at minor tracks daily. A small class edge, combined with sharp or improving form, is enough. In maiden-claiming races, fillies with an early-speed advantage can run away from the slower males, who are too untalented to catch up.

But the really attractive handicapping opportunity provided by the fillies vs. colts dichotomy is a traditional one. Whenever a filly or mare has been entered against females at the same claiming price for which it has recently delivered a good race against the males, the horse is a potential stickout. That is, $32,000 claiming is a much tougher proposition than Ⓕ $32,000 claiming. The higher the claiming price, the better.

At the lower claiming levels, a rise in claiming price may represent a drop in class. A hard-knocking mare that exits a sharp win in a $4000 claiming race open to males may be slumming if next entered in a $5000 claiming race restricted to females. The weaker sex is exactly that in sports, and in racing the weaknesses can be gripping at the bottom levels of competition.

Naturally, any drop from a good race against males to a lower claiming level against females is a huge descent. If the price is right, grab it.

The above stipulations excepted, fillies vs. colts is no fair bargain in American racing, and nothing unduly complicated for handicappers. Unless the females are clearly best, no play. An illustration serves the point, by dramatizing just how superior stakes-caliber females must be to prevail against stakes-caliber males in ordinary circumstances at middle distances.

The four horses whose past performances are presented below came together in a small five-horse field under classified allowance conditions during Del Mar 1989.

Review the past performances closely. Which should handicappers prefer, one of the mares, or one of the males?

8th Del Mar

1 MILE. (Turf). (1.34⅕) CLASSIFIED ALLOWANCE. Purse $60,000. 3-year-olds and upward which are non-winners of $18,000 twice other than closed or claiming at one mile or over in 1989. Weights, 3-year-olds, 116 lbs.; older, 121 lbs. Non-winners of such a race since June 1) allowed 2 lbs.; of such a race since March 1, 4 lbs.; of such a race in 1989 or such a race any distance since April 24, 6 lbs.

You're No Bargain — B. h. 5, by Riva Ridge—Suzest, by Fleet Nasrullah
PINCAY L JR — **115**
Br.—Bowen & Hancock & Peters (Ky) — 1989 8 0 3 1 $32,049
Tr.—Whittingham Charles — 1988 10 4 2 2 $109,140
Own.—Bowen & Hancock III — Lifetime 36 10 7 9 $380,759 — Turf 2 0 1 0 $11,000

24Jly89-3Hol	1	Ⓣ$:47^2$ $1:10^4$ $1:34^3$fm	3½	116	3^1	$3^{1½}$	$4^{1¼}$	2^{hd}	ValenzuelPA6	Aw55000	91-13	SilverCircus,You'reNoBrgin,Nrghile	6
4Jly89-7Hol	1	:44 $1:08^1$ $1:33^4$ft	16	116	$4^{2½}$	$5^{3¾}$	5^6	$5^{8½}$	Valenzuela PA10	HcpO	85-12	Rhy,PrmountJet,Don'sIrishMelody	10
4Jly89—Wide final 3/8													
17Jun89-6CD	6f	$:21^2$ $:44^4$ $1:10^3$ft	*9-5	118	4^3	4^3	$3^{1½}$	2no	McDowell M5	Aw29620	90-14	Sttr'sProspct,Yo'rNBrgn,RdndWht	6
30Mar89-8OP	1 1/16	$:48^3$ $1:13^4$ $1:45^1$gd	*9-5	120	$1^{1½}$	1^1	1^{hd}	2^1	Ardoin R1	Aw25000	74-23	ConwayChitty,You'reNoBrgin,Srhill	5
17Mar89-10OP	6f	$:22^2$ $:45^3$ $1:10^1$ft	7½	112	3^2	1^{hd}	$3^{1½}$	5^2	TrosclrAJ4	Barbizon S	87-22	NeverForgotten,BeAgnt,SlttthCrw	7
23Feb89-8OP	6f	$:21^4$:45 $1:09^2$ft	6-5	113	1^{hd}	3^1	$2^{1½}$	3^3	Snyder L2	Aw30000	90-15	SlutethCrw,Ltchburn,You'rNoBrgin	6
11Feb89-9OP	6f	$:21^4$ $:45^1$ $1:09^1$ft	20	121	3^{nk}	2^1	3^2	$5^{5¾}$	Snyder L6	H Springs	88-20	ProperRelty,Homebuilder,BeAgent	9
3Feb89-7OP	5½f	$:22^2$ $:46^2$ $1:04^3$ft	*9-5	112	$5^{1¼}$	$5^{2¼}$	4^4	$4^{3½}$	Day P 1	Aw22500	86-21	Be a Agent,SalutetheCrew Lopaka	12
3Feb89—Boxed in.													
22Dec88-9TP	6½f	$:22^3$ $:45^2$ 1:17 ft	*6-5	122	$4^{2½}$	4^6	3^5	3^{12}	Soto D J5	Aw16200	81-21	Tiger'sFinest,Pike,You'reNoBargin	6
4Nov88-8CD	7f	:23 :46 1:26 sy	*2½	118	4^3	$3^{2½}$	$8^{8¾}$	8^{10}	Garcia J J4	Hindoo H	66-32	The Red Rolls, Joel, Be a Agent	11

Aug 7 Dmr Ⓣ 5f fm 1:03 H (d) Aug 1 Dmr 3f ft $:36^4$ H ●Jly 20 Hol 6f ft $1:11^4$ H ●Jly 15 Hol 5f ft :59 H

Davie's Lamb B. m. 5, by Unpredictable—Davie Lady, by Bold and Brave
DAVIS R G **116** Br.—Meadowbrook Farms Inc (Fla) 1989 4 1 1 0 $42,250
Own.—Deals On Stable Tr.—Canani Julio C 1988 14 5 2 5 $323,190
Lifetime 39 11 4 12 $518,445 Turf 26 9 4 7 $488,890

27Jly89-8Dmr 1 Ⓣ:47^{2}1:12 1:37 fm 8½ 117 3^{2½} 3^{1½} 1^{½} 1^{½} Davis R G^3 ⒻAw55000 86-18 Dvie'sLmb,MriJesse,RintreeRenegd 7
28May89-11Cby 1 Ⓣ:48^{4}1:12 1:36 fm 14 117 4^2 3^2 3^1 7^{2¾} OlivresF^4 ⒻLdy Cby H 87-10 Down Again, Galunpe, InvitedGuest 9
21Apr89-8SA a6½f Ⓣ:21^4 :45^{2}1:16^{4}fm 3¼ 120 6^{4¾} 5^3 4^{3½} 2^{hd} ToroF^5 Ⓕ[R]Mt Wilson 75-25 DownAgin,Dvie'sLmb,ServeN'Volly 8
4Mar89-8SA 1 Ⓣ:48 1:11^{3}1:36^{2}gd 7½ 118 6^{2½} 6^{2¾} 5^3 7^{7¼} Toro F^5 ⒻBna Vsta H 82-11 Annoconnor, Daring Doone,Daloma 8
4Mar89—Rank backstretch
16Nov88-5Hol 1$\frac{1}{16}$ Ⓣ:46^{2}1:10^{3}1:42^{4}fm*6-5 118 5^9 4^{5½} 2^{hd} 1^{1¼} Toro F^7 ⒻAw40000 80-20 Davie'sLmb,Nture'sWy,GoldenGlxy 8
30Oct88-8SA 1 Ⓣ:46 1:09^{3}1:34^{4}fm 6½ 118 5^4 7^4 7^{2¾} 3^{5¼} Toro F^9 ⒻMdwk H 95-13 Balbonella, Choritzo, Davie'sLamb 10
30Oct88—Shuffled back turn
8Oct88-8BM a1⅛Ⓣ 1:46^{3}fm 8¼ 118 3^4 3^2 4^{3¼} 4^{2¾} OlivrsF^7 ⒻCa J C H 99-03 Brown Bess, JungleDawn,Choritzo 10
8Oct88—Grade III
4Sep88-8BM 1$\frac{1}{16}$ Ⓣ:49 1:13^{3}1:42^{3}fm*2-3 120 2^{½} 2^{hd} 1^{hd} 1no Toro F^5 ⒻTizna H 90-10 Davie'sLamb,BrownBess,HollyDonn 7
27Aug88-8Dmr 1$\frac{1}{16}$ Ⓣ:48^{3}1:12^{4}1:42^{3}fm 6½ 117 3^1 3^2 3^2 3^{2½} BlcCA^1 ⒻPalomar H 84-13 ChpelOfDrems,ShortSlvs,Dvi'sLmb 7
27Aug88—Grade II
15Aug88-8Dmr 1$\frac{1}{16}$ Ⓣ:46^{1}1:10^{2}1:42 fm 4½ 117 3^5 3^2 1^{hd} 2^{hd} Toro F^4 ⒻAw48000 90-10 Silent Arrival,Davie'sLamb,Galunpe 6
Aug 5 Dmr 3f ft :36^4 H Jly 20 Hol Ⓣ 5f fm 1:01^3 B Jly 13 Hol 4f ft :48^4 H Jly 4 Hol 6f ft 1:13^3 H

Down Again B. m. 5, by Encino—Dawn Is Breaking, by Import
BLACK C A **114** Br.—Schibbye & Nebbiolo Place (Ky) 1989 9 2 2 3 $185,430
Own.—Summa Stable Tr.—Cross Richard J 1988 11 4 2 0 $140,035
Lifetime 38 9 9 7 $454,771 Turf 36 9 9 6 $446,446

29Jly89-8Dmr 1$\frac{1}{16}$ Ⓣ:49 1:12^{3}1:43^{1}fm 11 115 5^5 5^{4¼} 5^{1¾} 5^{2½} Toro F^1 ⒻPlmr H 81-17 ClaireMarine,Galunpe,DaringDoone 8
29Jly89—Grade II;
12Jly89-8Hol 6f Ⓣ:23 :45^{3}1:08^{3}fm 3½ 122 4^4 3^2 3^{1½} 3^{1¼} Black C A^3 ⒻAw55000 93-09 WarningZone,HastyPsty,DownAgin 5
7Jun89-8Bel 7f Ⓣ:23^4 :48 1:27 sf 4½ 114 6^3 6^4 3^{3½} 3^4 Black C A^3 Jaipur 65-31 HarpIslet,Fourstardave,DownAgin 10
7Jun89—Grade III
28May89-11Cby 1 Ⓣ:48^{4}1:12 1:36 fm 10 115 6^{3½} 4^3 4^{1¼} 1^{nk} BlckCA^7 ⒻLdy Cby H 90-10 Down Again, Galunpe, InvitedGuest 9
28May89—Lacked room
7May89-8Hol 1$\frac{1}{16}$ Ⓣ:46 1:09 1:39 fm 3e 116 4^2 5^{4½} 5^4 5^{5¼} DlhssE^2 ⒻWlshr H 94-04 ClaireMarine,FitzwillimPlce,Glunpe 6
7May89—Grade II
21Apr89-8SA a6½f Ⓣ:21^4 :45^{2}1:16^{4}fm*6-5 114 5^{4¼} 2^1 2^{1½} 1^{hd} BlcCA^6 Ⓕ[R]Mt Wilson 75-25 DownAgin,Dvie'sLmb,ServeN'Volly 8
26Mar89-8SA a6½f Ⓣ:22^1 :45^{1}1:15^{3}gd *2 117 7^{4¼} 7^{3¼} 6^{3¼} 2^{hd} McCrrCJ^7 ⒻLs CngsH 81-20 ImperilStr,DownAgin,ServN'Volly 10
26Mar89—Bumped 3/8
17Mar89-8SA a6½f Ⓣ:21^2 :43^{3}1:14^{3}fm 4¾ 114 7^{5¾} 6^5 4^2 3^1 McCrrCJ^7 Sra Mdre H 85-14 Oraibi, Lordalik, Down Again 9
17Mar89—Grade III; Wide into stretch
28Jan89-3SA a6½f Ⓣ:22^1 :44^{3}1:14^{2}fm 2¼ 121 2^2 2^{2½} 2^{½} 2^{nk} McCrrnCJ^1 ⒻAw55000 87-13 GoldenGalaxy,DownAgin,Nture'sWy 6
6Aug88-8Dmr 1$\frac{1}{16}$ Ⓣ:46^{3}1:10^{2}1:41^{2}fm *2 120 5^5 5^{3½} 5^4 6^{3½} BlackCA^6 Ⓕ[R]Osnts H 89-09 Choritzo, My Virginia Reel, Fiara 6
6Aug88—Run in divisions; Wide into stretch
●Aug 6 Dmr 4f ft :47 Hg Jly 19 SA 6f ft 1:13^4 Hg Jly 5 SA 6f ft 1:13^3 Hg Jun 29 SA 4f ft :47^1 Hg

***Happy Toss** Dk. b. or br. c. 4, by Egg Toss—Hirosante, by Practicante
TORO F **115** Br.—Haras La Biznaga (Arg) 1989 3 2 1 0 $8,434
Own.—Bligh-de Burgh-Lima Tr.—Jones Gary 1988 9 3 1 1 $12,236
Lifetime 12 5 2 1 $20,670 Turf 5 1 2 0 $7,280

4Mar89♦9SanIsidro(Arg) a1 1:36^{3}sf *7-5 122 Ⓣ 2^{1½} VldvsoJ Cl America(Gr2) Rastafarian,HppyToss,HlconPotsio 7
12Feb89♦3Hipodromo(Arg) a1 1:34^{1}ft *2-5 122 1^{1½} VldivsoJ Cl Parguy(Gr3) HppyToss,HlconPotsio,AmricnToss 7
21Jan89♦9SanIsidro(Arg) a1 1:34^{4}fm*3-5 120 Ⓣ 1^{1½} VldivsoJ Cl Hrio Bstlo(Gr3) HappyToss,CapoMaximo,PndeLujo 4
30Dec88♦11Hipodromo(Arg) a1 1:36^{2}ft 2½ 119 1^6 VldivisoJ Cl Librtad(Gr3) HappyToss,CapoMaximo,MontePirt 7
11Dec88♦10SanIsidro(Arg) a1 3:21 gd 6 119 Ⓣ 7^{13} ShnP GP J S d Anchrn(Gr1) Companion, Fetichero, Bacache 10
6Nov88♦7Hipodromo(Arg) a1$\frac{3}{16}$ 2:33^{1}ft 7 126 9^{24} SahginP Gr Pr Ncnl(Gr1) Indalecio, Ultrasonido, Titiritero 14
14Oct88♦7Hipodromo(Arg) a1⅜ 2:15^{3}ft *2-3 126 1^2 ShginP Cl Edrdo Csy(Gr2) Happy Toss, Titiritero, Que Bravo 6
2Oct88♦7SanIsidro(Arg) a1¼ 2:02^{3}sf 8 123 Ⓣ 13^{50} ShginP Gr Pr Jky Clb (Gr1) Ultrasonido, SavageToss, Egineso 18
●Aug 3 Dmr Ⓣ 7f fm 1:28^2 H (d) Jly 28 Dmr 6f ft 1:11^1 H Jly 21 SA 6f ft 1:12^3 H Jly 16 SA 5f ft 1:01^2 H

The four records are difficult to decipher as to relative class, with the mare Davie's Lamb exiting a clever classified score, and both mares showing good races in a Grade 2 stakes.

The colt Happy Toss, from Argentina, is almost impossible

to classify, and the five-year-old You're No Bargain, while impressive, does not show a graded stakes in its record.

What to do? The odds at post time reflected the bettors' apprehensions.

You're No Bargain	7–5
Davie's Lamb	4–1
Down Again	7–2
Happy Toss	2–1

Happy Toss won, You're No Bargain finished second, and the males drew away from the females decisively in the lane.

In close nonclaiming situations, favor males over females. Only when the females look absolutely best, no reservations, do they figure to win.

EIGHTH RACE
Del Mar
AUGUST 10, 1989

1 MILE.(Turf). (1.34⅕) CLASSIFIED ALLOWANCE. Purse $60,000. 3-year-olds and upward which are non-winners of $18,000 twice other than closed or claiming at one mile or over in 1989. Weights, 3-year-olds, 116 lbs.; older, 121 lbs. Non-winners of such a race since June 10 allowed 2 lbs.; of such a race since March 1, 4 lbs.; of such a race in 1989 or such a race any distance since April 24, 6 lbs.

Value of race $60,000; value to winner $33,000; second $12,000; third $9,000; fourth $4,500; fifth $1,500. Mutuel pool $253,835. Exacta pool $193,822.

Last Raced	Horse	Eqt.A.Wt	PP	St	¼	½	¾	Str	Fin	Jockey	Odds $1
4Mar89 9Arg2	Happy Toss	4 115	4	5	5	5	5	5	1¹	Toro F	2.30
24Jly89 3Hol2	You're No Bargain	5 117	1	1	1¹½	1½	1½	1¹½	2¹½	Pincay L Jr	1.40
29Jly89 8Dmr5	Down Again	5 114	3	4	3½	3¹	4¹½	2½	3²½	Black C A	3.50
27Jly89 8Dmr1	Davie's Lamb	5 116	2	2	2½	2¹	2ʰᵈ	4½	4ⁿᵏ	Davis R G	4.10
31Jly89 8Dmr8	No Commitment	4 115	5	3	4²½	4¹½	3ʰᵈ	3ʰᵈ	5	Stevens G L	14.60

OFF AT 5:46 Start good. Won driving. Time, :24, :47⅘, 1:11⅘, 1:36⅕ Course firm.

$2 Mutuel Prices:

4–HAPPY TOSS	6.60	3.40	2.60
1–YOU'RE NO BARGAIN		3.20	2.40
3–DOWN AGAIN			2.40

$5 EXACTA 4–1 PAID $39.50.

Dk. b. or br. c, by Egg Toss—Hirosante, by Practicante. Trainer Jones Gary. Bred by Haras La Biznaga (Arg).

HAPPY TOSS, unhurried while trailing early after being slow to begin, came into the stretch five wide, accelerated once in the stretch for the drive to close with a rush, reached the front a little less than a sixteenth out and proved best. YOU'RE NO BARGAIN established the early pace without being hustled, had a clear advantage at the furlong marker, jumped course marks soon after passing the furlong marker to lose a bit of momentum, was overtaken by HAPPY TOSS not long thereafter but held on for the place. DOWN AGAIN, close up early, had to bide her time on the far turn when boxed in while still close up, looked dangerous a furlong out after getting a clear path but did not have the needed additional response in the final furlong. DAVIE'S LAMB forced the early pace without being hustled and gave way gradually in the last quarter. NO COMMITMENT, in contention early, moved up to lodge a bid at the quarter pole, could not sustain his bid in the last quarter and was four wide into the stretch.

THREE-YEAR-OLDS & UP

However the rumor began that three-year-olds can't beat their elders, the cost to the American horseplayer has been irreparable.

Gazing upon a field of paper contestants, 3up, grizzled railbirds cannot avoid the throwaway remark, "He's only a three-year-old," meaning, of course, no way can this horse win. In a more refined vernacular, the same attitude is expressed ad nauseam in the nation's turf clubs.

In fact, three-year-olds can beat older horses, and sometimes should be expected to, depending upon the conditions of eligibility. Or, to simplify, depending upon the kinds of races at hand.

If maidens of summer, 3up, will run, do handicappers prefer a four-year-old that has never won a race? How about a five-year-old? I think not.

Time of the season is also pertinent. Studies of the running times of races limited to three-year-olds reveal the typical times (pars) are slower by lengths than the typical times of older horses of comparable class, but the differences decrease as the season progresses.

In sprints, three-year-olds are slower by three fifths on January 1, by two fifths on April 15, and by one fifth on July 1. Not until November 1 do time differences disappear entirely.

At 1 1/16 miles, three-year-olds are slower by seven fifths on January 1, by a second on April 15, and by three fifths on July 1. Come November 1, three-year-olds at the route are still slower, by one fifth of a second, approximately a length.

These findings apply rigorously to claiming races. The inference that three-year-old claiming horses cannot challenge their elders successfully in spring, summer, and early fall is largely correct, notably at the route.

So the matter of three-year-olds & up is a mixed bag. The crucial variables are eligibility conditions and time of the season. Handicappers need to know in what kinds of races three-year-olds stand a greater or lesser chance. They must also know what month it is, a rather self-evident concern.

Regarding eligibility conditions, the laundry list below informs racegoers in what races open to 3up either the three-year-olds or older horses should be preferred. Clarifying comments are added, as necessary.

Maiden	three-year-olds

As intimated, any racehorse that reaches the summer of its four-year-old campaign winless is scarcely an attractive proposition today. Three-year-olds should be strongly preferred in maiden races for 3up, almost without exception.

In winter, when older maiden races are restricted to 4up, invoking similar logic, prefer only four-year-olds.

The logic does not extend to maiden-claiming races. Now age is irrelevant. The horses are not only winless, but also classless. If a five-year-old has run faster than the others, prefer the five-year-old.

Alw, NW1X2XMC	three-year-olds

The preliminary nonwinners allowance races are dominated by better nonclaiming three-year-olds en route to the stakes. These young tigers should be expected to maul older horses that have not yet won one or two allowance races, and do.

Toward the end of the year, mid-fall and later, the most talented three-year-olds will have progressed to advanced conditions. Leftover three-year-olds are less talented. Four-year-olds that have defeated older claiming horses at medium to high selling prices on the local schedules might revisit the preliminary nonwinners allowances, and succeed.

The prospect of a victorious return can be especially seductive in the nonwinners-twice allowance race, if attempted by a four-year-old that previously has won one allowance race, and since has beaten older claiming horses at high selling prices. These multiple winners boast a touch of class, enough to handle ordinary nonclaiming three-year-olds.

Of course, should a truly impressive, lightly raced three-year-old remain eligible for the preliminary nonwinners allowance races of fall, it goes to the head of the class. The races were written for precisely that kind of three-year-old, not for four-year-old claiming horses.

Alw, NW3X4XMC	better three-year-olds

The advanced nonwinners allowances require an extra dimension of class, ideally the well-connected, lightly raced, nicely bred three-year-old that has done everything asked of it, and might be any kind.

Handicappers credit the three-year-olds that already have annexed an open stakes, or finished close in any stakes. They discount any horse that has been entered for a claim. If the lightly raced, impressively improving three-year olds are absent, prefer four-year-olds of the same description.

Advanced nonwinners allowances are susceptible to the same late-season ramifications that complicate preliminary nonwinners races, with a twist. The truly talented three-year-olds have moved on. But now the claiming horses revisiting the allowances should have won a pair of allowance races themselves, and should be unadulterated gems in the claiming game. Stakesquality horses must be missing. So must those lightly raced, rampantly improving three-year-olds.

Classified allowance, three year olds
highly restricted

The exact conditions of eligibility here are critical. The conditions must bar any older horse that has won a single race offering a relatively moderate winner's share for approximately nine months. Older horses, notably stakes winners, that have accomplished anything in the nonclaiming division for a long time will be barred. The lightly raced, impressively improving three-year-olds gliding through the nonwinners allowances as if they might be something special will be eligible, the winning shares of the nonwinners races being less than the specified prices of the classified race. Those three-year-olds fit a highly restricted classified race superbly, and might trounce the opponents they find there.

A few cautions, however. A solid, older nonclaiming horse that has been lightly raced since the specified date of the classified race may be rounding into top form, and spank the three-year-olds.

So might an older stakes winner returning to the races following a long vacation, but warming-up noticeably. Claiming horses will also be eligible, and the highest-priced older claiming horses that once won allowance races and today will be particularly well-suited to the distance, footing, and probable pace, will be a handful for the improving three-year-olds.

So while certain three-year-olds can be preferred in highly restricted classified races, they may be outgunned, after all.

Classified allowance, older horses
minimally restricted

These classified races are not very restricted at all, barring only multiple stakes winners of recent months, and the best older horses on the grounds. Purses are large. The fields will be jammed with runners-up in open and graded stakes, a few recent open-stakes winners, and inveterate classified horses that earn a proud income in these races. Developing three-year-olds do not belong, notwithstanding their potential.

Stakes races   older horses

Until the middle of fall, three-year-olds do not mix well with older stakes horses. Most three-year-olds that brave these races get banged around badly.

An exception is the restricted stakes for 3up that bars former stakes winners, a soft spot for impressively improving three-year-olds. Restricted stakes limited to state-breds can be easy pickings as well for better three-year-olds previously preoccupied with Kentucky-breds and Florida-breds in the allowances and open stakes. In both situations, the latest numerical ratings earned by the three-year-olds will be clearly superior to anything in the field.

Obvious exceptions are the season's handful of super deluxe three-year-olds, distinguished already by their performances in the spring classics. By late summer or early fall, the truly outstanding three-year-olds will be challenging the stars of the older division in selected graded stakes. Their fate from season to season depends upon the quality of the older handicap division.

Under normal conditions, when the older handicap division is led by champions, near-champions, and classic winners of its own, a three-year-old must be genuinely supreme to defeat them. If the leaders of the older handicap division are talented but forgettable, ranking three-year-olds figure to upset.

But the bottom line for unexceptional three-year-olds in the stakes is harsh. Prefer older horses to three-year-olds in open, listed, and graded stakes of spring, summer, and fall.

Claiming races, older horses
all prices

If veteran railbirds would restrict the assertion that three-year-olds cannot beat older horses to claiming races, they would be correct more than 80 percent of the time. Three-year-olds will be outrun by older claiming horses in races of comparable class. No exceptions.

If three-year-olds plunge in class while challenging older claiming horses, they will probably lose anyhow.

The superior numerical ratings earned by three-year-olds in claiming races limited to that age group do not transfer well to comparable claiming races open to older horses. If a three-year-old entered against older claimers presents the high figure in the field, inspect the probable pace carefully. If the pace will quicken today, expect the three-year-old's numbers to decline. Next calculate turn times. If the three-year-old's turn times have been slower than other contenders', discard the three-year-old.

Anytime a three-year-old runs powerfully, or respectably, in a claiming race open to older horses, and resurfaces in a claiming race limited to three-year-olds, mark the horse up. That kind of three-year-old may be the best bet of the day, week, or month.

To less extent, the opportunity persists the next winter, when the three-year-olds turn four. If new four-year-olds impress against claiming horses 4up, they might stick out if rebounding in claiming races of comparable class but limited to new four-year-olds.

With so many three-year-olds scattered about the contemporary racing scene, it's long past the moment when handicappers should strive to know them better. An understanding of which racing conditions favor three-year-olds and which do not becomes a meaningful point of departure.

STATE-BREDS VS. OPEN COMPETITION

Statewide breeding programs have flourished in the past decade, state-breds now appearing daily on every major racing card in the nation. Most tracks have welcomed the horses, if less than enthusiastically, to support racing calendars that resisted the rampaging inflation of the 1970s by expanding to their end points.

To boost the state-bred programs, local owners and breeders have contributed to funds that pay premiums to the same owners and breeders whose horses win races. The state-bred premium awards are attached to local purses.

The mix of incentives that stimulates breeding in the home state has evolved into the anomaly whereby state-bred races run slower but pay better. The paradox has complicated, but not seriously, the practices of handicappers that rely upon earnings and relative class as bases for comparing horses.

Versatile handicappers have been sustained in their comparisons by the practical circumstance that state-breds run unmistakably slower than horses in open races of comparable class, or even of inferior class. Local handicappers rarely mistake a state-bred $20,000 claiming horse as superior to a legitimate $20,000 claiming horse, any superior earnings of the state-bred horse notwithstanding.

Time differences being as gross as they tend to be, handicappers generally can evaluate state-breds in relation to comparable open competition by numerical ratings—adjusted times, speed figures, pace ratings, turn times, and early speed. State-breds usually will be rated despairingly lower than counterparts exiting open races. As a general rule, too, state-breds switched to open races must be rated superior to other contenders to figure. This happens, but infrequently.

In addition, in claiming races limited to state-breds, numerical ratings carry the cause. Differences in running times of similar or comparable state-bred races can fluctuate wildly as well, and numerical ratings reflect the chaos. Recreational handicappers can take it for granted that effective figure handicapping unravels state-bred races exceedingly well. This book's pace ratings will perform more than adquately.

Handicappers of southern California and New York encounter unique headaches in comparing state-breds and open competition, New Yorkers having the worst of it.

In southern California, statewide breeding incentives have persevered for generations, but a dramatic change for the good transpired approximately a decade ago when breeders were permitted to send mares to Kentucky sires, drop the resulting foals in California, breed back to a California sire, and still register the Kentucky-sired horse as a Cal-bred. Prior to that, mares could not leave California without surrendering their progeny's eligibility to the Cal-bred premium programs, an insane policy that assured the improvement of the breed in California would be piecemeal and slow.

As more and more mares returned to California bearing Kentucky-sired foals, and productive sires were recruited to service those mares on the rebound, Cal-bred races improved. Cal-bred maidens and medium-scaled claiming horses run roughly one-fifth slower on average than comparable horses in open races. When Cal-bred maidens and claiming horses shift in and out of open and restricted races, southern California handicappers treat them interchangeably without a blink.

In contrast to southern California, the New York state-bred program is newborn, less than two decades old. But mares of New York were encouraged to ship to Kentucky from the outset. The early results have been predictably uneven, the majority of New York–bred races remaining significantly slower than comparable open races, but specific state-bred horses and fields quite impressive. New York handicappers must recognize specifically which state-bred races were comparable to open races, and which state-bred horses can upset under unrestricted conditions. In the Big Apple's comprehensive, richly funded program, it's a sticky problem.

As the competition stiffens, the disparity in all jurisdictions between state-bred performances and open performances grows more extreme. In the allowances and stakes, only specific state-bred races and specific state-bred horses qualify for comparable open competition, and not many do. As New Yorkers generally must adapt, local handicappers must know specifically which state-bred races and horses excel.

For example, the 1989 California Breeders' Champion Stakes, a seven-furlong state-bred sprint at Santa Anita, in January, purse of $125,000-added, was taken by a terrific son of Flying Paster named Past Ages. The adjusted times were splendidly fast at every call:

22.1   45   1:09.2   1:21.4

The seven-furlong stakes par at Santa Anita is 1:22 flat.

The California Breeders' Champion Stakes is normally completed seven fifths to two seconds slower. But Past Ages was not a typical Cal-bred, and neither were Flying Continental nor Very Personally, the runners-up in the January stakes. The three Cal-breds readily competed in open and graded stakes, and everyone in the southern California handicapping directory knew it. Two local handicappers, shrewdly competent each, even took the 100–1 odds on Past Ages proffered early in the Kentucky Derby Future Book.

The lesson generalizes to the several state-bred programs. In the allowances and stakes, certain state-bred races and specific state-bred horses transfer readily to open competition, and handicappers must grasp the particulars to adapt.

Not coincidentally, the sires of the top three finishers in the 1989 Breeders' Champion Stakes in southern California were leaders of the stateside pack:

Finishers	Sires
1. Past Ages	Flying Paster
2. Very Personably	Pretense
3. Flying Continental	Flying Paster

In most state-bred programs a handful of productive sires predominate. Local handicappers become attuned to the consistent local sires, and will be prone, rightly, to accept their offspring, not only in state-bred races, but also in comparable open competition.

Handicappers of southern California realize that anything deposited on the racetrack by Flying Paster, Desert Wine, Pretense, The Irish Lord, Pirate's Bounty, and a few other well-established brethren can excel beyond the customary Cal-bred boundaries, and that Flying Paster has been compiling a track record that soon may certify his national prestige.

To a less established degree, perhaps, the same is true of other state-bred programs. A handful of sires excel, and their progeny often perform well in open races. Recreational handicappers should commit the names of the most successful local sires to memory.

Certain class maneuvers from state-bred to open races, and vice versa, warrant special attention from handicappers.

The maneuver from open medium-priced claiming races to nonwinners allowance races restricted to state-breds can constitute a cleverly deceptive drop in class. If the claiming race were completed in respectable time, and the state-bred horse dispensed an acceptable performance, it's a legitimate contender, maybe a probable winner, in the state-bred allowance affair.

The converse does not hold. The transition from the state-bred allowances to mid-level open claiming competition represents a steep step-up for most state-breds. Unless the state-bred race looks atypically fast or contentious, the winner and close runners-up impressive, and the adjusted final time comparable to the typical times of comparable open races, discount the state-breds.

Drops from state-bred stakes to open overnight conditions can be trickier. The adjusted times of the state-bred stakes should be superior to the typical times (pars) of the overnight races. Lean on numerical ratings as best indicators. Subjective comparisons are often vague and indirect.

Class rises from overnight conditions to state-bred stakes can be treated similarly. Where numerical ratings have been comparable to those of state-bred stakes winners, the unrestricted overnight races were probably classier, perhaps decidedly better.

At all racetracks, all classes, the maneuver of greatest intrigue—up or down—is from open competition to state-bred restrictions. Class standouts reside here. If the open race looks better, and numerical ratings of any kind reinforce that perception, trust the open competition. A few mistakes each season may pinch, but the successes will keep the state-bred ledger comfortably in the black.

THE EARNINGS BOX

The earnings box has been a fatality of contemporary racing.

With purse inflation, a proliferation of stakes, state-bred premium programs, and the faster development of younger horses the trends of the times, money-won is no longer a reliable index of ability. It's just as much a happenstance of circumstance. Racegoers who continue to depend upon gross earnings, average earnings, and average purse values to make class distinctions have been out of step with a changing game.

The signals were clear on the matter as early as the late seventies. Probability studies revealed that gross earnings and average purse value correlated no better than randomly with race outcomes. Average earnings correlated significantly better, horses highest on average earnings winning better than half again as many races as probabilities would expect. Unfortunately, the horses also tossed substantial financial losses. The crowd over-bets top money-makers.

What, if anything, can modern handicappers do with the earnings box?

First, they can understand that earnings are not a valid measure of ability. Do not use earnings to evaluate class or to predict race outcomes.

But average purse value, or purse-size that horses have competed successfully for—meaning a good race, not necessarily a winning race—can be a fairly accurate measure of consistency. Consistent horses can be attractive as the undersides of exactas, notably at generous odds. Perhaps handicappers of today can resort to the earnings box to complete their exacta formulations.

In the mid-eighties, Bill Quirin demonstrated that the fashionable formulas for calculating average purse values actually measured consistency, not ability.

The formulas apply the purse-distribution percentages in the state to horses' numbers of wins, seconds, thirds, and fourths during a representative period of a season. Where this season's record is not representative, last season's is substituted.

In New York, for example, the winner receives 60 percent of the purse. A horse's number of wins would be multiplied by .60. New York gives 22 percent to second finishers, so the number of seconds is multiplied by .22. Thirds are multiplied by .12 and fourths by .06. When the products are summed and divided into gross earnings for the period, the quotient represents the average purse for which the horse has competed successfully.

Quirin showed that two horses having ten similar starts apiece, Horse A winning all ten races, Horse B running third in all ten, would be rated equally by the formula. In each race, the purse is assumed as $25,000. The arithmetic is persuasive:

Horse A	10–10–0–0	$150,000	($25,000 × .6 = 15,000)
Horse B	10–0–0–10	$ 30,000	($25,000 × .12 = 3,000)

To apply the average-purse-value formula, Horse A's wins (10) are multiplied by .6, to obtain a value of 6. Earnings ($150,000) divided by 6 equals an average purse value of $25,000.

Horse B's thirds (10) are multiplied by .12, to obtain a value of 1.2. Earnings ($30,000) divided by 1.2 equals an average purse value, you guessed it, of $25,000.

Thus a horse that wins all ten starts is rated equal to a horse that finishes third ten consecutive times. That's a measure of consistency, not ability.

A final step determines whether a horse's earning power qualifies it as a stronger or weaker candidate in today's exacta. Divide the horse's average purse value (APV) by today's purse. A quotient greater than 1 is positive, below 1 negative. Horses having APVs significantly greater than 1 can be included in exacta combinations. Their consistency in races bearing purses typically richer than today's suggests they have an unusually positive chance of finishing in-the-money.

To illustrate, we apply the APV formula to a pair of interesting contenders in an overnight handicap at Saratoga 1989, where the New York purse distribution again applies. Both horses won their last start. Which is likelier to complete the exacta?

5th Saratoga

1 1/16 MILES. (Turf). (1.39 2/5) HANDICAP. Purse $47,000. 3-year-olds and upward. Weights Wednesday, August 16. Declarations by 10:00 a.m. Thursday, August 17.

Turning For Home — B. g. 5, by Circle Home—Barbara's Reason, by Hail to Reason
Br.—ANW EnterprisesInc&Winick (Fla) — 1989 14 3 3 1 $108,100
Own.—Cedar Valle Stable — 114 — Tr.—Lenzini John J Jr — 1988 19 2 2 6 $80,580
Lifetime 67 11 14 14 $287,471 — Turf 34 7 4 8 $205,120

4Aug89-7Sar 1 1/16 (T):47 1:111 1:434fm 18 117 812 68 53 11 1/4 Antley C W 9 Aw47000 78-18 TrnngForHom,SvrgnJstc,RcngStr 10
24Jly89-3Bel 1 1/16 (T):473 1:112 1:421fm *2 122 42 1/2 42 1/2 44 54 3/4 Samyn J L 6 100000 80-19 SoverignJustic,MgntCov,Conquilot 8
1Jly89-5Bel 1 1/16 [T]:482 1:114 1:421fm 6 1/2 117 42 1/2 41 3/4 41 3/4 4 1/2 Cordero AJr 1 Aw47000 89-15 Major Beard, High Browser Win 7
1Jly89—Altered course
18Jun89-6Bel 1 :451 1:094 1:353ft 9 3/4 117 44 1/2 44 1/2 56 1/4 49 McCuleyWH 5 Aw37000 78-21 Fast Play, Cef's Miste Modes... 6
10Jun89-5Bel 1 1/16 (T):503 1:161 1:481sf *6-5e 113 62 1/4 62 3/4 65 47 1/4 Cordero A Jr 1 HcpO 46-43 AllHandsOnDeck,Whoom,Forest... 6
10Jun89—Poor start
29May89-4Bel 1 1/16 [T]:50 1:134 1:44 sf 2 3/4 119 52 31 1/2 1hd 2no McCuleyWH 6 Aw37000 81-21 LordBd,TrnngForHom,StrongRbuo 7
19May89-8Bel 1 :47 1:10 1:35 ft 18 112 43 1/2 33 1/2 54 64 Samyn J L 2 HcpO 86-16 TruendBlue,ForeverSilvr,ItsAcdmr 6
23Apr89-7Aqu 1 1/8 (T):472 1:121 1:501fm 3 120 63 51 1/4 1hd 1hd Cordero A Jr 6 95000 84-14 TrnngForHom,FrColony,ClsscMov 10
23Apr89—Came in drvng
Aug 15 Sar tr.t 5f ft 1:04 B — Jly 31 Sar (T) 4f fm :48 H — Jly 19 Aqu 4f ft :48 H — Jly 12 Aqu 4f ft :45 B

Wanderkin — Ch. g. 6, by Dewan—Plum's Sister, by Quadrangle
Br.—Flying Zee Stable (NY) — 1989 1 1 0 0 $28,200
Own.—Poma Stable — 122 — Tr.—O'Connell Richard — 1988 14 5 3 1 $313,916
Lifetime 41 15 5 5 $565,222 — Turf 26 12 4 3 $505,748

23Apr89-5Aqu 1 1/8 (T):47 1:112 1:433fm *1 122 43 21 1/2 1hd 1nk Antley C W 5 HcpO 87-14 Wnderkin,ClevrScrt,AllHndsOnDck 7
20Nov88-8Hol 1 1/8 (T):463 1:101 1:463fm 15 117 43 1/2 53 1011 1114 1/4 PncyLJr 11 Citation H 81-10 Forlitno,Prcisionist,SkipOutFront 11
20Nov88—Grade II
23Oct88-7Lrl 1 1/4 (T):474 1:374 2:03 fm 11 126 32 1/2 2 1/2 97 3/4 1116 1/4 PincayLJr 9 Bud Int'l 66-15 SunshineForevr,FrnklyPrfct,Squill 14
23Oct88—Grade I

80ct88-8Bel   1 ⊤:48⁴¹:144¹:42 sf 2¾ 119   2½ 42¼ 7¹⁵ 722¾ Davis R G⁴ Kelso H 32-60 Sn'stheShdow,Posen,Tinch'n'sPrinc 7
  80ct88—Grade III
30Sep88-9Med 1₁₆⊤:45 1:08³¹:39²fm 3 118   37¼ 3⁴ 2ʰᵈ 1ⁿᵏ Davis RG² Cliff Hgr H 103-05 Wnderkin,SlemDrive,Sn'stheShdow 9
  30Sep88—Grade III
18Sep88-3Bel 1₁₆⊤:49¹¹:131¹:433gd 9-5 122   3² 31½ 2ʰᵈ 11½ Antley C W⁸ HcpO 83-30 Wanderkin, Yucca, I Rejoice   8
3Sep88-9Mth 1⅛⊤:48 1:11⁴¹:494fm⁴4-5 117   31¼ 41¾ 21½ 2² SntsJA 2 Longfelow H 96-07 Tritemtri,Wnderkin,ArrivedOnTime 9
  3Sep88—Grade II; Jostled
14Aug88-8Sar 1⅛⊤:47 1:09⁴¹:46⁴fm 5¾ 115   5⁵ 44½ 42¼ 3¾ SntosJA ⁸ B Baruch H 92-14 My Big Boy, Steinlen, Wanderkin 9
  14Aug88—Grade I
 ●Aug 9 Sar ⑦ 6f fm 1:14³ H (d)   Aug 3 Sar ⑦ 6f fm 1:15¹ B (d)   Jly 27 Bel ⊤ 4f fm :49 B (d)   Jly 20 Bel ⊤ 4f sf :51³ B (d)

Using Turning For Home's 1989 earnings box, the arithmetic is $(3 \times .60) + (3 \times .22) + (1 \times .12) + (3 \times .06)$—note the three fourth-place finishes in the past performances—for a value of 2.76. When $108,100 is divided by 2.76, Turning For Home's APV is $39,166. When $39,166 is divided by today's purse of $47,000, the resulting APV index is 0.83. Turning For Home has been competing successfully for purses lower than today's. Its latest win at Saratoga amounts to an upset, as the odds indicate as well, and might not be repeated.

Using Wanderkin's 1988 earnings box, we get $313,916 divided by 3.78, or an APV of $83,046. When $83,046 is divided by today's purse of $47,000, the resulting APV index is 1.76.

Wanderkin has been competing successfully for purses significantly larger than today's. On earnings power, Wanderkin has been consistent at a richer level. The gelding is a stronger statistical bet to complete the Saratoga exacta than is Turning For Home.

If average purse value will be used at all, this is the way to do it. To honor consistency, not ability.

When evaluating claiming horses 4up, average earnings during the past season can be invoked as a measure of ability and consistency combined. If an older claiming horse's last qualifies as a good race, and it shows the highest average earnings in the field, the horses will finish first or second twice as often as probabilities would expect. Support these horses at attractive odds, and box them in exactas with other main contenders.

Be careful when analyzing the earning power of younger, lightly raced thoroughbreds. Rely upon the appropriate APV formula to evaluate developing horses' consistency, but do not confuse their consistency with their ability. Younger horses with attractive earnings do not figure to win for that reason alone.

PEAKING FORM

When can horses be expected to strut their absolute best?

The position that acceptable form accommodates the competitive requirements of a majority of races, as this book argues, does not mean handicappers should ignore the fine points of the form factor late in the decision-making process. Acceptable form is not interchangeable with improving form, or peaking form, among evenly matched contenders, the latter condition being almost irresistible.

The trick is to recognize peaking form before it has been expressed on the racetrack for everyone to behold. One highly identifiable pattern that precurses peak performance combines the twin elements of positive form.

First, significantly improved form in competition, or a much-improved race.

Second, significantly improved workouts in relation to prior workouts following the much-improved race.

Whenever this double-edged positive pattern appears, handicappers can expect a peaked performance to follow. Alerted handicappers, moreover, should not have undue difficulty in spotting peaking form, although experience can make a big difference.

Here's an excellent example:

Sewickley

B. c. 4, by Star De Naskra—Surgery, by Dr Fager
Br.—Evans Robert S (NJ)

Own.—Evans R S   **119**   Tr.—Schulhofer Flint S

Lifetime 16 7 3 0 $210,818

1989	9	4	2	0	$148,418
1988	5	2	1	0	$44,400
Turf	1	0	0	0	

15Jly89-8Bel 7f :23 :453 1:24 ft 3½ 119 66½ 45½ 21½ 13 RomrRP 5 Tom Fool 82-20 Sewickley, Houston,CrusaderSword 6
 15Jly89—Grade II
21Jun89-8Bel 1 ⊤:4521:1011:352gd 5 113 66½ 55 88½ 815½ Romero R P6 HcpO 73-18 Fourstardave, Closing Bid, War 10
20May89-7Bel 7f :221 :45 1:213ft 6½ 124 56 52½ 2½ 2nk • Romero R P1 Aw41000 94-17 SeekingtheGold,Swickly,CliffFlowr 5
6May89-8Aqu 7f :214 :434 1:212ft 10 111 74½ 63½ 75½ 63½ Bailey JD4 Carter H 91-19 OnTheLine,TruendBlu,Dr.Crrington 8
 6May89—Grade I
14Apr89-8Kee 7f :23 :454 1:222ft 5½ 115 65½ 88 2hd 1¾ RmrRP5 Com Brd Cup 94-15 Sewickley, IrishOpen,Danc'ngSpree 9
30Mar89-8Aqu 7f :23 :462 1:232ft *2-3 121 32 32 2½ 2½ Santos J A1 Aw41000 83-31 Phone Bid, Sewickley, WinterDrive 4
20Feb89-9GP 7f :224 :454 1:23 ft *3-2 117 63 42½ 1hd 1½ Romero R P8 Aw24000 89-32 Sewickley,NorthstrProspect,PrintII 8
11Feb89-5GP 1⅟₁₆:474 1:124 1:451ft 2½ 115 33—24½ 53½ 66½ Romero R P4 Aw29000 69-25 BoldMidwy,FstForwrd,RonStevens 7
 Aug 14 Sar 5f m 1:01 H   ● Aug 9 Sar 6f ft 1:114 H   Aug 4 Sar 5f ft 1:013 H   Jly 29 Sar 4f ft :502 B

In the ninth start of its four-year-old season, the undistinguished seven-furlong specialist Sewickley delivers a Big Win over the brilliant Houston in a Grade 2 stakes, after gaining striking position from behind a slow pace. Following that, the Belmont horses van to Saratoga, and Sewickley records a six-furlong best-of-morning workout in 1:11.4 seconds.

Sewickley certainly was no slouch prior to the Grade 2 smash, but the much-improved race, followed by the significantly improved workout, indicates a peak performance upcoming. Both conditions must be present, and associated. The much-improved race intensifies current form, and the much-improved workouts that follow both reflect peaking form and presage peak performance.

A somewhat different illustration:

After remaining an also-ran throughout the spring classics for three-year-olds of 1989, Hawkster glowed in its initial grass try. The conditioning pattern that followed included the fastest five-furlong workout of the season on Del Mar's deep turf, a best-of-morning 1:00.2 around the dogs.

Hawkster next appeared in the Grade 2 Del Mar Derby, on turf, and a peak performance was envisioned, publicly by the trainer and privately by form analysts. Hawkster romped by seven lengths and paid $8.20.

Peaking form can be recognized in claiming races as well, but the following example does not quite satisfy:

***Millero Y Medio *** B. g. 8, by Mr Long—Maria Blanca, by Blakemere
BLACK C A 116 Br.—Haras Santa Amelia (Chile) 1989 2 0 0 1 $3,900
Own.—Pulliam C N Tr.—Pulliam Vivian M $32,000 1988 17 1 2 1 $52,650
Lifetime 68 12 12 9 $132,147 Turf 34 3 3 3 $63,227
7Aug89-7Dmr 1 :454 1:11 1:364ft 12 117 58½ 58 47 35 Desilva A J 3 32000 77-20 SmrtGuy,PureExpense,Mil'roYMdio 5
7Aug89—Wide final 3/8
9Jly89-9Hol 1⅛ Ⓣ:4811:1241:49 fm 29 115 1013 108¾ 1012 1015¼ Sibille R5 Aw33000 68-14 Wrethm,ImpossibleStrem,Wroquir 10
14Oct88-5SA 1¼ Ⓣ:4531:3431:594fm 22 116 1218 1213 1215 1013½ Patterson A 7 80000 74-12 DysGoneBy,DefinitSigns,LckRson 12
5Sep88-8Dmr 1⅜ Ⓣ:5011:3912:154fm 85 109 86½ 116¾ 119¾ 1010¼ DmngRE 1 Dmr Iv H 80-15 SwordDnc,GrtCommnctor,BbKrm 11
5Sep88—Grade II
19Aug88-8Dmr 1⅜ Ⓣ:4911:3912:151fm 18 110 13 11 32½ 47½ Corral J R 5 HcpO 85-07 SirHarryLewis,BbKrm,CircusPrince 5
31Jly88-8Dmr 1⅛ Ⓣ:47 1:11 1:484fm 93 108 1012 129¼ 119¾ 1011 CorrlJR 12 E Read H 78-10 DptyGovrnor,SntllMc,Smp'yMjstc 12
31Jly88—Grade I; Wide
17Jly88-9Hol 1⅛ Ⓣ:47 1:11 1:463fm *3¼ 1135 119 118¾ 85¾ 86¾ Corral J R 6 Aw40000 88-03 McKnziPrinc,TblGlow,LmmonJuic 11
26Jun88-7Hol 1¼ Ⓣ:4841:3632:004fm 7¼ 111 21 1hd 2hd 2no Corral J R 1 Ⓡ HcpO 91-09 KnghtsLgnd,MllroYMdo,RussnRovr 6
12Jun88-9Hol 1⅛ Ⓣ:4711:1031:47 fm 12 1115 65 53¾ 31½ 14½ Corral J R 2 62500 93-07 MilleroYMedio,Clrmount,BeScenic 7
12Jun88—Wide 3/8 turn
1Jun88-5Hol 1 1/16 :461 1:104 1:43 ft 10 116 75½ 64½ 77½ 67¾ Pedroza M A 5 50000 77-15 Reland, Claramount, Aloma's Tobin 8
Aug 19 Dmr 4f ft :482 H Aug 14 Dmr 5f ft 1:012 H Jly 6 Hol 4f ft :50 H Jun 30 Hol 1 ft 1:442 H

The eight-year-old Millero Y Medio shows a much-improved race, and improved workouts following, but the workouts fall short of the eye-catching kind that trigger the pattern. Peaking form is a matter of degree. The improved race, and subsequent workouts, must be of the eye-popping tradition. Millero Y Medio's race and workout pattern indicates improving form, not peaking form.

A variation of the peaking pattern finds the much-improved performance in the afternoon followed by a quick return to the races, within five days, perhaps within three days. The trainer senses a peak performance in the offing. The fast turnaround substitutes for the customary workout. The pattern qualifies as a strongly positive sign of peaking form and trainer intentions in concert.

Routinely, it's the dramatically improved workouts that precede the peaked effort, often following a short series of improving races, the last looking much the best.

Fast workouts without the context of recent races can constitute slippery evidence for many handicappers. A common amateurish mistake overrates the substance, and effects, of fast morning drills.

The magnificent misconception about workouts is that they reflect relative class. Workouts are indicators of form, not class.

Moreover, training patterns reflect the habits of horsemen, or the idiosyncracies of horses, far more than real abilities. Faster workouts can be superfluous among horses 4up, claiming horses certainly. Younger horses should exercise smartly, to be sure, but the speed and ease of workouts does not transfer reliably to the races, any more than athletic practice transfers reliably to the games.

Horses recording average workouts demolish horses recording faster workouts every day at every track in the country. Positive form allows horses to express real abilities, but only occasionally turns the tables on more talented horses.

In addition, a poorly comprehended point—slow workouts should not be interpreted negatively. The speed and frequency of workouts are not nearly as meaningful as the distances and overall workout patterns. Longer workouts are invariably preferred.

In the peaking-form pattern, when the workouts following the much-improved race occur at five furlongs or longer, the distance is reassuring. Among sprinters, a blistering five-furlong workout is fortifying, especially at minor tracks. A blistering mile workout is ideal among routers, at any track.

Of the multitudinous workout patterns that handicappers encounter as standard fare, only a few are portentous, indicating a heightened degree of positive form:

1. Four workouts within 20 days, with one demonstrating authentic speed, preferably at five furlongs or longer.

2. In comparison with ordinary to sluggish works previously, a sharp workout from the gate with blinkers on.

3. A pair of improving grass works, prior to an improving horse's turf debut.

The trainer not only takes the trouble to familiarize his charge with the new surface, but also the horse acts as if he likes it.

4. A sharp workout by a shipper at an unfamiliar track.

If the stranger's workouts are faster than typical over an unfamiliar track, the shipper can be counted upon to dispense a solid performance in the race.

5. Improving form in competition, improved workouts following.

In the extreme, the latter pattern, indicative of improving form, qualifies as the author's harbinger of peaking form, to be forthcoming in the next outing.

The top pattern, four workouts in 20 days, is a reliable guide to positive form, however ordinary the times.

The great horseman Charles Whittingham is also a classicist with workout patterns. Regular workouts, spaced five or six days apart, is characteristic of Whittingham horses, virtually without exception.

Moreover, Whittingham organizes the workout pattern meticulously, paying careful attention to the speed and distance of every succeeding drill. The trainer's workouts are lessons in horsemanship. Whittingham notoriously subscribes to a pattern of four workouts within 20 days.

Consider how meticulously the undistinguished Bracoy was prepared for its initial allowance test of August 20, 1989.

7th Del Mar

1 ₁/₁₆ MILES. (1.40) ALLOWANCE. Purse $35,000. 3-year-olds and upward, which are non-winners of $3,000 other than maiden, claiming or starter. Weights, 3-year-olds, 115 lbs.; older, 120 lbs. Non-winners of a race other than claiming at one mile or over allowed 2 lbs.

Bracoy		B. c. 4, by Green Dancer—Huggle Duggle, by Never Bend						
MCCARRON C J	120	Br.—Spendthrift Farm (Ky)				1989 3 1 1 1	$24,600	
Own.—Bradley & McCoy		Tr.—Whittingham Charles				1988 3 M 0 0		
		Lifetime 7 1 1 1 $24,600				Turf 5 1 0 0	$15,400	
24Jly89-1Hol 1₁/₁₆ ⑦:47³ 1:11⁴ 1:42³fm *6-5 122	5³ 4² 1¹ 11¼	McCarron C J¹		Mdn 81-13 Bracoy,TheM.V.P.,RunawayRoberto	9
25Jun89-4Hol 1 :45¹ 1:10² 1:35⁴ft *3-5 122	1hd 1hd 1hd 3³	McCarron C J		Mdn 81-19 EdgyDiplomat,KingArmour,Brcoy	10
4Jun89-6Hol 1₁/₁₆:47 1:11 1:43¹ft 2½ 123	1hd 2hd 2½ 2nk	McCarron C J¹¹		Mdn 84-14 NjnskysGrndson,Brcoy,KngArmor	11
4Jun89—Broke in a tangle					
18Jly88◆3Pontefract(Eng) 1¼ 2:15⁴gd 2¾ 133	⑦ 6¹⁴	Cook P	WkfldCtnryH	GulfPlce,PrsinJoy,PrciousMmoris	12
27Jun88◆6Windsor(Eng) a1¼ 2:09²gd 5⁰ 123	⑦ 5⁴	CookP	KnghtsbrdgeGrad	BashfulBoy,Duke'sLodge,BalticBy	17
7Jun88◆4Goodwood(Eng) 1¼ 2:07²gd 3³ 126	⑦ 11	CP	Weald&DwnlndMsm(Mdn)	Mwzoon,WestrnFrontir,MrMinstrl	22
30Oct87◆1Newmarket(Eng) 1 1:43³gd 3³ 122	⑦ 15	Cook P	Soham House	Kahyasi, Assatis, Hillmead	19
Aug 16 Dmr 5f ft :59 H	Aug 11 Dmr 5f ft 1:00⁴ H	Aug 6 Dmr 5f ft 1:01 H	Jly 31 Dmr 8f ft :35⁴ H		

Seven days following her maiden victory, Bracoy trains at a short three furlongs, in ordinary time. A regular pattern of five-furlong workouts follow, each successive workout faster. Four days before the allowance start, Bracoy is urged for workout speed, and responds in 59H.

It's always the same. Whittingham horses are not asked for excessive speed until considerable stamina has been developed. A foundation built, the speed drill necessitates no exertion. Whittingham horses do not lose overnight races due to any shortfall of conditioning. In the stakes, Whittingham alternates preparatory races and workouts superbly, such that peak performance coincides with the main objective. No one else has ever done it better than Charlie in the morning.

Once peaked form has been attained, it can endure, and does. A short series of regular races finds the finely tuned horses at the top of their form. In between, workouts may be slow or irregular, to maintain condition, but race performance continues to peak. Eventually, form dulls, not severely perhaps, but the sharp edge is gone.

Performances in the afternoon are now not the same. Soon the horses will need to be rested. After a respite, the conditioning process begins anew. Acceptable form submits to improving form, and improving form to peaking form, handicappers watching to anticipate the peaked performance just before it happens.

OFF TRACKS

Traditional guidance about handicapping on off tracks, if it ever made sense, amounts to nonsense today. Mud does not favor closers. Neither do slow tracks that remain wet. Regardless of the official condition of the racing strip, wet surfaces favor speed.

Consider the results charts of two races run in the mud approximately a month apart at Santa Anita 1989. Note the running times in relation to par times in the margin.

SECOND RACE
Santa Anita
JANUARY 6, 1989

6 FURLONGS. (1.07⅗) CLAIMING. Purse $11,000. 4-year-olds and upward. Weights, 4-year-olds, 120 lbs.; older, 121 lbs. Non-winners of two races since November 7 allowed 3 lbs.; of a race since then, 5 lbs. Claiming price $10,000. (Races when entered for $8,500 or less not considered.)

Value of race $11,000; value to winner $6,050; second $2,200; third $1,650; fourth $825; fifth $275. Mutuel pool $283,875.

Last Raced	Horse	Eqt	A	Wt	PP	St	¼	½	Str	Fin	Jockey	Cl'g Pr	Odds $1
18Nov88 ^{9}Hol^{7}	Hillstark		4	115	10	1	$2^{1\frac{1}{2}}$	$1^{2\frac{1}{2}}$	$1^{2\frac{1}{2}}$	$1^{1\frac{3}{4}}$	Pedroza M A	10000	2.30
18Nov88 ^{2}Hol^{9}	D.D. The Kid	b	5	117	3	10	$8^{\frac{1}{2}}$	$7^{1\frac{1}{2}}$	$4^{\frac{1}{2}}$	2no	Pincay L Jr	10000	3.50
11Dec88 ^{4}Hol^{9}	Manhattan King	b	4	110	2	6	$7^{1\frac{1}{2}}$	8^{1}	$6^{1\frac{1}{2}}$	$3^{4\frac{1}{2}}$	Corral J R^{5}	10000	9.60
24Dec88 ^{1}Hol^{5}	Master Galaxy	b	5	116	4	5	4^{1}	3^{hd}	5^{1}	$4^{\frac{1}{2}}$	Olivares F	10000	10.10
11Dec88 ^{1}Hol^{7}	Don't Fight It		7	116	1	7	$3^{\frac{1}{2}}$	$4^{\frac{1}{2}}$	$3^{\frac{1}{2}}$	$5^{1\frac{1}{4}}$	Meza R Q	10000	18.80
26Dec88 ^{1}SA^{12}	Something For Kurt	b	4	112	8	2	1^{hd}	$2^{\frac{1}{2}}$	2^{hd}	$6^{1\frac{1}{2}}$	Garcia H^{5}	10000	37.60
21Dec88 ^{5}Hol^{7}	Falpar		4	115	6	3	6^{2}	6^{1}	7^{1}	$7^{1\frac{1}{4}}$	Solis A	10000	9.70
18Dec88 ^{2}Hol^{5}	King Of California		7	116	7	8	$5^{\frac{1}{2}}$	5^{1}	8^{1}	8^{nk}	Castanon A L	10000	3.30
10Dec88 ^{8}AC^{2}	Proud Day		4	115	5	9	10	$9^{1\frac{1}{2}}$	$9^{1\frac{1}{2}}$	$9^{2\frac{1}{2}}$	Baze R A	10000	14.40
30Dec88 ^{2}Hol^{11}	Native Forecast	b	6	116	9	4	9^{1}	10	10	10	Olguin G L	10000	54.80

OFF AT 1:02 Start good. Won ridden out. Time, :22, :45, :59⅘, 1:10⅕ Track muddy.

Pars
45.2
1:11.1

$2 Mutuel Prices:

10-HILLSTARK	6.60	4.20	3.40
3-D.D. THE KID		4.60	3.20
2-MANHATTAN KING			5.00

B. c, by Graustark—Northern Pine, by Far North. Trainer Canani Julio C. Bred by Galbreath D M (Ky).

HILLSTARK, away alertly, vied for the early lead, shook clear on the far turn and maintained a clear advantage through the stretch. D.D. THE KID, off last when breaking a bit awkwardly, rallied but could not catch HILLSTARK. MANHATTAN KING, outrun early and jostled soon after the start, came into the stretch six wide and was going strongly late. MASTER GALAXY, jostled soon after the start and in contention early, entered the stretch four wide and lacked the needed response in the drive. DON'T FIGHT IT, close up early, weakened in the drive. SOMETHING FOR KURT vied for the early lead, prompted the pace on the far turn, then also weakened in the drive. FALPAR was jostled in the initial strides and again soon after the start. KING OF CALIFORNIA, a bit slow to begin and wide down the backstretch, moved up in the opening quarter, gave way in the last quarter and was five wide into the stretch. PROUD DAY, jostled in the initial strides, was four wide into the stretch. NATIVE FORECAST was wide down the backstretch. All starters wore mud calks except DON'T FIGHT IT, MASTER GALAXY, FALPAR, NATIVE FORECAST and HILLSTARK.

Owners— 1, Medall & Summertime Stable; 2, Harrington L D; 3, Hogate H; 4, McGrue V L; 5, Halle & McWilliams; 6, Wagner K J; 7, McCleary E L; 8, Lewis Marjorie; 9, Howell & Lacy III; 10, Craigmyle J.

Trainers— 1, Canani Julio C; 2, Luby Donn; 3, West Ted; 4, Byrd Adolph; 5, Scolamieri Sam J; 6, Tetzlaff Terri; 7, Stute Melvin F; 8, Carbajal Sal; 9, Schiewe David; 10, Craigmyle Scott.

Overweight: D.D. The Kid 1 pound.

D.D. The Kid was claimed by Arredondo A; trainer, Martinez Richard.

Scratched—Twelfth Of Never (26Dec88 ^{1}SA^{9}).

FIFTH RACE
Santa Anita
FEBRUARY 11, 1989

€ FURLONGS. (1.07¾) ALLOWANCE. Purse $32,000. 3-year-olds. Bred in California which have never won two races. Weight, 120 lbs. Non-winners of a race other than claiming allowed 3 lbs.

Value of race $32,000; value to winner $17,600; second $6,400; third $4,800; fourth $2,400; fifth $800. Mutuel pool $340,950. Exacta pool $542,099.

Last Raced	Horse	Eqt.A.Wt	PP	St	¼	½	Str	Fin	Jockey	Odds $1
31Dec88 4SA1	Valiant Pete	3 120	2	3	1¹	11½	12½	1¾	Pincay L Jr	.60
18Jan89 4SA1	Maui's Eagle	b 3 117	3	5	6	6	41½	23½	Delahoussaye E	5.20
29Jan89 6SA1	Ole Hank McGill	b 3 120	1	6	2½	2ʰᵈ	22	32¾	Shoemaker W	3.10
22Jly88 4Hol1	El Gorrion	3 117	6	4	5⁶	4½	31	45	Fernandez A L	12.80
2Feb89 5SA7	Matthew C.	b 3 120	5	2	41½	3ʰᵈ	52½	5⁷	Sibille R	19.70
5Feb89 6GG5	Greek Myth	b 3 117	4	1	3½	53½	6	6	Solis A	14.50

OFF AT 2:37. Start good. Won driving. Time, :22, :45¾, 1:08½, 1:14 Track muddy.

Pars
44.4
1:10.1

$2 Mutuel Prices:

2-VALIANT PETE	3.20	2.60	2.20
3-MAUI'S EAGLE		3.60	2.40
1-OLE HANK MCGILL			2.40

$5 EXACTA 2-3 PAID $31.00.

Ch. g, by The Irish Lord—Courageous Girl, by Terresto. Trainer Sadler John W. Bred by Valenti & Coelho (Cal).

VALIANT PETE our sprinted his rivals for the early lead, drew well clear in the upper stretch, weakened slightly late but was able to last. MAUI'S EAGLE lagged far back while trailing early, closed strongly but could not get up. OLE HANK MCGILL forced the early pace while saving ground after being a bit slow to begin and weakened in the drive. EL GORRION was wide down the backstretch. MATTHEW C., close up early, gave way. GREEK MYTH, close up early, faltered. No starters wore mud calks.

Owners— 1, Coelho & Valenti; 2, Walker R & Bonnie J; 3, Foster W J; 4, J J J Stable; 5, House M; 6, Goldstein S.

Trainers— 1, Sadler John W; 2, French Neil; 3, Moerman Gerald C; 4, Orozco Salvador; 5, Feld Jude T; 6, Fanning Jerry.

Scratched—Spicy Yellowtail (1Feb89 5SA3); Damaskim (3Jun88 4GG1).

Tracks officially labeled muddy, heavy, slow, and good can be either wet or drying, but usually they will be wet. Sloppy surfaces are obviously wet. Speed horses will be advantaged.

That conclusion derives from the probability studies of the 1970s, conducted on a national sample of 5400 races. The studies revealed that on off-track surfaces of any kind, horses constituting the rear halves of the fields at the first-call positions won approximately half as many races as they should have. The lead horse at the first call on off tracks won at least twice as many races as probabilities would expect. And the leader on muddy tracks won three times as many races. Case closed.

Drying surfaces pose peculiar problems, but usually only after extended rains where tracks dry out slowly, as at Santa Anita. When the goo has turned to butterscotch pudding, frontrunners do tire. For a time, until normal firm conditions resurface, off-pace horses will be advantaged. Deep closers may be strongly advantaged, winning a disproportionate share of races.

Because track surfaces typically drain toward the inside, at these abnormal times the rail position may further complicate the speed horses' trips. Handicappers observe the speed horses stopping prematurely or tiring conspicuously, and the closers rallying impressively.

During these brief atypical intervals, handicappers benefit

by backing classy closers. They benefit later by observing now which frontrunners persevered willingly on the tiring surfaces. In a few weeks the same frontrunners will reappear, and now the track surface will not hinder them. Several will win at higher odds than they carried on the off tracks.

A nettlesome contemporary problem associated with off tracks attaches to a drastic change in routine track maintenance procedures. The trend began in the west, but is spreading east quickly enough. On the vaguest forecast of rain, Santa Anita, which dries slowly, seals the track surface. So do other tracks where the mud lingers.

In the east, if an important stakes race is scheduled but rain has been forecast, the track surface will likely be sealed.

Heavy rollers press over the track surface repeatedly, compressing the topmost soil. Instead of seeping underneath, the rain rolls off. The idea is to preserve a fast, honest surface, but unwanted consequences intrude. Sealing hardens track surfaces unfairly, such that front speed, including cheap speed, is less likely to tire than normally. Indeed, an opposite effect occurs. Running times improve extraordinarily.

Review the running times again of the pair of mud races at Santa Anita. The track had been sealed repeatedly prior to the January rains, but not enough prior to the February rains. If the February times are unrealistically slow, the January times are unrealistically fast.

Figure handicappers must remember to discount abnormally fast adjusted times recorded on muddy or sloppy surfaces when the track has been sealed. Variants will have been extreme, the resulting figures untenable. Do not rely upon numerical ratings of horses that impressed uncharacteristically on these surfaces. The ratings will be bogus. They cannot be repeated under normal conditions.

Naturally, a regular diet of surface sealing throws a handicapper's numbers terribly out of whack. During the 90-session winter season at Santa Anita 1989, track variants equaled or exceeded a full second, fast or slow, no less than 45 days, fully half the program. Local handicappers who received less nourishment than usual from the numerical ratings they bother to keep can point an accusing finger at track-maintenance procedures that strayed irrationally out of bounds.

Reliable indicators of which horses might move up surprisingly in the slop and mud include pedigree and strong performances on similar surfaces.

Of past performances, the *Daily Racing Form* symbol *, indicating "fair" performance in the mud, is virtually useless, but the *Form's* x designation, indicative of superior performance, is solid. Ignore the "fair" symbol, but trust the x horses in the slop and mud.

Only a few sires, such as Damascus, are prepotent for slop and mud racing. Several, however, have performed well enough. A selected list of stallions in the appendices identifies well-established sires whose progeny have won approximately 20 percent of their starts on sloppy, muddy, and slow tracks. Sons and daughters of the most productive mud sires might be acceptable statistical bets at odds of 5–1 or greater, but 10–1 and up will get more profitable long-haul results.

Given the modern alterations in track-surface composition, and especially in track-maintenance procedures, if it's raining today, the track surface most likely will be fast tomorrow. Regardless of the official track condition, speed horses will probably be advantaged, and several will win in a muddied romp. Final times will be the fastest of their careers.

CONTENTIOUS RACES

The race is contentious. Four horses, or more, share a legitimate chance. None wield a firm upper hand. If probabilities were estimated, none would exceed a 20 percent maximum. That indicates natural odds of 4–1, minimum. Overlay odds would be higher.

Recreational handicappers, and not a few practiced handicappers besides, commit either of two mistakes in these intriguing situations.

One, they pass the races altogether, arguing that because races are too contentious, they are unbeatable.

Two—and here lurks the real evil—handicappers spend another thirty to forty-five minutes fine-tuning the wealth of their considerable knowledge and skill, practically transfixed by the mental challenge of figuring out which horse is actually best. Humbly, I confess to the second misadventure for upward of a decade.

Of the first blunder, the assumption that contentious races are too tough ignores the reality that the art of handicapping is essentially a balancing of percentages, odds, probabilities, and decision-making, engaged successfully only when the odds favor the player. Contentious races can be perceived, and rightly, as fields filled with underlays and overlays. Why not consider the overlays?

The second blunder is merely adult fool's play. In a complicated game characterized by a sizable error factor, it's arrogant, egotistical, and delusional to imagine the individual can pinpoint the winners of contentious races frequently enough to amass profits.

More often than not, the finely tuned, in-depth handicapping of contentious races lands on the favorite, or co-favorite. These are precisely the horses that must be forsaken. The betting public determines that.

An intelligent strategy for coping successfully with contentious races can be summarized succinctly. Discard the favorite and other low-priced contenders. Support the outstanding overlays. Perhaps more than one in the same race. The greater the overlay, the better.

In the course of a season, or several seasons, the strategy rewards its devotees with magnificent profits. Alternatively, handicappers obsessed with picking the winners of contentious races will achieve nothing but unnecessary losses, unless splitting headaches associated with the jockey errors, bad trips, and rotten luck that upset their well-laid apple carts.

I recall a contentious race during the early weeks of Santa Anita 1989, where six $40,000 claiming sprinters should contest a sizzling early pace, and two off-pace stylists would be positioned to pick up the pieces. Literally eight horses of eleven stood a reasonable chance.

I wasted an extra 40 minutes on the race, my first mistake. After fine-tuning the race analysis to smithereens, at last I thought I knew which of the frontrunners should survive the early duel (Lucky Masadado), and which off-pace horse (Quip Star) would finish fastest. Arranged in order of my preference for each, and the odds the crowd was willing to offer me, are the inseparable eight (page 299).

No exacta was available.

What did I do? I bet $40 to win on Lucky Masadado, and $20 to win on Quip Star. Don't ask why.

Quip Star	7–2
Lucky Masadado	7–1
Golden Gauntlet	3–1
Cheyenne Tropic	5–1
Frere Jacques	8–1
Teddy Naturally	9–1
Pialor	28–1
Stan's Bower	17–1

What should I have done? Ah, that's the interesting question.

Putting first things first, I might have reminded myself the race was wildly contentious, and that favorites and low-priced contenders in highly contentious races belong in the dust bin.

By that reasoning, Golden Gauntlet is tossed and so is one of my heroes, Quip Star.

Second, I might have acknowledged the appropriate strategy in contentious races is to take the overlays. Take what they give you, so to speak, as in baseball and football. The bigger the overlay, the better.

If the eight were judged relatively even, each merits roughly a 12.5 percent chance. Fair odds on any is 7–1. Out goes Cheyenne Tropic, an underlay. At 7–1, 8–1, and 9–1, three horses are offered at the margin, not attractive enough in a field so contentious.

I might have either split a $50 investment on the two outstanding overlays, and protected with $10 to win on my preferred frontrunner, Lucky Masadado. In some variation, cover three real possibilities intelligently.

But I could not release my mental grip on Quip Star, and blew the play. The result chart reverberates as the kind of slap in the face that jolts someone into a rude awakening, even now.

SECOND RACE
Santa Anita
JANUARY 7, 1989

6 FURLONGS. (1.07⅗) CLAIMING. Purse $27,000. 4-year-olds and upward. Weights, 4-year-olds, 120 lbs.; older, 121 lbs. Non-winners of two races since November 7, allowed 3 lbs.; of a race since then, 5 lbs. Claiming price $40,000; if for $35,000, allowed 2 lbs. (Races when entered for $32,000 or less not considered).

Value of race $27,000; value to winner $14,850; second $5,400; third $4,050; fourth $2,025; fifth $675. Mutuel pool $484,587.

Last Raced	Horse	Eqt.	A.	Wt	PP	St	¼	½	Str	Fin	Jockey	Cl'g Pr	Odds $1
23Dec88 ^{7}Hol^{3}	Pialor	b	6	115	8	1	1^{1}	1^{1}	$1^{2\frac{1}{2}}$	$1^{1\frac{1}{4}}$	Castanon A L	35000	28.30
18Dec88 ^{6}Hol^{3}	Lucky Masadado	b	7	116	7	2	2^{hd}	$3^{1\frac{1}{2}}$	$2^{1\frac{1}{2}}$	2no	Pedroza M A	40000	7.00
3Dec88 ^{1}Hol^{1}	Quip Star		7	116	1	10	$7^{1\frac{1}{2}}$	6^{1}	5^{1}	3^{nk}	Stevens G L	40000	3.70
22Dec88 ^{7}Hol^{2}	Frere Jacques	b	6	117	5	7	6^{hd}	$4^{1\frac{1}{2}}$	3^{hd}	$4^{\frac{3}{4}}$	Pincay L Jr	40000	8.70
2Apr88 ^{5}SA^{6}	Dad's Quest		8	116	4	9	11	$9^{2\frac{1}{2}}$	$8^{1\frac{1}{2}}$	$5^{\frac{1}{2}}$	Delahoussaye E	40000	17.80
20Sep88 ^{12}Fpx^{7}	Golden Gauntlet	b	5	111	9	4	$8^{\frac{1}{2}}$	$8^{1\frac{1}{2}}$	7^{1}	$6^{1\frac{3}{4}}$	Corral J R^{5}	40000	3.40
29Dec88 ^{3}SA^{2}	Cheyenne Tropic		5	116	10	5	5^{1}	2^{hd}	4^{hd}	$7^{\frac{1}{2}}$	Sibille R	40000	5.10
29Dec88 ^{3}SA^{1}	Teddy Naturally		7	116	2	6	$3^{\frac{1}{2}}$	$5^{\frac{1}{2}}$	6^{1}	$8^{1\frac{1}{4}}$	Gryder A T	40000	9.50

20Oct88	7SA2	Just Never Mind		5 116	3	3		4½	7hd	93½	94	Black C A	40000	8.60
21Dec88	6BM2	Stan's Bower	b	7 111	6	11		10½	10½	10¹	10¹½	Olguin G L⁵	40000	17.80
26Dec88	5SA7	Write A Line		4 116	11	8		9²½	11	11	11	Philipperon M	40000	70.70

OFF AT 1:03. Start good for all but STAN'S BOWER. Won driving. Time, :21⅝, :44⅕, :56½, 1:09⅕ Track fast.

$2 Mutuel Prices:

8–PIALOR	58.60	23.40	9.60
7–LUCKY MASADADO		8.00	5.20
1–QUIP STAR			4.20

B. h, by Zoot Alers—Pia Mater, by Pia Star. Trainer Jackson Ronald D. Bred by Dollase & Duffel (Cal).

PIALOR went to the front at once, shook well clear in the upper stretch and had enough left late to prove best. LUCKY MASADADO prompted the issue throughout and gained the place. QUIP STAR, never far back, was steadied a bit when boxed in approaching the end of the backstretch, came on in the final quarter and just missed the place. FRERE JACQUES, also never far back, menaced on the turn, came into the stretch four wide, then finished willingly. DAD'S QUEST, devoid of early speed, entered the stretch five wide and was going well late. GOLDEN GAUNTLET outrun early and wide down the backstretch, lacked the necessary closing response and was four wide into the stretch. CHEYENNE TROPIC, close up early and wide down the backstretch, lacked the needed response in the drive. TEDDY NATURALLY, close up early, weakened in the drive. JUST NEVER MIND had no visible mishap. STAN'S BOWER broke in a tangle and was five wide into the stretch. WRITE A LINE, wide down the backstretch, was six wide into the stretch.

Owners— 1, Tomigal J T; 2, Hazan B; 3, Royal T Stable; 4, Roberts Racing Stables; 5, Dinges Clara; 6, Van Doren P & Andrena; 7, Alpert D & H; 8, Webb & West; 9, Marden & Wygod; 10, Poyer & Steinmann; 11, Moran & Sweeney.

Trainers— 1, Jackson Ronald D; 2, King Hal; 3, Lewis Craig A; 4, Marikian Charles M; 5, Dinges Vernon L. 6, Palma Hector O; 7, Stute Melvin F; 8, West Ted; 9, Ellis Ronald W; 10, Gerber Greg D; 11, Sweeney Brian.

Against all odds, Pialor, a gamester, bounced to the front unmolested and just scampered to the wire. Stan's Bower broke in a tangle. Lucky Masadado chased all the way. Quip Star had no suicidal pace to overtake. The overlay mutuel, $58.60, might have been snatched by any competent handicapper equipped with a rational strategy for dealing with contentious races.

Many generous mutuels await the competent handicappers of contentious races. In the nature of the events, some contenders will be underlays, some will be overlays, and some will be fabulous overlays. This strategy applies:

1. Eliminate the favorite
2. Eliminate low-priced contenders
3. Support the outstanding overlays to win
4. Support marginal overlays with smaller protective win bets

If exactas are offered, box key contenders in contentious fields with all other contenders that are attractive overlays.

If the exacta had been offered on the Santa Anita race, I should have keyed Lucky Masadado, and perhaps Quip Star, with other contenders that represented attractive overlays, which would have included Pialor, a happy ending. Outstanding overlays must be covered. The race is contentious and these are authentic contenders. Marginal overlays can be forsaken.

Contentious races pop up regularly, but the number of contenders usually will be four, five, or six. Outstanding overlays are more readily covered. Key horses (main contenders) should be coupled in generous exactas. Throw out favorites and low-priced contenders in the win pool, and in low-paying exactas too.

One kind of contentious race to which this strategy can be applied regards the phony favorite that shapes up as a definite underlay, but without a strong alternative. The situation develops often when trainers drop horses curiously in class following a good race. Not a small drop, for the win, but a big drop. The plunge in class makes no sense, except as the horse might have gone wrong, or is about to, and the trainer would like to rid himself of a nasty problem.

The crowd reacts to the good race against better, and the perplexing dropdown is sent to the post at 6–5, even money, or less. If another horse figures strongly as well, that presents handicappers with a low-priced overlay. But if no other horse adds up strongly, while a few look relatively even at long prices, the race should be considered contentious.

Thousands of recreational handicappers greatly desire to beat the phony favorites. Regrettably, they commit the same mistake as the finely tuned, in-depth handicappers of classically contentious races. They shop for the single best alternative. Usually, they miss. The financial losses accumulate, defeating the original lofty purpose. But if the race is judged contentious instead, now all outstanding overlays that are contenders can be backed, perhaps by varying amounts, in accord with the values available.

When the phony favorites lose, as almost always they do, enough of the outstanding overlays will inherit victory to ensure profits. Less the tearing up of well-intended tickets. But first, the proper strategy, please. The contention, and corresponding odds lines, dictate the action, not the all-knowing handicappers.

UNPREDICTABLE RACES

All things considered, no horse figures. The race is awful. The race is unpredictable. Therefore the race is unreliable. No play.

Fair enough.

Some races defy analysis. By all that is fundamental to effective handicapping, by any standard that counts, the race remains indecipherable.

By all means, regular handicappers should abstain. Most do.

But casual handicappers like to play, regardless. They've come to the track for the day. They want action.

In 1975, on a Thursday, I dragged a favorite companion to the races, and on both sides expectations ran high. The early portion of the program proved horrid, four awful, unpredictable races in a row.

I sat on my hands like a trooper.

As the horses appeared in the post parade for the fifth, the siren call went out, to me, from her, "I want some action."

The remainder of the day proved a total loss. Action bets, but no prime bets, no pet angles, not a sniff of success. The losses were mildly painful, but as one of us later remarked, "The fun was in the playing. . . ."

My companion has not yet returned to the races, but it's only been fifteen years, and no one can deny it's much more fun to play than sit.

Besides, the unpredictable races may be part of the pick-six sequence, or the serial triple, or the daily double, and everyone loves to dabble in the double, so to speak.

Because unpredictable races are so unreliable, forget the fundamentals. Unpredictable races are the province of handicapping angles. Angles consist of clusters of factors that tie together in statistically infrequent combinations. Positive angles have worked well in the past for the individual, well enough to toss profits at least occasionally.

Facing unpredictable races, recreational handicappers should look avidly for positive angles.

Uncommon trainer patterns are favorite angles of many casual handicappers. Puzzling races are absolutely the appropriate repository of trainer angles. Probe for them.

Other productive angles involve biases, early speed, and long shots noticeably sharp on body language. In unpredictable situations, lean to those pet factors.

A circumstance that must always accompany handicapping angles is generous odds, maybe high odds. Angles represent low-probability outcomes. Low odds nullifies any substantive edge an angle allows.

If no positive angles beckon, handicappers' best alternative is to favor personal strengths.

Speed handicappers should prefer the high-figure horse, however low the figure.

Class handicappers should prefer the class of the field, however dubious the basic ability.

Pace handicappers should prefer the horse having the fastest turn time, however slow the actual time.

Trip handicappers should prefer the horse returning from an excusable trip, however obvious the record.

Form analysts should prefer the horse in improving form, however pitiful the prospect of real success.

And so forth. Recreational handicappers best rely on their specialties, as best the methods can be implemented in a no-win predicament.

When all else fails, of course, it's standard operating procedure to pass unpredictable races. I recommend it to everyone.

SMALL FIELDS

The cruelest development of modern racing for racetrack bettors has been the institutionalization of the small field. Racegoers deposit more money than they withdraw at the races for two reasons.

One, a shortage of knowledge and skill in handicapping.

Two, they bet too many underlays.

An underlay is a horse whose actual chances of winning are not as good as its odds suggest. As the meager returns on winners cannot cancel the losses on losers, a steady diet of underlays guarantees the bettors will lose. The small field presents racegoers with precisely that kind of guarantee.

The five-horse stakes field is commonplace at major tracks. Year-round racing, promoting hundreds of big-ticket stakes events on the national calendar, encourages horsemen to shop for best values. Trainers pick their spots, which do not often include all-out efforts to dethrone the champions, near-champions, or division leaders. Sportsmanship cowers before greed.

So the barn's prized specimen goes elsewhere, to other races, at other places. In consequence, many of the nation's graded stakes present small fields consisting of a standout star at miserly odds, with a handful of lackluster others intended solely to pick up secondary awards. The runner-up in a $150,000-added stakes event collects $30,000. The third-place finisher claims $22,500, and smiles on the way to the bank.

To less extent, similar machinations have plagued the overnight allowances. Top-drawer competition is steadfastly avoided. As breeders of racehorses produce dozens of good ones and hundreds of bad ones annually, the typical racing card served up to modern racing's customers contains overflowing fields in the worst of races, and small fields in the best of races.

This is a dreadful situation. As these trends intensify, the quality of the competition erodes, the spectacle of the sport dims, and the plight of the small bettor worsens.

To stimulate wagering in noncompetitive races, racetracks offer the bettors exactas. The rationale is that bettors might win more seductive amounts by selecting the order of finish one-two, and after all, only five or six possibilities must be coupled.

The policy is seriously flawed. If racetrack customers could convert win underlays to exacta overlays in small fields, the practice would serve as a fantastic bailout. But the customers cannot, and the policy of attaching exacta wagering to small noncompetitive fields only exacerbates a deadening problem. Exacta underlays penalize the bettors just as harshly as do win underlays. More so, as combination betting normally extracts greater capital.

In 1989, exacta underlays accumulated in unprecedented numbers, as bettors struggled to manipulate profits from small noncompetitive fields. Less than a week ago, as this is written, Easy Goer trounced four forgettable opponents in the Grade 1 Travers Stakes at Saratoga at 1–5, and paid $2.40 to win. The $2 exacta paid $5.60.

Small bettors are unremittingly penalized by these circumstances. Exactas are low-probability events. A pair of 2–1 shots has a 10 percent probability of occurring in either direction. Thus a $2 exacta box on a pair of 2–1 shots, a $4 investment, encompasses 20 percent of the potential outcomes. In other words, bettors can expect to lose the investment 80 percent of the time. Small bankrolls cannot tolerate the loss skeins.

Moreover, the fair-value dollar return on a $2 exacta combination having a 10 percent chance of occurring is $20. A $24 return is better, yielding a 20 percent profit. Exacta underlays would return less than $20 on a pair of 2–1 shots, and many do.

What can recreational handicappers do to protect against the downside of small fields?

A few strategies can be contemplated. None attract hard-boiled racetrack bettors wholeheartedly.

If the favorite is overbet but solid, pass the race. No alternative exists, including keying the overbet favorite on top of overbet exactas. Skip the race. A bet on Easy Goer at 1–5 is a terrible, terrible wager.

If the favorite is overbet but vulnerable, key the favorite on the underside of exactas from any outstanding overlay having a reasonable chance. Of medium-priced contenders, or low-priced contenders, check the projected payoffs of exactas with the vulnerable favorite on the bottom. Only good bargains should be purchased. Do not use the risky overbet favorites on top, where they represent only additional underlays.

If a solid favorite is overbet to win but a fair value on top of an exacta coupling a strong second choice, with the others strictly outsiders, key that combination multiple times. Bettors must succeed with the top-two couplings repeatedly to earn real profits, so investments will be limited to the sturdy, reliable stakes-caliber horse looking primed on all the fundamentals. It's a conservative wager, and the risk must be relatively low.

Several small fields in the stakes and allowances feature two horses that tower above the rest. The two are closely matched on full-dress handicapping. If one is overbet, the other underbet, prefer the underbet horse—every time. If A is 8–5 and B is 5–2, bet B. If handicappers convert the opportunity four of ten times, profits can run high. On 5–2 shots, profits after ten wagers and four winners would total $8, or 40 percent on investment. Very nice, indeed!

If two horses in a small field are low-priced co-favorites in the betting but one is a fraud, key the genuine article in exactas with other overlays. If handicappers can be confident the phony favorite will finish up the course, several exactas should be overlays. If an overlay on top of the respectable co-favorite offers excellent value, take it.

Intelligent betting strategy is not the only impediment to finding happiness in small fields.

Small fields can wreak havoc on the probable pace. Trainers and jockeys routinely resort to cleverness in compact fields. The trainer of an outsider in a five-horse route tells the rider to steal the race. Suddenly the outsider pops into the lead. The others must adapt.

Or no horse possesses respectable early speed. Now five or six horses are unseemly bunched in a paceless race. Suddenly one horse takes off at the half-mile pole. Again, the others must adapt.

By methods strange and unpredictable, the pace of small fields can be abnormally fast or abnormally slow, severely contested or uncontested. Not all good horses are versatile. When funny things happen, events can veer out of control, of horse or jockey. To the chagrin of horseplayers who imagined the small field extended them a greater chance of backing a winner, balanced indelicately against lower odds, irritating upsets spoil the plot.

Nobody relishes the small field. Not racing fans, not track operators, not handicappers, not riders, and not bettors. Maybe horsemen, whose horses inherit a better chance of making money against fewer opponents.

For that reason, I'm afraid, the small field of the 1980s is unlikely to go away in the 1990s. The ennobling goals of the much-maligned racegoers will be more elusive than ever.

LOCAL INFORMATION SERVICES

Not a generation ago, authors of handicapping texts could blithely warn racing's customers to stay clear of anyone brandishing products and services on handicapping and be solidly on safe ground. The marketplace was cluttered then with hucksters, fast-buck artists, and quick-fix merchants who conspired to stamp the field with a blackened image it no longer deserves.

On this times have changed for the better.

The quick-fix merchants still abound, making daily appearances on the radio, the telephone, and the pages of the *Daily Racing Form*, but many of them have been squeezed out of the market by legitimate, state-of-the-art handicapping information services, promoted by honest professional handicappers who have a great deal to distribute to recreational handicappers, and at attractively low prices.

Until the racing industry—the local racetracks, in particular—elaborate a modern marketing strategy that emphasizes information services and customer education in handicapping—a natural, inevitable development of the information age—racing's customers must abide by a policy of buyer beware.

Thus the casual customers will confront the same disadvantage that prevents progress in the information and education arenas among racetracks—an inability to separate the wheat from the chaff.

To help in the discrimination, I shall present here an impressive array of handicapping information services strongly recommended to recreational handicappers in various regions of the country. I do not hesitate to endorse the high professional qualifications and personal character of the individuals that have developed the products and services and, against all odds, have promoted them effectively to small but grateful loyal markets of motivated horseplayers.

Before getting to the recommended material, certain handicapping services are reprehensible, of no value whatsoever, and should be steadfastly avoided by racing's casual audience, absolutely by anyone who cares to improve his or her knowledge and skill in handicapping.

As presently marketed, selection services, proffered by most irresponsible public and private selectors who offer to trade the day's selections for a fee, are irredeemably worthless. No adult of the slightest maturity, intelligence, or worldliness can possibly be baited by the hooks on which so-called handicapping experts are purportedly dangling enough winners to guarantee the consumer a profit. I implore recreational handicappers to do their own handicapping, make personal selections, and avoid the half-baked selection services of other handicappers.

Because public selectors are required to make a selection in every race, they all lose, and many of them lose abysmally. Thus, recreational handicappers have no way of knowing which of the maddening crowd are authentic winners.

Best bets suffer another mortal wound. Too many of them go postward as underlays. It's a mathematical truth that a series of wagers on underlays guarantees a long-term loss.

The unprofessional, unacceptable, unethical aspect of virtually every selection service crowding the marketplace is the failure of the promoters to provide a fair-value betting line by which consumers can determine whether the horses will be underlays or overlays. Without the fair-value odds clearly stated, no one can tell whether the selections should actually be bet. And no one can determine how talented the self-styled experts really are.

The only way for professional selection services to become

legitimized and credible is that authentically talented handicappers (winners) identify the key horses on a card having a strong probability of winning as overlays, and to establish for each a fair-value betting line, such that continuous records of success and failure can be monitored closely and evaluated. And none of the services do that.

Telephone selection services, computer services that supply selections disguised as complicated output, and the traditional selection cards hawked at the entrances to racetracks, all fall down on the odds criterion, and should be abandoned.

Day-of-the-races seminars are not strictly selection services, although the vast majority suffer the shortcomings of (a) inauthentic experts, (b) making a selection to win in every race, and (c) not defining the fair-value odds lines.

Yet the seminars can be possessed of a redeeming social value. They can represent a case-study approach, if you will, to customer education, assuming the experts can articulate the reasons for their selections and eliminations, explained in terms of fundamental handicapping principles. Too, the handicapping personalities can supply information and insights otherwise inaccessible to the occasional customer.

If an impressive, responsible handicapper conducts a day-of-the-races seminar, recreational handicappers can usually benefit from the discussion.

But the outstanding contribution of professional handicappers to recreational handicappers has been the publication of information reports, commonly newsletters, at affordable prices. The newsletters distribute performance ratings, trip and bias notes, details of workouts, trainer data, daily track variants, horses to watch, and other assorted information that bring recreational handicappers up to snuff on every race at the local tracks.

The following handicapping information services supply information and data that can be considered no less than state of the art. I strongly recommend the services to casual handicappers wanting every edge. We begin in southern California, where the trend to handicapping information services began some fifteen years ago.

Selected Information Services

Handicapper's Report, published biweekly by Bob Selvin and Jeff Siegel of Los Angeles. Good performance ratings that embrace pace as well as final times, and feature the handicapping skill of Siegel. Also emphasizes workouts, of first-starters, layoff types, and improving horses, a result of hiring staff clockers to obtain the information. Available for the entire southern California circuit.

    Handicapper's Report also markets various selection services over the telephone and by special-delivery mail, but the selections should not be confused with the information services. The information services are recommended, the selection services are not.

Today's Racing Digest, published daily by William Archer and associates of San Diego. A massive array of data and information about every horse and every race on the card. Something of value for everyone. Sold at numerous retail outlets and at the entrances to local tracks. Available for the entire southern California circuit.

Daily Track Variants and Horses to Watch, published weekly by Tom Brohamer of Long Beach. Brohamer uses projected times, instead of pars, at both the pace call and final call, to produce arguably the best track variants anywhere. His horses-to-watch list has produced at a 50 percent rate, or better, for several seasons. It is based strictly on overachieving performances. The service is low-cost and highly recommended for handicappers who wish to make their own figures but need daily variants to proceed. Available for southern California tracks, excepting Fairplex.

The Northern California Track Record, published weekly by Ron Cox of Pleasanton, California. Pace figures, final figures, extensive trip and bias notes, daily track variants, key workouts, horses to follow, the whole ball game. Available for Bay Meadows and Golden Gate Fields, but not the northern California fair circuit.

The Northwest Track Review, published weekly by Paul Braseth of Seattle. Figures, trips and biases, variants, workouts, and so forth, the regular menu, but especially outstanding on trainer performance data and trainer patterns. Braseth is unexcelled on trainers, a factor that can predominate at smaller tracks. Available for Longacres and Portland Meadows.

Inside Edge, published weekly by Dave Maycock of Omaha, Nebraska. Provides speed figures, the usual trip and bias information attached, for Ak-Sar-Ben customers. Maycock also provides accurate figures for as many as twenty racetracks in the midwest. Another weekly, called *Win Facts*, and limited to Ak-Sar-Ben racing, features local studies of handicapping factors, trainer patterns, or situations that have been successful recently. Available for Ak-Sar-Ben, feeder tracks, and regional tracks.

The Professor's Speed Service, as well as *Trainer & Class Update*, published biweekly by M. Scott McMannis of Chicago. The speed service includes not only excellent speed and pace figures, but trip and bias notes. The updates on class and trainers provide other basic information resources, either to handicappers with those preferences or to versatile types who want access to everything.

McMannis also publishes *Chicago Trainer Profiles* annually. All services are available for Arlington Park, Sportsman's Park, and Hawthorne.

In addition, at all three Chicago tracks, McMannis conducts day-of-the-races seminars on-site at the handicapping information centers, provided specifically for recreational handicapping purposes.

The Thoroughbred Speculator, published weekly by Bill Olmsted of Maryland. Speed and pace figures, Quirin-style, for the eight states surrounding Maryland racing, including New Jersey, West Virginia, and Pennsylvania. The out-of-state figures give local handicappers at Pimlico and Laurel a leg up on the continuous shipping that characterizes the daily programs on the eastern seaboard.

The Speculator also presents interesting feature articles and timely news updates on the national scene.

Thoro-Graph, published daily by Jerry Brown and associates of New York. An upscale speed-figure service for savvy New Yorkers. For every horse on the card, a complete history of speed figures is presented on a columnar page, such that recurring patterns might be identified. Good figures, but pricey for recreational bettors. Available in southern California too.

The Handicapper's Data Base, published daily, by Bloodstock Research of Lexington, Kentucky. A computerized report presenting Beyer-style speed figures, trip notes, and trainer information. Only accessed by personal computer and modem. Upscale. Good figures and information, but pricey for recreational bettors.

Recreational handicappers interested in computer applications of merit can consult Cynthia Publishing of Los Angeles, publisher Dick Mitchell; and Com-Cap of Omaha, Nebraska, publisher George Kaywood. Com-Cap, in particular, offers low-priced software of an introductory ambience, nicely suited to recreational handicapping. In 1990 Com-Cap began selling Sharp handheld computers for $100, and each is nicely stocked with handicapping software. Cynthia Publishing's programs are more advanced, and more expensive, but first-rate. Handicapping videos have entered the marketplace too. The best, especially a visually stimulating treatment of horses' body language by the late Bonnie Ledbetter, have been produced by Greg Lawlor, of Lawlor Enterprises, near San Diego, CA.

As the quality of objective, no-nonsense handicapping information has improved, so have the lines of supply. At the same time, the collection, storage, and retrieval of the relevant handicapping information now requires an outlay of time and effort by the individual well beyond the interest of all but the most dedicated of handicappers.

The twin developments form an obvious nexus. For a modest fee, recreational handicappers in the well-served markets can now resort to the same information resources obtained by their professional counterparts. The information can only lead to additional winners, several at juicy mutuels, a cost-effective bargain.

CHAPTER VIII

Familiar Situations that Recreational Handicappers Misjudge

CERTAIN RECURRING SITUATIONS can be troublesome for recreational handicappers, resulting in recurring mistakes, not to mention recurring financial losses.

To be fair, the situations become troublesome for understandable reasons. They fall outside of general handicapping principles, or normal handicapping practice. The races offer subtle variations, nuances, opposite logics, and nonstandard applications that only thoughtful experience can comprehend.

In this section I have selected a couple of dozen interesting situations that illustrate many fine points of handicapping. Several of the races occurred during the winter season of Santa Anita 1989, because I play that meeting from beginning to end. Yet the situations and handicapping guidelines they represent generalize well to all major tracks.

The examples do not exhaust the possibilities by any means. Selecting intriguing handicapping situations is the kind of endeavor that never concludes. Experience remains the practitioner's continuing education. But the situations that follow have been carefully picked, and can be considered salient. The lessons to be learned should be comprehended well.

Most of the past performances to be presented are marked, to an extent, as recommended earlier in this book. Other personal notations of the author have been deleted, to reduce the distractions.

Let's begin with a truly perplexing situation, a play consistently bungled badly, not only by recreational handicappers, but by regulars, the media, and almost all public selectors.

GRADE 1 WINNERS IN CLASSIFIED ALLOWANCE FIELDS

Let's begin with a fine point of handicapping well within the grasp of the casual racegoer.

Whenever a Grade 1 stakes winner is entered under classified allowance conditions, handicappers should expect the horse to lose. There are no exceptions.

The reason is elementary. No Grade 1 stakes winner is prepared or intended to win any allowance race. The objective makes no sense. Grade 1 horses are prepared and intended to win additional stakes races, and preferably additional graded stakes. Minor races offer minor money, no prestige, and no breeding value. Graded stakes offer major money, prestige, and tremendous breeding value. Any premature or ill-advised exertion to win minor races with important horses is not happily indulged.

A common scenario finds Grade 1 winners returning to the races following lengthy layoffs in classified allowance races. The handicapper's assumption must inevitably be that the classy horses are prepping for future stakes. Regardless of the trainer, jockey, workouts, or other seductive circumstances, the Grade 1 horses should be discounted. Few racegoers comprehend the point, as the Grade 1 horses routinely become the betting favorites, a convenient circumstance for savvy handicappers who recognize the situation for what it is.

On Day 2 of Santa Anita's 1988–89 winter season, the seventh was a classified allowance race. Scheduled overnight for the turf, the 6½-furlong sprint was switched to the dirt due to recent rains. Read the conditions of the race carefully.

7th Santa Anita

ABOUT 6 ½ FURLONGS. (Turf). (1.11⅘) CLASSIFIED ALLOWANCE. Purse $55,000. Fillies and mares. 3–year–olds and upward, which are non–winners of $17,000 twice other than closed or claiming since July 25. Weights, 3–year–olds, 119 lbs.; older, 121 lbs. Non–winners of two such races since April 20, allowed 2 lbs.; of such a race since October 1, 4 lbs.; since June 1, 6 lbs. (Claiming races not considered).

The conditions bar any horse that since July 25—five months—has won two races where first money equalled $17,000 or more. As California pays 55 percent of the purse to the winner, the $17,000 first prize translates roughly to a purse size of $31,000. These are minor awards for better horses at Santa Anita.

Yet horses that have won one graded stakes since July 25 might also remain eligible. Whenever classified races allow the eligible horses to have won a stakes race since a date within six months of today, handicappers can emphasize class; that is, expect a relatively classy animal to win. But not a Grade 1 horse.

Handicappers should prefer (a) runners-up in graded stakes, or (b) winners once since the specified date of a classified race having a purse equal to or higher than today's, or (c) horses that have accomplished each of the above since the specified date.

The better the overall record, the brighter the prospects today. The fewer the attempts since the specified date, the better, though five, six, or seven starts is entirely normal and acceptable. Also, in any classified allowance race, horses particularly well-suited to the distance deserve extra credit. Ditto for horses particularly well-suited to the footing and probable pace.

Now examine three interesting prospects entered in the Santa Anita classified race on December 28.

Queen Forbes — past performance chart

Flying Julia — past performance chart

```
5Aug87-5Dmr    6f :221 :452 1:101ft    9-5 117    42½ 44   32  32½    StevensGL⁶ ⒻAw24000 84-20 IrshLord'sMss,YoursAnytm,Flyng.JI 7
1Jan87-3SA   . 6f :213 :451 1:111ft    2½ 116    66   63¾ 73½ 73½    StevensGL² ⒻAw29000 78-19 BlconyPss,SeDoubyRun,LuckySilvr 9
2Nov86-5SA     6f :212 :441 1:102ft    2½ 117    56½ 55½ 53½ 31½    StevensGL² ⒻAw28000 84-10 StridingEsy,LoversNtive,FlyingJuli 9
12Oct86-2SA    6½f:22  :45 1:164ft     2½ 114    52  31  11½ 16½    StevensGL⁴ ⒻAw25000 86-21 FlyingJulia,HirlessHeiress,CrestLdy 9
31May86-4Hol   6f :223 :454 1:11 ft   *4-5 121    5³  6⁶  6⁷  6⁸     StevensGL 3ⒻAw20000 81-16 Argentrio,PromiseMeLuck,CrstLdy 8
   31May86—Bobbled start
   Dec 21 SA 5f gd :594 H        Dec 15 SA 6f ft 1:134 H        Dec 10 SA 6f ft 1:14 H        Dec 3 SA 5f ft 1:003 H
```

Rose's Record

```
                                       B. f. 4, by Cougar II—In Full Bloom, by Fleet Nasrullah
BAZE R A                               Br.—Bally Glen Partnership (Ky)      1988  8 2 1 1      $72,890
                              115      Tr.—Mandella Richard                 1987  5 2 2 0      $35,725
Own.—Ringler Mr–Mrs D·V                Lifetime  13 4 3 1  $108,575         Turf  4 1 1 1      $43,850
30Dec88-5Hol   6f ⊕:223 :453 1:09 fm  8½ 115   33  33  33  21½   Baze R A² ⒻAw35000 90-11 GoldenGalaxy,Rose'sRecord,Mdrug 7
5Nov88-9SA     7f :22  :444 1:222ft   14 116   106½108½109½ 89   Toro F9 ⒻⒷEmmia H 79-13 Valdemosa,NtivePster,QueeeBebe 10
29May88-3Hol   6½f:22  :444 1:162ft    3 118   22  31½ 44½ 412   McCrrnCJ² ⒻAw55000 84-13 Annoconnor,SilntArrivl,MssSprnklt 4
14May88-8Hol   7f :222 :451 1:23 ft   9½ 116   31  42½ 44  45    ToroF² ⒻA Gleam H 84-15 Integr,BehindTheScns,Crol'sWondr 5
   14May88—Grade III
26May88-9SA'  a6½f⊕:212 :441 1:15 fm  5½ 116   107½117½118½107½ McHrDG¹¹ ⒻLsCngsH 77-12 HirlessHirss,ChickOrTwo,Aromcor 12
1Mar88-8SA   a6½f⊕:213 :441 1:15 fm  *2½ 117   75  87  65½ 1hd  Toro F8 ⒻAw55000 84-15 Rose'sRecord,SilentArrivl,Aromcor 8
   1Mar88—Wide in stretch
10Feb88-7SA    1 ⊕:462 1:112 1:373 fm 4½ 115   65½ 63½ 32  31½  Toro F² ⒻAw44000 85-13 SlyChrmer,GoldenGlxy,Rose'sRcord 9
   10Feb88—Lacked room 3/8
2Jan88-3SA     6f :214 :444 1:101ft    6 116   43  44  21½ 1½   Toro F3 ⒻAw35000 87-15 Ros'sRcord,Crol'sWondr,GoldnGlxy 7
24May87-4Hol   6½f:221 :452 1:17 ft    4 115   21½ 32  45½ 512  Toro F1 ⒻⒷTrlnga H 83-13 MissSprinkleL,LdyyNskr,YoungFlyr 5
9May87-5Hol    6f :221 :453 1:102ft   11 117   3⁴  2hd 11½ 12½  Toro F4 ⒻAw22000 91-10 Rose's Record,RaiseYou,FleetRoad 7
   ● Dec 23 Hol 5f m :594 H    ● Dec 16 Hol 3f sy :354 H    Nov 26 Hol 5f m 1:013 H    Nov 17 SA 4f ft :481 B
```

Which horse do racegoers prefer?

As usual, most preferred Flying Julia, sending the mare postward the 2–1 favorite, because she had won a Grade 1 event February 21, ten months ago, and had not raced since. Flying Julia was perceived as a multiple stakes winner that could also sprint with the best of them, returning to competition against classified horses with a set of regular, sharp workouts.

Fair enough. But the mare should be short of winning form, will not be abused or overexerted today, and at low odds does not figure to prevail. To repeat, an assumption of defeat is the crucial analysis whenever Grade 1 winners show up under classified conditions. The odds will be low, the horses unintended. Eliminate them.

Notice Queen Forbes's record of six races since the specified date of July 25, when the filly won a closed* sprint at Hollywood Park. It is practically prototypical of the kind of relatively classy individual that shines in these races.

Next out, July 31, Queen Forbes finished second in a Grade 3 sprint at Del Mar.

On October 15, at Santa Anita, Queen Forbes won a classified turf sprint in sharp time. First money that day was $27,500 (55 percent of $50,000). The filly remained eligible today for a similar purse versus similar horses.

---

*A closed race is an allowance race that bars horses that have already won a specified number of allowance or stakes races. They are commonly called nonwinners allowance races.

Queen Forbes's overall record is impressive, and she performs at her best in long sprints.

In only two starts since July 25, Rose's Record had not won, but the filly exhibited much-improved form last out in a classified turf sprint at Hollywood Park. This kind of form reversal often precedes victory under classified conditions, and handicappers know the third start following a lengthy layoff is often a thoroughbred's best.

The overall record is fine, Rose's Record having won a classified turf sprint March 1 at Santa Anita.

Improved workouts following the much-improved race December 3, a highly positive pattern of improving form, gains the filly added respect.

Yet handicappers prefer the classier article in these minimally restricted classified events, and Queen Forbes outclasses Rose's Record. Flying Julia excepted, Queen Forbes held a class edge on the field here, exactly the kind of classified prospect handicappers want. Queen Forbes was 5–1 in the betting with ten minutes to post, but final odds on the three we've examined looked like this:

Flying Julia	2–1
Queen Forbes	3–1
Rose's Record	9–2

In an extra-game effort, Queen Forbes contested the pace from the rail, and dueled with other contenders every step of the way. She needed the class edge she enjoyed, and prevailed.

Flying Julia never seriously contended, finished out of the money.

SEVENTH RACE
Santa Anita
DECEMBER 28, 1988

6 ½ FURLONGS. (1.14) CLASSIFIED ALLOWANCE. Purse $55,000. Fillies and mares. 3–year–olds and upward, which are non–winners of $17,000 twice other than closed or claiming since July 25. Weights, 3–year–olds, 119 lbs.; older, 121 lbs. Non–winners of two such races since April 20, allowed 2 lbs.; of such a race since October 1, 4 lbs.; since June 1, 6 lbs. (Claiming races not considered).(ORIGINALLY CARDED TO BE RUN ON THE TURF.)

Value of race $55,000; value to winner $30,250; second $11,000; third $8,250; fourth $4,125; fifth $1,375. Mutuel pool $322,283. Exacta pool $362,800.

Last Raced	Horse	Eqt.A.Wt	PP	St	¼	½	Str	Fin	Jockey	Odds $1
5Nov88 ^{9}SA^{5}	Queen Forbes	b 4 119	1	6	$2^{1\frac{1}{2}}$	$2^{\frac{1}{2}}$	$1^{1\frac{1}{2}}$	1^{hd}	Delahoussaye E	3.20
30Oct88 ^{8}SA^{5}	Daloma	4 114	4	3	$4^{\frac{1}{2}}$	$4^{1\frac{1}{2}}$	$2^{\frac{1}{2}}$	$2^{1\frac{3}{4}}$	Valenzuela F H^{5}	3.70
3Dec88 ^{5}Hol^{4}	Silent Arrival	5 121	3	5	$6^{2\frac{1}{2}}$	6^{5}	4^{1}	3^{hd}	McCarron C J	8.50
3Dec88 ^{5}Hol^{2}	Rose's Record	4 115	6	2	3^{hd}	3^{hd}	$3^{\frac{1}{2}}$	$4^{2\frac{1}{2}}$	Baze R A	4.90
21Feb88 ^{8}SA^{1}	Flying Julia	5 115	7	1	5^{1}	5^{hd}	6^{7}	$5^{1\frac{1}{4}}$	Olivares F	2.40
31Dec87 ^{8}SA^{9}	Sari's Heroine	5 115	2	4	1^{hd}	1^{hd}	5^{2}	6^{8}	Stevens G L	5.60
26Jun88 ^{5}Hol^{9}	Munchkin Michele	4 115	5	7	7	7	7	7	Toro F	45.80

OFF AT 3:48. Start good. Won driving. Time, :21⅗, :44⅕, 1:08⅘, 1:15 Track fast.

$2 Mutuel Prices:

1-QUEEN FORBES	8.40 4.00	3.00
5-DALOMA	4.20	3.20
3-SILENT ARRIVAL		4.60

$5 EXACTA 1-5 PAID $88.50.

Dk. b. or br. f, by Air Forbes Won—Artistic Queen, by Vested Power. Trainer Jordan James. Bred by Artistic Queen Syndicate (Va).

QUEEN FORBES, a bit slow to begin, engaged for the lead from along the inside rail soon after the start, vied for the lead around the far turn, had a clear advantage at the furlong marker, drifted out to brush slightly with DALOMA In the closing yards and prevailed by a narrow margin. DALOMA, close up early, pressed the issue on the far turn, kept to her task in the drive, brushed slightly with QUEEN FORBES In the closing yards and could not quite get up. A claim of foul against QUEEN FORBES by the rider of DALOMA for alleged interference in the stretch drive was not allowed by the stewards when they ruled that the incident nearing the finish was minor and had no bearing on the order of finish. SILENT ARRIVAL, outrun early, finished willingly. ROSE'S RECORD, close up early and wide down the backstretch, pressed the issue on the far turn, came into the stretch four wide and lacked the needed response in the drive. FLYING JULIA, outrun early but not far back and wide down the backstretch after an alert beginning, failed to generate the necessary response in the last quarter and was five wide into the stretch. SARI'S HEROINE vied for the lead to the stretch and weakened. MUNCHKIN MICHELE was slow to begin. TOULANGE (4) AND MOST PRESTIGIOUS (8) WERE SCRATCHED BY THE STEWARDS. ALL WAGERS ON THEM IN THE REGULAR AND EXACTA POOLS WERE ORDERED REFUNDED AND ALL OF THEIR PICK NINE AND LATE TRIPLE SELECTIONS WERE SWITCHED TO THE FAVORITE, FLYING JULIA (9).

Owners— 1, Crowley & Downey; 2, Enemy Stbs & Mandysland Fm; 3, Coelho-Fields-Valenti; 4, Ringler Mr-Mrs D V; 5, Marino J; 6, Rochelle B; 7, Black Chip Stable & Levy.

Trainers— 1, Jordan James; 2, Whittingham Charles; 3, Stute Melvin F; 4, Mandella Richard; 5, Luby Donn; 6, Stute Melvin F; 7, Jones Gary.

Scratched—Golden Galaxy (3Dec88 5Hol¹); Toulange (3Dec88 5Hol⁶); Bragora (6Oct88 8SA¹⁰); Jungle Dawn (12-Nov88 8BM⁴); Debby Kay (26Nov88 6BM⁶); Most Prestigious (26Nov88 6Hol²); Abstract Energy (3Dec88 5Hol⁷); Valdemosa (17Dec88 7Hol³).

Postscript. Occasionally, Grade 1 winners that have been racing regularly, but exhibiting dull or puzzling form, will be lowered to classified allowance conditions, or to minor stakes. Form has become a mystery, and trainers need to know whether the stars require a rest. The trainers know Grade 1 horses should pulverize classified horses, and now intend to win.

But form has become problematic, odds will be paltry, and handicappers should abandon the horses. Grade 1 winners do not belong in classified races, period.

If other relatively classy classified or stakes horses look inviting, and the odds beckon, play. Otherwise, pass the races.

Notwithstanding all of the above, Grade 1 horses returning from layoffs do enter classified races, and sometimes win waltzing. Innate ability tells. Racegoers should not be upset. Grade 1 dropdowns may win as underlays, but they lose as underlays, too, often enough that handicappers in the know can profit by betting against them.

ONE-TURN MILE TO SPRINT

With a pair of simple adjustments, handicappers can obtain reliable pace ratings for sprints from the running lines of one-turn miles.

Ordinarily, pace ratings are best obtained from recent representative races at related distances—a distance related to today's—thus, sprint ratings best derive from sprint races. But when circumstances conspire against us, handicappers adapt by becoming resourceful.

The 4YO gelding below was entered December 28 at 6F versus $10,000 claiming horses 3up. Review its past performances and identify the representative pace lines.

Naked Jaybird — Dk. b. or br. g. 4, by Ruken—French Jay, by Barbizon
STEVENS G L — 116 — Br.—Dietrich-Dietrich-Doty (Cal) — 1988 17 2 4 1 $28,675
Tr.—Timphony Vincent $10,000 — 1987 12 1 1 5 $20,975
Own.—Neumann & Timphony — Lifetime 29 3 5 6 $49,650

4Dec88-2Hol	1	:45^3	1:11	1:37 ft	4	115	$2^{2\frac{1}{2}}$	$3^{1\frac{1}{2}}$	1^{hd}	$2^{1\frac{1}{4}}$	Stevens G L^6	10000	77-13	Silor'sTle,NkedJybird,BoldDecree	12
26Nov88-1Hol	6f	:22^1	:45^3	1:11^1 m	8¾	115	11^{14}	8^{12}	$6^{8\frac{1}{2}}$	$4^{5\frac{3}{4}}$	Ortega L E^3	10000	80-25	Romx,SundncSqur,KingOfCliforni	12
11Nov88-5Hol	6f	:22^1	:45	1:09^4 ft	26	114	12^{17}	12^{16}	$12^{9\frac{1}{4}}$	$11^{6\frac{1}{4}}$	Ortega L E^6	14000	87-11	IndinSignII,RysARumbl,ShowrDcr	12
21Oct88-3SA	6½f	:21^4	:45	1:17^1 ft	*2½	114	7^4	$7^{4\frac{3}{4}}$	$6^{5\frac{1}{4}}$	$6^{4\frac{1}{4}}$	Meza R Q^4	[S] c10500	80-18	Mel O'C., Roll A Natural, City View	9
21Oct88—Wide final 3/8															
6Oct88-1SA	6½f	:21^3	:45^1	1:16^3 ft	7	118	3^6	$3^{4\frac{1}{2}}$	3^4	$2^{2\frac{3}{4}}$	Valenzuela P A^3	10000	84-18	NobleNthn,NkedJybird,HijoElToro	11
25Sep88-9Fpx	6f	:22^1	:45^3	1:10^2 ft	3½	119	10^6	7^7	$5^{6\frac{1}{2}}$	$6^{8\frac{1}{2}}$	Patterson A^{10}	12500	86-06	StrOrphn,JustTheFcts,RdwoodBoy	10
25Sep88—Wide to stretch															
15Sep88-9Fpx	6½f	:22^1	:45^3	1:17^3 ft	*7-5	119	4^3	$3^{3\frac{1}{2}}$	1^{hd}	$1^{1\frac{1}{4}}$	Pedroza M A^6	c8000	88-15	NkdJybrd,RdwoodBoy,MschvsMtt	10
15Sep88—Bumped rear quarters stretch															
19Aug88-1Dmr	6f	:22^1	:45	1:10^1 ft	3	118	$5^{3\frac{1}{2}}$	4^5	4^5	$2^{4\frac{1}{2}}$	Pedroza M A^3	10000	82-15	WeWnnWinner,NkdJybird,MsoBlu	10
19Aug88—Lugged out 3/8															
11Aug88-9Dmr	6½f	:22	:45^1	1:17^3 ft	*3¼	116	$8^{3\frac{1}{2}}$	$5^{2\frac{1}{2}}$	$3^{1\frac{1}{2}}$	1^{hd}	Pedroza M A^8	10000	84-21	NkdJybird,LuckyAdvnc,WldPursut	12
9Jly88-2Hol	6½f	:22^1	:45^1	1:17 ft	12	116	$10^{7\frac{1}{2}}$	$7^{5\frac{1}{2}}$	$6^{6\frac{3}{4}}$	$6^{7\frac{1}{4}}$	Meza R Q^2	c25000	86-13	FrlyOmn,EmotonlFlyr,Ppy'sCnsl	12

Dec 21 SA 5f gd 1:03^4 H   Dec 15 SA 5f ft 1:01^3 H   Nov 21 SA 4f ft :52^1 H

Off-form since claimed October 21, Naked Jaybird suddenly snapped to life last out, in a one-turn mile. Up close at every call, and working out noticeably since, the gelding could be expected to show its good stuff again today.

How to rate Naked Jaybird for pace?

Three pace lines look representative: December 4, October 6, and September 15.

Fairplex Park (September 15) is a bullring. Pace ratings at bullrings do not transport well to mile ovals.

The October 6 race occurred at Santa Anita 83 days ago. Confronted with a distance change, mile to 6F, handicappers can avoid the switches by rating the October 6 performance. This is perfectly acceptable procedure. Yet recency is preferred in claiming races, if possible.

My bias is to rate both races, and rely on the higher rating as the best estimate of Naked Jaybird's pace ability.

The adjustments to the one-mile times are these:

1. No adjustment to the 4F fractional time
2. Subtract two fifths from the 6F fractional time
3. Divide the beaten lengths at 6F by one half

Convert the adjusted times to a pace rating by the standard procedure. Rate the pace of the race, the final time of the race, and the final position of the horse.

Applied to Naked Jaybird's line of December 4, handicappers get:

Actual times	45.3	1:11	beaten 1½ lengths
Adjusted times	45.3	1:10.3	beaten ¾ lengths
Pace ratings	45.3	=92	
	1:10.3	=87	
	beaten 1	=86	
	Pace rating	=265	

Handicappers who rated the October 6 sprint as well, obtained figures of 94–87–84. The pace rating is 265. The procedure requires less than thirty seconds.

Unusual circumstances baffle racetrack crowds. When horses switch from one-turn miles to sprints, racegoers cannot compare the running lines. In the 6F sprint December 28, Naked Jaybird was rated comparable to the 9–5 favorite, whose two recent pace ratings were 265 and 267. Form analysis indicated the favorite's rating might decline, Naked Jaybird's improve.

At 5–1, Naked Jaybird challenged the favorite strongly approaching the quarter pole, won handily, and paid $13.60, a definite overlay. As expected, Naked Jaybird's pace rating improved, to an impressive 270.

HAPPY NEW YEAR

On January 1, 1989, at Santa Anita, the fifth was carded for horses 4up that had never won two races.

Any horse that has arrived at age four without winning two races, or any race except a maiden or claiming race, had better present a legitimate excuse, such as few attempts.

Any horse age five or older still eligible to these events can be viewed as a washout and eliminated without mercy. The past performances will reveal records of futility, such as 1 for 18, 1 for 23, and 1 for 20.

Recreational handicappers can cut to the guts of these races quickly and reliably. First, track through the past performances hastily and eliminate any horse older than four. Spare no horse, unless it shows a half-dozen starts or fewer. For practice, run through the past performances for the Santa Anita New Year's race and pare the field of older chronic losers.

The eliminations include Mispu, Winnerwald, Spirit Bay, Dhaleem, and Exceller's Special.

Secret Selection, age five, is spared for completing only six races. But not for long. Any lightly raced 5YO should be forsaken if its only victory was gained against maiden-claiming horses. Maiden-claiming graduates do not often survive in allowance fields. Throw out Secret Selection.

The surviving 4YOs can be separated utilizing the PDQ pace ratings. In the Santa Anita race, handicappers would rate Jokers Jig, Sky High, Awesome Bud, Crackedbell, and Malo Malo.

5th Santa Anita

1 ¼ MILES. (1.40½) ALLOWANCE. Purse $34,000. 4-year-olds and upward which have never won two races. Weights, 4-year-olds, 119 lbs.; older, 120 lbs. Non-winners of a race other than claiming at one mile or over allowed 2 lbs.; such a race any distance, 4 lbs.

Mispu U-N
PINCAY L JR
Own.—Brimasea Crop
Ch. g. 5, by Miswaki—Heeria (Ire), by Habitat
Br.—Esterhazy Countess Maryann (Ky)
Tr.—Lukas D Wayne
120
1988 7 0 1 2 $13,579
1987 8 1 3 2 $34,990
Lifetime 18 1/4 4 $48,569 Turf 18 1 4 4 $48,569

Winnerwald *
SOLIS A J-
Own.—Wald & Winner
Gr. c. 4, by Private Account—Promised Woman, by Promised Land
Br.—Gentry T (Cal)
Tr.—Aguilera Humberto
119
1988 12 1 5 0 $80,900
1987 3 0 1 0 $8,400
Lifetime 23 1/7 3 $117,425 Turf 3 0 1 0 $8,400

10Apr88-4SA 1 :46² 1:12³ 1:39²ft 3 117 75¾ 2½ 2hd 2no Pincay L Jr 5 ⓈMdn 71-18 RcklssOn,Wnnrwld,Knndy'sKnockt 8
10Apr88—Troubled trip
Dec 27 Hol 5f gd 1:03⁴ H Nov 25 Hol 5f m 1:03² H Nov 18 Hol 7f ft 1:30¹ H Nov 11 Hol 5f ft 1:02¹ H

Jokers Jig B. c. 4, by Vigors—Cute n' Pretty, by Lucky Debonair
STEVENS G L 115 Br.—West S III (Ky) 1988 8 1 1 0 $19,725
Own.—Southern Cross RacingStable Tr.—Mitchell Mike 1987 0 M 0 0
Lifetime 8 1 1 0 $19,725

18Dec88-9Hol 1 1/16 :47¹ 1:12² 1:45¹sy *3½ 115 11 11 12½ 2¾ Stevens G L 1 Aw25000 73-23 AffirmdAffction,JokrsJig,Silvrstp 10
3Dec88-8Hol 1 :45 1:09⁴ 1:36 ft 7½ 115 85½ 107¼ 108½ 107¼ Stevens G L 11 Aw25000 75-12 HisLegacy,ParmountJet,AdiosGirl 12
5Jun88-7Hol 1 :45 1:10¹ 1:36 ft 3 114 31 2hd 33 44¾ Stevens G L 9 Aw35000 78-13 Lin, McKenzie Prince, RecklessOne 9
22May88-8GG 1 1/16 :45⁴ 1:09¹ 1:40⁴ft 5¾ 113 42 54 810 813 Diaz A L 5 Gold Rush H 82-13 PrspctrsGmbl,OnnMstr,GrnJdmnt 10
29Apr88-3Hol 1 1/16 :46¹ 1:10³ 1:42 ft 4½ 114 31½ 12 17 111 Stevens G L 6 M50000 90-17 Jokers Jig, Attesa, Proud Legacy 9
6Apr88-4SA 1 1/16 :47¹ 1:12¹ 1:45¹ft *2 117 94¾ 53 43½ 55¼ Hawley S 10 Mc40000 70-17 NorthernVal,GranjaAmigo,MloMlo 12
6Apr88—Lugged out, wide into stretch, lugged in
12Mar88-6SA 6f :21² :44² 1:10 ft 11 118 55 55¾ 88½ 910 Hawley S 9 Mdn 78-19 Perfecting, Elkman, Lin 11
12Mar88—Wide into stretch
28Feb88-6SA 6f :21¹ :44¹ 1:11 gd 40 118 811 77½ 76½ 51¼ Hawley S 8 Mdn 81-18 DamscusCommnder,RonBon,Coch 11
Dec 27 Hol 4f gd :49² H ●Dec 14 Hol 7f ft 1:27³ H Nov 28 Hol 7f ft 1:27³ H Nov 20 Hol 7f ft 1:27⁴ H

Sky High Ch. c. 4, by Limit to Reason—High Strung, by High Echelon
DELAHOUSSAYE E 119 Br.—Ashwood Thoroughbreds Inc (Ky) 1988 5 1 1 1 $24,050
Own.—Dollase-Duckett-Jhayare Stb Tr.—Dollase Wallace 1987 1 M 0 0
Lifetime 6 1 1 1 $24,050 Turf 1 0 0 0

3Dec88-8Hol 1 :45 1:09⁴ 1:36 ft 7½ 118 12¹⁴ 97½ 64¾ 62¼ DelhoussyE 10 Aw25000 80-12 HisLegacy,ParmountJet,AdiosGirl 12
4Aug88-7Dmr 1 1/16 Ⓣ:48² 1:13¹ 1:43³fm 6½ 120 10¹³ 106½ 97¼ 96¾ Solis A 1 Aw30000 75-16 Truly Met, TheBrazilian,MaloMalo 10
4Aug88—Wide 3/8 turn
25Jly88-2Hol 1 :45² 1:10² 1:35⁴ft 3½ 115 84¾ 53½ 32½ 1no Solis A 6 Mdn 84-16 SkyHigh,HotOpertor,Mikeylikeshim 8
25Jly88—Wide
24Jan88-4SA 1 1/16 :47² 1:12⁴ 1:44³ft *9-5 117 53½ 52½ 45 310¼ Solis A 3 Mdn 68-18 Bel AirDancer,Addie'sBro,SkyHigh 12
24Jan88—Rank early
10Jan88-6SA 1 1/16 :46⁴ 1:11¹ 1:43²ft 12 117 86½ 64½ 33 22¼ Solis A 2 Mdn 81-15 Stalwars, Sky High, Major Man 9
26Dec87-6SA 6f :22² :45² 1:10³ft 9½ 118 12¹⁶ 12¹⁴ 811 69 Solis A 5 Mdn 76-16 Joe Nasr, Peace, Din's Dancer 12
26Dec87—Wide in stretch
Dec 29 SA 4f ft :46⁴ H Dec 23 SA 4f ft :48² H Dec 18 Hol 4f m :51⁴ H ●Nov 27 Hol 7f m 1:27⁴ H

Awesome Bud B. c. 4, by Cox's Ridge—Kathleen's Girl, by Native Charger
GRYDER A T 119 Br.—Kentucky Select BloodstockI (Ky) 1988 6 1 0 0 $8,525
Own.—Garrison W & Pam Tr.—Van Berg Jack C 1987 0 M 0 0
Lifetime 6 1 0 0 $8,525

18Dec88-9Hol 1 1/16 :47¹ 1:12² 1:45¹sy 5 118 31½ 21 32½ 64 Gryder A T 7 Aw25000 70-23 AffirmdAffction,JokrsJig,Silvrstp 10
3Dec88-8Hol 1 :45 1:09⁴ 1:36 ft 12 118 33 66 87¾ 86½ Gryder A T 3 Aw25000 77-12 HisLegacy,ParmountJet,AdiosGirl 12
20Nov88-7Hol 1 1/16 :46² 1:11 1:43¹ft 8½ 118 — — — — Baze R A 3 Aw25000 — — SplendorCatch,Amtr,InfiniteMgic 10
20Nov88—Pulled up
19Oct88-7SA 1 :45³ 1:10³ 1:36 ft 5½ 117 85½ 86½ 64¾ 59 Stevens G L 1 Aw29000 79-16 HtOprtr,TmFrAccrc,DmscsCmmndr 8
19Oct88—Bumped start
12Mar88-10OP 1 :46² 1:11⁴ 1:37³ft 3½ 120 — — — — Smith M E 3 Aw14000 — — SmckoverCreek,RmboPhil,FoxCrek 8
12Mar88—Pulled up
15Feb88-6OP 1 :47² 1:13¹ 1:40¹ft *6-5 118 53¾ 2hd 11½ 12¼ Smith M E 4 Mdn 71-22 AwsomBd,Gnt'sAgrmnt,HnrryRgnt 9
15Feb88—5 wide.
●Dec 29 Hol 5f ft :59⁴ H ●Dec 10 Hol 1 ft 1:39² H Nov 30 Hol 4f ft :47¹ H ●Nov 24 Hol 6f m 1:11⁴ H

Crackedbell Dk. b. or br. g. 4, by Private Account—Belle O' Belgium, by Amarullah
BLACK C A 119 Br.—Gentry T (Ky) 1988 5 1 1 0 $20,620
Own.—Koosa & Pineda Tr.—Anderson Joe 1987 0 M 0 0
Lifetime 5 1 1 0 $20,620

18Dec88-9Hol 1 1/16 :47¹ 1:12² 1:45¹sy 8 118 914 96¾ 65¾ 51½ Castanon A L 4 Aw25000 72-23 AffirmdAffction,JokrsJig,Silvrstp 10
18Dec88—Wide into stretch
3Dec88-4Hol 1 :45⁴ 1:10⁴ 1:36²ft 8½ 118 2½ 2hd 1½ 1no Castanon A L 3 Mdn 81-12 Crackedbell, Quavo, Winivor 9
4Nov88-6SA 1 1/16 :46² 1:11 1:43²ft 8 117 66½ 87½ 78½ 57 Sorenson D 4 Mdn 77-18 LondonFix,Knndy'sKnockout,Shrk 12
4Nov88—Wide into stretch
5Sep88-5Bel 7f :23² :46⁴ 1:24¹m 23 118 75½ 46 36 25 Carter T 3 Mdn 76-22 SecretClaim,Crckedbell,DilyReview 8
26Aug88-2Sar 6f :22³ :45² 1:10³sy 30 117 76¾ 77½ 46 47½ Carter T 2 Mdn 80-20 Current Voyage, Poulpe, Deck 7
Dec 28 SA 4f ft :46⁴ H Dec 13 SA 5f ft :59 H Nov 30 SA 3f gd :38 H Nov 19 SA 1 ft 1:43² H

Spirit Bay — B. h. 5, by Sir Ivor—Ocean Choir, by Foolish Pleasure
SHOEMAKER W — 118 — Br.—Kinghaven Farms Limited (Ont-C) — 1988 8 0 3 3 $19,763
Own.—Kinghaven Farm — Tr.—Attfield Roger — 1987 3 1 0 0 $3,000
Lifetime 11 1 3 3 $22,763

8Dec88-7Grd 1 1/16 :484 1:403 2:142ft *2¼ 117 813 66 35 33½ Seymour D J 9 Aw20500 78-27 NobleImperator,NttyDred,SpiritBy 10
1Dec88-9Grd 1 :462 1:111 1:384ft 5½ 119 87½ 45 3½ 32 Seymour D J 9 Aw24000 84-20 Subtle Chaos,IronStrike,SpiritBay 11
6Nov88-8Grd 6½f :233 :473 1:212m 3½ 119 911 88½ 45 2¾ SymourDJ 2 Ⓢ Aw20500 78-30 AdmirlMcFrln,SpirtBy,PlmrSprngs 10
23Oct88-9WO 1 1/16 :474 1:131 1:454sy 7½ 121 68½ 65½ 35½ 24½ SymourDJ 4 Ⓢ Aw22600 75-24 GoldenVigor,SpiritBy,HloStonbridg 6
15Oct88-4WO 6½f :223 :46 1:174ft 2¾ 117 75½ 88½ 43 3½ Seymour D J 6 19000 83-21 Moon Compass, EcuD'Or,SpiritBay 8
22Sep88-7WO 6f :223 :461 1:112ft 3½ 118 42 2½ 21½ 2nk Seymour D J 2 16000 86-24 ShrwoodForst,SpiritBy,GlryStorm 8
5Sep88-10WO 7f :224 :453 1:252m 8½ 119 62½ 53½ 48 65 Seymour D J 10 20000 77-17 CoolMrg,AccssCod,IMsprsombody 11
18Aug88-7WO 7f :232 :462 1:234ft 12 118 63¾ 54½ 48½ 49½ Seymour D J 5 25000 80-22 TopWarrior,BellLap,KeepWhistling 8
22Aug87-4FE 5½f :223 :464 1:061ft *1 115 54¾ 31 2hd 1¾ Standring J S 9 Mdn 89-22 SpiritBy,DiplomticMn,DonrPcome 10
22Aug87—Sluggish start
16Aug87-4WO 6f :222 :454 1:114ft 6 120 95½ 88½ 79¾ 65 Platts R 8 Ⓢ Mdn 79-18 Andy's Prince,That'sABet,LtSting 10
Dec 29 SA 6f ft 1:011 H Dec 24 SA 3f ft :361 H ●Nov 27 WO tr.t 4f gd :481 H Nov 3 WO tr.t 5f ft 1:053 B

Dhaleem — B. h. 6, by Lyphard—Patia, by Don
OLIVARES F — 120 — Br.—de Chambure-Ouaki Est-Ades (Ky) — 1987 17 0 3 2 $26,900
Own.—Six-S Racing Stable — Tr.—O'Hara John — 1986 3 1 0 0 $3,869
Lifetime 20 1 3 2 $30,769 — Turf 16 1 3 2 $30,069

24Dec87-9Hol 1⅛ :47 1:113 1:49 ft 14 115 45½ 55½ 59½ 710½ FernndezAL 4 Aw36000 81-10 Fiction, The Great Prize, Sinforoso 7
12Nov87-7SA 1¼ Ⓣ :481 1:383 2:041fm 3 117 86½ 83¾ 86¾ 77¾ Toro F 4 Aw30000 58-34 Convincing, Proud Cat. Unicopia 8
12Nov87—Steadied 3/16
14Oct87-5SA 1¼ Ⓣ :492 1:374 2:041fm 12 118 87 98¾ 85 31 DelhoussyeE 8 Aw30000 65-34 Rough Passage, Feraud, Dhaleem 9
14Oct87—Wide in stretch
19Sep87-10Fpx 1 1/16 :48 1:133 1:451ft 17 118 106½ 96½ 98 109½ FernndezAL 1 Aw27000 75-18 Bugarian, Proving Spark, Shrewdy 10
6Sep87-7Dmr 1 1/16 Ⓣ :471 1:12 1:424fm 14 118 87 86¾ 67 78½ Kaenel J L 2 Aw24000 77-16 Rufus Dawes, Ima Bullet,ChiefPal 10
6Sep87—Rank 1/8
29Aug87-5Dmr 1⅜ Ⓣ :494 2:171fm 18 117 35 53¾ 54 74¾ Ortega L E7 62500 79-18 Migrator, Solidified, CuttingWind 10
10Aug87-5Dmr 1⅛ Ⓣ :474 1:122 1:493fm 15 118 811 67 56½ 54¼ Meza R Q6 Aw23000 81-11 L'Empire, Ima Bullet, First Dibs 9
29Jly87-9Dmr 1 1/16 Ⓣ :474 1:122 1:431fm 7½ 118 76½ 73½ 43¼ 43¾ Ortega L E6 Aw23000 80-13 Quietly Bold, L'Empire, Table Glow 9
19Jun87-5Hol 1 1/16 Ⓣ :46 1:094 1:403fm 7½ 117 75½ 74½ 45½ 54¼ Ortega L E 10 Aw24000 87-09 Forlaway,TableGlow,ContactGame 10
19Jun87—Bumped 1/16
6Jun87-11GG 1⅜ Ⓣ :491 1:392 2:18 fm *2 119 31 2hd 1hd 23 Ortega L E 2 Aw16000 72-20 De Soto,Dhaleem,LonesomeDancer 9
Dec 28 SA 4f ft :481 H Dec 20 SA 6f ft 1:14 H Dec 11 SA 7f ft 1:253 H Dec 5 SA 5f ft 1:01 H

Secret Selection — B. g. 5, by Convincingly—Proof Tested, by Olden Times
MCCARRON C J — 116 — Br.—Proctor J & W L (Tex) — 1988 6 1 2 1 $24,950
Own.—Sutton H E — Tr.—Proctor Willard L — 1987 0 M 0 0
Lifetime 6 1 2 1 $24,950

4Dec88-7Hol 6f :221 :451 1:10 ft 59 113 1011 95½ 76½ 55 Kimes C9 Aw24000 87-13 SnstionlStr,FrontlinFbl,SnowPrch 10
2Jun88-3Hol 6½f :22 :45 1:162ft 9 119 711 79½ 48 36¾ DelahoussayeE6 25000 89-13 Alitak, LansManus,SecretSelection 7
22Apr88-6SA 1 1/16 :462 1:12 1:453gd *1 118 45 31½ 31½ 1½ Gryder A T9 M45000 73-20 SecretSelction,SuprJimmy,SolrGuy 9
2Apr88-4SA 6f :222 :462 1:112ft 2½ 118 61¾ 84½ 43 45¼ Black C A1 M45000 75-19 MuscatKid,SocialMan,FirstHolidy 12
2Apr88—Crowded 3/8 to 1/4; wide into stretch
5Mar88-4SA 6f :22 :453 1:102ft 3½ 118 76 44½ 46½ 24½ Black C A10 M45000 81-14 HechizrDOro,ScrtSlction,VryDoubl 12
19Feb88-6SA 6f :214 :452 1:114ft 26 117 86½ 107¾ 75 2½ Black C A7 M45000 78-23 Vysotsky, Secret Selection, Trask 12
19Feb88—Broke slowly; very wide in stretch
Dec 31 SA 3f ft :37 H Dec 24 SA 6f ft 1:124 H Dec 19 SA 4f ft :472 H Nov 27 Hol 6f m 1:162 H

Exceller's Special — Dk. b. or br. h. 5, by Exceller—Keys Special, by Chieftain
SIBILLE R — 116 — Br.—Reverie Knoll Farm (Fla) — 1988 6 1 2 0 $27,125
Own.—Ippolito S — Tr.—Ippolito Steve — 1987 2 M 0 0
Lifetime 9 1 3 0 $27,849 — Turf 3 0 1 0 $724

15Dec88-6Hol 1 :45 1:101 1:361gd *2½ 121 13 12 13 12 Sibille R 10 M50000 82-18 Excllr'sSpcl,CorondBy,MjstcSght 10
14May88-6Hol 1 1/16 :462 1:113 1:451ft 4½ 1195 43½ 54 44 47½ Corral J R 8 Mdn 66-15 PrExpns,ExcptonlTlnt,PrvSmthng 12
17Apr88-6SA 1 1/16 :46 1:11 1:432ft 9 1185 2½ 12 21½ 24 Corral J R 7 Mdn 80-17 Delegant,Exceller'sSpecil,Dupond 10
30Mar88-6SA 6½f :22 :45 1:164ft 2½ 120 53 56 47 49¾ Meza R Q 7 Mdn 76-18 WllNWylon,ExcptnlTlnt,MrkOfCzr 10
27Feb88-4SA 1 1/16 :471 1:113 1:443ft *2 119 65 45 49½ 413 Meza R Q4 Mdn 65-17 ThirtyGrand,Daloma,FortunteHour 10
27Feb88—Broke slowly; lugged in stretch
14Jan88-6SA 6f :213 :444 1:10 ft *2½ 119 53 41½ 31½ 21¾ Meza R Q10 Mdn 86-21 UndrAndOvr,Ecllr'sSpcl,InfltnHdg 12
17Jly87♦5N'wmarket(Eng) 1 1:424gd 16 126 Ⓣ 611 SnbrnW GlnIntl(Mdn) Just Mine, No Sleuth, KristalAir 11
15Jun87♦6Windsor(Eng) a1¼ 2:144sf 5 123 Ⓣ 510 EddryP BrnEndGrdtn Mccubbin, Proud Crest,ClassicTale 8
27Oct86♦4Lingfield(Eng) 7f 1:274sf 10 126 Ⓣ 21½ Mcd R Willow(Mdn) Lyphento,Excellr'sSpcil,Thornfild 16
Dec 26 SA 5f ft 1:004 H Dec 3 SA 5f ft 1:002 H Nov 27 SA 5f m 1:043 H Nov 19 SA 5f ft 1:003 H

```
Malo Malo                              Gr. c. 4, by Valdez—Wickedly, by Decidedly
 VALENZUELA F H               1105   Br.—Pope Mrs G A Jr (Cal)            1988 12 1 2 5    $42,950
Own.—Ettlinger J A or Greta           Tr.—Wiseheart Larry                  1987  2 M 0 1     $3,100
                                      Lifetime   14 1 2 6   $46,050        Turf  4 0 0 3    $15,375
3Dec88-8Hol  1    :45  1:094 1:36 ft     14 115  106½ 43½ 34 41    ValenzuelFH2 Aw25000 82-12 HisLegacy,ParmountJet,AdiosGirl 12
7Oct88-5SA   1    :451 1:094 1:372ft     9½ 115  711 713 45 21¼    Gryder A T5    40000 80-19 Lot'sCuriosity,MaloMlo,SpekHigh 10
   7Oct88—Took up sharply 3/8
14Sep88-5Dmr 1   Ⓣ:4731:1121:36 fm     *3½ 116  73½ 74¾ 66½ 56¼   Baze R A7    Aw33000 85-12 TnkerPort,Scobey,Gntlmn'sHonor 10
   14Sep88—Wide final 3/8
22Aug88-7Dmr 1 1/16Ⓣ:4831:1331:45 fm    4¼ 116  52¼ 42 31½ 31¾    Gryder A T6  Aw32000 73-25 Clev, Gunnabeasaint, Malo Malo 10
4Aug88-7Dmr  1 1/16Ⓣ:4821:1311:433fm    3½ 117  32 3nk 1hd 31½    Gryder A T10 Aw30000 80-16 Truly Met, TheBrazilian,MaloMalo 10
24Jun88-5Hol 1 1/8Ⓣ:48 1:12 1:483fm     17 114  53½ 52¼ 31½ 31    Gryder A T6  Aw35000 84-13 JustAsLucky,TwiceElegnt,MloMlo 10
16Jun88-7Hol 1 1/16 :454 1:103 1:431ft    8 114  56 55 58 511      Gryder A T8  Aw35000 73-15 IzASros,PureExpense,Intensitizer 10
4May88-6Hol  1 1/8 :474 1:122 1:501ft    2¼ 112  31 21 1hd 1½      Gryder A T4   M35000 86-19 MaloMlo,RecittionSpin,RodToWin 10
6Apr88-4SA   1 1/16 :471 1:121 1:451ft    6 117  74½ 75½ 63¾ 33½   Gryder A T2   M40000 71-17 NorthernVal,GranjaAmigo,MloMlo 12
9Mar88-4SA   1 1/16 :46  1:103 1:452ft   2¼ 117  59½ 59½ 28 23½    Gryder A T6   M40000 70-19 FnHostg,MloMlo,WngOutThWorld 11
 Dec 27 SA 5f ft 1:002 H      Dec 19 SA 6f ft 1:132 H      Dec 13 SA 4f ft :49 H      ●Nov 29 SA tr.t 4f gd :484 H
```

If one horse possesses a clearly superior pace rating, the handicapping is finished.

If numerical ratings are unclear or too close for comfort, look for the improving 4YO. The fewer its attempts, and misses, the better.

In the sample race, Malo Malo has a significantly higher rating than its foes. Notwithstanding its fourteen races, Malo Malo figures, and deserves the handicapper's nod. Happily, the colt won, at 6–1, and paid $14.60.

The trick is getting to the nub of the real competition by eliminating mercilessly the older chronic losers, including 4YOs with too many losses, such as more than fifteen. Why would anyone expect these horses will reverse form and win today?

A variation of this type of field is an allowance race for nonwinners of a race other than maiden or claiming, or nonwinners of two races other than maiden or claiming. A race for nonwinners of two races, 4up, bars horses that have won claiming races. Many 4YOs and 5YOs have won several claiming races, but not a single allowance race. Early in the calendar year especially these consistent claiming-race winners can enter allowance fields for nonwinners other than maiden or claiming, and shine.

A CLEAR LOOK BACK

The fifth at Santa Anita on January 5 was a 6F sprint for $25,000 claiming horses, 4up. Below are the speed points, PDQ pace ratings (variants applied), recent class levels, and odds for the ten entrants.

Which do you prefer? Why?

	Speed Pts.	PDQ Pace	Class Level	Odds
Eighty Below Zero	8	271	$16,000	13–1
Superb Moment	5	260	20,000	5–1
John's Retreat	5	267	25,000	10–1
Dance For Lee	0	273	Alw,NW2X	5–2
Silent Impact	1	270	20,000	12–1
Biscayne Boy	6	NR	25,000	41–1
Gossarone	0	266	25,000	8–1
Boo Boo's Buckaroo	1	NR	20,000	4–1
Tranzor	1	264	20,000	6–1
Rays A Rumble	7	260	20,000	13–1

The track, officially labeled muddy, was muddy-wet-hard instead, and had played evenly, favoring no particular running style, during the first four races.

I played this race, as did the pair of professionals sitting alongside me this rainy day. I bet to win on Dance For Lee, the favorite, and in the exacta I boxed Dance For Lee and Eighty Below Zero, and used Dance For Lee on top only of Silent Impact and Tranzor.

Why Tranzor, racegoers wonder? The gelding earned a low pace rating for the field, to be sure, but last out had been haltered by one of the leading claiming trainers in southern California, Noble Threewitt. These kind normally improve following the claim, and Tranzor represented an exacta overlay with the favorite on top. Tranzor finished third.

Nonetheless, taking a clear look back, I misplayed the race, and inexcusably.

Eighty Below Zero won wire to wire by three lengths, setting fractions of 21.2, 44.0, 56.1, and 1:08.4. Dance For Lee, devoid of speed and shuffled back in the initial strides, finished a dull fourth. The winner paid $29.20.

Eighty Below Zero had three advantages:

1. A clear early-speed edge, combined with a post-position advantage versus its only early threat, Rays A Rumble.

Moreover, deeper inspection of the past performances showed Rays A Rumble had never broken 22 flat, and usually ran 22 and change to the first call. Eighty Below Zero normally ran faster than 22 flat to the first call, and at times, as he would today, went 21.2.

2. A pace rating within a length (two points translates to a length) of the favorite.
3. Good races at a class level one bracket removed from to-day's, a rise in claiming class that should trouble nobody.

Dance For Lee possessed little early speed, and had not raced since October 29.

At the odds on the two high-rated horses, the correct wager would have backed Eighty Below Zero to win, plus an exacta box with Dance For Lee.

None of the professionals in the box supported Eighty Below Zero to Win. All three bet Dance For Lee to win. The bets re-sulted in part from a troubled trip in a fast $32,000 claiming sprint Dance For Lee might have won otherwise during Oak Tree at Santa Anita in October.

The lesson to be learned anew regards the importance of early speed. When suited to the class and probable pace, the juxta-position of early speed and high odds is always a prime consid-eration.

In fact, early speed is more preferable at high odds than low odds. At low odds, early-speed horses win far more than their rightful share of the races, but return dollar losses. Too many customers bet the obvious early speed. At high odds, the early speed not as apparent to the crowd, or for some reason dis-counted, the early-speed horses win fewer races, but clearly enough to toss substantial profits.

Racegoers need remember only that when all tracks, all classes, all distances, are considered, early-speed horses win approximately 2½ times the number of races probabilities would expect, and pay off at average odds of as high as 9–2.

Eighty Below Zero is exactly the type of early-speed horse that contributes to the 9–2 payoff, and makes underbet early-speed leaders among the best risks at the races. Recreational handicappers who take the trouble to calculate speed points can find similar opportunities virtually every other racing day.

Don't let them steal away, as I did this time.

BOUNCE

And on the fourteenth day of racing, two early winners at the Santa Anita meeting returned as potential repeaters. Each was entered under allowance conditions, for horses that had never won an allowance race.

In the fifth the crowd supported Book Collector with abandon. In the eighth, It's Not My Job got heavy late action, went off a solid favorite. Below are the past performances for both, alongside the records of the main contention.

Examine the records closely. What parallels between Book Collector and It's Not My Job might a savvy racegoer observe that the public can be expected to overlook?

5th Santa Anita

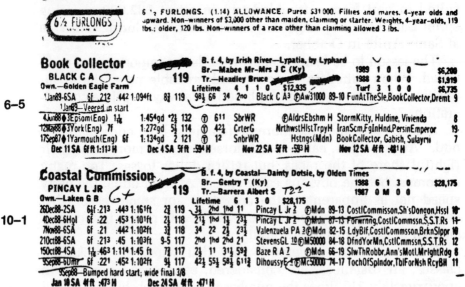

Book Collector and It's Not My Job have slightly better figures than their foes. But will they repeat their impressive comeback performances? Is either horse a decent wager at the odds?

8th Santa Anita

Form analysis becomes a tricky art at times, but neither Book Collector nor It's Not My Job represent sensible bets at the odds. Each horse is part of a pattern that fools the crowd repeatedly, but offers alert handicappers opportunities for outstanding overlays.

Recreational handicappers should notice the following:

1. Book Collector lost by a nose following a six month absence from competition, not to mention shipment from England.

2. It's Not My Job won by three handy lengths following a 5½ month absence from competition.

Anytime ordinary horses (nonstakes horses) win or finish within a length in rapid time following layoffs of five months or longer, the comeback efforts should be regarded as overexertions, which can trigger the phenomenon called the "bounce" pattern. The strenuous comeback races take too much energy too soon, tax the muscles, and suggest the horses might regress in their conditioning if they return to the races too soon, as long as 30 days later.

The horses often perform below expectation, falling back, or bouncing, when the going gets tough in the late stages. Moreover, because the comeback races were impressive, the public overbets the horses next out. They "bounce" at low odds, a pattern handicappers surely wish to avoid.

In the comeback races, Book Collector almost upset at 8–1, and It's Not My Job surprised at 14–1. Next out, Book Collector never threatened at 6–5, It's Not My Job collapsed at the quarter pole at 2–1. Who needs it?

A particularly optimistic aspect of the bounce pattern is precisely that the horses lose as underlays, but bounce back, and often win, next time, as overlays. Because the horses have disappointed at low odds, the public discounts them. But in the third start following a layoff, any effects of overexertion in the comeback effort have been nullified by continuous training and a second race.

At Santa Anita on January 12 the rush to Book Collector resulted in part from a troubled trip out of the gate, which the filly almost overcame.

It's Not My Job was being handled by Bobby Frankel, arguably the finest claiming-race trainer ever. The horse had won handily, Frankel raised it to allowance conditions, and a draw into post-position No. 1 afforded an easy run and good position around the clubhouse turn.

All of the above is true enough, but superfluous. All-out efforts following long layoffs automatically qualify the horses as candidates to bounce. At paltry odds, ignore them. Wait for the third race in the comeback. If the horses have bounced, the odds next time will be sweeter. Bet then, provided the horses figure on the fundamentals and numbers.

Regarding the fundamentals, recreational handicappers are urged to appreciate that It's Not My Job is a seven-year-old still eligible to a race that bars any horse that has won a single allowance race. Seven-year-olds that have not yet won an allowance race are not exactly superb bets to do so today, bounce or no bounce.

WHEN A FILLY BEATS THE COLTS

Occasionally fillies challenge colts, and handicappers must determine their fate.

The golden rule is simple.

Where fillies and colts appear evenly matched, the females can be discounted.

But where fillies look clearly superior, they can throttle the boys, and do.

Sensible horsemen adhere to the same fundamental guidelines. When Charles Whittingham or Neil Drysdale, of southern California, enters a filly against colts, handicappers on the scene understand the ladies probably enjoy a class edge. D. Wayne Lukas will be a greater risk-taker, but when Lukas spots his fillies against males, the females undoubtedly will be talented.

The crowd notes that a female is tackling real men, and backs away in a traditional chauvinistic reaction. The odds creep up, at times higher than warranted. If the fillies look better, and the odds beckon, make the play.

The situation arises in distance races, under allowances for nonwinners once, twice, or three times other than maiden or claiming, or in stakes, notably for two-year-olds. Below is an outstanding illustration from the 1989 winter season at Santa Anita.

Review the records of the filly entered against colts and horses, along with two of the interesting four-year-old colts that remained lightly raced and still unclassified. It's January 28.

7th Santa Anita

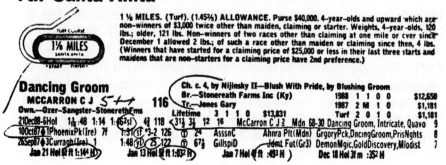

The filly Lyphka, trained by careful Neil Drysdale, last out finished sixth of twelve, beaten only 4 ½ lengths, in the Grade 1 Yellow Ribbon Stakes, an invitational, and arguably the premier turf event for older fillies and mares in the nation. Yellow Ribbon runners-up Nastique and No Review had already won subsequent graded stakes attempts. Lyphka's French form looked superb, including a win in a listed stakes (Lilas), and a second in the Grade 2 Prix d'Astarte.

Listed-stakes winners that have finished second in Grade 2 company are virtually slumming when entered against older horses that have not yet won two allowance races. The class advantage is palpable. I trust recreational handicappers can appreciate that.

Now examine the two colts of interest here.

Dancing Groom is entered above its conditions. The colt is eligible for allowances, nonwinners once other than maiden or claiming. By Nijinsky II, world's leading sire, this colt exits a romp on a slow surface versus maidens. Beautifully bred, well-trained, lightly raced, it might be any kind. With the exacta in the offering, handicappers can protect an investment on Lyphka with an exacta box between the two.

Malkhatoun has come to Santa Anita from France as well, and has been entered above its eligibility conditions also. But

Malkhatoun's recent starts overseas occurred in unlisted stakes (overnight races), and in its solitary Grade 2 test, the colt was thumped by twelve lengths. At 2–1, no play.

With Neil Drysdale announcing loudly his filly possesses some class, handicappers need not hesitate at 3–1. The filly was 4–1 with two minutes left to wager, but got knocked down a point in the end.

Recreational handicappers will want to know, what about the layoff since November 6?

If the class edge is pronounced, accept the short form. A peak performance is not required to win. Only an ordinary performance is required, and this is readily dispensed when good horses return from vacation. Moreover, Lyphka shows the standard five-furlong workout or longer within 14 days, the conditioning norm for horses returning from long layoffs. Form may not be extra sharp, but it's acceptable.

When the gates opened Lyphka sped to the front and stayed there. It was a facile victory. Malkhatoun chased the filly all the way, but never got closer than a length. Lyphka paid $8.40 when she might have been 6–5.

ONE-RACE WONDERS?

You find them in maiden races. I call them one-race wonders. The horses show one terrible race. They have been distanced and uncompetitive at every call. Still, handicappers wonder what might happen today.

Examine the three below. They were entered in a route for 3YO maidens at Santa Anita, March 5, 1989.

6th Santa Anita

1 1-16 MILES. (1.40½) MAIDEN. Purse $29,000. 3-year-olds. Weight, 117 lbs. (Non-starters for a claiming price of $32,000 or less in their last three starts preferred.)

Grand Piano 2+
VALENZUELA P A
Own.—Gann E A

B. c. 3, by Fappiano—Screenland, by Silent Screen
Br.—Sltzr&AmrivstThbdPrtnrsNo2 (Ky) 1989 1 M 1 0 $5,400
Tr.—Frankel Robert 1988 0 M 0 0
117 Lifetime 1 0 1 0 $5,400
18Feb89-6SA 7f :223 :454 1:241ft 6½ 117 42½ 42½ 2hd 2nk Valenzuela P A 3 Mdn 79-19 MutinyOnIc,GrndPino,KingArmour 8
18Feb89—Wide 3/8 turn
Feb 14 SA 5f gd 1:01 H   Feb 7 SA tr.t 4f gd :492 H   Feb 1 SA 5f ft 1:011 H   Jan 25 SA 4f ft :50 H

Stylish Believer

Ch. c. 3, by Believe It—Lots of Flair, by Bold Native'

STEVENS G L   117

Br.—Clark B C & Indian Creek (Ky)   1989 2 M 1 1 $10,150

Own.—Siegel M-Jan-Samantha

Tr.—Mayberry Brian A   1988 4 M 0 1 $6,800

Lifetime 6 0 1 2 $16,950

19Feb89-6SA 1¹⁄₁₆:464 1:114 1:453ft 4½ 117 911 76¾ 32½ 2½ Stevens.G L 10 Mdn 72-21 RolIngDont,StylshBlvr,NrthrnDrm 11
19Feb89—Bumped 3/16; crowded 1/8

22Jan89-6SA 1¹⁄₁₆:464 1:113 1:44¹ft 9 117 10⁷ 84½ 63¾ 3⁴ Solis A10 Mdn 76-14 SuperRedy,Hrmonic,StylishBelievr 12
22Jan89—Wide 7/8 turn. into stretch; lugged in late

26Dec88-6SA 1:47¹ 1:112 1:37 ft 20 117 42½ 3² 3³ 31½ Solis A¹ Mdn 82-13 FirstLoylty,SuperRedy,StylishBlivr 9
26Dec88—Lugged in late

27Nov88-6Hol 1¹⁄₁₆:472 1:131 1:454gd 44 118 109¾ 96½ 54½ 49¾ Baze R A11 Mdn 61-24 Stphn'sSnr,SvnRvrs,NjnsksGrndsn 12
27Nov88—Wide 7/8

13Nov88-6Hol 1 :464 1:114 1:362ft *9-5e118 8³ 88½ 88½ 813¾ Pincay L Jr7 Mdn 67-13 ExemplryLeder,SevenRivers,RcrRx 9
13Nov88—Lugged in drive

16Oct88-6SA 1¹⁄₁₆:462 1:113 1:454ft 26 117 6⁸ 67¾ 59½ 511½ Solis A11 Mdn 60-16 SnowsInPris,Pster'sImge,RcerRex 12

Feb 13 SA 5f gd 1:01³ Hg   Jan 17 SA 5f ft 1:02⁴ H   Jan 13 SA 3f ft :36¹ H

Advocate Training   ?

B. c. 3, by Desert Wine—Desire, by Graustark

MCCARRON C J   117

Br.—Mabee Mr-Mrs J C (Cal)   1989 1 M 0 0 $675

Own.—Golden Edge Farm

Tr.—Jones Gary   1988 0 M 0 0

Lifetime 1 0 0 0 $675

10Feb89-6SA 6f :221 :461 1:123m 5 117 81² 813 6⁹ 510 Hawley S 2 ⑤Mdn 65-25 PiedsPromise,IrishDrmin,SrosTown 8
10Feb89—Rough start

Feb 23 Hol 5f ft :59² H   Feb 18 Hol 4f ft :47⁴ H   ●Feb 3 SA 6f ft 1:12⁴ H   Jan 29 Hol 6f ft 1:14¹ Hg

Betting favorites were Grand Piano and Stylish Believer. Grand Piano would be stretching out following a par performance at seven furlongs. Stylish Believer was returning from a sub-par race he blew due to an awful trip. Stylish Believer had not run a par time for the class in six attempts.

Now glance at Advocate Training. If handicappers do not dart past the awful line, a number of plus factors combine to make the colt intriguing. Consider the signs:

1. The poor line occurred in the mud and followed a "rough start."
2. The workouts before and after the debut are regular and sharp, and the last is a fast five-furlong turn, a definite positive.
3. The trainer is national leader Gary Jones.
4. The rider is national leader Chris McCarron.
5. The colt is a son of Desert Wine, a son himself of the leading sire Damascus.

These circumstances are virtually prototypical. One ugly race, surrounded by positive signs.

Yet another circumstance is indispensable; generous odds. For most of the prerace betting Advocate Training was offered at 15–1. The odds near posttime on the three contenders:

Grand Piano	5–2
Stylish Believer	3–1
Advocate Training	12–1

Advocate Training became irresistible at the odds, an attractive value bet. At 5–1 I would have dismissed the colt. The overlay must be plain.

Sometimes horses having one poor line and several vital signs and positive angles are strongly bet. The connections believe the horse has a future, and the leak has flowed. Abandon these. As underlays, they must be deserted. If they triumph by half a furlong, it's no matter. By backing potential, not performance, at low odds, handicappers lose in the long run.

SIXTH RACE **Santa Anita** **MARCH 5, 1989**

1 1/16 MILES. (1.40⅗) MAIDEN. Purse $29,000. 3-year-olds. Weight, 117 lbs. (Non-starters for a claiming price of $32,000 or less in their last three starts preferred.)

Value of race $29,000; value to winner $15,950; second $5,800; third $4,350; fourth $2,175; fifth $725. Mutuel pool $932,825.

Last Raced	Horse	Eqt.	A.	Wt	PP	St	¼	½	¾	Str	Fin	Jockey	Odds $1
10Feb89 6SA5	Advocate Training	b	3	117	11	5	3^{1}	$3^{\frac{1}{2}}$	$3^{1\frac{1}{2}}$	$1^{\frac{1}{2}}$	$1^{5\frac{1}{2}}$	McCarron C J	12.80
5Feb89 6SA	Nijinskys Grandson	b	3	117	3	1	$1^{\frac{1}{2}}$	$1^{\frac{1}{2}}$	$1^{\frac{1}{2}}$	2^{2}	2^{nk}	Hawley S	16.60
18Feb89 4SA2	Grand Piano	b	3	117	4	7	4^{1}	4^{2}	$4^{1\frac{1}{2}}$	$3^{\frac{1}{2}}$	3^{nk}	Valenzuela P A	2.70
19Feb89 6SA3	Northern Drama	b	3	117	10	3	2^{1}	2^{1}	$2^{\frac{1}{2}}$	4^{1}	$4^{1\frac{1}{4}}$	Solis A	13.40
19Feb89 6SA4	Event		3	112	6	10	9^{hd}	$10^{3\frac{1}{2}}$	8^{hd}	6^{hd}	$5^{\frac{3}{4}}$	Valenzuela F H5	8.70
19Feb89 6SA2	Stylish Believer	b	3	117	7	11	10^{2}	7^{hd}	5^{hd}	$5^{1\frac{1}{2}}$	$6^{\frac{3}{4}}$	Stevens G L	3.20
12Feb89 6SA7	Damask Star		3	117	8	4	$6^{1\frac{1}{2}}$	6^{1}	6^{1}	7^{3}	7^{3}	Santos J A	13.30
18Feb89 4SA4	Devil's Walk		3	117	2	6	$7^{1\frac{1}{2}}$	8^{1}	9^{1}	$8^{1\frac{1}{2}}$	8^{2}	Pincay L Jr	4.20
18Feb89 6SA3	Try Trust	b	3	117	9	9	$5^{\frac{1}{2}}$	5^{1}	7^{1}	9^{hd}	9no	Delahoussaye E	8.80
18Feb89 4SA5	Campaign Promise	b	3	112	1	2	11	11	11	10^{4}	10^{7}	Garcia H J5	99.80
12Feb89 6SA9	Smart Dollars		3	117	5	8	8^{1}	9^{1}	$10^{1\frac{1}{2}}$	11	11	Black C A	101.60

OFF AT 3:54. Start good. Won ridden out. Time, :22⅖, :46, 1:10⅖, 1:35⅖, 1:41⅗ Track fast.

$2 Mutuel Prices:			
11–ADVOCATE TRAINING	27.60	13.80	7.60
3–NIJINSKYS GRANDSON		13.60	7.20
4–GRAND PIANO			4.00

B. c, by Desert Wine—Desire, by Graustark. Trainer Jones Gary. Bred by Mabee Mr–Mrs J C (Cal).

ADVOCATE TRAINING, close up early and five wide into the clubhouse turn, took over approaching the quarter pole raced a bit greenly early in the drive and drew out in the final furlong. NIJINSKYS GRANDSON set the early

PEAKING FORM IN CLAIMING RACES

When analyzing claiming races, improved workouts following an improved race signals peaking form.

The six-year-old gelding in the chart on page 334 was entered March 8, 1989, same class, same distance as its most recent race.

Where's Machias — Dk. b. or br. g. 6, by Domineering—Sue Ann, by Truly Tempered
PINCAY L JR 4+ — 115 — Br.—Grooms H (Wash) — Tr.—Murphy Marcus J — $16,000
Own.—Redman L & Ida — Lifetime 58 5 15 12 $54,650
1989 5 0 0 1 $4,650
1988 18 1 4 5 $17,152
Turf 1 0 1 0 $640

24Feb89-9SA 1⅛ :46² 1:10³ 1:50 ft 8½ 117 22½ 23½ 23 41¼ Pincay L Jr 2 16000 77-16 OurBrndX.,SirTyson,Mischifinmnd 12
10Feb89-9SA 1 1/16 :47² 1:12⁴ 1:46 m 21 116 87½ 65 45½ 34 Pedroza M A7 16000 66-25 FriskMeNot,SirTyson,Whr'sMchis 10
4Feb89-1SA 6½f :21⁴ :45¹ 1:17⁴ sy 50 116 63¾ 65 87¼ 69¾ Solis A11 16000 71-30 RunCougrRun,MuiMelody,LsForvr 12
4Feb89—Wide final 3/8
25Jan89-2SA 1 1/16 :46³ 1:11² 1:44² ft 4½ 116 53 53½ 42½ 43¼ Stevens G L5 c12500 76-17 Bold Reach, Tricky Lad, Siraluovat 9
25Jan89—Wide into stretch
14Jan89-5SA 1 1/16 :45⁴ 1:10³ 1:44 ft 16 116 55½ 77½ 68 75¼ Stevens S A5 16000 76-11 CrystlCttr,LstCommnd,ExtcArbtr 11
31Dec88-1SA 6½f :21² :44¹ 1:16¹ ft 14 116 111 119½ 1112 97½ Stevens G L 1 16000 81-10 Pppy'sConsul,MuiMlody,KingClyd 12
31Dec88—Rank 5/8, 4 1/2
7Dec88-5Hol 1 1/16 :47¹ 1:12 1:44 ft 4 115 21½ 22 31½ 42¾ Stevens G L 3 16000 78-17 Chili Hill, Kamp Out, Tablado 9
7Dec88—Veered out start
27Nov88-2Hol 1 1/16 :47² 1:12³ 1:45¹ gd 7½ 115 42 21½ 21 21¼ Stevens G L 5 12500 72-24 Extrnix,Wher'sMchis,BrgirStndrd 12
27Nov88—Altered path 1/16
11Nov88-5Hol 6f :22¹ :45 1:09⁴ ft 14 114 95¼ 108¾ 96½ 103¾ Stevens G L 10 14000 89-11 IndinSignII,RysARumbl,ShowrDcr 12
11Nov88—Wide 3/8
23Oct88-1SA 6f :21² :44⁴ 1:10⁴ ft 8½ 120 66¼ 78 55½ 32¾ Stevens G L 1 10000 81-16 Mr.Edlwss,Emprr'sTrn,Whr'sMchs 12
23Oct88—Awarded second purse money; Drifted out, bumped start
●Mar 2 Hol 4f ft :45³ H Jan 8 SA 4f ft :47² H

Following the claim January 25, this infrequent winner ran improving races for trainer Marcus Murphy. Last out it chased a fast pace, staying close at every call. Six days following that good effort, Where's Machias worked 4F in a best-of-morning 45.3H.

Improved form on the track, followed by improved workouts in the morning, followed by a return to similar competition, amounts to a peak effort today. The lower the claiming bracket, the better. All claiming horses exhibiting the pattern become notable, but the cheaper horses can only show their best stuff when peaking in form.

Where's Machias had been a nondescript nonwinner at the lower claiming levels at Santa Anita as far back as the eye can see. The gelding had won 1 of 23 starts versus similar during 1988–89. But the improved race, and improved workout pattern, indicated it would race in peaking form now. Leading rider Laffit Pincay stayed aboard, not insignificant in this context.

At 9–2 Where's Machias again dogged the pace, overcame traffic trouble on the far turn, and drew clear in mid-stretch to win handily. This kind wins handily only in razor-sharp form.

Recreational handicappers must look for the vital signs of improving and declining form among the claimers, particularly among the inconsistent horses near the bottom. A clearly improved workout following an improved performance is telltale positive.

3YO CLM TO 3YO ALW

Three-year-olds of winter that have triumphed impressively in high-priced claiming races will be tested under allowance conditions for nonwinners once other than maiden or claiming. Their times will be fast. Their victories will look sharp. The connections will often be leading trainers, leading jockeys. So the crowd will be fooled. The step-up usually results in failure. Excepting in fall, the rise from 3YO claiming to 3YO allowance is among the most difficult in major-league racing.

The crowd's confusion is understandable. In winter, four-year-olds and older that have won impressively in high-priced claiming races can step into the nonwinners allowance division and score. But older (4up) nonwinners of allowance races represent either chronic losers or poor prospects. Impressive high-priced older claiming horses can trounce them, and do.

Three-year-olds entered in nonwinners allowance races of winter represent the fanciest prospects on the grounds. Their claiming-race counterparts have already been branded as relatively cheap. They have been for sale as young racehorses. No one should confuse the $40,000 claiming race for 4up (or 3up) with the $40,000 claiming race limited to 3YOs. The pair resemble one another not a bit.

When 3YOs that have won with claiming tags try allowance runners, they normally confront horses that run a faster pace while expending less energy. Pressed to keep abreast early, the claiming graduates regularly fall apart when the late running begins. This is particuarly true if the race is a route.

The illustration below, from Santa Anita, March 29, 1989, is typical. Try to find the crowd's favorite. Can you pick the eventual winner?

7th Santa Anita

1 MILE (1.33⅗) **ALLOWANCE. Purse $36,000. Fillies. 3–year–olds, which are non–winners of $3,000 other than maiden or claiming. Weight, 120 lbs. Non–winners of a race other than claiming at one mile or over allowed 2 lbs.; of such a race any distance, 4 lbs.**

Formidable Lady

			B. f. 3, by Silver Hawk—Hey Mama, by High Tribute		
VALENZUELA P A S~N		120	Br.—Jones B C (Ky) Tr.—Manzi Joseph	1988 7 1 2 1	$73,150
Own.—FstFrndsSt–Lvtn–TanngmEtl			Lifetime 7 1 2 1 $73,150		

10Oct88-8SA	1⅛:464 1:113 1:44 ft	13 116	32 43 54 68¾	VlnlPA2 ⑥Oak Leaf 72-16 Une UTAKlein,StocksUp,LadyLister /
10Oct88-Grade I				
24Sep88-9Cby	170:474 1:121 1:423ft	5¼ 120	21 1hd 1hd 21	VlenzulPA4 ⑥Cby Deb 87-09 LeLucind,Formidbll.dy,NorthrnWif 9
4Sep88-8Dmr	1 :453 1:101 1:362ft	7 116	76¼ 53¼ 54 44	DlhssE5 ⑥Dmr Deb 82-10 ‡ApprovdToFly,LLucnd,BwrOfThCt 8
4Sep88-Grade II; Wide final 3/8				

8Aug88-6Dmr 1 :464 1:121 1:373ft 3 116 33 31½ 1hd 14 DelahoussyeE4 ⒻMdn 80-15 FrmdblLd,BrvAndQck,Dlght'sTrbt 10
10Jly88-4Hol 6f :213 :444 1:094ft 4½ 117 911 79¾ 510 411 DelahoussyeE5 ⒻMdn 82-10 WndrsDlght,ChnChn,PrncssPnnch 11
22Jun88-4Hol 5½f :221 :46 1:044ft *1 117 67 65 45 37½ DelahoussyeE3 ⒻMdn 82-13 LeaLucinda,ChnChn,FormidbleLdy 10
22Jun88—Bumped at start
27May88-4Hol 5f :221 :453 :581ft 8½ 117 55½ 45 34 25 DelahoussyeE7 ⒻMdn 90-15 DistnctvSs,FormdblLdy,BwrOfThCt 8
Mar 27 SA 4f ft :474 H Mar 22 SA 1 ft 1:443 H Mar 17 SA 1 ft 1:401 H Mar 12 SA 1 ft 1:414 H

Serena Blake
VALENZUELA F H **1115**
Own.—Weissman & Whittingham
Ch. f. 3, by In Tissar—Tina's Cat, by Zanthe
Br.—Weissman S B (Cal) **1989 3 1 0 1 $23,550**
Tr.—Whittingham Charles **1988 2 1 0 0 $10,450**
Lifetime 5 2 0 1 $34,000
17Mar89-3SA 1$\frac{1}{16}$:453 1:103 1:45 ft 8½ 1115 36 35 34 32 VlenzulFH4 ⒻAw36000 74-20 Kelly, Bel Darling, Serena Blake 7
20Feb89-2SA 1 :471 1:123 1:382ft 5 1115 23 2hd 12½ 11¾ ValenzuelFH9 Ⓕ 50000 76-19 SerenBlk,Ms.Dimpls,FillAFirPockt 10
15Jan89-3SA 6f :213 :442 1:10 ft 55 115 99¼ 99¼ 78½ 65¼ GrydrAT1 ⒻⓈAw31000 83-11 MyGlmorosOn,RgosRos.VrosRsons 9
25Aug88-6Dmr 6½f :22 :453 1:184ft 17 117 98 64 31½ 1hd Solis A7 ⒻM50000 78-18 SerenBlke,CrystlBounty,IceTruffls 12
25Aug88—Wide 3/8
17Jly88-4Hol 6f :214 :453 1:121ft 34 117 813 811 710 79¼ Baze R A1 ⒻⓈMdn 72-13 Mtt'sGenie,Ms.Dimpls,CrystlBounty 8
17Jly88—Broke slowly
Mar 27 Hol 3f ft :362 H Mar 14 SA 3f ft :364 H Mar 9 SA 1 ft 1:43 H Mar 4 Hol 5f ft 1:031 H

Reluctant Guest
DELAHOUSSAYE E **118**
Own.—Folsom R S
B. f. 3, by Hostage—Vaguely Royal, by Vaguely Noble
Br.—Hillstead Farm (Ky) **1989 2 1 1 0 $20,800**
Tr.—Mandella Richard **1988 0 M 0 0**
Lifetime 2 1 1 0 $20,800
12Mar89-4SA 6f :213 :444 1:102ft 4½ 117 62½ 31½ 3nk 11¾ Stevens G L11 ⒻMdn 86-14 ReluctntGuest,FncyGirl,DebsAngl 12
26Feb89-4SA 6f :213 :451 1:11 ft 14 117 54¾ 42½ 21½ 21 Stevens G L7 ⒻMdn 82-14 RadintStr,ReluctntGuest,FncyGirl 11
Mar 23 SA 6f ft 1:134 H Mar 9 SA 4f ft :474 H Feb 20 SA 6f ft 1:13 Hg Feb 15 SA 6f ft 1:161 Hg

Beautiful Gold
STEVENS G L **120**
Own.—Calumet Farm Inc
B. f. 3, by Mr Prospector—Before Dawn, by Raise a Cup
Br.—Calumet Farm (Ky) **1989 3 1 2 0 $27,550**
Tr.—Lukas D Wayne **1988 3 M 0 1 $3,900**
Lifetime 6 1 2 1 $31,450
25Feb89-3SA 1 :464 1:11 1:373ft *3-5 117 11 1½ 12 14¼ Stevens G L1 ⒻMdn 80-14 BeutifulGold,MyGidget,FortuntFlyr 7
25Feb89—Lugged out backstretch, 3/8 turn
28Jan89-6SA 1$\frac{1}{16}$:462 1:11 1:434ft *4-5 117 33 2hd 1½ 2no Stevens G L8 ⒻMdn 82-14 BigCityMiss,BeautifulGold,Voclized 8
14Jan89-6SA 1 :46 1:104 1:363ft 4 117 1½ 2hd 2hd 2nk Stevens G L1 ⒻMdn 85-11 ToTheAltr,BeutifulGold,OldCpeCod 7
14Jan89—Lugged out backstretch; bumped at intervals in stretch
31Dec88-6SA 6f :211 :441 1:093ft 4½ 117 76½ 67¼ 68½ 811¼ Stevens G L9 ⒻMdn 79-10 StormyBtVld,DbsAngl,TncosTgrss 12
9Jly88-8Hol 6f :213 :444 1:104ft *7-5e114 86 66 68½ 710 StnsGL 10 ⒻLndlc 78-13 DistinctivSis,LLucind,ExcutivRow 11
9Jly88—Grade III; Broke poorly
3Jly88-6Hol 6f :221 :452 1:112ft 5½ 117 3nk 2hd 21½ 33¼ McCarron C J6 ⒻMdn 82-14 DuchssGrg,Mhmt'sPrncss,BtflGold 8
Mar 23 Hol 5f ft 1:022 H Mar 16 Hol 4f ft :482 H Mar 10 Hol 4f ft :484 H Feb 18 Hol 5f ft 1:01 H

Super Keeper
DAVIS R G **118**
Own.—Brown R
Dk. b. or br. f. 3, by Super Moment—Keeper, by Prince John
Br.—Elmendorf Farm Inc (Ky) **1989 5 2 0 1 $41,200**
Tr.—Lewis Craig A **1988 1 M 1 0 $3,400**
Lifetime 6 2 1 1 $44,600
16Mar89-3SA 1 :454 1:104 1:362ft *1 117 12 11½ 13 19 Pincay L Jr 7 Ⓕ 50000 86-16 SuperKeeper,GalxyCilin,KeptSecret 7
22Feb89-3SA 6½f :212 :45 1:164ft 3½ 117 2½ 2½ 23½ 37 Pincay L Jr 5 Ⓕ 62500 79-18 Pointedly,RoylPrimDonn,SuperKpr 8
2Feb89-7SA 1 :46 1:112 1:37 ft 5 116 1½ 63¾ 912 922¾ Hawley S3 ⒻAw35000 60-18 GnrlChrg,RodToRomnc,ExcllntLdy 9
2Feb89—Lugged out backstretch; took up sharply 3/8
26Jan89-7SA 6f :212 :442 1:092ft *3-2 118 51¾ 54¾ 56½ 49¼ StevensGL3 ⒻAw32000 82-16 StormyButValid,Kiss'EmAgin,BldL 6
26Jan89—Wide into stretch
8Jan89-4SA 6½f :213 :442 1:153ft 2½ 117 1½ 2hd 1½ 12 Stevens G L7 ⒻMdn 92-13 SuperKeeper,JetStStr,BllrinPrincss 8
9Dec88-4Hol 6½f :22 :453 1:172ft 5½ 118 32 11 21½ 21¾ Sibille R5 ⒻMc50000 86-16 RoylPrimDonn,SuperKepr,ChnChn 12
Mar 23 SA 5f ft 1:021 H Mar 1 SA 4f ft :493 H Feb 12 SA 4f m :493 Hg

At even-money, March 16, Super Keeper humiliated a field of $50,000 three-year-olds by nine lengths in good time. The class hierarchy presented on page 365 indicates $50,000 claiming-race winners can be accepted under allowance conditions, for nonwinners twice other than maiden or claiming. Today's allowance race is limited to nonwinners once other than maiden or claiming. Isn't Super Keeper a good thing here?

No.

The class hierarchy refers to races open to older horses, or

124 to races for 3up. Three-year-olds are distinct. Look again at Super
125 Keeper's earlier allowance attempts. Woeful. The filly may be
126 much improved. But the rise from claiming to allowance com-
127 petition for young threes is dramatic. Most cannot change
128 divisions successfully. If today's race is a route, or the three-
129 year-old was offered for sale as a two-year-old as well, discard
130 the horse, surely at low odds.

131 As always, certain exceptions must be considered. Stables
132 do make mistakes with young horses, entering them prema-
133 turely for a claim. If a high-priced 3YO claimer has run faster
134 speed and pace figures than any other horse in the allowance
135 race, professional handicappers will accept it.

136 The pace ratings are especially significant. Against allow-
137 ance competition, the rising 3YOs will be forced to run faster
138 for longer. Those that have done it before are most likely to do
139 it again versus better.

140 In addition, some nonwinners fields for 3YOs appear empty
141 of quality. Nothing has impressed in a stakes. The few allow-
142 ance performances of others have been nondescript. The maiden
143 graduates look uninteresting. A high-priced claiming-race win-
144 ner that contested a rapid pace can step ahead and survive, es-
145 pecially in sprints. Fair odds is essential. Do not buy the
146 underlays.

147 Finally, in late fall, November-December, 3YOs having a
148 future in nonclaiming races will have graduated from the non-
49 winners allowance series. The leftovers are common. Three-year-
50 olds that have won medium-prized claiming races open to older
51 horses can step up to minor allowance competition and shine.

52 In the sample race, Formidable Lady returned from a 5½
53 month layoff and handled this nonwinners-once group, paying
54 $11.20, after a troubled trip. Super Keeper attended the pace for
55 six furlongs but could not keep up late. She finished fourth,
56 beaten two lengths. Examine the pace of today's race in com-
57 parison to Super Keeper's nine-length claiming-race romp of
58 March 16.

59 A faster pace versus nonclaiming horses with greater re-
60 serves of stamina and competitiveness spells defeat for claiming

Alw, NW1XMC	22.2	45.1	1:10.0
Clm, $50,000	22.2	45.4	1:10.4

horses. Do not be fooled by improving three-year-olds that win big against claimers and next try to duplicate the exploit against attractive allowance runners.

THE POWER SPRINTERS

Until 1990, the Breeders' Cup Sprint aside, only one sprint stakes in the United States came adorned with the Grade 1 label. It's the Vosburgh Handicap, contested at Belmont Park during fall. All other sprint stakes were Grade 2 or below, an inducement to horsemen to run their fastest horses over ground.

Any horse that has won a Grade 2 sprint qualifies as an elite sprinter. If that horse has also won Grade 1 or Grade 2 events at middle distances, it deserves marquee billing as a sprinter whenever it runs the shorter distances. The stamina it has displayed in routes means it can repulse any sprinter that depends ultimately on brilliance alone.

As this was written, the classiest sprinter in the U.S. looked like this in the past performances:

On The Line had proved repeatedly he could carry his swift up to nine furlongs against Grade 1 opposition. In sprints, he was monstrous on the front end. Regardless of the pace, On The Line would draw off effortlessly at the eighth pole, just as the fastest sprinters without comparable endurance began to feel the effects of tired blood.

In the 6½ furlong Grade 3 Potrero Grande Handicap, run April 5, 1989, at Santa Anita, On The Line's main foes looked like this:

Oraibi — Ch. c. 4, by Forli—Dancing Liz, by Northern Dancer
PINCAY L JR — 122 — Br.—Todd R E & Aury (Ky) — 1989 3 1 1 0 $89,400
Tr.—Mandella Richard — 1988 5 4 0 0 $117,200
Own.—Todd R E & Aury — Lifetime 8 5 1 0 $206,600 — Turf 1 1 0 0 $49,400

17Mar89-8SA	a6½f Ⓣ:212	:433	1:143fm	*2	120	3½	1hd	1½	1½	PncyLJr8	Sra Mdre H	86-14	Oraibi, Lordalik, Down Again	9
17Mar89—Grade III														
20Feb89-10Lrl	7f :221	:452	1:224ft	8	119	32	2hd	13	2½	CstndM10	Gen George	96-15	LittleBoldJohn,Oribi,Findr'sChoic	13
15Jan89-8SA	1⅛:464	1:101	1:472ft	4¼	120	2½	53¼	45	1112¾	PincyLJr8	Sn Frndo	79-11	MiPreferido,Spdrtic,PrcivArrognc	12
15Jan89—Grade I														
26Dec88-8SA	7f :22	:44	1:213ft	6	117	41	1hd	11½	1¾	PincayLJr3	Malibu	92-13	Oraibi,PerceiveArrognce,Speedrtic	13
26Dec88—Grade II														
13Nov88-5Hol	1 :442	1:092	1:351ft	*3-2	113	33	1½	12	1hd	Pincay L Jr4	Aw27000	87-13	Oraibi, Monte Simon, Vysotsky	10
13Nov88—Bumped start														
29Oct88-3SA	6f :212	:442	1:09 ft	*1-2	117	52½	2½	1hd	1hd	Pincay L Jr6	Aw27000	93-12	Oraibi, Phone Bid, Silverstep	8
6Oct88-6SA	6f :213	:442	1:091ft	*8-5	117	1hd	1hd	12½	15½	Pincay L Jr11	Mdn	92-18	Oraibi, Toe River, Khaled's Radar	11
3Apr88-4SA	6f :213	:443	1:104ft	5¾	118	56½	68	57	45¾	Pincay L Jr8	Mdn	78-18	Elkman, Wildridge, Toe River	8
3Apr88—Broke very slowly; wide final 3/8														

Apr 1 SA 5f ft 1:002 B — Mar 27 SA 4f ft :492 B — Mar 16 SA 3f ft :39 B — Mar 12 SA Ⓣ 5f fm 1:011 H (d)

Ron Bon — B. c. 4, by Halo—Confirm, by Proudest Roman
SOLIS A — 116 — Br.—North Ridge Farm (Ky) — 1989 5 3 0 0 $68,750
Tr.—Boyce Neil — 1988 5 2 2 0 $39,050
Own.—Hvens-Lmb-N-MBoyceStInc — Lifetime 10 5 2 0 $107,800 — Turf 1 0 0 0

10Mar89-8SA	6½f :214	:441	1:143ft	4	114	1½	1hd	11½	1¾	Solis A1	Aw50000	97-17	Ron Bon,Jamoke,Don'sIrishMelody	6
25Feb89-8SA	1 Ⓣ:471	1:104	1:361fm	9¾	113	11	1hd	52½	79¾	Solis A7	Arcadia H	80-10	BlloHorzont,Srhoob,PtchyGrondfg	7
25Feb89—Grade II; Checked at 1/8														
5Feb89-9RP	6½f :221	:454	1:153ft	*2-5	117	2hd	2hd	89¾	819	Solis A7	Centennial	71-13	Cold Trail, Illustrious High,Overage	8
14Jan89-3SA	6f :212	:44	1:082ft	*4-5	120	1½	11½	13	13½	Baze R A5	Aw40000	96-11	RonBon,WesterlyWind,LagunNtive	6
4Jan89-5SA	6f :211	:44	1:084ft	4	118	1hd	1½	2hd	12	Solis A7	Aw35000	94-12	RonBon,IcyAmber,BeyondTheWall	12
24Nov88-7Hol	6½f :22	:45	1:164gd	3½	119	2½	1hd	12½	14½	Toro F3	Aw24000	91-16	Ron Bon, Angle Arc, MagicLeader	12
27Aug88-7Dmr	6f :213	:443	1:094ft	2	116	3nk	2½	3nk	73½	DelhoussyeE6	Aw31000	85-16	ReasonbleRj,OurNtiveWish,JetPro	12
13Aug88-3Dmr	6f :213	:443	1:102ft	*3-5	116	21½	2½	21½	2½	Toro F6	Aw30000	85-17	SecretMeting,RonBon,Circumstntil	9
20Mar88-4SA	6f :211	:44	1:091ft	3	118	12½	12½	16	19	Toro F2	Mdn	92-15	RonBon,DevineBoy,TimeFcrShmns	8
28Feb88-6SA	6f :211	:441	1:11 gd	10	118	53½	34	22	2hd	Toro F11	Mdn	83-18	DamscusCommnder,RonBon,Coch	11

●Mar 31 SA 5f ft :574 H — Mar 25 SA tr.t 4f gd :502 H — ●Mar 5 SA 5f ft :581 H — ●Feb 20 SA 6f ft 1:123 H

Oraibi had won the Grade 2 Malibu Stakes, limited to 3YOs, to open the Santa Anita season. A savagely contested seven furlongs, the Malibu had proved productive throughout the Santa Anita season, several horses exiting the race to win or impress in stakes competition successively. Oraibi had lasted at a mile against overnight allowance horses as well, and last out had won a long sprint on the grass under Grade 3 conditions. Can Oraibi survive in a graded stakes at a middle distance? No one knew as yet. But the colt's endurance remained doubtful.

Ron Bon is a brilliant frontrunner in sprints. In a long sprint last out, the four-year-old outran a blistering pace and nearly toppled the track record for the distance. But Ron Bon is exactly the kind of sprinter more powerful sprinters like On The Line ultimately gobble up. Ron Bon lacks the combination of brilliance and endurance that amounts to power.

When comparing speedsters such as Ron Bon with versatile powerful horses such as On The Line, recreational handicappers should ask whether the speedster can outrun stakes horses at middle distances. If the answer is negative or doubtful, the versatile powerful types get the nod. Not the come-from-behind kind of sprint power. Brilliant power. The kind that can participate in the front duel, and switch into second and third gears during the late stages.

On The Line stumbled badly out of the gate in the Potrero Grande. Ron Bon shot to the lead unmolested. On The Line righted itself and quickly dispensed a tremendous performance. He reached Ron Bon's rear approaching the three-eighths pole, refused to let go around the turn, and stuck his head in front entering the stretch, just as Oraibi had moved up boldly from slightly behind the torrid pace.

Oraibi fooled announcer Trevor Denman totally, the race caller prematurely intimating the Forli colt was primed to make mincemeat of On The Line. On The Line switched gears again, and in a few strides Oraibi quit.

Remember this: the very best sprinters are the brilliant types that can carry the brilliance at middle distances versus graded stakes stars. The Ron Bons and Oraibis of the thoroughbred world cannot do that. Few horses can. Weight does not defeat the power sprinters. On The Line carried 125 in the Potrero Grande. Ron Bon carried nine pounds less.

Interestingly, when horses like On The Line lose sprinting, it's usually to middle-distance stakes horses dropping back in distance. Their considerable endurance serves them well, and they prevail in the lane, often following a furious pace.

My education here began early. When I started as a handicapper in 1971, the great Ack Ack was king of the land. Ack Ack that year carried 134 pounds and won the 1¼ mile Grade 1 Hollywood Gold Cup wire to wire, without tiring. Months later Ack Ack set the still-standing track record at Del Mar for 5½ furlongs (1:02.1). Horse of the Year for his feats of brilliance on the front of classic routes, when Ack Ack sprinted, no horse stood a chance against him. Ack Ack was also voted best sprinter that year. He devastated the fastest sprinters on the grounds like flicking insects away.

Which are the greatest sprinters? The horses having the strongest combination of brilliance and endurance; the power sprinters, I call them, like On The Line.

BIG MOVE, BIG WIN ON THE TURF

Whenever a thoroughbred runs the second quarter at a middle distance on the grass in 23 seconds, and extends that move to a Big Win, notably in good time, that horse can be expected to repeat versus the same caliber or slightly better.

Below are the two main contenders in a classified allowance mile on turf, run at Santa Anita, April 6, 1989. Read the eligibility conditions carefully. Examine the horses' records.

8th Santa Anita

TURF COURSE

1 MILE.
SANTA ANITA

1 MILE. (Turf). (1.34½) CLASSIFIED ALLOWANCE. Purse $60,000. 4-year-olds and upward which are non-winners of $19,250 other than closed or claiming at one mile or over since September 25. Weight, 121 lbs. Non-winners of two such races since April 25 allowed 2 lbs.; of such a race since June 1, 4 lbs.; of such a race since April 25, 6 lbs.

Astronaut Prince
B. h. 5, by Majestic Light—Flying Above, by Hoist the Flag
Br.—Clark S C Jr (Ky)
Tr.—Drysdale Neil
PINCAY L JR   115
Own.—Mauladad Stable

	1989	3	2 0 0	$29,710
	1988	3	1 1 0	$20,375
Lifetime 13 5 2 0 $60,341	Turf	13	5 2 0	$60,341

Roi Normand
Dk. b. or br. h. 6, by Exclusive Native—Luth de Saron, by Luthier
Br.—S C E A Haras du Mezeray (Ky)
Tr.—Frankel Robert
VALENZUELA P A   121
Own.—Sann Mr–Mrs E A

	1988	8	3 0 0	$336,260
	1987	2	1 0 1	$25,931
Lifetime 16 5 1 1 $381,530	Turf	13	4 1 1	$298,530

Roi Normand has not raced since September 25, the specified date in the conditions. Prior to that, the six-year-old competed in three of this nation's Grade 1 turf classics, winning the Sunset Handicap at Hollywood Park, and finishing within three lengths (good race) in the Arlington Million. No wonder Roi Normand was favored at 6–5 to whip classified horses at Santa Anita.

Astronaut Prince had raced five times since September 25, winning twice. Each winner's share was less than the specified amount of $19,250, or Astronaut Prince would be ineligible here. When last entered for a $60,000 classified purse at Santa Anita, Astronaut Prince ran well, beaten three lengths at a mile by Mazillier, a top turf miler in southern California. Up in class, Astronaut Prince fits today's conditions nicely, combining sharp form and a liking for the distance and footing. Under restricted classified conditions, as a rule, handicappers should prefer sharp horses particularly well-suited to the distance, footing, and probable pace, in opposition to classier types burdened by shortcomings on the form, distance, footing, and pace factors.

Look at Astronaut Prince's last line again. Shipped to minor Turf Paradise for an event billed as the Governor's Handicap, Astronaut Prince not only sets the track record for the distance, but completes the second quarter of the mile in 23 seconds, passing six horses with the big move. The horse proceeds to win by seven lengths in record time. Trained by the meticulous Neil Drysdale, to be ridden today by leading rider Pincay, at 4–1 Astronaut Prince represents an excellent bet against the comebacking Roi Normand.

To appreciate the situation further, glance again at Roi Normand's past performances.

Roi Normand is not a miler. The excellent workouts notwithstanding, Roi Normand's running style has been better suited to longer distances. On the turf, handicappers should prefer horses at exact or closely related distances. Sprinters do not stretch out well on grass. Milers do not stretch out well, either, though many of them can get 1⅛ miles. Middle-distance and classic types do not easily shorten up to a mile or seven furlongs. Often a favorable change of class will be needed to assist turf horses attempting to stretch out or shorten up.

Consider the classified horse that follows, also entered in the Santa Anita turf mile of April 6.

*Romantic Prince
Ch. h. 5, by Henbit—Supremely Royal, by Crowned Prince

STEVENS G L 115

(Past performance data table for Romantic Prince)

Romantic Prince runs best on turf in long sprints, but has won twice against older horses at 1⅛ miles. The difference is class. The victories at nine furlongs came at the expense of non-winners allowance competition; that is, nonwinners of one, two, or three allowance races. Against lower forms of nonclaiming competition, Romantic Prince endured at middle distances.

Now ineligible to nonwinners conditions, Romantic Prince must face classified and stakes types. Against the better horses, Romantic Prince does not possess enough endurance to survive the late speed duels throughout the stretch. He fades. Romantic Prince cannot handle Roi Normand, Astronaut Prince, and the like, at a middle distance. Handicappers should pause to understand that. As distances lengthen on grass, endurance counts more than speed. Late speed counts the most.

A fourth horse in the Santa Anita classified race appears below.

No Commitment ✳
B. g. 4, by Search for Gold—Premarital, by Impressive

DELAHOUSSAYE E 115

(Past performance data table for No Commitment)

Two for two in overnight handicaps at a mile on turf, and placed last out at the same distance in a Grade 3 stakes, No Commitment has shipped from Golden Gate Fields to Santa Anita for today's feature. How strongly does No Commitment figure here?

The record remains unconvincing. The December 17 turf handicap was limited to three-year-olds and completed in inordinately slow time at every call. Similarly, the January 16 handicap was limited to new four-year-olds. The purse was $22,000. The March 25 mile against Grade 3 older horses looks impressive, but occurred on a yielding course. Again, the fractions and final time were slow. Unless the odds are large, the proposition that No Commitment can take Santa Anita stakes horses wire to wire on grass does not have lasting appeal. No Commitment was offered at 4–1; not enough.

If Astronaut Prince can throw a 23-second quarter mile at this field between the four-furlong call and the finish, and sustain that momentum, the horse should prevail. The public offered 7–2 on that proposition, a good bet.

EIGHTH RACE
Santa Anita
APRIL 6, 1989

1 MILE.(Turf). (1.34⅕) CLASSIFIED ALLOWANCE. Purse $60,000. 4-year-olds and upward which are non-winners of $19,250 other than closed or claiming at one mile or over since September 25. Weight, 121 lbs. Non-winners of two such races since April 25 allowed 2 lbs.; of such a race since June 1, 4 lbs.; of such a race since April 25, 6 lbs.

Value of race $60,000; value to winner $33,000; second $12,000; third $9,000; fourth $4,500; fifth $1,500. Mutuel pool $282,456. Exacta pool $268,474.

Last Raced	Horse	Eqt.	A.	Wt	PP	St	¼	½	¾	Str	Fin	Jockey	Odds $1
12Mar89 10TuP1	Astronaut Prince		5	117	1	6	$6^{1/2}$	$6^{1\,1/2}$	$5^{1\,1/2}$	4^{1}	$1^{1\,3/4}$	Pincay L Jr	3.60
17Sep88 8Bel7	Roi Normand		6	121	4	4	4^{1}	3^{hd}	3^{1}	2^{1}	$2^{2\,3/4}$	Valenzuela P A	1.30
24Mar89 8SA6	Happyasalark Tomas	b	4	116	7	2	2^{4}	2^{3}	1^{hd}	1^{hd}	$3^{1\,1/4}$	Valenzuela F H5	13.50
24Mar89 8SA4	Romantic Prince		5	115	3	5	$5^{1\,1/2}$	4^{1}	4^{hd}	$5^{1\,1/2}$	$4^{1\,1/4}$	Stevens G L	8.20
24Mar89 8SA3	Neshad		5	115	2	7	7	7	6^{2}	6^{4}	$5^{4\,1/2}$	McCarron C J	5.60
25Mar89 8GG2	No Commitment		4	116	6	1	$1^{2\,1/2}$	$1^{3\,1/2}$	2^{1}	3^{hd}	$6^{1\,3/4}$	Delahoussaye E	4.10
19Mar89 5SA8	Nasib		7	115	5	3	3^{1}	5^{1}	7	7	7	Dominguez R E	52.20

OFF AT 4:37. Start good. Won driving. Time, :22⅗, :46, 1:10⅕, 1:22⅖, 1:34⅘ Course firm.

$2 Mutuel Prices:				
	1-ASTRONAUT PRINCE	9.20	4.00	3.60
	4-ROI NORMAND		3.20	3.00
	7-HAPPYASALARK TOMAS			5.00
	$5 EXACTA 1-4 PAID $63.00.			

B. h, by Majestic Light—Flying Above, by Hoist the Flag. Trainer Drysdale Neil. Bred by Clark S C Jr (Ky).

ASTRONAUT PRINCE, unhurried while devoid of early speed, commenced rallying in earnest after a half, gained strongly to reach the front in the final sixteenth and was going away at the end. ROI NORMAND, patiently handled while being outrun early, moved up to get into an easy striking position on the far turn, came on to get the lead between calls in midstretch but could not resist ASTRONAUT PRINCE'S rally. HAPPYASALARK TOMAS prompted the early pace, wrested the lead approaching the quarter pole but weakened in the last furlong. ROMANTIC PRINCE, patiently handled while being outrun early, advanced to get within close range of the lead with three furlongs remaining, continued close up on the far turn but gave way in the drive. NESHAD, devoid of early speed and wide down the backstretch after he broke slowly, failed to generate the necessary rally and was four wide into the stretch. NO COMMITMENT, the early pacesetter, faltered. NASIB was four wide into the stretch.

Owners— 1, Mauladad Stable; 2, Gann Mr-Mrs E A; 3, Thomas J W; 4, Charles & Clear Valley Stables; 5, Currie D & Trish; 6, Northgate Ranch & Hagan; 7, Frdrcks-Flmer-MLM Stb

Trainers— 1, Drysdale Neil; 2, Frankel Robert; 3, Van Berg Jack C; 4, Shulman Sanford; 5, Goodin Mike; 6, Mason Lloyd C; 7, Mulhall Richard W

Overweight: Astronaut Prince 2 pounds; No Commitment 1

THE TWO-SPRINT STRETCHOUT FOLLOWING LAYOFFS

Handicappers become bedeviled by horses' form cycles following layoffs. Can horses win fresh? Should they improve on the second start? If so, why do so many of them regress? What about class drops following layoffs; good sign or bad? What about changes of distance?

None of these questions can be answered unequivocally, but certain facts are well known.

While many horses win fresh after a layoff of 90 days or longer, the majority do not. The vital signs are (a) a win following a similar layoff in the past, and (b) a trainer that strikes quickly, or one that bears down all the time. Both conditions should be present.

The knowledge here is specific. Handicappers must know enough about the horse and trainer in question to draw a conclusion. An intriguing fact lost to handicappers is that routers win following layoffs more frequently than do sprinters. Casual handicappers share the tendency to accept sprinters returning from layoffs but not routers. This is backward. Apparently, the slower pace of routes conserves energy. The energy so reserved can be released in one long late run.

Elsewhere we have discussed the bounce pattern pertinent to horses' form following layoffs. If horses spend too much energy too soon, winning or running close in a rapid, contested finish, the overextension strains muscles, saps stamina. The conditioning process is impeded. The horses disappoint next time, often when favored.

The bounce pattern excepted, horses should run better the second start following a layoff. Usually, however, they do not win. The crucial starts following layoffs are the third and fourth, the third especially.

Accept these guidelines:

- In sprints, the third start following a layoff is best, provided the second start was a sprint and a good race.
- In routes, the third start following a layoff is best when preceded by a pair of improving sprints.

The guideline for routes is instructive. Statistics have revealed the two-sprint combination is the most successful stretchout pattern following layoffs of 90 days or longer. The least successful is one sprint and a route. Second best is a sprint, a route, and another route.

The illustration below relates the two-sprint stretchout to considerations of class. The race was a 1¹⁄₁₆ mile route for older fillies and mares, to be claimed for $12,500 to $10,500.

3th Santa Anita

1 1/16 MILES. (1.40⅘) CLAIMING. Purse $14,000. Fillies and mares. 4-year-olds and upward. Weight, 121 lbs. Non-winners of two races at one mile or over since February 1 allowed 3 lbs.; of such a race since then, 5 lbs. Claiming price $12,500; if for $10,500 allowed 2 lbs. (Claiming and starter races for $10,000 or less not considered.)

Video Pirate
Dk. b. or br. f. 4, by Pirate's Bounty—Stone Lily, by Stonewalk
GARCIA H J 1115 Br.—Wygod M J (Cal) 1989 5 2 0 1 $16,550
Tr.—Ravin Robert $12,500 1988 10 3 1 0 $21,353
Own.—Chila-Maiden-Mariucci Lifetime 15 5 1 1 $37,903

30Mar89-9SA 1 1/16 :46 1:104 1:433ft 3½ 1135 42 1hd 11 14½ Garcia H J 6 Ⓕ c10000 83-16 VideoPirate,T.V.Tussle,OurOleLdy 12
30Mar89—Rank 7/8 turn, backstretch lugged out 3/8 turn
15Mar89-1SA 6f :213 :451 1:112ft 9¾ 1135 96 73¾ 74½ 52¾ Garcia H J 2 Ⓕ 10000 78-14 GoldDcr,FrdmInMyEys,ClmntsCrk 12
15Mar89—Took up 3/16
15Feb89-9SA 1 :471 1:121 1:384ft 3¾ 1095 54 63¼ 31 1hd Garcia H J 3 Ⓕ 10000 74-17 Video Pirate, Kris'sPeach,OneDrum 8
15Feb89—Erratic
29Jan89-1SA 6½f :222 :461 1:184ft 58 1105 63 74¼ 52½ 32¼ Garcia H J 1 Ⓕ 12500 74-16 PrisosQueen,MostDrmtic.VidoPirt 11
29Jan89—Lugged out backstretch; checked 3 1/2
13Jan89-3SA 6f :22 :452 1:111ft 35 115 103½118¼119 1110¼ CastnonAL 12 Ⓕ c10000 72-15 FlyingHighr,EngginBu,AcAllginc 12
13Jan89—6-wide into drive
30Dec88-9SA 1 1/16 :463 1:111 1:433ft 13 115 22½ 23 816 921 Bazan J 5 Ⓕ 16000 62-12 BrvstStr,AncintLdy,Coloni'Trchry 10
21Dec88-8TuP 6½f :221 :45 1:17 ft *8-5 116 55½ 45½ 63½ 54¼ Bazan J 3 Ⓕ 18000 82-16 Orleanna,WaltzingFran,NoMissTalk 7
17Dec88-10TuP 6f :214 :441 1:093ft 44 116 84¾1211128¼124 Bazan J 4 ⒻMly Btlr H 82-15 KpOnTop,SkyFthr.Goldin'sDoctor 12
6Nov88-1SA 1 1/16 :471 1:12 1:444ft *3 116 31 2½ 43 88 CastanonAL 7 Ⓕ c12500 69-17 Softscape, Raise You, Plumpetra 11
6Nov88—Wide 7/8
13Oct88-9SA 1 1/16 :464 1:113 1:451ft 8 115 41¼ 21½ 2½ 11¾ Castanon AL 3 Ⓕ 18000 75-19 VdoPrt,Explodd'sGrl,SpctculrBold 12
13Oct88—Bumped start

Lady Charmin
Ch. f. 4, by Commissioner—Lady Kit Kat, by Majestic Prince
SIBILLE R 116 Br.—Taylor Mr-Mrs (Cal) 1989 2 0 0 0 $975
Tr.—Dorfman Leonard $12,500 1988 7 2 1 0 $14,550
Own.—Taylor Thelma Lee Lifetime 9 2 1 0 $15,525

16Mar89-1SA 6f :22 :451 1:11 ft 14 116 42 53 42½ 41¾ Sibille R 8 ⒻⓈ 12500 81-16 SilvrSbin,JklinAndHid,DynmitKiss 12
20Feb89-1SA 6½f :214 :451 1:18 ft 76 115 106¾117½128¼119¼ Sibille R 11 ⒻⓈ 16000 71-19 MostDrmtc,AShdFstr,RbrtsRglGrl 12
20Feb89—Wide
20Nov88-2Hol 6f :22 :452 1:111ft 28 115 107¼ 87¼ 78 76½ Meza R Q 9 Ⓕ 20000 79-12 Valhall,NobleBrndy,HeedToSpeed 12
20Nov88—Wide 3/8
7Nov88-3SA 6f :212 :443 1:094ft 47 114 76½ 87 811 813¼ Meza R Q 5 Ⓕ 35000 76-15 FunAtTheSale,RunwyBlues,MyFirst 8
14Sep88-3Dmr 6f :222 :452 1:101ft 8 118 66½ 65¼ 76½ 59½ Black C A 3 Ⓕ 40000 77-14 WandaWiggins,MayFirst,BoldyLuck 7
14Sep88—Broke in a tangle
2Sep88-7Dmr 1 :45 1:103 1:363ft 27 113 35½ 86 87¼ 714½ Gryder AT 6 ⒻAw33000 70-15 HalloweenBby,Pribor,ComedyCourt 8
12Aug88-1Dmr 6½f :221 :454 1:181ft 22 118 51¾ 41½ 22 1¾ Black C A 1 Ⓕ 32000 81-18 Lady Charmin, Boldy Luck, MissLiz 8
16Jly88-1AC 6f :231 :454 1:102ft *2-3 119 32½ 42½ 2½ 11½ Alferez J O 4 ⒻAlwM 87-17 LadyCharmin,ChelliCordil,AllExlted 6
3Jly88-3AC 6f :23 :451 1:104ft 4½ 119 53 42½ 43¼ 22 Alferez J O 2 ⒻAlwM 83-15 LoveNTII,LdyChrmin,Womn'sWork 7
Apr 11 SA 4f ft :494 H Apr 4 SA 6f ft 1:16 H Mar 26 SA 5f gd 1:012 H Mar 14 SA 4f ft :483 H

Cherokee Gladys
Dk. b. or br. m. 5, by Cherokee Fellow—Dol's Gladys K, by Assagai Jr
PINCAY L JR 116 Br.—Just A Farm (Fla) 1989 2 0 0 0
Tr.—Ippolito Steve $12,500 1987 9 1 0 1 $10,970
Own.—Beall & Mancini Lifetime 13 1 0 1 $10,970 Turf 3 0 0 0 $1,800

24Mar89-1SA 7f :222 :454 1:251ft 70 113 119¾1113 89½ 65¾ DomnguzRE 10 Ⓕ 13000 68-20 RobertsRegIGirl,Vlhll,NoSePorque 12
24Mar89—Wide into stretch
8Mar89-1SA 6f :214 :453 1:111ft 18 116 118¼1211107¾ 68¼ DomnguzRE 11 Ⓕ 10000 74-15 NlliMlb,OurCoqutt,Priscill'sCrown 12
8Mar89—6 wide into drive
18Sep87-10Fpx 1 1/16 :46 1:121 1:461ft 24 1075 76½ 88¾ 813 817½ MagallonP 9 ⒻAw27000 62-18 ProfitIsland,LadyKell,LyricalPirte 10

31Aug87-5Dmr 1 1/16 ①:4821:13 1:444fm 15 1125 42½ 65 96½ 99¾ MagallonP6 ⒻAw24000 66-18 NrobExprss,BoldlyDrvn,TmForHrt 10
17Aug87-9LA 6½f :21 :442 1:171ft 16 1095 37 38½ 45½ 34 MagallonP4 ⒻAw16000 87-12 FunLoving,AprilMriEln,ChrokGldys 6
23Jly87-9Hol 1 1/16 ①:4711:1111:424fm 34 1095 2hd 32½ 42½ 44½ MagallonP1 ⒻAw24000 76-20 AmrcnDrm,Grn'sGllry,HollywdGlttr 6
20Jun87-6Hol 6f :213 :45 1:102ft 70 112 99 1010 912 812 Solis A3 Ⓕ 35000 79-11 Hoofer's Brew,Folja,MyProperGal 10
12Apr87-2SA a6½f ①:211 :4411:151fm 66 116 77¾ 75¾ 86¼ 89¾ CstnonAL3 ⒻAw29000 73-15 Solany, Texas Wild, La Sierra 9
17Mar87-6GG 1 1/16 :464 1:114 1:451ft 9¾ 117 21½ 33 57 511½ CastnedM3 ⒻAw18000 65-21 NvrDncAlon,FrulnLbr,PlyngThrogh 6
7Mar87-7GG 6f :213 :442 1:102ft 4½ 117 612 615 613 610½ Baze R A1 ⒻAw17000 76-16 PrettyPrestigious,RiverBll,FinllyFr 6
Apr 9 SA 5f ft 1:033 H Apr 2 SA 4f ft :483 H Mar 18 SA 4f ft :474 H Mar 3 SA 5f m 1:001 H

Yes Miss Helen Ch. m. 5, by Be a Native—Girlish Laughter, by Father John
DOMINGINEZ R E Br.—Dominguez M M (Cal) 1989 2 0 0 0
116 Tr.—Martinez Rafael A $12,500 1988 5 0 0 1 $3,450
Own.—Dominguez M M Lifetime 12 1 0 3 $16,300
29Mar89-1SA 6f :22 :453 1:113ft 33 116 118 117¾ 107 64 DomngzRE1 ⒻⓈ 10000 76-17 MissLiz,HiddenPast,SparkleBright 11
8Mar89-1SA 6f :214 :453 1:111ft 37 116 1211 108¾ 85¾ 911½ Meza R Q5 Ⓕ 10000 70-15 NiftyMib,OurCoqutt,Priscill'sCrown 12
31Mar88-9SA 1 1/16 :471 1:122 1:461ft 13 1115 99½ 108¼ 106¼ 1111¼ Sherman A B3 Ⓕ 12500 59-20 DrmticElegnc,LunSol,MistyFbrury 11
3Mar88-9SA 1 1/16 :462 1:114 1:46 ft 7 116 911 76½ 76 85 Gryder A T8 Ⓕ 12500 66-19 ScarletLake,DramaticElegnce,Fye 12
3Mar88—Veered out start
5Feb88-9SA 1 1/16 :464 1:124 1:46 ft 4¾ 115 88 4nk 1hd 42½ Velasquez J7 Ⓕ 12500 68-20 AssumdTrts,MxmumPropht,Zythm 12
5Feb88—Broke slowly
21Jan88-1SA 6f :22 :454 1:122ft 8 117 107¾ 66¼ 52½ 33½ DlhoussyE10 ⒻⓈ 12500 72-19 Hash, Bold Rumor, Yes MissHelen 12
21Jan88—Wide
2Jan88-1SA 6f :22 :452 1:104gd 9½ 117 1210 99 79 813½ DlhoussyE3 ⒻⓈ 16000 70-15 JklinAndHide,HvyWthr,ThirdMrrig 12
10Dec87-1Hol 6f :221 :45 1:093ft 12 118 129 1212 1022 1018 DlhoussyE9 ⒻⓈ 25000 76-11 LaSierra,Divest,SweetExpecttions 12
10Dec87—Wide
25Nov87-4Hol 6½f :221 :453 1:181ft *3-2 119 43½ 43 22 12¼ DlhossyE10 ⒻⓈM32000 87-13 YesMissHelen,SwetKtin,Dublinique 11
6Nov87-4SA 6½f :213 :443 1:184m 2¾ 118 1119 1115 54½ 43 DlhossyE7 ⒻⓈM32000 73-24 PetiteVlntin,Olympi'sSpy,SwtKtin 11
Apr 8 Hol 5f ft 1:032 H Mar 26 Hol 3f gd :364 H Mar 19 Hol 6f ft 1:151 H Mar 5 Hol 3f ft :36 Hg

Lady Charmin, Cherokee Gladys, and Yes Miss Helen each were stretching out following a layoff and a pair of sprints. Which figured best?

At this juncture knowledge of the class hierarchy at the local track and the form factor helps enormously. Handicapping data is relational, as many have pointed out.

At Santa Anita the seemingly minor class rise from $10,000 claiming to $12,500, and the corresponding drop, prove significant, but the drop from $16,000 claiming to $12,500 means little.

Video Pirate's rise following a four-length win at $10,000 might be repeated at $12,500, but was hardly automatic.

Of the three horses stretching out following the pair of sprints and a layoff, only Lady Charmin exits a good race.

Cherokee Gladys shows an acceptable race at $16,000 claiming, and the jockey switch from Dominguez to Pincay signals a dedicated try today. But the layoff here stretches from September 1987 to March 1989, some eighteen months. Handicappers should consider layoffs of a year or longer seriously problematic, notably among claiming horses. With a single win in the full record, and not a single good race in its past performances, Cherokee Gladys should improve under Pincay, but cannot be backed with confidence.

Yes Miss Helen shows similar shortcomings. Away roughly

a year, she shows only an acceptable second sprint at the $10,000 claiming level. The mare is up in class and stretching out simultaneously. Having beaten maiden claimers at age three, but nothing since, Yes Miss Helen can be tossed.

Recreational handicappers may counter that Lady Charmin is moving from state-bred $12,500 claiming to open $12,500 claiming, a tougher race. The point is not well taken here. At California tracks, state-bred to open claiming is not meaningful at the lowest price levels. These represent catchall brackets, top-heavy with dismal horses. An example is the $10,000 claiming level at Santa Anita, the bottom of the barrel there, jammed with slow, unreliable runners. Thus the drop from $12,500 to $10,000 claiming at Santa Anita frequently pays off. The order of competition has changed for much the worse.

At minor tracks the change from state-bred to open claiming at even the lowest levels can be meaningful. It depends. Handicappers must be acquainted with the local competition.

In sum, be alert for the two-sprint stretchout following a lengthy layoff. It's a positive pattern. If the horse deserves a class edge besides, award extra credit. If the price is right, make the bet.

NINTH RACE
Santa Anita
APRIL 13, 1989

1 $\frac{1}{16}$ MILES. (1.40⅕) CLAIMING. Purse $14,000. Fillies and mares. 4–year–olds and upward. Weight, 121 lbs. Non–winners of two races at one mile or over since February 1 allowed 3 lbs.; of such a race since then, 5 lbs. Claiming price $12,500; if for $10,500 allowed 2 lbs. (Claiming and starter races for $10,000 or less not considered.)

Value of race $14,000; value to winner $7,700; second $2,800; third $2,100; fourth $1,050; fifth $350. Mutuel pool $260,509. Exacta pool $439,812.

Last Raced	Horse	Eqt.	A.	Wt	PP	St	¼	½	¾	Str	Fin	Jockey	Cl'g Pr	Odds $1
16Mar89 $^{1}SA^{4}$	Lady Charmin	b	4	116	8	7	$6^{1\frac{1}{2}}$	$6^{2\frac{1}{2}}$	3^{4}	$1^{1\frac{1}{2}}$	$1^{\frac{1}{2}}$	Sibille R	12500	4.20
30Mar89 $^{9}SA^{3}$	Our Ole Lady	b	4	116	7	1	5^{2}	$3^{\frac{1}{2}}$	$2^{\frac{1}{2}}$	3^{3}	$2^{2\frac{1}{2}}$	Davis R G	12500	10.20
24Mar89 $^{1}SA^{10}$	Tamtulia		5	116	2	8	$8^{1\frac{1}{2}}$	8^{1}	$4^{1\frac{1}{2}}$	$4^{1\frac{1}{2}}$	3^{2}	Corral J R	12500	34.10
24Mar89 $^{1}SA^{6}$	Cherokee Gladys		5	117	10	9	9^{5}	9^{4}	$6^{1\frac{1}{2}}$	5^{2}	4^{nk}	Pincay L Jr	12500	4.90
30Mar89 $^{9}SA^{1}$	Video Pirate	b	4	111	6	2	1^{2}	$1^{2\frac{1}{2}}$	1^{2}	$2^{\frac{1}{2}}$	$5^{2\frac{3}{4}}$	Garcia H J^{5}	12500	1.40
30Mar89 $^{9}SA^{2}$	T. V. Tussle	b	4	116	5	11	10^{1}	$10^{1\frac{1}{2}}$	$10^{\frac{1}{2}}$	$6^{2\frac{1}{2}}$	6^{3}	Black C A	12500	16.50
23Mar89 $^{3}SA^{6}$	Colonial Treachery	b	4	116	4	12	12	12	12	$7^{1\frac{1}{2}}$	$7^{\frac{3}{4}}$	Solis A	12500	8.40
29Mar89 $^{1}SA^{6}$	Yes Miss Helen		5	116	11	10	11^{5}	$11^{3\frac{1}{2}}$	$11^{2\frac{1}{2}}$	$9^{1\frac{1}{2}}$	$8^{2\frac{1}{2}}$	Dominguez R E	12500	42.50
24Mar89 $^{1}SA^{9}$	Sweetness	b	6	111	1	5	7^{2}	7^{1}	7^{1}	$8^{\frac{1}{2}}$	9^{4}	Valenzuela FH^{5}	12500	19.00
25Mar89 $^{8}AC^{1}$	Miss Palton		6	118	12	4	3^{1}	$2^{1\frac{1}{2}}$	5^{hd}	10^{2}	$10^{1\frac{1}{4}}$	Meza R Q†	12500	23.00
22Mar89 $^{2}SA^{4}$	Raposa		5	116	3	6	$4^{\frac{1}{2}}$	5^{hd}	9^{1}	11^{2}	11^{6}	Bazan J	10500	104.90
11Mar89 $^{1}Ril^{1}$	M. D. Charge		5	114	9	3	2^{hd}	$4^{1\frac{1}{2}}$	$8^{\frac{1}{2}}$	12	12	Patterson A	10500	153.40

OFF AT 5:11. Start good. Won driving. Time, :22⅗, :46, 1:11⅕, 1:37⅗, 1:44⅖ Track fast.

$2 Mutuel Prices:			
8–LADY CHARMIN	10.40	7.40	6.40
7–OUR OLE LADY		11.00	6.20
2–TAMTULIA			9.80

$5 EXACTA 8–7 PAID $261.50.

Ch. f, by Commissioner—Lady Kit Kat, by Majestic Prince. Trainer Dorfman Leonard. Bred by Taylor Mr–Mrs (Cal).
LADY CHARMIN, outrun early, came on to get the lead after six furlongs, had a clear lead at the furlong marker and bested OUR OLE LADY. The latter, never far back, threatened through the last quarter and gained the place in a good try. TAMTULIA lacked early speed, entered the stretch four wide and was going well late. CHEROKEE GLADYS, devoid of early speed, came into the stretch four wide and found her best stride too late. VIDEO PIRATE, the early pacesetter, weakened in the drive. COLONIAL TREACHERY, wide down the backstretch, was five wide into the stretch. YES MISS HELEN, wide down the backstretch, was six wide into the stretch. SWEETNESS bobbled at the break. MISS PALTON, close up early and four wide into the clubhouse turn, faltered. RAPOSA, in contention early, was through after six furlongs and entered the stretch five wide. M. D. CHARGE, close up early, faltered badly and was four wide into the stretch.
Owners— 1, Taylor Thelma Lee; 2, Argonaut Stable; 3, Fritts R E & Maria J; 4, Beall & Mancini; 5, Chila-Madden-Mariucci; 6, Youst H A; 7, Lima Mr or Mrs M; 8, Dominguez M M; 9, Roberts Racing Stables; 10, Virissimo A R & Louise B; 11, Cordova A; 12, Zimmerman Debbie.
Trainers— 1, Dorfman Leonard; 2, Friday Charles; 3, Fourzon Howard; 4, Ippolito Steve; 5, Ravin Robert; 6, Needham Lloyd; 7, Carava Jack; 8, Martinez Rafael A; 9, Marikian Charles M; 10, Magana Rene; 11, Juarez Clare A; 12, Zimmerman Jon.
† **Apprentice allowance waived:** Miss Palton 5 pounds. **Overweight:** Cherokee Gladys 1 pound; Raposa 2.
Video Pirate was claimed by Segal–Segal–Xitco; trainer, Canani Julio C.
Scratched—Lady Kell (22Mar89 ²SA²); Face The King (29Mar89 ⁴GG¹).

IMPROVING MAIDENS

Well-backed maidens that disappoint but improve tremendously in their second start, still losing while supported, are excellent propositions the third time around.

The key is major improvement from the debut to the second chance. Examine the two efforts of Yugo Marie.

Clear in the slop on February 4 and ahead by three at the eighth pole, this Cal-bred filly tires and loses to other Cal-breds.

The second time, Yugo Marie contests a sizzling pace for the first three calls and holds well, beaten two lengths in a much faster sprint.

The experience counts, and lots. If the second race features a rapid pace and a second-place finish, award extra credit. A third-place finish deserves notice, too, if the time is quick and the beaten lengths two or less.

The third race should be better still. A facile victory is common. Because the maiden has lost twice at low odds, the odds today will be fair, perhaps generous if a sharp-working first-starter with leading connections has been entered. But first-starters 3up lose far more frequently than probabilities would expect. Inexperience defeats them. Stick with the improving maiden in its third attempt.

An exception to respect is the first-starter from a barn whose trainer wins repeatedly with first-starters, but recreational race-goers do not have that information. If the maiden is three years old or older, and the betting action is strong, forget it. The insiders will be wrong far more often than correct. If the odds allow, stay with the improving maidens.

And look longingly for that maiden having its third round, following a much-improved second try.

9661—FOURTH RACE. 6-1/2 furlongs. 3 year old maiden fillies. Cal bred. Purse $28,000.

Index	Horse and Jockey	Wt.	PP	ST	¼	½	¾	Str.	Fin.	To $1
9472	Yugo Marie, Davis	117	5	4	2^1	$1^{1½}$	-	1^4	1^6	2.80
9472	Conclaire, Black	117	9	3	$4^{3½}$	3^2	-	3^3	$2^½$	7.50
9571	Betsy's Theme, Stevens	117	4	1	1^{hd}	2^1	-	$2^½$	3^3	6.40
——	Alas De Oro, Delahoussaye	117	6	5	5^1	$5^{2½}$	-	4^{hd}	$4^{1¼}$	3.50
9571	Grandpa's Image, F. Vinzl	x112	10	6	$6^{1½}$	$6^{1½}$	-	6^1	5^2	29.40
9571	Scottish Brat, Garcia	117	8	2	3^{hd}	4^2	-	$5^{1½}$	6^{nk}	7.80
6130	Aunt Tecla, Solis	117	2	8	9^1	$8^{1½}$	-	7^3	$7^½$	12.80
9472	Play Dancer, Baze	117	11	7	7^1	$7^{3½}$	-	$8^{3½}$	$8^{1¼}$	41.00
——	Imperial Gem, Pincay	117	1	10	$8^½$	$9^½$	-	$9^{1½}$	9^4	4.70
——	Flying Sneakers, Olivares	117	3	11	10^3	10^5	-	10^9	10	44.10
——	Courage To Dream, Sblle	117	7	9	11	11	-	11^9	11	76.00

Scratched—Night Lily, Matti's Cabaret, Tuppence A Dance, Roberta Lin.

    5—YUGO MARIE 7.60   4.40   3.20
  10—CONCLAIRE 6.40   4.40
    4—BETSY'S THEME 6.00

Time—21 4/5, 44 2/5, 1.09 4/5, 1.16 3/5. Clear & fast. Winner—b.f 86 Ruffinal—Libya. Trained by Gary Jones. Mutuel pool—$814,810.

9662—FIFTH RACE. About 6.5 furlongs (turf). 4 year olds & up. Fillies & mares. Allowance. Purse $37,000.

LONG LONG AGO HE WAS GOOD

Several times a season handicappers are revisited by horses away longer than a calendar year. A few will have stayed away two years or longer. The resurrection will be accompanied by a drop in class. Workouts may be steady and sharp. The barn may be effective. A top jockey may be aboard.

What to do?

Pass.

Not the race necessarily, but the horse. The example that follows is typical. It's April 20, 1989.

Calvinist, age five, is dropping into a maiden-claiming affair, where, as all now know, the competition is slow. Maiden drop-downs regularly win.

6th Santa Anita

But Calvinist has not raced since January 11, 1987, twenty-seven months ago. Ineligible for a stall at Santa Anita, the horse has been working impressively at the Galway Downs training site, though a gap in training from February 21 until April 4 unfurls a red flag.

No matter.

Workouts notwithstanding, trainer patterns notwithstanding, the drop in class notwithstanding, Calvinist and his ilk should not be supported. The layoff extending beyond a year indicates serious injury. The longer the absence, the worse.

In the Calvinist situation at Santa Anita, the drop to maiden-claiming conditions misled a savvy crowd. The horse was backed down to 7–5, an unequivocal favorite.

Without doubt, when odds are low on these repatriates, ignore them. Few horses rebound from serious injuries to win at first crack. A drop in class, however large, does not redeem them.

Calvinist attended a rapid pace after being inactive for twenty-seven months, and faded.

SIXTH RACE
Santa Anita
APRIL 20, 1989

6 FURLONGS. (1.07⅗) MAIDEN CLAIMING. Purse $21,000. 4-year-olds and upward. Weight, 120 lbs. Claiming price $50,000; if for $45,000 allowed 2 lbs.

Value of race $21,800; value to winner $11,550; second $4,200; third $3,150; fourth $1,575; fifth $525. Mutuel pool $346,508.

Last Raced	Horse	Eqt.A.Wt PP St	¼	½	Str	Fin	Jockey	Cl'g Pr	Odds $1
23Jly88 4Hol7	Going Easy	b 4 115 6 2	2hd	1½	11½	11	Valenzuela FH5	50000	25.40
23Mar89 6SA2	Oh Dat Fox	b 4 120 7 6	51	3½	21½	2no	Valenzuela P A	50000	2.00
23Mar89 6SA3	Career Day	b 5 118 11 10	9½	5hd	4½	34	Solis A	45000	6.10
11Jan87 8SA11	Calvinist	5 118 2 4	31	41½	3½	41	Corral J R	45000	1.40
9Mar89 6SA8	On Easy Street	b 4 118 1 3	11½	22½	52	51½	Olivares F	45000	6.50
9Mar89 6SA11	High Ego	b 4 118 5 5	41	61½	62	6nk	Davis R G	45000	15.00
23Mar89 6SA5	Wined Out	b 5 118 10 1	7½	7hd	7hd	71½	Dominguez R E	45000	59.40
23Mar89 6SA9	Barn Burning	b 5 118 4 9	6hd	81	82	82	Patterson A	45000	59.40
2Mar89 6SA8	Buoyant Lyphard	b 4 118 8 8	104	9½	9hd	9½	Meza R Q	45000	173.60
7Sep88 4Dmr6	Beer Wagon	b 4 113 3 7	81	104	106	1012	Garcia H J5	45000	29.50
	Bonlou	4 118 9 11	11	11	11	11	Sinne H A†	45000	244.20

UP, UP, UP THE CLAIMING LADDER

A troublesome circumstance for handicappers involves horses rising in claiming class, perhaps dramatically, following good races or unexceptional victories. Most instinctively will discount any claiming horse moving ahead by too many levels. Confusion on the matter can be dissipated by adhering closely to this book's guidelines.

To illustrate, examine the main contention of a 6½-furlong claiming sprint open to $62,500 horses, 4up, at Santa Anita, April 21, 1989. Specifically, is the gelding Desperate outclassed, or does the horse fit the competition?

7th Santa Anita

6½ FURLONGS. (1.14) CLAIMING. Purse $36,000. 4-year-olds and upward. Weight, 122 lbs. Non-winners of two races since February 1 allowed 2 lbs.; of a race since then, 4 lbs.; since December 25, 6 lbs. Claiming price $62,500; for each $2,500 to $55,000 allowed 1 lb. (Races when entered for $50,000 or less not considered.)

Decore — B. g. 6, by Secretariat—Sight, by Gallant Romeo
PINCAY L JR 115 — Br.—Claiborne Fm & Gamely Corp (Ky) — 1989 3 0 1 0 $10,150
Tr.—Mitchell Mike $62,000 — 1988 5 1 0 0 $36,250
Own.—Alxndr-Fschng-Ustn Et al — Lifetime 26 6 9 1 $171,875 — Turf 6 0 2 0 $9,400

7Apr89-7SA 1 :453 1:10 1:353ft *2¾ 117 65¼ 63¾ 53 42 Pincay L Jr4 80000 88-19 He'sACajun,Shigamba,CaptainValid 9
7Apr89—Wide
30Mar89-8SA a6½f Ⓣ:22 :443 1:142fm 8¼ 115 44 54½ 69½ 69¼ Sibille R2 Aw55000 78-13 Ofanto, Pinecutter, Half A Year 6
30Mar89—Wide entering main track
1Mar89-3SA 6½f :214 :44 1:15 ft 3¾ 116 32 34½ 37 25 Sibille R2 62500 90-14 LimitedPrâctice,Decore,MgicLeder 6
9Dec88-8Hol 6f Ⓣ:222 :444 1:084fm 5 117 117¼ 108 106¼ 93¼ Gryder A T8 100000 90-07 Thrgs,RcordTurnout,ArbinFlconil 11
9Dec88—Wide
4May88-8Hol 1⅛Ⓣ 1:472fm 16 117 74¾ 99½ 911 917½ Gryder A T2 Aw52000 73-09 WorldCourt,Lordalik,Nostalgia'sStr 9
4May88—Bobbled 3/4, 3/8
22Apr88-8SA 1 1/16 :462 1:103 1:421gd 4¾ 118 74 31½ 42¼ 43¼ Gryder A T6 Aw60000 87-20 MarkChip,Epidurus,HotAndSmoggy 8
22Apr88—Bobbled start; wide 7/8 turn
6Mar88-3SA 7f :22 :442 1:213ft 2¼ 116 45½ 56½ 43½ 52¾ DlhossyE5 Vkng Spt H 89-13 HighBrit,ErnYourStrips,MyGllntGm 7
25Feb88-8SA 6f :22 :451 1:10 ft *3-2 1145 54½ 31½ 21½ 11½ Gryder A T2 Aw55000 88-22 Decore, Paisano Pete, Bid Us 5
15Nov87-3SA 1 1/16 :454 1:111 1:441ft 4½ 1095 33½ 3½ 1hd 1½ Gryder A T3 Aw48000 80-18 Decore, Forkintheroad, NativePriss 6
15Nov87—Erratic 7/8 turn
10Oct87-3SA 6f :213 :443 1:092ft 4½ 1146 56½ 43½ 31½ 11½ Gryder A T4 Aw34000 91-17 Decore,HotSauceBaby,CabllоDeOro 6
10Oct87—Wide 3/8 turn
Apr 12 SA 4f ft :49 H Mar 24 SA 4f ft :491 H Mar 18 SA 5f ft 1:02 H Mar 11 SA 4f ft :494 H

Desperate — B. g. 5, by Lucy's Axe—Darling Despot, by Mr Leader
GUERRA W A — 113 — Br.—Owens R (Ariz) — Tr.—Shulman Sanford — $55,000
Own.—Success Stables
Lifetime 15 8 0 2 $78,681 — 1989 5 3 0 1 $38,900 — 1988 2 2 0 0 $5,700 — Turf 2 1 0 1 $4,183
12Apr89-5SA 6½f :211 :434 1:151ft 4 116 32 21½ 1hd 13½ DelahoussayeE 5 32000 94-14 Desperte,KevinsDefense,Mgnifico 12
2Apr89-2SA 6f :214 :45 1:102ft *3 116 53 2½ 1hd 11½ Baze R A 7 c25000 86-15 Desperte,Mcemobile,UnderAndOver 8
25Mar89-1SA 6f :212 :442 1:09 gd 3½ 116 1hd 1½ 1hd 12 Baze R A 9 c20000 93-13 Desperate, Amazing Courage,FillUp 9
18Mar89-1SA 6f :212 :443 1:102ft 6½ 116 2½ 3½ 32 76¾ Black C A 3 25000 79-15 SuperbMomnt,RidrMrcus,HdlinNws 9
18Mar89—Bumped start
18Feb89-2SA 6½f :213 :443 1:171ft 9½ 114 2hd 21½ 21 32¼ Black C A 2 22500 82-19 UnderAndOvr,NoMonyDown,Dsprt 12
18Dec88-10TuP 7½f Ⓣ:24 :472 1:312fm *8-5 113 12 11½ 15 15 Martinez F III 5 16000 92-08 Desperate,NtiveFell,Robert'sLuck 12
4Dec88-7TuP 6f :221 :444 1:092ft 3 115 1½ 12½ 13 1½ Martinez F III 8 12500 87-17 Desperate,BellaRullah,BlueGreene 10
3Jly87-8Cby 1 :474 1:13 1:393ft 5 120 1½ 1hd 41¼ 75¾ Montoya D 4 Indep 77-19 RuffofthRibs,CptinSkff,ArrowSport 8
6Jun87-9Cby 7½f Ⓣ:231 :454 1:292fm *3½ 120 11 1hd 1hd 31¼ Kutz D 4 Aw11300 97-02 Arrow Sport, Feudal, Desperate 9
17May87-10Cby 5½f :221 :451 1:033ft *2½ 120 42 44½ 48½ 410¾ Allen R DJr 3 Scot Cty 91-15 Rat's Ruler, Farmer Mac, QueMeIn 6
Mar 13 SA 5f ft :593 H — Mar 7 SA 4f ft :482 H

Smart Guy — Ch. g. 4, by Perrault—Raise a Luv, by Raise a Native
VALENZUELA P A — 116 — Br.—Birdsell J (Ky) — Tr.—Jory Ian — $62,500
Own.—Banche Mr-Mrs N C
Lifetime 14 4 0 3 $90,950 — 1989 3 0 0 0 $2,850 — 1988 8 3 0 2 $75,300 — Turf 2 0 0 0
7Apr89-7SA 1 :453 1:10 1:353ft 16 1115 51¾ 43 42½ 53 Valenzuela F H 2 80000 87-19 He'sACajun,Shigamba,CaptainValid 9
7Apr89—Checked 3/8
18Mar89-9GG 6f :214 :44 1:083sy 6 116 56½ 55¾ 46 44½ Hansen R D 3 HcpO 91-14 RobrtoGrnd,ExclsvPtrt,Dncllthdncs 6
18Mar89—Steadied start
13Jan89-8SA 1 Ⓣ:481 1:124 1:374gd 26 113 32½ 62¾ 710 713½ Black C A 2 Aw48000 68-18 Vallotton, Ofanto, Bello Horizonte 8
26Dec88-8SA 7f :22 :44 1:213ft 10f 114 118¼ 96½ 75 106¼ Toro F 8 Malibu 86-13 Oraibi,PerceiveArrognce,Speedrtic 13
26Dec88—Grade II
26Nov88-8Hol 1 :45 1:10 1:362m 22 115 63¾ 53¼ 23½ 31¾ Toro F 7 Affrmd H 79-25 Speedratic,BldeOfTheBll,SmrtGuy 10
26Nov88—Grade III; Steadied 3/16
5Nov88-11BM 1 :464 1:113 1:362ft *3-2 116 2hd 2½ 1½ 1½ Doocy T T 7 HcpO 86-18 Smart Guy, Chillon, Buck Sweeper 7
13Oct88-8SA 1⅛ Ⓣ:462 1:104 1:48 fm 8 116 32½ 54½ 75½ 65½ DelhoussyeE 2 Aw43000 81-13 MircleHorse,PlesntVriety,Eliminnte 7
1Oct88-11Fpx a1⅛ :472 1:121 1:50 ft 3½ 122 2hd 3nk 43½ 57¾ Black C A 9 Pom Dby 85-09 PercivArrognc,BlAirDncr,Ship'sLog 9
5Sep88-7Dmr 1 1/16 :451 1:094 1:421ft 2¾ 114 31½ 1hd 1½ 11½ McCarronCJ 5 Aw36000 89-12 SmartGuy,RecittionSpin,RedobleII 6
21Aug88-3Dmr 1 :461 1:103 1:362ft 6 115 41¾ 42 34 31 McCarronCJ 4 Aw35000 85-12 ExoticEagle,FieldOfView,SmartGuy 9
21Aug88—Hopped start, bumped 1/16
Apr 2 Hol 6f ft 1:134 H — Mar 11 Hol 5f ft 1:00 H — Mar 6 Hol 4f ft :491 H

Having won by 3½ lengths versus $32,000 horses on April 12, nine days later Desperate tackles $62,500 claimers, a caliber the five-year-old has not confronted before.

How many class levels is Desperate actually leap-frogging?

To answer that question, reconsider this book's claiming-class hierarchy at major tracks. The ladder at Santa Anita looks in part like this:

$32,000–40,000
$50,000–62,500

Desperate is moving up a single class level, or bracket, according to this hierarchy. That is, one bracket equals one level. Statistics persuade us claiming horses can move up or down one level and win their expected share of the races.

In this book's scheme, Desperate is acceptable on class at

$62,500 claiming. Instead of jumping ahead by three class levels, Desperate can be accepted as moving ahead just one level.

Moreover, at $32,000 claiming April 12, Desperate recorded a Big Win and a turn time of 22.3 seconds. Prior to the $32,000 race, Desperate had beaten $25,000 claiming and $20,000 claiming horses. The step-ups following those triumphs were required as a result of two claims, but would have been acceptable regardless. Recall the relevant price brackets in the claiming-class hierarchy:

$20,000–25,000
$32,000–40,000

By this book's scheme, on April 2 Desperate was not moving ahead in class a bit, changing from $20,000 to $25,000 in selling price, a lateral move. The horse moved up one level April 12, rising from $25,000 to $32,000 horses. As steep as the next escalation appears, a rise from $32,000 to $62,500 claiming represents a step-up of one level following a Big Win, a perfectly acceptable class maneuver.

Modern speed handicappers use speed figures to predict which claiming horses can withstand a rise in price, one of the most reliable applications of the figures. To avoid the grossest kinds of confusion, recreational handicappers can evaluate the last representative running line in the context of the claiming-class ladder promoted here. Following a good race, one bracket up is suitable.

Desperate won the $62,500 claiming sprint at Santa Anita rather handily and paid $9.80. The uprising five-year-old, entered four months ago for $16,000 at Turf Paradise, was obviously not outclassed. Casual handicappers need to recognize that, and can.

THE CHAMPION RETURNS

It was April 29, 1989. Six months had elapsed since the brilliant filly Winning Colors had lost the Breeders' Cup Distaff by a nose to the marvelous champion Personal Ensign, becoming champion three-year-old of 1988 herself a few weeks later. A year had passed since Winning Colors had bested the leading males of her generation in the 114th Kentucky Derby.

Trainer D. Wayne Lukas had entered his champion in the seven-furlong A Gleam Handicap (Grade 3) at Hollywood Park, purse of $75,000-added.

The moment Winning Colors's name appeared in the entries, she shaped up as the underlay of the month. Every savvy handicapper in southern California should have realized that, but few did. Among the public selectors of the *Daily Racing Form* Winning Colors was set forth in bold type as the best bet of the day. Every correspondent picked her to win, from Trackman to Sweep. Special racing correspondent Jay Hovdey wrote in the *Los Angeles Times* that Winning Colors was primed to win and surely would. Taking cheap shots at the predictions of public selectors after the horses lose is low ball, but certain tendencies cannot be ignored.

No experienced handicapper should have touted Winning Colors to win A Gleam Handicap on the comeback, and those that did should commence some soul-searching until they find the answers they seemingly lack.

Winning Colors carried the following record into the A Gleam Handicap.

Against minor stakes opposition, Winning Colors was sent to the post in the A Gleam at 2–5.

Let's lay down a golden rule. Under no circumstances is a champion returning to competition after a vacation in a race below Grade 1 to be bet. No exceptions, unless the odds become irresistible, which they rarely do.

The workout pattern is impressive. The horse looks sturdier and more muscular than ever. The trainer announces the champ is fit and ready. The opposition is clearly inferior. Every public selector in town concedes the outcome.

Do not bet on the champion regardless. The horse is simply not intended to win. The comeback race is part of the conditioning process. It's worse than silly to go all-out with a champion for meaningless rewards. The overexertion of a winning effort might delay the stable's preparations for another season of Grade 1 triumphs. That would be mindless. So the champ is permitted to tire and lose, and that's what handicappers should expect. If the distance, footing, or probable pace will be other than ideal, the champion's chances are even less. In that regard, Winning Colors had not sprinted since her two-year-old season.

This logic extends as well, if not as compellingly, to the comebacks of all Grade 1 stakes winners. Champions, division leaders, and authentic Grade 1 horses are not primed to win unimportant stakes when returning from lengthy layoffs. Avoid the temptation to bet, and the underlay odds normally proffered.

Look instead for the logical alternatives to the champ or stakes star, which might be generous overlays today. The logical alternatives to Winning Colors on April 29, 1989, were not altogether persuasive, but they did finish one-two and yielded $123 for a $2 exacta when the champion tired and finished fourth. Both were exiting solid performances in minor stakes, which is customarily the case. Daloma paid $14.80 to win.

Survive B. m. 5, by Pass the Glass—Elite Khaled, by Prince Khaled
DELAHOUSSAYE E **113** Br.—Coffee Dessie F or J (Cal)
Tr.—Coffee John
Own.—Coffee Dessie F or J
Lifetime 19 5 6 2 $159,500

1989	6	2	2	0	$68,800
1988	10	1	4	2	$60,450
Turf	3	0	1	0	$9,000

19Apr89-8GG	1	$:45^{1}$	$1:09^{3}$	$1:36^{1}$ft	3¾	117	8^{7}	$6^{7\frac{1}{2}}$	2^{4}	$2^{1\frac{1}{2}}$	CpTM^{3}	(F)(S)Cal GirlsH	82-20	LyricalPirate,Survive,HlloweenBby	8
19Apr89—Forced wide 1/4															
26Mar89-8SA	a6½f (T)	$:22^{1}$	$:45^{1}$	$1:19^{3}$gd	11	116	$4^{1\frac{3}{4}}$	$4^{1\frac{1}{2}}$	4^{3}	6^{4}	Baze RA^{9}	(F)Ls Cngs H	77-20	ImperilStr,DownAgin,ServN'Volly	10
3Mar89-8SA	6½f	$:21^{4}$	$:44^{3}$	$1:16^{2}$gd	7½	115	$6^{6\frac{1}{2}}$	$5^{6\frac{1}{2}}$	$5^{1\frac{3}{4}}$	1^{2}	Baze R A^{3}	(F)Aw55000	88-19	Survive, Invited Guest, Saros Brig	6
3Mar89—Wide into stretch															
9Feb89-8SA	6f	$:21^{4}$	:45	$1:10^{3}$sy	3¾	118	6^{5}	$5^{5\frac{1}{2}}$	2^{3}	1no	DlhoussyE^{2}	(F)Aw41000	85-24	Survive, Humasong, Hasty Pasty	7
26Jan89-8SA	1	$:45^{3}$	$1:10^{1}$	$1:36^{2}$ft	6½	117	$5^{3\frac{3}{4}}$	5^{4}	$8^{7\frac{1}{4}}$	$8^{12\frac{1}{2}}$	Baze R A^{7}	(F)Aw45000	73-16	SettlSmooth,LdyBrunicrdi,SdiB.Fst	8
11Jan89-7SA	6f	$:21^{2}$	$:44^{1}$	$1:08^{3}$ft	4	119	$8^{6\frac{1}{4}}$	$8^{5\frac{3}{4}}$	3^{3}	$2^{3\frac{1}{2}}$	Baze R A^{1}	(F)Aw40000	91-14	Warning Zone, Survive, HastyPasty	8
30Dec88-5SA	a6½f (T)	$:21^{4}$	:45	$1:18^{1}$gd	3½	118	6^{7}	$6^{6\frac{1}{2}}$	4^{4}	$2^{2\frac{3}{4}}$	Baze R A^{7}	(F)Aw40000	75-22	Madruga,Survive,Marian'sCourage	12
30Dec88—Wide into stretch															
15Dec88-8Hol	6½f	$:21^{3}$	$:44^{3}$	$1:16^{3}$sy	16	115	8^{9}	7^{7}	$4^{1\frac{1}{4}}$	$1^{1\frac{3}{4}}$	Baze R A^{1}	(F)Aw27000	92-13	Survive, Young Flyer, Little BarFly	8
15Dec88—Boxed in 1/8															
16Jly88-7Hol	1	$:45^{4}$	$1:10^{1}$	$1:35^{2}$ft	3½	118	$8^{5\frac{1}{2}}$	$7^{5\frac{1}{4}}$	$5^{4\frac{3}{4}}$	$3^{6\frac{1}{4}}$	Baze R A^{7}	(F)Aw40000	80-15	Little Bar Fly, Flying Hill, Survive	9
16Jly88—Wide 3/8 turn															
19Jun88-4Hol	1	:45	$1:09^{4}$	$1:35^{2}$ft	*2	118	$4^{1\frac{1}{2}}$	$3^{1\frac{1}{2}}$	3^{2}	2^{4}	McCrrnCJ^{2}	(F)Aw40000	82-12	RenissncLdy,Surviv,Lt'sDrinkDinnr	7

Apr 17 SA 3f ft $:36^{2}$ B Apr 12 SA 6f ft $1:12^{3}$ H Apr 5 SA 3f ft $:35^{3}$ B Mar 24 SA 3f ft $:35^{4}$ H

When Winning Colors lost at 2–5, the same prognosticators who predicted an easy victory looked for an explanation from the principals.

"She just got tired," said Jeff Lukas, assistant to father Wayne.

Rodney Rash, assistant trainer to Charlie Whittingham, whose mare got the upset, told it exactly as it is: "If Winning Colors was going to get beat, it made sense that this might be the spot.

"She was making her first start in six months, and she was sprinting for the first time in more than a year.

"We also figured that they had bigger plans for Winning Colors farther down the line, and that maybe she wouldn't be cranked up all the way for this race."

I should think not. Perhaps the last segment of Rash's quote should be memorized. Champions are never, never, never cranked up for races like the A Gleam Handicap. Handicappers should remember that forever. So should the working press. Here is the memorable chart:

1035—EIGHTH RACE. 7 furlongs. 3 year olds & up. Fillies & mares. A Gleam Handicap. Purse $75,000.

9755	Daloma, McCarron	115	7	3	3^{hd}	$2^{\frac{1}{2}}$	-	1^{hd}	$1^{1\frac{3}{4}}$	6.40
9620	Survive, Delahoussaye	116	6	2	6^{1}	7	-	4^{1}	$2^{2\frac{3}{4}}$	18.30
9705	Behind The Scenes, P.Vinzi	116	1	7	7	6^{1}	-	$5^{2\frac{1}{2}}$	3^{hd}	6.50
——	Winning Colors, Stevens	123	4	4	$2^{1\frac{1}{2}}$	$1^{\frac{1}{2}}$	-	2^{3}	$4^{1\frac{3}{4}}$	.40
9584	Hot Novel, Guerra	107	5	1	$4^{1\frac{1}{2}}$	$4^{2\frac{1}{2}}$	-	3^{1}	$5^{1\frac{1}{4}}$	6.60
9606	Never Cee Miss, F.Valenzuela	112	3	6	5^{4}	$5^{1\frac{1}{2}}$	-	$6^{\frac{1}{2}}$	6^{5}	30.60
9527	Tomorrow's Child, Davis	111	2	5	1^{hd}	3^{1}	-	7	7	39.80

Scratched—Sadie B. Fast.

7—DALOMA	**14.80**	**6.20**	**3.80**
6—SURVIVE		**11.00**	**6.80**
1—BEHIND THE SCENES			**3.80**

Time—21 4/5, 44 2/5, 1.09, 1.21 3/5. Clear & fast. Winner—gr.m.84 Bellypha—Ricabie Trained by Charles Whittingham. Mutuel pool—$361,798. $2 Exacta pool—$436,362. Daily Triple pool—$469,926.

$2 EXACTA (7-6) PAID $123.00
$3 DAILY TRIPLE (5-6-7) PAID $433.50

DALOMA, close up early, forced the issue around the far turn without being hard ridden, took the lead a furlong out, responded when roused with the whip once right handed leaving the furlong marker to draw clear, then was shown the whip left handed in the final sixteenth while maintaining a clear advantage. SURVIVE lacked early speed, came into the stretch four wide and closed strongly. BEHIND THE SCENES also lacked early speed after breaking a bit awkwardly, was wide down the backstretch, entered the stretch five wide, failed to threaten in the drive but got up for the show. WINNING COLORS, away in good fashion, vied for the early lead without being hustled, set the pace around the far turn without being hard ridden, remainedin front in the upper stretch when roused with the whip once left handed leaving the three sixteenths marker and once more nearing the furlong marker, relinquished command a furlong out and weakened in the last furlong while being shown the whip right handed. HOT NOVEL, close up early, was difficult to handle in the run down the backstretch when trying to lug out while inside DALOMA, continued close up on the far turn and in the upper stretch, then gave way in the final furlong. TOMORROW'S CHILD had early speed and faltered.

EXCUSES, EXCUSES

Mispu was a fraud. The sort that finished second and third persistently at low odds without winning, earning the handicapper's scorn. A five-year-old in 1989, Mispu had been 1 for 24 and had failed when favored in three of his latest four races. The past performances looked like this:

Numerous thoroughbreds qualify as imitators of Mispu. They run well enough to attract the customers' money, without paying dividends. Handicappers learn to use the horses on the bottom sides of exactas, but do not support them to win.

Yet a variation of the pattern is less obvious to most handicappers, and Mispu fits the description.

When does a chronic loser figure to win?

When its losses have accumulated against clearly superior opposition, and now it faces stock it can defeat.

Out of the D. Wayne Lukas barn, Mispu had confronted minor stakes horses while in France and older nonwinners allowance types in four disappointing starts in the States. Competitive races under nonwinners-once allowance conditions translate to medium-range claiming races, roughly the $32,000 to $40,000 bracket at Santa Anita.

Lowered to $20,000 claiming on March 31, Mispu was facing his kind or worse at last. True to form, Mispu has lost twice when favored versus the lower claiming company, but zero for two is not the same as 1 for 24.

The point is plain. When chronic nonwinners have been consistently thwarted by horses of a clearly superior order, do not hold them unduly accountable for the woeful record once the level of opposition softens. Rate them solely off the record against the cheaper brand.

This guideline can become advantageous when two additional conditions present themselves, as with Mispu. One, the horse has showed competitive efforts recently against better. Two, the horse belongs to a leading stable.

The Lukas barn contains superior horseflesh. Not many cheapies. Some horses do not perform as expected, but top barns remain patient. So some horses continue to disappoint while outclassed. Finally, the barn gives up and drops. Soon the horses win at last. To repeat, if the dropdown of a chronic nonwinner from a top barn signals a new order of opposition, forgive the dismal record.

Some additional comments about horses like Mispu put their situation in a broader context.

Entered for $12,500 claiming on April 30, 1989, Mispu actually figured strongly against lackluster opposition. Examine the five-year-old's latest past-performance line, the $16,000 race on April 19.

Mispu broke from the far outside at a middle distance that day. As the *Form* trouble comment suggests, Mispu was forced wide on the clubhouse turn. The trip was far more problematic than that, however, and recreational handicappers are urged to pay attention to the point. It represents one of the worst trips a racehorse can encounter.

Normally an off-pace type, Mispu raced forwardly from the outside April 19 under Pat Valenzuela, a rider who prefers the front. The horse was forced extra wide while engaging for forward position. Mispu continued to race wide down the backside and around the far turn, all the while attempting to force the pace.

A frontrunner forced wide all the way at a middle distance while struggling for the lead is an awful trip that not only must be excused, but can be converted to profits next time. Wide all the way at the route is the worst trip for frontrunners, but among the best for handicappers to exploit.

Mispu had a legitimate excuse for finishing third at 2–1 on April 19. He might have won with a smooth trip. The winner, Ono Gummo, also returned April 30, and was favored at 7–5 against $20,000 horses. He won handily, and Kamp Out, second on April 19, again finished second.

With a legitimate trip excuse April 19, and legitimate class excuses for the 1 for 24 record, Mispu figured to defeat the $12,500 horses he lined up against April 30. Excuses, excuses, I know, but legitimate excuses nonetheless. Here's what happened in the race:

1039—THIRD RACE. 1-1/16 miles. 4 year olds & up. Claiming prices $12,500-$10,500. Purse $12,000.

Index	Horse and Jockey	Wt.	PP	ST	1/4	1/2	3/4	Str.	Fin.	To $1
9765	Mispu, P.Valenzuela	116	8	3	3$^{1\frac{1}{2}}$	2^2	1^{hd}	1$^{1\frac{1}{2}}$	1^4	2.40
9585	Prince Hoedown, Solis	116	9	8	8^5	8^6	6$^{1\frac{1}{2}}$	3^1	2^2	4.70
9675	Well In The Air, Davis	116	6	1	2$^{1\frac{1}{2}}$	1^{hd}	2^3	2^2	3^4	4.60
9788	Shams Ego, R.Meza	116	5	7	7$^{1\frac{1}{2}}$	7$^{1\frac{1}{2}}$	7$^{1\frac{1}{2}}$	5^1	4^4	20.60
9775	Debonair Aidan, Stevens	116	1	2	1$^{1\frac{1}{2}}$	3$^{1\frac{1}{2}}$	3^2	4^2	5^2	4.70
1001	Fill Up, Guerra	116	2	5	5$^{2\frac{1}{2}}$	5$^{2\frac{1}{2}}$	5^{hd}	6$^{3\frac{1}{2}}$	6$^{1\frac{1}{2}}$	4.20
9779	Me And The Drummer, H.Grc	x111	7	9	9	9	9	7$^{1\frac{1}{2}}$	7$^{1\frac{1}{2}}$	34.80
9779	F.H. King, Pedroza	118	4	6	6^1	6$^{1\frac{1}{2}}$	8^6	8^3	8^9	12.10
9783	Miami Bound, Fernandez	114	3	4	4^{hd}	4^{hd}	4^{hd}	9	9	33.90

Scratched—None.
Claimed—Well In The Air by Madden, Madden & Risoldi (trainer William Spawr), for $12,500; Mispu by F Malorrus (trainer John Sadler), for $12,500.

8—MISPU	6.80	3.40	2.60
9—PRINCE HOEDOWN		4.60	3.60
6—WELL IN THE AIR			3.60

Time—23 1/5, 46 3/5, 1.11, 1.36 3/5, 1.43 1/5 Clear & fast. Winner—ch.g 84 Miswaki—Heeria. Trained by D Wayne Lukas. Mutuel pool—$303,050. $2 Exacta pool—$422,094.

$2 EXACTA (8-9) PAID $33.00

Unfortunately, the predictable victory did not warrant a handicapper's support. At 2–1 on the board, Mispu must be forsaken. Although his record of futility has been forgiven, it cannot be forgotten. With two other contenders in the $12,500 field, and six noncontenders (which win at least 20 percent of all races), Mispu figured no better than 2–1, and the public offered no better than 2–1. No value.

More often than not, horses like Mispu will be offered at attractive odds when finally dropped to spots where they can survive. Having been dumped repeatedly by the horse, the bettors abstain. The horse not only has an honest chance, it walks to the post at 5–1. That's a profitable bet. But not this time. Not 2–1.

The contradictions inherent in Mispu's situation—weak record, strong chance, poor bet—represent the subtle variations characteristic of successful handicapping. No logical contradictions exist, but real contradictions do.

THREE-YEAR-OLD PACESETTERS ON THE GRASS

The good three-year-old Music Merci skipped the 1989 Kentucky Derby and on Derby Day entered instead the Listed stakes below.

5th Hollywood

1 MILE. (Turf). (1.32¾) 11th Running of THE SPOTLIGHT HANDICAP. $75,000 added. 3-year-olds. By subscription of $100 each, which shall accompany the nomination. $750 additional to start, with $75,000 added, of which $15,000 to second, $11,250 to third, $5,625 to fourth and $1,875 to fifth. Weights Monday, May 1. Starters to be named through the entry box by closing time of entries. Hollywood Park reserves the right not to divide this race. Should this race not be divided and the number of entries exceed the starting gate capacity, xppghweights on the scale will be preferred and an also eligible list will be drawn. Total earnings in 1989 will be used in determining the order of preference of horses assigned equal weight on the scale. Failure to draw into this race at scratch time cancels all fees. A trophy will be presented to the owner of the winner. Closed Wednesday, April 26, 1989 with 30 nominations.

Limited to three-year-olds at a mile on the turf, the $75,000-added purse smelled like easy-picking roses to the crowd at Hollywood Park. It was not. Examine Music Merci's record. Do handicappers notice any danger signs?

The crowd sent Music Merci to the gate at 1–2, an odds-on favorite.

Music Merci shaped up this May day on the turf as an underlay the equal of Easy Goer in the mud. Music Merci was a pacesetter, and handicappers should accept the following guideline as a maxim.

> When three-year-old pacesetters first try the turf, the percentage of energy expended to the prestretch call will be too high, and the horses will usually be defeated in the late stages by off-pace types that could not catch them on the dirt.

Good speed horses are especially vulnerable first time on grass, and many will be overbet. Running style aside, three-year-olds that cannot be rated kindly ordinarily will perish on the grass. Throw them out without mercy.

To appreciate the situation, consider the early-energy output to the second call of the winners at Hollywood Park 1989 in three kinds of races:

Sprints on dirt	52.8%
Routes on dirt	51.9%
Routes on grass	50.2%

The difference in lengths between routes on dirt and turf is roughly fifteen. In other words, turf-course winners run significantly slower early. They win with late speed. Three-year-olds that spend too much energy to the second call normally will be doomed in the stretch on grass. It happens everywhere. As frontrunners and pace-pressers become accustomed to expending their energies early, frontrunning styles will require some fine tuning when first switched to the turf. Horses cannot change running styles abruptly. The pacesetters should be expected to lose at first and regularly do.

Music Merci finished a tired second in his grass debut, and no finer illustration of the pattern can be brandished to unaware handicappers.

An exception is the forward-running three-year-old that has learned to relax for the rider on command. These horses can be snugged back without tension or restraint. They can be maneuvered into a relaxed stride on the lead as well. Their early speed can be converted to late speed. So they can win on the turf at first asking. Handicappers must respect this minority. If the odds are low, play it safe regardless.

The colt that defeated Music Merci in the Spotlight Handicap underscores another poorly understood pattern among the three-year-olds. Examine the past performances of Hollywood Reporter, who was jumping from a preliminary nonwinners allowance mile on dirt to a Listed stakes on grass. Why might handicappers consider the colt a legitimate contender?

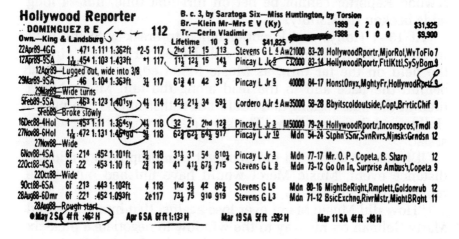

This is the impressively improving three-year-old that might be any kind, or if that assertion is too bold, a colt that might become better than its three-year-old past suggests.

Handicappers must pay attention whenever a three-year-old begins to soar. Three-year-olds can improve tremendously, and regularly do. Hollywood Reporter's improving record contains a twist that warrants another handicapping guideline.

> Whenever a three-year-old is claimed by a competent trainer and next out improves dramatically while up in class, handicappers should expect further improvement still, probably against better.

It's not unusual that a good trainer will find the key to an improving three-year-old. If a three-year-old impresses versus better following a claim, the best is probably yet to come.

Hollywood Reporter won by four, was claimed by a competent barn, and won by thirteen next in a nonwinners allowance race. Shipping from Santa Anita to Golden Gate Fields, the colt went 2–5 against the allowance field, but won, as the odds predicted.

Hollywood Reporter's young sire, Saratoga Six, is unknown as a turf sire. Successful turf sires distinguish three-year-olds when first they try the grass. Unknown does not mean ineffective, however. Without sire support, and another colt absolutely possessing the pace-pressing running style, an improving Hollywood Reporter cannot be bet on turf first time, unless long odds beckon irresistibly.

At 15–1 Hollywood Reporter failed to break with the field in the Spotlight Handicap. The colt lagged far back. It circled the field on the far turn, as Music Merci edged up from just behind the pace and to the lead along the rail. Music Merci tired in the final furlong and could not withstand the late punch Hollywood Reporter threw. The slow start probably deserves an assist.

It happens often. Had the Spotlight Handicap been a middle-distance event, Music Merci would have finished out of the money, and well beaten.

"How did Music Merci ever lose against that bunch?" asked Marty Gelman on his way to the window to negotiate a pick-six ticket that had five winners on it, but also Music Merci as a single. Gelman concurred with the explanation his acquaintance provided, but in the end could not resist restating the obvious.

"Yeah, but he just looked like he was so much better than the others. He should have won anyway."

MAIDEN-CLAIMING GRADUATES

When should last-out winners of maiden-claiming races be expected to beat previous winners or close runners-up in open competition?

The circumstance hounds even the best of handicappers. Maiden-claiming races feature the cheapest horses on the grounds in the slowest races on the cards. The traditional guideline has been conservative, and rightfully so. Expect maiden-claiming graduates to win at selling prices roughly 50 percent below the maiden-claiming price.

Recreational handicappers without numerical ratings should

cling to the traditional standard. Maiden-claiming graduates normally lose next time, in part because they cannot run as swiftly as prior open-claiming winners, in part because stables tend to enter them against winners too ambitiously. Conservative practice protects against the downside.

Recreational handicappers in possession of the pace ratings promoted by this book can proceed differently. They can support maiden-claiming graduates when they are entered for a claim and possess higher pace ratings than any other horse in the field. It's crucial, too, that the maiden-claiming win reveal a turn time at least equal to par. The early pace of open-claiming races regularly defeats maiden-claiming graduates, who cannot speed up early and still repeat the maiden-claiming final time.

For an outstanding example, let's tackle the past performances of the seventh race at Hollywood Park, May 10, 1989. Using the PDQ pace ratings, modified by track variants based upon the par variants for Santa Anita (17) and Hollywood Park (13), we can rank the seven entrants from high to low on pace. Examine the past performances below.

7th Hollywood

6 ½ FURLONGS. (1.15) CLAIMING. Purse $20,000. 3-year-olds. Weight, 122 lbs. Non-winners of two races since March 19, allowed 3 lbs.; a race since then, 6 lbs. Claiming price $40,000; for each $2,500 to $35,000, allowed 2 lbs. (Races when entered for $32,000 or less not considered).

Chief Runnin Blaze

DAVIS R G
Own.—R N H Racing Stable

Dk. b. or br. c. 3, by Hula Chief—Indi's Fluff, by Khal Me Indi
Br.—RNH Racing Stable (Tex)
Tr.—Threewitt Noble $40,000

116

1989 1 1 0 0 $8,800
1988 6 1 0 0 $13,928
Lifetime 7 2 0 0 $22,728

Jazz

SOLIS A
Own.—Meredith Mr-Mrs J S

Ch. c. 3, by Messenger of Song—Circle the Day, by Walker's
Br.—Goemans Peg (Cal)
Tr.—McAnally Ronald $40,000

116

1989 1 1 0 0 $9,900
1988 2 M 1 0 $3,450
Lifetime 3 1 1 0 $13,350

Burnt Twice
DELAHOUSSAYE E 116
Own.—Downey J
Ch. c. 3, by J Burns—Annie Arf, by Figonero
Br.—Downey J (Okla) 1989 2 1 0 0 $9,350
Tr.—Jordan James $40,000 1988 0 M 0 0
Lifetime 2 1 0 0 $9,350
17Mar89-7SA 6f :212 :444 1:094ft 11 1125 64½ 67 811 813¼ ValenzuelFH5 Aw32000 76-20 RomanAvie,BigConviction,Jotcaro 10
17Mar89—Rough start
23Feb89-2SA 6f :214 :453 1:11 ft 3½ 118 3½ 2hd 11½ 15 DelahoussyeE7 M32000 83-20 BurntTwic,ClostClown,AugustWst 12
23Feb89—Bumped hard start
May 5 SA 4f ft :473 Hg Apr 28 SA 5f ft 1:013 H Apr 22 SA 4f ft :471 H Apr 17 SA 5f ft 1:012 H

Colorful Hitter
PEDROZA M A 116
Own.—Fmiglietti–Selvin–ThreeMSts
B. c. 3, by Color Bearer—Lavish Affair, by Bold Hitter
Br.—3 M Stbs & Carrieri (Cal) 1989 4 0 0 1 $6,450
Tr.—Cenicola Lewis $40,000 1988 6 1 0 2 $21,935
Lifetime 10 1 0 3 $28,385
29Mar89-9SA 1 :46 1:104 1:363ft 4¾ 114 31 62½ 64½ 75¾ Pedroza M A9 40000 79-17 HonstOnyx,MghtyFr,HollywodRprtr 9
1Mar89-7SA 1 :472 1:12 1:374ft 5½ 113 65¼ 62¼ 52¼ 42¼ Pedroza M A7 40000 77-14 Dime Time, HourFinder,MightyFair 7
1Mar89—Rough start; 6 wide into stretch
15Feb89-5SA 6f :213 :45 1:103ft 27 116 53 42 43½ 32½ Pedroza M A8 40000 82-17 Pttn'ForEgl,MgcJohnson,ClrflHttr 8
15Feb89—Wide
1Feb89-5SA 6f :22 :451 1:101ft 11 117 86 1014 1019 1024 Pincay L Jr10 50000 63-15 GntlmnsStyl,MgcJhnsn,SpcyYlltl 10
16Dec88-5Hol 1 :454 1:111 1:38 sy *3¼ 116 43 63¾ 62½ 35 Pedroza M A5 40000 68-24 Lord'sLns,Prt'sAdvntr,ColorflHttr 11
23Nov88-7Hol 1 :45 1:10 1:353ft 6½ 117 41¾ 41¾ 43½ 49 Pedroza MA5 Aw25000 76-14 RisAStnz,VryPrsonbly,SnowsInPris 6
29Oct88-8SA 1 :461 1:102 1:351ft 20 114 53 55¾ 58¾ 513¼ PedrozMA 1 Ⓢ B J Rdr 79-12 Endow,FlyingContinental,BoldBryn 6
29Oct88—Rank at 7 1/2
12Oct88-2SA 6f :212 :443 1:103ft 3¼ 114 66 47 36 31 Pedroza M A9 40000 84-19 SkyVrdict,Michlbrry,ColorfulHittr 12
16Sep88-8Fpx 6½f :22 :463 1:171ft 5¾ 116 67 53½ 66½ 410¼ Sibille R3 Aw33000 80-14 Shipping Time, Loaded Juan, Irish 8
25Aug88-2Dmr 6f :223 :454 1:11 ft 5¼ 117 41½ 11½ 14 14 PedrozMA10 ⓈM32000 83-18 Colorful Hitter, Try Raja, Latour 12
Apr 26 Hol 7f ft 1:251 H ●Apr 20 Hol 6f ft 1:13 H ●Apr 14 Hol 5f ft 1:00 H Apr 8 Hol 4f ft :492 H

Waltzing Sass
SIBILLE R 112
Own.—Smith & Yount
Ch. c. 3, by Sassafras (Fra)—Waltzing Blade, by Blade
Br.—Cassidy–Cassidy Partnership (Ky) 1989 8 1 1 1 $20,400
Tr.—Miller Grace A $35,000 1988 7 2 0 2 $27,650
Lifetime 15 3 1 3 $48,050
20Apr89-1SA 6f :214 :451 1:094ft 4¼ 118 43 21½ 2½ 32¼ Cedeno A 2 c20000 87-16 GrkMyth,LightningPort,WltzingSss 7
7Apr89-5SA 6f :22 :46 1:113ft 6½ 116 95¼ 95¾ 54 43¼ Cedeno A 3 25000 77-19 GrkMyth,SpcyYllowtl,PcktflOfAcs 10
7Apr89—Took up, wide
23Mar89-1SA 6½f :213 :45 1:183ft 4¾ 116 83¾ 34 2hd 1½ Cedeno A 8 20000 77-19 WltzngSss,MgcJhnsn,LghtngPrt 11
10Mar89-2SA 6f :213 :444 1:102ft 5¼ 115 75 74½ 64 63½ Black C A 7 25000 82-17 RstlssGlxy,Triptomu,HombrHombr 12
10Mar89—Steadied at 5/8
16Feb89-1SA 6f :214 :451 1:111ft 21 115 62½ 43 22 23½ Black C A 2 25000 78-21 MiracleMystery,WaltzingSss,Trgo 12
2Feb89-5SA 6f :213 :45 1:111ft 5½ 114 109¾ 108 99½ 910¼ Stevens G L 5 32000 72-18 GingrSocks,Ptzcuro,HombrHombr 11
2Feb89—Broke in, stumbled, bumped start; 6 wide into drive
19Jan89-5SA 1 :462 1:12 1:39 ft *2½ 114 62¾ 42 42½ 45 Stevens G L 6 32000 68-23 Dime Time,Bargainaul,Caro'sRuler 10
6Jan89-5SA 1 :46 1:113 1:381m 7½ 1105 66 84¾ 98 910¾ ValenzuelaFH 10 40000 66-20 AgnKing,Prt'sAdvntur,John'sRvng 10
6Jan89—Bumped early drive
26Oct88-3SA 6f :214 :452 1:111ft 6 118 63¾ 32 21½ 1½ Stevens G L 6 c32000 82-16 Waltzing Sass, Rip Curl, Morlando 9
26Oct88—Bumped start
16Oct88-7SA 6f :21 :442 1:103ft 52 116 811 811 78¾ 810 Pedroza MA 1 Aw31000 75-16 BetOnTheBlurr,Irish,ManstshRidge 9
May 7 Fpx 4f ft :48 H ●May 2 Fpx 5f ft 1:012 H Mar 30 SA 5f ft 1:014 H Mar 20 SA 5f ft 1:003 H

Shelter Us
MCCARRON C J 116
Own.—Bacharach B
B. c. 3, by Shelter Half—School Play, by Halo
Br.—Blue Seas Music Inc (Md) 1989 2 1 0 0 $8,250
Tr.—Jones Gary $40,000 1988 0 M 0 0
Lifetime 2 1 0 0 $8,250
26Apr89-4Hol 6f :214 :444 1:09 ft 7 115 31½ 1hd 12 11½ McCarron C J 3 M32000 96-10 ShltrUs,CourgoußPirt,GoldnVision 12
26Apr89—Lugged in stretch
22Mar89-6SA 6f :213 :444 1:104ft 5 118 1½ 2hd 45½ 1112¾ McCarron C J 9 M50000 71-17 Skisit, Number One Tuto,WayWild 12
May 4 Hol 4f ft :473 H Apr 21 Hol 5f ft 1:003 H Apr 16 Hol 4f ft :484 H Apr 9 Hol 5f ft 1:024 H

Triptomaui
GARCIA H J 1075
Own.—Carlesimo J C
Ro. g. 3, by Kamehameha—Stone Jumper, by Stonewalk
Br.—Newmarket Stables Inc (Va) 1989 2 1 1 0 $8,350
Tr.—Tinsley J E Jr $35,000 1988 1 M 0 0
Lifetime 3 1 1 0 $8,350
10Mar89-2SA 6f :213 :444 1:102ft 5 116 1½ 1½ 11 2hd ValenzuelaPA1 c25000 86-17 RstlssGlxy,Triptomu,HombrHombr 12
26Jan89-5GG 6f :22 :451 1:101ft 30 118 53¼ 34½ 33 1½ Mills J W6 M20000 88-17 Triptomaui, Raketmensch,KidOWar 9
26Jan89—Bumped 3/16
9Sep88-6Lga 6f :22 :46 1:122ft 5¾ 120 42½ 42½ 65½ 1010 Arias J D 11 Mc25000 64-27 TroysFriend,MerriNot,NvrbnCptin 11
May 7 Hol 4f ft :492 H Apr 30 Hol 6f ft 1:14 H Apr 24 Hol 4f ft :492 H Apr 16 SA 5f ft 1:021 H

First let's identify the track variant for the ratable races, which have been underlined. The procedure, to recall, obtains the deviation between the track's par variant and the *Daily Racing Form*'s daily track variant.

Horse	Class	Track	Par Variant	Form Variant	Difference	Track Variant
Chief Runnin Blaze	Clm 40	Hol	13	15	S2	S2
Jazz	MdnClm 32	SA	17	14	F3	F3
Burnt Twice	Alw 32	SA	17	20	S3	S3
Colorful Hitter	Clm 40	SA	17	17	0	even
Waltzing Sass	Clm 20	SA	17	16	F1	F1
Shelter Us	MdnClm 32	Hol	13	10	F3	F3
Triptomaui	Clm 25	SA	17	17	0	even

To obtain PDQ pace ratings, handicappers apply half the track variant to the race's fractional time, the full variant to the race's final time. This converts actual times to adjusted times and reflects the influences of track-surface speed, as below.

Horse	Date	Actual Times		Track Variant	Adjusted Times	
Chief Runnin Blaze	May 3	45.1	1:10.4	S2	45	1:10.2
Jazz	Apr 12	45.2	1:11.1	F3	45.4	1:11.4
Burnt Twice	Feb 23	45.3	1:11	S3	45.1	1:10.2
Colorful Hitter	Feb 15	45	1:10.3	0	45	1:10.3
Waltzing Sass	Apr 20	45.1	1:09.4	F1	45.2	1:10
Shelter Us	Apr 26	44.4	1:09	F3	45.1	1:09.3
Triptomaui	Mar 10	44.4	1:10.2	0	44.4	1:10.2

To obtain pace ratings from adjusted times, subtract 1 point for each one-fifth second the adjusted times are slower than the mythical 100-point times. To recall, the 100-point standard times are:

6F	1:08	1M	1:33
6½F	1:14	1⅟₁₆M	1:40
7F	1:20	1⅛M	1:46

Now handicappers simply rate the race's fractional time and final time, plus the horse's final time, subtracting 1 for each beaten length from the race's final-time rating. Add the three ratings. If handicappers prefer, they can rate each horse's position at the pace call, instead of its final position. Either procedure satisfies here.

Horse	Fractional Rating	Final Rating	Beaten Lengths	Horse's Final Rating	PDQ Pace Ratings
Chief Runnin Blaze	95	88	won	88	271
Jazz	91	81	won	81	253
Burnt Twice	94	88	won	88	270
Colorful Hitter	95	87	2½	84	266
Waltzing Sass	93	90	2¼	88	271
Shelter Us	94	92	won	92	278
Triptomaui	96	88	hd	88	272

Two horses, Jazz and Shelter Us, represent last-out maiden-claiming graduates. Jazz shows the weakest pace rating in the field. Shelter Us shows the strongest.

Chief Runnin Blaze and Waltzing Sass have beaten open-claiming competition, Triptomaui almost. Colorful Hitter has demonstrated good races against today's $40,000 competition. Burnt Twice returns to a claiming race from allowance conditions, following his facile score at $32,000 maiden-claiming.

Which horse figures to win?

The pace ratings give Shelter Us a clear-cut five-point advantage. With no other horse in the field even close, Shelter Us cannot be denied on the numbers here. Check the turn time of Shelter Us in the maiden-claiming win. It's a splendid 22.3 seconds. The Hollywood Park claiming par is 23.3. The cold facts stand out, and the race should be regarded that way, notwithstanding the rise from maiden-claiming competition.

Examine the result chart for the race, before a few final comments.

SEVENTH RACE	6 ½ FURLONGS. (1.15) CLAIMING. Purse $20,000. 3-year-olds. Weight, 122 lbs. Non-winners of two races since March 19, allowed 3 lbs.; a race since then, 6 lbs. Claiming price $40,000; for each $2,500 to $35,000, allowed 2 lbs. (Races when entered for $32,000 or less not considered).
Hollywood	
MAY 10, 1989	

Value of race $20,000; value to winner $11,800; second $4,000; third $3,000; fourth $1,500; fifth $500. Mutuel pool $252,904. Exacta pool $318,571.

Last Raced	Horse	Eqt.A.Wt	PP	St	¼	½	Str	Fin	Jockey	Cl'g Pr	Odds $1
26Apr89 4Hol1	Shelter Us	b 3 116	6	2	1hd	11	12	12¾	McCarron C J	40000	1.50
17Mar89 7SA8	Burnt Twice	b 3 116	3	4	22½	32	2hd	2no	Delahoussaye E	40000	3.10
29Mar89 9SA7	Colorful Hitter	3 116	4	3	4hd	2hd	33½	32	Pedroza M A	40000	6.40
10Mar89 2SA2	Triptomaui	3 107	7	1	6½½	4½	4hd	4hd	Garcia H J5	35000	7.30
20Apr89 1SA3	Waltzing Sass	b 3 116	5	7	7	7	52	56½	Sibille R	35000	19.40
3May89 5Hol1	Chief Runnin Blaze	3 116	1	6	5½	61	6hd	6no	Davis R G	40000	10.50
12Apr89 4SA1	Jazz	3 116	2	5	3hd	5hd	7	7	Solis A	40000	5.30

OFF AT 4:39. Start good. Won ridden out. Time, :22, :45, 1:09⅘, 1:16 Track fast.

$2 Mutuel Prices:

6-SHELTER US	5.00	2.60	2.40
3-BURNT TWICE		3.00	2.40
4-COLORFUL HITTER			2.80

$2 EXACTA 6-3 PAID $15.80.

B. c, by Shelter Half—School Play, by Halo. Trainer Jones Gary. Bred by Blue Seas Music Inc (Md).

SHELTER US vied for the early lead without being hustled, drew clear after a half and remained clear through the final furlong. BURNT TWICE vied for the early lead after being jostled in the initial strides, remained close up through the drive and nipped COLORFUL HITTER for the place. COLORFUL HITTER, close up early after being jostled in the opening strides, forced the issue on the far turn, remained close up through the drive and just miss the place. TRIPTOMAUI was wide down the backstretch. WALTZING SASS, wide early, was four wide into the stretch. JAZZ, close up early after being jostled in the initial strides, faltered.

Owners— 1, Bacharach B; 2, Downey J; 3, Famiglietti-Selvin-ThreeMSts; 4, Carlesimo J C; 5, Smith & Yount; 6, R N H Racing Stable; 7, Meredith Mr-Mrs J S.

Trainers— 1, Jones Gary; 2, Jordan James; 3, Cenicola Lewis; 4, Tinsley J E Jr; 5, Miller Grace A; 6, Threewitt Noble; 7, McAnally Ronald.

Overweight: Waltzing Sass 4 pounds.

$2 Pick Six (11–6–7–7–7–6) Paid $43,590.80 for 6 Wins. Including $305,786.32. 16 Tickets. 5 Wins Paid $546.20; 694 Tickets. Pool $980,151.

First, three-year-old claiming horses are best distinguished numerically by pace ratings. Not speed figures. Not class ratings. Three-year-olds move up and down the claiming ranks for most of the sophomore season. They improve. They decline. They improve again, decline again. Maturation, seasoning, and the relative quality of the competition interact constantly, and the results can be confounding. The kind of pace they have handled in the past three months is the best clue as to what claiming three-year-olds might do today. This is especially true in winter and spring, before the three-year-olds begin to mix it up with older claiming horses. All of this applies to maiden-claiming graduates. If these exhibit the best pace ratings, they figure, and notably so, against other three-year-olds of winter and spring.

The same will be true, by the way, of two-year-old maiden-claiming graduates of fall.

When maiden-claiming graduates next enter a nonwinners

allowance race, the logic shifts. Now pace ratings are indicative but inconclusive. Burnt Twice in the sample race followed a powerful maiden-claiming win having a strong pace rating with an allowance try, but was humbled. Even superior pace ratings do not translate easily to an allowance win. That's because allowance horses possess reserves of speed and energy claiming horses do not. The allowance runners can turn up the tempo, or pace, and persevere. When they do, the vast majority of maiden-claiming winners cannot stay with them.

Would Shelter Us have won against an allowance field, non-winners of a race other than maiden or claiming?

Possibly. Probably not.

Even more: with its fancy pace rating, Shelter Us might have been overbet against allowance horses. When that happens, handicappers should abstain. I have observed a few of the nation's top figure handicappers using speed figures or pace ratings to support maiden-claiming graduates under allowance conditions. More often than not, the professionals squander the bets. Recreational handicappers cannot cash these bets either, and should not try.

THE INSIDE SPEED BIAS

Recreational handicappers can benefit from cursory analyses of the post-position studies published by the *Daily Racing Form* astride the past performances for the first race at the local track.

Look for severe track biases favoring one or two posts, either inside or outside. If inside posts have been winning a vastly disproportionate share of the races, assume the early-speed horses have been galloping unmolested. To confirm the assumption, pay attention to the early races. If an inexplicable long shot goes wire to wire after exiting the one- or two-hole, prepare to back other overlays exiting the same posts for the rest of the day.

During Preakness week 1989 I arrived at the Race Book of the Frontier Hotel in Las Vegas for five days of frenzied recreational handicapping, playing multiple cards simultaneously, which I like to do a few outings each year. On Wednesday morning I surveyed the Central edition of the *Form*, and fastened on the following post-position tabulation for Louisiana Downs.

Winners by Post Positions

	SPRINTS (Under One Mile)			ROUTES (One Mile & Over)		
P.P.	**STS**	**WINS**	**PCT.**	**STS**	**WINS**	**PCT.**
1	96	21	.22	40	15	.38
2	96	17	.18	40	4	.10
3	96	13	.14	40	5	.13
4	96	8	.08	40	4	.10
5	96	11	.11	40	4	.10
6	95	9	.09	40	2	.05
7	90	6	.07	36	1	.03
8	81	6	.07	25	5	.20
9	66	3	.05	18	0	.00
10	50	1	.02	16	0	.00
11	45	0	.00	11	0	.00
12 & UP	33	1	.03	5	0	.00

LOUISIANA DOWNS
(April 28 to May 14, Inclusive)
(Main Track)

The post-position bias favoring the number-one hole at the route looked irresistible. Would it persist?

The two inside posts looked clearly biased in sprints as well, though not nearly as much as the rail in routes.

The first two races that Wednesday were sprints, and each was won by a horse exiting post 2 and running near the lead. The third was a route. The 8–5 favorite would exit post No. 1. He lost by a head to a 4–1 contender exiting post 4. But he throttled the third finisher by eleven lengths.

The fourth sprint on the program, race five, was won on the front by a long shot out of the two-hole. The horse paid $45.80. Named Sharon Searcher, its past performances appear below, along with those of the inside horse. The two maiden-claiming fillies look eerily alike:

5th La. Downs

6 FURLONGS. (1.08⅔) MAIDEN. CLAIMING. Purse $6,500. Fillies. 3 and 4-year-olds, accredited Louisiana–bred. Weight, 3-year-olds, 112 lbs.; 4-year-olds, 123 lbs. Claiming price $15,000; if for $12,500 allowed 3 lbs.

Maybeon Tuesday   120   Dk. b. or br. f. 4, by Take the Floor—Gamblet's Sabbath, by Poker
HOWARD D L   7-N   Br.—Franks John (La)   1989 2 M 0 0
Own.—River Ridge Farm   Tr.—Balthazar Andrew $12,500   1988 2 M 0 0
                            Lifetime, 4 0 0 0

28Apr89-2LaD 7f :22³ :46³ 1:26¹ft   6½ 119   1½ 2½ 10¹⁷¹ 1¹³⁷   Romr̥SP ²ⓕ⑤M12500 40-17 DelingAtEse,JillDncr,SomtimsJuli 12
4Mar89-4LaC   6f :22² :47⁴ 1:14⁴ft   7⁷ 1155⑂13 13 2² 8¹⁰   JourdnₘJ̤⑧ⓕ⑤M25000 61-23 CndinSunrise,GryMrker,Nn'sAngel12
20Nov88-4LaD 6f :22 :46⁴ 1:13⁴ft   12 110⁵ 2½ 7⁴¹2¹9¹2²²   SctchPW⑨ⓕ⑤M17500 51-18 Bit of Guile,‡BellCity,Silk'sDancer 12
20Nov88—Placed eleventh through disqualification
16Jly88-3LaD 6f :22³ :46² 1:23⁴ft   6² 113   1ʰᵈ 5⁴³¹11512261½   CrawfordKE⑧ⓕ⑤Mdn 53-16 TruPrsonlity,WlcomArrst,Tchukon 12

Sharon Searcher
FAUL J H ⌐ ○
Own.—Feeback Glen

B. f. 3, by Reef Searcher—Pink Lemonade, by Cannonade
Br.—Franks John (La)   1989 3 M 0 0
112 Tr.—Creighton Brett $15,000   1988 0 M 0 0
Lifetime 3 0 0 0

18Apr89-10P   6f :22¹ :47 1:13⁴ft   2⁶ 118   1¹½ 1½ 87½ 91⁷½ Foster D E⁸ ⓕM13000 53-23 Cntrvill̄L dy,DMri,Z,‡SunOksShdy!n 12
28Mar89-50P   6f :22⁴ :47 1:13²sy   17 116   7⁵ 86³10¹⁴10¹⁷½ Foster D E¹¹ ⓕM13000 55-24 Irish Draft, Zeugram'sGirl,Tishaka 11
28Mar89—Wide.
16Mar89-70P   6f :22 :46¹ 1:13¹ft   19 111⁷ 86½ 7⁴¹10¹311114½ Davis K⁷ ⓕM25000 59-29 Chunter, Court tne Boys, Kisham 12
May 9 LaD 4f ft :50² B   Apr 13 0P 5f ft 1:04⁴ Hg   Mar 25 0P 3f ft :36³ H

At 5–1 I preferred Maybeon Tuesday. This state-bred four-year-old had raced against the post-position bias at Louisiana Downs from the seven-hole on April 28 before expiring. Inside now, she might get clear and trot around.

But Maybeon Tuesday could not outrun Sharon Searcher early. The winner was a three-year-old exiting an open maiden-claiming sprint at Oaklawn Park, a more reliable play on conventional handicapping. Handicappers at Louisiana Downs who had experienced the post-position bias for two weeks might have supported both horses here. Those that did profitted nicely.

Following the fifth, I determined to play any underbet speed types out of 1–2 posts in sprints and any horse exiting the one-hole in routes.

The second route was the seventh. It was another maiden-claiming affair for three- and four-year-old fillies. The filly in the one-hole looked like this:

7th La. Downs

1 ₁/₁₆ MILES. (1.42⅖) MAIDEN. CLAIMING. Purse $5,500 (includes $700 OTB supplement). Fillies. 3 and 4-year-olds. Weight, 3-year-olds, 113 lbs.; 4-year-olds, 124 lbs. Claiming price $15,000; if for $12,500 allowed 4 lbs.

Big Weep Out
POYADOU B E
Own.—Udouj Herman Mrs

Dk. b. or br. f. 3, by Diabolo—Tiny Tears, by Ingrained
Br.—Mitchell Robert S (Ark)   1989 2 M 0 0 $480
113 Tr.—Fite Walter $15,000   1988 0 M 0 0
Lifetime 2 0 0 0 $480

3May89-2LaD 6½f :22⁴ :46² 1:19¹ft   11 114   98¾ 99½10¹³ 81³¾ PoyadouBE⁷ ⓕM15000 65-21 PrivateSquw,Penill,Timo'sDynstic 12
14Apr89-10P   6f :22 :46⁴ 1:13 sy   15 112   10¹³ 9¹⁵ 68½ 47   TrosclairAJ⁵ ⑤M15000 68-24 GnRom,PossumJuncton,ButflBtty 12

Here is the result chart.

SEVENTH RACE
La. Downs
MAY 17, 1989

1 1/16 MILES. (1.42⅘) MAIDEN. CLAIMING. Purse $5,500 (includes $700 OTB supplement). Fillies. 3 and 4-year-olds. Weight, 3-year-olds, 113 lbs.; 4-year-olds, 124 lbs. Claiming price $15,000; if for $12,500 allowed 4 lbs.

Value of race $5,500; value to winner $3,300; second $1,100; third $605; fourth $330; fifth $165. Mutuel pool $48,373. Exacta pool $55,147.

Last Raced	Horse	Eqt.A.Wt	PP	St	¼	½	¾	Str	Fin	Jockey	Cl'g Pr	Odds $1
3May89 ^{2}LaD^{8}	Big Weep Out	b 3 114	1	2	$1^{1\frac{1}{2}}$	$1^{1\frac{1}{2}}$	1^{2}	$1^{2\frac{1}{2}}$	1^{2}	Poyadou B E	15000	10.90
19Apr89 ^{10}RP^{2}	Obsessed With Gold	3 114	6	7	$7^{1\frac{1}{2}}$	6^{2}	$3^{1\frac{1}{2}}$	2^{hd}	2^{2}	Whited D E	15000	2.70
3May89 ^{7}LaD^{3}	Kathy's First	b 4 115	8	8	9^{3}	7^{4}	4^{hd}	4^{4}	3^{1}	Scotch P W^{5}	12500	*2.70
25Mar89 ^{7}FG^{9}	A Dublin Rising	b 3 113	2	10	3^{hd}	2^{1}	$2^{1\frac{1}{2}}$	$3^{1\frac{1}{2}}$	4^{8}	Borel C H	15000	13.20
3May89 ^{2}LaD^{5}	Camellia Ann	b 3 112	11	5	5^{1}	5^{hd}	5^{1}	$5^{1\frac{1}{2}}$	5^{1}	Romero S P	12500	9.70
13Apr89 ^{1}OP^{3}	My Pretty Papillon	3 113	7	6	$8^{1\frac{1}{2}}$	8^{3}	6^{4}	6^{4}	6^{3}	Rini W	15000	6.10
3May89 ^{7}LaD^{7}	Ten Spot Lady	b 4 120	3	12	12	12	9^{3}	$7^{1\frac{1}{2}}$	$7^{3\frac{1}{2}}$	Frazier R L	12500	16.70
3May89 ^{2}LaD^{4}	Shower Scene	4 120	12	3	$2^{2\frac{1}{2}}$	$3^{2\frac{1}{2}}$	$7^{1\frac{1}{2}}$	8^{5}	8^{4}	Ardoin R	12500	11.00
3May89 ^{2}LaD^{12}	Reva Shane	b 3 110	5	9	$10^{1\frac{1}{2}}$	9^{4}	10^{5}	$9^{\frac{1}{2}}$	$9^{1\frac{1}{2}}$	Sonnier T J	12000	42.80
4Apr89 ^{5}OP	Gee Admiral Girl	4 120	10	11	11^{4}	10^{1}	11	11	10^{2}	Leblanc K P	12500	75.70
12Apr89 ^{3}OP^{3}	Banshee Magic	b 3 114	4	1	4^{hd}	4^{hd}	$8^{2\frac{1}{2}}$	10^{hd}	11	Roberts T D	15000	10.20
20Apr89 ^{1}OP^{10}	Diabolo's Luv	3 112	9	4	$6^{2\frac{1}{2}}$	11^{hd}	—	—	—	Court J K	12500	46.20

Diabolo's Luv, Distanced.

***—Actual Betting Favorite.**

OFF AT 3:48. Start good. Won driving. Time, :24, :49, 1:15⅕, 1:43, 1:50⅘ Track muddy.

$2 Mutuel Prices:				
	1-BIG WEEP OUT	23.80	10.20	6.00
	6-OBSESSED WITH GOLD		4.80	3.40
	8-KATHY'S FIRST			2.80
	$5 EXACTA (1-6) PAID $335.00.			

Dk. b. or br. f, by Diabolo—Tiny Tears, by Ingrained. Trainer Fite Walter. Bred by Mitchell Robert S (Ark).

BIG WEEP OUT sprinted clear to set the pace and maintained a clear lead under steady urging. OBSESSED WITH GOLD made a run inside after a half, steadied briefly and was angled out around A DUBLIN RISING then finished willingly for the place. KATHY'S FIRST advanced inside after a half, came three wide into the stretch but lacked a late bid. A DUBLIN RISING, close up inside, weakened. CAMELLIA ANN, wide into the first turn, tired. MY PRETTY PAPILLON made a good gain while wide after a half but could not sustain the bid. SHOWER SCENE, closest to the early pace, faded. BANSHEE MAGIC tired. DIABOLO'S LUV, four wide on the first turn, stopped and was outdistanced.

Owners— 1, Udouj Herman Mrs; 2, King Happy; 3, Timphony V et al; 4, Morreale Jake V; 5, Cutshaw Randy lessee; 6, Steger O L Jr; 7, Fussell Robert; 8, Zent June-Shapiro H; 9, Bankston Patti T; 10, Peek Judy; 11, Strube J L; 12, McGinness Leland.

Trainers— 1, Fite Walter; 2, Wallerstedt Mark; 3, Karlin W C; 4, Morreale Jake V; 5, Oxley John; 6, Holthus Paul E; 7, Luce Michael J; 8, Ciavaglia Gilbert; 9, Gilbert Riley M III; 10, Peek Martin; 11, Lothinger Roy; 12, Jackson R D.

Corrected weight: Kathy's First 115 pounds. **Overweight:** Big Weep Out 1 pound; Obsessed With Gold 1; Camellia Ann 3; Reva Shane 1; Banshee Magic 1; Diabolo's Luv 3.

Scratched—Chancy Weather (3May89 ^{2}LaD^{9}); Blazing Spruce (3May89 ^{7}LaD^{4}); Sure Judgement (30Apr89 ^{10}EvD^{2}); Crawford's Delite (4May89 ^{4}LaD^{2}).

A long shot that has never flashed speed at any call runs away from the field and wins. The explanation is often a strong bias. The bias produces a victory otherwise implausible. Alert racegoers can size up similar opportunities and capitalize.

Later that Wednesday at Louisiana Downs the inside-post bias prevailed easily in the eighth and tenth, a pair of sprints. Examine the charts. They contain a vital sign that a powerful bias exists.

EIGHTH RACE
La. Downs
MAY 17, 1989

6 FURLONGS. (1.08⅘) CLAIMING. Purse $5,300 (includes $500 OTB supplement). Fillies and mares. 4-year-olds and upward. Weight, 122 lbs. Non-winners of two races since March 17 allowed 4 lbs.; a race since then, 6 lbs. Claiming price $6,250; if for $6,000 allowed 3 lbs. (Races where entered for $5,000 or less not considered.)

Value of race $5,300; value to winner $3,180; second $1,060; third $583; fourth $318; fifth $159. Mutuel pool $52,999. Exacta pool, $63,320.

Last Raced	Horse	Eqt.	A.	Wt	PP	St	¼	½	Str	Fin	Jockey	Cl'g Pr	Odds $1
7May89 ^{1}LaD^{8}	Earl's Honey	b	4	116	1	6	1^{2}	$1^{2\frac{1}{2}}$	1^{2}	1^{4}	Frazier R L	6250	4.10
3May89 ^{5}JnD^{4}	Victory Design	b	5	110	12	1	$5^{\frac{1}{2}}$	2^{2}	2^{4}	2^{6}	Howard D L	6000	28.20
10May89^{10}LaD^{2}	Loco Native	b	4	114	8	5	3^{hd}	3^{1}	3^{hd}	3^{nk}	Poyadou B E	6000	9.30
4May89 ^{7}LaD^{8}	First Accountant	b	4	113	4	3	4^{1}	5^{1}	$4^{1\frac{1}{2}}$	$4^{1\frac{1}{2}}$	Sonnier T J	6000	13.40
3May89^{10}LaD^{8}	Pacific Stop		5	110	10	10	$11^{\frac{1}{2}}$	10^{2}	$7^{1\frac{1}{2}}$	5^{hd}	Gonzalez C V	6000	26.40
7May89 ^{1}LaD^{7}	Ididarod		4	116	3	12	7^{1}	7^{4}	5^{2}	6^{1}	Romero S P	6250	*3.20
14Apr89^{11}OP^{3}	Bennys Lightning	b	4	108	5	9	$10^{\frac{1}{2}}$	8^{1}	6^{2}	7^{1}	Scotch P W^{5}	6000	3.20
6May89^{11}LaD^{11}	Miss A Moment	b	5	113	7	11	12	$11^{\frac{1}{2}}$	9^{4}	8^{hd}	Griffin E D	6000	88.40
3May89^{10}LaD^{2}	Nalees Chomp	b	4	113	11	8	8^{1}	9^{hd}	8^{hd}	9^{8}	Walker B J Jr	6250	6.60
3May89^{10}LaD^{9}	Atolloyah		5	113	2	4	9^{1}	12	12	10^{nk}	Court J K	6000	26.10
3May89^{10}LaD^{4}	Exclusive Luck		4	113	6	7	$2^{1\frac{1}{2}}$	4^{hd}	$10^{1\frac{1}{2}}$	11^{nk}	Ceballos O F	6000	8.40
6May89^{11}LaD^{12}	Shecky Weekend	b	5	113	9	2	6^{3}	6^{hd}	$11^{\frac{1}{2}}$	12	Ardoin R	6000	51.20

***—Actual Betting Favorite.**

OFF AT 4:14. Start good. Won driving. Time, :22⅖, :46⅗, :59⅗, 1:13⅕ Track muddy.

$2 Mutuel Prices:

1–EARL'S HONEY	10.20	7.60	5.20
12–VICTORY DESIGN		23.40	9.60
8–LOCO NATIVE			6.20

$5 EXACTA (1–12) PAID $545.50.

Dk. b. or br. f, by Khatango—Pot of Honey, by Crozier. Trainer Holthus Robert E. Bred by Bramble R & Bucci R (Fla).

EARL'S HONEY sprinted clear soon after the start, set the pace off the inside and increased her lead under steady urging. VICTORY DESIGN made a run five wide into the turn to reach closest to the winner on the turn but lacked a late bid. LOCO NATIVE, a forward factor, tired. FIRST ACCOUNTANT steadied in the initial quarter when in tight and again on the turn when lacking room, got through inside approaching the stretch but could not menace. PACIFIC STOP improved her position in the middle of the strip IDIDAROD was not a threat. BENNYS LIGHTNING was not a factor. ATOLLOYAH steadied in the initial furlong when in tight then was not a factor. EXCLUSIVE LUCK tired. SHECKY WEEKEND was wide.

Owners— 1, Hickerson Earl; 2, Valene Farms; 3, Cox Robert J; 4, Halter Racing Stable; 5, Lucas Lane; 6, Young Allen Jr; 7, Tart Joe; 8, King A R & A R Jr; 9, April Fools Racing Partnership #1; 10, Watkins Gracie; 11, Lafevers John; 12, Wahman Darlene.

Trainers— 1, Holthus Robert E; 2, Guenther Freddy; 3, Waldie Jack; 4, Johnson Thomas M; 5, Wiggins Hal R; 6, Young Allen Jr; 7, Tart Joe; 8, Wallack Patrick; 9, Hebert Eldridge; 10, Rose Paul; 11, Ellison Robert; 12, Wahman Jeff.

Overweight: Loco Native 1 pound.

Scratched—Little Ira Annie (10May89^{10}LaD^{3}); Personal Doll (10May89^{10}LaD^{5}).

$2 Super Six (5–4–2–2–1–1). Consolation Super Six Paid $659.20. 4 Wins, 9 Tickets. Super Six Pool $26,368 Carryover Pool $13,843.20.

TENTH RACE
La. Downs
MAY 17, 1989

6 FURLONGS. (1.08⅘) CLAIMING. Purse $5,000. 4-year-olds and upward, which have not won two races in 1989. Weight, 122 lbs. Non-winners since March 17 allowed 3 lbs.; since February 17, 6 lbs.; since January 17, 9 lbs. Claiming price $5,000.

Value of race $5,000; value to winner $3,000; second $1,000; third $550; fourth $300; fifth $150. Mutuel pool $42,189. Trifecta pool $58,402.

Last Raced	Horse	Eqt.	A.	Wt	PP	St	¼	½	Str	Fin	Jockey	Cl'g Pr	Odds $1
29Apr89^{11}LaD^{4}	Hubas Avenger		4	113	1	2	1^{2}	$1^{1\frac{1}{2}}$	1^{3}	1^{5}	Trosclair A J	5000	1.90
5May89 ^{8}LaD^{7}	Pine Manor		8	122	4	4	$5^{1\frac{1}{2}}$	$3^{\frac{1}{2}}$	$2^{\frac{1}{2}}$	$2^{\frac{1}{2}}$	Borel C H	5000	3.60
10Dec88 ^{4}DeD^{1}	Half Ruby	b	5	113	5	3	3^{hd}	2^{4}	$3^{2\frac{1}{2}}$	$3^{1\frac{1}{2}}$	Guillory D	5000	15.70
6May89 ^{4}LaD^{4}	Noisy Axe	b	4	113	8	6	$6^{1\frac{1}{2}}$	$5^{1\frac{1}{2}}$	4^{4}	$4^{5\frac{1}{2}}$	Romero S P	5000	8.60
29Apr89^{11}LaD^{10}	Spectabuleaux	b	4	113	6	7	8	7^{1}	5^{hd}	5^{1}	Snyder L	5000	6.50
15Jan89^{11}TuP^{4}	Contrabass		4	113	3	5	$2^{\frac{1}{2}}$	4^{hd}	$6^{1\frac{1}{2}}$	6^{5}	Simington D E	5000	13.00
6May89 ^{4}LaD^{7}	Delta Sting	b	5	107	2	8	7^{hd}	8	$7^{1\frac{1}{2}}$	7^{2}	Scotch P W^{5}	5000	11.00
19Apr89 ^{6}RP^{11}	Fast Focus	b	4	113	7	1	4^{1}	$6^{\frac{1}{2}}$	8	8	Howard D L	5000	3.80

OFF AT 5:04. Start good. Won driving. Time, :22⅖, :46⅖, :59⅗, 1:13⅗ Track muddy.

$2 Mutuel Prices:

1–HUBAS AVENGER	5.80	4.20	3.00
5–PINE MANOR		4.40	4.00
6–HALF RUBY			6.00

$3 TRIFECTA (1–5–6) PAID $343.80.

B. g, by **Staunch Avenger—La Belle Vitesse, by Clev Er Tell. Trainer Herndon Hoot W. Bred by Hukill C & Bass M H (Tex).**
HUBAS AVENGER sprinted clear to set the pace and was not menaced while under steady urging. PINE MANOR moved between rivals on the turn but lacked a solid late bid. HALF RUBY made a run at the winner approaching the stretch but weakened in the drive. NOISY AXE was not a serious threat. SPECTABULEAUX failed to menace. CONTRABASS tired. FAST FOCUS was through early.
Owners— 1, Herndon H W; 2, J.E.L. Farm; 3, Kelso H F Jr; 4, Henson F Juanita; 5, Thomas Sue; 6, Stockseth W & Norma Lee; 7, Ellison J R; 8, Stoddard R W Jr.
Trainers— 1, Herndon Hoot W; 2, Edwards Larry D; 3, Eddings Larry; 4, Hardin Jerry K; 5, Switzer Daniel G; 6, Culver Edward L; 7, Ellison Robert; 8, Wiggins Hal R.
Overweight: Delta Sting 2 pounds.
~~Scratched~~—P. Tonker (4May89 2LaD6); Tetou (1Apr89 12FG3); Kings Ex (23Apr89 2RP3); Social Diamond (4May89 2LaD10).

The large margin of victory is part and parcel of a positive inside speed bias. The horses just draw away relentlessly.

Later that week at Louisiana Downs, as the muddy track slowly dried, the bias prevailed less decisively. Yet several sprinters exiting the No. 1 and No. 2 posts won literally by half a furlong.

In sum, here are a few guideposts to a positive inside speed bias.

- Post-positions 1 and 2 have won a significantly disproportionate share of the races.
- Horses that otherwise do not figure to win will romp home on the lead from the inside posts.
- In routes, either the No. 1 post dominates, or horses that speed immediately to the rail do.
- In routes, the horses resemble a string of pearls while racing down the backside. Few horses change position between calls. The lead horses continue to widen the gap. A horse in the front flight consistently wins.

A cautionary note regards frontrunners in sprints that win from the inside posts but figure to impress nonetheless. This is a coincidence, not a bias. Too many casual handicappers observe the first two races have been won by frontrunners, or by horses exiting the rail slot. They conclude the track surface is biased in favor of early speed on the inside.

Positive biases help contenders dominate and move noncontenders up.

In situations where biases persevere, any horse that has run strongly against an inside speed bias when exiting outside posts figures that much more if situated inside next out. And any horse helped by an inside speed bias but defeated regardless hardly figures when shifted to the outside next start.

The inside speed bias has an opposite number, a negative rail bias. This tires frontrunners on the inside. The advantage shifts to speed on the outside, at least in front-speed duels.

During the period the rail was propelling the speed at Louisiana Downs, it was strangling the speed at Hollywood Park. Examine the post-position tabulations below:

HOLLYWOOD PARK
(April 26 to May 17, Inclusive)

	(Main Track)							(Turf Track)					
	....SPRINTS.....			.....ROUTES......				....SPRINTS.....			.....ROUTES......		
	(Under One Mile)			(One Mile & Over)				(Under One Mile)			(One Mile & Over)		
P.P.	STS	WINS	PCT.	STS	WINS	PCT.	P.P.	STS	WINS	PCT.	STS	WINS	PCT.
1	74	4	.05	47	4	.09	1	0	0	.00	23	2	.09
2	74	4	.05	47	5	.11	2	0	0	.00	23	3	.13
3	74	4	.05	47	7	.15	3	0	0	.00	23	2	.09
4	74	9	.12	47	3	.06	4	0	0	.00	23	4	.17
5	74	10	.14	47	4	.09	5	0	0	.00	23	2	.09
6	73	9	.12	45	5	.11	6	0	0	.00	23	4	.17
7	66	10	.15	43	7	.16	7	0	0	.00	20	1	.05
8	60	2	.03	30	7	.23	8	0	0	.00	17	3	.18
9	46	7	.15	20	0	.00	9	0	0	.00	10	1	.10
10	38	5	.13	13	4	.31	10	0	0	.00	5	0	.00
11	32	7	.22	10	0	.00	11	0	0	.00	3	1	.33
12 & UP	19	3	.16	5	1	.20	12 & UP	0	0	.00	2	0	.00

Inside speed in sprints at Hollywood Park confronted a post-position bias that should predictably stop it.

Negative rail biases cannot be exploited as directly as positive rail biases, though outside speed at Hollywood obviously would appeal to handicappers. The time to exploit negative rail biases is later. Any frontrunner that runs impressively against a negative rail bias is strongly advantaged if wheeled back when the bias has disappeared. If the bias persists but one of its front-running victims returns in a favorable post position following a strong effort, the odds might be delectable. Whenever they are, make the play.

THE TWO-HORSE RACE

In the middle seventies I routinely ridiculed a handicapping associate who could not refrain from alluding to much of the competition as "two-horse races."

"This is a two-horse race," he would allege, even when the field was far more contentious than that. He would then name the two contenders forcefully, implying that any dissension reflected only a confused mentality. The assertions represented the insecurity of a journeyman handicapping talent more than the actual depth of the races' contention. Not many races could be reduced by fundamental handicapping to two contenders.

But nowadays many races can.

Handicappers are trapped in the era of the small field. In stakes and featured allowances, the five- or six-horse field has become commonplace. Two of the horses stand apart. The two are clearly superior to the others. Even journeymen handicappers can arrive at the guts of the competition quickly. So the odds offered on each horse will be low.

The tricky question is, which horse should be bet to win, if either?

Below is a featured allowance route on the grass run at Hollywood Park on May 24, 1989. Read the conditions of eligibility. Examine the past performances briefly. Identify the two-horse race. Which horse should win? How should handicappers bet the race?

8th Hollywood

1 ⅛ MILES. (Turf). (1.38⅘) ALLOWANCE (Stretch Start). Purse $45,000. 4-year-olds and upward. Non-winners of $13,500 other than closed or claiming at a mile or over since December 1. Weight, 121 lbs. Non-winners of two such races of $19,500 since September 15, allowed 3 lbs.; $19,000 twice at a mile or over since July 27, 5 lbs.; such a race of $22,000 since September 15, 7 lbs. (Claiming races not considered.)

Gallant Sailor

B. g. 6, by Gallant Best—Sailing Joy, by Sailing Along
Br.—Jones K & Sheryl (Wash)
Tr.—Jones Kenneth G
Lifetime 56 5 8 5 $212,725

NAKATANI C S — 1095
Own.—Jones K G

1989	4	0	0	0	$3,500
1988	17	2	3	1	$144,925
Turf	18	1	0	2	$54,750

Pasakos

B. c. 4, by Nureyev—Cendres Bleues, by Charlottesville
Br.—Cahan M & Meltzer W (Ky)
Tr.—Whittingham Charles
Lifetime 9 2 3 1 $182,237

MCCARRON C J — 114
Own.—Duchossois R L

1988	6	0	2	1	$106,874
1987	3	2	1	0	$75,363
Turf	9	2	3	1	$182,237

5Jun88♦3Chantilly(Fra) a1½ 2:332yl 6¼ 128 Ⓣ 13 Head F Px Jky Clb(Gr1) HoursAfter,GhostBusters,Emrrson 16
15May88♦3Longchamp(Fra) a1 5/16 2:082gd 5¾ 128 Ⓣ 2no Head F Px Lupn(Gr1) ExactlySharp,Pasakos,SoftMachine 9
24Apr88♦6Longchamp(Fra) a1⅛ 1:564gd 2 128 Ⓣ 31¾ Head F Px D Gche(Gr3) InExtremis,DrapeauTricolore,Pskos 7
11Oct87♦3Longchamp(Fra) a1 1:451sf 3¼ 123 Ⓣ 22 Head F Grd Crtrm(Gr1) FijarTango, Pasakos, MostPrecious 6
13Sep87♦2Longchamp(Fra) a1 1:411gd *4-5 121 Ⓣ 1hd Head F PxLaRchtt(Gr3) Pasakos, BabaCool, Preston 10
11Aug87♦2Deauville(Fra) a6½f 1:202yl *4-5 123 Ⓣ 12 HeadF Px d Tncarville(Mdn) Pasakos, ColdBid, MaitreA Bord 6
●May 18 Hol Ⓣ 6f fm 1:141 H (d) May 13 Hol 1 ft 1:39 H May 8 Hol 7f ft 1:273 H May 3 Hol 6f ft 1:131 H

Loyal Double
B. h. 6, by Nodouble—Saygood, by Royal Ascot
SOLIS A 114
Br.—Lasater D R (Fla) 1989 10 0 1 0 $9,575
Tr.—Sweeney Brian 1988 2 0 0 0
Own.—Hoffman-Kruse-Sweeney
Lifetime 30 4 2 1 $94,933 Turf 26 4 1 1 $87,033
10May89-8Hol 1 Ⓣ:4621:1011:343fm 14 114 86¼ 85¾ 54 43 Solis A7 Aw45000 88-09 Crimson Slew, Neshad, PurdueKing 9
10May89—Blocked early
24Apr89-8SA 1¼Ⓣ:4621:3542:013fm 85 113 75½ 94¼ 75 73¼ Solis A1 ⓇSn Jcnt H 75-19 MsterTrety,SilentPrinceII,ThMdic 10
24Apr89—Crowded 1/4, wide into stretch
8Apr89-8SA 1¼Ⓣ:4741:3622:013fm 110 113 21½ 2½ 21 63¾ Solis A9 ⓇSta Grts H 75-21 Delegant,Academic,PleasantVriety 11
2Apr89-8GG 1 1/16Ⓣ:4811:12 1:431fm 22 112 54 64½ 65¼ 65¼ Patton D B4 HcpO 81-19 Ev'sError,ChplOfDrms,GrnJudgmnt 8
19Mar89-8GG 1¼:482 1:373 2:02 gd 3¼ 111 2hd 1hd 21½ 22½ Patton D B4 HcpO 78-19 ChessSet,LoylDouble,PirdAndPintd 4
5Mar89-5SA 1⅛Ⓣ:4621:11 1:474fm 61 116 1013107¾ 78¾ 55½ Pedroza M A9 80000 82-12 PlsntVrity,PointD'Artos,ClshOfIds 10
15Feb89-7SA 1 1/16:461 1:101 1:411ft 114 114 812 813 814 816¾ Solis A4 Aw60000 78-17 GoodTste,StylishWinner,NoCnLose 8
15Feb89—Checked start
28Jan89-10TuP 1⅛Ⓣ:4731:1131:483fm 73 112 42½ 43¼ 65½ 79¾ Ortiz M F Jr9 Tu P H 87-03 PatchyGroundfog,Reincarnte,Kdil 11
22Jan89-8SA 1¼Ⓣ:47 1:36 2:02 fm 167 110 21½ 56 510 712½ CorralJR8 Sn Mrcs H 64-23 Trokhos,Vallotton,Roberto'sDancer 8
22Jan89—Grade III; Bumped start
15Jan89-7SA 1⅛Ⓣ:4721:1211:503gd 45 116 75 86¼ 810 712½ DominguezRE8 125000 61-24 Patchy Groundfog,Havildar,Wolsey 8
May 22 SA 3f ft :352 H May 17 SA 3f ft :374 H May 8 SA 3f ft :352 H May 3 SA 5f ft 1:023 H

Fair Judgment
B. h. 5, by Alleged—Mystical Mood, by Roberto
STEVENS G L 114
Br.—Farish-Hudson-Hudson Jr (Ky) 1988 7 1 2 0 $90,609
Tr.—Mettee Richard C 1987 4 2 0 0 $68,639
Own.—Tsurumaki T
Lifetime 11 3 2 0 $159,248 Turf 11 3 2 0 $159,248
5Nov88♦5StCloud(Fra) a1 1:424yl 5 128 Ⓣ 42¾ Reid J Prix Perth(Gr3) FrenchStress,Somorumujo,Mlspin 14
23Oct88♦4Longchamp(Fra) a7f 1:24 yl *4-5 138 Ⓣ 55½ Reid J Px d lForet(Gr1) Salse, Gabina, Big Shuffle 13
30Sep88♦3Goodwood(Eng) 7f 1:293gd *9-5 124 Ⓣ 11½ Reid J Supreme(Gr3) FairJudgement, Alquoz, Luzum 8
4Sep88♦4PhoenixPk(Ire) 1¼ 2:082gd 16 132 Ⓣ 65½ Reid J Phnx Champ (Gr1) IndinSkimmer,ShdyHights,Triptych 9
14Jun88♦1Ascot(Eng) 1 1:47 fm 20 131 Ⓣ 43¼ Reid J QueenAnne(Gr2) Waajib, Soviet Star, Then Again 5
14May88♦5Curragh(Ire) 1¼ 2:083gd 2¼ 127 Ⓣ 2½ Reid J TttrsllsRgrsCp(Gr2) ShdyHeights,FirJudgmnt,HzyBird 10
23Apr88♦2Curragh(Ire) 1¼ 2:161gd *1-2 135 Ⓣ 2no Reid J Mooresbridge HzyBird,FirJudgement,HwiinPece 13
6Sep87♦4PhoenixPk(Ire) 1¼ 2:063yl 12 123 Ⓣ 926 AssnC Phnx Chmpn(Gr1) Triptych, Entitled, Cockney Lass 11
29Jly87♦4Goodwood(Eng) 1 1:384gd 9 122 Ⓣ 42¾ AsmssnC Sussex (Gr1) Soviet Star, Star Cutter, Hadeer 7
4Jly87♦4PhoenixPk(Ire) 1 : gd *2 119 Ⓣ 1¾ AsssnC Pcemakr Int(Gr2) FairJudgment, StatelyDon, Waajib 6
4Jly87—No time taken
May 18 Hol Ⓣ 7f fm 1:292 H (d) May 11 Hol Ⓣ 7f fm 1:25 H (d) May 4 Hol Ⓣ 7f fm 1:283 H (d) Apr 28 Hol 5f ft :593 H

***Romantic Prince**
Ch. h. 5, by Henbit—Supremely Royal, by Crowned Prince
PINCAY L JR 114
Br.—Allen I (Ire) 1989 6 0 1 0 $20,300
Tr.—Shulman Sanford 1988 6 3 1 2 $89,050
Own.—Charles & ClearValleyStables
Lifetime 19 4 3 3 $131,536 Turf 19 4 3 3 $131,536
24Apr89-8SA 1¼Ⓣ:4621:3542:013fm 27 115 43 83¾1011 914½ GurrWA2 ⓇSn Jcnt H 64-19 MsterTrety,SilentPrinceII,ThMdic 10
24Apr89—Crowded 3/8 turn
6Apr89-8SA 1 Ⓣ:46 1:1011:344fm 8¼ 115 46½ 42 52¼ 45¾ Stevens G L3 Aw60000 91-03 AstrontPrnc,RNrmnd,HppyslrkTms 7
24Mar89-8SA 1 Ⓣ:4721:1041:353fm 5 115 2½ 21 21½ 43 Stevens G L2 Aw60000 90-12 PoliticalAmbition,TheMedic,Neshd 6
17Mar89-8SA a6½f Ⓣ:212 :4331:143fm 6 114 54½ 76 75¼ 76¾ PdrzMA 6 Sra Mdre H 79-14 Oraibi, Lordalik, Down Again 9
17Mar89—Grade III; Wide into stretch
24Feb89-8SA a6½f Ⓣ:213 :4431:15 fm 7¾ 114 42 43 21 2¾ Pedroza MA2 Aw55000 83-16 CblloDOro,RomntcPrnc,HppyInSpc 7
29Jan89-7SA 1 Ⓣ:4521:0931:351fm 8¾ 115 64 52½ 64¼ 79¼ Hawley S8 Aw60000 86-05 Mzilier,DncCrdFilld,NorthrnProvidr 8
29Jan89—Veered in, stumbled start
1Jly88-9Hol 1⅛Ⓣ:4731:1111:471fm *8-5 116 42½ 31½ 1hd 11¾ Stevens G L6 Aw46000 92-05 RomnticPrince,Rfel'sDncr,KingHill 6
18Jun88-8Hol 1¼Ⓣ:4731:3622:004fm *2¼ 114 11 1½ 11 31 Stevens G L4 Aw46000 90-09 Uptothhilt,ArctcBlstII,RomntcPrnc 6
5Jun88-9Hol 1⅛Ⓣ:4721:1011:471fm 2¼ 116 1½ 2hd 1hd 32 Stevens G L6 Aw46000 90-07 RussinRovr,PlsntVrity,RomntcPrnc 6
5Jun88—Jumped mirror reflection 1st time around
9Apr88-2SA 1⅛Ⓣ:4731:1131:483fm *2¼ 114 21 1hd 11½ 12½ Stevens G L3 Aw42000 84-08 RomnticPrince,BrekfstTbl,StrtPrty 9
May 19 Hol Ⓣ 5f fm 1:014 H (d) Apr 20 SA Ⓣ 4f fm :50 H (d)

Neshad
. h. 5, by Sharpen Up—Nasseem, by Zeddaan
VALENZUELA P A 114
Br.—H H Aga Khan (Ky) 1989 6 0 1 1 $23,500
Tr.—Goodin Mike 1988 14 1 3 3 $120,835
Own.—Currie D & Trish
Lifetime 29 5 4 4 $198,186 Turf 28 5 4 4 $198,186
10May89-8Hol 1 Ⓣ:4621:1011:343fm 3¼ 116 64¾ 63¼ 43 21 ValenzuelPA5 Aw45000 90-09 Crimson Slew, Neshad, PurdueKing 9
10May89—Crowded stretch

6Apr89-8SA 1 Ⓣ:46 1:1011:344fm 5¼ 115 710 63¾ 63¾ 57 McCarronCJ2 Aw60000 90-03 AstrontPrnc,RNrmnd,HppyslrkTms 7
6Apr89—Steadied start
24Mar89-8SA 1 Ⓣ:4721:1041:353fm 9¼ 116 62¾ 62¾ 64½ 31½ ValenzuelPA6 Aw60000 91-12 PoliticalAmbition,TheMedic,Neshd 6
24Mar89—Bumped 3/16
25Feb89-8SA 1 Ⓣ:4711:1041:361fm 23 112 54½ 51¾ 31½ 54¼ VlnzulFH5 Arcadia H 86-10 BlloHorzont,Srhoob,PtchyGrondfg 7
25Feb89—Grade II; Wide 3/8 turn
29Jan89-7SA 1 Ⓣ:4521:0931:351fm 9¾ 115 87 83¼ 74¼ 56¼ McCarronCJ5 Aw60000 89-05 Mzilier,DncCrdFilld,NorthrnProvidr 8
29Jan89—Crowded 5/16, took up sharply 3/16
1Jan89-7SA 6½f :212 :44 1:141ft 15 115 75 55½ 69 712¼ Baze R A 6 Aw55000 87-10 Sunny Blossom, Jamoke, Sabona 8
12Nov88-7Hol 1 1/16 Ⓣ:4621:1021:411fm*8-5 115 44 53 32 33¼ McCarronCJ5 Aw40000 84-16 Five Daddy Five, Lordalik, Neshad 8
23Oct88-8SA 1 Ⓣ:4641:1031:342fm 6¼ 116 74¾ 42¼ 33 44¾ VlnzulPA2 Col Kstr H 97 — MohmedAbdu,Mzilir,DputyGovrnor 7
7Oct88-8SA 1 Ⓣ:46 1:0941:344fm 4 116 62¾ 31½ 43 66 Black C A1 Aw60000 94 — PatchyGroundfog,Mazilier,Forlitno 9
7Oct88—Crowded backstretch
14Sep88-8Dmr 1 1/16 Ⓣ:4821:1141:42 fm 2¾ 118 77½ 66½ 54 2½ McCarronCJ2 Aw45000 89-12 Havildar, Neshad, Jungle Dawn 8
14Sep88—Rank early
May 5 SA 5f ft 1:003 H   May 1 SA 6f ft 1:17 H   Apr 26 SA 5f ft 1:013 H   ●Apr 21 SA Ⓣ 5f fm 1:001 H (d)

The imports Pasakos and Fair Judgment tower over an otherwise lackluster six-horse classified field. Anyone unable to sort the group of six in this way needs a refresher course on the class factor.

But which horse should win?

Full-dress handicapping lands on Pasakos, a four-year-old that twice finished second in important Group 1 stakes in France, where the best racing of Europe proceeds. Yet the two imports are reasonably close on past class, both have been away for more than six months, and each will be exiting competent turf stables while showing regular sharp workouts.

Thus the pair contribute to a useful guideline for betting two-horse races intelligently.

Take the higher-priced horse.

Let the odds dictate the bet.

Usually, one horse will be an underlay, the other a low-priced overlay. If both possibilities are underlays, pass.

In the example, Pasakos was 4–5 and Fair Judgment 5–2. Handicappers can consider each horse in any two-horse field to have a relatively equal chance, and the rest of the field some chance. By this reasoning, either of the two horses is a fair bet at 2–1, an underlay below 2–1, and an overlay at 5–2 or greater.

If handicappers apply these guidelines, they will limit betting action in two-horse situations to 5–2 shots or greater, and thereby stand a chance of accumulating profits for the season.

A bet on Pasakos at 4–5 is obviously nonsense. A bet on Fair Judgment at 5–2 is acceptable.

If exactas are bet, the overlay should be placed on top of the underlay multiple times, the underlay atop the overlay only as a saver. Do not use the underlay on top. Exacta underlays penalize the bettors just as cruelly as do underlays in the win pool.

In two-horse races, exactas often make sense, as straight bets do not. The exacta must be an overlay. That's the point of betting exactas in the first place: to convert underlays to win to overlays in predictable exactas.

A variation of the two-horse exacta bet is even more enticing. If the public judges the field a two-horse race, but one of the two looks suspicious or vulnerable on fundamental handicapping, the exacta procedure changes.

Throw out the suspicious or vulnerable—and therefore overbet—horse, and play the legitimate contender on top of other attractive overlays. The small field reduces the chances of a juicy score, but where an underlay can be tossed and a few overlays supported on the bottom, the exactas can return profits, and handicappers can employ the tactic. It copes with the oppression of small fields handicappers suffer nowadays.

If Pasakos had been 4–5 but Fair Judgment a fake, handicappers might have discarded Fair Judgment altogether, and keyed Pasakos in exactas on top of Loyal Double and Neshad, with multiple tickets on top of the higher-priced Loyal Double.

To repeat, in two-horse races, bet the overlays only, either to win or in exacta combinations. Handicappers who handled Pasakos and Fair Judgment by these guidelines got a fair return on investment.

EIGHTH RACE
Hollywood
MAY 24, 1989

1 1/16 MILES.(Turf). (1.39⅘) ALLOWANCE (Stretch Start). Purse $45,000. 4-year-olds and upward. Non-winners of $18,500 other than closed or claiming at a mile or over since December 1. Weight, 121 lbs. Non-winners of two such races of $19,500 since September 15, allowed 3 lbs.; $19,000 twice at a mile or over since July 27, 5 lbs.; such a race of $22,000 since September 15, 7 lbs. (Claiming races not considered).

Value of race $45,000; value to winner $24,750; second $9,000; third $6,750; fourth $3,375; fifth $1,125. Mutuel pool $259,642. Exacta pool $241,532.

Last Raced	Horse	Eqt.A.Wt	PP	St	¼	½	¾	Str	Fin	Jockey	Odds $1
5Nov88 ^{5}Fra^4	Fair Judgment	b 5 114	4	5	6	6	6	2^{hd}	1½	Stevens G L	2.70
10Oct88 ^{4}Fra^4	Pasakos	4 115	2	6	5^1	5^2	$5^{1½}$	1½	2^4	McCarron C J	1.40
10May89 ^{8}Hol^4	Loyal Double	6 114	3	1	4^2	2^{hd}	3½	4^{hd}	$3^{1¼}$	Solis A	21.20
24Apr89 ^{8}SA^9	Romantic Prince	5 117	5	2	1^1	1^1	1½	3^1	4½	Pincay L Jr	4.30
10May89 ^{8}Hol^7	Gallant Sailor	6 109	1	4	2^{hd}	3½	2½	5½	5^2	Nakatani C S^5	38.00
10May89 ^{8}Hol^2	Neshad	5 116	6	3	3½	4^1	4^{hd}	6	6	Valenzuela P A	3.00

OFF AT 5:06. Start good. Won driving. Time, :24⅘, :46, 1:11⅘, 1:35⅕, 1:41 Course firm.

$2 Mutuel Prices:			
4-FAIR JUDGMENT	7.40	3.80	2.60
2-PASAKOS		3.40	2.60
3-LOYAL DOUBLE			3.40

$2 EXACTA 4–2 PAID $18.40.

B. h, by Alleged—Mystical Mood, by Roberto. Trainer Mettee Richard C. Bred by Farish–Hudson–Hudson Jr (Ky).
FAIR JUDGMENT, trailed early, closed with a rush to engage for the lead leaving the furlong marker, ba'tled for command the rest of the way with PASAKOS and had the necessary late response to prevail. PASAKOS, outrun early while being patiently handled, moved up to get closer going into the far turn, was boxed in all the way around the far turn while full of run and was steadied nearing the quarter pole, swung down to the inner rail to find a clear path entering the stretch, accelerated to reach the front approaching the furlong marker, battled for command with FAIR JUDGMENT from just inside the furlong marker to the finish and gained the place. LOYAL DOUBLE, close up early, lacked the needed response in the drive. ROMANTIC PRINCE established a leisurely early pace, continued as a pace factor to the furlong marker, then weakened. GALLANT SAILOR, close up to the furlong marker, weakened. NESHAD, close up early and four wide into the far turn, lacked the needed response in the last quarter.

THREE-YEAR-OLD MAIDENS AT A MILE

The one-mile maiden event for three-year-olds profiled here contains a half-dozen lessons for occasional racegoers. The two top-consensus choices were Birthday Roses and Bally Well. Neither figured firmly. But the gelding Modern Classic did, and he was sent to the post at 4–1.

Examine the past performances briefly.

First, during winter and spring especially, three-year-old maidens will regularly be switched from sprints to routes. Recreational handicappers need not be fooled by the changes. Sprinters do stretch out effectively. Yet certain misconceptions should be corrected.

Let's begin with Hoofer and Modern Classic, the pair of sprinters being stretched out to a mile.

Many recreational handicappers prefer horses having running styles like Hoofer's. They note the stretch gain at six furlongs, and expect an even stronger close at the mile. The reasoning is faulty. Closers in sprints should not be expected to finish as strongly in routes. The longer distance frequently softens the punch the horses retain at six furlongs.

Even more: horses like Hoofer cannot catch horses like Modern Classic at a mile, provided the latter types possess enough stamina to get the distance. A simple test solves the riddle reliably. Any three-year-old maiden that runs the turn time of a sprint faster than par, and continues to carry that swift to the wire, can be accepted at a flat mile. The majority will get the distance handily.

1st Golden Gate

 1 MILE. (1.33) MAIDEN. Purse $17,000. 3-year-olds. Weight, 118 lbs.

Hoofer
B. c. 3, by Wavering Monarch—In Review, by Reviewer
Br.—Glencrest Farm (Ky) 1989 1 M 0 1 $2,400
CHAPMAN T M 118 Tr.—Specht Steve 1988 0 M 0 0
Own.—Bell S J Lifetime 1 0 0 1 $2,400
6May89-5GG 6f :211 :434 1:092ft 4¾ 118 68 67 59½ 35½ Chapman T M8 Mdn 86-14 Private Jet,ModernClassic,Hoofer 12
May 16 GG 4f ft :49 H May 3 GG 4f ft :492 Hg ●Apr 25 GG 6f ft 1:114 H Apr 19 GG 6f ft 1:144 Hg

Interbend
B. g. 3, by Interco—Indian Bend, by Triple Bend
Br.—Warwick G M (Cal) 1989 5 M 2 1 $11,475
DOOCY T T 118 Tr.—Vince James J 1988 3 M 0 0 $350
Own.—Warwick G M Lifetime 8 0 2 1 $11,825
4May89-1GG 1 :474 1:121 1:37 ft 3½ 118 43 42 31 32½ Doocy T T 6 Mdn 77-16 CremToThTop,BirthdyRoss,Intrbnd 6
6Apr89-7GG 1 :462 1:12 1:40 ft 11 118 74¾ 42½ 1½ 2nk Steiner J J 3 Mdn 65-26 MjorRole,Interbend,Hugo'sMillion 10
23Mar89-7GG 1 :454 1:104 1:362ft 10 118 41½ 31 43 46¼ Espindola M A 2 Mdn 77-19 OcensEleven,RglNrv,BrookstownLd 9
11Mar89-7GG 6f :214 :451 1:114m 11 118 66¾ 57 47 410½ Espindola M A 4 Mdn 69-25 PitinoBll,WdesMn,CremToTheTop 11
11Mar89—Bumped start
20Feb89-5GG 1 :462 1:113 1:372ft 69 118 45 31½ 24 27 Espindola M A 6 Mdn 71-21 Mock Modesty, Interbend, Janjoni 9
20Feb89—Steadied start
12Nov88-6BM 1 1/16 :462 1:112 1:442ft 59 118 913 913 813 811 Maple S1 Mdn 59-18 SilentAlrm,MeNBobbyLe,OrnryGust 9
12Nov88—Bumped start
29Oct88-3BM 1 :454 1:103 1:363ft 24 118 511 512 616 520½ Maple S6 Mdn 64-17 BaseCamp,ArcOfTawa,OrneryGuest 8
29Oct88—Broke slowly
22Oct88-4BM 6f :224 :454 1:102ft 45 118 1217 1215 1115 1112¼ Warren R J Jr12 [S]Mdn 75-16 Bu'sAllinc,Notlotttlk,BrghtstGlxy 12
22Oct88—Broke slowly
May 17 GG 4f ft :49 H Apr 29 GG 5f ft 1:034 H Apr 22 GG 4f ft :484 H Apr 15 GG 4f ft :491 H

Modern Classic
B. g. 3, by Chivalry—Kamila, by Keenly
Br.—Wilson Constance S (Cal) 1989 2 M 2 0 $4,500
MAPLE S 118 Tr.—Kiesner James R 1988 0 M 0 0
Own.—Wilson Constance S Lifetime 2 0 2 0 $4,500
6May89-5GG 6f :211 :434 1:092ft *3¾ 118 78½ 45½ 25 24 Maple S10 Mdn 88-14 Private Jet,ModernClassic,Hoofer 12
19Apr89-2GG 6f :22 :443 1:101ft 8½ 118 1½ 1½ 1½ 2nk Maple S4 [S]M12500 88-20 PlusOrMinus,ModrnCissic,Muskrt 12
19Apr89—Broke slowly
Apr 28 GG 5f ft 1:023 H Apr 14 GG 3f ft :37 Hg Apr 8 GG 6f ft 1:141 H Mar 28 GG 5f ft 1:014 H

Flying Revenge
B. c. 3, by Flying Paster—Revered, by In Reality
Br.—Cardiff Stud Farm (Cal) 1989 5 M 1 0 $9,625
WARREN R J JR 118 Tr.—Hilling J M 1988 3 M 0 0
Own.—Cardiff Stud Farm Lifetime 8 0 1 0 $9,625
6May89-5GG 6f :211 :434 1:092ft 6¼ 118 57½ 56 47½ 46 Doocy T T 7 Mdn 86-14 Private Jet,ModernClassic Hoofer 12
1Apr89-4SA 1 :464 1:113 1:371ft 11 117 21½ 22 34 47¼ Sibille R 3 [S]Mdn 75-16 AnotherSros,IntercoJoe,RoylAction 8
3Mar89-6SA 1 1/16 :462 1:111 1:45 gd 5½ 118 1hd 21½ 44½ 710¾ Sibille R 2 M50000 65-19 StrungUp,LightTheWorld,Drmtizd 12
11Feb89-6SA 1 :474 1:143 1:424m 2¾ 117 2hd 2hd 2hd 43 Sibille R 4 [S]Mdn 51-31 PrinceOfAck,PtThTnor,TrtEnough 7
19Jan89-4SA 1 1/16 :462 1:114 1:452ft 3 117 21½ 21 3nk 21¼ Sibille R 2 M50000 73-23 RacerRex,FlyingRevenge,Drmtized 11
2Dec88-6Hol 6f :214 :443 1:104ft 14 118 76 65 67 63¾ Sibille R 4 [S]Mdn 84-15 DistntPowr,BluEydDnny,BggrBoy 10
5Nov88-8SA 6f :213 :443 1:092ft 33 117 76½ 98¾ 912 814¾ Sorenson D 7 [S]Mdn 76-13 Mr.Bolg,DonutsToDollrs,FistDISol 12
23Oct88-6SA 6f :214 :45 1:102ft 17 118 65 66¼ 912 915 Solis A 8 [S]Mdn 71-16 Pt'sPocktful,Mr.Bolg,VryPrsonbly 11
Apr 30 GG 4f gd :484 H Apr 19 GG 5f ft 1:004 H Apr 14 GG 4f ft :492 H Mar 27 Hol 4f ft :482 H

Bally Well
B. c. 3, by Well Decorated—Bally Bis (Ire), by Windjammer
Br.—Eaton & Thorne (NY) 1989 3 M 0 0
CASTANON A L 118 Tr.—Whittingham Michael 1988 0 M 0 0
Own.—Duchossois R L Lifetime 3 0 0 0
15Apr89-6SA 1 1/16 :463 1:114 1:434ft 4½e 114 21 2hd 88¼ 915 Olivares F 6 Mdn 67-15 Presidentil,DesseZenny,MindMstr 10
2Apr89-6SA 1 1/16 :46 1:104 1:434ft 99 1125 67 89¼ 711 714½ Valenzuela F H 10 Mdn 67-15 PrncClny,NjnskysGrndsn,DssZnny 12
2Mar89-6SA 6f :22 :444 1:094ft 64 1135 1010 1011 915 1016¼ Valenzuela F H6 Mdn 73-14 JungleRidge,AbacoIsland,Picehart 12
May 15 Hol 5f ft 1:011 H May 10 Hol 4f ft :473 H May 5 Hol 7f ft 1:272 H May 1 Hol 5f ft 1:024 H

Birthday Roses
B. c. 3, by Nostalgia—Laura's Bouquet, by Beau's Eagle
Br.—Mabee Mr-Mrs J C (Cal) 1989 4 M 2 1 $7,250
KAENEL J L 118 Tr.—Jenda Charles J 1988 0 M 0 0
Own.—Golden Eagle Farm Lifetime 4 0 2 1 $7,250
4May89-1GG 1 :474 1:121 1:37 ft 2½ 118 31 31½ 2hd 2no Kaenel J L 1 Mdn 80-16 CremToThTop,BirthdyRoss,Intrbnd 6
4May89—Bumped late
20Apr89-4GG 1 :454 1:101 1:352ft 6 117 51½ 3nk 32 39½ Kaenel J L 6 Mdn 79-13 Fruitziq,AMnToRmmbr,BrthdyRoss 7

23Mar89-7GG   1 :454 1:104 1:362ft   10 118   53 72¼ 65¼ 69¾   Hummel C R⁹   Mdn 73-19 OcensEleven,RglNrv,BrookstownLd 9
23Mar89—Steadied 1st turn
3Mar89-2GG   1⅟₁₆ :463 1:12 1:452ft   6¼ 118   53¼ 31¼ 2¹ 2¾   Hummel CR⁹ Ⓢ M12500 71-23 JimPrice,BirthdyRoses,PintdDrms 12
3Mar89—Bumped 1/16
May 12 GG 4f ft :511 H   Apr 29 GG 4f ft :503 H   Apr 15 GG 4f ft :474 H   Apr 8 GG 4f ft :47 H

Wave To Flo   Dk. b. o⁷ br. g. 3, by Faliraki (Ire)—Hello Flo, by Fleet Allied
HUBBARD N J   Br.—Metz–Heller–Heller (Cal)   1989 3 M 1 1 $7,025
          1135   Tr.—Sherman Art   1988 0 M 0 0
Own.—R G M' Stb Inc Heller or Heller   Lifetime   3 0 1 1 $7,025
4May89-1GG   1 :474 1:121 1:37 ft *7-5 118   2¹ 2¼ 4³ 49¼   Gryder A T⁴   Mdn 70-16 CremToThTop,BirthdyRoss,Intrbnd 6
4May89—Ducked out, bumped
22Apr89-4GG   1 :471 1:111 1:362ft   5¾ 117   3¹ 2² 25 313¼   Kaenel J L⁶   Aw21000 69-20 HollywoodRportr,MjorRol,WvToFlo 7
5Apr89-6GG   6f :223 :461 1:104ft   9 118   66¼ 44 42¼ 2¹   Kaenel J L ¹   M32000 84-17 NturlGlss,WveToFlo,RoyllyDecortd 7
5Apr89—Broke slowly
May 14 GG 5f ft 1:004 H   Apr 14 GG 7f ft 1:274 B   Apr 2 GG 3f ft :361 Hg   Mar 27 GG 7f ft 1:28 H

Modern Classic completed the second quarter of his May 6 sprint in a sizzling 22 seconds flat. It then ran evenly to the wire in rapid time, finishing second of twelve. Modern Classic that day was moving from a maiden-claiming race to confront straight maidens, a difficult rise in class. The gelding was favored by the Golden Gate bettors. Its PDQ pace rating, unadjusted, is 283, a huge rating for a maiden.

Hoofer exits the same fast race. But to repeat the point for the emphasis it deserves, a Hoofer cannot catch a Modern Classic at the mile unless the speedier horse tires on its own and fades. Three-year-old maidens that come from behind gradually will win at the route only when the more brilliant types expire. At a mile, maidens with sparkling turn times that have been extended sharply to the finish should not be expected to tire. More likely, these types will grab the lead and extend it at each point of call.

Modern Classic did exactly that. The gelding won by five, paid $10.40.

Interbend has finished close in his previous two starts, but the races were slow both at the fractional and final calls. Now zero for eight, Interbend cannot keep apace of Modern Classic, and will spend himself trying.

Bally Well illustrates a situation regularly misapprehended by recreational handicappers. The colt was well-supported at Golden Gate because it had been shipped from Santa Anita following a handy six furlongs in a maiden route. But Bally Well should have been discarded instantly by the bettors at Golden Gate. Turf racing excepted, maidens shipped from major tracks to medium-sized tracks, or to minor tracks, are sent because they cannot withstand the tougher competition. If the shipper's record looks awful or nondescript, as does Bally Well's, the local customers should not imagine dramatic improvement will occur. Usually, it will not.

Look again at Birthday Roses, the probable favorite. Whenever a three-year-old maiden finishes up the course in fast races (March 23 and April 20) but close in slow races (March 3 and May 4), mark it down. After tracking a pace of 47.1 and 1:12.1 at a mile May 4, Birthday Roses was behind by a head at the stretch call, perfectly poised to win. It lost by a nose. Or, to put it precisely, the colt did *not* win.

Can Birthday Roses possibly track the fast pace of a Modern Classic and overtake that horse in the stretch? Very, very unlikely. Do not expect slow horses to run faster and then finish strongly. They cannot do it.

The same reasoning applies to the chances of Wave To Flo.

This mile for maidens has been presented to Modern Classic to win or lose, and the improving gelding obliged with an easy score.

TROUBLED TRIPS AND PRIOR RACE RATINGS

A large number of figure handicappers modify the basic figures with trip adjustments, a procedure that often introduces an additional source of error in the figures. The more rational approach juxtaposes numerical ratings and trip notes, and examines the information analytically.

Here's a tip to a topsider of a play for recreational handicappers in possession of the PDQ pace ratings promoted in this book. If several horses in a field show similar pace ratings (within a point) but one of them suffered a troubled trip, and in its prior race ran even more impressively, check the PDQ race rating for the prior race, and prepare to bet on the horse if the rating stands out.

The situation arises whenever several horses return at a comparable class after finishing within arm's length of one another last out. The fifth at Hollywood Park, June 24, 1989, was a $50,000 claiming race, 4up, at seven furlongs. The four main contenders exited a one-turn mile when entered for a similar claiming price 14 days ago. Scan the past performances and obtain the PDQ ratings of each for either the June 10 mile or the previous start.

5th Hollywood

START — 7 FURLONGS — HOLLYWOOD PARK — FINISH

7 FURLONGS. (1.20⅘) CLAIMING. Purse $25,000. 4-year-olds and upward. Weight, 122 lbs. Non-winners of two races since May 7 allowed 3 lbs.; a race since then, 5 lbs. Claiming price $50,000; for each $2,500 to $45,000 allowed 2 lbs. (Races when entered for $40,000 or less not considered.)

Pricey Mac — Ch. g. 4, by Proud Appeal—Beautiful You, by Bold Native

VALENZUELA P A — 117 — Br.—Hough Stanley (Fla) — 1989 6 1 0 1 $23,175

Tr.—Mayberry Brian A — $50,000 — 1988 14 1 3 2 $31,455

Own.—Siegel M-Jan-Samantha — Lifetime 25 4 5 3 $77,207 — Turf 3 0 0 0 $825

DQ 276

10Jun89-7Hol 1 :451 1:10 1:35 ft 9 116 2½ 2hd 31 76¼ Black C A 5 50000 82-13 GoodDelivernc,Dcor,RoylCmronin 11

14May89-5Hol 1 :45 1:094 1:343ft 6½e 116 41½ 1hd 1hd 32¾ Black C A 1 50000 87-09 Decore, Momentus, Pricey Mac 9

14May89—Veered out

21Apr89-7SA 6½f :22 :444 1:153ft 7½ 116 78 78¾ 77½ 62 Black C A 5 62500 90-17 Desperate, Tranzor, Smart Guy 8

21Apr89—Wide into drive

15Mar89-7SA 6½f :214 :441 1:154ft 10 114 34 66¾ 67 42½ Black C A 2 75000 88-14 Presidents Summit, Tranzor, Order 6

15Mar89—Lugged out backstretch; wide into drive

22Feb89-7SA a6½f Ⓣ:213 :4441:16 fm 8½ 114 64½ 64 84½ 62½ Solis A 3 75000 77-21 Rufjan, Rockard, Vistasun 12

22Feb89—Troubled trip

21Jan89-5SA 6½f :213 :434 1:153ft 53 114 62¾ 34½ 33 1nk Black C A 9 50000 92-12 PrcyMc,DonnrPrty,PrsdntsSummt 10

21Jan89—Lugged out 3/8

13Nov88-7Hol 1 1/16 :46 1:103 1:422ft 52 113 2½ 2½ 37 613½ Solis A 8 Aw30000 74-13 Payant, Olympic Native, Galba 9

13Nov88—Lugged out late

4Nov88-8SA a6½f Ⓣ:22 :4511:162fm 34 115 74½ 77½ 77 54½ Solis A 3 Aw33000 72-14 RsonblRj,MobiusStrip,WhtADplomt 8

20Oct88-7SA 1 :451 1:094 1:343ft 9¾ 113 89 68¼ 47½ 510¼ Solis A 8 c50000 85-14 L.A.Fire,JustNeverMind,Sissy'sHlr 8

20Oct88—Wide

23Sep88-9Crc 7f :224 :46 1:25 ft 4½ 113 32½ 31½ 42½ 22¾ Velez J A Jr 5 Aw17700 88-18 PositionLeader,PriceyMac,LordGut 5

May 31 Hol 5f ft 1:013 B   May 10 Hol 5f ft 1:002 H

Tranzor * — ✓. g. 5, by Native Charger—Our Laura, by Ace of Aces

STEVENS G L — 117 — Br.—Fredericks F L (Ky) — 1989 10 4 2 2 $75,976

DQ 275

Tr.—Shulman Sanford — $50,000 — 1988 17 1 2 3 $20,510

Own.—Katayama Nancy & Tracy — Lifetime 53 7 7 8 $111,732

10Jun89-7Hol 1 :451 1:10 1:35 ft 7 118 62½ 41½ 62½ 43½ Stevens G L 3 50000 85-13 GoodDelivernc,Dcor,RoylCmronin 11

17May89-7Hol 1 :451 1:094 1:35 ft 3½ 115 42 42 53½ 56½ ValenzuelFH 1 Aw30000 81-11 Henbne,GoodDelivernce,ScrtMting 8

4May89-7Hol 1 :45 1:093 1:344ft 3 114 31½ 2hd 11 1½ Stevens G L 8 c47500 89-15 Tranzor, Decore, Ascension 10

21Apr89-7SA 6½f :22 :444 1:153ft 7¾ 1125 56 54¾ 32½ 21 Valenzuela F H 1 55000 91-17 Desperate, Tranzor, Smart Guy 8

8Apr89-6SA 6f :212 :44 1:092ft 3¾ 1135 78¾ 47 45½ 33½ Valenzuela F H 2 50000 88-12 EightyBelowZero,SnowPrch,Trnzor 8

8Apr89—Wide 3/8 turn

23Mar89-5SA 6½f :212 :443 1:161ft 5 1115 118 85¾ 42 1¾ VlenzuelFH 11 Aw32000 89-19 Tranzor, Our Native Wish, Script 11

15Mar89-7SA 6½f :214 :441 1:154ft 8½ 1115 64½ 55¾ 34 21½ Valenzuela F H 2 75000 90-14 Presidents Summit, Tranzor, Order 6

15Mar89—Bumped 3/16

25Jan89-5SA 6½f :214 :444 1:164ft 3¾ 1105 95 64½ 53 12 Valenzuela F H 7 30000 86-17 DnceForLee,Trnzor,PrintsChrming 11

25Jan89—Wide into stretch; lugged in badly final 1/8; Dead heat

11Jan89-3SA 6½f :214 :442 1:151ft 3½ 1115 73½ 52½ 21½ 12 Valenzuela F H 4 20000 94-14 Trnzor,Peppy'sConsul,ToB.ARuler 10

11Jan89—Wide on turns

5Jan89-5SA 6f :212 :44 1:084m 6¾ 116 65 44 34 33¾ Stevens G L 2 25000 90-17 EghtyBlowZro,SprbMommt,Trnzor 10

Jun 2 Hol 5f ft 1:003 H   Apr 29 Hol 5f ft 1:003 H

Royal Cameronian — B. g. 6, by Temperence Hill—Lucinda Light, by Laser Light

GUERRA W A — 113 — Br.—Hill 'N' Dale Farms (Ont-C) — 1989 3 1 0 2 $15,800

DQ 275

Tr.—Luby Donn — $45,000 — 1988 12 1 1 1 $21,425

Own.—Brook-Lovett-Noren et al — Lifetime 35 5 7 7 $111,535 — Turf 6 0 1 1 $13,070

10Jun89-7Hol 1 :451 1:10 1:35 ft 11 112 72¾ 52 52½ 32¾ Guerra W A 8 45000 85-13 GoodDelivernc,Dcor,RoylCmronin 11

19May89-5Hol 1 :451 1:092 1:342ft 6½ 115 21½ 2hd 12 11¾ Guerra W A 9 25000 91-08 RoylCmronn,OnoGmmo,Alm'sTbn 12

DQ 283

6May89-2Hol 6f :213 :443 1:092ft 16 117 67½ 57 43½ 33½ Guerra W A 4 25000 90-09 HrdToMiss,KvinsDfns,RoylCmronin 9

7Aug88-2Dmr 6½f :213 :444 1:16 ft 7¾ 116 1111 97 67½ 48 Olivares F 7 c16000 84-13 Gerril,Gypsy'sProphecy,WstBoyII 12

7Aug88—Wide into stretch

31Jly88-1Dmr 7f :224 :451 1:221ft 5 116 43 21½ 1½ 11½ Pedroza M A 7 10000 91-07 RoylCmronin,IndinSignII,D.D.ThKd 9

12Jun88-2Hol 6½f :22 :45 1:17 ft 5¾ 116 98 96¼ 76¾ 95¼ Gryder A T 4 16000 88-09 Lark'sLegacy,AngleArc,StarOrphn 12

5Jun88-2Hol 7f :223 :453 1:234ft 5¼ 1115 96¾ 53 42½ 21½ Corral J R 10 12500 84-13 Mr.Edlwiss,RoylCmronin,DncnKid 11

5Jun88—Wide 3/8 turn

12May88-9Hol 1 :451 1:102 1:37 ft 6¾ 116 77½ 57 54 54¾ Stevens G L 4 20000 73-21 ImprousSprt,Bshop'sRngII,InBold 11

1May88-7Hol 6f :22 :451 1:102ft 14 116 710 78¾ 78½ 76¾ Pedroza M A 3 40000 83-13 BoldJade,LuckyMasddo,Cliff'sPlce 7

13Apr88-5SA a6½f Ⓣ:22 :4441:153fm 68 116 109¾ 96 53 41¾ Sibille R 3 70000 79-16 FbulousSond,QpStr,H'sADncngMn 10

Jun 4 Hol 6f ft 1:13 H   May 29 Hol 5f ft :59 H   May 14 Hol 5f ft :593 H   Apr 30 Hol 5f ft 1:014 Hg

Delightful Doctor * Dk. c. 4, by Dr Blum—Debra's Delight, by The Axe II
MCCARRON C J 117 Br.—Glen Crest Fm&MorguelanSL (Ky) 1989 5 1 1 0 $19,950
Tr.—Hronec Philip $50,000 1988 8 1 0 1 $58,427
PDQ 276 Own.—Ridgewood Racing Stable Lifetime 22 4 4 3 $126,857 Turf 2 0 0 0

10Jun89-7Hol	1	:451	1:10	1:35 ft	19	116	1½	1hd	42	89¼	Davis R 6 1		50000	79-13	GoodDelivernc,Dcor,RoylCmronin	11
29May89-3Hol	1 1/16	:463	1:103	1:43 ft	2½	116	2½	1½	12	11¾	ValenzuelaFH 1		c40000	85-13	DelightfulDoctor,KmikzeSn,HesBr	6
4May89-7Hol	1	:45	1:093	1:344ft	7	116	41½	42½	51¾	74	Black C A 4		50000	85-15	Tranzor, Decore, Ascension	10
8Mar89-7SA	1 1/16	:463	1:103	1:412ft	18	116	1½	1hd	32½	48	DelhoussyeE 3		Aw46000	86-15	Bosphorus,RcittionSpin,PrmountJt	7
16Feb89-8GG	1 1/16	:461	1:093	1:413ft	7½	117	33	32½	22	22	ChapmanTM 2		Aw22000	89-22	RovingFree,DlightfulDoctcr,Slwbop	5
2Oct88-6Bel	1¼ T	:48	1:36	2:004fm	76	114	45½	66¼	1016	1017	Vasquez J 4		Aw33000	73-13	ThreeEngins,FrColony,ClosingBid	10
22Sep88-8Bel	1 1/16 T	:46	1:094	1:412fm	34	113	1hd	32½	1119	1123¼	Santos J A 9		Aw33000	66-13	MstrModsty,RomntcTn,ThrEngns	12
11Jun88-6Bel	1⅛	:46	1:101	1:484ft	39	119	95	67	718	821	Bailey J D 5		Colin	62-13	Gay Rights, Tejano, Parlay Me	9
28Apr88-8Kee	1⅛	:483	1:13	1:521ft	40	121	78	99½	915	919¼	MigliorR 7	Blue Grass		54-22	Grncus,IntensiveCommnd,RglClssic	9
28Apr88—Grade I																
2Apr88-11TP	1⅛	:463	1:112	1:504m	28	121	43	64¼	77	79½	HrnndzR 1	Jim Beam		81-15	Kingpost, Stalwars, Brian's Time	
2Apr88—Grade II; Lugged in 2d turn																

Jun 21 SA 4f ft :49 H May 25 Hol 5f ft 1:001 H May 20 Hol 5f ft :584 H May 15 Hol 4f ft :48 H

Unless they observed the action, recreational handicappers could not know that Royal Cameronian had been boxed in, without running room, for roughly a furlong of the June 10 mile. No mention of the mishap appears in the *Daily Racing Form*. In its prior start, at two class levels lower, the six-year-old smashed its opposition in rapid fractions throughout.

Trainer Donn Luby jumped the horse confidently following the May 19 win, and does not drop Royal Cameronian off the June 10 trip.

The recent PDQ pace ratings for the four contenders are impressive, and vary by a point only. The PDQ pace rating for Royal Cameronian's May 19 romp tells why trainer Luby would not lower the horse after a troubled trip for $50,000. The May 19 rating is a huge 283, three to four lengths superior to the June 10 competition.

Be alert to this pattern. A troubled trip last out, but a comparable pace rating, preceded by a more highly rated race. If the horse shows an improvement pattern, or even regular racing, assume the horse can approach the prior rating. A competent trainer is a plus factor. The pattern tosses overlays, always another plus.

FIFTH RACE
Hollywood
JUNE 24, 1989

7 FURLONGS. (1.20$\frac{1}{5}$) CLAIMING. Purse $25,000. 4-year-olds and upward. Weight, 122 lbs. Non-winners of two races since May 7 allowed 3 lbs.; a race since then, 5 lbs. Claiming price $50,000; for each $2,500 to $45,000 allowed 2 lbs. (Races when entered for $40,000 or less not considered.)

Value of race $25,000; value to winner $13,750; second $5,000; third $3,750; fourth $1,875; fifth $625. Mutuel pool $386,220. Exacta pool $457,981.

Last Raced	Horse	Eqt.A.Wt	PP	St	¼	½	Str	Fin	Jockey	Cl'g Pr	Odds $1
10Jun89 ^{7}Hol^{3}	Royal Cameronian	6 113	8	5	4^{hd}	$3^{1\frac{1}{2}}$	1^{1}	$1^{1\frac{3}{4}}$	Guerra W A	45000	4.20
10Jun89 ^{7}Hol^{8}	Delightful Doctor	b 4 117	9	3	$3^{\frac{1}{2}}$	4^{2}	3^{2}	$2^{2\frac{1}{2}}$	McCarron C J	50000	4.20
14Jun89 ^{8}GG^{2}	High Hook	7 117	2	6	6^{2}	6^{1}	4^{1}	3^{hd}	Delahoussaye E	50000	4.00
10Jun89 ^{7}Hol^{7}	Pricey Mac	b 4 117	1	4	1^{hd}	$1^{\frac{1}{2}}$	$2^{1\frac{1}{2}}$	$4^{1\frac{3}{4}}$	Valenzuela P A	50000	8.20
29May89 ^{5}Hol^{2}	Mehmetski	4 117	3	7	$7^{\frac{1}{2}}$	$7^{\frac{1}{2}}$	$5^{\frac{1}{2}}$	5^{nk}	Solis A	50000	15.90
10Jun89 ^{7}Hol^{4}	Tranzor	b 5 117	6	1	$5^{\frac{1}{2}}$	5^{2}	6^{3}	6^{3}	Stevens G L	50000	3.80
26Feb88 ^{3}SA^{4}	Key Purchase	6 117	4	8	$8^{2\frac{1}{2}}$	$8^{1\frac{1}{2}}$	$7^{1\frac{1}{2}}$	$7^{1\frac{1}{4}}$	Meza R Q	50000	30.30
14May89 ^{5}Hol^{2}	Momentus	b 5 112	5	9	9	9	9	8^{3}	Nakatani C S^{5}	50000	11.90
26May89 ^{7}Hol^{5}	Knight Regent	b 4 117	7	2	$2^{2\frac{1}{2}}$	2^{hd}	8^{1}	9	Baze R A	50000	11.20

OFF AT 3:43. Start good. Won driving. Time, $:22\frac{4}{5}$, :45, $1:09\frac{4}{5}$, 1:22 Track fast.

$2 Mutuel Prices:			
8–ROYAL CAMERONIAN	10.40	4.80	3.20
9–DELIGHTFUL DOCTOR		6.60	3.80
2–HIGH HOOK			4.00

$2 EXACTA 8–9 PAID $48.80.

B. g, by Temperence Hill—Lucinda Light, by Laser Light. Trainer Luby Donn. Bred by Hill 'N' Dale Farms (Ont–C).

ROYAL CAMERONIAN, in contention early, reached the front soon after going a half and remained in the lead through the stretch while kept to a drive. DELIGHTFUL DOCTOR, close up early, was boxed in going into the far turn and had enough of a response in the drive to gain the place. HIGH HOOK, outrun early but not far back, dropped farther back after a quarter, came into the stretch four wide, gained some ground in the drive but did not have the needed late kick. PRICEY MAC vied for the lead to the furlong marker and weakened. MEHMETSKI, devoid of early speed, could not gain the necessary ground in the drive. TRANZOR had no apparent mishap. MOMENTUS, wide down the backstretch after he broke slowly, was five wide into the stretch. KNIGHT REGENT, a pace factor for a half, faltered.

CLASS STANDOUTS

In any nonclaiming race, the conditions of eligibility must be comprehended without oversight or apology. The conditions define the class boundaries of the eligible horses, absolutely in the nonwinners allowance series, where the basic purpose is to provide a kind of restricted competition for younger, still-developing prospects.

To qualify on class, nonclaiming horses should be nicely suited to the conditions. At times a particular horse fits the conditions of eligibility so snugly, class handicappers have alleged the race was written for him.

That's exactly the situation below, a seven-horse state-bred allowance sprint for fillies and mares. In relation to eligibility conditions, one of the seven stands out. The race is loaded with additional handicapping lessons besides.

Read the eligibility conditions carefully. Ignore the weight allowances. Which horse sticks out as the probable class of the field?

BELMONT

6 FURLONGS

6 FURLONGS. (1.07½) ALLOWANCE. Purse $28,000. Fillies and Mares, 3-years-old and upward foaled in New York State and approved by the New York State-bred registry which have never won two races other than maiden, claiming or starter. Weight, 3-year-olds, 116 lbs. Older, 122 lbs. Non-winners of a race other than maiden or claiming since July 1 allowed 3 lbs. Of such a race since June 15, 5 lbs.

Happy Dapple

Gr. f. 4, by Lejoli—Dapples, by Hunters Creek
Br.—Dutch Acres Enterprises Inc (NY)
Tr.—Odintz Jeff

Own.—Jewel E Stables

117

Lifetime	1989	13	1	3	3	$36,800
31 3 6 5	1988	13	1	3	2	$25,470
$102,976						

LATEST WORKOUTS   Jun 20 Aqu 3f fst :35½ H   ●May 31 Aqu 5f fst 1:01 H

Ying N' Yang

B. f. 4, by Star Gallant—Reason to be Bold, by Bold Reason
Br.—Connelly Lawrie & Imperio (NY)
Tr.—Imperio Dominick A

Own.—Behman S E

117

Lifetime	1989	4	0	0	0	$39,300
16 2 1 2	1988	10	2	0	2	
$45,740						

LATEST WORKOUTS   Jly 27 Bel ⊺ 5f fm 1:02½ B (d)   Jly 13 Bel 4f fst :48¾ H   Jly 8 Bel 4f fst :49⅜ B   Jly 1 Bel 4f fst :48¾ H

Oh Betty

Dk. b. or br. f. 4, by Pace Jean—Acceptor, by Accipiter
Br.—Rence Bay Stables (NY)
Tr.—Nesky Kenneth A

Own.—Rence Bay Stable

117

Lifetime	1989	8	1	0	1	$31,440
17 2 3 1	1988	9	1	3	0	$35,460
$54,900						

LATEST WORKOUTS   ●Jly 6 Aqu 4f my :48½ H (d)   May 29 Aqu 3f fst :36½ H

Super Appeal

B. f. 3(Mar), by Proud Appeal—Superlative Gal, by Royal Consort
Br.—Timber Bay Farm (NY)
Tr.—Baillie Sally A

Own.—Timber Bay Farm

111

Lifetime	1989	4	2	1	0	$36,760
4 2 1 0	1988	M	0	0	0	
$36,760						

LATEST WORKOUTS   Jly 11 Bel 4f fst :48½ B   Jly 2 Bel 4f fst :51 B   Jun 21 Bel 4f fst :49 B   ●Jun 16 Bel 5f sly 1:01 H

Iron's Advance

Dk. . or br. f. 3(Mar), by Iron Constitution—Advance Reason, by Limit Reason
Br.—Mangurian Mr-Mrs H T Jr (NY)
Tr.—Root Thomas F Jr

Own.—Mangurian H T

111

Lifetime	1989	5	1	2	1	$28,440
5 1 2 1	1988	0	M	0	0	
$28,440						

LATEST WORKOUTS   Jun 2 Bel 5f fst 1:00½ H

Hit The Bell

Ch. m. 6, by Sir Wimborne—Toll O' Bells, by One For All
Br.—Wimpfheimer Jacques D (NY)
Tr.—Sedlacek Woodrow C

Own.—Sedlacek W C

107 10

Lifetime	1989	13	0	1	0	$4,000
61 2 3 6	1988	15	0	1	0	$9,460
$80,046	Turf	21	1	1	4	$36,110

LATEST WORKOUTS   May 31 Aqu 4f fst :52 B

Miss Norma Jean — Ch. f. 3(Jan), by Poster Prince—Miss Sarah Jean, by Warm Front
Own.—L'Ilusion Stable
Br.—Old Westbury Farms Inc (NY)
Tr.—Barrera Guillermo S
111
Lifetime 17 2 2 3 $45,020 | 1989 16 2 2 3 $45,020 | 1988 1 M 0 0 | Turf 1 0 0 0

1Jly89- 7Bel	fm	1¼	T :46⅕	1:37⅖	2:03⅕	3+ⒻⓈAlw 31000	1	9	97¾	1014	1015	1021½	Rojas R I	b 111	13.20	57-15	Sa Marche 117½ MarineBand1173¾MaggieTonight1171½	Slow early	10
19Jun89- 7Bel	fst	1⅛	:46⅘	1:11⅘	1:53	3+ⒻⓈAlw 31000	5	1	3nk	1hd	33½	45¾	Ortega P Jr	b 110	6.90	56-25	Twixt Appeal 110¾ Maggie Tonight 1122 Herblue 1193	Weakened	6
26May89- 7Bel	fst	7f	:22⅗	:45⅘	1:24	3+ⒻⓈAlw 28000	4	5	31½	3½	44½	610¼	Cordero A Jr	b 115	3.30	72-17	Tim's Lady 1121½ Twixt Appeal 1154 Nit Pic 119nk	Tired	9
18May89- 7Bel	fst	1 1/16	:45⅖	1:10⅘	1:44⅘	3+ⒻⓈAlw 31000	3	1	12	11	1½	31	Santos J A	b 110	*2.20	78-17	FmilyFrud114nkShinnecockLssi119¾MissNormJn1101½	Drifted out	10
10May89- 5Bel	my	1 1/16	:45⅗	1:10⅗	1:44⅕	ⒻAlw 29000	6	1	11½	11	14	15½	Santos J A	b 116	9.60	81-19	Miss Norma Jean 1165½ Tremolos 1162¾ Aria 1164	Driving	6
14Apr89- 5Aqu	fst	1	:45⅗	1:11⅕	1:38⅘	3+ⒻⓈAlw 29000	2	7	711	77½	47	35½	Velasquez J	114	6.20	67-31	Semideity 1135½ Star Circle 113nk Miss Norma Jean 1142¾	Rallied	9
8Apr89- 8Aqu	fst	1⅛	:47⅕	1:11⅗	1:50⅘	3+ⒻAlw 29000	5	5	617	511	33½	47	Velasquez J	113	8.50	74-14	Samra 121nk Charming Fappiano1126½LadyProfessional121½	Wide	8
25Mar89- 7Aqu	fst	1	:46⅕	1:11⅗	1:39	ⒻⓈAlw 29000	2	10	97¼	99	67	53¼	Hernandez R Z	116	12.50	68-23	Gate Lady 116hd Wise Woman 111no Twixt Appeal 1161½	Outrun	10
11Mar89- 3Aqu	fst	170	⊡:48⅘	1:14	1:45⅘	ⒻClm 35000	7	8	89	67½	32½	2nk	Hernandez R Z	116	19.50	71-18	PerfectGin116nkMissNormaJean1161½MyGallantStar111nk	Rallied	8
4Mar89- 3Aqu	fst	170	⊡:49⅕	1:15	1:46	ⒻClm 50000	5	7	99½	911	613	513½	Hernandez R Z	116	34.40	57-30	Cherlindre1129MoonlightMiss112nkBelieveinDstiny1091	No factor	9

LATEST WORKOUTS Jly 24 Bel 4f fst :48 H Jun 16 Bel tr.t 4f sly :55 B

To frame the handicapping properly, recreational handicappers are reminded that in any nonwinners allowance race the conditions are most hospitable to younger, lightly raced horses that have impressed in few attempts and might be any kind. That means three-year-olds are preferred to older nonwinners, and horses having fewer than a dozen races are preferred to horses still eligible despite numerous attempts.

Although the New York–bred race under study contains no potential champions, only two of the fillies are three-year-olds that remain lightly raced, each starting fewer than a half dozen times. Most impressive in recent races, a positive sign, the two form the guts of this restricted state-bred allowance affair.

That narrows the handicapping task conveniently, but which of the pair actually stands out under today's conditions, Super Appeal or Iron's Advance?

Two back, Super Appeal thrashed a state-bred allowance field at Belmont Park, and last out finished second under conditions of eligibility the same as today's. The filly is two for four under state-bred conditions, and surely will win its second state-bred allowance race soon.

But Iron's Advance is a filly altogether different. This New York–bred three-year-old has battled open competition at Belmont Park from the outset, and impressively, with a conspicuous exception two races back.

In that exceptional race, a maiden sprint limited to New York–breds, Iron's Advance scooted wire to wire in a romp, winning by eight uncontested lengths at 9–5. It followed with a third-place rally in an open allowance race.

Open allowance competition at any major track, Belmont Park absolutely, is leagues removed from the state-bred contests. Iron's Advance's tour de force in its single state-bred experience testifies eloquently to that point.

Now Iron's Advance is entered anew under restricted state-bred allowance conditions. Not only that, the filly has been entered above the allowance conditions for which it remains eligible. Having never won an allowance race, Iron's Advance is eligible for nonwinners once other than maiden or claiming.

Yet the filly's handlers confidently confront horses that already have won an allowance race, although allowance races restricted to New York–breds. Perhaps trainer Thomas Root believes this developing filly will simply run away from state-breds under any preliminary nonwinners allowance conditions, as it did against state-bred maidens. A pace handicapper would notice, too, that Iron's Advance can travel the first quarter in 22.2 seconds under no pressure, a speed outlay unmatched by its opponents.

How many recreational handicappers noticed that Iron's Advance had been entered above its eligibility conditions? Those that did not might be more alert, more careful in the future.

In fact, Iron's Advance's brief record contains an unusual combination of handicapping elements, each of which signals an impending victory against inferior opposition:

1. The filly is moving from a good performance under open allowance conditions to the state-bred kind, now facing a quality of competition it has devastated in its only state-bred try, at a class level one step lower.
2. The filly has been entered above its eligibility conditions, suggesting the trainer is confident his horse outclasses the state-bred competition at the lower level.
3. The filly possesses the best early lick in a lackluster field devoid of authentic speed.
4. The filly is precisely the younger, lightly raced, improving commodity that can be expected to shine in preliminary nonwinners allowance contests.

Unless Super Appeal can improve its latest effort, Iron's Advance should triumph against this bunch in a runaway.

The filly has provided evidence it might outclass preliminary state-bred nonwinners allowance races, and handicappers that recognize the situation for what it is can participate in the celebration.

The result chart reveals how easily Iron's Advance thwarted state-bred opponents that had already won a state-bred allowance race.

FOURTH RACE
Belmont
JULY 28, 1989

6 FURLONGS. (1.07⅘) ALLOWANCE. Purse $28,000. Fillies and Mares, 3-year-old and upward foaled in New York State and approved by the New York State-bred registry which have never won two races other than maiden, claiming or starter. Weight, 3-year-olds, 116 lbs. Older, 122 lbs. Non-winners of a race other than maiden or claiming since July 1 allowed 3 lbs. Of such a race since June 15, 5 lbs.

Value of race $28,000; value to winner $16,800; second $6,160; third $3,360; fourth $1,680. Mutuel pool $263,927. Exacta Pool $488,588. Quinella Pool $120,818.

Last Raced	Horse	Eqt.	A.	Wt	PP	St	¼	½	Str	Fin	Jockey	Odds $1
21Jly89 7Bel3	Iron's Advance		3	111	5	1	$1^{1\frac{1}{2}}$	1^{3}	1^{5}	1^{3}	Thibeau R J Jr	2.20
15Jly89 9Bel3	Happy Dapple	b	4	117	1	3	$3^{1\frac{1}{2}}$	5^{hd}	$3^{2\frac{1}{2}}$	2^{3}	Maple E	4.10
15Jly89 9Bel2	Super Appeal	b	3	111	4	7	6^{3}	3^{1}	2^{2}	$3^{4\frac{1}{2}}$	Migliore R	1.10
15Jly89 9Bel5	Ying N' Yang		4	117	2	2	$4^{1\frac{1}{2}}$	$4^{1\frac{1}{2}}$	$4^{1\frac{1}{2}}$	$4^{1\frac{1}{2}}$	Cruguet J	19.50
3Jly89 4Mth5	Hit The Bell		6	107	6	5	7	7	6^{3}	5^{3}	Singh D10	35.70
1Jly89 7Bel10	Miss Norma Jean	b	3	111	7	6	$2^{1\frac{1}{2}}$	2^{1}	5^{1}	6^{3}	Rojas R I	8.10
15Jly89 9Bel6	Oh Betty	b	4	117	3	4	5^{2}	6^{4}	7	7	Castillo R E	16.30

OFF AT 2:34 Start good, Won driving. Time, :22⅗, :45⅘, 1:12⅗ Track fast.

$2 Mutuel Prices:			
5-(E)-IRON'S ADVANCE	6.40	3.00	2.20
1-(A)-HAPPY DAPPLE		4.20	2.40
4-(D)-SUPER APPEAL			2.10

$2 EXACTA 5-1 PAID $24.80. $2 QUINELLA 1-5 PAID $14.60.

Dk. b. or br. f, by Iron Constitution—Advance Reason, by Limit Reason. Trainer Root Thomas F Jr. Bred by Mangurian Mr-Mrs H T Jr (NY).

IRON'S ADVANCE raced slightly out from the rail while making the pace, drew away after entering the stretch and was under pressure to hold sway. HAPPY DAPPLE, carefully handled while bearing out approaching the stretch, finished well when straightened away for the drive. SUPER APPEAL, off slowly, made a run along the inside leaving the turn but lacked a late response. YING N' YANG tired. MISS NORMA JEAN was used up prompting the pace. OH BETTY was finished early while racing wide.

Owners— 1, Mangurian H T; 2, Jewel E Stables; 3, Timber Bay Farm; 4, Behman S E; 5, Sedlacek W C; 6, L'Ilusion Stable; 7, Rence Bay Stable.

Trainers— 1, Root Thomas F Jr; 2, Odintz Jeff; 3, Bailie Sally A; 4, Imperio Dominick A; 5, Sedlacek Woodrow; 6, Barrera Gasper S; 7, Nesky Kenneth A.

Corrected weight: Super Appeal 111 pounds.

OPEN CLAIMING RACES TO STATE-BRED ALLOWANCE RACES

Recreational handicappers should understand that horses switching from claiming races open to all runners to allowance races limited to horses bred in the home state may actually be dropping in class.

At major tracks, any horse that has run a good race versus open claiming competition valued at $25,000 or higher can be accepted on class in an allowance race restricted to nonwinners of one or two allowance races. If the claiming race were restricted to 3YOs, the claiming price of the good race should be $35,000 or higher.

If the state-bred allowance race is restricted to nonwinners of two races other than maiden, claiming, or starter, contenders should have won a state-bred allowance race in the past six starts. The best pattern is a win in a state-bred allowance race a while ago, and a win or good races versus open claimers recently. The higher the recent claiming prices, the better.

New York handicappers face the toughest challenges in these situations but also find the best opportunities, as the New York state-bred program is the most comprehensive in the nation. A typical illustration from Aqueduct frames the issues well. It's December 8.

Let's browse through the entries, identifying the logical contenders. Read the eligibility conditions.

In preliminary nonwinners allowance races (nonwinners once or twice), recall that handicappers prefer 3YOs to older horses, and lightly raced horses to horses that have been afforded many attempts, but have failed.

5th Aqueduct

6 FURLONGS. (InnerDirt). (1.08⅗) ALLOWANCE. Purse $24,000. 3-year-olds and upward. Foaled in New York State and approved by the New York State-Bred Registry which have never won two races other than Maiden, Claiming or Starter. Weights: 3-year-olds, 120 lbs.; older, 122 lbs. Non-winners of a race other than maiden or claiming since November 15 allowed 3 lbs.; of such a race since November 1, 5 lbs.

```
The Real Virginian              Ro. g. 3, by The Cool Virginian—Easter Moment, by For The Moment
                                Br.—Rence Bay Stables (NY)              1988 17 3 1 3   $69,864
Own.—Beach Boy Stables 5-N+ 115 Tr.—Nesky Kenneth A — N                 1987  2 M 0 0    $1,740
                            Lifetime 19 3 1 3 $71,604                   Turf  1 0 0 0
3Dec88-8Aqu  6f :22  :452 1:103ft  24 113  1½  31½ 712 719   MglorR2 [S]Joe Palmer 68-25 Notebook,ScottishMonk,Fourstrdv 7
13Nov88-9Aqu 6f :221 :452 1:102sy  15 113  13½ 12½ 13½ 13    McCauley W H1 30000   88-20 TheRelVirginin,Sekr'sJourny,Histd 12
22Oct88-5Aqu 6f :221 :454 1:11 gd   6 114  42½ 43  711 713¾  Vega A6  [S]Aw28000  71-18 Agnoble, Banquo, Jiltavo 7
5Oct88-5Bel  6f :223 :461 1:104ft  13 109  1½  1½  44  59¼   Castillo R E1  35000   76-25 Dale's Folly, Fast Jack, Hot Amber 7
23Sep88-9Bel 6f :222 :451 1:103ft  23 117  33  37½ 812 810½  Romero R P5     50000  75-19 DncingPrtns,Skr'sJourny,TizComc 11
28Aug88-6Sar 6f :222 :453 1:094ft  12 112  21  31½ 45  59¼   Day P5   [S]Aw28000  82-11 CrftyNorth,NowBonny,CrftyReply 10
29Jly88-6Bel 6½f :224 :453 1:162gd 19 113  42½ 69½ 819 829¼  Romero R P8     75000  64-17 Hayes'Hope,Tulipark,CleverChristin 8
23Jun88-7Bel 6f :224 :462 1:102ft  6½ 109  22  2½  1½  11½   Day P8   [S]Aw27000  87-16 TheRealVirginian,Bnquo,Cndensis 10
   ●Nov 30 Aqu 4f ft :474 H    ●Nov 10 Aqu 3f ft :35 H    Nov 5 Aqu 5f ft 1:00 H    ●Oct 31 Aqu 5f ft 1:004 H

Scottie's Partner               Dk. b. or br. g. 6, by Distinctpartner—Dear Scottie, by Go Marching
                                Br.—Nocella V (NY)                      1988 14 1 1 0   $29,140
Own.—Nocella V R 1-0        117 Tr.—Nocella Vincent — N                 1987 18 1 4 1   $47,880
                            Lifetime 47 2 9 1 $100,820                  Turf  2 0 0 0
20Nov88-9Aqu 1                  sy 14 117  — — — 513½          Baird E T6 [S]Aw31000 — — Ogle, Katie's Noblest, Banquo 9
    20Nov88—Running positions omitted because of weather conditions; No time available due to fog
22Oct88-5Aqu 6f :221 :454 1:11 gd  28 117  67  65  55¾ 56¼     Velez R I3  [S]Aw28000 78-18 Agnoble, Banquo, Jiltavo 7
15Sep88-9Bel 1 :463 1:111 1:372ft  37 117  43  54  610 68¾     ThibeauRJ2 [S]Aw31000 69-16 ClerCtrcts,MkeSttemnt,WonLump 10
1Aug88-5Bel  1 :464 1:11 1:361ft   26 1125 32  59  617 727     Peck B D7  [S]Aw31000 57-18 Whodam, Won Lump, Silver Pass 7
17Jly88-7Bel 1⅛ T:47 1:1141:441fm  78 1125 55  106½ 1114 1113¼ Peck B D4 [S]Aw31000 62-29 ClosingBid,Mr.Beutiful,Don'tGivIn 11
24Jun88-6Bel 7f :221 :453 1:241ft  48 117  612 612 710 68½     BelmontJF8 [S]Aw28000 72-18 Achenar, Ivory Trade, Hallen 9
12Jun88-1Bel 1⅛ :471 1:114 1:441ft 39 117  55½ 816 823 829¼    Baird E T5 [S]Aw31000 52-17 DeAcuerdo,MakeaSttement,Tenner 8
21May88-10Bel 1⅛ :453 1:104 1:43 ft 37 124 77½ 96¾ 912 1020    Baird E T3 [S]Aw31000 67-11 Tina's Dewan, Silver Pass, Tenner 11
   Nov 27 Bel tr.t 4f ft :482 H    Oct 20 Bel tr.t 3f ft :36 H    Oct 11 Bel tr.t 4f ft :511 B

Beyond all Odds                 B. c. 3, by What Luck—Beyond Reasoning, by Hurry to Market
                                Br.—Mihovich M (NY)                     1988  8 2 0 0   $35,080
Own.—Mitto Stable 5-N       115 Tr.—Picou James E — N                   1987  2 M 0 0
                            Lifetime 10 2 0 0 $35,080
18Nov88-6Aqu 7f :224 :454 1:273gd  3½e115 42  79½ 715 724¾   Vega A2      Aw28000 58-38 RedScmper,RocktPrinc,RltivlySmrt 7
    18Nov88—Lacked room
24Jly88-9Pha 7f :22  :443 1:281gd  17 116  31  41½ 612 618¾   Capanas S1 [R]Fescue 72-16 MySwtMusic,TddyDron,ChrgthCstl 8
3Jly88-7Bel  7f :222 :46  1:242ft  33 1065 1hd 1½  66  613    Peck B D5     Aw30000 67-25 SecrtFlotill,CrusdrSword,PlcidWtrs 7
3Jun88-7Bel  6f :223 :461 1:11 ft  5½ 112  52½ 52½ 43  45½   Santos J A5 [S]Aw28000 79-21 CavanghSpecil,ClerCtrcts,Dr.TimVil 9
21May88-10Bel 1⅛ :453 1:104 1:43 ft 26 113 3½  31  77½ 715   Santos J A4 [S]Aw31000 72-11 Tina's Dewan, Silver Pass, Tenner 11
8May88-6Aqu  6f :22  :45  1:104ft  27 116  53½ 31  2½  1nk   Santos J A6 [S]Aw30000 86-14 BeyondllOdds,CrftyReply,AtomBlde 8
21Apr88-6Aqu 6f :231 :473 1:131ft  4½ 115  1½  1½  12  1¾    Krone J A6  [S]Mdn    74-26 BeyondllOdds,Shcky'sLst,LJzzHot 12
30Mar88-4Aqu 7f :224 :453 1:254ft  20 115  31  3½  31  55    Krone J A2  [S]Mdn    67-22 BraveBest,PineIslndPt,KnickPress 10
    30Mar88—In tight
   Dec 2 Bel tr.t 4f ft :492 H    Nov 26 Bel 5f ft 1:024 B    Nov 14 Bel 5f gd 1:014 Bg    Nov 9 Bel 6f ft 1:153 H
```

Dr. Tim Vail 3-0
Own.—Krohn Deborah 117
Dk. b. or br. h. 5, by Great Neck—Brazil Nut, by Hard Work
Br.—Krohn & Kaswell & Stein (NY) 1988 6 1 1 1 $27,960
Tr.—Krohn Nat – O 1987 5 1 2 2 $32,760
Lifetime 19 2 4 6 $71,520
3Nov88-1Aqu 6f :223 :462 1:114ft 30 117 85¾ 86¼ 76½ 99 Fox W I Jr5 25000 72-25 CttngAppl,DcortdEmpror,Rdccho 10
24Jun88-6Bel 7f :221 :453 1:241ft 14 1125 36 37½ 58½ 810½ Peck B D1 SAw28000 70-18 Achenar, Ivory Trade, Hallen 9
3Jun88-7Bel 6f :223 :461 1:11 ft 13 1125 2½ 41¼ 3½ 33 Peck B D3 SAw28000 81-21 CavanghSpecil,ClerCtrcts,Dr.TimVil 9
17Apr88-7Aqu 6f :22 :453 1:121ft 8½ 121 1½ 2hd 1hd 12¼ Davis R G2 SAw30000 79-25 Dr.TimVail,Where'sBilly,Canadensis 8
3Mar88-6Aqu 6f ⊡:23 :4631:12 ft 25 117 42 44 23½ 25¾ Nuesch D8 SAw30000 78-22 Jiltavo,Dr.TimVail,FleetfootedPsser 9
20Feb88-7Aqu 6f ⊡:224 :4541:11 gd 21 117 32 33 34 67¼ Nuesch D9 SAw30000 81-15 ClerCtrcts,Cordin,FleetfootedPssr 10
11Sep87-9Bel 6f :231 :463 1:123ft 3 1175 1½ 1½ 12 1hd Nuesch D9 SMdn 76-18 Dr.TimVil,KickYourHels,NoblWish 12
17Jly87-9Bel 6f :223 :453 1:13 ft *2 122 2½ 1hd 2hd 34½ Venezia M9 SMdn 70-28 IvoryTrade,Wizrd'sSlick,Dr.TimVil 11
Dec 3 Bel tr.t 3f ft :364 H Oct 31 Bel 4f ft :51 B Oct 18 Bel tr.t 3f ft :36 H

London Lassa O-N
Own.—Spataro J M 1075
Dk. b. or br. f. 4, by London Company—Antilassa, by Anticipating
Br.—Villani Eileen G (NY) 1988 19 7 2 0 $51,112
Tr.—Aquilino Joseph – N 1987 15 1 3 1 $6,612
Lifetime 43 10 6 1 $90,574 Turf 1 0 0 0
4Dec88-2Aqu 7f :233 :48 1:28 ft *3 1125 910 108¾ 98¾ 66½ Castillo R E1 17500 54-36 HarvrdImp,DizzyDixie,FoundJewel 10
28Nov88-2Aqu 7f :232 :471 1:263sy 5 1085 79 77 77¼ 47 Carle J D3 Ⓕ 20000 61-29 TrnishMiss,CrmellSwets,StrBrillint 9
21Nov88-9Aqu 7f :233 :47 1:243ft 5 1125 95 78½ 1½ 14 Castillo R E8 Ⓕ c14000 78-30 London Lassa,AprilJovee,Brevolly 11
29Oct88-4Aqu 7f :23 :46 1:244ft 2¼e 115 84¾ 912 914 811½ Fox W I Jr2 Ⓕ 22500 65-24 TooBobsRtrn,GccGl,OhHwWDncd 10
8Oct88-1Bel 6f :22 :453 1:122sy 6½ 10710 514 510 35½ 21 Carle J D1 Ⓕ 17500 76-21 SucyVoyge,LondonLss,ChngeblQun 8
26Sep88-6Bel 1⅟₁₆ Ⓣ:4721:1211:424fm 19 10710 53 95 78 68¾ Carle J D6 ⒻSAw31000 73-17 Sweet BlowPop,LadyTalc,Overrule 12
19Sep88-3Bel 6f :221 :454 1:114ft 7½ 10510 79 55 21½ 12¾ Carle J D1 Ⓕ 16500 80-18 LondonLss,ChngblQun,Wht'sHrNm 7
12Sep88-9Bel 6f :23 :471 1:124ft 15 10710 32 1½ 11½ 12 Carle J D11 Ⓕ 14000 75-20 LondonLss,FireDimond,DizzyDixie 12
Nov 15 Bel tr.t 3f ft :37 B Oct 21 Bel tr.t 3f ft :36 H

Pour Moi 1-N
Own.—Yagoda S 117
Gr. g. 3, by Jolly Johu—Elsada, by Iron Warrior
Br.—Yagoda Stanley (NY) 1988 21 3 4 2 $83,780
Tr.—Galimi Paul – N 1987 5 M 0 1 $3,120
Lifetime 26 3 4 3 $86,900 Turf 7 1 0 1 $18,490
Entered 7Dec88- 8 AQU
25Nov88-6Aqu 1⅛ :482 1:132 1:514ft 15 115 55 31 32 23½ Imparato J3 Aw31000 72-27 Ucncontonm,PorMo,John'sConcord 7
4Nov88-7Aqu 7f :224 :46 1:241ft 7 115 76 75½ 1½ 11¼ Imparato J1 SAw27000 80-16 Pour Moi, Forecart,YonkelYonkel 11
28Oct88-7Aqu 1⅛ Ⓣ:4941:1541:552fm 4½ 114 42½ 41½ 21 33½ Imparato J9 SAw29000 54-36 HorseplayerJoy,SaMrche,PourMoi 10
12Oct88-9Bel 1⅟₁₆ :463 1:112 1:434ft 16 114 76¼ 46½ 46½ 27½ Samyn J L3 SAw29000 75-21 DmondAnchor,PrM,HrrVnKnnchn 12
1Oct88-5Bel 7f :232 :473 1:253ft 33 115 1013 86½ 77 811 Lovato F Jr1 SAw27000 63-21 Agnoble,HerrVonKninchn,ActivWr 11
7Aug88-9Sar 1⅛ Ⓣ:5021:15 1:524fm 9¾ 112 118¾ 107¼ 117¾ 106¼ Cordr A Jr11 SAw29000 70-21 BrWtnss,UltmtAthorty,BowdnStrt 11
7Aug88—Very wide
17Jly88-7Bel 1⅟₁₆ Ⓣ:47 1:1141:441fm 16 112 98½ 62¼ 44 55½ Bailey J D10 SAw31000 69-29 ClosingBid,Mr.Beutiful,Don'tGivIn 11
7Jly88-7Bel 1⅜ Ⓣ:48 1:3632:153fm 27 113 711 816 76½ 57½ Velasquez J4 Aw29000 71-23 StrongRbound,LordLsr,PlcInThSun 9
Nov 15 Aqu 4f ft :503 B

Jiltavo 4-0
Own.—Trampe Patricia a 117
Ch. g. 4, by Octavo—Jilly's Rose, by Knightly Manner
Br.—Byrne Vincent Exec of (NY) 1988 14 2 1 1 $49,860
Tr.—Veitch Leo H – N 1987 5 M 3 1 $22,400
Lifetime 20 2 4 2 $72,260
24Nov88-4Aqu 6f :223 :462 1:114ft 20 117 61¾ 54½ 56½ 57 McCauley W H6 25000 74-26 Sutblforkng,Rdccho,OurHppyWrror 7
16Nov88-9Aqu 1 :45 1:094 1:354ft 50 117 1hd 2½ 97½ 1011½ Santagata N4 35000 75-14 RodGmJohnny,RodToPndr,FxyZd 12
10Nov88-1Aqu 6f :222 :45 1:111ft 21 115 62½ 66 812 814½ Arellano S2 45000 69-24 Temper Tanthem, Fugie, Cardenas 8
22Oct88-5Aqu 6f :221 :454 1:11 gd 18 117 11½ 11½ 1hd 33½ Arellano S1 SAw28000 82-18 Agnoble, Banquo, Jiltavo 7
3Jun88-7Bel 6f :223 :461 1:11 ft 20 117 64 83¾ 77 79¾ Doran K1 SAw28000 75-21 CavanghSpecil,ClerCtrcts,Dr.TimVil 9
28May88-9FL 6f :214 :444 1:094ft 18 119 22½ 21½ 33 711¼ Doran K 9 SGeo Barker 87-17 Kick Kahana, Hallen, Bold Mein 9
20Apr88-7Aqu 6f :23 :47 1:12 ft 5¼ 121 3nk 3½ 45½ 46½ Samyn J L 1 SAw32000 73-26 IKnewThat,MyPalooka,ClearCtrcts 7
23Mar88-6Aqu 7f :224 :454 1:234ft *2 122 2½ 2hd 24 49 Romero R P 5 SAw32000 73-24 PattiesBoy,LeadMan,ArcadeDncer 11
Dec 2 Bel tr.t 5f ft 1:031 B Oct 20 Bel 4f ft :484 H Oct 16 Bel 4f ft :49 H

Waterzip 5-N+
Own.—Paparo I 115
B. g. 3, by Herb Water—Northern Zip, by Norcliffe
Br.—Paparo Irving (NY) 1988 7 2 1 0 $37,520
Tr.—Imperio John M – + 1987 1 M 0 0
Lifetime 8 2 1 0 $37,520 Turf 2 0 0 0
24Sep88-9Bel 1⅟₁₆ Ⓣ:4641:1021:421fm 11 113 34 42¾ 75 99 Pezua J M3 SAw31000 76-15 ClosngBd,Jmmy'sBronc,GrndShkr 12
11Sep88-7Bel 6f :231 :463 1:11 ft 5¾ 113 11 1hd 12½ 13 Pezua J M2 SAw27000 84-21 Waterzip, Ivory Trade, Agnoble 9
17Jly88-7Bel 1⅟₁₆ Ⓣ:47 1:1141:441fm 30 111 2½ 1hd 66 68¾ Belmonte J F1 SAw31000 67-29 ClosingBid,Mr.Beutiful,Don'tGivIn 11
29Jun88-6Bel 1⅛ :464 1:121 1:523ft *2¼ 114 2½ 1hd 2½ 1nk Belmonte J F11 SMdn 64-22 Waterzip, ClassiWhip,BearWitness 12
20Jun88-2Bel 6f :23 :472 1:124ft *2 114 2hd 51¼ 64½ 55 Belmonte J F1 SMdn 70-20 Mr.Frosty,Mr.Vesuvio,DncforLions 11
22May88-6Bel 1⅟₁₆ :463 1:12 1:45 ft 43 115 11 1½ 13 2nk Belmonte J F10 SMdn 77-19 BowdoinStreet,Wtrzip,Don'tGivIn 11
14Apr88-2Aqu 6f :222 :462 1:123ft 7¾ 115 75½ 79½ 913 914½ Belmonte J F4 SMdn 63-21 CraftyReply,LoversVow,Sflverbck 11
21Sep87-4Bel 6f :224 :462 1:12 ft 19 1135 96½ 89½ 87 94 Ortega P Jr5 SMdn 75-15 Whodm,EnjoyTheMomnt,ThrGifts 14
21Sep87—Off slowly
Dec 4 Bel tr.t 4f ft :492 B ●Nov 23 Bel tr.t 3f ft :354 H ●Nov 15 Bel tr.t 5f ft 1:003 H Nov 10 Bel tr.t 4f ft :492 H

Late in the season, October to December, if no improving
3YOs can be found, handicappers prefer consistent older performers exiting open, higher-priced claiming races. Especially
impressive 4YOs.

Now to the Aqueduct field.

The Real Virginian. A 3YO, but not lightly raced, with nine-
teen starts, but not yet two allowance victories. But this gelding
beat open $30,000 claiming horses wire-to-wire in good time
November 13, and five days ago showed high early speed in a
state-bred stakes won by the multiple stakes winner Notebook.
It last won a state-bred allowance race June 23 at Belmont Park,
but has lost only two state-bred attempts since, while racing
well enough against high-priced open New York claiming horses.
Contender.

Scottie's Partner. A 6YO with 47 attempts is never a contender in a nonwinners allowance race. Out.

Beyond all Odds. This 3YO has a state-bred allowance win
in good time May 8. It has lost only two races under today's
conditions since, and ran well enough to merit consideration
June 3. It showed acceptable early speed (within two lengths)
versus open allowance company last out, before lacking room
and dropping out of it suddenly. Doubtful, but let's rate the horse
for pace.

Dr. Tim Vail. A 5YO away 35 days without an acceptable
5F workout since, this horse does not fit the conditions. Out.

London Lassa. A 4YO filly with 43 starts and ten wins, but
not even two allowance wins. Its open claiming-race victories
have been too cheap to qualify here. It returns to the races four
days after running horribly as the 3–1 favorite versus open
claimers, a positive sign. But the filly's basic class is low-grade,
and it lacks early speed. Out.

Pour Moi. This 3YO won its first allowance race two back,
in its twenty-fifth try. Hardly the lightly raced type handicappers prefer. Yet it came back with a surprising second-place
route finish under open allowance conditions. Let's give it the
benefit of serious doubts, and rate its 7F win November 4.

Jiltavo. This 4YO has been trying open high-priced claiming
horses, but with miserable returns. Nothing to recommend a
further look. Out.

Waterzip. A lightly raced 3YO away 75 days, this gelding
qualifies on form with a steady workout pattern that includes a

best-of-morning 5F drill on the Belmont training track November 15. We'll rate its front-running win at Belmont September 11. Contender.

Handicappers now survey the field for early-speed advantages. No horse has earned more than 5 speed points. When this happens, handicappers scan the fractional times of the high-point horses, The Real Virginian and Waterzip. The Real Virginian has a clear advantage on its rival, reaching the first and second calls of its key race a full second faster than Waterzip. The same advantage can be found consistently among several races at various tracks.

Now handicappers check the turn times of the key races. The Real Virginian has gone 23.1 on the turn, Waterzip 23.2. Notice that in its key race, Beyond All Odds traveled the turn in a sharp 22.3, another reason to rate the horse for pace.

Here are the unadjusted pace ratings for the four 3YOs we want to separate:

The Real Virginian	269	(Nov. 13)
Beyond All Odds	246	(June 3)
Pour Moi	248	(Nov. 4)
Waterzip	257	(Sept. 11)

With a decisive pace advantage, the best early speed, and the recent telltale win against open claiming horses, The Real Virginian shapes up as a highly probable winner. Trainer Kenneth Nesky has brought the gelding back in five days for this spot, a plus factor, to be sure.

As a final check, let's pace-rate the sharp May 8 Aqueduct win of Beyond All Odds. The rating is 267, two points below The Real Virginian's rating in the claiming-race win, a better field.

FIFTH RACE

Aqueduct

DECEMBER 8, 1988

6 FURLONGS.(InnerDirt). (1.08⅘) ALLOWANCE. Purse $24,000. 3-year-olds and upward. Foaled in New York State and approved by the New York State-Bred Registry which have never won two races other than Maiden, Claiming or Starter. Weights: 3-year-olds, 120 lbs.; older, 122 lbs. Non-winners of a race other than maiden or claiming since November 15 allowed 3 lbs.; of such a race since November 1, 5 lbs.

Value of race $24,000; value to winner $14,400; second $5,280; third $2,880; fourth $1,440. Mutuel pool $198,848. Exacta Pool $391,849.

Last Raced	Horse	Eqt.A.Wt	PP	St	¼	½	Str	Fin	Jockey	Odds $1
3Dec88 8Aqu7	The Real Virginian	3 115	1	3	12	13	14½	17	Migliore R	1.80
3Nov88 1Aqu9	Dr. Tim Vail	5 117	4	2	21	22	22½	2nk	Fox W I Jr	15.70
20Nov88 9Aqu5	Scottie's Partner	6 117	2	1	5½	42	3hd	32	Baird E T	23.80
25Nov88 6Aqu2	Pour Moi	3 117	5	7	4hd	3hd	46	412½	Imparato J	2.40
18Nov88 6Aqu7	Beyond all Odds	b 3 115	3	4	3hd	52½	52	5hd	Vega A	11.50
24Nov88 4Aqu5	Jiltavo	b 4 117	6	5	6½	63	63	63	Santagata N	5.70
24Sep88 9Bel9	Waterzip	3 115	7	6	7	7	7	7	Thibeau R J	3.20

OFF AT 2:17. Start good. Won driving. Time, :23⅘, :47⅘, 1:12 Track fast.

$2 Mutuel Prices:

1–(A)–THE REAL VIRGINIAN		5.60	3.60	2.80
4–(D)–DR. TIM VAIL			10.20	6.00
2–(B)–SCOTTIE'S PARTNER				7.60

$2 EXACTA 1–4 PAID $52.60.

Ro. g. by The Cool Virginian—Easter Moment, by For The Moment. Trainer Nesky Kenneth A. Bred by Rence Bay Stables (NY).

THE REAL VIRGINIAN opened a clear advantage shortly after the start to make all the pace, then drew off through the stretch while being kept to pressure. DR. TIM VAIL raced in the attending position but could make no gain on the top one. SCOTTIE'S PARTNER saved ground. POUR MOI was wide. JILTAVO and WATERZIP were outrun.

Post-race script. If horses are moving from open claiming races to state-bred stakes competition, the standards should be tightened. Now the claiming races should reveal victories at the $35,000 level or higher. Moreover, the horses should show multiple allowance wins under state-bred conditions, not just one.

And importantly, now older horses, 4YOs and 5YOs especially, may hold a decisive edge against the younger 3YOs, notably if the 3YOs' claiming-race wins have occurred in races restricted to 3YOs. The exception can be 3YOs whose pace ratings at the distance, or a related distance, are significantly higher (10 points) than the older contenders'.

CHAPTER IX

Recreational Betting

AN ASPECT OF the racetrack experience that chimes loudly with peoples' ringing approval is the individual freedom it condones.

To be one's own master, free to pursue ideas, free to implement personal methods, free to indulge tastes, free to make choices, free to take risks, even free to commit mistakes, serves as an almost hallucinating antidote to the broadly conformist and restrictive world at large.

If the practice of handicapping qualifies as a greatly individual endeavor—and it does—the habits of recreational betting constitute intensely personal and intimate acts. The racetrack bet, in fact, arouses the individual's innate sense of privacy, a territory marked private property, which others should not dare to invade.

The betting windows are not only everyone's private domain, but unscientific parimutuel wagering is perfectly compatible with the recreational motives of racetrack participation. Recreational betting, after all, consists of wagering exactly as one pleases, and nothing more, hardly an unimportant thread weaving its seam along a day at the races. It's nobody's business how a person bets.

There is, however, an unsavory downside. The racetrack would personify an unmatched haven of adult recreation if the participants did not lose so much money on their occasional excursions there.

For the short run—of a season, of two seasons, or three—it must be unhesitatingly conceded, it does not much matter. Recreational racetrack bettors can tolerate recreational losses—the price, if you will, of playing the game.

But as the seasons extend into years, the years into decades, the decades into adult lifetimes, recreational racetrack losses accumulate in an increasingly annoying way. In the aggregate, small steady financial losses amount to significant personal losses. A narrow but unrelenting, unforgiving stream of losing racetrack bets creates simultaneously an inexorably dulling enthusiasm for the recreation that results in the losses.

In consequence, many recreational bettors leave the racetrack, desert the sport. The same people who so exult in individual freedom—young adults especially—do not as much like playing a difficult risk-decision game in which they take a repeated financial thrashing.

Business organizations that have monitored racetrack markets have estimated a turnover among racing's casual customers of approximately 20 percent per year. That is, one of five recreational bettors depart the scene annually. Within five years the recreational market virtually regenerates itself. The explanation is a natural attrition among recreational customers haplessly unversed on the intricacies of effective handicapping and parimutuel wagering.

It's instructive to pursue the racetrack-betting realities a little further.

Imagine the upscale customer—educated, affluent, independent, upwardly mobile, a member of the professional-managerial-technical classes, with regular intervals of leisure time but with varied personal interests to engage. The racetrack appeals as one activity among several.

If upscale per capita wagering can be estimated at $300 a day, on average this kind of recreational bettor can expect to lose roughly $50 a trip. That amount reflects the typical racetrack take (16 percent), the crowd's aggregate losses during the day. Untutored individuals should do no worse long-term.

If the upscale customer attends the races twenty outings a year, he loses $1000.

On gas, parking, admission, the *Daily Racing Form*, track program, and refreshments, the track's customer spends another $12, minimum. Annual cost, $320. A family head spends more, and loses more. So does a couple.

Parimutuel wagering only, within five years the upscale customer loses $5000, a negligible cost for an exciting hobby. The upscale customer who bets $500 daily loses $75 a day minimum, $1500 a year, and $7500 within five years, still a tolerable sum.

But something else has happened. The pastime is no longer so exciting. The sweet smell of success is gone. Nobody enjoys losing money. A defensive, protective betting shield begins to envelop the proceedings.

As recreational bettors learn they cannot cope well enough by applying their limited knowledge and skill, long shots look increasingly tempting, the exotics irresistibly inviting. From that impulsively defensive threshold, matters deteriorate more rapidly. The customer falls hopelessly behind. Occasional windfalls only interrupt an irreversibly negative cash flow.

The upscale customer inevitably feels beaten back. Many quit the game.

The saving alternative is so simple, so ironic.

So often unformful and apparently unpredictable, horse racing long-term is an amazingly formful game of percentages, probabilities, and patterns. A pedestrian accumulation of knowledge and skill, of handicapping and parimutuel wagering—a few brief courses of study, so to speak—can transform a seemingly complex sport into a lively intellectual challenge game at which skillful practitioners can win, sometimes unexpectedly large amounts of money. It pays to learn how to play this game.

The irony attaches to the dual requirements of effective handicapping and successful parimutuel wagering.

But while the art of handicapping is perceived by racegoers as a relatively static discipline that might be mastered by interested parties as a function of time and experience, money management and betting at the races are seen as rarefied elusive pursuits that defy the best efforts of all comers.

The reality is just the opposite.

Effective handicapping is a highly dynamic mental challenge characterized by numerous factors that interact in multitudinous ways, depending in part on the abilities and capacities of horses, in part on the talents and maneuvers of horsemen, and in part on the circumstances of races. No situation is the same as the preceding situation, however similar. Every race presents a slightly different puzzle.

Methods and techniques of handicapping must be continuously amplified and refined, as must the tools of any dynamic discipline.

In comparison, effective money management and betting at the races is practically cut and dried. Once handicapping decisions have been contemplated, the same wagering principles, guidelines, and techniques apply over and over. The old saw that once racetrack fans learn how to handicap, their level of success depends on how well they manage their money, is desperately wrong-headed. It turns reality upside down.

The cliché is true only in the sense that foolish betting can subvert effective handicapping. Anyone who cares can learn quickly enough how to manage money and how to bet intelligently at the races. The principles, guidelines, and techniques to be presented here can be accepted as maxims. The sources of instruction are incontrovertible: mathematical truth and empirically validated fact.

As mathematician and handicapping author Dick Mitchell has observed, "The fundamental principles of horse-race wagering derive from mathematical truth. They are absolute, and should not be violated. The good news is that racegoers need only learn them once. What was true a thousand years ago is true today. What is true today will be true a thousand years from now."

The bad news is that not all the principles, guidelines, and techniques of racetrack betting will prove compatible with individual temperament, or recreational betting, which, as we have admitted, consists of whatever the individual prefers to do.

The traditional resistance of the racetrack customer to instruction on money management and parimutuel betting is based on firm adherence to the essential character of the recreational approach—unfettered individual freedom. But a middle ground appears tenable, and desirable.

If racing's customers can suspend belief in the merits and desirability of individual enterprise, suspend disbelief in the oppression and undesirability of formal guidance in trackside money matters, then not only might demonstrably effective betting techniques be incorporated into individual style, but the individual might also continue to practice much of what he most enjoys.

At the least, the principles, guidelines, and techniques promoted in the discussion to follow will cut losses in the long run. In a positive situation, where knowledge and skill have reached a threshold that begs success, they will maximize seasonal profits and optimize the rate of growth of the bankroll.

The overwhelming change in racetrack betting, of course, has been the advent of exotic wagering. To suggest this guide is sanguine about the possibilities of exotic wagering for recreational handicappers is bald understatement. Combination bets like the exacta, the quinella, and the serial triple extend to casual customers the greatest wagering opportunities in the history of the sport.

Now the recreational bettor not only stands a legitimate chance to accumulate consistent but moderate profits in the win pools, but a few times each season the same recreational bettor can expect to supplement those profits with unexpected windfalls.

To amplify an engaging trend of thought, it's entirely feasible nowadays that a deliberate hobbyist can end the racing season upward of $10,000 in the black, and without risking the budget. Excellent recreational handicappers repeat the achievement regularly.

Before leaping to the types of racetrack wagers, and the best ways to come to terms with each, recreational bettors should exercise patience with the following section. Of the several laws of parimutuel wagering, the first should be axiomatic among recreational customers. Professional handicappers too. Never bet the underlays.

UNDERLAYS AND OVERLAYS

A shocking omission from the popular discourse on thoroughbred racing has been the distinction between a handicapper's selection and the actual bet.

"Who do you like in the fifth?" is familiar parlance to anyone that has visited a racetrack more than once.

I like so-and-so, ushers an immediate response.

Why?

Because of these very reasons.

Only rarely does a racetrack inquisitor bother to wonder whether so-and-so will be a fair or unfair bet at the probable odds.

Official and unofficial handicapping information services

contribute mightily to the same vicious paradox. All offer selections, but none define the acceptable odds.

As a result, racegoers bet too much money on too many underlays, which is the main reason intelligent, well-informed, competent handicappers are unable to beat the races.

An underlay is simply an overbet horse. The horse's real chances to win are not as strong as the odds suggest. More money is squandered at the races annually on this kind of miscue than on any other half-dozen.

What recreational handicappers must understand—and the notion apparently is awfully difficult to grasp—is that even when underlays win, the bettors lose.

Consider again our upscale racing customer, now $50 in arrears for the day, but determined to recoup with a $50 win bet on an absolutely good thing at even-money in the feature.

The even-money shot wins by a half length in a driving finish. The delighted bettor collects 50 bucks in profit, and assures his buddies post-haste he is dead-even for the day.

That horse was an underlay, snaps a friend, in a tone intimating the successful bettor had actually made a mistake.

Nothing's an underlay if horses win, comes the snappy retort, in a tone presupposing the matter is closed to further debate.

For discussion's sake, let's assume the even-money favorite was one of three contenders, but possessed a clear edge in the past performances, a quite typical racetrack scenario. An oddsmaker assigns a 40 percent probability to the even-money shot, and approximately 20 percent apiece to the other main contenders.

Fair odds on a horse having a 40 percent chance to win is 3–2. The fair odds are calculated by dividing 40 into 100 (2½), and subtracting one (1½, or 3–2).

But the public overbets the horse, offering 1–1 when the fair odds are 3–2.

By betting $50 at even-money, the upscale bettor has won $50, when he should have won $75, the profit on a legitimate 3–2 shot for a $50 wager. By taking even-money, the bettor surrendered fully one third ($25) of the fair-value profit on that horse.

Now consider what has happened after our upscale bettor has repeated that kind of wager twenty times.

On each occasion the horse has a legitimate 40 percent chance to win, meaning the horse can be expected to win two of five attempts long-term. In 20 attempts, the horse wins 8 races, loses 12.

At $50 to win, the eight successes gross $800, a net of $400. The twelve losses cost $600.

The bottom line is a $200 loss after twenty wagers. On a $1000 investment ($50 × 20), the rate of loss is 20 percent.

I hope recreational handicappers can appreciate the bottom line. But do they?

What happens as a result of any particular race is merely a part of a pattern that will have positive or negative long-term consequences. If handicappers are willing to assume the same types of bets will be repeated frequently throughout the season, the upscale bettor who imagined he got even for an afternoon by taking even-money on a legitimate 3–2 shot actually fell further behind for the season.

When that type of wager has been repeated 100 times, the bettor has won 40 races, a $2000 profit, but has lost 60 races, a $3000 loss.

The bottom line is a $1000 loss.

Never bet the underlays. It's the first axiom of parimutuel wagering. The more frequently underlays are bet, the larger the long-term loss. No matter how expert the handicapping, only a disastrous fate awaits bettors who play too many underlays. It's a crucial argument. Betting underlays explains why talented handicappers lose. Betting underlays explains why expert handicappers win less than they are capable of winning.

How do recreational handicappers learn to recognize underlays?

They do not learn the skill mathematically, with formulas, charts, slide rules, and math paraphernalia, which in the best of circumstances provide imprecise estimates of accurate odds.

The skill develops intuitively, with know-how and experience.

A key step is merely to ask, hypothetically, if the race were run a hundred times, how often would this horse win? A victory rate greater than 50 percent is disallowed arbitrarily, such that no horse can be expected to win more than half the races (few do).

A horse that is expected to win half the hundred races has a 50 percent probability of winning each race. The fair-value odds each time will be 1–1, or even money. Anytime the horse is offered at less than even money, that's an underlay, and no bet.

Here are several win probabilities and fair-value odds that recreational handicappers can rely upon as betting lines. Commit the values to memory.

Win Probabilities	Fair-Value Odds
50%	1–1
40%	3–2
33%	2–1
28%	5–2
25%	3–1
20%	4–1
15%	6–1
10%	9–1
5%	19–1

The win probabilities are estimates and contain error, but are not wild guesses. Handicappers depend upon the sum of their knowledge, information, and experience to set personal betting lines.

If handicappers believe the favorite should be expected to beat today's field under today's racing conditions about one third of the time (33 percent), the fair-value odds will be 2–1. If the favorite is offered at 8–5, no play; at 2–1, maybe; at 5–2, an overlay, and a sensible bet.

The estimates provided above are gross, but serve the purpose. Finer estimates can be intuited, as handicappers prefer. If handicappers believe a horse should win less than 25 percent of the races but more than 20 percent, the fair-value odds would be 7–2. If greater than 33 percent but less than 40 percent, 8–5 or 9–5 would be acceptable.

Once a win probability has been estimated, fair-value odds can be calculated simply, by dividing the win probability into 100 and subtracting 1. The habit is easily formed, with practice.

Estimating fair odds and identifying underlays in rather predictable races—where two, three, or four horses form the main contention—can be sticky, as the contenders will not often be evenly matched. One may have a fine edge on another, the second an edge on the leftovers. But what edge?

Best estimates err on the conservative side. In predictable races, underestimates of horses' winning chances are better than overestimates. Fair-value odds will be slightly higher. Underlays will be more frequently avoided. If handicappers are uncertain whether horses enjoy a 33 percent chance of winning, or a 28 percent chance, choose the lower estimate. Acceptable odds will be 5–2, not 2–1.

Where win probabilities and odds lines support recreational handicapping especially well are the contentious races. By definition, in a contentious field four, five, or six horses have a relatively equivalent chance to win.

The predicament erects certain betting barriers that should not be violated.

Where four or five horses share an equitable chance of winning, none deserves more than a 20 percent slice of the probability pie. Minimum acceptable odds on any will be 4–1. In contentious races containing four or five major contenders, the favorite is invariably an underlay. No bet.

In fact, no horse offered below 4–1 in a contentious race should be bet. As a rule, main contenders at odds of 8–1 or better should be bet. Multiple bets are appropriate if the odds allow. Split the normal bet size in two, or bet 60 percent of a normal amount on the higher-odds horse, 40 percent on the lower odds horse. Or, split the normal wager in three parts, 50 percent on the highest odds horse, 30 percent on the second highest, and 20 percent on the third highest.

If a contentious race contains six contenders, none warrants more than 15 percent of the probabilities. So none is acceptable at odds below 6–1. Favorites and low-priced contenders should be eliminated.

Contentious races elicit a wider variation in opinion among the bettors, such that some horses will be underlays, some overlays. Recreational handicappers can beat these races only by avoiding the underlays persistently and taking the overlays intelligently.

An overlay is an underbet horse. Now the horse's real chances are better than the odds suggest.

Although handicappers beat the races only by backing overlays consistently, that means low-priced overlays, from 8–5 to 8–1, and thousands of recreational handicappers abuse the principle by jumping to a wrong conclusion.

A longshot is not an overlay.

Almost invariably, longshots are horses with extremely low probabilities of winning. Longshots may be overlays, but most are underlays. Numerous empirical studies have demonstrated the point. The crowd has a tendency to overbet its longshots. Even when they win, many longshots pay less than they should. So betting overlays must not be confused with betting longshots.

Moreover, longshots that are overlays win too infrequently to be supported regularly. In the short run, longshot overlays are impractical overlays.

Among horses having a middling chance to win, fair-value odds from 7–1 to 15–1, recreational handicappers should insist on a 50 percent overlay.

A legitimate 8–1 shot should be offered at 12–1 or thereabouts. A 15–1 horse should bring more than 20–1.

The horses are lower-probability types, or higher risks, and win less than frequently. Good value replaces fair value. Fortunately, the crowd makes its most glaring betting blunders on medium-priced horses.

If horses have only a Chinaman's chance—a 5 percent probability, or such—then demand gigantic odds, say 30–1. These probabilities arise infrequently, but they do occur. As the losing streaks can be ghastly, secure top value from the occasional winners.

If a handicapper's main selection has roughly a 20 percent chance of winning (4–1), and the public offers 8–1, that's a 100 percent overlay, and a terrific bet. At lower odds, below 6–1, a 20 percent overlay is adequate.

Juxtaposing winning chances and betting odds is the ultimate decision-making problem of comprehensive handicapping. Few recreational handicappers, and not many regulars, are especially proficient at it, as the overwhelming tendency at the races has been toward making selections, not decisions.

Making selections should not be abandoned, as picking winners is the fine art of handicapping, but when selections become underlays, they must be forsaken. The most likely winner of the season is not a good bet if it is not a fair price.

On those everyday occasions when underlays surface, effective decision-making makes all the difference. Competent handicappers who learn how to spot strong-probability overlays, as well as how to bet them shrewdly, have the odds in their corner.

If they persist in avoiding underlays and betting overlays without letup, eventually recreational handicappers will be among the winners. Only good things can happen long-haul.

A blunt reminder here is appropriate.

No method of money management or parimutuel wagering is capable of transforming a losing game into a winning game. That's a mathematical truth. In other words, a deficient handicapper, but excellent bettor, equals an eventual loser.

So guidance on recreational betting must be carefully couched.

Never bet the underlays.

Bet the high-probability overlays as smartly as know-how and experience allows.

Make decisions, not merely selections.

But become a proficient handicapper before all else.

THE ONLY TWO WAYS TO BEAT THE RACES

The heading portends no sensational revelations. No great secrets. No shortcuts.

By all that is rational, elegant, and wise about the great game of handicapping, there are but two ways to beat the races:

1. Prime bets to win on outstanding selections at acceptable odds.
2. Value bets in the exotics, and to less extent in the win pool, combining key horses and other attractive contenders.

The first is a long-term investment strategy, based upon established handicapping proficiency.

The second is a short-term risk-value decision strategy, dependent upon handicapping expertise, situational factors, and sheer fortune in combination.

The trick, if there is one, is to implement both strategies concurrently.

The integration of win wagering and exotic betting satisfies complementary purposes. The first of these is the competent handicapper's ability to accumulate substantial profits in both directions. The second sets the practitioner on a parallel course with racing's realities; on any afternoon's program a couple of races offer outstanding win bets, and several others extend attractive possibilities in the exotics.

To engage one slice of that reality but not the other puts handicappers on a collision course with the game; the inevitable crash causes debilitating mental and psychological distress. A prime bet to win is combined in exotic combinations only, and all is lost as the horse wins but the combinations fail. Or a potential key horse in extravagant exotic combinations is fully supported to win instead, and a truly exotic combination materializes, paying boxcars.

A complementary strategy of win wagering and exotic betting supports all the affirmative purposes of playing the races, and protects bettors simultaneously from the ruinous implications of an incomplete plan.

Separate bankrolls are preferred but unnecessary. A single bankroll, however, should be realistically large, and separated from income—even discretionary income—a tactic not one recreational horseplayer in fifty follows.

For recreational bettors, I recommend a minimal bank of $1500, set aside for racetrack speculations before the season begins. Twenty-five hundred dollars would be preferable. Of the bankroll, approximately two thirds should be targeted for exotic wagering, one third for systematic win betting. This is a radical departure from traditional strategy, but not only has exotic wagering overtaken the game, that's where recreational bettors will find the bulk of a good season's profits.

The cost of the hobby is sizable, no doubt, but certainly no greater than the annual expenses of golf, sailing, skiing, traveling, or other leisure pursuits. Racetrack hobbyists enjoy the singular advantage of indulging in a game where, as a result of performing well, they might win double or triple the costs of playing.

How much money can proficient handicappers expect to earn in a season? The question falls from the lips of recreational bettors almost instinctively.

It depends. And in the age of exotic wagering, seasonal profits depend on a confluence of factors not readily sorted into neatly stacked piles.

Recreational handicappers must understand that while the profits derived from competent win wagering on outstanding selections can be predicted reliably, profits from exotic wagers cannot.

The reason should be plain. Profits associated with win wagering on prime selections derive directly from knowledge and skill in handicapping, and systematic betting. If the knowledge base remains relatively stable and the betting controlled, the profit margin should stay predictable.

Profits associated with exotic wagering result not only from knowledge and skill in handicapping, but also from situational factors, unpatterned betting, and sheer fortune. Next season this year's prosperous handicappers may experience somewhat altered situations and a heavier dose of bad fortune. Exotic profits will dwindle and may disappear. Every once in a while the best efforts of proficient handicappers cannot withstand the caprice of exotic wagering.

Although systematic win wagering on prime selections cannot approach the heady profits exotic combinations supply, recreational handicappers should not abandon it. The profits win wagering does supply will be steady and predictable for competent handicappers. When the season's outcomes of exotic betting have proved perverse, a negative flow, the profits obtained by successful win wagering will be greatly reinforcing.

When handicappers are hitting on all cylinders for a significant portion of the core season, the profit stream literally rushes like the tide. Happily, it happens.

The remainder of this section treats the various types of parimutuel wagers in practical ways. The emphases will be on tactics and techniques, with some explanatory discussion. As the betting habits of recreational handicappers in the exotics have been as a rule little short of awful, just about everybody might consider the material a point of departure for making a change.

PRIME BETS TO WIN

A standard of excellence in handicapping is the ability to earn a 20 percent rate of profit on prime bets to win. A prime bet means a high-probability contender that has a clear decisive edge on the field and has been offered at a fair price. Numerous handicappers are talented enough to satisfy the 20 percent standard, but few do.

Consider the following performance standards:

Win %	Avg. Odds	Edge	Dollar Return
30	5–2	5%	$1.05
33	5–2	15%	1.15
35	5–2	22.5%	1.22
40	2.3–1	32%	1.32

These are the attainable goals achieved by successful handicappers in the win pools.

Handicappers who win 30 percent of their prime bets at average odds of 5–2 share a 5 percent edge on the game. For every dollar wagered to win, they receive $1.05 in return, a 5 percent profit.

A handicapper who can win as frequently as the crowd—33 percent—but at 5–2 odds (the public averages 1.6–1), boasts a splendid 15 percent edge on the game. As Dick Mitchell has pointed out, by improving handicapping proficiency 10 percent, profits triple. This is the attainable goal all recreational handicappers should set sails to achieve: 33 percent winners, average odds of 5–2, a 15 percent edge and profit margin. The reality for the casual majority is closer to 30 percent winners at odds of 5–2, a mere 5 percent profit margin.

The column marked "Edge" is important. A handicapper's true edge on the game suggests the optimal bet-size. It's the edge divided by the odds to $1.00. If the handicapper has a 5 percent and the horse is 5–2, the optimal bet is 5/2.5, or 2 percent.

To bet more is to bet too much in relation to actual proficiency, and guarantees a long-term loss. Overly aggressive betting is ruinous in horse racing. To bet less is to win at a rate of profit less than actual proficiency allows, a sad but not desperate circumstance.

The realities of win wagering can be converted to a betting plan for recreational handicappers willing to assume 30 percent proficiency on prime selections. Proceeding cautiously, those handicappers can bet 4 percent of a $500 win bank. First bet is $20. Better still, pretend the $500 is $1000, a 50 percent margin, and bet 4 percent of $1000. First bet is $40.

The win bank is recalculated every racing day, and the betting plan continued.

Each win wager will be 4 percent of the win bank, until handicappers have collected enough data to indicate win proficiency has been underestimated and the bet-size can be raised.

If recreational handicappers have demonstrated they can convert 33 percent of their prime bets at average odds of 5–2, the new bet-size becomes one half the edge (15 percent), rounded down, or 7 percent. It's safer to underestimate proficiency than to overestimate it. Overestimation, as we have seen, leads ultimately to ruin.

Profits for the season will depend upon actual proficiency, number of bets, and bet-size. Regrettably, the initial profits will not be huge. If three prime horses a day are supported, on average, and handicappers attend 50 days, 150 bets will be placed. Profits will equal the total amount wagered multiplied by the handicapper's edge.

A practical alternative to fixed-percentage wagering to win has been suggested by the indomitable Andrew Beyer, and the strategy is strongly associated with the individual's confidence in his handicapping judgment.

Beyer argues that handicapper's opinions range from strong to weak on various horses, and the corresponding bets should range from strong to weak.

In Beyer's formulations, the ceiling bet is equal to the largest amount the handicapper has invested in the past year, to be risked a few times a season, when the horses and all the circumstances of the race appear to be ideal. From the ceiling bet, bets are scaled downward in accord with the strength of the bettor's opinions.

Beyer's strategy assumes recreational handicappers can distinguish best bets from riskier bets fairly consistently. Those who can will collect greater profits in the win pools by Beyer's approach. Handicappers who too often lose the big bets but win the small ones will end as long-suffering losers, even though overall handicapping proficiency may be satisfactory.

Recreational handicappers who have experienced persistent problems with money management in win wagering are encouraged to implement the fixed-percentage approach for a year.

Maintain accurate records of the prime bets. Profits may prove less than provocative, but handicappers will have begun to bet with discipline, and will have learned valuable lessons about their actual handicapping proficiency.

They will know at last whether they are betting a winning hand. If not, bettors can improve their knowledge and skill in handicapping, and try again.

If actually winning systematic profits, the win bank can be enlarged, and the bet-size will be greater. Those recreational handicappers will not only be gathering the profits they are capable of making, the amounts will be meaningful at last. As the seasons slide by, proceedings in the win pools should only improve, an ideal state of affairs.

VALUE BETS TO WIN

Value bets to win involve horses having a handicapper's reasonably good chance, but at conspicuously generous odds. The odds will be twice as great as expected, or longer than that. Instead of fair value, the handicapper perceives excellent value, perhaps outrageous value.

The horses do not figure convincingly, and many will not be first choices. Betting decisions remain equivocal, but the price exerts an undeniable pull.

In certain situations, as in contentious races, the horses may be mild first choices offered upward of 8–1. That's value, as the horses can be expected to win at least once in eight attempts, probably more than once.

Or, the value bets may be unexpected overlays at 10–1 or better in contentious fields where lukewarm first and second choices have been overbet.

In predictable races, first choices may be severely overbet, as public choices, too, leaving the handicapper's second or third alternative as an outstanding board attraction.

Or false favorites may be ridiculously overbet, such that a pair of reasonable alternatives go to the post at very attractive prices.

Or an angle horse in a relatively unpredictable race may be offered at irresistible odds.

Value bets are characterized by lower probabilities of winning than prime bets, so losing runs can be extended. If a horse has roughly a 20 percent chance (4–1), actual odds should be 6–1. A horse that has a 15 percent chance (6–1), should be 10–1 on the board, or better. A horse having a 10 percent chance (9–1) should be 15–1, minimum.

Bet-size should be a portion of the prime bet to win, not an equivalent amount. Following Beyer, stronger opinions can receive 50 percent of prime, weaker opinions 10 to 20 percent.

If a fixed percentage win-wagering strategy has been employed for prime bets, slice the percentage bet in half. If multiple horses are win values, distribute the respective betting amounts after 50 percent of the prime bet has been determined.

It's an amateurish mistake to risk as much capital on low-probability horses as successful handicappers invest on high-probability horses. The larger numbers of losses will cut the profit margin on prime bets irrationally.

The greater the public odds, the likelier horses having the handicapper's reasonable chance should be perceived as value bets in the win pool, and not merely as contenders in exotic combinations. Authentic longshots, odds of 13–1 upward, should invariably be supported to win. If recreational handicappers prefer a 25–1 shot enough to key the outsider in multiple exacta combinations, the horse warrants a value bet to win as well. As noted, exacta combinations containing longshots are regularly overbet, and pay less than bettors desire. With value bets to win, what you see is what you get.

How will recreational handicappers know whether value bets to win are tossing real winnings, or losses?

It's strictly an empirical question. Handicappers must keep a record of the value bets and study the results. A year's worth of results on 8–1 shots, or greater, reveals the trend. Two year's data tell a fairly accurate story.

The log-keeping on value bets is not especially inconveniencing, but most recreational handicappers probably will be too busy, distracted, or uninterested to bother.

Most will remain curious on the issue, but will never really know.

BETTING TO PLACE AND SHOW

Whether expert or novice, mass confusion thwarts veritably all attempts to earn money at the races in the place and show holes, which is possible but improbable.

Which of the following two horses is a decent place bet? Show bet?

	Horse A	Horse B	Totals
Odds	4–5	11–1	
Win	8293	1251	18,223
Place	2560	903	9214
Show	1570	712	6558

At 11–1 to win, Horse B is a terrible bet to place or show, but is exactly the prospect racetrack bettors forever are supporting as potential runners-up.

If the odds-on favorite runs out, they assert, Horse B will be a great place and show price. Nonsense. If Horse A finishes last, B remains an awful bet to place or show.

On close inspection, the odds-on favorite here is an outstanding bet to place or show.

The correct math compares a horse's percentage of the total win pool to its percentages of the total place and show pools. If the place and show percentages are significantly lower than the win percentage, the conclusion is that the crowd has committed egregious mistakes in the runners-up pools.

The technique is based upon the public's well-documented ability to estimate a horse's winning chances exceedingly well. But the crowd makes glaring errors in the place and show pools. Handicappers are encouraged to capitalize on precisely those extravagant blunders.

Horse A has 44 percent of the win pool, but just 27 percent of the place pool, and 23 percent of the show pool.

Horse B has only 7 percent of the win pool, but 10 percent of the place pool, and 11 percent of the show pool.

Horse A is underbet to place and show. Horse B is overbet to place and show.

Horse B is prototypical of longshots in the place and show pools. Longshots are notoriously overbet there. Anything above 8–1 is almost universally an awful bet to place or show.

The message is plain. Recreational handicappers should not bet longshots to place or show. They are probably underlays in those pools.

Alternately, low-priced favorites can often become overlays to place and show. Look for horses like A in the illustration. The discrepancies between their percentages of win money and place-show monies will be obviously large. Approximately a 15 to 20 percent discrepancy will be large enough. The more extreme the discrepancy, the more money handicappers should wager. Discrepancies to show are more frequent and more sizable than discrepancies to place.

The real reason many competent handicappers bet to place— few bother betting to show—is unrelated to the math. It's strictly psychological.

Competent handicappers learn soon enough that when best bets do not win, they regularly finish second. It's fun, and reassuring, to cash, notably on selections especially well liked. The regular cashing also interrupts loss skeins.

When key horses do finish second, place bets recoup win bets, with some spillage of profit. Records might indicate that much more money would be collected if handicappers bet to win exclusively, but cash flow counts, and may be next to everything for handicappers operating on too thin a budget.

Recreational handicappers generally bet to place and show for defensive, protective reasons. This is perfectly acceptable, of course, the proper motive for place-show wagering among truly casual customers. As long as the intent is not confused with making profits, it's noble enough. No one likes to part with the pocket money.

But for recreational handicappers who engage in handicapping as a hobby, attending the races on weekends as a matter of routine, defensive betting in the place-show pools betrays a pathos best eradicated. The dual purposes of recreational handicapping are fun and profits. Profits are equally soothing to the spirit as having fun. The objective is to win.

And that's the real reason place-show wagering should be abandoned by all but the occasional visitors. For recreational handicappers, it's simply impractical. Only negligible profits are feasible, even in the long run, unless unusually large sums are risked. Defensive betting will not limit losses, as intended, but it will reduce potential profits.

Who needs it?

Besides, a few interesting studies of exotic wagering have already demonstrated that where handicapping proficiency can produce profits by betting to place or to show, the same proficiency can produce significantly greater profits by coupling the horses in exactas, a topic that best signifies the times, and to which we delightedly turn.

EXACTAS

Professional handicappers may meddle with exactas or not, as a matter of individual style or temperament. But for recreational handicappers the exacta represents the greatest advance in a lifetime of racetrack speculation. Racegoers should gaze on a menu of exactas fondly, knowing the combination bets will be the source of their most delectable financial bonanzas.

Because exactas have emerged as critical to the recreational handicapper's game, racegoers should determine to master the intricacies of the wager as best they can. The plea is hardly idle conversation, as some of the dumbest betting practices at the races surround exacta wagering.

First, the exacta supports the following crucial handicapping and betting purposes:

1. Converts underlays in the win pool to overlays in the combination pools, when key horses are combined intelligently with other attractive contenders.
2. Supports the use of a wide array of handicapping information to analyze the same race in various ways.
3. Permits the accumulation of substantial profits in the short run, of a day, a week, a few weeks, a month, or a race meeting.
4. At relatively small risk, allows competent handicappers to cover all the real possibilities in contentious races.
5. Provides recreational customers the complementary rewards they seek during a day at the races, high action and potentially high mutuels.

That's a dynamite list. Exotic wagering opportunities have literally altered the character of the racetrack experience, and in positive ways never before approached.

The exacta first appeared at Hollywood Park in 1969. Multiple exactas on a card soon followed. So did subspecies of the innovative wager, including the quinella, the trifecta, and the pick-six. New exotic wagers are merely a matter of time and imagination.

The newness of exacta wagering has created its own peculiar downside for racing's faithful customers. Few of them know how to attack the bet. Popular strategies are disastrous. The ignorance is costing racing's customers unnecessary bundles. Characteristically, little has been done by a reluctant industry to educate its attendance base. The omission assures more customers will continue to squander more money in exacta combinations than they should.

What follows can be accepted by recreational handicappers as acceptable bylaws of exacta wagering. Bylaws are not fixed, but regulatory. Out of chaos and ignorance, bylaws bring order and discipline. That facilitates positive developments, helping members of the group to conduct their business in more rational, orderly ways.

Exacta bettors commit three mortal mistakes every racing day.

The put too many overbet favorites on top, thereby creating numerous exacta underlays as well.

They buy exacta boxes connecting three horses—baseballs—routinely, usually a nonsense bet.

They bet exacta wheels, absolutely a nonsense bet.

From the maladies spring the remedies.

1. Overbet favorites should be used primarily on the bottom of exacta combinations.
2. Exacta boxes make sense only when both sides represent overlays.
3. Key horses should be coupled in partial wheels only, limited to other contenders that are overlays.

To recall, if favorites are overbet, their prospects are not as favorable as the odds indicate. The underlay generalizes to exacta combinations as well. Exactas are low probability events. Underlays must be avoided.

Not only that, in exotic wagering, good value substitutes for fair value. The overbet favorite on the bottom often provides precisely that serving of generous value. Overbet favorites regularly finish a disappointing second, notably in full fields.

Three-horse baseballs and exacta wheels collapse under the same crushing disadvantage. Too many of the combinations will be underlays, and others will offer negligible value. In low-probability events, underlays and value-poor combinations are akin to swallowing tiny dosages of poison. Another slow, painful passing.

As we have seen before, a pair of 2–1 shots has slightly less than a 10 percent chance of occurring in either direction. A pair of 3–1 shots occurs just 5 percent of the time. A coupling having a 5–1 horse atop a 5–2 horse occurs only three times in one hundred races.

Exacta reversals must promise positive value both ways. Partial wheels can include all the tantalizing overlays having a handicapper's fair chance, but no pushes, no underlays.

If recreational handicappers will abandon the baseballs, wheels, and overbet favorites on top, at least seven exacta strategies regularly contribute a generous compensation.

1. Pairs of medium-priced horses represent the best exacta overlays of all.

Pairs of longshots are severely overbet in exacta wagering, but pairs of medium-priced horses are normally underbet. Many of the combinations pay extraordinary sums. In wide-open races, box the middle-class horses whenever they rate as reasonably strong contenders.

If a first choice in a contentious field is medium-priced, it's a natural exacta key in boxes covering other underbet contenders. Whenever the key horses finish first or second, shrewd handicappers register keen profits.

2. If three horses form the main contention in a close analysis but one is severely overbet, box the remaining two and play each on top of the overbet favorite.

Recreational handicappers will relish this betting tactic. It gets a steady stream of winners and juicy mutuels. Four combinations cover the main contention amazingly well. If the overbet favorite suffers a disadvantage on any handicapping fundamental, the recommended exactas exploit the opportunity, and should not be neglected.

3. If the favorite is bogus but the second choice solid, key the second choice in exactas, top and bottom, with other outstanding overlays having a handicapper's fair chance.

Presumably, the phony favorite will finish out of the picture, but the second choice has an extraordinarily strong chance to be first or second. If coupled with another overlay in a winning exacta, the prices should be extra fine.

4. If an unbettable low-priced favorite figures absolutely to win, eliminate the second and third betting choices, and couple

the favorite (on top) multiple times with the fourth, fifth, and perhaps sixth choices in the wagering.

The rationale is persuasive. When low-priced favorites look rock solid, the second and third betting choices will usually be overbet in relation to real chances. The crowd is overbetting the most obvious exacta combinations, eager to take aim on sitting ducks. But the fourth, fifth, and sixth betting choices figure almost as strongly on the undersides of exactas, and might be grossly underbet.

The tactic serves handicappers nicely whenever they find handicapping cracks in the second and third betting choices.

5. If the handicapping has been complex and unresolved, with several dissimilar outcomes rated equally probable, use multiple keys in exactas coupling the overlays in each outcome scenario.

Maybe the speed horse will get loose and coast, or it might not, and perish.

Maybe the intriguing outsider representing a successful trainer pattern will jump up and surprise.

Maybe the class horse returning from a long layoff will blow them down.

Because the probable outcomes are several and distinct, the betting should be widely distributed. Handicappers might exploit the exacta pools utilizing multiple keys. Each key horse is linked to other attractive contenders in a particular outcome scenario. Multiple keys are not coupled with one another.

If any of the probable outcomes occurs, handicappers can benefit from underbet exacta combinations. As multiple combinations will be covered—as many as six or seven—only generous overlays qualify for support. A few unrewarding combinations will be left out, and sometimes these will interfere with extensively well-laid plans. So be it. When the correct combinations click, payoffs will be ripe. Naturally, the size of several payoffs must compensate for the wider coverage and occasional mishaps. Several combinations usually will.

6. If pace and running style figure prominently to win, a contrasting running style often completes the exacta.

The classic situation involves a hotly contested early pace, the probable winner emerging either from the lead group or from directly behind the front. A closer can easily overhaul tired horses to trigger the exacta. Find the bravest closer and stick it in the place hole.

Another scenario develops in routes. A sluggish early pace is predictable, yet an off-pace runner is expected to win. Include the likeliest frontrunner in the exacta. Following slow fractions, the pacesetter can save second.

7. In full claiming fields, or almost full, favorites below 2–1 should be covered in exactas on the bottom sides only.

If form is less than peaked, the typical case, claiming horses are peculiarly vulnerable to the vicissitudes of racing. Full fields exaggerate the fates. From traffic, trouble, and jockey errors, claiming favorites may bounce back, not to win but to finish second. It happens all the time.

Moreover, the situation is consistent with the proposition that low-priced favorites generate profits in exactas only when anchored on the undersides.

In predictable races, where favorites and low-to-moderate priced horses form the guts of the contention, recreational handicappers will lean automatically toward exacta kills. The instinct is laudable, but the mutuel must be equally laudable. Underlays and fair-value payoffs are meaningless.

If infield tote boards do not flash exacta probables, handicappers must resign themselves to intermittent walks to the nearby monitors. There they can observe potential exacta payoffs and compare them to the values below.

Table 2 presents the cutoff values at 15 to 20 percent profit for the $2 and $5 exactas, respectively, at odds from 6–5 to 8–1, based upon empirical studies of exacta wagering in New York and southern California. The column heads indicate the odds of the horse on top.

In using the cutoff values, handicappers can substitute personal odds for public odds. If the public gives 8–1 but handicappers judge the horse 4–1, use the column marked 4–1. Also, toward the high end of the chart, handicappers can reduce the cutoff values by 20 percent and still receive good value. Be strict toward the low end of the chart. Demand top value there or no bet.

Exacta bettors must realize the nature of the exotic risk opens the possibility of extended losing runs. Low-probability events can happen infrequently over longer periods, certainly throughout the run of a race meeting. If recreational handicappers club

Table 2. Cutoff Dollars at 15 to 20 Percent Profit for $2 and $5 Exacta Wagering at Odds of 6–5 to 8–1. Odds of Horses to Win are Atop the Columns.

	6–5	7–5	8–5	9–5	2–1	5–2	3–1	7–2	4–1	9–2	5–1	6–1	7–1	8–1
6–5 ($2)		11	13	14	17	20	24	28	32	37	43	51	59	67
($5)		27	31	34	40	48	59	69	79	90	106	125	145	165
7–5	11	13	14	16	18	22	26	31	35	40	47	56	65	74
	26	30	33	37	44	53	65	76	87	99	116	137	159	181
8–5	12	13	15	17	20	24	28	33	38	44	51	60	70	80
	28	32	36	40	47	57	70	82	94	107	125	148	172	195
9–5	13	14	16	18	21	25	31	36	41	47	55	65	75	86
	30	35	39	43	50	61	75	88	101	115	134	159	184	210
2–1	14	16	18	20	24	29	34	40	46	52	61	73	84	96
	33	39	43	48	57	68	84	98	113	128	150	178	206	235
5–2	16	19	21	23	27	33	39	46	53	60	70	83	97	110
	39	45	50	56	65	79	97	113	130	148	173	205	238	271
3–1	19	22	24	27	31	38	45	53	61	69	81	96	112	127
	44	51	58	64	75	91	111	130	150	170	199	236	274	312
7–2	21	24	27	30	36	43	52	60	69	79	92	109	127	144
	50	58	65	73	85	103	126	148	170	193	226	268	311	354
4–1	24	28	31	34	40	48	58	68	78	89	104	123	143	162
	57	65	74	82	96	116	142	166	191	217	254	301	349	398
9–2	27	31	34	38	45	54	65	76	87	99	116	137	159	181
	63	73	82	91	107	129	158	185	213	242	283	336	389	443
5–1	30	35	39	44	51	62	74	87	100	113	132	157	182	207
	72	84	94	104	122	148	181	212	244	277	324	385	446	508
6–1	35	41	46	51	60	72	86	101	116	132	154	183	212	241
	84	97	109	121	142	172	211	247	284	322	377	447	518	590
7–1	40	47	52	58	68	82	98	115	132	150	176	209	242	275
	96	111	125	138	162	196	241	282	324	368	431	511	592	674
8–1	45	53	59	65	77	92	111	130	149	169	198	235	272	310
	108	125	140	156	182	220	271	317	365	414	485	575	666	758

the exactas into submission for two, three, and four consecutive seasons, the next year might bring famine. The dry spell may reflect only a statistical fluctuation. No reason to panic. If handicapping skill and sound judgment have kept intact, the upswing will recur.

No need to understate it. The exacta is the competent contemporary handicapper's best friend. It affords the occasional customer a chance for meaningful profits in the short run, as win wagering does not. If recreational handicappers respect the bet and play it smartly, they should do all right much of the time, and sometimes reel in the big ones.

DAILY DOUBLES

Thoroughbred racing's traditional gimmick bet is the daily double.

In recent years the double has become an increasingly invisible wager. With the exacta, the quinella, the trifecta, and the pick-six dangling racing's plums in front of bettors, the daily double has receded in the hearts of racegoers.

I ponder my personal relationship with the daily double, and discover the memory bank oddly empty. Last season survives for its salutary effects, nice recollections not yet lost in the morass.

Also, in my rookie year, fully half the profits for the season at Hollywood Park were accounted for by a fancy $319 double I captured ten times. In the second half, Bill Shoemaker opened a fifteen-length lead on a 30–1 shot upon entering the stretch, and lasted over the even-money favorite by a disappearing 1¼ lengths.

On watching the replay, I noticed the favorite stumble badly at the start, reaching its knees, and not recovering well. I realized I should have lost, but nonetheless dumped the profits that night on an eating table in full view of seven college friends in a particularly adolescent display.

In between, late one season—again at Hollywood Park—I recall imagining after a painful ending of the second race that I had played the double rather foolishly that season. That night I checked my copious records. I stood in arrears of the daily double by $1640. I was astonished. Aware only that I had been dabbling, I cut out daily doubles for the duration. I can think of little else across the years.

Yet the daily double retains its elementary charm. It gets the racing day started on a hopeful charge. Unfamiliar guests and loved ones cherish the double. It's as if they cannot wait to rush the windows with the magical numbers. It's a cheery, optimistic escort into the afternoon, brimming with a sense of adventure and vaguely tainted fun.

But I suspect that for repeat customers the daily double's lasting allure relates to its capacity for dealing abruptly with a discordant slice of the race day. Inevitably, at least one half of the double dispatches a repulsively unattractive horse race, and on many days both halves are ugly. Rather than sit silently at the outset, handicappers can choose to dabble in the double. Customarily, they mix up a handful of hopefuls in each half, and manage to win a fair share of the bets.

On occasion, the daily double will be alluring for all the appropriate reasons. Two betting strategies facilitate long-term success.

First, if one half of the daily double is predictable and the other contentious, key the probable winner to all the probable overlays in the contentious half. Ignore the favorite and any low-priced contenders.

If the other half of a daily double having a predictable race is unfathomable, follow one of two tactics. If a successful trainer pattern or other pet angle points to a longshot, hook the longshot and predictable winner in multiple doubles.

If no successful pattern or pet angle rescues the unpredictable half, a partial wheel of attractive overlays hooked to the probable winner of the predictable half is the practical alternative to a pass. Under no circumstance should favorites or low-priced contenders in unpredictable races be linked in daily doubles.

Second, if both halves are contentious, criss-cross a pair of attractive overlays in each. Once again, favorites and low-priced contenders in contentious races are taboo. These generate underlays in the double, another low-probability event.

Whenever each half of the daily double is predictable, handicappers can scrape added value from the opportunities by connecting the most probable winners in multiple tickets. If strong second and third choices in either half will be seriously underbet, cover these bases in predictable doubles as well. If pairs of favorites are hooked in predictable doubles, insist the tandem pay more than would a win parlay. It normally will.

The future of the daily double has been secured by its tradition, no doubt, but a positive change in the day's programming might be urged by racing's loyal fans.

Del Mar, the summer resort track near San Diego, in a generally enlightened program of parimutuel wagering attractions, offers its patrons a late daily double. Outstanding handicappers relish the late double and can plunder it for profits not often available earlier.

The eighth and ninth races at Del Mar are far more amenable to conventional handicapping skill than the first and second. At all major tracks the same circumstance generally presides. Handicappers can usually challenge the late double intelligently, but the early double only capriciously.

No need to upset hallowed tradition here. An add-on, as at Del Mar, carries the cause.

THE SERIAL TRIPLE AND OTHER EXOTICS

Truly exotic parimutuel wagers are characterized by extremely low probabilities but extravagantly high payoffs. Raffles such as the pick-nine and pick-six appeal variously to the lowbrow bettor reaching for the moon and to big-money betting syndicates scheming to buy success.

Small bettors are inevitably chewed to pieces by the natural odds against scoring—the pick-six at Del Mar on Labor Day of 1989 presented 62 horses and 1,088,644 possible combinations. Larger syndicates usually do not appropriate enough profit when successful, in relation to the risk.

If members of either group persist in chasing these parimutuel pots of gold, the probabilities eventually will prevail, and a decimated bankroll is a virtual certainty.

But a happy medium has rushed to the rescue of exotic bettors. In 1987 Santa Anita Park introduced a gimmick wager that combines rational probabilities of winning with extravagant overlay payoffs. The new bet is the serial triple, or pick-three, and this is the sweetest bettor-friendly development so far in the age of exotic wagering.

Bettors must pick the winners of three consecutive races, a difficult but not irrational proposition. Whenever nonfavorites dominate the series, payoffs soar. Upset winners that are longshots can propel the payoffs toward the tips of annual salaries. Occasionally, payoffs exceed $20,000. Once, at Del Mar 1989, the pick-three paid $41,000. Numerous times a major meeting, payoffs range from $5000 to $10,000. One thousand dollars is routine.

Because the normal payoff is merely generous, not fabulous, the big-betting syndicates do not trifle with the serial triple. Smaller bettors who are excellent handicappers have found a friendly retreat. Several times a season the odds will beckon them. Probabilities will be good, the potential payoffs huge. A few successes equate to sizable profits. The successes, furthermore, can be repeated—irregularly, but absolutely.

Because the serial triple is relatively novel, bettors are still adjusting to the wager. As events proceed and bettors adapt, payoffs will drop, regrettably. A handicapping colleague swears by data he collected during the inaugural year of the serial triple that showed whenever three nonfavorites won, they combined for payoffs upward of $1500, even when the nonfavorites were low-priced contenders.

That is no longer true. Three low-priced nonfavorites may pay well enough, but not $1500.

Other corrections will be forthcoming, but the adjustments will not alter the essential character of the wager: reasonable probabilities and excellent payoffs. Recreational handicappers can flourish from season to season by playing the serial triple shrewdly.

Two betting strategies will be especially rewarding over time. But the prerequisite decision is whether to engage the serial triple at all.

A recreational approach to the gimmick (a) stresses overlays as key horses and (b) avoids overbetting both in predictable and unpredictable races.

Unless a nonfavorite can be singled, or a favorite can be combined with a pair of medium-priced overlays, the serial triple will be best forgotten. Do not combine a trio of favorites. Do not combine a pair of favorites with long shots in the remaining race. Do not combine favorites with other low-priced contenders only.

Moreover, if favorites and low-priced contenders are preferred in the pick-three by full-dress handicapping, pass. Payoffs will be unfavorable in relation to the risk. No long-term gain.

A potentially positive situation arises whenever handicappers prefer a nonfavorite in any of the pick-three races. The greater the odds, the better.

Strategy No. 1 says that horse should be singled. Cover the contention in the other two races. Higher-priced contenders deserve stronger support, notably in contentious races. Lower-priced contenders warrant less support, unless multiple tickets connecting the same highly predictable combinations will be purchased.

If a nonfavorite is singled in a parlay consisting of two contentious races besides, the higher-priced contenders might be covered multiple times, the lower-priced contenders once, as savers. Only the genuine contenders should be covered. Minimize the risk.

A second strategy is rarely implemented, but highly recommended. If three selections in the serial triple will be nonfavorites, single each in separate parlays. Cover the main contention in the other two races to complete each parlay. The outlay will be costlier but the risk cost-effective. If any of the nonfavorites wins, and the contention of the remaining races has been doped out properly, a fine profit results.

If two of the nonfavorites win, and the contention of the remaining race has been doped out properly, two parlays will have succeeded and profits will be double. If the winner of the leftover race in the series is a higher-priced contender, a couple of windfalls will be collected. For competent handicappers, it happens several times a season.

At Del Mar, on Labor Day 1989, the late triple included the sixth, seventh, and eighth races. Top picks, contenders, and morning lines of the three races looked to me like this:

6th	7th	8th
Selection	Selection	Selection
Silver Torque (7–2)	Runaway Prince (6–1)	Payant (4–1)
Contenders	Contenders	Contenders
She's a V. P. (5–2)	Harmonic (15–1)	Saratoga Passage (3–1)
Temperence Gift (6–1)	Kentucky Star (5–2)	

The following three parlays were formed in the serial triple. Each combination costs $3.

Parlay 1 ($18)	Parlay 2 ($18)	Parlay 3 ($27)
6th Silver Torque	6th Silver Torque	6th Silver Torque
7th Runaway Prince	She's a V. P.	She's a V. P.
Harmonic	Temperence Gift	Temperence Gift
Kentucky Star	7th Runaway Prince	7th Runaway Prince
8th Payant	8th Payant	Harmonic
Saratoga Passage	Saratoga Passage	Kentucky Star
		8th Payant

And the winners were:

6th   She's a V. P.
7th   Runaway Prince
8th   Payant

The serial triple paid $1100. As two main selections won, a pair of live parlays depended upon identifying the contention of the sixth race. When morning-line favorite She's a V.P. survived in the sixth, a $63 investment resulted in a pair of convertible triples worth $2200. A single successful parlay would have secured the day, and normally does.

Whenever handicappers prefer nonfavorites across the board in the serial triple, implement the strategy above.

Whenever a prime bet to win can be singled in the serial triple besides, it makes sense to increase the exotic investment. If that horse is a nonfavorite, by all means hype the exotic bet. Payant above qualified as a prime bet to win. The parlay Payant keyed in the serial triple might have merited twice the basic amount.

The trifecta, where bettors predict the order of finish one, two, three, generally succumbs to the same disadvantages as plague unintelligent exacta wagering. Baseballs, combinations of longshots, wheels, and favorites on top produce negative results. Overlays, combinations of medium-priced horses, and favorites in the place and show holes get optimum results long-haul.

The pick-six is not hospitable to recreational handicappers. The six-race parlay requires the inclusion of too many low-priced contenders that are marginal. Costs escalate, but probabilities remain minuscule.

If recreational handicappers can single three horses in the sequence, with one an attractive overlay, a minor investment sometimes should be considered. If the contention of the three remaining races can be isolated and covered, lightning might strike. The opportunity gathers steam if a carryover pool exists. Carryovers stimulate significantly extra betting. The consolation prize for picking five winners in the parlay can be generous, perhaps thousands.

But the trifecta and the pick-six cannot compare to the charms of the serial triple. If recreational handicappers long to make a memorable score in racing's exotics, let them concentrate their energies in the serial triple. It's the best exotic game in town.

Betting Artistry

A dangerous chasm separates the racegoer's allegiance to the fundamental principles of parimutuel wagering and betting artistry. The former is a cognitive learning skill within the grasp of everyone, the latter an intuitively learned skill within the grasp of a few.

The awful betting habits of racegoers as a group suggest some kind of grossly miscalculated leap from the fundamental to the arty, resulting ordinarily in a tragic plunge to the depths. It's convenient to master the fundamentals before attempting the death-defying leap to the artistic.

The sad truth that haunts even excellent handicappers everywhere is that few of them have bothered to develop themselves as proficient bettors. Expert handicappers are rarely expert bettors. They therefore win significantly less profit than they are capable of winning. In the worst-case scenario, not uncommon, proficient handicappers lose money for the season due to incompetent wagering.

Surely a kind of first principle holds that handicappers should determine to become fundamentally sound bettors before they become artistic bettors. Competent horseplayers who overbet underlays or escalate bets when losing or chase losses or ignore attractive overlays or bet too aggressively or sacrifice prime bets in exotic gambles or butcher the exotic combinations or risk big money on losers and much less on winners, should as a matter of routine retreat to square one, where they might learn eventually to do exactly the opposite.

Where basic betting proficiency has been evident, the transition to betting artistry is possible. Indeed, the successful leap can make a tremendous difference, especially for recreational handicappers. In the short run of a season, competent handicapping and proficient betting add up to moderate profits. Artistic betting represents the likeliest chance for substantial profits in the same short term.

Needless to say, where incompetent handicapping endures, artistic betting will be meaningless.

Betting artistry depends upon an awareness of the intuitive skills associated with a variety of identifiable betting situations that arise numerous times a season. Of the opportunities that follow, the top three might occur anytime. When the final two do occur, how handicappers respond tells the tale of the financial tape for the season underway.

1. Backing strong contenders that are overlays, whenever two horses, or three, have roughly comparable chances to win.

If Horse A has a slight edge over Horse B, but A is 9–5 and B is 5–1, Horse B deserves the wager. It's an incredibly crucial point. The situation develops regularly. Go to the overlay every time. Among horses having relatively equivalent chances to win, take the conspicuous overlays. This book has stressed the point variously, but it cannot be overemphasized. Effective recreational handicapping cannot be reduced to the art of picking winners. Rather, it's extensively the art of appraising the relative chances to win of the horses in the field, notably the main contenders.

2. Finding outstanding overlays in exactas.

As low-probability bets, exactas must provide good value, not just fair value. Good value means a minimum 20 percent overlay. But frequently, exactas connecting key horses and contenders provide overlays of 50 to 100 percent. Those combinations represent outstanding overlays.

A little detective work will be required. Recreational handicappers must examine the monitors for the exacta probables. The gambit is imperative whenever the prime horse is a nonfavorite. If the prime horse can be coupled in overly generous exactas as well, recreational handicappers can exploit a bettable race for added value.

Sharp detectives who are clever handicappers can exploit similar exacta opportunities for exaggerated profits numerous times a season, without a corresponding risk to the bankroll.

3. Sensing when a maximum bet is appropriate.

Knowing when to risk a maximum bet is strictly an intuitive skill. It develops only with repetitive prior success. Normally, the prime horse and all the circumstances of the race will be ideal, and the odds will be seductive. Suddenly, as if impulsively, an overwhelming intuition envelops the situation. Yet the intuition has sprung from a rational base having a relentless emotional force. Handicappers feel the moment is ripe for the kill, and the mental sensation is undeniable.

Trust the overwhelming intuition. Instead of making a normal wager, up the ante. The uncommon confidence is no false alert. It's rooted in past experience, past success. The situation embodies major handicapping strengths, and a major bet is the rational response.

4. During losing runs, reduce the bet-size to a bare-bones minimum.

Practically everyone, it seems, realizes that handicappers should bet more when winning and less when losing. All handicapping texts unite on the principle. Fixed-percentage betting methods are predicated upon it.

But during losing runs that have become abnormal or extended, handicappers benefit by stretching the principle to the extreme. Bet-size should be reduced to a bare-bones minimum. The objective during losing runs is to minimize losses. The moment a losing trend has been spotted, a defeatist attitude sensed, bet only a token amount if anything. Quitting for a time is a pragmatic alternative.

Minimum bets remain standard fare until normal win-loss patterns emerge.

Most handicappers develop this negative intuitive skill through the hard lessons of bitter experience. Once is enough. Next time, normal bets should be scaled down, all the way down. Obsessive chasers excepted, casual racegoers can learn how to cope with losing runs well enough.

A contrasting intuition and skill is a vastly different phenomenon. The skill qualifies as the ultimate wagering weapon, the most advanced style of betting artistry, but not one regular racegoer or competent handicapper in a hundred can perform it well.

5. Press a winning streak by escalating the bet-size.

Unreproducible windfalls aside, if recreational handicappers intend to make substantial profits at the races during the course of a single season, this is the only way. The best of racetrack bettors have learned how to press a winning streak, and do.

Winning streaks develop when sharp handicapping, excellent opportunities, and good fortune coincide. The streaks last for a few days to a few weeks. They occur once or twice a season. The earlier a winning run is sensed, the better. Bet-size should be increased, routinely by 20 to 50 percent of the normal amount, to the limit occasionally.

Competent handicappers intuit a winning run as surely as they do a losing run, but few of them are prepared to capitalize on the favorable circumstances. The deep instinct is conservative, to protect profits, to defend the status quo.

Fair enough.

But these friendly, fortunate runs occur just once or twice a season. The artistic bettor exploits them confidently. The competent bettor makes a normal profit. The difference is enormous.

Recently I watched the storied Andrew Beyer press an unanticipated winning streak at Hollywood Park. Beyer netted a thousand dollars at least for each of eight consecutive racing days. In town for three weeks of handicapping action, Beyer had begun with a lowered bet-size, intent on staying afloat at a strange course.

On the eighth day Beyer had been losing early. He was down approximately a thousand dollars following the fifth-race exacta. The afternoon's results would depend on a typical top-figure horse in the seventh, morning-line odds of 5–2. Playing well and confidently now, Beyer pressed an exacta combination he preferred. Naturally, the figure horse won, at 8–5, and the exacta combo clicked too. The day's profit to Beyer was roughly $1200. Nice comeback!

On the ninth day Beyer liked a nicely priced trip playback in the second race. Sensing a potential kill, he hooked his top-figure horse in the first half of the daily double to the trip overlay in the second on a $250 ticket, his steepest double investment of the abbreviated stay.

The figure horse survived in a hard drive, and the trip horse won smartly at 9–2. The daily double paid $93. Beyer's net on investment was $11,625.

The next afternoon, a Saturday, Beyer won slightly less than a thousand dollars, the winning run persevering.

On the eleventh day Beyer again liked the second race, this one an angle horse that would be bet, surprisingly, by insiders, but walked to the post nonetheless at 8–1.

Beyer pressed the moment as he characteristically does. He bought huge doubles from three contenders in the first half, and sure enough, one won. He then singled the 8–1 shot in the early serial triple, and in the pick-six as well, taking comprehensive coverage of each exotic. He finished optimistically with a prime bet to win.

"If this horse wins," said Beyer with confident enthusiasm between races, "I'm a rich man."

The 8–1 angle showed high early speed out of the gate, and took a short lead into the Hollywood stretch, but was outrun to the wire by a 30–1 shot that made no handicapping sense whatsoever. Beyer's rich-man angle horse had finished second.

"Well, that's the end of the streak, I suppose," said a dejected Beyer. "But it's been nice enough."

Beyer's winning run did end, and it had been "nice enough"— $19,000 in profits during eleven racing days.

I recount the incidents because Beyer practices the ultimate parimutuel betting skill, pressing a winning streak, as well or better than anyone else. His reputation as a big bettor, and big winner, is hinged absolutely to the "crushing" skill, as he so aptly has labeled it.

Recreational handicappers cannot imitate Beyer on the practice and should not try. But they can press uncommon winning streaks by escalating wagers in their own inimitable styles—and must, if they intend to convert their considerable handicapping prowess into meaningful profits at the races.

CHAPTER X

Making Selections,
Making Decisions

ELSEWHERE I HAVE URGED regular handicappers to make decisions, not selections. I now confess to mild overstatement.

Probably the most personally rewarding aspect of the handicapping experience is making selections that figure to win. When, in fact, the selections do win, the feeling of accomplishment that swells within the individual's breast is not to be denied.

No one, certainly not me, wants to encourage a practice, as the cliché holds, that would take the fun out of the game. I am not a bogeyman.

Thus my new position. I urge racegoers everywhere to make selections and decisions.

Where horses hold a strong probability of winning and the odds will be fair to generous, make selections.

Where horses hold a shaky probability of winning, or races will be contentious, unpredictable, or indecipherable, forget about making selections. Make decisions.

The best decisions will embrace contending horses having a reasonably strong chance of winning, but at relatively spicy odds. The stronger the chances, and the higher the odds, the two forces coming together like magnetic fields, the better.

When making decisions, and with no exceptions, a first principle of parimutuel wagering imposes itself on the proceedings: avoid the underlay; take the overlay. The principle should never be violated.

On the typical nine-race program, maybe three races, more often two, lend themselves to making selections.

433

The other six, sometimes seven, lend themselves to making decisions.

When races lend themselves to making decisions, then making selections—and here I must insist—is simply and irredeemably wrong. This qualifies as an ineluctable imperative among recreational handicappers, who have scarcely a gnat's chance of beating the races for meaningful money by adhering to mere selections, but might do surprisingly well for the season by making solid selections and cunning decisions in concert.

As a sort of supreme illustration of the power of making decisions at the races, I leave you with four contenders for the second half of the double at Santa Anita last weekend (October 14, 1989). It was an awful race, a maiden-claiming sprint for older fillies and mares, to be claimed, if anyone dared, for $32,000.

So that handicappers might play along in the situation, please understand I rarely attempt to unravel maiden-claiming affairs, except to notice the horses dropping from straight maiden competition, and at times to support the fastest of these, provided the price is right.

As the par times are several lengths apart, in the past two seasons at Santa Anita I sometimes have indulged dropdowns from maiden-claiming $50,000 to maiden-claiming $32,000, although a definite advantage as to speed or pace is prerequisite.

Given that framework, review the past performances of the four fillies below. By whatever means, make a selection.

2nd Santa Anita

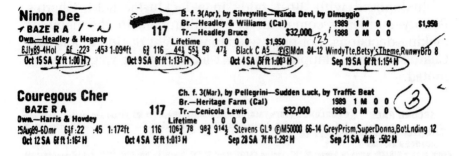

Ninon Dee
B. f. 3(Apr), by Silveyville—Nanda Devi, by Dimaggio
✓ BAZE R A
117
Br.—Headley & Williams (Cal)
1989 1 M 0 0 $1,950
Own.—Headley & Hegarty
Tr.—Headley Bruce $32,000 1988 0 M 0 0
Lifetime 1 0 0 0 $1,950
6Jly89-4Hol 6f :22³ :45³ 1:09⁴ft 6½ 116 44½ 55½ 58 47¼ Black C A⁵ ⒻⓈMdn 84-12 WindyTte,Betsy'sTheme,RunwyBrb 8
Oct 15 SA 5f ft 1:00 H Oct 9 SA 6f ft 1:13³ H Oct 4 SA 8f ft 1:00³ H Sep 19 SA 6f ft 1:15⁴ H

Couregous Cher
Ch. f. 3(Mar), by Pellegrini—Sudden Luck, by Traffic Beat
BAZE R A
117
Br.—Heritage Farm (Cal)
1989 1 M 0 0
Own.—Harris & Hovdey
Tr.—Cenicola Lewis $32,000 1988 0 M 0 0
Lifetime 1 0 0 0
25Aug89-6Dmr 6¼f:22 :45 1:17²ft 8 116 106¾ 7⁸ 98¾ 9¹⁴½ Stevens GL⁹ ⒻM50000 66-14 GreyPrism,SuperDonna,Bo'tLnding 12
Oct 12 SA 6f ft 1:16² H Oct 4 SA 5f ft 1:01³ H Sep 28 SA 7f ft 1:29² H Sep 21 SA 4f ft :50² H

Couregous Cher was getting Lasix for the first time while dropping from maiden-claiming $50,000 to maiden-claiming $32,000. The filly attracted hot action on the tote early in the betting, but had not shown the speed or pace tendencies I demand of pitiable horses, and I dismissed her.

Of the maiden dropdowns, Ninon Dee was clearly best on speed, pace, and turn time. Form was acceptable, the workout pattern rather impressive for bottom-of-the-barrel runners. Zjena looked second best, Charo's Bounty a third call.

Whether other handicappers would prefer Ninon Dee here, or something else, the conventional output of handicapping has been represented precisely. The selection is Ninon Dee, or something else. End of preparation, end of discussion.

Then the betting begins.

With less than five minutes to go in the wagering, the odds on the maiden dropdowns looked like this:

Ninon Dee	8–5
Zjena	5–2
Charo's Bounty	30–1

Handicappers in the business of making selections might insist that Ninon Dee figures best and bet that horse to win. Thousands at Santa Anita did.

Handicappers in the business of making decisions in unpredictable circumstances would surely desert Ninon Dee at 8–5 and Zjena at 5–2, and just as surely would take another careful look at Charo's Bounty.

On second glance, those handicappers would notice improved early speed at the Fairplex bullring, a sign of improving form, reinforced by four workouts within 16 days, another positive pattern, the final two trials attractive.

Juxtaposed with 30–1 odds in a lackluster field, Charo's Bounty suddenly comes alive. Handicappers in the habit of making decisions, not only selections, might decide to support Charo's Bounty. Happily, I did. At least a minor wager is warranted.

SECOND RACE
Santa Anita
OCTOBER 21, 1989

6 FURLONGS. (1.07⅗) MAIDEN CLAIMING. Purse $17,000. Fillies and mares. 3–year-olds and upward. Weights, 3–year-olds, 117 lbs.; older, 120 lbs. Claiming price $32,000; if for $29,000 allowed 2 lbs.

Value of race $18,000; value to winner $9,900; second $3,600; third $2,700; fourth $1,350; fifth $450. Mutuel pool $424,949.

Last Raced	Horse	Eqt.A.Wt PP St	¼	½	Str	Fin	Jockey	Cl'g Pr	Odds $1
24Sep89 5Fpx5	Charo's Bounty	b 3 117 6 3	3¹½	3¹	2¹½	12¾	Dominguez R E	32000	31.60
8Jly89 4Hol4	Ninon Dee	3 117 10 4	4hd	4hd	42½	2½	Nakatani C S	32000	1.60
25Aug89 6Dmr9	Couregous Cher	3 117 11 1	1¹	1¹	1¹	34½	Baze R A	32000	9.70
22Dec88 2Hol10	Natalie's Mint	3 117 7 6	6¹	6¹½	6½	4hd	Delahoussaye E	32000	5.80
24Sep89 5Fpx3	Zjena	b 3 117 3 9	9²½	9¹½	7¹½	5no	Flores D R	32000	2.90
25Aug89 4Dmr12	Evening Angel	3 117 12 2	2½	2¹½	3¹	6¹½	Meza R Q	32000	31.50
28Aug89 2Dmr8	More Than Native	b 3 117 9 7	8¹	5hd	5¹	7¾	Solis A	32000	10.60
4Aug89 9LA6	Lovely Adrano	4 120 1 8	7hd	8hd	8¹½	8¼	Patton D B	32000	58.90
25Aug89 4Dmr7	Cris And Kim	b 3 117 5 11	11⁵	10²½	9½	9³	Ortega L E	32000	50.90
23Jly89 1Hol6	Care Free Caper	3 117 4 10	10¹	113½	114	101¾	Toro F	32000	9.50
	Parada	b 3 117 2 5	5¹	7¹	10¹	114½	Black C A	32000	64.30
	Stormy Trend	3 112 8 12	12	12	12	12	Jauregui L H5	32000	65.80

OFF AT 1:35. Start good. Won driving. Time, :22, :45⅘, :58⅘, 1:11⅘ Track fast.

$2 Mutuel Prices:

6-CHARO'S BOUNTY	65.20	17.60	9.00
10-NINON DEE		4.60	3.40
11-COUREGOUS CHER			5.60

Dk. b. or br. f, (May), by Pirate's Bounty—Charo, by Bagdad. Trainer Dinges Vernon L. Bred by Klein Mr-Mrs E V (Cal).

CHARO'S BOUNTY, close up early after being bumped in the initial strides, got the lead a sixteenth out and drew clear. NINON DEE, outrun early and wide down the backstretch, came into the stretch four wide and had enough of a response in the drive to gain the place. COUREGOUS CHER established the early pace and weakened a bit in the final furlong. NATALIE'S MINT, outrun early after being bumped in the opening strides, lacked the needed response in the drive. ZJENA, devoid of early speed, improved her position in the last quarter but failed to threaten and was four wide into the stretch. EVENING ANGEL, wide early, pressed the pace to the stretch and gave way. MORE THAN NATIVE, quite wide down the backstretch, was five wide into the stretch. CHRIS AND KIM was five wide into the stretch. CARE FREE CAPER was four wide into the stretch. PARADA, in contention early, was through after a half. STORMY TREND was wide down the backstretch.

Owners— 1, Chila-Chila-Dinges Et al; 2, Headley & Hegarty; 3, Harris & Hovdey; 4, Friendly Natalie B; 5, Samarzich L & R; 6, Zeilinger D J; 7, Gonzalez F; 8, GoldenGreenFm&VanDenBock; 9, Jam Stable & Sears; 10, Daley M-R-Jean; 11, Senzell H; 12, Denholm R A.

Trainers— 1, Dinges Vernon L; 2, Headley Bruce; 3, Cenicola Lewis; 4, Fulton Jacque; 5, Garcia Victor; 6, Jackson Bruce L; 7, Stute Melvin F; 8, Hundley Robert; 9, Mazzone Paul A; 10, Mandella Richard; 11, Soriano Morris; 12, Needham Lloyd.

Natalie's Mint was claimed by Asistio L A; trainer, Seguin Yves M.

Scratched—Fairly Level; Farrell (28Aug89 2Dmr6); Daddy's Doll (14Aug89 2Dmr2); Monologue (24Sep89 5Fpx4).

$2 Daily Double (5–6) Paid $1,273.60. Daily Double pool $414,399.

The ability to make similar decisions as the situations arise depends in part on the handicapper's awareness of the appropriate odds, based upon horses' records in relation to other horses in the field.

Mathematics need not apply. An intuitive grasp of the appropriate odds is all that is necessary. The intuition derives largely from experience, but first from a mental set that forming a betting line is part and parcel of the handicapping regimen.

The betting line for the sample race might be intuited as below:

Horse	Betting Line	Actual Odds
Ninon Dee	5–2	8–5
Zjena	4–1	5–2
Charo's Bounty	8–1	30–1
Couregous Cher	10–1	9–1
Others	2–1	x

To digress briefly, in setting betting lines, the noncontenders (others) should invariably be assigned a minimal 20 percent chance (4–1), an optimal 33 percent chance (2–1), depending upon the size of the field, the degree of authentic contention, and the reliability of the race.

From this vantage point, a value orientation, it's clear Charo's Bounty deserves to be bet, while the others do not. Final decisions rest, as always, on a balancing beam connecting a horse's chances to win and the odds the crowd will extend.

If a handicapper's estimates of the relative odds make sense, a function of sound handicapping, effective decision-making can only result in long-term profits.

In the example, Charo's Bounty should win roughly once in nine attempts. If she wins that frequently or thereabouts, the payoff at 30–1 greatly overcompensates for the losses. Long dry spells are entirely feasible when backing 8–1 shots, of course, but when they surprise as underbet longshots, like 30–1, the decision to bet looks uncommonly smart indeed.

No one predicts with confidence that Charo's Bounty should win, of course, a not unimportant concession. Local experts do not pop up on a morning radio show touting the possibility (they instead like Ninon Dee to win). Selection sheets do not steer the customers to Charo's Bounty either.

The wager on Charo's Bounty does not reflect a selection, but a decision. Yet the decision makes perfect sense, even as a bet on Ninon Dee at the price amounts to nonsense. I implore recreational handicappers to wrestle with the vital distinction, and to begin making decisions at the racetrack, as well as selections.

Just as importantly, when horses like Charo's Bounty do win, with money down, no one of civilized deportment claims to have picked the horse. The bragging rights that remain so unduly important to public selectors and to handicappers as a species should not confuse one's selections and decisions.

On reveling in the fabulous result, handicappers should admit to the proper explanation, that they backed the horse because it had earned a handicapper's reasonable chance to upset and the odds had drifted too far out of line. How much better that than a specious account about making a superb selection, which is not only usually untrue, but also reinforces the conventional wisdom about making selections that figure to win.

Unfortunately, making decisions is a far more complicated art than making selections. Selections emerge from systematic methods. Almost any rational arrangement of rating procedures will suffice.

The selections that emerge fit the method's procedures remarkably well. Speed methods produce speed horses. Class methods produce classy horses. Form methods produce improving horses. And so forth.

But much is lost. Horses that do not fit the method's parameters very well have an awfully good chance of being ignored and forgotten. Of these, they are great in number. Needless to say, several of the outcasts win regardless.

Excellent method players, to be sure, make excellent selections. If their methods emphasize the fundamentals of handicapping—speed, class, pace, form—and the indecipherable races are bypassed, no doubt the most outstanding of method handicappers can actually beat the races.

Yet handicappers that complement excellent selections with similarly excellent decisions will have earned the best—and most numerous—opportunities to finish ahead of the horses.

This is the case for recreational handicappers, who attend irregularly and rarely depend upon systematic methods for the composite of their racetrack portfolios. Recreational handicappers diversify, but without much thought, and outrageously at the windows.

Of the minority that do cling to systematic methods, few recreational handicappers, however talented, however motivated, can beat the races with unswerving reliance on stepwise procedures and the occasional prime selections these contribute. Not enough prime selections materialize, and even when they do, not enough of the horses will win at satisfactory mutuels. The more-than-occasional overlays represent the practical alternative, even the practical imperative.

Finally, all should understand the ability to make effective decisions at the races evolves over a relatively lengthy stretch of experience. Where the experience has been informed by knowledge and surrounded by information resources, effective decisions are much more likely to occur with some consistency. Expertise is not a commodity to be gathered in the short run, no matter the subject.

Of the three well-documented sources of expertise—knowledge, information resources, and experience—the last, thoughtful experience, makes the ultimate difference.

Devouring useful books on handicapping, and consulting useful information resources on race days, are necessary, but insufficient preparation for making successful decisions. Most necessary is actual playing time. Only by playing the races repetitively do the diverse applications and fine distinctions that never cease to matter accumulate in organized patterns that might be recognized more clearly in the future.

Recreational handicappers still in the learning stages will be wisely urged to play the races as frequently as schedules and conflicting interests permit.

When at the track they should make selections, and make decisions too.

When the selections have won approximately one third of the time, at odds of 5–2 on average, recreational handicappers can take a well-deserved bow.

When spontaneous decisions have been correct enough of the time to reveal a clear and substantial profit for the season, repeated twice for good measure, recreational handicappers have arrived as fully accredited practitioners of the art.

Whatever racing's future brings, a valuable portion will be theirs for the taking.

Appendices

HOW TO READ THE PAST PERFORMANCES

The *Daily Racing Form* regularly provides users denotative explanations of the symbols and numerals that appear in the past performance tables. Racegoers unable to read the tables should consult those explanations.

Here we discuss several key symbols and numbers for handicapping purposes, emphasizing meanings and basic interpretations.

Review the past performances of the champion Sunday Silence, below.

By the numbers, handicappers can interpret the data items as follows.

440

1. Age and sex. Sunday Silence is a three-year-old colt.

2. Sire. The colt was sired by Halo. Sires are most important in turf racing, to less extent in mud racing, and to less extent in stakes races among developing horses. Also, sires can be influential in dashes for juveniles.

3. Trainer. The colt's trainer is Charles Whittingham. Trainers are never unimportant, and often very important in handicapping.

4. Final time and internal fractional times for the distance. At 1¼ miles, the first call—or first fractional time—appears after the horses have run four furlongs (47.1). The second call appears after one mile (1:37.4). Final time appears as 2:03.1 seconds, that is, two minutes, three and one-fifth seconds.

Notice the April 8 race of Sunday Silence, where another numeral 4 identifies the internal fractions for a race at 1⅛ miles. At middle distances of a mile to 1³⁄₁₆ miles, the first call appears after four furlongs (45.3) and the second call appears after six furlongs (109.3).

Notice the November 13 race of Sunday Silence, where another numeral 4 identifies the internal fractions of a race at six furlongs. For sprints of six to seven furlongs, the first call appears after two furlongs (22) and the second call appears after four furlongs (44.4).

Final times are used to calculate adjusted final times and speed figures. Final times and fractional times in combination are used to calculate adjusted pace times and pace ratings.

5. The points of call by position and beaten lengths. These always correspond to the fractional times to the left. Thus, after four furlongs on September 24 at Louisiana Downs, Sunday Silence was fourth, beaten 2½ lengths. After one mile, the colt was first, leading by a head. The next point of call is always the same, regardless of distance, one eighth of a mile from the finish, and is termed the stretch call. Sunday Silence at this point of call was first, leading by four lengths. Sunday Silence finished first, leading by six lengths.

Notice now the points of call for the colt's races on April 8 and November 13, respectively. Where was Sunday Silence after the second call on April 8? The colt was second, beaten one-half length. After the first call on November 13, Sunday Silence was second, beaten 1½ lengths.

The first call is used to assess early speed. The second call is used to assess early pace. Turn time equals the difference in time between the first and second calls, modified by lengths gained or lost.

6. Class of the race. Stakes are identified by name, as is the Super Derby of September 24. Purses are not identified. Notice the numeral 6 astride the March 2 race. This is an allowance race (Aw). Allowance

purses are identified. On March 2 Sunday Silence competed for a $32,000 purse. Purse values can be used to assess relative track class, with several qualifications.

7. Speed rating and track variant. Calculated as the deviation between the horse's running time today and the best running time at the distance at the track across the past three years, the speed rating can sometimes be used to compare maidens and two-year-olds competing at the same track.

The track variant is calculated as the average deviation from best times for sprint times and route times, respectively, on that specific day.

8. Speed index. A measure of how fast a horse has run in relation to the typical winner on a specific day. Is calculated for today's distance and footing, using the most recent race of the same distance and footing as today's. The speed index is calculated by summing the speed rating and track variant, and comparing the sum to a figure of 100. Thus a sum (of a horse's speed rating plus track variant) above 100 will be a plus and a sum below 100 will be a minus. A plus means the horse ran faster than the typical winner that day, and the numeral by how many lengths. A minus means the horse ran slower than the typical winner that day, and the numeral by how many lengths.

In his last race at today's distance and on today's footing, which was the September 24 start at Louisiana Downs, Sunday Silence earned a speed index of 0.0, meaning he ran as fast that day as the typical route winner.

The speed index has limited value for handicappers, and can be terribly misleading. But if relatively cheap horses show a plus in relation to the typical winners at the distance for the day, or relatively classy horses show a minus in relation to the typical winners at the distance for the day, mark the horses up and down, respectively.

9. Official track condition. On March 2, at Santa Anita, Sunday Silence ran on a sloppy track surface.

10. Workouts. The heavy black dot in front of the workout indicates a best-of-the-morning time at the distance.

Workouts are indicators of form, not class. Approximately 12 seconds a furlong represents average time, so a five-furlong drill of one minute should be interpreted as typical, or average. Fast or slow workouts may be meaningful or may not, depending upon other circumstances.

Workouts out of the gate are typically slower by a second than breezing workouts, or works designated as handily (H). So are workouts around the "dogs" on the turf, indicated by the symbol D.

11. A mud mark. The symbol X means Sunday Silence has shown he is a good mud runner. The X symbol is reliable as an indicator of mud-running ability, but the symbol * (fair) is not.

12. Trouble line (and gradings of stakes). Remarks under a horse's last running line will describe the kinds of trouble or mishaps the horse experienced in the race. On July 23 Sunday Silence "lugged out late." If the running line occurred in a graded stakes, as with the Super Derby (Grade 1), the trouble line also tells the grade designation.

13. Number of horses in the field.

The above table is standard for users of the Central and Western editions of the *Daily Racing Form*. The Eastern edition, however, has a slightly different arrangement of data items, plus a few of interest the other editions lack.

Review the past performances of the claiming horse Any Alibi.

1. Eligible ages. The ages of horses eligible to race; specifically, whether three-year-olds were competing against older horses (3 ↑).

A crucial piece of handicapping information, not available to Central and Western users, except in results charts.

When evaluating claiming races and stakes races, and to less extent maiden and allowance races, handicappers need to know whether three-year-olds competed effectively versus older horses. Those that did, and today will face only their own age group, might have a decisive advantage.

On September 14 Any Alibi ran evenly throughout the late stages against $28,000 older claiming horses. He beat half the field. If today Any Alibi faces $20,000 three-year-olds, as indicated, he might just win waltzing. Handicappers need to know that. The information is indispensable.

2. Post position and position at the start. Any Alibi exited the No. 5 post and started eighth of eight on September 14 in the slop at The Meadowlands.

A glance down the post position/start column indicates Any Alibi usually starts slowly, regardless of post position. Nice to know, especially among frontrunners and pace-pressers.

3. Blinkers. The symbol b means the horse raced with blinkers on. Any Alibi always wears blinkers, but among horses that do not, it's nice to know when blinkers were added, and how horses performed when they were—or were taken off. Only in the Eastern form does the b appear. In the Central and Western editions a solid line under the post position above the jockey's name provides the same information about blinkers on, blinkers off.

4. Lengths ahead of the next horse. On September 14 the second-place finisher, I Don't Tell, beat the third finisher Assault Leader by four (4) lengths. Also nice to know. Only available in charts in the midwest and west.

5. Trip comment. Any Alibi managed just a "mild bid" on September 14, according to the chart-maker. The comments at times can be helpful.

HOW TO READ THE RESULTS CHARTS

Not many recreational handicappers collect results charts and refer to them during the handicapping routine.

Racegoers of the middle and western regions of the country would especially benefit. The charts contain nuggets of information the past performance tables do not. Consider the chart below:

①

EIGHTH RACE — 7 FURLONGS. (1.20) 4th Running of THE CASCAPEDIA HANDICAP. $75,000 added. Fillies and mares. 3-year-olds and upward. By subscription of $75 each, $750 additional to start, with

Santa Anita — $75,000 added, of which $15,000 to second, $11,250 to third, $5,625 to fourth and $1,875 to fifth. ②

OCTOBER 25, 1989 — Weights, Friday October 20. Starters to be named through the entry box by the closing time of entries. A trophy will be presented to the owner of the winner. Closed Wednesday, October

18, 1989 with 12 nominations.

Value of race $82,650; value to winner $48,900; second $15,000; third $11,250; fourth $5,625; fifth $1,875. Mutuel pool $313,047.

Exacta Pool $302,606.

Last Raced	Horse	Eqt.A.Wt	PP	St	¼	½	Str	Fin	Jockey	Odds $1
11Oct89 5SA1	Akinemod ③	3 115	6	1	1½	11½	13	12¾	Stevens G L	1.70
25Sep8912Fpx1	Miss Tawpie	5 117	7	2	5¹	52½	21	2½	Flores D R	6.10
11Oct89 8SA7	Hasty Pasty	4 118	4	4	41	41	41	3¹½	Pincay L Jr	9.40	④
29Sep8912Fpx3	Survive	5 118	5	5	63½	61½	6hd	4½	Baze R A	2.80
29Sep8912Fpx1	Corvettin	b 4 116	8	3	87	86	71½	5hd	Nakatani C S	13.70
29Sep8912Fpx6	Behind The Scenes	5 115	1	9	9	9	9	6¾	Solis A	'8.90
8Sep89 8Dmr4	Linda Card	b 3 115	2	8	22½	21½	3hd	71½	Toro F	16.80
9Sep89 7Dmr1	A Penny Is A Penny	4 115	3	7	3hd	3½	51½	8½	Sibille R	26.60
6Oct89 7SA5	Seattle Meteor	3 116	9	6	7hd	7½	81	9	Delahoussaye E	8.30

⑤ — OFF AT 4:43. Start good. Won ridden out. Time, :22⅕, :44⅘, 1:09⅖, 1:22⅖ Track fast. — ⑥

$2 Mutuel Prices:	6–AKINEMOD	5.40	3.80	3.20
	7–MISS TAWPIE		6.60	5.00
	4–HASTY PASTY			7.00

$5 EXACTA 6–7 PAID $83.00.

B. f, (Apr), by Time to Explode—Lady Paese, by Sir Gaylord. Trainer Fanning Jerry. Bred by Klugman J (Cal).

AKINEMOD, off alertly but bumped hard in the initial strides, moved back in front before going a quarter after LINDA CARD had led for a time between calls early, drew well clear in the upper stretch and was not in jeopardy in the final sixteenth when being shown the whip right handed. MISS TAWPIE, also away alerty but bumped hard in the opening strides, was outrun early, saved ground into the stretch, could not catch AKINEMOD in the last furlong but gained the place. HASTY PASTY, never far back, came into the stretch four wide and was going well — ⑦ late. SURVIVE, outrun early, could not gain the necessary ground in the drive. CORVETTIN, well back early after she veered inward and bumped hard with MISS TAWPIE in the initial strides, bettered her position after a half but failed to threaten. BEHIND THE SCENES, far back while trailing early, gained her best stride too late. LINDA CARD rushed up to get the lead between calls just before going a furlong, lost the advantage to AKINEMOD before going a quarter, forced the pace to the stretch and gave way. A PENNY IS A PENNY, close up early, gave way. SEATTLE METEOR, devoid of early speed and wide down the backstretch, failed to rally.

Owners— 1, El Rancho De Jaklin; 2, Saiden A; 3, Spelling A & Candy; 4, Allred & Hubbard; 5, Hudon E A; 6, Alpert D & H; 7, Hi Card Ranch; 8, Hughes & Yedor; 9, Buckland Farm.

Trainers— 1, Fanning Jerry; 2, Barrera Lazaro S; 3, Lukas D Wayne; 4, Mandella-Richard; 5, Luby Donn; 6, Stute Melvin F; 7, Dutton Jerry; 8, Vogel George; 9, Speckert Christopher. — ⑧

Overweight: Linda Card 1 pound; Seattle Meteor 2.

Once again, by the numbers:

1. Purse values of stakes races. Open, listed, and graded stakes below Grade 1 are fairly evaluated as to competitive quality by relative purse sizes. The higher the purse, the better the race—normally.

2. Exact conditions of eligibility. This is crucial to know among allowance races. How restricted or unrestricted were they? Also, any restrictions in claiming races or stakes races will be specified. The Cascapedia Handicap, for 3up females, was open to all comers.

3. Ages of horses in order of finish. In the Cascapedia Handicap, Akinemod, a three-year-old, defeated a five-year-old (second) and a four-year-old. Very important to know. Notice the pair of remaining three-year-olds in the field were soundly drubbed. In open stakes, three-year-olds are disadvantaged against older horses, a condition flattering the performance here of Akinemod.

4. Running lines at the various points of call, including the post position and start of the race. Unlike the past performance tables, which describe by how many lengths each horse trailed the leader at each point of call, the charts describe by how many lengths each horse has led the horse succeeding it at each point of call.

Miss Tawpie started second from post position 7. At the first call (one-quarter), she was fifth, one length ahead of the sixth horse. After a half mile, Miss Tawpie was still fifth, but now 2-1/2 lengths ahead of the sixth-place horse. At the stretch call Miss Tawpie was second, one length ahead of the third horse. She finished second, one-half length ahead of the third-place finisher.

5. Start comment/Manner of victory. Here the start was good for all horses and Akinemod won ridden out. If any horse had broken badly

enough to warrant chart comment, that horse's name would have been identified here. Concerning poor starts, chart comment is significantly more meaningful than the trouble comments in the past performances.

6. Complete fractional times. Includes the two-furlong times of routes and the times at the stretch calls of all races; that is, with one furlong to run.

7. Running lines. Descriptions of the trips, troubles, and biases of horses and racetracks. If detailed, as in the Western edition of the *Daily Racing Form*—courtesy of the excellent Jon White—descriptions of running lines can be amazingly helpful. They illuminate numerous dull finishes and interior moves.

Biases can be inferred at times from the running lines. If horses are constantly moving up strongly along the rail on the far turn, a positive rail bias is evident. The same if horses move up strongly on the outside.

Speed biases are evident when horses continually win on the lead at every call. If horses uncharacteristically win from the rear at the early stages, maybe a closer's bias is operating.

8. The names of trainers in the complete order of finish. If horses have been claimed, trainers of record will be named.

Recreational handicappers who collect results charts and learn to use them intelligently, will enjoy a precious edge that will reward them numerous times a season. The practice is strongly recommended.

SELECTED SIRES WHOSE PROGENY WIN ON THE TURF

Astray	Dancing Count	High Steel
Auction Ring	Daniel Boone	Hy Swaps
Beau Buck	Danzig	Imapuncher
Big Jess	Daryl's Joy	Irish River
Bob Mathias	Decimator	Jahan
Bold Bidder	Determined Cosmic	Jet Diplomacy
Brazen Brother	Doonesbury	J.O. Tobin
Brilliant Sandy	Dr. Marc R.	King's Bishop
Canmore	Flag Officer	Kohoutek
Canonero II	Fortunate Harbor	La Quinta King
Champagne Charlie	Gentleman Gene	Lefty
Circle	Gleaming	Long Position
Circle Home	Great Nephew	Lord Gaylord
Crafty Drone	Gunflint	Lyphard
Curra Boy	Hall of Reason	Lyphard's Wish
Dactylographer	Haveago	Majestic Light

Malinowski
Master Willie
Miswaki
Mitey Prince
Montparnasse II
More Horsepower
Mr. Tal
Muscovite
Nain Bleu
Nalees Man
National Zenith
Nijinsky II
Noble Descent
Noble Saint
No No Billy
Northern Baby
Northern Bay
Northern Dancer
Nureyev
Ole Bob Bowers
Olympiad King
Painted Wagon

Pas Seul
Persian Bold
Pontifex
Private Thoughts
Qui Native
Regal and Royal
Restless Native
Rich Cream
Riverman
Round Table
Royal Ski
Ruritania
Saber Thrust
Salt Spray
San Feliou
Seattle Slew
Semi Royal
Sette Bello
Silent Screen
Silver Series
Singular
Somethingfabulous

Spectacular Bid
Stage Door Johnny
St. Bonaventure
Sunny Clime
Syncopate
Taylor's Falls
Terrible Tiger
Thatching
The Bart
Thurloe Square
Traffic Beat
Transworld
Truxton King
Tyrant
U Pos Ent
Vatza
What A Threat
Wolfgang
Yrrah Jr.
Zanthe
Zen

SELECTED SIRES WHOSE PROGENY WIN IN THE MUD

Ace II
Ack Ack
Affirmed
Aldershot
Alhambra
Alleged
Always Gallant
Alydar
American Native
Another Practice
Arctic Flash
Avatar
Baederwood
Banner Sport
Barrera
Batonnier
Be A Prospect
Believe A Little
Believe It

Bel Sorel
Best Turn
Better Gallant
Big Burn
Big John J.
Big Kohinoor
Blushing Groom
Bold Conquest
Bold Josh
Bold Laddie
Bold Ruckus
Bold Victor
Borzoi
Brave Emperor
Bravest Roman
Breezy Lane
Broadway Forli
Buck Private
Buck's Bid

Capacitator
Captain Cee Jay
Captain Seaweed
Century Prince
Champagne Supper
Charles Elliot
Child Of Clay
Coastal
Cojak
Commissioner
Cormorant
Country Boy Jim
Court Ruling
Crafty Drone
Creme De La Creme
Crystal Ruler
Cyane
Czaravich
Damascus

Dangblastit
Danzig
Darby Creek Road
Dark Eagle
Debonair Roger
Delaware Chief
Delta Flag
Devoted Ruler
Dewan Keys
Diamond Black
Distant Land
Doc Scott J.
Doonesbury
Double Hitch
Double Letter
Double Quote
Dr. Blum
Dr. Jarrell
Drum Fire
Dumpty Humpty
Edziu
Elegant Prince
Eustace
Executioner
Executive Order
Eye of the Morn
Fappiano
Faraway Son
Farnsworth
Father Elmer
First Albert
Five Star Flight
Flashy Image
Fleet Burn
Fly Ash
Flying Paster
Foggy Road
Fort Prevel
Forty Bye Two
Frankie's Nod
Full Intent
Full Partner
Gallant Best
Gallent Knave
Georgeandthedragon

Gigli Saw
Ginistrelli
Gold and Myrrh
Golden Singer
Gold Stage
Good Rob
Grannys Boy
Greatest Roman
Gregorian
Gunter
Hagley
Harry's Secret Joy
Hidden World
Hoist The Silver
Honest Pleasure
Icecapade
I'ma Hell Raiser
Imperial Native
In A Trance
In Reality
Inverness Drive
Irish Tower
Iron Glove
Island Sultan
Ivorson
Ja Aglo
Jacinton
Jacques Who
Jatski
Jerry Crow
John Gaylord
Just The Time
King Rolf
Kirrary
Klassy Flight
Knights Choice
Kokomo Jimmy
Land of Eire
Lawmaker
Leonato
L'Heureux
Lines of Power
Little Current
Lombardi
Lord Gaylord

Lord Treasurer
Mac Corkle
Magesterial
Magnificent Mickey
Majestic Man
Matsadoon
Mombo Jombo
Monetary Crisis
Mr. Prospector
Mr. Ralph
Nantequos
Nasty And Bold
Native Jungle
Native Uproar
Neater
Night Invader
Nijinsky II
No Excuses
No House Call
Northern Supremo
North Tower
Nostrum
Notable Square
Our Gary
Pappagallo
Pas Seul
Paternity
Pay The Toll
Permian
Pitso Casello
Play Boy
Pleasant Colony
Pleasure Bent
Pledge Allegiance
Plugged Nickel
Plum Bold
Pocket Coin
Pollinize
Prince Astro
Princely Game
Princely Native
Princely Song
Prince of Reason
Prince's Last
Prodigo

Quantum Jump
Queen City Lad
Raise A Man
Raise A Regal
Raised Socially
Raise Your Glass
Raja Baba
Real Reason
Reb's Policy
Recitation Rectory
Red Monk
Red Wing Bold
Reflected Glory
Relaunch
Reviewer
Rexson
Right Mind
Rip The Candy
Roanoke Island
Rollicking
Romantic Lead
Round Table Jr.
Royal Consort
Royal Ski
Ruritania
Sabor Cat
Salem
Salesman Sam
Satan's Hills
Sauce Boat
Scotchman
Search For Gold
Seattle Slew
Seclusive
Secretariat
Sensitive Prince
Sharp Kid
Shredder
Silent Screen
Singh

Sinister Purpose
Sir Earl
Sirlad
Sir Raleigh
Sir Sizzling Jim
Skookum
Smarten
Solar Salute
Solo Performance
Somethingfabulous
Sovereign Dancer
Spanish Riddle
Spear Carrier
Spectacular Bid
Speedy Jim
Spellcaster
Spinonin
Spirit Rock
Splendid Courage
Springhill
Squire
Stage Door Johnny
Stalwart
Stanstead
Star De Naskra
Star Spangled
Stephanos
Stopgap
Stop The Music
Stutz Blackhawk
Such A Rush
Sun Hunter
Sunny Clime
Sunny North
Surgeon Sam
Swaps Again
Sweet Medic
Swift Don
Swift Pursuit
Sylarian

Tai
Taylor's Falls
T. Brooke
Temperence Hill
Thaliard
The Astonisher
The Irish Lord
Thin Slice
Third World
Timeless Moment
Tinajero
Tonkaton
Topsider
Transatlantic
Travelling Music
Tri Jet
Trimlea
Trojan Bronze
True To Life
Turn Of Coin
Underwood
Upper Nile
Upton
Valdez
Valid Appeal
Victorian Heritage
Victory Lap
Victory Stride
Vigors
Wild Rose
Wild Wind
Will Hays
Willie Pleasant
Winged Brook
Yaba
Yukon
Zoot Aloors
Zulu Tom
Zuppardo's Prince

LISTED STAKES IN U.S. RACING

Stakes races that appear on this list can be considered superior in quality and prestige to open unlisted stakes, purse size notwithstanding. Relative quality of Listed and Grade 3 stakes is best estimated by purse values.

If a Listed stakes is also restricted, the symbol (R) so designates. Open stakes that are Listed can be considered superior to the restricted kind.

Purse values and eligible ages are provided here. Distance and racetrack can be found in the past-performance tables of the *Daily Racing Form*.

Abrogate H.	$ 50,000	3up	Bay Meadows—Bud-		
Affirmed S. (R)—			weiser Breeders		
Florida stallions	140,000	2yo	Cup H.	50,000	3up
Ak-Sar-Ben—Budweiser			Bay Meadows Debutante	50,000	2yo
Breeders Cup H.	50,000	3up	Bay Meadows Lassie	50,000	2yo
Ak-Sar-Ben H.	75,000	3up	Beaumont S.	50,000	3yo
Albany H.	50,000	3up	Bedside Promise—Fall		
Albany S. (R)—NY Bred	100,000	3yo	Sprint Championship	50,000	3up
Alex M. Robb S. (R)—			Begonia H.	75,000	3yo
NY Bred	63,750	3up	Bell Roberts H.	100,000	3up
All Along S.	250,000	3up	Ben Franklin S.	50,000	3yo
All Brandy H. (R)—MD			Benecia H. (R)	50,000	3up
Bred	75,000	3up	Berlo H.	60,000	3up
Americana H.	75,000	3up	Berkeley H. (R)	50,000	3up
American Beauty H.	50,000	4up	Bertram F. Bongard H.—		
Ancient Title H.	75,000	3up	(R) NY Bred	85,000	2yo
Annapolis S.	60,000	3yo	Best of Ohio Distaff—		
Anne Arundel H.	60,000	3yo	Championship (R)	125,000	3up
A Phenomenon S.	75,000	3up	Best of Ohio Endur-		
Aprisa H.	50,000	3up	ance—Championship		
Arkansas Traveler	50,000	4up	(R)	150,000	3up
Ashley T. Cole S. (R)—			Best of Ohio Juvenile—		
NY Bred	75,000	3up	Championship H. (R)	125,000	2yo
Aspidistra H.	75,000	3up	Best of the West H.	50,000	3up
Au Revoir H.	50,000	3yo	Bird of Paradise H.	50,000	3up
Autumn Days H.	75,000	3up	B. J. Ridder S. (R)—Cal		
Azalea H.	50,000	3yo	Bred	100,000	2yo
			Blue Chip S. (R)—Ohio		
			Bred	60,000	3up
Bachelor S.	50,000	3yo	Blue Delight H.	50,000	3up
Baldwin S.	56,200	3yo	Blue Larkspur S.	60,000	3up
Balmoral Derby	100,000	3yo	Blue Ribbon Classic—		
Balmoral Sprint S.	50,000	3up	Thor. Futurity	50,000	2yo
Bangles & Beads S.	50,000	3up	Bold Bidder	50,000	3up
Barksdale H.	50,000	3up	Bold Favorite H.	50,000	3yo
Bashford Manor S.	50,000	2yo	Bold Reason H.	75,000	3up
Bassinet S.	150,000	2yo	Bolsa Chica S. (R)	75,000	3yo

Bouwerie S.—(R) NY Bred	75,000	3yo
Bradbury S. (R)	75,000	3yo
Broad Brush	50,000	3yo
Broadway H. (R)—NY Bred	75,000	3up
Broward H.	50,000	3up
Brown & Williamson H.	50,000	4up
B. Thoughtful S.	60,000	4up
Buckeye H.	50,000	3up
Buckram Oak H.	50,000	3up
Budweiser Maryland— Classic (R)	200,000	3up
Buena Vista H.	75,000	4up
Burlingame S.	50,000	2yo
Busanda S.	60,000	3yo
Busher H.	60,000	3yo
Caballero H.	75,000	3up
Caesar's Wish S. (R)— MD Bred	60,000	3yo
Calder—Budweiser— Breeders Cup H.	50,000	3up
Calder H.	50,000	3up
California Breeders— Champion S. (R)	125,000	3yo
Canterbury Debutante	150,000	2yo
Canterbury Juvenile	150,000	2yo
Canterbury Queen H.	50,000	3up
Capital H.	50,000	3up
Capital Holding Twin— Spires	50,000	3yo
Cardinal H.	50,000	3up
Carmel H.	50,000	3yo
Carousel H.	50,000	4up
Carry Back H.	50,000	3yo
Catskill S. (R)—NY Bred	75,000	3yo
Cavalier S. (R)	50,000	2yo
C. B. Afflerbaugh (R)	50,000	3up
Cedar Key	50,000	3up
Calledon H. (R)	50,000	3up
Challenger S.	50,000	3yo
Chapman S.	50,000	3up
Charles H. Russell H.	50,000	3up
Charles W. Bidwell—Sr. Memorial	100,000	4yo
Chaucer Cup H.	150,000	3up
C.H.B.P.A. Invitational H. (R)	50,000	3up
Chicago H.	50,000	3up

Chicagoland H. (R)—Ill. Bred	50,000	3up
Chief Pennekeck H.	50,000	3up
Chieftain H.	60,000	3up
Children's Hospital	50,000	3up
Churchill Downs H.	50,000	4up
Cicada S.	60,000	3yo
Cicero H.	50,000	4yo
City of Miami S.	50,000	3yo
Cleveland Gold Cup H.(R)—OH Bred	100,000	3yo
Clipsetta S.	75,000	2yo
Coaltown S.	75,000	4up
Colfax Maid S.	50,000	3yo
Colin S.	100,000	3yo
Colleen S.	50,000	2yo
Columbia S.	100,000	3yo
Commonwealth—Bud- weiser Breeders Cup	50,000	3up
Congressional H.	100,000	3up
Conniver H. (R)	50,000	3up
Convenience S. (R)	50,000	3yo
Coral Gables H.	50,000	3up
Coronado S. (R)	60,000	2yo
Coronet H.	50,000	3up
Correction H.	60,000	3up
Corte Madera S.	50,000	2yo
Count Fleet S.	60,000	3yo
Courtship S. (R)—Cal Bred	50,000	2yo
Crowning Glory (R)	60,000	3yo
Crusader H.	75,000	3up
C.T.B.A. S. (R)	60,000	2yo
C.T.B.A. Marion S. (R)	50,000	3yo
Damon Runyon S. (R)— NY Bred	75,000	2yo
Dancealot S.	50,000	3yo
Davona Dale H.	60,000	3up
De Anza S.	60,000	2yo
Debonair S.	75,000	3yo
Debutante S.	50,000	2yo
Delray H.	50,000	3yo
Deputed Testimony S. (R)—MD Bred	60,000	3yo
Derby Trial S.	50,000	3yo
Desert Vixen S. (R)— Fla. Stallion	85,000	2yo
Determine H.	50,000	3yo
Devil's Bag S.	60,000	2yo

Dewitt Clinton H. (R)—			Gay Matilda S.	50,000	3yo	
NY Bred	100,000	3yo	Geisha H. (R)	75,000	3up	
Divot Digger S.	50,000	3up	Gen. Douglas Mac-			
Dogwood S.	50,000	3yo	Arthur H. (R)	100,000	3up	
Don Benito S.	50,000	3up	General George S.	100,000	3yo	
Don Leon S.	50,000	2yo	Genuine Risk S.	50,000	3yo	
Don Riley H.	50,000	3up	Glass House H.	50,000	4up	
Doublerab H.	75,000	4up	Golden Bear S.	50,000	3yo	
Dr. Fager S. (R)	85,000	2yo	Golden Grass S.	50,000	3yo	
Duck Dance H.	50,000	3up	Gold Rush H.	100,000	3yo	
Durazna S.	50,000	2yo	Goss L. Stryker S. (R)	50,000	3yo	
			Governor's Buckeye Cup			
East View S. (R)	75,000	2yo	H. (R)	100,000	3up	
Eatontown H.	50,000	3up	Governor's Cup	50,000	3up	
E. B. Johnston S. (R)	50,000	3up	Governor's H.	100,000	3yo	
Edgewood S.	50,000	3yo	Governor's H.	50,000	3up	
El Cajon S.	60,000	3yo	Governor's Lady H. (R)	50,000	4up	
El Conejo H.	75,000	4up	Graduation S. (R)	60,000	2yo	
El Rincon H.	100,000	4up	Grassland H.	75,000	3up	
Emmamia H. (R)	60,000	3up	Gulfstream Park—Bud-			
Empire S. (R)—NY Bred	75,000	2yo	weiser Breeders			
Escondido H. (R)	60,000	3up	Cup H.	50,000	3up	
Evan Shipman S. (R)	75,000	3up	Gulfstream Sprint—			
Explorer H.	50,000	3yo	Championship	60,000	3up	
			Gus Fonner H.	50,000	3up	
Fair Star S.	50,000	2yo				
Fairway Fun S.	55,000	4up	Haddonfield H.	50,000	3up	
Find H.	75,000	3up	Hallendale H.	50,000	3up	
Finger Lakes—Bud-			Harbor Place S.	60,000	3yo	
weiser Breeders			Harrison E. Johnson—			
Cup H.	50,000	3up	Memorial H.	50,000	3up	
First Nat'l Bank of			Hawthorne—Budweiser	50,000	3up	
Maryland—Ladies H.	150,000	3up	Hawthorne Heritage S.			
Flashy Mac Futurity	100,000	2yo	(R)	50,000	3yo	
Florida Oaks	100,000	3yo	Hawthorne Juvenile	100,000	2yo	
Foolish Pleasure S.	50,000	2yo	Heavenly Cause S. (R)	60,000	2yo	
Foothill S.	50,000	3yo	H.B.P.A. Handicap	50,000	3up	
Ford Juvenile S. (R)	50,000	2yo	Henry P. Russel H.	75,000	3up	
Fort McHenry S.	60,000	3up	Herecomesthebride S.	50,000	3yo	
Friendship S. (R)—			Heritage S.	50,000	2yo	
Texas Bred	100,000	2yo	Hilltop S.	50,000	3yo	
Full Pocket S.	50,000	3yo	Hindoo H.	50,000	3up	
			H. J. Hardenbrook—			
Gala Feete H.	50,000	3up	Memorial H. (R)	50,000	3up	
Gala Lil H.	50,000	3up	Hollie Hughes H. (R)	75,000	3up	
Gardenia S.	200,000	2yo	Holly S.	50,000	2yo	
Garden State Park—			Hollywood Park—Bud-			
Budweiser Br. Cup H.	50,000	3up	weiser Breeders Cup	50,000	3up	
Gateway to Glory S.	50,000	2yo	Hollywood Turf Express	75,000	3up	
Gator H.	50,000	3up	Honeybee H.	75,000	3yo	

Hot Springs S.	50,000 4up	Lady Canterbury H.	150,000 3up
Hudson H. (R)	75,000 3up	Lady Hallie H.	75,000 4up
Humphrey S. Finney S.		Lady Mannequin H.	50,000 3up
(R)—MD Bred	60,000 3yo	Lafayette H.	50,000 3yo
Hurricane H.	50,000 3up	La Habra S.	56,000 3yo
Hyde Park H. (R)	75,000 3up	Lakes & Flowers H.	75,000 3up
		Land of Lincoln S. (R)	50,000 3yo
Illinois Heritage S.	50,000 3yo	La Puente S. (R)	75,000 3yo
Illinois Oaks (R)	50,000 3yo	Las Cienegas H.	75,000 4up
Imp H.	50,000 3up	Las Madrinas H.	100,000 3up
Independence Day H.	50,000 3up	Las Palmas S.	50,000 3up
Indian Maid H.	50,000 3up	La Troienne S.	50,000 3yo
Inner Harbor S.	50,000 2yo	Laurel—Budweiser	
In Reality S. (R)	400,000 2yo	Breeders Cup H.	50,000 3up
Iroquois S. (R)	50,000 2yo	Laurel Dash H.	250,000 3up
		Leland Stanford H.	50,000 3yo
Jack R. Johnson—		Level Best S.	60,000 3yo
Memorial H.	50,000 4up	Life's Magic H.	75,000 3up
Jacob France H.	50,000 3up	Lincoln H.	75,000 3up
Jameela S. (R)	50,000 3yo	Little Silver H.	60,000 3yo
Japan Racing Assoc. H.	60,000 3yo	Locust Grove H.	75,000 4up
Jefferson Cup S.	75,000 3yo	Longacres—Budweiser	
Jennings H. (R)	75,000 3up	Breeders Cup S.	50,000 3up
Jersey Belle S.	50,000 3yo	Los Altos Invitational H.	
Jet Pilot S.	50,000 2yo	(R)	50,000 3up
Jiffy Lube Maryland—		Los Feliz S. (R)	75,000 3yo
Sprint H. (R)	100,000 3up	Louisiana Breeders	
Jim Beam Breeders—		Derby (R)—LA Bred	75,000 3yo
Classic H. (R)	125,000 3up	Louisiana Breeders—	
Joe Gottstein—Futurity		Oaks (R)	75,000 3yo
(R)	75,000 2yo	Louisiana Downs—Bud-	
Joe Palmer S. (R)	75,000 3up	weiser Breeders Cup	50,000 3up
John D. Hertz H. (R)	50,000 3yo	Louisville H.	75,000 3up
John R. Macomber H.	50,000 3yo	Lucky Draw S.	100,000 3yo
Junior Miss S.	60,000 2yo		
Juvenile S.	50,000 2yo	Magnolia S.	50,000 3yo
Juvenile S. (R)	100,000 2yo	Majorette H.	75,000 3up
		Mambo Dancer H.	50,000 3up
Keeneland—Budweiser		Manalapan H.	75,000 3yo
Breeders Cup H.	75,000 3up	Marica S.	50,000 2yo
Kensington S.	100,000 3up	Marie P. Debartolo—	
Kentahten S.	50,000 3yo	Memorial H.	100,000 3up
Kindergarten S.	50,000 2yo	Marion H. Van Berg—	
King Cotton S.	50,000 4up	Memorial S.	50,000 4up
Kings Point H. (R)	75,000 3up	Martha Washington S.	75,000 3yo
Kingston S. (R)	100,000 3up	Maryland—Budweiser	
		Breeders Cup H.	50,000 3up
Lace Garter H.	50,000 4yo	Maryland City H.	100,000 3yo
La Centinela S. (R)	75,000 3yo	Maryland Juvenile (R)—	
Lady Baltimore H.	60,000 3up	MD Bred	125,000 2yo

Maryland Nursery S. (R)	100,000	2yo
Maryland Oaks (R)	100,000	3yo
Maryland Turf H. (R)	100,000	3yo
Massachusettes—Breeders Derby	50,000	3yo
Massachusettes H.	250,000	3up
Mata Hari H.	50,000	3yo
Maxwell G. H.	50,000	3yo
Mayflower S.	100,000	2yo
Meadowbrook Farm H.	50,000	3up
Melreese H.	50,000	3up
Memorial Day H.	50,000	3up
Miami Beach H.	75,000	3up
Michigan Breeders'— Governor's Cup	50,000	3up
Michigan Futurity (R)	50,000	2yo
Michigan Sire S.	114,030	2yo
Midwest Championship H.	50,000	3up
Midwest Derby	100,000	3yo
Midwest H.	50,000	3up
Midwick H.	100,000	3up
Mike Lee H. (R)	100,000	3yo
Minnesota Breeders'— Derby (R)	80,000	3yo
Minnesota Breeders' Oaks	80,000	3yo
Mint Julip H.	50,000	3up
Miramar H.	50,000	3up
Miss America H.	100,000	3up
Miss California S. (R)	50,000	3yo
Miss Dade H.	75,000	3up
Miss Florida H.	50,000	3yo
Miss Musket H.	50,000	3yo
Miss Ohio H. (R)	60,000	2yo
Miss Prosperity H.	50,000	3up
Miss Tropical H.	50,000	3up
Miss Woodford S.	50,000	3yo
Mister Diz S. (R)	50,000	3yo
Moccasin S.	50,000	3yo
Moccasin S.	75,000	2yo
Mod S. (R)—OH Bred	50,000	2yo
Mohawk S. (R)—NY Bred	75,000	2yo
Monrovia H.	75,000	4up
Montauk S. (R)—NY Bred	75,000	3yo
Monterey H.	50,000	3up
Morvich H.	75,000	3up
Mountain Valley S.	50,000	3yo
Mount Vernon S. (R)	100,000	3up
Mt. Harvard S.	50,000	3up
Mutual Savings Life— Derby	100,000	3yo
Mutual Savings Life— Gold Cup H.	100,000	3up
Mutual Savings Life— Ladies H.	100,000	3up
Mutual Savings Life— Sprint Championship	100,000	3up
My Dear Girl S. (R)	400,000	2yo
My Juliet S.	50,000	3up
National Jockey Club— Oaks	100,000	3yo
Native Dancer H.	50,000	3up
Nebraska Stallion Derby	75,000	3yo
Nebraska Stallion S. (R)	75,000	2yo
Needles H.	50,000	3yo
Never Bend H.	50,000	3up
New Jersey Futurity (R)	83,662	2yo
New Mexico State Fair H.	70,000	3up
New York Breeders'— Futurity	70,000	2yo
New York Derby (R)	200,000	3yo
New York Stallion (R)	100,000	2yo
Nodouble H.	50,000	3up
Northern Dancer S. (R)—MD Bred	75,000	3yo
Northern Lights—Debutante S. (R)	80,000	2yo
Northern Lights Futurity (R)	80,000	2yo
NYRA Mile H.	500,000	3up
Oaklawn—Budweiser Breeders Cup H.	50,000	3up
Oakland H. (R)	50,000	3up
Oceanside S.	60,000	3up
Office Queen H.	50,000	3yo
Oil Capitol H.	75,000	3yo
Old South H.	50,000	3up
On Trust H. (R)—CA Bred	100,000	3up
Orange County—Centennial S.	50,000	3up
Orange County Derby	50,000	3yo
Orange County Handicap	100,000	3up

Orange County Matron S.	50,000	3up
Orinda H.	50,000	3up
Osunitas H.	60,000	3up
Pacifica Invitational H. (R)	50,000	3yo
Palisades H.	50,000	3yo
Palm Beach H.	50,000	3yo
Palo Alto H.	50,000	3yo
Parasol H.	60,000	3up
Pasadena S.	75,000	3yo
Pat O'Brien H.	60,000	3up
Paumonok H.	75,000	3up
Pearl Necklace S. (R)— MD Bred	60,000	3yo
Pembroke Lakes H.	50,000	3up
Pembroke Pines H.	50,000	3yo
Petrify H.	60,000	3up
Petticoat S.	50,000	4yo
Phil D. Shepperd S.	50,000	3up
Phoenix H.	50,000	3up
Piedmont S.	50,000	3yo
Pimlico Special S.	500,000	4up
Pinafore H.	50,000	3up
Pink Pigeon S.	75,000	3up
Pippin S.	50,000	4up
Piston S.	50,000	3yo
Plantation H.	50,000	3up
Playpen S.	50,000	2yo
Pocahontas S.	50,000	2yo
Poinsetta S.	65,000	3yo
Politely S. (R)	50,000	3yo
Polynesian H.	100,000	3up
Pomona Derby	100,000	3yo
Pomona Invitational	150,000	3up
Prelude S.	100,000	3yo
President's Cup S.	50,000	3yo
Prima Donna S.	50,000	3yo
Primer S.	50,000	2yo
Princessnessian H.	50,000	3up
Princess Rooney H.	50,000	3up
Protagonist H.	60,000	3up
Providencia S. (R)	75,000	3yo
Queen City Oaks (R)	100,000	3yo
Queen Empress S.	75,000	2yo
Quickstep H.	50,000	3up
Rainbow Miss S.	50,000	3yo
Rainbow S. (R)	50,000	3yo
Rancho Santa Fe (R)	60,000	2yo
Rebel S.	100,000	3yo
Regret S.	50,000	3yo
Remington Cup H.	50,000	3up
Remington Park—Sprint Championship	100,000	3up
Resolution H.	50,000	3up
Revidere H.	75,000	3up
River Cities—Budweiser Breeders Cup	50,000	3up
Riviera S.	50,000	2yo
Rochester Cup H.	100,000	3up
Rollicking S.	50,000	2yo
Rolling Hills H.	50,000	3up
Roman Brother S. (R)	50,000	3yo
Roman H.	50,000	3up
Rose DeBartolo—Memorial H. (R)	100,000	3up
Round Table H.	100,000	3up
Round Table H.	50,000	3yo
Royal Glint S.	50,000	2yo
Ruffian H.	200,000	3up
Rumson H.	50,000	3up
Ruthless S.	60,000	3yo
Sacramento H.	100,000	3up
Sag Harbor S. (R)	75,000	3yo
San Clemente H.	75,000	3yo
San Francisco H.	100,000	3up
San Jacinto H. (R)	100,000	4up
San Joaquin Invitational H. (R)	50,000	3yo
San Jose H.	50,000	3yo
San Marino H. (R)	75,000	4up
San Mateo Mile S.	50,000	2yo
San Miguel S.	75,000	2yo
Santa Anita—Budweiser Breeders Cup H.	50,000	3up
Santa Catalina S. (R)	75,000	3yo
Santa Clara Invitational H. (R)	50,000	3yo
Santa Gertrudes H. (R)	75,000	4up
Santa Lucia H. (R)	75,000	4up
Santa Ysabel S. (R)	75,000	3yo
Saratoga H.	50,000	3up
Sausalito S.	50,000	3yo
Schnectady H.	75,000	3-5
Seabiscuit Claiming S.	60,000	3up
Senorita S.	75,000	3yo
Sensational S.	50,000	3yo

Shiskabob H. (R)	50,000	3up
Silky Sullivan Invita-		
tional H. (R)	50,000	3up
Sir Ivor S.	60,000	3yo
Smart Angle S. (R)	50,000	2yo
Snow Goose H.	50,000	3up
Songstress S.	50,000	3yo
Sooner H.	50,000	3up
Sorority S. (R)	50,000	3yo
Southwest S.	50,000	3yo
Spectacular Bid S.	50,000	3yo
Spectacular H.	50,000	3up
Spicy Living S.	100,000	3up
Sport City H.	50,000	3up
Sporting Plate H.	100,000	3up
Sport of Kings Futurity	75,000	2yo
Spotlight H.	75,000	3yo
Squan Song H.	50,000	3up
Star Ball Invitational H.		
(R)	50,000	3up
Star De Naskra (R)	50,000	3yo
State of Maryland—		
Distaff H. (R)	100,000	3up
Stickney S.	50,000	4yo
Straight Deal H.	50,000	3up
Summertime S.	50,000	3yo
Sun and Snow H.	50,000	3up
Sun Beau H.	50,000	3up
Sunny Isle H.	100,000	3up
Super Derby—Debutante		
S.	50,000	2yo
Super Derby Juvenile	50,000	2yo
Super Moment H.	50,000	3up
Susan's Girl S. (R)	140,000	2yo
Southern-Accent S.	50,000	3up
Swale S.	50,000	3yo
Sweet Audrey S. (R)	75,000	3yo
Temperence Hill H.	75,000	3yo
The Bart Invitational	50,000	3up
Thistledown—Bud-		
weiser Breeders		
Cup H.	50,000	3up
Thomas D. Nash Memo-		
rial	75,000	3yo
Thomas Edison H.	50,000	3up
Thomas P. Scott H.	75,000	4yo
Tiburon S.	50,000	2yo

Ticonderoga H. (R)	63,750	3up
Timely Writer H.	50,000	3yo
Tizna H.	50,000	3up
Torrey Pines S. (R)	60,000	3yo
Tropical Park—Bud-		
weiser Breeders		
Cup H.	50,000	3up
Tropical Park H.	200,000	3up
Tropical Park Oaks	50,000	3yo
Turf Paradise Futurity	100,000	2yo
Turf Paradise H.	100,000	3up
Turfway Park—Bud-		
weiser Breeders		
Cup H.	50,000	3up
Turnberry Isle S.	50,000	2yo
Twixt S. (R)—MD Bred	75,000	3yo
USF&G Maryland Lassie	100,000	2yo
Valkyr H. (R)	100,000	3up
Vallejo S.	50,000	3yo
Valnor H.	50,000	3up
Vanlandingham S.	75,000	2yo
Viking Spirit S.	60,000	3up
Violet S.	50,000	3yo
Virginia Belle H.	50,000	3up
Virginia H.	100,000	3up
Vizcaya H.	50,000	3up
Walter Haight H.	60,000	3up
Walter R. Cluer H.	50,000	3up
Washington Oaks	50,000	3yo
Weston H.	50,000	3up
West Point H. (R)	100,000	3up
West Virginia Derby	100,000	3yo
What a Pleasure S.	100,000	3yo
What a Pleasure S.	50,000	2yo
What a Summer S. (R)	60,000	2yo
Whirlaway S.	75,000	3yo
Whitemarsh H.	50,000	3up
William Hal Bishop H.	60,000	3up
Winona H.	50,000	3up
Winter Quarters H.	50,000	3yo
Wintergreen S. (R)	50,000	2yo
Woodlawn S.	50,000	3yo
Yaddo S. (R)—NY Bred	100,000	3up
Yo Tambien H.	50,000	3up

References

Several latter-day books on thoroughbred handicapping have altered the general practice sufficiently, or might, to be regarded as standards. Recreational handicappers motivated to increase their knowledge and skill are urged to consult the following list.

Fundamental Knowledge, Basic Methods

Ainslie, Tom. *Ainslie's Complete Guide to Thoroughbred Racing*. Rev. ed. New York: Simon & Schuster, 1986.
Quinn, James. *The Best of Thoroughbred Handicapping*. New York: William Morrow, 1987.
Quirin, William L. *Winning at the Races: Computer Discoveries in Thoroughbred Handicapping*. New York: William Morrow, 1979.

Speed Handicapping

Beyer, Andrew. *Picking Winners*. Boston: Houghton Mifflin Company, 1975.
Quirin, William L. *Winning at the Races: Computer Discoveries in Thoroughbred Handicapping*. New York: William Morrow, 1979.

Class Handicapping

Davidowitz, Steven. *Betting Thoroughbreds*. Rev. ed. New York: E. P. Dutton, 1984.
Quinn, James. *The Handicapper's Condition Book*. Rev. ed. New York: William Morrow, 1986.

Pace Analysis

Brohamer, Tom. *Modern Pace Handicapping*. New York: William Morrow, 1991 (in press).
Quirin, William L. *Thoroughbred Handicapping: State of the Art*. New York: William Morrow, 1984.

Form Analysis

Ainslie, Tom. *Ainslie's Complete Guide to Thoroughbred Racing*. Rev. ed. New York: Simon & Schuster, 1986.
Cramer, Mark. *Thoroughbred Cycles*. New York: William Morrow, 1990.
Scott, William L. *How Will Your Horse Run Today?* Baltimore: Amicus Press, 1984.

Trips, Biases, and Trainers

Beyer, Andrew. *The Winning Horseplayer*. Boston: Houghton Mifflin Company, 1984.
Davidowitz, Steven. *Betting Thoroughbreds*. Rev. ed. New York: E. P. Dutton, 1984.

Money Management and Betting Strategy

Beyer, Andrew. *The Winning Horseplayer*. Boston: Houghton Mifflin Company, 1984.
Mitchell, Dick. *Winning Thoroughbred Strategies*. New York: William Morrow, 1989.